SIXTH EDITION

ECONOMICS

A Contemporary Introduction

SIXTH EDITION

ECONOMICS
A Contemporary Introduction

William A. McEachern

Professor of Economics

University of Connecticut

THOMSON

SOUTH-WESTERN

Australia · Canada · Mexico · Singapore · Spain · United Kingdom · United States

THOMSON
SOUTH-WESTERN

Interactive Text

Economics: A Contemporary Introduction, 6e

William A. McEachern

Editor-in-Chief:
Jack Calhoun

VP/Team Director:
Michael P. Roche

Acquisitions Editor:
Michael Worls

Executive Marketing Manager:
Lisa L. Lysne

Sr. Developmental Editor:
Susanna C. Smart

Sr. Production Editor:
Elizabeth A. Shipp

Manufacturing Coordinator:
Sandee Milewski

Media Technology Editor:
Vicky True

Media Developmental Editor:
Peggy Buskey

Media Production Editor:
Pam Wallace

Production Houses:
Monarch Media;
Orr Book Services

Compositor:
Parkwood Composition Service, Inc.

Internal and Cover Designer:
Michael H. Stratton

Cover Photographer/Illustrator:
Digital Vision

Printer:
Courier Kendallville, Inc.

Library of Congress Cataloging-in-
Publication Data

McEachern, William A.
  Economics : a contemporary
introduction / William A. McEachern.
— 6th ed.
      p. cm.
Includes bibliographical references
and index.
  ISBN 0-324-17697-X (Interactive
ed. : alk. paper)
1. Economics. I. Title
  HB171.5 .M475 2002
  330—dc21   2002007707

William A. McEachern began teaching large sections of economic principles when he joined the University of Connecticut in 1973. In 1980, he started offering teaching workshops around the country. In 2000, the University of Connecticut Alumni Association conferred on him its Faculty Excellence in Teaching Award.

He has published books and monographs in public finance, public policy, and industrial organization. His research has also appeared in a variety of journals, including *Economic Inquiry, National Tax Journal, Journal of Industrial Economics, Kyklos,* and *Public Choice.* He is Founding Editor of *The Teaching Economist,* a newsletter that focuses on teaching economics at the college level, and is Founding Editor of *The Connecticut Economy: A University of Connecticut Quarterly Review.*

Professor McEachern has advised federal, state, and local governments on policy matters and directed a bipartisan commission examining Connecticut's finances. He has been quoted in media such as the *New York Times, London Times, Wall Street Journal, Christian Science Monitor, USA Today,* and *Reader's Digest.*

He was born in Portsmouth, N.H., earned an undergraduate degree with honors from Holy Cross College, spent three years in the army, and earned an M.A. and Ph.D. from the University of Virginia.

To Pat

CONTENTS

PART 2

INTRODUCTION TO THE MARKET SYSTEM

PART 3

MARKET STRUCTURE AND PRICING

PART 6

INTERNATIONAL MICROECONOMICS

PART 8

FISCAL AND MONETARY POLICY

PART 9

INTERNATIONAL MACROECONOMICS

WHAT IS *INTERACTIVE TEXT?*

Interactive Text offers students a new way to learn and instructors a new way to teach. *Interactive Text* combines a traditional textbook with rich multimedia, real-time updates, exercises, self-assessment tests, note-taking tools, and much more. Students benefit from the ability to move beyond the words on the page to use the best resources available to learn a concept, carefully integrated into the text where students need the resource most. Students can adapt their learning to their preferred learning style and learn better and more efficiently. Instructors benefit from having a complete teaching package that integrates all of the media together in one seamless package – no "assembly" is required to put the pieces together. Instructors save time and effort organizing their course and can instead focus on teaching.

Specifically, *Interactive Text* consists of a Print Companion and an Online Companion.

PRINT COMPANION

The Print Companion is a paperback text that includes the content from the original textbook. However, time-sensitive pedagogical features and materials at the end of chapters have been moved to the Online Companion to (a) provide a briefer textbook, and (b) take advantage of the Web to provide a more interactive, real-time experience with these examples and exercises. The Print Companion marks these features (along with additional features not from the original textbook) in the Online Companion with unique icons, to enable students and instructors to quickly see what additional resources are available while they are reading the text.

ONLINE COMPANION
http://interactivetext.swlearning.com/

The Online Companion, found at **http://interactivetext.swlearning.com/**, is a dedicated Web Site featuring unique "views," or versions, for instructors and students. The Online Companion contains all of the text from the Print Companion, along with a rich collection of interactive, multimedia learning resources. These resources consist of the time-sensitive pedagogical materials extracted from the Print Companion, as well as a wealth of additional multimedia and interactive features. Furthermore, the Online Companion offers self-assessment through Pre- and Post-Tests. These tests tie into topics in the chapter and, in the test results, directly link students to the section of the text relevant to the questions missed or answered correctly. The scores from these tests are then saved and tracked for students and instructors to keep a record of progress on these tests. Students may also take notes, bookmark their most recent page, find a specific topic, and call upon additional resources like a glossary. In addition, instructors have the opportunity to manage a syllabus and track student test scores, broadcast notes to their students (or keep private annotations to their text), and send electronic messages to their students. Finally, students and instructors receive a subscription to InfoTrac College Edition, which provides 24-hour access to over ten million full-text articles from over 3,800 scholarly and popular periodicals.

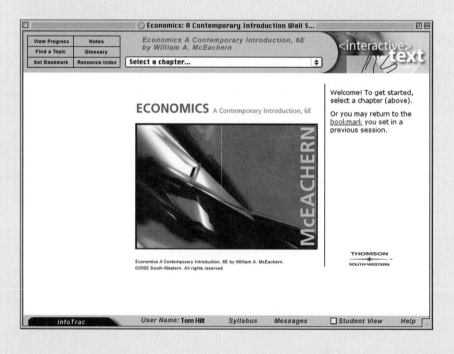

WHAT MAKES *INTERACTIVE TEXT* "INTERACTIVE"?

Interactive Text integrates in the Online Companion the core text with real-time updates, examples, exercises, multimedia, and self-assessment tests. By tying all of these pieces together into one learning solution, students and instructors now have at their fingertips new content, resources, and media with which to learn and to teach. Moreover, these new teaching and learning tools enable students and instructors to interact with the instructional materials in ways not easily done before. A few examples follow.

Learn through Interactive Self-Assessment – Students have the opportunity to take a Pre-Test at the start of each chapter. Students then receive the results of these pre-tests, with direct feedback tied to each answer explaining why the question was answered correctly or incorrectly. Students then receive a link to the exact content covered by the question. This enables students to launch directly to the part of the test relevant to what students need to know. Students can take the Pre-Test as often as they like, each time receiving feedback and unique and specific links into the topics of the text to study the relevant content.

Each chapter also provides a more comprehensive Post-Test that features the same advantages as the Pre-Test. The Post-Test, however, offers the added benefit of randomizing the questions with each attempt, so students have a "new" test every time they try.

These self-assessment tests enable students to thoroughly and repeatedly gauge how well they are learning the key concepts and ideas in the chapter. The rich feedback helps to point out what specific mistakes the students are making. And the topic links tied to each missed question create a unique prescription for the students addressing which exact topics need additional study. Students, therefore, have the ability to study more efficiently and effectively.

Learn through Interactive Study – As students read through the text in the Online Companion, they have the ability to annotate the text using the Notes feature. This feature enables students to place a marker in the text indicating a note, and then type in further explanations, questions, comments or ideas. Instructors also can create annotations and send these notes to every student in the class. In essence, every student and instructor can customize their *Interactive Text* with additional hints, questions, and comments to create a personalized study guide. For any particular chapter, students and instructors can then save these customized notes to their computers, edit them further if desired, and print them through a word processing program.

Learn through Interactive Exploration – Unique features in the Online Companion, such as Interactive Examples and Interactive Updates, provide links into the Web's richest sources of learning information. These features provide students with a roadmap to see in action and work with concepts and ideas from the text. These features are carefully placed within the flow of the text to bring the example or update to the attention of students at exactly the right moment. Students then have the opportunity to leave the text, explore the application of the concept or idea at hand, and then return to the text. Because these examples and updates are links, however, students also are able to simply read through the examples and updates, and return to these at a later time.

FEATURES OF *INTERACTIVE TEXT*

Interactive Text provides much more than the text from the book. Numerous interactive features, discussed below, are integrated throughout the Online Companion. The textbook, then, provides indicators to what features can be found online, and where these features reside within the flow of the text. By providing these features in the Online Companion, the textbook becomes briefer and features only the essential content. The following list highlights the unique features found in this *Interactive Text*.

Pre- and Post-Test – Each chapter offers a Pre-Test, typically consisting of 10 static objective questions, and a Post-Test, consisting of 15-20 randomly generated objective questions. Students have the opportunity to take these self-assessment tests to assess or review their knowledge of key ideas in the chapter. At the completion of each test, students receive a score and instructive feedback on how they answered each question. As well, students receive a direct link to the topic in the chapter addressed in the question. Students can take the tests as often as they need to – a record of their progress for each attempt is kept for them to revisit and gauge their improvement. As well, instructors have access to these progress reports. The Pre- and Post-Test are provided only in the Online Companion.

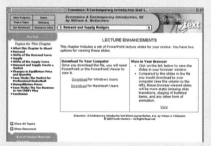

Lecture Enhancements – Lecture Enhancements provide materials, such as PowerPoint Lecture Review Slides, that complement the classroom lectures. Because these materials span entire chapters, these are collected in a unique location for easier studying. The Lecture Enhancements are provided only in the Online Companion.

Interactive Text **includes the following:**
✗ Microsoft PowerPoint Lecture Review Slides

End-of-Chapter Materials – End-of-Chapter Materials gather all of the questions, problems, terms, and summaries found at the end of the textbook and provide these online. Students benefit from enhancements made to these resources, such as direct links back to the relevant text. The End-of-Chapter Materials are provided only in the Online Companion.

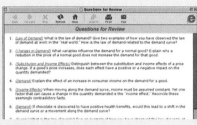

> *Interactive Text* **includes the following:**
> ✗ Summary
> ✗ Questions for Review
> ✗ Problems and Exercises
> ✗ Experiential Exercises
> ✗ Wall Street Journal Exercises
> ✗ Graphing Workshop: Apply It!

InfoTrac College Edition – Students receive a free, exclusive subscription to InfoTrac College Edition. InfoTrac is an online library, updated daily, featuring over ten million articles from 3,800 full-text journals and periodicals. These articles, available 24 hours a day, 7 days a week, range over 22 years, from 1980 until the present. InfoTrac is available wherever students go in the Online Companion, ensuring this research tool is available whenever students need it.

Interactive Example – Interactive Examples offer real-life demonstrations of the key concepts and ideas in the text. Often these examples are drawn from periodical articles, Web resources, interviews with academics and practitioners, among other sources.

> *Interactive Text* **includes the following:**
> ✗ NetBookMark

Interactive Exercise – Interactive Exercises provide opportunities to apply the concepts and ideas in the chapter through structured activities. Typically, these draw upon resources from the Web and other information sources.

> *Interactive Text* **includes the following:**
> ✗ Reading It Right: Wall Street Journal Exercise
> ✗ eActivity
> ✗ EconData Online

Interactive Graph – Interactive Graphs extend the static graphs in the text through animation, audio, and interactive drawing tools to enable students to understand key graphs better. By drawing upon South-Western's successful *Graphing Workshop*, Interactive Graph offers two different types of instruction. "See It" graphs provide an animated demonstration, with audio narration, of how key graphs are constructed and how they change under different conditions. "Try It" graphs pick up on the graphs from "See It," but enable students, at the prompting of questions, to draw the graphs themselves (using online drawing tools) and check the accuracy of their answers.

Interactive Update – Interactive Updates offer the latest happenings, examples and information in a discipline from news, government, industry, and academic institutions. These updates are highly focused to the text and closely related to the concept or idea being presented.

Interactive Text **includes the following:**
✗ EconNews Online
✗ EconDebate Online
✗ EconLinks Online

Interactive Video – Interactive Videos provide a variety of brief (2-5 minute) video clips that serve to integrate news, instruction, and/or business examples into the text.

Interactive Text **includes the following:**
✗ CNN News Clips
✗ Ask the Instructor

THE COURSE TOOLS IN *INTERACTIVE TEXT*

The Online Companion features more than just the text and interactive resources. Instructors and students can take advantage of key course tools included with *Interactive Text*, such as the ability to track the progress of each student's pre- and post-test scores, take notes, provide a unique course syllabus, broadcast messages, bookmark the text, and more. However, because not every instructor wants or needs to use all of these tools, the instructor version of Interactive Text provides the flexibility wherever possible to not use these tools, and not have them appear for students. A convenient "student view" button is always available to instructors to review exactly what the student sees. Here is a listing of the course tools found in *Interactive Text*.

Syllabus – Instructors have the ability to create a syllabus for their course directly in Interactive Text. This tool enables instructors to provide course information, such as course name, title, and policies, as well as add custom information. Further, instructors can create a course schedule that provides students with assignments, homework, and other information based around schedule that provides students with assignments, homework, and other information based around the course calendar. The course schedule is completely customizable.

Should instructors already have a syllabus created, or wish to use another tool to build a course syllabus, the *Interactive Text* syllabus tool provides the option to link instead directly to what the instructors have already created. Finally, should instructors wish not to have any syllabus present, this tool can be turned off, and the students will not see any reference to the syllabus in *Interactive Text*.

Messages – The Messages tool enables instructors to broadcast text messages to individual students, groups of students, or to every student in the class. Instructors can create a message and send it immediately, or they can indicate a future date at which time to broadcast the message. The Messages tool will remember this request and send the message automatically at the specified time. These messages then arrive automatically to the student or students and are visible upon logging into the Online Companion of the *Interactive Text*.

Notes – The Notes tool enables students and instructors to place a marker in the text indicating a note, and then type in further explanations, questions, comments or ideas. Instructors also can create annotations and send these notes to every student in the class. Specifically, with the Notes tool students and instructors can do the following:

    ✗ Read notes that were previously recorded;
    ✗ Change or delete notes that were previously recorded;
    ✗ Read notes that the instructor has broadcast;
    ✗ View all notes (student and instructor notes) for the
       entire chapter, and then download these notes to a file
       to print or revise further in a word processing program.

View Progress – Students who take the Pre- and Post-Test have their scores recorded within the View Progress gradebook. When students take these tests, the results are presented with feedback directly relevant to each answer to each question. This feedback also includes a direct link to the content in the chapter specific to the topic of the question. These records of the results are then saved within the View Progress gradebook, up to five test results per test per student. As well, this gradebook tracks all of the overall test scores by student and by chapter.

Instructors have the ability to change the presentations of these scores in the View Progress gradebook, either presenting all test scores for a student by chapter, or all test scores for a chapter by student. As well, instructors have the option to download the scores in their gradebook into a spreadsheet-ready format, to provide further ability to organize and manage the scores.

Glossary – The glossary provides a collection of all defined terms in the *Interactive Text*, organized alphabetically. The glossary is always present to make it easy to use when needed. Also, key terms within the text are also linked to the definitions from the glossary, and appear in pop-up boxes when clicked.

Bookmarking – The Bookmarking tool enables students and instructors to "bookmark," or create a direct link to the last topic visited in the *Interactive Text*. This link is then presented at the start of the next visit into the product, to jump back to where the instructor or student left off.

Find a Topic/Resource Index – The Find a Topic tool is a useful way to quickly locate and jump to a specific topic in the *Interactive Text*. A content expert has carefully compiled all of the topics in the text, as well as alternate ways in which the typical students would search for the topic. These topics and alternate topics are then indexed alphabetically.

The Resource Index, conversely, provides listing of all the major features, such as Interactive Updates and Interactive Videos. The Resource Index provides a quick way to find specific types of resources, located throughout the *Interactive Text*.

Technical Support – Technical support for *Interactive Text* is available through Thomson Learning Academic Resource Center and Technology Services. To contact a technical support representative, call 1-800-423-0563 or email support@kdc.com.

1

The Art and Science of Economic Analysis

Why are comic-strip characters like Hagar the Horrible, Hi & Lois, Cathy, Monty, and Fox Trot missing a finger on each hand? And where is Dilbert's mouth? Why does Japan have twice as many vending machines per capita as the United States does? In what way are people who pound on vending machines relying on a theory? What's the big idea with economics? Finally, how can it be said in economics that "what goes around comes around"? These and other questions are answered in this chapter, which introduces the art and science of economic analysis.

You have been reading and hearing about economic issues for years—unemployment, inflation, poverty, the federal budget, college tuition, airfares, stock prices, computer prices, gas prices. When explanations of these issues go into any depth, your eyes may glaze over and you may tune out, the same way you do when a weather forecaster tries to provide an in-depth analysis of high-pressure fronts colliding with moisture carried in from the coast.

What many people fail to realize is that economics is livelier than the dry accounts offered by the news media. Economics is about making choices, and you make economic choices every day—choices about whether to get a part-time job or focus on your studies, live in a dorm or off campus, take a course in accounting or one in history, pack a lunch or buy a Big Mac. You already know much more about economics than you realize. You bring to the subject a rich personal experience, an experience that will be tapped throughout the book to reinforce your understanding of the basic ideas. Topics discussed in this chapter include:

- The economic problem
- Marginal analysis
- Rational self-interest
- Scientific method
- Normative versus positive analysis
- Pitfalls of economic thinking

\<interactive\>exercise

- **ECONDEBATE ONLINE: SUPPLY AND DEMAND**
- **ECONDEBATE ONLINE: SCARCITY, CHOICE, AND OPPORTUNITY COST**

\<interactive\>update

- **ECONDATA ONLINE: SUPPLY AND DEMAND**
- **ECONDATA ONLINE: SCARCITY, CHOICE, AND OPPORTUNITY COST**
- **ECONLINKS ONLINE: ECONOMICS WEB LINKS**
- **ECONNEWS ONLINE: SUPPLY AND DEMAND**
- **ECONNEWS ONLINE: SCARCITY, CHOICE, AND OPPORTUNITY COST**

THE ECONOMIC PROBLEM: SCARCE RESOURCES, UNLIMITED WANTS

Would you like a new car, a nicer home, better meals, more free time, a more interesting social life, more spending money, more sleep? Who wouldn't? But even if you can satisfy some of these desires, others will pop up. *The problem is that, although your wants, or desires, are virtually unlimited, the resources available to satisfy these wants are scarce.* A resource is *scarce* when it is not freely available—that is, when its price exceeds zero. Because resources are scarce, you must choose from among your many wants and, whenever you choose, you must forgo satisfying some other wants. The problem of scarce resources but unlimited wants exists to a greater or lesser extent for each of the 6 billion people around the world. Everybody—taxicab driver, farmer, brain surgeon, shepherd, student, politician—faces the problem.

Economics examines how people use their scarce resources to satisfy their unlimited wants. The taxicab driver uses the cab and other scarce resources, such as knowledge of the city, driving skills, gasoline, and time, to earn income. The income, in turn, buys housing, groceries, clothing, trips to Disney World, and thousands of other goods and services that help satisfy some of the driver's unlimited wants.

Let's pick apart the definition of economics, beginning with resources, then examining goods and services, and finally focusing on the heart of the matter—economic choice, which arises from scarcity.

Resources

Resources are the inputs, or factors of production, used to produce the goods and services that humans want. *Goods and services are scarce because resources are scarce.* We can divide resources into four general categories: labor, capital, land, and entrepreneurial ability. **Labor** is the broad category of human effort, both physical and mental. It includes the effort of the cab driver and the brain surgeon. Labor itself comes from a more fundamental resource: *time.* Without time we can accomplish nothing. We allocate our time to alternative uses: we can *sell* our time as labor, or we can *spend* our time doing other things, like sleeping, eating, studying, playing sports, going online, or watching TV.

Capital includes all human creations used to produce goods and services. We often distinguish between physical capital and human capital. *Physical capital* consists of factories, machines, tools, buildings, airports, highways, and other manufactured items employed to produce goods and services. Physical capital includes the taxi driver's cab, the surgeon's scalpel, the farmer's tractor, the interstate highway system, and the building where your economics class meets. *Human capital* consists of the knowledge and skill people acquire to enhance their productivity, such as the taxi driver's knowledge of city streets and the surgeon's knowledge of human biology.

Land includes not only land in the conventional sense of plots of ground but all other natural resources—all so-called *gifts of nature,* including bodies of water, trees, oil reserves, minerals, and even animals.

A special kind of human skill called **entrepreneurial ability** is the talent required to dream up a new product or find a better way to produce an existing one. The entrepreneur tries to discover and act on profitable opportunities by hiring resources and assuming the risk of business success or failure. Every large firm in the world today, such as Ford, Microsoft, and Intel, began as an idea in the mind of an entrepreneur.

Resource owners are paid **wages** for their labor, **interest** for the use of their capital, and **rent** for the use of their land. The entrepreneur's effort is rewarded by **profit,** which equals the *revenue* from sales minus the *cost* of the resources employed. The entrepreneur claims what is left over after paying other resource suppliers. Sometimes the entrepreneur suffers a loss. Resource earnings are usually based on the *time* these resources are employed. Resource payments therefore have a time dimension, as in a wage of $10 *per hour,* interest of 6 percent *per year,* rent of $600 *per month,* or profit of $10,000 *per year.*

Goods and Services

Resources are combined in a variety of ways to produce goods and services. A farmer, a tractor, 50 acres of land, seeds, and fertilizer come together to grow the good: corn. One hundred musicians, musical instruments, chairs, a conductor, a musical score, and a music hall combine to produce the service: Beethoven's Fifth Symphony. Corn is a **good** because it is something you can see, feel, and touch; it requires scarce resources to produce; and it is used to satisfy human wants. The book you are now holding, the chair you are sitting in, the clothes you are wearing, and your next meal are all goods. The performance of the Fifth Symphony is a **service** because it is intangible, yet it uses scarce resources to satisfy human wants. Lectures, movies, concerts, phone calls, online computer services, guitar lessons, dry cleaning, and haircuts are all services.

Because goods and services are produced using scarce resources, they are themselves scarce. A good or service is scarce if the amount people desire exceeds the amount available at a zero price. Since we cannot have all the goods and services we would like, we must continually choose among them. We must choose among more pleasant living quarters, better meals, nicer clothes, more reliable transportation, faster computers, and so on. Making choices in a world of **scarcity** means we must pass up some goods and services.

A few goods and services seem *free* because the amount freely available (that is, available at a zero price) exceeds the amount people want. For example, air and seawater often seem free because we can breathe all the air we want and have all the seawater we can haul away. Yet, despite the old saying "The best things in life are free," most goods and services are scarce, not free, and even those that appear to be free come with strings attached. For example, *clean* air and *clean* seawater have become scarce. *Goods and services that are truly free are not the subject matter of economics. Without scarcity, there would be no economic problem and no need for prices.*

Sometimes we mistakenly think of certain goods as free because they involve no apparent cost to us. Subscription cards that fall out of magazines appear to be free. At least it seems we would have little difficulty rounding up about three thousand if necessary! Producing the cards, however, absorbs scarce resources, resources drawn away from competing uses, such as producing higher-quality magazines. You may have heard the expression "There is no such thing as a free lunch." There is no free lunch because all goods and services involve a cost to someone. The lunch may seem free to us, but it draws scarce resources away from the production of other goods and services, and whoever provides a free lunch often expects something in return. A Russian proverb makes a similar point but with a bit more bite: "The only place you find free cheese is in a mousetrap." Albert Einstein said, "Sometimes one pays the most for things one gets for nothing."

Economic Decision Makers

There are four types of decision makers, or participants, in the economy: households, firms, governments, and the rest of the world. Their interaction determines how an economy's resources are allocated. *Households* play the leading role. As consumers, households demand the goods and services produced. As resource owners, households supply labor, capital, land, and entrepreneurial ability to firms, governments, and the rest of the world. *Firms, governments,* and *the rest of the world* demand the resources that households supply and then use these resources to supply the goods and services that households demand. The rest of the world includes foreign households, firms, and governments that supply resources and products to U.S. markets and demand resources and products from U.S. markets.

Markets are the means by which buyers and sellers carry out exchange. Bringing together the two sides of exchange, demand and supply, markets determine price and quantity. Markets are often physical places, such as supermarkets, department stores, shopping malls, or flea markets. But markets also include other mechanisms by which buyers and sellers communicate, like classified ads, radio and television ads, telephones, bulletin boards, the Internet, and face-to-face bargaining. These market mechanisms provide information about the quantity, quality, and price of products offered for sale. Goods and services are bought and sold in **product markets;** resources are bought and sold in **resource markets.** The most important resource market is the labor, or job, market. Think of your own experience looking for a job, and you get some idea of that market.

A Simple Circular-Flow Model

Now that you have learned a bit about economic decision makers, let's see how they interact. Such a picture is conveyed by the **circular-flow model,** which describes the flow of resources, products, income, and revenue among economic decision makers. The simple circular-flow model focuses on the primary interaction in a market economy—that between households and firms. Exhibit 1 shows households on the left and firms on the right; please take a look.

Households supply labor, capital, land, and entrepreneurial ability to firms through resource markets, shown in the lower portion of the exhibit. In return, households demand goods and services from firms through product markets, shown on the upper portion of the exhibit. Viewed from the business end, firms supply goods and services to households through product markets, and firms demand labor, capital, land, and entrepreneurial ability from households through resource markets.

The flows of resources and products are supported by the flows of income and expenditure—that is, by the flow of money. So let's add money flows to the picture. The supply and demand for resources come together in resource markets to determine wages, interest, rents, and profits, which flow as *income* to households. The supply and demand for products come together in product markets to determine the prices for goods and services, which flow as *revenue* to firms. Resources and products flow in one direction—in this case, counterclockwise—and the corresponding payments flow in the other direction—clockwise. What goes around comes around. Take a little time now to trace the various flows.

THE ART OF ECONOMIC ANALYSIS

An economy results from the choices that millions of individuals make in attempting to satisfy their unlimited wants. Because these choices lie at the very heart of the economic problem—coping with scarce resources but unlimited wants—they deserve a closer look. Learning about the forces that shape economic choice is the first step toward mastering the art of economic analysis.

Rational Self-Interest

A key economic assumption is that individuals, in making choices, rationally select alternatives they perceive to be in their best interests. By *rational,* economists mean simply that people try to make the best choices they can, given the available information. People may not know with certainty which alternative will turn out to be the best. They simply select the alternatives they *expect* will yield the most satisfaction and happiness. *In general, rational self-interest means that individuals try to maximize the expected benefit achieved with a given cost or to minimize the expected cost of achieving a given benefit.*

Rational self-interest should not be viewed as blind materialism, pure selfishness, or greed. We all know people who are tuned to radio station WIIFM (What's In It For Me?). For most of us, however, self-interest often includes the welfare of our family, our friends, and perhaps the poor of the world. Even so, our concern for others is influenced by the cost of that concern. We may readily volunteer to drive a friend to the airport on Saturday afternoon but are less likely to offer a ride if the plane leaves at 6:00 A.M. When we donate clothes to an organization like Goodwill Industries, they are more likely to be old and worn than brand new. We tend to

EXHIBIT 1

The Simple Circular-Flow Model for Households and Firms

Households earn income by supplying resources to the resource market, as shown in the lower portion of the model. Firms demand these resources to produce goods and services, which they supply to the product market, as shown in the upper portion of the model. Households spend their income to demand these goods and services. This spending flows through the product market to become revenue to firms.

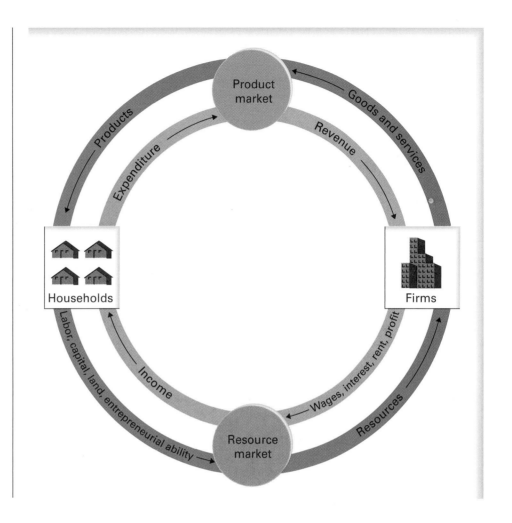

give more to our favorite charities if our contributions are tax deductible. TV stations are more likely to donate airtime for public-service announcements during the dead of night than during prime time (in fact, 80 percent of such announcements air between 11:00 P.M. and 7:00 A.M.[1]). *The notion of self-interest does not rule out concern for others; it simply means that concern for others is to some extent influenced by the same economic forces that affect other economic choices.* The lower the personal cost of helping others, the more help we offer.

NETBOOKMARK: ADOBE ACROBAT READER

Choice Requires Time and Information

Rational choice takes time and requires information, but time and information are scarce and valuable. If you have any doubts about the time and information required to make choices, talk to someone who recently purchased a home, car, or personal computer. Talk to a corporate official deciding whether to introduce a new product, sell over the Internet, build a new factory, or buy another firm. Or think back to your own experience of selecting a college. You

[1]Sally Goll Beatty, "Media and Agencies Brawl Over Do-Good Advertising," *Wall Street Journal,* 29 September 1997.

probably talked to friends, relatives, teachers, and guidance counselors. You likely used school catalogues, college guides, and Web sites. You may have visited campuses to meet with the admissions staff and anyone else willing to talk. The decision took time and money, and it probably involved aggravation and anxiety.

Because information is costly to acquire, we are often willing to pay others to gather and digest it for us. The existence of markets for college guidebooks, stock analysts, travel agents, real estate brokers, career counselors, restaurant critics, movie reviewers, specialized Web sites, and *Consumer Reports* magazine indicates our willingness to pay for information that will improve our economic choices. As we'll see next, *rational decision makers will continue to acquire information as long as the additional benefit expected from that information exceeds the additional cost of gathering it.*

Economic Analysis Is Marginal Analysis

Economic choice usually involves some adjustment to the existing situation, or status quo. Amazon.com must decide whether to add an additional line of products. The school superintendent must decide whether to hire another teacher. Your favorite jeans are on sale, and you must decide whether to buy another pair. You are wondering whether you should carry an extra course next term. You have just finished dinner and are deciding whether to have dessert.

Economic choice is based on a comparison of the *expected marginal cost* and the *expected marginal benefit* of the action under consideration. **Marginal** means incremental, additional, or extra. Marginal refers to a change in an economic variable, a change in the status quo. *You, as a rational decision maker, will change the status quo as long as your expected marginal benefit from the change exceeds your expected marginal cost.* For example, Amazon.com compares the marginal benefit expected from adding a new line of products (the added sales revenue) with the marginal cost (the added cost of the resources required). Likewise, you compare the marginal benefit you expect from eating dessert (the added pleasure and satisfaction) with its marginal cost (the added money, time, and calories).

Typically, the change under consideration is small, but a marginal choice can involve a major economic adjustment, as in the decision to quit school and get a job. For a firm, a marginal choice might mean building a plant in Mexico or even filing for bankruptcy. By focusing on the effect of a marginal adjustment to the status quo, the economist is able to cut the analysis of economic choice down to a manageable size. Rather than confront a bewildering economic reality head-on, the economist can begin with a marginal choice and then see how this choice affects a particular market and shapes the economic system as a whole. Incidentally, to the noneconomist, *marginal* usually means relatively inferior, as in "a movie of marginal quality." Forget that meaning for this course and instead think of *marginal* as meaning incremental, additional, or extra.

Microeconomics and Macroeconomics

Although you have made thousands of economic choices, you probably have seldom thought about your own economic behavior. For example, why are you reading this book right now rather than doing something else? **Microeconomics** is the study of your economic behavior and the economic behavior of others who make choices about such matters as what to buy and what to sell, how much to work and how much to play, how much to borrow and how much to save. Microeconomics examines the factors that influence individual economic choices and how markets coordinate the choices of various decision makers. For example, microeconomics explains how price and output are determined in individual markets—for breakfast cereal, sports equipment, or used cars, for instance.

You have probably given little thought to what influences your own economic choices. You have likely given even less thought to how your choices link up with those made by hundreds of millions of others in the U.S. economy to determine economy-wide sums such as total production, employment, and economic growth. **Macroeconomics** studies the performance of the economy as a whole. Whereas microeconomics studies the individual pieces of the economic puzzle, as reflected in particular markets, macroeconomics puts all the pieces together to focus on the big picture.

To review: The art of economic analysis focuses on how individuals use their scarce resources in an attempt to satisfy their unlimited wants. Rational self-interest guides individual choice. Choice requires time and information, and choice involves a comparison of the marginal cost and marginal benefit of alternative actions. Microeconomics looks at the individual pieces of the economic puzzle; macroeconomics fits the pieces together to get the big picture.

THE SCIENCE OF ECONOMIC ANALYSIS

Economists use scientific analysis to develop theories, or models, that help explain economic behavior. An **economic theory,** or **economic model,** is a simplification of economic reality that *is used to make predictions about the real world.* A theory, or model, such as the circular-flow model, captures the important elements of the problem under study; it need not spell out every detail and interrelation. In fact, the more details a theory contains, the more unwieldy it becomes and the less useful it may be. The world we live in is so complex that we must simplify if we want to make any sense of things, just as comic strips simplify characters—leaving out fingers or a mouth, for instance. You might think of economic theory as a stripped-down, or stream-lined, version of economic reality.

ASK THE INSTRUCTOR: WHY ARE ECONOMISTS ALWAYS TALKING ABOUT MONEY AND WEALTH?

ECONNEWS ONLINE: NO NET TAXES

The Role of Theory

Many don't understand the role of theory. Perhaps you have heard, "Oh, that's fine in theory, but in practice it's another matter." The implication is that the theory provides little aid in practical matters. People who say this fail to realize that they are merely substituting their own theory for a theory they either do not believe or do not understand. They are really saying, "I have my own theory that works better."

All of us employ theories, however poorly defined or understood. Someone who pounds on the Pepsi machine that just ate a quarter has a crude theory about how that machine works and what went wrong. One version of that theory might be "The quarter drops through a series of whatchamacallits, but sometimes the quarter gets stuck. *If* I pound on the machine, *then* I can free up the quarter and send it on its way." Evidently, this theory is so pervasive that many people continue to pound on machines that fail to perform (a real problem for the vending machine industry and one reason why newer machines are fronted with glass). Yet, if you asked any of these mad pounders to explain their "theory" about how the machine operates, he or she would look at you as if you were crazy.

The Scientific Method

To study economic problems, economists employ a process of theoretical investigation called the *scientific method,* which consists of four steps, as outlined in Exhibit 2.

Step One: Identify the Question and Define Relevant Variables. The first step is to identify the economic question and define the variables that are relevant to the solution. For example, the question might be "What is the relationship between the *price* of Pepsi and the *quantity* of Pepsi purchased?" In this case, the relevant variables are price and quantity. A **variable** is a measure that can take on different values. The variables of concern become the elements of the theory, so they must be selected with care.

Step Two: Specify Assumptions. The second step is to specify the assumptions under which the theory is to apply. One major category of assumptions is the **other-things-constant assumption**—in Latin, the *ceteris paribus* assumption. The idea is to identify the variables of interest and then focus exclusively on the relations among them, assuming that nothing else of importance will change—that other things will remain constant. Again, suppose we are interested in how the price of Pepsi influences the amount purchased. To isolate the relation between these two variables, we assume that there are no changes in other relevant variables such as consumer income, the price of Coke, and the average temperature.

EXHIBIT 2

The Scientific Method: Step by Step

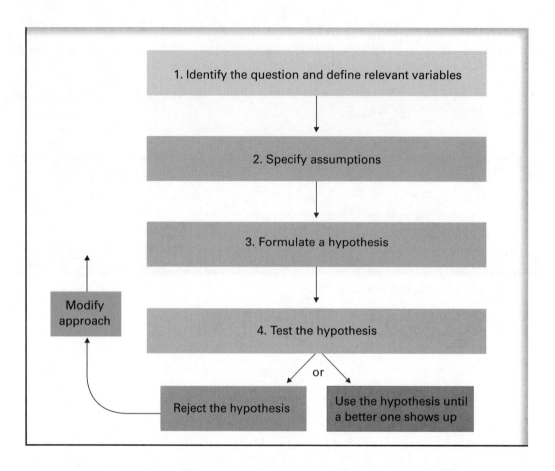

1. Identify the question and define relevant variables

2. Specify assumptions

3. Formulate a hypothesis

4. Test the hypothesis

or

Reject the hypothesis

Use the hypothesis until a better one shows up

Modify approach

We also make assumptions about how people will behave; these we call **behavioral assumptions.** Perhaps the most basic behavioral assumption is rational self-interest. Earlier we assumed that individual decision makers pursue their self-interest rationally and make choices accordingly. Rationality implies that each consumer buys the products expected to maximize his or her level of satisfaction. Rationality also implies that each firm supplies the products expected to maximize that firm's profit. These kinds of assumptions are called behavioral assumptions because they specify how we expect economic decision makers to behave—what makes them tick, so to speak.

Step Three: Formulate a Hypothesis. The third step is to formulate a **hypothesis,** a theory about how key variables relate to each other. For example, one hypothesis holds that *if* the price of Pepsi goes up, other things constant, *then* the quantity purchased will decline. The hypothesis becomes a prediction of what will happen to the quantity purchased if the price goes up. *The purpose of this hypothesis, like that of any theory, is to help make predictions about cause and effect in the real world.*

Step Four: Test the Hypothesis. By comparing its predictions with evidence, we test the validity of a hypothesis. To test a hypothesis, we must focus attention on the variables in question, while carefully controlling for other effects assumed not to change. The test will lead us either to (1) reject the hypothesis, or theory, if it predicts worse than the best alternative theory or (2) use the hypothesis, or theory, until a better one comes along. If we reject it, we can go back and modify our approach in light of the results. Spend a moment reviewing the steps in Exhibit 2.

Normative Versus Positive

Economists usually try to explain how the economy works. Sometimes they concern themselves not with how the economy *does* work but how it *should* work. Compare these two statements: "The U.S. unemployment rate is 5.1 percent" and "The U.S. unemployment rate should be lower." The first is called a **positive economic statement** because it is an assertion about economic reality that can be supported or rejected by reference to the facts. The second is called a **normative economic statement** because it reflects an opinion. And an opinion is merely that—it cannot be shown to be true or false by reference to the facts. Positive statements concern what *is;* normative statements concern what, in someone's opinion, *should be.* Positive statements need not necessarily be true, but they must be subject to verification or refutation by reference to the facts. Theories are expressed as positive statements such as "If the price increases, then the quantity demanded will decrease."

Most of the disagreement among economists involves normative debates—for example, the appropriate role of government—rather than statements of positive analysis. To be sure, many theoretical issues remain unresolved, but economists largely agree on most fundamental theoretical principles—that is, about positive economic analysis. For example, in a survey of 464 U.S. economists, only 6.5 percent disagreed with the statement "A ceiling on rents reduces the quantity and quality of housing available." This is a positive statement because it can be shown to be consistent or inconsistent with the evidence. In contrast, there was much less agreement on normative statements such as "The distribution of income in the United States should be more equal." Half the economists surveyed "generally agreed," a quarter "generally disagreed," and a quarter "agreed with provisos."[2]

Normative statements, or value judgments, have a place in a policy debate such as the proper role of government, provided that statements of fact are distinguished from statements of opinion. In such policy debates, you are entitled to your own opinion, but you are not entitled to your own facts.

Economists Tell Stories

Despite economists' reliance on the scientific method for developing and evaluating theories, economic analysis is perhaps as much art as science. Formulating a question, isolating the key variables, specifying the assumptions, proposing a theory to answer the question, and devising a way to test the predictions all involve more than simply an understanding of economics and the scientific method.

Carrying out these steps requires good intuition and the imagination of a storyteller. Economists explain their theories by telling stories about how they think the economy works. To tell a compelling story, an economist relies on case studies, anecdotes, parables, the personal experience of the listener, and supporting data. Throughout this book, you will hear stories that bring you closer to the ideas under consideration. The stories, such as the one about the Pepsi machine, breathe life into economic theory and help you personalize abstract ideas. As another example, here is a case study about the popularity of vending machines in Japan.

CASE**STUDY**	A Yen for Vending Machines
	● *The World of Business*

In recent decades, the rate of unemployment in Japan has usually been lower than in other countries. Japan faces a steady drop in the number of people of working age, because of (1) a birth rate that reached a record low in 1999, (2) virtually no immigration—only 2 of every 1,000 workers in Japan are foreigners, and (3) an aging population. Since labor is relatively scarce in Japan, it is relatively costly. To sell products, Japanese retailers rely on capital, particularly vending machines, which obviously eliminate the need for sales clerks.

Japan has more vending machines per capita than any other country on the planet—more than twice as many as the United States has and nearly ten times as many as Europe. Also, vending machines in Japan are highly sophisticated. For example, through phone links, some vending machines tell vendors when more product or more change is needed, thereby eliminating unnecessary restocking trips. Vending machines that sell cigarettes or alcohol can now verify the purchaser's age using a driver's license. And some vending machines for cold drinks automatically raise their prices in hot weather.

Robo Shop Super 24, a convenience store in Tokyo, is completely automated. After browsing long display cases, a customer can make selections by punching product numbers on a

[2]Richard M. Alston, et al., "Is There a Consensus Among Economists in the 1990s?," *American Economic Review* 82 (May 1992): pp. 203–209, Table 1.

keyboard. A bucket whirs around the store, rounding up the selections. Robo Shop is a giant vending machine.

We already discussed how it is common practice in the United States to shake down vending machines that malfunction. Such abuse increases the probability that the machines will fail, leading to yet more abuse. In Japan, vending machines are rarely mistreated, in part because they are more sophisticated and more reliable and in part because the Japanese generally have greater respect for property and, consequently, a lower crime rate (the automobile theft rate in Japan is one-twentieth the U.S. rate).

Japanese consumers use vending machines with great frequency. For example, 40 percent of all soft-drink sales in Japan are through vending machines, compared to only 12 percent of U.S. sales. Sales per machine in Japan are double the U.S. level. Vending machines in Japan also sell a wider range of products, including videos, eggs, boxer shorts, stuffed animals, hot pizza, liquor, even dating services. Research shows that Japanese consumers prefer dealing with anonymous machines rather than having to exchange greetings and pleasantries with a real person. Despite the relative abundance of vending machines in Japan, their use is projected to grow even more, spurred on by technological innovations, a shrinking labor pool, and a wider acceptance of machines there.

\<interactive\>exercise

eACTIVITY: A YEN FOR VENDING MACHINES

Sources: Peter Hadfield, "Public Sold on Ugly, Wasteful Vending Machines," *South China Morning Post,* 14 February 2001; "Coke Testing Vending Unit That Can Hike Prices in Hot Weather," *New York Times,* 28 October 1999; and "Sales Per Vending Machine Accelerates in Japan," *Beverage Digest,* 29 August 1999. Pictures and descriptions of Robo Shop 24 can be found at http://www.theimageworks.com/Robo/roboftur.htm.

This case study makes two points. First, producers combine resources in a way that conserves, or economizes on, the resource that is more costly—in this case, labor. Second, the customs and conventions of the marketplace can differ across countries, and this can result in different types of economic arrangements, such as the more extensive use of vending machines in Japan.

Predicting Average Behavior

The task of an economic theory is to predict the impact of an economic event on economic choices and, in turn, the effect of these choices on particular markets or on the economy as a whole. Does this mean that economists try to predict the behavior of particular consumers or producers? Not necessarily, because any individual may behave in an unpredictable way. But the unpredictable actions of numerous individuals tend to cancel one another out, so the *average behavior* of groups can be predicted more accurately. For example, if the federal government cuts personal income taxes, certain households may decide to save the entire tax cut. On average, however, household spending in the economy will increase. Likewise, if Burger King cuts the price of Whoppers, the manager can better predict how much Whopper sales will increase than how a given customer will respond. *The random actions of individuals tend to offset one another, so the average behavior of a large group can be predicted more accurately than the behavior of a particular individual.* Consequently, economists tend to focus on the average, or typical, behavior of people in groups—for example, as average taxpayers or Whopper consumers—rather than on the specific behavior of an individual.

Some Pitfalls of Faulty Economic Analysis

Economic analysis, like other forms of scientific inquiry, is subject to common mistakes in reasoning that can lead to faulty conclusions. We will discuss three possible sources of confusion.

The Fallacy That Association Is Causation. In the last two decades, the number of physicians specializing in cancer treatment increased sharply. At the same time, the incidence of most cancers increased. Can we conclude that physicians cause cancer? No. To assume that event A caused event B simply because the two are associated in time is to commit the **association-is-causation fallacy,** a common error. The fact that one event precedes another or that the two events occur simultaneously does not necessarily mean that one causes the other. Remember: *Association is not necessarily causation.*

The Fallacy of Composition. Standing up at a football game to get a better view does not work if others stand as well. Arriving early to buy concert tickets does not work if many others have the same idea. These are examples of the **fallacy of composition,** which is an erroneous belief that what is true for the individual, or the part, is also true for the group, or the whole.

The Mistake of Ignoring the Secondary Effects. In many cities, public officials have imposed rent controls on apartments. The *primary effect* of this policy, the effect on which policy makers focus, is to keep rents from rising. Over time, however, fewer new apartments get built because the rental business becomes less profitable. Moreover, existing rental units deteriorate because owners have no incentive to pay for maintenance since they have plenty of customers anyway. Thus, the quantity and quality of housing may decline as a result of what appears to be a reasonable measure to control rents. The mistake was to ignore the **secondary effects,** or the *unintended consequences,* of the policy. Economic actions have secondary effects that often turn out to be more important than the primary effects. Secondary effects may develop more slowly and may not be obvious, but good economic analysis takes them into account.

\<interactive\>exercise

ECONDEBATE ONLINE: DO SLAVE REDEMPTION PROGRAMS REDUCE THE PROBLEM OF SLAVERY?

If Economists Are So Smart, Why Aren't They Rich?

Why aren't economists rich? Well, some of them are, earning as much as $25,000 per appearance on the lecture circuit. Others earn thousands a day as consultants. Economists have been appointed to cabinet positions, such as Secretaries of Commerce, Defense, Labor, State, and Treasury, and to head the Federal Reserve. Economics is the only social science and the only business discipline for which the prestigious Nobel Prize is awarded, and pronouncements by economists are reported in the media daily.

A columnist for the *New York Times* wrote that business owners "employ economists in large numbers or consult them at high fees, believing that their cracked crystal balls are better than none at all. The press pursues the best-known seers. While many laymen may be annoyed by economists, other social scientists *hate* them—for their fame, Nobel Prizes, and ready access to political power."[3] A recent article in *The Economist,* a widely respected news weekly from London, argues that economic ideas have influenced policy "to a degree that would make other social scientists drool."[4]

Despite its critics, the economics profession thrives because its models usually do a better job of making economic sense out of a confusing world than do alternative approaches. But not all economists are wealthy, nor is personal wealth the objective of the discipline. In a similar vein, not all doctors are healthy, not all carpenters live in perfectly built homes, not all marriage counselors are happily married, and not all child psychologists have well-adjusted children. Still, those who study economics do reap rewards, as discussed in this closing case study, which looks at the link between earnings and the choice of a college major.

CASE**STUDY**	College Major and Career Earnings
	● *The Information Economy*

Earlier in the chapter, you learned that economic choice is based on a comparison of expected marginal benefit and expected marginal cost. Surveys show that students go to college because they believe a college diploma is the ticket to better jobs and higher pay. Put another way, for about two-thirds of high school graduates, the expected marginal benefit of college seems to exceed its expected marginal cost. We'll discuss the cost of college in the next chapter and focus here on the benefits of college, particularly expected earnings.

Among college graduates, all kinds of factors affect earnings, such as general ability, choice of occupation, personal characteristics, college attended, college major, and highest degree

[3]Leonard Silk, *Economics in Plain English* (New York: Simon and Schuster, 1978), p. 17 (emphasis in original).
[4]"The Puzzling Failure of Economics," *The Economist* 23 August 1997, p. 11.

earned. Until recently, there was little systematic evidence linking earnings to college major, but then the National Science Foundation sponsored a huge survey of college graduates to examine that relationship. To isolate the effects of college major on earnings, the survey focused on people in specific age groups who worked full time and had earned a bachelor's as their highest degree.

Exhibit 3 shows the median earnings in 1993 by major for men and women aged 35 to 44. As a point of reference, the *median* annual earnings for men was $43,199 (half earned more and half earned less). The median earnings for women was $32,155, only 74 percent of the median for men. Among men, the top median pay was the $53,286 earned by engineering majors; that pay was 23 percent above the median for all men aged 35 to 44. Among women, the top median pay was the $49,170 earned by economics majors; that pay was 53 percent above the median for all surveyed women aged 35 to 44.

Incidentally, men who majored in economics earned a median of $49,377, ranking them seventh among 27 majors and 14 percent above the median for all men aged 35 to 44 in the survey. Thus, even though the median pay for all women was only 74 percent of the median

EXHIBIT 3

Median Annual Earnings in 1993 of 35- to 44-Year-Olds with Bachelor's as Highest Degree by Major

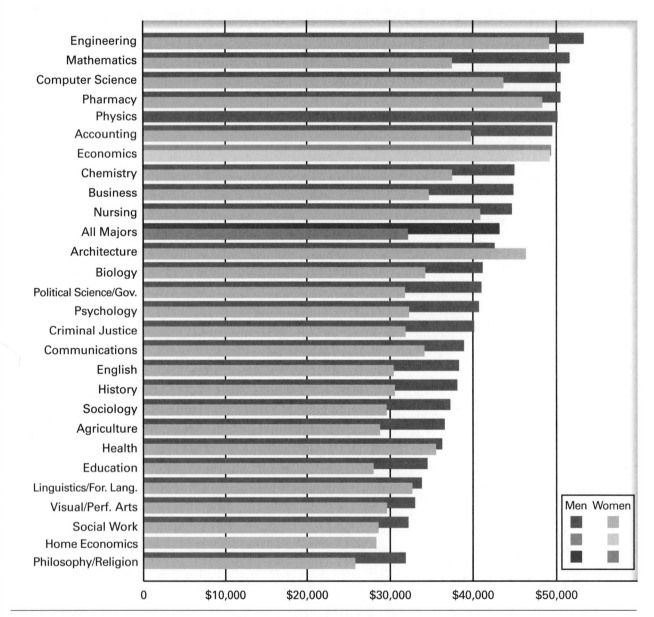

Source: Earnings based on figures reported by Daniel Hacker in "Earnings of College Graduates, 1993," *Monthly Labor Review,* December 1995, pp. 3–17.

pay for all men, women who majored in economics earned about the same as men. We can say that economics majors earned more than most, and they experienced no pay difference based on gender.

Notice that among both men and women, the majors ranked toward the top of the list tend to be the most quantitative and analytical. According to the study's author, "Employers may view certain majors as more difficult and may assume that graduates in these fields are more able and hard working, whereupon they offer them higher salaries."[5] The selection of a relatively more challenging major such as economics sends a favorable signal to future employers.

The study also examined the kinds of jobs different majors actually found. Those who majored in economics became top and mid-level managers, executives, and administrators. They also found jobs in sales, computer fields, financial analysis, and economic analysis. Remember, the survey was limited to those whose highest degree was the baccalaureate, so it excluded the many economics majors who went on to pursue graduate studies in law, business administration, economics, public administration, journalism, and other fields.

A number of world leaders majored in economics, including three of the last six U.S. presidents, Supreme Court Justice Sandra Day O'Connor, and Philippines President Gloria Macapagal Arroyo, who earned a Ph.D. in the subject. Other well-known economics majors include actor Arnold Schwarzenegger, aging rocker Mick Jagger, high-tech guru Esther Dyson, and Scott Adams, creator of the mouthless wonder, Dilbert.

\<interactive\>exercise

- eACTIVITY: COLLEGE MAJOR AND CAREER EARNINGS
- READING IT RIGHT: WALL STREET JOURNAL EXERCISE

Source: Daniel E. Hacker, "Earnings of College Graduates, 1993," *Monthly Labor Review,* December 1995. For a survey of employment opportunities, go to the U.S. Labor Department's *Occupational Outlook Handbook* at http://www.bls.gov/oco/.

CONCLUSION

This textbook describes how economic factors affect individual choices and how all these choices come together to shape the economic system. Economics is not the whole story, and economic factors are not always the most important. But economic considerations have important and predictable effects on individual choices, and these choices affect the way we live.

Sure, economics is a challenging discipline, but it is also an exciting and rewarding one. The good news is that you already know a great deal about economics. To use this knowledge, however, you must cultivate the art and science of economic analysis. You must be able to simplify the world to formulate questions, isolate the relevant variables, and then tell a persuasive story about how these variables relate.

An economic relation can be expressed in words, represented as a table of quantities, described by a mathematical equation, or illustrated as a graph. The Appendix to this chapter provides an introduction to the use of graphs. You may find the Appendix unnecessary. If you are already familiar with graphs—such as relations among variables, slopes, tangents, and the like—you can probably just browse. If you have little recent experience with graphs, you might benefit from a more careful reading with pencil and paper in hand.

In the next chapter, we will introduce some key tools of economic analysis. Subsequent chapters will use these ideas to explore economic problems and to explain economic behavior that may otherwise seem puzzling. You must walk before you can run, however, and in the next chapter, you will take your first wobbly steps.

endofchaptermaterial

- **Summary**
- **Questions for Review**
- **Problems and Exercises**

- **Experiential Exercises**
- **Wall Street Journal Exercise**
- **Appendix Questions**

[5]Daniel E. Hacker, "Earnings of College Graduates, 1993," *Monthly Labor Review* (December 1995): p. 15.

Take the Post-Test to assess your overall understanding of the key ideas in this chapter. The Post-Test provides a comprehensive selection of exam-style questions addressing the main topics and concepts of the chapter. At the completion of each Post-Test, you will receive a score and instructive feedback on how you answered each question, and a direct link to the part of the chapter addressed in the question. Take the Post-Test as often as you need to—a record of your progress for each attempt is kept for you to revisit and gauge your improvement. And each Post-Test is randomly generated, so every attempt is new.

APPENDIX

UNDERSTANDING GRAPHS

Take out a pencil and a blank piece of paper. Go ahead. Put a point in the middle of the paper. This is your point of departure, called the **origin.** With your pencil at the origin, draw a straight line off to the right. This line is called the **horizontal axis.** The value of the variable x measured along the horizontal axis increases as you move to the right of the origin. Now mark off this line from 0 to 20, in increments of 5 units each. Returning to the origin, draw another line straight up. This line is called the **vertical axis.** The value of the variable y measured along the vertical axis increases as you move upward. Now mark off this line from 0 to 20, in increments of 5 units each.

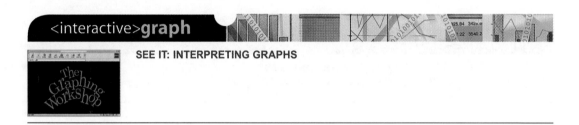

SEE IT: INTERPRETING GRAPHS

Within the space framed by the two axes, you can plot possible combinations of the variables measured along each axis. Each point identifies a value measured along the horizontal, or x, axis *and* a value measured along the vertical, or y, axis. For example, place point a in your graph to reflect the combination where x equals 5 units and y equals 15 units. Likewise, place point b in your graph to reflect 10 units of x and 5 units of y. Now compare your results with points shown in Exhibit 4.

A **graph** is a picture showing how variables relate, and a picture can be worth a thousand words. Take a look at Exhibit 5, which shows the U.S. annual unemployment rate since 1900. The year is measured along the horizontal axis and the unemployment rate along the vertical axis. Exhibit 5 is a *time-series graph,* which shows the value of a variable, in this case the unemployment rate, over time. If you had to describe the information presented in Exhibit 5 in

EXHIBIT 4

Basics of a Graph

Any point on a graph represents a combination of particular values of two variables. Here point *a* represents the combination of 5 units of variable *x* (measured on the horizontal axis) and 15 units of variable *y* (measured on the vertical axis). Point *b* represents 10 units of *x* and 5 units of *y.*

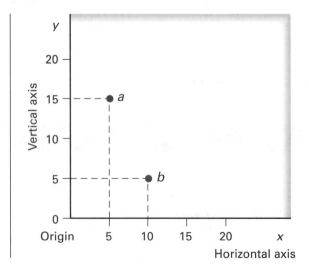

EXHIBIT 5

U.S. Unemployment Rate Since 1900

A time-series graph depicts the behavior of some economic variable (here, the unemployment rate) over time.

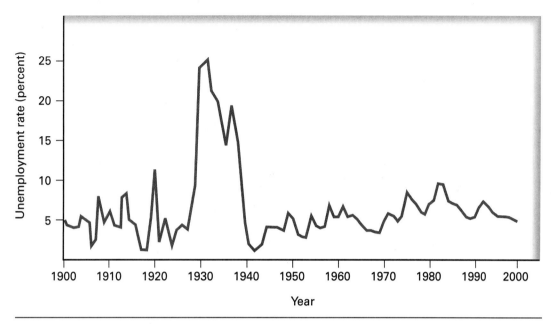

Sources: *Historical Statistics of the United States,* 1970, and *Economic Report of the President,* January 2001.

words, the explanation could take pages and would be mind numbing. The picture shows not only how one year compares to the next but also how one decade compares to another and how the rate trends over time. Your eyes can wander over the hills and valleys to observe patterns that would be hard to convey in words. The sharply higher unemployment rate during the Great Depression of the 1930s is unmistakable. *Graphs convey information in a compact and efficient way.*

This appendix shows how graphs express a variety of possible relations among variables. Most of the graphs of interest in this book reflect the relationship between two economic variables, such as the year and the unemployment rate, the price of a product and the quantity demanded, or the price of production and the quantity supplied. Because we focus on just two variables at a time, we usually assume that other relevant variables remain constant.

We often observe that one variable appears to depend on another. The time it takes you to drive home depends on your average speed. Your weight depends on how much you eat. The amount of Pepsi people buy depends on its price. A *functional relation* exists between two variables when the value of one variable *depends* on the value of another variable. The value of the **dependent variable** depends on the value of the **independent variable.**

The task of the economist is to isolate economic relations and determine the direction of causality, if any. Recall that one of the pitfalls of economic thinking is the erroneous belief that association is causation. We cannot conclude that, simply because two events relate in time, one causes the other. There may be no relation between the two events.

DRAWING GRAPHS

Let's begin with a simple relation. Suppose you are planning to drive across country and want to determine how far you will travel each day. You plan to average 50 miles per hour. Possible combinations of driving time and distance traveled appear in Exhibit 6. One column lists the hours driven per day, and the next column lists the number of miles traveled per day, assuming an average speed of 50 miles per hour. The distance traveled, the *dependent* variable, depends on the number of hours driven, the *independent* variable. We identify combinations of hours driven and distance traveled as *a, b, c, d,* and *e.* As shown in Exhibit 7 we can plot these combinations as a graph, with hours driven per day measured along the horizontal axis and distance traveled along the vertical axis. Each combination of hours driven and distance traveled is represented by a point in Exhibit 7. For example, point *a* shows that if you drive for 1 hour, you

EXHIBIT 6 |

Schedule Relating Distance Traveled to Hours Driven

	Hours Driven per Day	Distance Traveled per Day (miles)
a	1	50
b	2	100
c	3	150
d	4	200
e	5	250

EXHIBIT 7 |

Graph Relating Distance Traveled to Hours Driven

Points *a* through *e* depict different combinations of hours driven per day and the corresponding distances traveled. Connecting these points creates a graph.

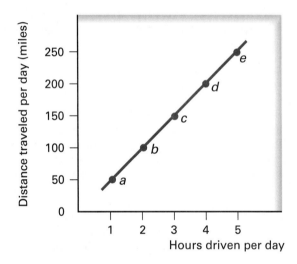

travel 50 miles. Point *b* indicates that if you drive for 2 hours, you travel 100 miles. By connecting the points, or combinations, we create a line running upward and to the right. This makes sense, because the longer you drive, the farther you travel. Assumed constant along this line is your average speed of 50 miles per hour.

Types of relations between variables include the following:

1. As one variable increases, the other increases—as in Exhibit 7; this is called a **positive,** or **direct, relation** between the variables.
2. As one variable increases, the other decreases; this is called a **negative,** or **inverse, relation.**
3. As one variable increases, the other remains unchanged; the two variables are said to be *independent,* or *unrelated.* One of the advantages of graphs is that they easily convey the relation between variables. We do not need to examine the particular combinations of numbers; we need only focus on the shape of the curve.

THE SLOPES OF STRAIGHT LINES

A more precise way to describe the shape of a curve is to measure its slope. The **slope of a line** indicates how much the vertical variable changes for a given increase in the horizontal variable. Specifically, the slope between any two points along any straight line is the vertical change between these two points divided by the horizontal increase, or

$$\text{Slope} = \frac{\text{Change in the vertical distance}}{\text{Increase in the horizontal distance}}$$

Each of the four panels in Exhibit 8 indicates a vertical change, given a 10-unit increase in the horizontal variable. In panel (a), the vertical distance increases by 5 units when the horizontal distance increases by 10 units. The slope of the line is therefore 5/10, or 0.5. Notice that the slope in this case is a positive number because the relation between the two variables is positive, or direct. This slope indicates that for every 1-unit increase in the horizontal variable, the vertical variable increases by 0.5 units. The slope, incidentally, does not imply causality; the increase in the horizontal variable does not necessarily *cause* the increase in the vertical variable. The slope simply indicates in a uniform way the relation between an increase in the horizontal variable and the associated change in the vertical variable.

In panel (b) of Exhibit 8, the vertical distance declines by 7 units when the horizontal distance increases by 10 units, so the slope equals –7/10, or –0.7. The slope in this case is a negative number because the two variables have a negative, or inverse, relation. In panel (c), the vertical variable remains unchanged as the horizontal variable increases by 10, so the slope equals 0/10, or 0. These two variables are unrelated. Finally, in panel (d), the vertical variable can take on any value, although the horizontal variable remains unchanged. Again, the two variables are unrelated. In this case, any change in the vertical measure, for example a 10-unit change, is divided by 0, because the horizontal value does not change. Any change divided by 0 is infinitely large, so we say that the slope of a vertical line is infinite.

EXHIBIT 8

Alternative Slopes for Straight Lines

The slope of a line indicates how much the vertically measured variable changes for a given increase in the variable measured on the horizontal axis. Panel (a) shows a positive relation between two variables; the slope is 0.5, a positive number. Panel (b) depicts a negative, or inverse, relation. When the *x* variable increases, the *y* variable decreases; the slope is –0.7, a negative number. Panels (c) and (d) represent situations in which two variables are unrelated. In panel (c), the *y* variable always takes on the same value; the slope is 0. In panel (d), the *x* variable always takes on the same value; the slope is infinite.

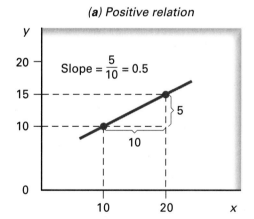

(a) Positive relation

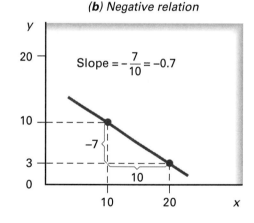

(b) Negative relation

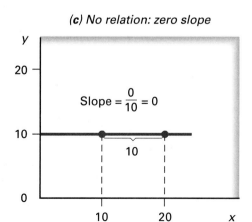

(c) No relation: zero slope

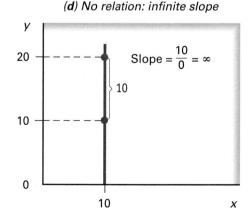

(d) No relation: infinite slope

THE SLOPE, UNITS OF MEASUREMENT, AND MARGINAL ANALYSIS

The mathematical value of the slope depends on the units of measurement on the graph. For example, suppose copper tubing costs $1 a foot to produce. Graphs depicting the relation between output and total cost are shown in Exhibit 9. In panel (a), total cost of production increases by $1 for each 1-foot increase in the amount of tubing produced. Thus, the slope equals 1/1, or 1. If the cost remains the same but the unit of measurement is not *feet* but *yards*, the relation between output and total cost is as depicted in panel (b). Now total cost increases by $3 for each 1-*yard* increase in output, so the slope equals 3/1, or 3. Because different units were used to measure the copper tubing, the two panels reflect different slopes, even though the cost of tubing is $1 per foot in each panel. Keep in mind that *the slope will depend in part on the units of measurement.*

Economic analysis usually involves *marginal analysis,* such as the marginal cost of producing one more unit of output. The slope is a convenient device for measuring marginal effects because it reflects the change in total cost along the vertical axis for each 1-unit change along the horizontal axis. For example, in panel (a) of Exhibit 9, the marginal cost of another *foot* of copper tubing is $1, which also equals the slope of the line. In panel (b), the marginal cost of another *yard* of tubing is $3, which again is the slope of that line. Because of its applicability to marginal analysis, the slope has special relevance in economics.

THE SLOPES OF CURVED LINES

The slope of a straight line is the same everywhere along the line, but the slope of a curved line is different at different points along the curve, as shown in Exhibit 10. To find the slope of a curved line at a particular point, draw a straight line that just touches the curve at that point but does not cut or cross the curve. Such a line is called a **tangent** to the curve at that point. The slope of the tangent is the slope of the curve at that point. Look at the line *A*, which is tangent to the curve at point *a*. As the horizontal value increases from 0 to 10, the vertical value drops along A from 40 to 0. Thus, the vertical change divided by the horizontal change equals –40/10, or –4, which is the slope of the curve at point *a*. This slope is negative because the curve slopes downward at that point. The line *B*, a line tangent to the curve at point *b*, has the slope –10/30, or –0.33. As you can see, the curve depicted in Exhibit 10 gets flatter as the horizontal variable increases, so the value of its slope approaches zero.

Other curves, of course, will reflect different slopes as well as different changes in the slope along the curve. Downward-sloping curves have a negative slope, and upward-sloping curves, a positive slope. Sometimes curves, such as those in Exhibit 11, are more complex, having both

EXHIBIT 9

Slope Depends on the Unit of Measure

The value of the slope depends on the units of measure. In panel (a), output is measured in feet of copper tubing; in panel (b), output is measured in yards. Although the cost of production is $1 per foot in each panel, the slope is different in the two panels because copper tubing is measured using different units.

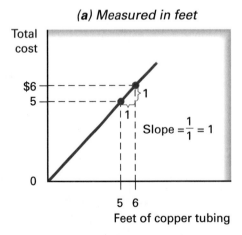

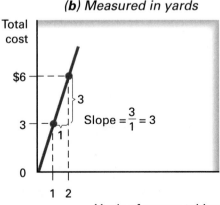

EXHIBIT 10

Slopes at Different Points on a Curved Line

The slope of a curved line varies from point to point. At a given point, such as *a* or *b,* the slope of the curve is equal to the slope of the straight line that is tangent to the curve at that point.

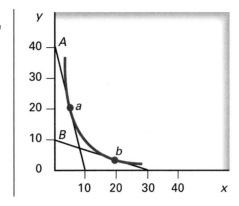

EXHIBIT 11

Curves with Both Positive and Negative Ranges

Some curves have both positive and negative slopes. The hill-shaped curve has a positive slope to the left of point *a,* a slope of 0 at point *a,* and a negative slope to the right of that point. The U-shaped curve starts off with a negative slope, has a slope of 0 at point *b,* and has a positive slope to the right of that point.

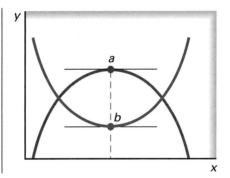

positive and negative ranges. In the hill-shaped curve, for small values of *x,* there exists a positive relation between *x* and *y,* so the slope is positive. As the value of *x* increases, however, the slope declines and eventually becomes negative. We can divide the curve into two segments: (1) the segment between the origin and point *a,* where the slope is positive; and (2) the segment of the curve to the right of point *a,* where the slope is negative. The slope of the curve at point a is 0. The U-shaped curve in Exhibit 11 represents the opposite relation: *x* and *y* are negatively related until point *b* is reached; thereafter, they are positively related. The slope equals 0 at point *b.*

LINE SHIFTS

Let's go back to the example of your cross-country trip, where we were trying to determine how many miles you traveled per day. Recall that we measured hours driven per day on the horizontal axis and miles traveled per day on the vertical axis, assuming an average speed of 50 miles per hour. That same relation is shown as line *T* in Exhibit 12. What if the average speed is not 50 miles per hour but slows to 40 miles per hour? The entire relation between hours driven and distance traveled would change, as shown by the shift to the right of line *T* to *T'*. With a slower average speed, any distance traveled per day now requires more driving time. For example, 200 miles traveled requires 4 hours of driving when the average speed is 50 miles per hour (as shown by point *d* on curve *T*), but 200 miles takes 5 hours when your speed averages 40 miles per hour (as shown by point *f* on curve *T'*). Thus, *a change in the assumption*

EXHIBIT 12

Shift in Line Relating Distance Traveled to Hours Driven

Line *T* appeared originally in Exhibit 7 to show the relation between hours driven per day and distance traveled per day, assuming an average speed of 50 miles per hour. If the average speed is only 40 miles per hour, the entire relation shifts to the right to *T'*, indicating that each distance traveled requires more driving time. For example, 200 miles traveled takes 4 hours of driving at 50 miles per hour, but that distance takes 5 hours at 40 miles per hour.

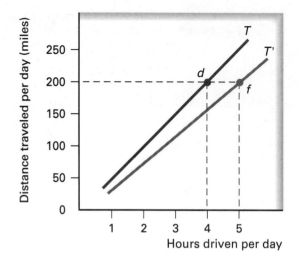

about average speed changes the relationship between the two variables observed. This changed relationship is expressed by a shift in the line that shows how the two variables relate.

With that we close our once-over of graphs. Return to this appendix when you need a review.

Some Tools of Economic Analysis

Why are you reading this book right now rather than doing something else? What is college costing you? Why will you eventually major in one discipline rather than continue to take courses in different ones? Why is fast food so fast? Why is there no sense crying over spilt milk? These and other questions are addressed in this chapter, which introduces some tools of economics—some tools of the trade.

Chapter 1 introduced the idea that scarcity forces us to make economic choices, but the chapter said little about how to make choices. In this chapter, we develop a framework for evaluating economic alternatives. First, we consider the cost involved in selecting one alternative over others. Next, we develop tools to explore the production choices available to individuals and to the economy as a whole. Finally, we examine the questions that different economies must answer—questions about what goods and services to produce, how to produce them, and for whom to produce them. Topics discussed in this chapter include:

- Opportunity cost
- Production possibilities frontier
- Division of labor
- Three economic questions
- Comparative advantage
- Economic systems
- Specialization

<interactive>exercise

ECONDEBATE ONLINE: SCARCITY, CHOICE, AND OPPORTUNITY COST

<interactive>update

- ECONDATA ONLINE: SCARCITY, CHOICE, AND OPPORTUNITY COST
- ECONDATA ONLINE: PRODUCTION POSSIBILITY FRONTIERS
- ECONLINKS ONLINE: SCARCITY, CHOICE, AND OPPORTUNITY COST
- ECONNEWS ONLINE: SCARCITY, CHOICE, AND OPPORTUNITY COST
- ECONNEWS ONLINE: PRODUCTION POSSIBILITY FRONTIERS

CHOICE AND OPPORTUNITY COST

Think about a decision you just made: the decision to read this chapter right now rather than use your time to study for another course, play sports, watch TV, go online, get some sleep, or do something else. Suppose your best alternative to reading right now is getting some sleep. The cost of reading is passing up the opportunity to sleep. Because of scarcity, whenever you make a choice, you must pass up another opportunity; you must incur an *opportunity cost.*

<interactive>update

ECONNEWS ONLINE: CHILL OUT AND DON'T COOK IN

Opportunity Cost

What do we mean when we talk about the cost of something? Isn't it what we must give up—must forgo—to get that thing? The **opportunity cost** of the chosen item or activity is *the value of the* best *alternative that is forgone.* You can think of opportunity cost as the *opportunity lost.* Sometimes opportunity cost can be measured in terms of money, although, as we shall see, money is usually only part of opportunity cost.

How many times have you heard people say they did something because they "had nothing better to do"? They actually mean they had no alternatives as attractive as the choice they selected. Yet, according to the idea of opportunity cost, people *always* do what they do because they have nothing better to do. The choice selected seems, at the time, preferable to any other possible choice. You are reading this chapter right now because you have nothing better to do. In fact, you are attending college for the same reason: College appears more attractive than your best alternative, as discussed in the following case study.

CASE**STUDY**	The Opportunity Cost of College
	● *Bringing Theory to Life*

What is your opportunity cost of attending college full time this year? What was the most valued alternative you gave up to attend college? If you had a job, you have a good idea of the income you gave up to attend college. Suppose you expected to earn $16,000 a year, after taxes, from a full-time job. As a full-time college student, you plan to work part time during the academic year and full time during the summer, earning a total of $7,000 after taxes. Thus, by attending college this year, you are giving up after-tax earnings of $9,000 (= $16,000 − $7,000).

There is also the direct cost of college itself. Suppose you are paying $5,000 this year for tuition, fees, and books at a public college (paying out-of-state rates would add $5,000 to that, and attending a private college would add about $13,000). This money is unavailable to you or your family to spend elsewhere. So the opportunity cost of paying for tuition, fees, and books is the value of the goods and services that money could have purchased.

How about room and board? Expenses for room and board are not necessarily an opportunity cost because, even if you were not attending college, you would still need to live somewhere and eat something, though these costs could be higher at college. Likewise, whether or not you attended college, you would still incur outlays for items such as movies, CDs, clothing, toiletries, and laundry. Such expenses are not an opportunity cost of attending college; they are personal upkeep costs that arise regardless of what you do. So for simplicity, we'll assume that room, board, and personal expenses are the same whether or not you attend college. The forgone earnings of $9,000 plus the $5,000 for tuition, fees, and books yield an opportunity cost of $14,000 this year for a student paying in-state rates at a public college. The opportunity cost jumps to about $19,000 for students paying out-of-state rates and to about $27,000 for those at private colleges. Scholarships, but not loans, would reduce your opportunity cost.

This analysis assumes that all other things are constant. But if, in your view, attending college is more of a pain than you expected the best alternative to be, then the opportunity cost of attending college is even higher. In other words, if you are one of those people who find college difficult, often boring, and in most ways more unpleasant than a full-time job, then the cost in money terms understates your opportunity cost. Not only are you incurring the expense of college, but you are also forgoing a more pleasant quality of life. If, on the other hand, you think the wild and crazy life of a college student is more enjoyable than a full-time job, then the above figures overstate your opportunity cost, because the next best alternative involves a less satisfying quality of life.

Evidently, you view college as a wise investment in your future, even though it is costly and perhaps even painful. College graduates on average earn about twice as much per year as high school graduates. These pay gains from college have encouraged a growing fraction of college students to pile up debts to finance their education. Some students, even those attending public institutions, graduate with debts exceeding $25,000.

Still, college is not for everyone. Some find the opportunity cost too high. For example, Tiger Woods, once an economics major at Stanford, dropped out after two years to earn a fortune in professional golf, including a $100 million five-year endorsement deal with Nike. Some high school seniors who believe they are ready for professional basketball skip college altogether, as do most pro tennis players and many singers and actors (Tom Cruise even dropped out of high school).

<interactive>exercise

eACTIVITY: THE OPPORTUNITY COST OF COLLEGE

Sources: Jonathan Kaufman, "At Elite Universities, a Culture of Money Highlights Class Divide," *Wall Street Journal*, 8 June 2001; and Mary Beth Marklein, "Toll Goes Up on Road to Higher Salary," *USA Today*, 17 October 2000. For information about how to pay for college, go to the College Board Web site, http://www.collegeboard.com/.

Opportunity Cost Is Subjective

Opportunity cost is subjective. Only the individual making the choice can select the most attractive alternative. And the chooser seldom knows the actual value of the best alternative forgone, since that alternative is "the road not taken." If you give up an evening of pizza and conversation with friends to work on a term paper, you will never know the exact value of what you gave up. You know only what you *expected*. Evidently, you expected the value of working on that paper to exceed the value of the best alternative. (Incidentally, focusing on the best alternative forgone makes all other alternatives irrelevant.)

Calculating Opportunity Cost Requires Time and Information. We have assumed that people rationally choose the most valued alternative. This does not mean they exhaustively calculate the value of all possible alternatives. Because acquiring information about alternatives is costly and time consuming, people usually make choices based on limited or even incorrect information. Indeed, some choices may turn out to be poor ones (you went for a picnic but it rained; the movie you rented stunk; your new shoes hurt). Regret about lost opportunities is captured in the common expression "coulda, shoulda, woulda." At the time you made the choice, however, you thought you were making the best use of all your scarce resources, including the time required to gather and evaluate information about your alternatives.

Time Is the Ultimate Constraint. The sultan of Brunei is among the world's richest people, with wealth estimated at $16 billion in 2001 based on huge oil revenues that flow into his tiny country. He has two palaces, one for each wife. The larger palace has 1,788 rooms, with walls of fine Italian marble and a throne room the size of a football field. The royal family owns 2,000 cars, including 150 Rolls-Royces (though some have been put up for sale).[1] Supported by such wealth, the sultan appears to have overcome the economic problem caused by scarcity. But though he can buy just about whatever he wants, he lacks *time* to enjoy his stuff. If he pursues one activity, he cannot at the same time do something else, so each activity he undertakes has an opportunity cost. Consequently, the sultan must choose from among the competing uses of his scarcest resource, time. Although your alternatives are less exotic, you face time constraints too, especially toward the end of the college term.

Opportunity Cost May Vary with Circumstance. Opportunity cost depends on the value of your alternatives. This is why you are more likely to study on a Tuesday night than on a Saturday night. On a Tuesday night, the opportunity cost of studying is lower because your alternatives are less attractive than on a Saturday night, when more is happening. Suppose you go to a movie on Saturday night. Your opportunity cost is the value of your best alternative forgone, which might be attending a game. For some of you, studying on Saturday night may be well down the list of alternatives—perhaps ahead of reorganizing your closet but behind doing your laundry.

Opportunity cost is subjective, but in some cases, money paid for goods and services is a reasonable approximation. For example, the opportunity cost of the new DVD/CD player you bought is the value of spending that $300 on the best forgone alternative. The monetary-cost definition may leave out some important elements, however, particularly the value of the time involved. For example, renting a movie costs you not just the $4 rental fee but the time and travel expense required to get it, watch it, and return it.

Sunk Cost and Choice

Suppose you have just finished shopping for groceries and are wheeling your grocery cart toward the checkout counters. How do you decide which line to join? You pick the one you think will involve the least time. Suppose, after waiting 10 minutes in a line that barely moves, you notice that a cashier has opened another register and invites you to check out. Do you switch to the open line, or do you think, "Since I've already spent 10 minutes in this line, I'm going to stay here"? The 10 minutes you waited represents a **sunk cost,** which is a cost that has already been incurred and cannot be recovered, regardless of what you do now. You should ignore sunk cost in making economic choices. Hence, you should switch to the newly opened register. *Economic decision makers should consider only those costs that are affected by the choice. Sunk costs have already been incurred and are not affected by the choice, so they are irrelevant.* Likewise, you should walk out on a boring movie, even if it cost you $10 to get in. The irrelevance of sunk costs is underscored by the proverb "There's no sense crying over spilt milk." The milk has already spilled, so what you do now cannot change that.

Now that you have some idea about opportunity cost, let's apply this idea to the problem of how best to use scarce resources to help satisfy unlimited wants.

COMPARATIVE ADVANTAGE, SPECIALIZATION, AND EXCHANGE

Suppose you live in a dormitory. You and your roommate have such tight schedules that you each can spare only about an hour a week for mundane tasks like ironing shirts and typing papers (granted, in reality you may not iron shirts or type papers, but this example will help you understand some important points). Each of you must turn in a typed three-page paper every week, and you each prefer to have your shirts ironed when you have the time. Let's say it takes you a half hour to type your handwritten paper. Your roommate is from the hunt-and-peck school and takes about an hour to type a handwritten paper. But your roommate is a talented ironer and can iron a shirt in 5 minutes flat (or should that be, iron it flat in 5 minutes?). You take twice as long, or 10 minutes, to iron a shirt.

During the hour set aside each week for typing and ironing, typing takes priority. If you each do your own typing and ironing, you type your paper in a half hour and iron three shirts in the remaining half hour. Your roommate takes the entire hour to type the paper and so has no time left for ironing. Thus, if you each do your own tasks, the combined output is two typed papers and three ironed shirts.

[1]Wayne Arnold, "Brunei and Its Leader Try Economic Discipline," *New York Times,* 6 March 2001.

SEE IT: COMPARATIVE ADVANTAGE

The Law of Comparative Advantage

Before long, you each realize that total output would increase if you did all the typing and your roommate did all the ironing. In the hour available for these tasks, you type both papers and your roommate irons 12 shirts. As a result of specialization, total output increases by 9 shirts! You strike a deal to exchange your typing for your roommate's ironing, so you each end up with a typed paper and 6 ironed shirts. Thus, *each of you is better off as a result of specialization and exchange.* By specializing in the task that you each do best, you both employ the **law of comparative advantage,** which states that the individual with the lowest opportunity cost of producing a particular output should specialize in producing that output. You face a lower opportunity cost of typing than does your roommate, because in the time it takes to type a paper, you could iron 3 shirts whereas your roommate could iron 12 shirts. And if you face a lower opportunity cost of typing, your roommate must face a lower opportunity cost of ironing.

Absolute Advantage versus Comparative Advantage

The gains from specialization and exchange in the previous example are obvious. A more interesting case arises if you are not only a faster typist but also a faster ironer. Suppose the example changes in one way: your roommate takes 12 minutes to iron a shirt compared with your 10 minutes. You now have an *absolute advantage* in both tasks, meaning each task takes you less time than it does your roommate. More generally, having an **absolute advantage** means being able to produce a product using fewer resources than other producers require.

Does your absolute advantage in both activities mean specialization is no longer a good idea? Recall that the law of comparative advantage states that the individual with the *lower opportunity cost* of producing a particular good should specialize in producing that good. You still take 30 minutes to type a paper and 10 minutes to iron a shirt, so your opportunity cost of typing a paper is still ironing three shirts. Your roommate takes an hour to type a paper and 12 minutes to iron a shirt, so your roommate could iron five shirts in the time it takes to type a paper. The opportunity cost of typing a paper for you is ironing three shirts, and for your roommate it is ironing five shirts. *Because your opportunity cost of typing is still lower than your roommate's, you still have a comparative advantage in typing.* Consequently, your roommate must have a comparative advantage in ironing (try working this out to your satisfaction). Therefore, you should do all the typing and your roommate, all the ironing. Although you have an absolute advantage in both tasks, your **comparative advantage** calls for specializing in the task for which you have the lower opportunity cost—in this case, typing.

If neither of you specialized, you could type one paper and iron three shirts; your roommate could still type just the one paper. Your combined output would be two papers and three shirts. If you each specialized according to comparative advantage, in an hour you could type both papers and your roommate could iron five shirts. Thus, specialization increases total output by two ironed shirts. Even though you are better at both tasks than your roommate, you are comparatively better at typing. Put another way, your roommate, although worse at both tasks, is not quite as poor at ironing as at typing.

Don't think that this is simply common sense. Common sense would lead you to do your own ironing and typing, since you are more skilled at both. *Absolute advantage focuses on who uses the fewest resources, but comparative advantage focuses on what else those resources could have been used to produce—that is, on the opportunity cost of those resources.* Comparative advantage is the better guide to who should do what.

The law of comparative advantage applies not only to individuals but also to firms, regions of a country, and entire nations. Individuals, firms, regions, or countries with the lowest opportunity cost of producing a particular good should specialize in producing that good. Because of such factors as climate, workforce skills, natural resources, and capital stock, certain parts of the country and certain parts of the world have a comparative advantage in producing particular goods. From Apple computers in California's Silicon Valley to oranges in Florida, from DVD/CD players in Taiwan to bananas in Honduras—*resources are allocated most efficiently across the country and around the world when production and trade conform to the law of comparative advantage.*

Specialization and Exchange

In the previous example, you and your roommate specialized and then exchanged your output. No money was involved. In other words, you engaged in **barter,** a system of exchange in which products are traded directly for other products. Barter works best in simple economies where there is little specialization and few types of goods to trade. But for economies with greater specialization, *money* plays an important role in facilitating exchange. Money—coins, bills, and checks—serves as a *medium of exchange* because it is the one thing that everyone is willing to accept in return for all goods and services.

Because of specialization and comparative advantage, most people consume little of what they produce and produce little of what they consume. People specialize in particular activities, such as plumbing or carpentry, and then exchange their products for money, which in turn is exchanged for goods and services. Did you make anything you are wearing? Probably not. Think about the degree of specialization that went into your cotton shirt. Some farmer in a warm climate grew the cotton and sold it to someone who spun it into thread, who sold it to someone who wove it into fabric, who sold it to someone who sewed the shirt, who sold it to a wholesaler, who sold it to a retailer, who sold it to you. Your shirt was produced by many specialists.

Division of Labor and Gains from Specialization

Picture a visit to McDonald's: "Let's see, I'll have a Big Mac, an order of fries, and a chocolate shake." Less than a minute later your order is ready. It would take you much longer to make a homemade version of this meal. Why is the McDonald's meal faster, cheaper, and—for some people—tastier than one you could make yourself? Why is fast food so fast? McDonald's takes advantage of the gains resulting from the **division of labor.** Each worker, rather than preparing an entire meal, specializes in separate tasks. This division of labor allows the group to produce much more.

How is this increase in productivity possible? First, the manager can assign tasks according to *individual preferences and abilities*—that is, according to the law of comparative advantage. The worker with the toothy smile and pleasant personality can handle the customers up front; the one with the strong back but few social graces can do the heavy lifting in the back. Second, a worker who performs the same task again and again gets better at it (experience is a good teacher). The worker filling orders at the drive-through window, for example, learns how to deal with special problems that arise. Third, there is no time lost in moving from one task to another. Finally, and perhaps most importantly, the **specialization of labor** allows for the introduction of more sophisticated production techniques—techniques that would not make sense on a smaller scale. For example, McDonald's large shake machine would be impractical in the home. The specialization of labor allows for the introduction of specialized machines, and these machines make each worker more productive.

To review: The specialization of labor takes advantage of individual preferences and natural abilities, allows workers to develop more experience at a particular task, reduces the time required to shift between different tasks, and permits the introduction of labor-saving machinery. Specialization and the division of labor occur not only among individuals but also among firms, regions, and indeed entire countries. The shirt production mentioned earlier might involve growing cotton in one country, turning it into cloth in another, making the shirt in a third, and selling it in a fourth.

We should also note the downside of specialization. Doing the same thing all day can become tedious. Consider, for example, the assembly-line worker whose sole task is to tighten a particular bolt. Such a job could drive that worker bonkers and lead to injury caused by repetitive motion. Thus, the gains from dividing production into individual tasks must be weighed against the problems caused by assigning workers to repetitive and tedious jobs.

Specialization is discussed in the following case study.

CASESTUDY | Evidence of Specialization Abounds

● *Bringing Theory to Life*

Evidence of specialization is all around us. Look at the extent of specialization in higher education. A large university may house a dozen or more schools and colleges—agriculture, architecture, business, drama, education, engineering, law, fine arts, liberal arts and sciences, medicine, music, nursing, pharmacy, social work, and more. Some of these include a dozen or more departments. And each department may offer courses in a dozen or more fields of specialization. Economics, for example, offers courses in micro, macro, development, econometrics, economic history, health, industrial organization, international finance, international trade, labor, law, money and banking, poverty, public finance, regulation, urban and regional, and more. Altogether, a university may offer courses in thousands of specialized fields.

Specialization is abundant in production and sales. Specialty shops range from luggage to lingerie. Restaurants can be quite specialized—from subs to sushi. Let your fingers do the walking through the *Yellow Pages*, and you find thousands of specializations. Under "Physicians" alone, you uncover dozens of specialties. Without moving a muscle, you can witness the division of labor within a single industry by watching the credits roll at the end of a movie. There you will see scores of specialists—from gaffer (lighting electrician) to assistant location scout. Magazines also offer fine degrees of specialization. One Web site lists over 200,000 different magazines from around the world—something for everyone.

The extent of specialization is perhaps most obvious on the Web, where the pool of potential customers is so vast that individual sites can be extremely specialized. For example, there are individual sites specializing in miniature furniture, paper airplanes, musical bowls, prosthetic noses, tongue studs, toe rings, brass knuckles, mouth harps, ferret toys, juggling equipment, and bug visors (for motorcycle helmets)—just to name a few of the hundreds of thousands of specialty sites. Because each is so narrowly focused, you will not find such specialists at the mall, but they apparently can survive in the virtual world.

<interactive>exercise

eACTIVITY: EVIDENCE OF SPECIALIZATION ABOUNDS

Source: The magazine subscription site is http://www.asiasmart.com. You can find online versions of the *Yellow Pages* at http://www.yellowpages.com/ and http://www.superpages.com/. Any search engine will turn up the specialty sites reported above.

THE ECONOMY'S PRODUCTION POSSIBILITIES

Our focus to this point has been on how individuals choose to use their scarce resources to satisfy their unlimited wants or, more specifically, how they specialize based on comparative advantage. This emphasis on the individual has been appropriate because the economy is shaped by the choices of individual decision makers, whether they are consumers, producers, or public officials. Just as resources are scarce for the individual, they are also scarce for the economy as a whole (no fallacy of composition here). An economy has millions of different resources that can be combined in all kinds of ways to produce millions of possible goods and services. In this section, we step back from the immense complexity of the real economy to develop our second model, which presents the economy's production options.

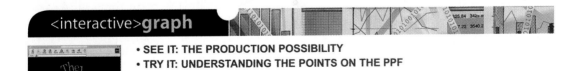

<interactive>graph

- **SEE IT: THE PRODUCTION POSSIBILITY**
- **TRY IT: UNDERSTANDING THE POINTS ON THE PPF**

Efficiency and the Production Possibilities Frontier

Let's develop a model to get some idea of how much an economy can produce with the resources available. What are the economy's production capabilities? Here are the model's simplifying assumptions:

Chapter 2 Some Tools of Economic Analysis

1. To reduce the analysis to manageable proportions, we limit the output to just two broad classes of products: consumer goods, such as pizzas and haircuts, and capital goods—physical capital, such as a machine, and human capital, such as a college education.
2. The focus is on production during a given period—in this case, a year.
3. The resources available in the economy are fixed in both quantity and quality during that period.
4. Society's knowledge about how these resources can be combined to produce output—that is, the available *technology*—does not change during the year.

The point of these assumptions is to freeze the economy in time so we can focus on the economy's production alternatives based on the resources and technology available during that time.

Given the resources and the technology available in the economy, the **production possibilities frontier,** or **PPF,** identifies the various possible combinations of the two types of goods that can be produced when all available resources are employed fully and efficiently. *Resources are employed fully and efficiently when there is no change that could increase the production of one good without decreasing the production of the other good.* **Efficiency** involves getting the maximum possible output from available resources.

The economy's PPF for consumer goods and capital goods is shown by the curve *AF* in Exhibit 1. Point *A* identifies the amount of consumer goods produced per year if all the economy's resources are used efficiently to produce consumer goods, and *F* identifies the amount of capital goods produced per year if all the economy's resources are used efficiently to produce capital goods. Points along the curve between *A* and *F* identify possible combinations of the two goods that can be produced when *all* the economy's resources *are used efficiently.*

Inefficient and Unattainable Production

Points inside the PPF, including *I* in Exhibit 1, represent combinations that do not employ resources fully, employ them inefficiently, or both. Note that point *C* yields more consumer goods and no fewer capital goods than *I*. And point *E* yields more capital goods and no fewer consumer goods than *I*. Indeed, any point along the PPF between *C* and *E*, such as point *D*, yields both more consumer goods and more capital goods than *I*. Hence, point *I* is *inefficient.* By using resources more efficiently or by using previously idle resources, the economy can produce more of at least one good without reducing the production of the other good.

Points outside the PPF, such as *U* in Exhibit 1, represent *unattainable* combinations, given the resources and the technology available. Thus *the PPF not only shows efficient combinations of*

EXHIBIT 1

The Economy's Production Possibilities Frontier

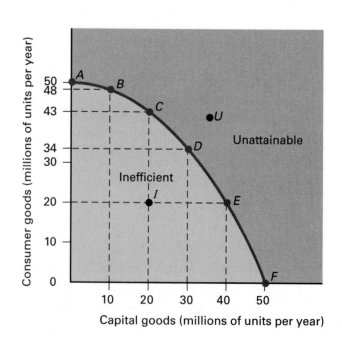

If the economy uses its available resources and technology fully and efficiently in producing consumer goods and capital goods, it will be on its production possibilities frontier curve *AF.* The PPF is bowed out to illustrate the law of increasing opportunity cost: additional units of capital goods require the economy to sacrifice more and more units of consumer goods. Note that more consumer goods must be given up in moving from *D* to *E* than in moving from *A* to *B,* although in each case the gain in capital goods is 10 million units. Points inside the PPF, such as *I,* represent inefficient use of resources. Points outside the PPF, such as *U,* represent unattainable combinations.

production but also serves as the border between inefficient combinations inside the frontier and unattainable combinations outside the frontier.

The Shape of the Production Possibilities Frontier

Focus again on point *A* in Exhibit 1. Any movement along the PPF involves giving up some of one good to get more of the other. Movement down the curve indicates that the opportunity cost of more capital goods is fewer consumer goods. For example, moving from point *A* to point *B increases* the amount of capital goods produced from none to 10 million units and *reduces* production of consumer goods from 50 million to 48 million units, a decline of only 2 million units. Increasing production of capital goods to 10 million units causes the production of consumer goods to fall only a little. Capital production initially employs resources (such as heavy machinery used to build factories) that add little to production of consumer goods but are quite productive in making capital goods.

As shown by the dashed lines in Exhibit 1, each additional 10 million units of capital goods reduces consumer goods by successively larger amounts. As more capital goods are produced, the resources drawn away from consumer goods are those that are increasingly better suited to producing consumer goods. *Opportunity cost increases as the economy produces more capital goods, because the resources in the economy are not all perfectly adaptable to the production of both types of goods.* The shape of the production possibilities frontier reflects the **law of increasing opportunity cost.** If the economy uses all resources efficiently, the law of increasing opportunity cost states that each additional increment of one good requires the economy to sacrifice successively larger and larger increments of the other good.

The PPF derives its bowed-out shape from the law of increasing opportunity cost. For example, whereas the first 10 million units of capital goods have an opportunity cost of only 2 million units of consumer goods, the final 10 million—that is, the increase from point *E* to point *F*—have an opportunity cost of 20 million units of consumer goods. Notice that the slope of the PPF shows the opportunity cost of an increment of capital. As the economy moves down the curve, the curve becomes steeper, reflecting the higher opportunity cost of capital goods in terms of forgone consumer goods. The law of increasing opportunity cost also applies when moving from the production of capital goods to the production of consumer goods. If resources were perfectly adaptable to alternative uses, the PPF would be a straight line, reflecting a constant opportunity cost along the PPF.

SEE IT: THE PRODUCTION POSSIBILITY

ECONNEWS ONLINE: DRUG DEBATE

What Can Shift the Production Possibilities Frontier?

When we construct the production possibilities frontier, we assume that resources available in the economy and the level of technology are fixed. Over time, however, the PPF may shift as a result of changes in resource availability or in technology. An outward shift of the PPF reflects **economic growth,** which is an expansion in the economy's ability to produce goods and services.

Changes in Resource Availability. If people decide to work longer hours, the PPF shifts outward, as shown in panel (a) of Exhibit 2. An increase in the size or health of the labor force, an increase in the skills of the labor force, or an increase in the availability of other resources, such as new oil discoveries, also shifts the PPF outward. In contrast, a decrease in the availability or quality of resources shifts the PPF inward, as depicted in panel (b). For example, in 1990 Iraq invaded Kuwait, setting oil fields ablaze and destroying much of Kuwait's physical

capital, thereby shifting Kuwait's PPF inward. In West Africa the encroaching sands of the Sahara cover and destroy thousands of square miles of productive farmland each year, shifting the PPF of that economy inward.

The new PPFs in panels (a) and (b) appear to be parallel to the original PPFs, indicating that the resources that changed could produce either good. For example, an increased supply of electrical power can be used in the production of both consumer goods and capital goods. If, however, a resource (such as farmland) is suited only to the production of consumer goods, then an increase in the supply of that resource shifts the PPF more along the consumer goods axis than along the capital goods axis, as shown in panel (c). Panel (d) shows the effect of an increase in the supply of a resource (such as construction equipment) that is suited only to capital goods.

Increases in the Capital Stock. An economy's PPF depends in part on the stock of human and physical capital. The more capital an economy produces during one period, the more output can be produced in the next period. Thus, producing more capital goods this period (for example, more machines in the case of physical capital or better education in the case of human capital) shifts the economy's PPF outward the next period. The choice between consumer goods and capital goods is really between present consumption and future production. Again, *the more capital goods produced this period, the greater the economy's production possibilities next period.*

EXHIBIT 2

Shifts in the Economy's Production Possibilities Frontier

When the resources available to an economy change, the PPF shifts. If more resources become available, the PPF shifts outward, as in panel (a), indicating that more output can be produced. A decrease in available resources causes the PPF to shift inward, as in panel (b). Panel (c) shows a change affecting consumer goods production. More consumer goods can now be produced at any given level of capital goods. Panel (d) shows a change affecting capital goods production.

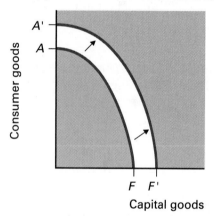

(a) Increase in available resources

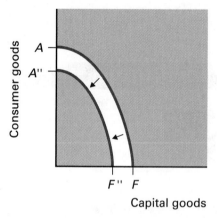

(b) Decrease in available resources

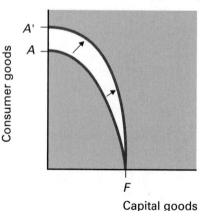

(c) Increase in resources or technological advance that benefits consumer goods

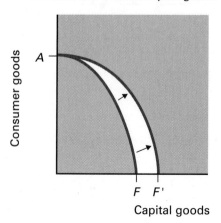

(d) Increase in resources or technological advance that benefits capital goods

Technological Change. Another type of change that could shift the economy's PPF outward is a technological discovery that employs available resources more efficiently. Some discoveries enhance the production of both products, as shown in panel (a) of Exhibit 2. For example, the Internet has increased the efficiency of resource markets by enhancing each firm's ability to identify resource suppliers. The effect of a technological advance in the production of consumer goods, such as genetically altered seeds that increase crop production, is reflected by a rotation outward of the PPF along the consumer goods axis, as shown in panel (c) of Exhibit 2 (note that point *F* remains unchanged because the technological breakthrough does not affect the production of capital goods). Panel (d) shows the result of a technological advance in the production of capital goods, such as improved software that reduces the cost of designing and manufacturing heavy machinery.

ASK THE INSTRUCTOR: DO ECONOMISTS AND THE GENERAL PUBLIC ATTACH DIFFERENT MEANINGS TO THE TERM "INVESTMENT"?

ECONNEWS ONLINE: THE WEALTH OF NATIONS, PART II

What Can We Learn from the PPF?

The PPF demonstrates several ideas introduced so far. The first is *efficiency:* The PPF describes the efficient combinations of outputs that are possible, given the economy's resources and technology. The second is *scarcity:* Given the stock of resources and technology, the economy can produce only so much. The PPF slopes downward, indicating that, as the economy produces more of one good, it must produce less of the other good. This trade-off demonstrates *opportunity cost.* The bowed-out shape of the PPF reflects the *law of increasing opportunity cost;* it arises because not all resources are perfectly adaptable to the production of each good. And a shift outward in the PPF reflects *economic growth.* Finally, because society must somehow choose a specific combination of output—a single point—along the PPF, the PPF also underscores the need for *choice.* That choice will determine not only current consumption but also the capital stock available next period. One thing the PPF does not tell us is which combination to choose; the PPF tells us only about the costs, not the benefits, of the two goods. To make a selection, we need information on both costs *and* benefits. How society goes about choosing a particular combination depends on the nature of the economic system, as we will see in the next section.

Three Questions Every Economic System Must Answer

Each point along the economy's production possibilities frontier is an efficient combination of outputs. Whether the economy produces efficiently and how the economy selects the most preferred combination depends on the decision-making rules employed. Regardless of how decisions are made, each economy must answer three fundamental questions: What goods and services will be produced? How will they be produced? And for whom will they be produced? An **economic system** is the set of mechanisms and institutions that resolve the *what, how,* and *for whom* questions. Some criteria used to distinguish among economic systems are (1) who owns the resources, (2) what decision-making process is used to allocate resources and products, and (3) what types of incentives guide economic decision makers.

What Goods and Services Will Be Produced? Most of us take for granted the incredible number of choices that go into deciding what gets produced—everything from which new kitchen appliances are introduced and which aspiring novelists get published to which roads are built. Although different economies resolve these and millions of other questions using different decision-making rules and mechanisms, all economies must somehow make such choices.

How Will Goods and Services Be Produced? The economic system must determine how output is to be produced. Which resources should be used, and how should they be combined to produce each product? How much labor should be used and at what skill levels? What kinds of machines should be used? What type of fertilizer should be applied to grow the best strawberries? Should the factory be built in the city or closer to the interstate highway? Millions of individual decisions determine which resources are employed and how these resources are combined.

For Whom Will Goods and Services Be Produced? Who will actually consume the goods and services produced? The economic system must determine how to allocate the fruits of production among the population. Should equal amounts be provided to everyone? Should the weak and the sick get more? Should those willing to wait in line the longest receive more? Should goods be allocated according to height? Weight? Religion? Age? Gender? Race? Appearance? Strength? Political connections? The value of resources supplied? The question "For whom will goods and services be produced?" is often referred to as the *distribution question.*

ECONOMIC SYSTEMS

Although we discussed the three economic questions separately, they are closely interwoven. The answer to one depends very much on the answers to the others. For example, an economy that distributes goods and services in uniform amounts to all will, no doubt, answer the what-will-be-produced question differently than an economy that somehow allows each person to choose. Laws about resource ownership and the extent to which the government attempts to coordinate economic activity determine the "rules of the game"—the set of conditions that shape individual incentives and constraints. Along a spectrum ranging from the freest to the most regimented type of economic system, *capitalism* would be at one end and the *command system* at the other.

READING IT RIGHT: WALL STREET JOURNAL EXERCISE

Pure Capitalism

Under **pure capitalism,** the rules of the game include the private ownership of all resources and the coordination of economic activity based on the price signals generated in free, unrestricted markets. Any income derived from supplying labor, capital, land, or entrepreneurial ability goes exclusively to the individual owners of those resources. Owners have *property rights* to the use of their resources and are therefore free to supply those resources to the highest bidder. Producers are free to make and sell whatever they think will be profitable. Consumers are free to buy whatever goods they can afford. All this voluntary buying and selling is coordinated by unrestricted markets, where buyers and sellers make their intentions known. Market prices guide resources to their most productive use and channel goods and services to the consumers who value them the most.

Under capitalism, markets answer the what, how, and for whom questions. Markets transmit information about relative scarcity, provide individual incentives, and distribute income among resource suppliers. No single individual or small group coordinates these activities. Rather, it is the voluntary choices of many buyers and sellers responding only to their individual incentives and constraints that direct resources and products to those who value them the most. According to Adam Smith (1723–1790), one of the first to explain the allocative role of markets, market forces coordinate as if by an "invisible hand"—an unseen force that harnesses the pursuit of self-interest to direct resources where they earn the greatest payoff. According to Smith, *although each individual pursues his or her self-interest, the "invisible hand" of markets promotes the general welfare.* Capitalism is sometimes called *laissez-faire;* translated from the French, this phrase means "to let do," or to let people do as they choose without government intervention. Thus, under capitalism, voluntary choices based on rational self-interest are made in unrestricted markets to answer the questions what, how, and for whom.

As we will see in later chapters, pure capitalism has its flaws. The most notable market failures are:

1. No central authority protects property rights, enforces contracts, and otherwise ensures that the rules of the game are followed.
2. People with no resources to sell can starve.
3. Some producers may try to monopolize markets by eliminating the competition.
4. The production or consumption of some goods generates by-products, such as pollution, that affect people not involved in the market transaction.

5. Private firms do not produce so-called *public goods,* such as national defense, because private firms cannot prevent nonpayers from enjoying the benefits of public goods.

Because of these limitations, countries have modified pure capitalism to allow a role for government. Even Adam Smith believed government should play a role. The United States is one of the most market-oriented economies in the world today.

NETBOOKMARK: THE CENTER FOR INTERNATIONAL COMPARISONS AT THE UNIVERSITY OF PENNSYLVANIA

Pure Command System

In a **pure command system,** resources are directed and production is coordinated not by markets but by the "command," or central plan, of government. At least in theory, there is public—communal—ownership of property. Government planners, as representatives of all the people, answer such questions through *central plans* spelling out how much steel, how many cars, and how many homes to produce. They also decide how to produce these goods and who gets them.

In theory, the pure command system incorporates individual choices into collective choices, which, in turn, are reflected in central plans. In practice, the pure command system also has flaws, most notably:

1. Running an economy is so complicated that some resources are used inefficiently.
2. Since nobody in particular owns resources, people have less incentive to employ them in their highest-valued use, so some resources are wasted.
3. Central plans may reflect the preferences of central planners more than they do those of society.
4. Because government is responsible for all production, the variety of products tends to be more limited than it does in a capitalist economy.
5. Each individual has less personal freedom in making economic choices.

Because of these limitations, countries have modified the pure command system to allow a role for markets. North Korea is perhaps the most centrally planned economy in the world today.

Mixed and Transitional Economies

No country on earth exemplifies either type of economic system in its pure form. Economic systems have grown more alike over time, with the role of government increasing in capitalist economies and the role of markets increasing in command economies. The United States represents a **mixed system,** with government directly accounting for about one-third of all economic activity. What's more, government regulates the private sector in a variety of ways. For example, local zoning boards determine lot sizes, home sizes, and the types of industries allowed. Federal bodies regulate workplace safety, environmental quality, competitive fairness, and many other activities.

Although both ends of the spectrum have moved toward the center, capitalism has gained more converts in recent decades. Perhaps the benefits of markets are no better illustrated than where countries were divided by ideology into capitalist economies and command economies: Taiwan and China, West Germany and East Germany before unification, and South Korea and North Korea. In each case, the economies began with similar human and physical resources, but income per capita diverged sharply, with the capitalist economies outperforming the command economies. For example, Taiwan's income per capita in 2000 was 4 times that of China's, and South Korea's income per capita was 13 times that of North Korea's.

Recognizing the incentive power of markets, some of the most die-hard central planners now reluctantly accept some free-market activity. For example, about 20 percent of the world's population is in China, which grows more market oriented each day. More than a decade ago, the former Soviet Union dissolved into 15 independent republics; most are trying to privatize what had been state-owned enterprises. From Hungary to Mongolia, the transition to mixed economies now under way in former command economies will shape economies of the 21st century.

Economies Based on Custom or Religion

Finally, some economic systems are molded largely by custom or religion. For example, caste systems in India and elsewhere restrict occupational choice. Family relations also play significant roles in organizing and coordinating economic activity. Even in the United States, some occupations are still dominated by women, others by men, largely because of tradition. Your own pattern of consumption and choice of occupation may be influenced by some of these factors.

CONCLUSION

Although economies can answer the three economic questions in a variety of ways, this book will focus primarily on the mixed market system, such as exists in the United States. This type of economy blends *private choice*, guided by the price system in competitive markets, with *public choice*, guided by democracy in political markets. The study of mixed market systems grows more relevant as former command economies try to develop markets.

If you were to stop reading right now, you would already know more economics than most people. But to understand market economies, you must learn how markets work. You will do so in the next chapter, which introduces demand and supply.

endofchaptermaterial

- **Summary**
- **Questions for Review**
- **Problems and Exercises**

- **Experiential Exercises**
- **Wall Street Journal Exercise**

Take the Post-Test to assess your overall understanding of the key ideas in this chapter. The Post-Test provides a comprehensive selection of exam-style questions addressing the main topics and concepts of the chapter. At the completion of each Post-Test, you will receive a score and instructive feedback on how you answered each question, and a direct link to the part of the chapter addressed in the question. Take the Post-Test as often as you need to—a record of your progress for each attempt is kept for you to revisit and gauge your improvement. And each Post-Test is randomly generated, so every attempt is new.

Post-Test

CHAPTER 3

Demand and Supply Analysis

Why do roses cost more on Valentine's Day than during the rest of the year? Why do TV ads cost more during the Super Bowl ($1.6 million for 30 seconds) than during *Nick at Nite* reruns? Why do hotel rooms in Phoenix cost more in February than in August? Why do surgeons earn more than butchers? Why do pro basketball players earn more than pro hockey players? Why do economics majors earn more than most other majors? Answers to these and most economic questions boil down to the workings of demand and supply—the subject of this chapter.

This chapter introduces the underpinnings of demand and supply and shows how they interact in competitive markets. *Demand and supply are the most fundamental and the most powerful of all economic tools*—important enough to warrant their own chapter. Indeed, some believe that if you program a computer to respond "demand and supply" to every economic question, you could put many economists out of work. An understanding of the two ideas will take you far in mastering the art and science of economic analysis. As you will see, fruitful analysis of demand and supply takes skill and care. This chapter uses graphs extensively, so you may want to refer to the appendix in Chapter 1 for a refresher. Topics discussed in this chapter include:

- Demand and quantity demanded
- Movement along a demand curve
- Shift of a demand curve
- Supply and quantity supplied
- Movement along a supply curve
- Shift of a supply curve
- Markets and equilibrium
- Disequilibrium

\<interactive\>exercise

ECONDEBATE ONLINE: SUPPLY AND DEMAND

\<interactive\>update

- ECONDATA ONLINE: SUPPLY AND DEMAND
- ECONLINKS ONLINE: ECONOMICS WEB LINKS
- ECONNEWS ONLINE: SUPPLY AND DEMAND

DEMAND

How much Pepsi will consumers buy each week if the price per six-pack is $3? If the price is $2? If it's $4? The answers reveal the relationship between the price of Pepsi and the quantity purchased. Such a relationship is called the *demand* for Pepsi. **Demand** indicates how much of a good consumers are both *willing* and *able* to buy at each possible price during a given period, other things remaining constant. Because demand pertains to a specific period—a day, a week, a month—think of demand as the *planned rate of purchase per period* at each possible price. Also, notice the emphasis on *willing* and *able*. You may be *able* to buy a Harley-Davidson for $8,000 because you can afford one, but you may not be *willing* to buy one if motorcycles don't interest you.

\<interactive\>example

NETBOOKMARK: INOMICS SEARCH ENGINE

\<interactive\>video

CNN VIDEO: RED LIGHT FOR MEXICAN DRUG TRAFFICKERS

The Law of Demand

In 1962, Sam Walton opened his first store in Rogers, Arkansas, with a sign that read: "Wal-Mart Discount City. We sell for less." The rest is history. Wal-Mart now sells more than any other retailer in the world because prices there are the lowest around. As a consumer, you have little trouble understanding that people will buy more at a lower price. Sell for less, and the world will beat a path to your door. Wal-Mart, for example, on average sells about 20,000 pairs of shoes *an hour.*[1]

This relation between the price and the quantity demanded is an economic law. The **law of demand** says that quantity demanded varies inversely with price, other things constant. Thus,

[1]Leslie Kaufman, "Its Prices, and Its Reach, Push Wal-Mart to Top," *New York Times,* 22 October 2000.

the higher the price, the smaller the quantity demanded; the lower the price, the greater the quantity demanded.

Demand, Wants, and Needs. Consumer *demand* and consumer *wants* are not the same thing. As we have seen, wants are unlimited. You may *want* a new Mercedes SL600, but the $130,000 price tag is probably beyond your budget (that is, the quantity you demand at that price is zero). Nor is *demand* the same as *need*. You may *need* a new muffler for your car, but if the price is $200, you may decide, "I am not going to pay a lot for this muffler." Apparently, you have better uses for your money. If, however, the price of mufflers drops enough—say, to $100— then you become both willing and able to buy one.

The Substitution Effect of a Price Change. What explains the law of demand? Why, for example, is more demanded when the price is lower? The explanation begins with unlimited wants confronting scarce resources. Many goods and services are capable of satisfying particular wants. For example, you can satisfy your hunger with pizza, tacos, burgers, chicken, or hundreds of other items. Similarly, you can satisfy your desire for warmth in the winter with warm clothing, a home-heating system, a trip to Hawaii, or in many other ways. Clearly, some ways of satisfying your wants will be more appealing than others (a trip to Hawaii is more fun than warm clothing). In a world without scarcity, everything would be free, so you would always choose the most attractive alternative. Scarcity, however, is a reality, and the degree of scarcity of one good relative to another helps determine each good's *relative* price.

Notice that the definition of *demand* includes the other-things-constant assumption. Among the "other things" assumed to remain constant are the prices of other goods. For example, if the price of pizza declines while other prices remain constant, pizza becomes relatively cheaper. Consumers are more *willing* to purchase pizza when its relative price falls; they tend to substitute pizza for other goods. This is called the **substitution effect of a price change.** On the other hand, an increase in the price of pizza, other things constant, causes consumers to substitute other goods for the now higher-priced pizza, thus reducing their quantity of pizza demanded. Remember that *it is the change in the relative price—the price of one good relative to the prices of other goods—that causes the substitution effect.* If all prices changed by the same percentage, there would be no change in relative prices and no substitution effect.

The Income Effect of a Price Change. A fall in the price of a product increases the quantity demanded for a second reason. Suppose you clear $30 a week from a part-time job, so your money income is $30 per week. **Money income** is simply the number of dollars received per period, in this case, $30 per week. Suppose you spend all your income on pizza, buying three a week at $10 each. What if the price drops to $6? At that price you can now afford five pizzas a week. Your money income remains at $30 per week, but the decrease in the price has increased your **real income**—that is, your income measured in terms of what goods and services it can buy. The price reduction, other things constant, increases the purchasing power of your income, thereby increasing your *ability* to buy pizza. The quantity of pizza you demand will likely increase because of this **income effect of a price change.** You may not increase your quantity demanded to five pizzas, but you could. If you purchase four pizzas a week when the price drops to $6, you have $6 left to buy other goods.

Thus, the income effect of a lower price increases your real income and thereby increases your ability to purchase all goods. Because of the income effect of a price decrease, other things constant, consumers typically increase their quantity demanded. Conversely, an increase in the price of a good, other things constant, reduces real income, thereby reducing the *ability* to purchase all goods. Because of the income effect of a price increase, consumers typically reduce their quantity demanded as the price increases. Again, note that money income is assumed to be constant along a demand curve.

The Demand Schedule and Demand Curve

Demand can be expressed as a *demand schedule* or as a *demand curve*. Panel (a) of Exhibit 1 shows a hypothetical demand schedule for pizza. When we describe demand, we must specify the units being measured and the period considered. In our example, the price is for a 12-inch regular pizza and the period is a week. The schedule lists possible prices, along with the quantity demanded at each price. At a price of $15, for example, consumers demand 8 million pizzas per week. As you can see, the lower the price, other things constant, the greater the quantity demanded. If the price drops as low as $3, consumers demand 32 million per week. As the price falls, consumers substitute pizza for other goods. And as the price falls, the real income of consumers increases, causing them to increase the quantity of pizza they demand.

The demand schedule in panel (a) appears as a **demand curve** in panel (b), with price on the vertical axis and the quantity demanded per week on the horizontal axis. Each combination

EXHIBIT 1

The Demand Schedule and Demand Curve for Pizza

Market demand curve *D* shows the quantity of pizza demanded, at various prices, by all consumers.

(a) Demand schedule

	Price per Pizza	Quantity Demanded per Week (millions)
a	$15	8
b	12	14
c	9	20
d	6	26
e	3	32

(b) Demand curve

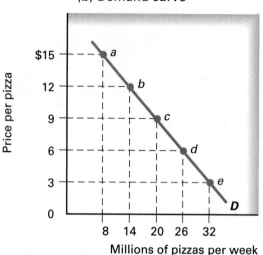

of price and quantity listed in the demand schedule in the left panel becomes a point in the right panel. Point *a*, for example, indicates that if the price is $15, consumers demand 8 million pizzas per week. These points connect to form the demand curve for pizza, labeled *D*. Note that some demand curves are straight lines and some are curved lines, but we refer to all of them as demand *curves*. The demand curve slopes downward, reflecting the *law of demand:* Price and quantity demanded are inversely related, other things constant. Assumed to be constant along the demand curve are the prices of other goods. Thus, along the demand curve for pizza, the price of pizza changes *relative to the prices of other goods*. The demand curve shows the effect of a change in the *relative price* of pizza—that is, relative to other prices, which do not change.

Take care to distinguish between *demand* and *quantity demanded*. The *demand* for pizza is not a specific quantity, but rather the *entire relation* between price and quantity demanded—represented by the demand schedule or the demand curve. An individual point on the demand curve shows the **quantity demanded** at a particular price. For example, at a price of $12, the quantity demanded is 14 million pizzas per week. If the price decreases to, say, $9, this change is shown in Exhibit 1 by *a movement along the demand curve*—in this case from point *b* to point *c*. Any movement along a demand curve reflects a *change in quantity demanded,* not a change in demand.

The law of demand applies to the millions of products sold in grocery stores, department stores, clothing stores, drugstores, music stores, bookstores, travel agencies, and restaurants, as well as through mail-order catalogues, the *Yellow Pages,* classified ads, the Internet, stock markets, real estate markets, job markets, flea markets, and all other markets. The law of demand applies even to choices that seem more personal than economic, such as whether or not to own a pet. For example, after New York City passed an anti-dog-litter law, owners had to follow their dogs around the city with scoopers, plastic bags—whatever would do the job. Because the law raised the cost, or price, of owning a dog, the quantity demanded decreased. Many owners simply abandoned their dogs, raising the number of strays in the city. The number of dogs left at animal shelters doubled. The law of demand predicts such behavior.

It is useful to distinguish between **individual demand,** which is the demand of an individual consumer, and **market demand,** which is the sum of the individual demands of all consumers in the market. In most markets, there are many consumers, sometimes millions. Unless otherwise noted, when we talk about demand, we are referring to market demand, as in Exhibit 1.

SHIFTS OF THE DEMAND CURVE

A demand curve isolates the relation between the price of a good and the quantity demanded when other factors that could affect demand remain unchanged. What are those other factors, and how do changes in them affect demand? Variables that can affect market demand are

(1) the money income of consumers, (2) prices of related goods, (3) consumer expectations, (4) the number or composition of consumers in the market, and (5) consumer tastes. Let's see how a change in each influences demand.

Changes in Consumer Income

Exhibit 2 shows market demand curve D for pizza. This demand curve assumes a given level of money income. Suppose income increases. Some consumers will then be willing and able to buy more pizza at each price, so market demand increases; the demand curve shifts to the right from D to D'. For example, at a price of $12, the amount of pizza demanded increases from 14 million to 20 million per week, as indicated by the movement from point b on demand curve D to point f on demand curve D'. In short, *an increase in demand—that is, a rightward shift of the demand curve—means that consumers are willing and able to buy more pizza at each price.*

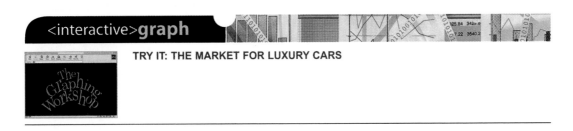

<interactive>graph

TRY IT: THE MARKET FOR LUXURY CARS

We classify goods into two broad categories, depending on how the demand for the good responds to changes in money income. The demand for a **normal good** increases as money income increases. Because pizza is a normal good, the demand curve for pizza shifts rightward when consumer income increases. Most goods are normal. In contrast, the demand for an **inferior good** actually decreases as money income increases, so the demand curve shifts leftward. Examples of inferior goods include bologna sandwiches, used furniture, used clothing, trips to the Laundromat, and bus rides. As money income increases, consumers tend to switch from consuming these inferior goods to consuming normal goods (like roast beef sandwiches, new furniture, new clothing, a washer and dryer, and automobile or plane rides).

EXHIBIT 2

An Increase in the Market Demand for Pizza

An increase in the demand for pizza is reflected by a rightward shift of the demand curve. After the increase in demand, the quantity of pizza demanded at a price of $12 increases from 14 million (point b) to 20 million (point f).

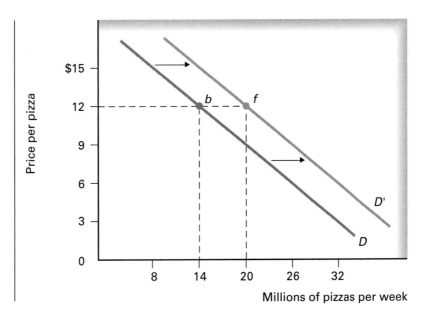

Changes in the Prices of Related Goods

As we've seen, the prices of other goods are assumed to be constant along a given demand curve. Now let's bring these other prices into play. There are various ways of trying to satisfy any particular want. Consumers choose among substitutes partly on the basis of their relative prices. For example, pizza and tacos are substitutes, though not perfect ones. Yet an increase in the price of tacos, other things constant, reduces the quantity of tacos demanded along a given demand curve and shifts the demand curve for pizza right. Two goods are **substitutes** if an increase in the price of one shifts the demand for the other rightward and, conversely, if a decrease in the price of one shifts demand for the other leftward.

Certain goods are sometimes used in combination. Pizza and Coke, milk and cookies, computer hardware and software, and airline tickets and rental cars are complements. Two goods are **complements** if a decrease in the price of one shifts the demand for the other rightward. For example, a decrease in the price of pizza shifts the demand curve for Coke rightward. But most pairs of goods selected at random are *unrelated*—for example, pizza and socks, or milk and housing.

Changes in Consumer Expectations

Another factor assumed to be constant along a given demand curve is consumer expectations about factors that influence demand, such as the future income of consumers and the future price of the good. A change in consumer expectations can shift the demand curve. For example, a consumer who learns about a future pay increase might increase demand well before that pay increase occurs. In anticipation of a steady paycheck, a college senior who lands that first job may buy a new car even before graduation. Changes in price expectations can also shift demand. For example, if you expect pizza prices to jump next week, you may buy an extra one now for the freezer, shifting the demand for pizza rightward. Or if consumers come to believe that home prices will climb next year, some will increase their demand for housing this year, shifting the demand for housing rightward. On the other hand, expectations of lower housing prices in the future will encourage some consumers to postpone purchases, thereby shifting housing demand leftward.

Changes in the Number or Composition of Consumers

As mentioned earlier, the market demand curve is the sum of the individual demand curves of all consumers in the market. If the number of consumers in the market changes, the demand curve will shift. For example, if the population grows, the demand curve for pizza will shift rightward. Even if the total population remains unchanged, demand could shift as a result of a change in composition of the population. For example, a bulge in the teenage population could shift pizza demand rightward. A baby boom would shift rightward the demand for car seats and baby food.

Changes in Consumer Tastes

Do you like anchovies on your pizza or sauerkraut on your hot dog? How about tattoos and body piercing? Is music to your ears more likely to be rock, country, heavy metal, hip-hop, reggae, jazz, new age, or classical? Choices in food, body art, music, clothing, reading, movies, TV—indeed, all consumer choices—are influenced by consumer tastes. **Tastes** are nothing more than your likes and dislikes as a consumer. What determines tastes? Who knows? Economists certainly don't, nor do they spend much time worrying about the question. They recognize, however, that tastes are important in shaping demand.

For example, although pizza is a popular food, some people just don't like it and others are lactose intolerant so they can't stomach the cheese topping. Thus, some people like pizza and some don't. In our analysis of consumer demand, *we will assume that tastes are given and are relatively stable.* Tastes are assumed to be constant along a demand curve. We know, for example, that young people usually prefer rock music, whereas older people also like other kinds of music. The music piped into shopping malls tends to be so-called easy-listening music, encouraging older, higher-income shoppers to stay longer, be at ease, and spend more, while at the same time discouraging young people from hanging out any longer than necessary to shop.

A change in the tastes for a particular good shifts the demand curve. For example, a discovery that the combination of cheese and tomato sauce on pizza promotes overall health could affect consumer tastes, shifting the demand for pizza to the right. But because a change in tastes is so difficult to isolate from other economic changes, we should be reluctant to attribute a shift of demand to a change in tastes.

Before we move on, you should remember the distinction between a **movement along a given demand curve** and a **shift of a demand curve.** A change in price, other things constant, causes a *movement along a demand curve,* changing the quantity demanded. A change in one of the determinants of demand other than price causes a *shift of a demand curve,* changing demand. So a change in price, other things constant, changes quantity demanded along a given demand curve, and a change in a determinant of demand other than the price of the good—such as money income, the prices of related goods, consumer expectations, the number or composition of consumers, or consumer tastes—shifts the demand curve.

SUPPLY

Just as demand is a relation between price and quantity demanded, supply is a relation between price and quantity supplied. **Supply** indicates how much of a good producers are *willing and able* to offer for sale per period at each possible price, other things constant. The **law of supply** states that the quantity supplied is usually directly related to its price, other things constant. Thus, the lower the price, the smaller the quantity supplied; the higher the price, the greater the quantity supplied.

The Supply Schedule and Supply Curve

Exhibit 3 presents the market *supply schedule* and market **supply curve** *S* for pizza. Both show the quantities of pizza supplied per week at various possible prices by the thousands of pizza makers in the economy. As you can see, price and quantity supplied are directly, or positively, related. Producers offer more for sale at a higher price than at a lower price, so the supply curve slopes upward.

There are two reasons producers tend to offer more for sale when the price rises. First, as the price increases, other things constant, a producer becomes more *willing* to supply the good. Prices act as signals to existing and potential suppliers about the rewards for producing

EXHIBIT 3

The Supply Schedule and Supply Curve for Pizza

Market supply curve *S* shows the quantity of pizza supplied, at various prices, by all pizza makers.

(a) Supply schedule

Price per Pizza	Quantity Supplied per Week (millions)
$15	28
12	24
9	20
6	16
3	12

(b) Supply curve

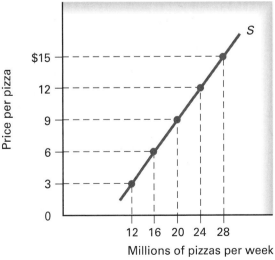

various goods. An increase in the price of pizza, with other prices constant, provides suppliers a profit incentive to shift some resources from producing other goods, for which the price is now relatively lower, and into pizza, for which the price is now relatively higher. *A higher pizza price attracts resources from lower-valued uses.*

Higher prices also increase the producer's *ability* to supply the good. The law of increasing opportunity cost, as noted in Chapter 2, states that the opportunity cost of producing more of a particular good rises as output increases—that is, the *marginal cost* of production increases as output increases. Since producers face a higher marginal cost for additional output, they must receive a higher price for that output to be *able* to increase the quantity supplied. A *higher price makes producers more able to increase quantity supplied.* As a case in point, a higher price for gasoline increases oil companies' ability to explore in less accessible areas, such as the remote jungles of the Amazon, the stormy waters of the North Sea, and the frozen tundra above the Arctic Circle. On the other hand, a decade-long slide in the price of gold means producers are no longer able to mine as much gold.

Thus, a higher price makes producers more *willing* and more *able* to increase quantity supplied. Producers are more *willing* because production of the higher-priced good is now more profitable than the alternative uses of the resources involved. Producers are more *able* because the higher price allows them to cover the higher marginal cost that typically results from a greater rate of output.

As with demand, we distinguish between *supply* and **quantity supplied.** *Supply* is the entire relation between the price and quantity supplied, as reflected by the supply schedule or supply curve. *Quantity supplied* refers to a particular amount offered for sale at a particular price, as reflected by a point on a given supply curve. We also distinguish between **individual supply,** the supply of an individual producer, and **market supply,** the sum of individual supplies of all producers in the market. Unless otherwise noted, when we talk about supply, we are referring to market supply.

SHIFTS OF THE SUPPLY CURVE

The supply curve isolates the relation between the price of a good and the quantity supplied, other things constant. Assumed constant along a supply curve are the determinants of supply other than the price of the good, including (1) the state of technology, (2) the prices of relevant resources, (3) the prices of alternative goods, (4) producer expectations, and (5) the number of producers in the market. Let's see how a change in each affects the supply curve.

Changes in Technology

Recall from Chapter 2 that the state of technology represents the economy's stock of knowledge about how to combine resources efficiently. Along a given supply curve, technology is assumed to remain unchanged. If a more efficient technology is discovered, production costs will fall; so suppliers will be more willing and more able to supply the good at each price. Consequently, supply will increase, as reflected by a rightward shift of the supply curve. For example, suppose a new high-tech oven bakes pizza in half the time. Such a breakthrough would shift the market supply curve rightward, as from *S* to *S'* in Exhibit 4, where more is supplied at each possible price. For example, if the price is $12, the amount supplied increases from 24 million to 28 million pizzas, as shown in Exhibit 4 by the movement from point *g* to point *h*. In short, *an increase in supply—that is, a rightward shift of the supply curve—means that producers are willing and able to sell more pizza at each price.*

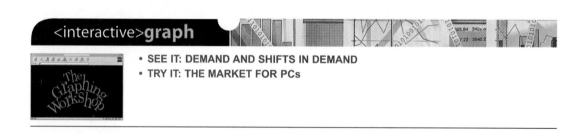

<interactive>**graph**

• SEE IT: DEMAND AND SHIFTS IN DEMAND
• TRY IT: THE MARKET FOR PCs

Changes in the Prices of Relevant Resources

Relevant resources are those employed in the production of the good in question. For example, suppose the price of mozzarella cheese falls. This reduces the cost of pizza production. Producers are therefore more willing and better able to supply pizza. The supply curve for

EXHIBIT 4 |

An Increase in the Supply of Pizza

An increase in the supply of pizza is reflected by a rightward shift of the supply curve, from *S* to *S'*. After the increase in supply, the quantity of pizza supplied at a price of $12 increases from 24 million pizzas (point *g*) to 28 million pizzas (point *h*).

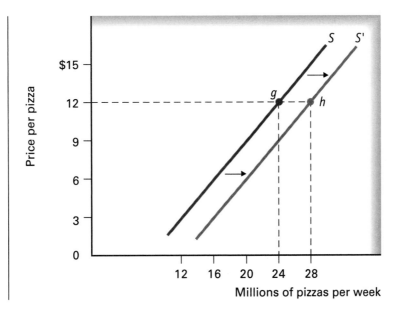

pizza shifts rightward, as shown in Exhibit 4. On the other hand, an increase in the price of a relevant resource reduces supply, meaning a shift of the supply curve leftward. For example, a higher cheese price increases the cost of making pizzas. Higher production costs decrease supply, so pizza supply shifts leftward, as from *S'* to *S* in Exhibit 4.

Changes in the Prices of Alternative Goods

Nearly all resources have alternative uses. The labor, building, machinery, ingredients, and knowledge needed to run a business could produce other products besides pizza, such as baked goods. **Alternative goods** are those that use some of the same resources employed to produce the good under consideration. For example, as the price of bread increases, so does the opportunity cost of making pizza. Some pizza makers may bake more bread and less pizza, so the supply of pizza decreases, or shifts to the left. On the other hand, a fall in the price of an alternative good, such as bread, makes pizza production relatively more attractive. As resources shift from making bread to making pizza, the supply of pizza increases, or shifts to the right.

Changes in Producer Expectations

Changes in producer expectations can change current supply. For example, a pizza maker expecting higher pizza prices in the future may begin expanding her pizzeria today, thereby shifting the supply of pizza rightward. When a good can be easily stored (crude oil, for example, can be left in the ground), expecting higher prices in the future might prompt some producers to *reduce* their current supply while awaiting the higher price. Thus, an expectation of higher prices in the future could either increase or decrease current supply, depending on the good. More generally, any change expected to affect future profitability, such as a change in business taxes, could shift the supply curve.

Changes in the Number of Producers

Since market supply sums the amounts supplied at each price by all producers, market supply depends on the number of producers in the market. If that number increases, supply will increase, shifting supply to the right. If the number of producers decreases, supply will decrease, shifting supply to the left. As an example of increased supply, the number of gourmet coffee bars more than quadrupled in the United States during the last decade (think Starbucks), shifting the supply curve of gourmet coffee to the right.

Finally, note again the distinction between a **movement along a supply curve** and a **shift of a supply curve.** A change in *price,* other things constant, causes *a movement along a supply curve,* changing the quantity supplied. A change in one of the determinants of supply other than price causes a *shift of a supply curve,* changing supply. So a change in price, other things constant, changes quantity supplied along a given supply curve, and a change in a determinant of supply other than the price of the good—such as technology, the prices of relevant resources, the prices of alternative goods, producer expectations, and the number of producers—shifts the entire supply curve.

We are now ready to put demand and supply together.

DEMAND AND SUPPLY CREATE A MARKET

Demanders and suppliers have different views of price, because demanders pay the price and suppliers receive it. Thus, a higher price is bad news for consumers but good news for producers. As the price rises, consumers reduce their quantity demanded along the demand curve and producers increase their quantity supplied along the supply curve. How is this conflict between producers and consumers resolved?

Markets

A market sorts out the conflicting price perspectives of individual participants—demanders and suppliers. A *market,* as you know from Chapter 1, includes all the arrangements used to buy and sell a particular good or service. Markets reduce **transaction costs**—the costs of time and information required for exchange. For example, suppose you are looking for a summer job. One approach might be to go from employer to employer looking for openings. But this would be time consuming and could involve running around for days. A more efficient strategy would be to pick up a copy of the local newspaper and read through the help-wanted ads or go online and look for openings. Classified ads and Web sites, which are elements of the job market, reduce the transaction costs required to bring workers and employers together.

The coordination that occurs through markets takes place not because of some central plan but because of Adam Smith's "invisible hand." For example, the auto dealers in your community tend to locate together, usually on the outskirts of town, where land is cheaper. The dealers congregate not because someone told them to or because they like one another's company but because each wants to be where customers shop for cars—that is, near other dealers. Similarly, stores group downtown and in shopping malls to be where shoppers shop. From Orlando theme parks to Broadway theaters to Las Vegas casinos, suppliers gather where demanders are. Some groups of suppliers can be quite specialized. For example, shops selling dress mannequins cluster along Austin Road in Hong Kong.

Market Equilibrium

To see how a market works, let's bring together market demand and supply. Exhibit 5 shows the market for pizza, using schedules in panel (a) and curves in panel (b). Suppose the price initially is $12. At that price, producers supply 24 million pizzas per week, but consumers demand only 14 million, resulting in an *excess quantity supplied,* or a **surplus,** of 10 million pizzas per week. This surplus and suppliers' desire to eliminate it put downward pressure on the price, as symbolized by the arrow pointing down in the graph. As the price falls, producers reduce their quantity supplied and consumers increase their quantity demanded. As long as quantity supplied exceeds quantity demanded, the surplus forces the price lower.

- SEE IT: MARKET EQUILIBRIUM
- TRY IT: THE MARKET FOR DAIRY PRODUCTS
- TRY IT: THE MARKET FOR CIGARETTES

Alternatively, suppose the price is initially $6 per pizza. You can see from Exhibit 5 that at that price, consumers demand 26 million pizzas but producers supply only 16 million, resulting in an *excess quantity demanded,* or a **shortage,** of 10 million pizzas per week. Producers quickly notice that the quantity supplied has sold out and those customers still demanding pizzas are grumbling. Frustrated consumers and profit-maximizing producers create market pres-

EXHIBIT 5

Equilibrium in the Pizza Market

Market equilibrium occurs at a price at which the quantity demanded by consumers is equal to the quantity supplied by producers. This is shown at point *c*. At prices above the equilibrium price, the quantity supplied exceeds the quantity demanded; at these prices there is a surplus, and there is a downward pressure on the price. At prices below equilibrium, quantity demanded exceeds quantity supplied; the resulting shortage puts upward pressure on the price.

(a) Market schedules

Millions of Pizzas per Week

Price per Pizza	Quantity Demanded	Quantity Supplied	Surplus or Shortage	Effect on Price
$15	8	28	Surplus of 20	Falls
12	14	24	Surplus of 10	Falls
9	20	20	Equilibrium	Remains the same
6	26	16	Shortage of 10	Rises
3	32	12	Shortage of 20	Rises

(b) Market curves

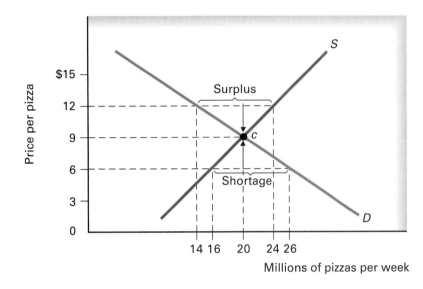

sure for a higher price, as symbolized by the arrow pointing up in the graph. As the price rises, producers increase their quantity supplied and consumers reduce their quantity demanded. The price continues to rise as long as quantity demanded exceeds quantity supplied.

Thus, a *surplus creates downward pressure on the price, and a shortage creates upward pressure.* So long as quantity demanded and quantity supplied differ, this difference forces a price change. Note that a shortage or a surplus must always be defined at a particular price. There is no such thing as a general shortage or a general surplus.

When the quantity that consumers are willing and able to buy equals the quantity that producers are willing and able to sell, that market reaches equilibrium. In **equilibrium,** the independent plans of both buyers and sellers exactly match, so market forces exert no pressure to change price or quantity. In Exhibit 5, the demand and supply curves intersect at the *equilibrium point,* identified as point *c.* The *equilibrium price* is $9 per pizza, and the *equilibrium quantity* is 20 million per week. At that price and quantity, the market *clears.* Since there is no shortage and no surplus, there is no longer any pressure for the price to change.

A market finds equilibrium through the independent actions of thousands, or even millions, of buyers and sellers. In one sense, the market is personal because each consumer and each producer makes a personal decision regarding how much to buy or sell at a given price. In another sense, the market is impersonal because it requires no conscious coordination among consumers or producers. *Impersonal market forces synchronize the personal and independent decisions of many individual buyers and sellers to achieve equilibrium price and quantity.*

CHANGES IN EQUILIBRIUM PRICE AND QUANTITY

Equilibrium is the combination of price and quantity at which the intentions of demanders and suppliers exactly match. Once a market reaches equilibrium, that price and quantity will prevail until one of the determinants of demand or supply changes. A change in any one of these determinants usually changes equilibrium price and quantity in a predictable way, as you'll see.

<interactive>video

ASK THE INSTRUCTOR: DO PRICES ADJUST MORE QUICKLY IN SOME MARKETS THAN IN OTHERS?

Shifts of the Demand Curve

In Exhibit 6, demand curve *D* and supply curve *S* intersect to yield the initial equilibrium price of $9 and the initial equilibrium quantity of 20 million 12-inch regular pizzas per week. Now suppose that one of the determinants of demand changes in a way that increases demand, shifting the demand curve to the right from *D* to *D'*. Any of the following could shift the demand for pizza rightward: (1) an increase in the money income of consumers (since pizza is a normal good); (2) an increase in the price of a substitute, such as tacos, or a decrease in the price of a complement, such as Coke; (3) a change in expectations that encourages consumers to buy more pizzas now; (4) a growth in the number of pizza consumers; or (5) a change in consumer tastes—based, for example, on a discovery that the tomato sauce on pizza has antioxidant properties that improve overall health.

After the demand curve shifts rightward to *D'* in Exhibit 6, the amount demanded at the initial price of $9 is 30 million pizzas, which exceeds the amount supplied of 20 million by 10 million pizzas. This shortage puts upward pressure on the price. As the price increases, the quantity demanded decreases along the new demand curve *D'*, and the quantity supplied increases along the existing supply curve *S* until the two quantities are equal once again. The new equilibrium price is $12, and the new equilibrium quantity is 24 million pizzas per week. Thus, given an upward-sloping supply curve, an increase in demand, meaning a rightward shift of the demand curve, increases both equilibrium price and quantity. A decrease in demand, meaning a leftward shift of the demand curve, would lower both equilibrium price and quantity. We can summarize these results as follows: *Given an upward-sloping supply curve, a rightward shift of the demand curve increases both equilibrium price and quantity and a leftward shift of the demand curve decreases both equilibrium price and quantity.*

EXHIBIT 6

Effects of an Increase in Demand

After an increase in demand shifts the demand curve from *D* to *D'*, quantity demanded exceeds quantity supplied at the old price of $9 per pizza. As the price rises, quantity supplied increases along supply curve *S*, and quantity demanded falls along demand curve *D'*. When the new equilibrium price of $12 is reached, the quantity demanded once again equals the quantity supplied. Both price and quantity are higher following the increase in demand.

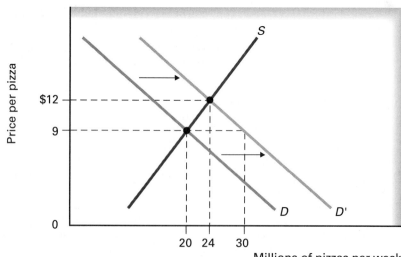

Shifts of the Supply Curve

Let's look now at the impact of shifts of the supply curve. In Exhibit 7, as before, we begin with demand curve *D* and supply curve *S* to yield the initial equilibrium price of $9 and the initial equilibrium quantity of 20 million pizzas per week. Suppose one of the determinants of supply changes, increasing supply from *S* to *S'*. Changes that could shift the supply curve rightward include (1) a technological breakthrough in pizza ovens; (2) a reduction in the price of a relevant resource, such as mozzarella cheese; (3) a decline in the price of an alternative good, such as Italian bread; (4) a change in expectations that encourages pizza makers to expand production now; or (5) an increase in the number of pizzerias.

After supply increases in Exhibit 7, the amount supplied at the initial price of $9 increases from 20 million to 30 million, so producers are willing and able to supply 10 million more pizzas than consumers demand. This surplus forces the price down. As the price falls, the quantity supplied declines along the new supply curve and the quantity demanded increases along the existing demand curve until a new equilibrium point is established. The new equilibrium price is $6, and the new equilibrium quantity is 26 million pizzas per week. The rightward shift of supply reduces the equilibrium price but increases the equilibrium quantity.

On the other hand, a decrease in supply—that is, a shift of the supply curve to the left—increases equilibrium price but decreases equilibrium quantity. Thus, *given a downward-sloping demand curve, a rightward shift of the supply curve decreases price but increases quantity, and a leftward shift increases price but decreases quantity.* An easy way to remember this is to picture the supply curve shifting along a given downward-sloping demand curve. If supply shifts to the right, price decreases but quantity increases. If supply shifts to the left, price increases but quantity decreases.

Simultaneous Shifts of Demand and Supply Curves

As long as only one curve shifts, we can say for sure what will happen to equilibrium price and quantity. If both curves shift, however, the outcome is less obvious. For example, suppose both demand and supply increase, or shift rightward, as in Exhibit 8. Note that in panel (a), demand shifts by more than supply, and in panel (b), supply shifts more than demand. In both panels, equilibrium quantity increases. The change in equilibrium price, however, depends on the shift of demand relative to the shift of supply. If the shift of demand is greater, as in panel (a), equilibrium price increases from *p* to *p'*. For example, in the last decade, the demand for housing has increased more than the supply, so both price and quantity have increased. If the shift of supply is greater, as in panel (b), equilibrium price decreases from *p* to *p"*. For example, in the last decade, the supply of personal computers has increased more than the demand, so price has decreased and quantity increased.

EXHIBIT 7

Effects of an Increase in Supply

An increase in supply is depicted as a shift to the right of the supply curve, from *S* to *S'*. At the new equilibrium, quantity is greater and price is lower than before the increase in supply.

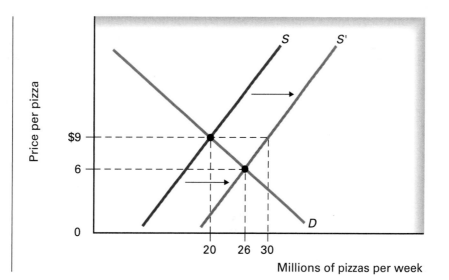

EXHIBIT 8

Indeterminate Effect of an Increase in Both Supply and Demand

When both supply and demand increase, the quantity exchanged—the equilibrium quantity—also increases. The effect on price depends on which curve shifts farther. In panel (a), the shift in demand is greater than the shift in supply; as a result, the price rises. In panel (b), the shift in supply is greater, so the price falls.

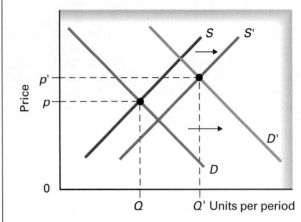

(a) Shift in demand dominates

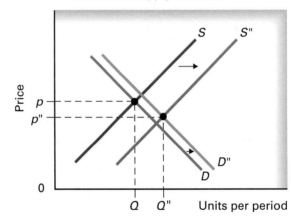

(b) Shift in supply dominates

Conversely, if both demand and supply decrease, or shift leftward, equilibrium quantity decreases; but again we cannot say what will happen to equilibrium price unless we examine relative shifts. (You can use Exhibit 8 to consider decreases in demand and supply by viewing D' and S' as the initial curves.) If the shift of demand exceeds the shift of supply, the price will fall. If the shift of supply exceeds the shift of demand, the price will rise.

If demand and supply shift in opposite directions, we can say what will happen to equilibrium price. *Equilibrium price will increase if demand increases and supply decreases; equilibrium price will decrease if demand decreases and supply increases.* Without reference to particular shifts, however, we cannot say what will happen to equilibrium quantity.

These results are no doubt confusing, but Exhibit 9 summarizes the four possible combinations of changes. For example, the results just depicted in Exhibit 8 are shown in the upper-left box of Exhibit 9. Using Exhibit 9 as a reference, please take the time right now to work through some hypothetical shifts of demand and supply to develop an intuitive understanding of the results. Then, in the following case study, evaluate changes in the market for professional basketball.

<interactive>**exercise**

READING IT RIGHT: WALL STREET JOURNAL EXERCISE

EXHIBIT 9

Effects of Changes in Both Supply and Demand

When the supply and demand curves shift in the same direction, equilibrium quantity also shifts in that direction; the effect on equilibrium price depends on which curve shifts more. If the curves shift in opposite directions, equilibrium price will move in the same direction as demand; the effect on equilibrium quantity depends on which curve shifts more.

	Change in demand	
	Demand increases	Demand decreases
Supply increases	Equilibrium price change is indeterminate. Equilibrium quantity increases.	Equilibrium price falls. Equilibrium quantity change is indeterminate.
Supply decreases	Equilibrium price rises. Equilibrium quantity change is indeterminate.	Equilibrium price change is indeterminate. Equilibrium quantity decreases.

(Change in supply)

CASE**STUDY** | The Market for Professional Basketball

● *The World of Business*

Toward the end of the 1970s, the National Basketball Association (NBA) seemed on the verge of collapse. Game attendance had sunk to little more than half of capacity. Some teams were nearly bankrupt. Championship games didn't even merit prime-time television coverage.

In the 1980s, however, three superstars turned things around. Michael Jordan, Larry Bird, and Magic Johnson brought new life to the sagging league and attracted millions of new fans. Now a new generation of stars, including Allen Iverson, Vince Carter, and Kobe Bryant, continue to fuel interest in the league. Since 1980, game attendance has doubled, the number of teams has increased from 22 to 29 (with new franchises selling for record amounts), and, most importantly, the value of television rights jumped *35-fold* from $76 million in 1978–1982 to $2.6 billion in 1998–2002. Celebrities such as Jack Nicholson and Spike Lee have become courtside fixtures (Lee's seat costs $1,350 per game). Basketball's popularity has also increased around the world. The NBA formed global marketing alliances with Coca-Cola, McDonald's, and IBM; and the 2001 NBA final games topped the weekly TV ratings and were televised around the world.

Players are the key resource in the production of NBA games. Exhibit 10 shows the market for NBA players, with demand and supply in 1980 as D_{1980} and S_{1980}, yielding an average pay that year of $170,000, or $0.17 million, for the 300 or so players in the league. During the next two decades, the pool of available talent expanded somewhat, shifting the supply curve a bit rightward from S_{1980} to S_{2001} (almost by definition, the supply of the top few hundred players in the world is limited). But the demand for talented players exploded from D_{1980} to D_{2001}. The greater demand, with supply relatively fixed, boosted average NBA pay to $3.2 million in 2001 for the 400 or so players in the league.

Such pay attracts younger and younger players, because top players who remain in school risk a career-ending injury. For example, Kevin Garnett, who entered the NBA in 1995 right out of high school, signed a seven-year contract in 1997 worth $121 million. The top two picks in the 2001 NBA draft of players had just graduated from high school. The high pay earned by top players stems from the scarcity of those with such talent, combined with a large and growing demand for that talent. But rare talent alone is not enough. For example, top rodeo riders, top bowlers, and top women basketball players also possess rare talent, but the demand for their talent is not great enough to support pay anywhere close to NBA levels. NBA players are now the highest-paid team professionals in the world—earning 60 percent more than pro baseball's

EXHIBIT 10|

Change in the Market for NBA Players Between 1980 and 2001

Because the supply of the top few hundred basketball players in the world is relatively fixed by definition, the big jump in the demand for such talented players caused average league pay to explode. Between 1980 and 2001 average pay increased from $170,000 to $3,200,000. Because the number of NBA teams increased, the number of players in the league grew from about 300 to 400.

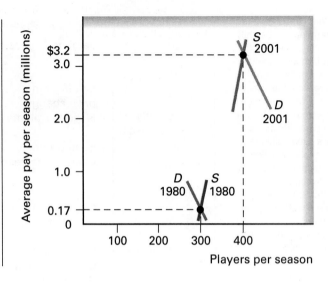

average and at least double that for pro football and pro hockey. Both demand *and* supply determine average pay.

<interactive>exercise

eACTIVITY: THE MARKET FOR PROFESSIONAL BASKETBALL

Sources: Stefan Fatsis, "Allen Iverson Has Recharged the NBA, But Can He Pitch to the Mainstream?" *Wall Street Journal,* 8 June 2001; Mike Wise, "High School Star Taken No.1 in N.B.A. Draft," *New York Times,* 28 June 2001; Frazier Moore, "NBC: Slam Dunk," *Hartford Courant,* 20 June 2001; U.S. Census Bureau, *Statistical Abstract of the United States: 2000,* http://www.census.gov/prod/www/statistical-abstract-us.html; and http://sportsillustrated.cnn.com/.

DISEQUILIBRIUM PRICES

A surplus exerts downward pressure on the price, and a shortage exerts upward pressure. Markets, however, do not always reach equilibrium quickly. During the time required for adjustment, the market is said to be in disequilibrium. **Disequilibrium** is usually temporary as the market gropes for equilibrium. Sometimes, often as a result of government intervention in markets, disequilibrium can last a while, as we will see next.

Price Floors

Sometimes public officials set prices above their equilibrium values. For example, the federal government often regulates the prices of agricultural commodities in an attempt to ensure farmers a higher and more stable income than they would otherwise earn. To achieve higher prices, the federal government sets a **price floor,** or a *minimum* selling price that is above the equilibrium price. Panel (a) of Exhibit 11 shows the effect of a $2.50 per gallon price floor for milk. At that price, farmers supply 24 million gallons per week, but consumers demand only 14 million gallons. Thus, the price floor results in a surplus of 10 million gallons. This surplus milk will pile up on store shelves, eventually souring. So, as part of the price support program, the government usually agrees to buy the surplus milk to take it off the market. The federal government, in fact, has spent billions buying and storing surplus agricultural products.

EXHIBIT 11

Effects of a Price Floor and a Price Ceiling

If a price floor is established above the equilibrium price, a permanent surplus results. A price floor established at or below the equilibrium price has no effect. If a price ceiling is established below the equilibrium price, a permanent shortage results. A price ceiling established at or above the equilibrium price has no effect.

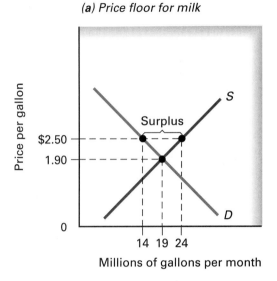

(a) Price floor for milk

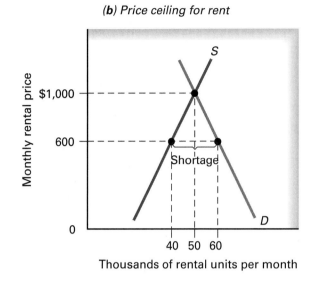

(b) Price ceiling for rent

Price Ceilings

Sometimes public officials try to keep prices below their equilibrium levels by establishing a **price ceiling,** or a *maximum* selling price. For example, concern about the rising cost of rental housing in some cities prompted legislation to impose rent ceilings. Panel (b) of Exhibit 11 depicts the demand and supply for rental housing in a hypothetical city. The vertical axis shows the monthly rent, and the horizontal axis shows the quantity of rental units. The equilibrium, or market-clearing, rent is $1,000 per month, and the equilibrium quantity is 50,000 housing units.

Suppose the government sets a maximum rent of $600 per month. At that ceiling price, 60,000 rental units are demanded, but only 40,000 supplied, resulting in a housing shortage of 20,000 units. Because of the price ceiling, the rental price no longer rations housing to those who value it the most. Other devices emerge to ration housing, such as waiting lists, personal connections, and the willingness to make under-the-table payments, such as "key fees," "finder's fees," high security deposits, and the like.

To have an impact, a price floor must be set above the equilibrium price and a price ceiling must be set below the equilibrium price. Effective price floors and ceilings distort markets. Floor prices above equilibrium prices create surpluses, and ceiling prices below equilibrium prices create shortages. Various nonprice allocation devices emerge to cope with the disequilibrium resulting from the market interference.

Government intervention in the market is not the only source of disequilibrium. Sometimes, when new products are introduced or when demand changes suddenly, it takes a while to achieve equilibrium. For example, popular toys, best-selling books, and chart-busting CDs often sell out and are temporarily unavailable. On the other hand, some new products attract few customers and pile up unsold on store shelves, awaiting a "clearance sale." Disequilibrium is discussed in the following case study.

<interactive>**exercise**

- **ECONDEBATE ONLINE: DOES AN INCREASE IN THE MINIMUM WAGE RESULT IN A HIGHER UNEMPLOYMENT RATE?**
- **ECONDEBATE ONLINE: HAS DEREGULATION CAUSED THE ENERGY SHORTAGE IN CALIFORNIA?**

● *The World of Business*

U.S. toy sales exceeded $25 billion a year in 2001, but the business is not much fun for toy makers. Most toys don't make it from one season to the next, turning out to be costly duds. A few have staying power, like G.I. Joe, who could retire after more than 30 years of military service; Barbie, who is pushing 40; and the Wiffle Ball, still a hit after 40 years.

Most store buyers must order in February for Christmas delivery. Can you imagine the uncertainty of this market? Who, for example, could have anticipated the phenomenal success of Tickle Me Elmo, Beanie Babies, Teletubbies, Furbies, Pokémon, or PlayStation 2? A few years ago, the Mighty Morphin Power Rangers were hot. Within a year, the manufacturer increased production tenfold, with 11 new factories churning out nearly $1 billion in Rangers. Still, at a selling price of $13, quantity demanded exceeded quantity supplied.

Why don't toy manufacturers simply let the price find equilibrium? Suppose, for example, that the market-clearing price for Power Rangers was $26, twice the actual price. Consumers may have resented paying so much for such a small toy. Toy manufacturers usually make a variety of toys and may not want to be viewed as "profiteering price gougers." After all, a firm's reputation is important, and surveys indicate that consumers consider some price hikes as unfair. Suppliers who hope to retain customers over the long haul may want to avoid appearing greedy. That may be why Home Depot doesn't raise the price of snow shovels after the first winter storm, why Wal-Mart doesn't jack up prices of air conditioners during the dog days of summer, and why DaimlerChrysler prefers long waiting lists to raising prices still higher for its new sports utility vehicles.

To sum up, uncertainty abounds in the market for new products. Suppliers can only guess what the demand will be, so they must feel their way in deciding what price to charge and how much to produce. Eventually, markets do achieve equilibrium. For example, DaimlerChrysler doubled production of utility vehicles, which erased the shortage. But because achieving equilibrium takes time, some markets are temporarily in disequilibrium.

<interactive>**exercise**

eACTIVITY: THE TOY BUSINESS IS NOT CHILD'S PLAY

Sources: Raymond Gorman and James Kehr, "Fairness as a Constraint on Profit Seeking," *American Economic Review,* 82 (March 1992): pp. 355–58; Joe Pereira, "Hasbro Trims 5% of Work Force," *Wall Street Journal,* 13 October 2000; "Retailers Predict Hot Toys," Associated Press, 17 October 2000; the Toy Industry Association Web site http://www.toy-tma.com/index.html; and Pokémon World http://www.pokemon.com/.

CONCLUSION

Demand and supply are the foundation of a market economy. Although a market usually involves the interaction of many buyers and sellers, few markets are consciously designed. Just as the law of gravity works whether or not we understand Newton's principles, market forces operate whether or not participants understand demand and supply. These forces arise naturally, much the way car dealers cluster on the outskirts of town.

Markets have their critics. Some observers are troubled, for example, that Shaquille O'Neal's annual salary could fund a thousand new schoolteachers, or that U.S. consumers spend billions each year on pet food when people in the world are starving. On your next trip to the supermarket, notice how much shelf space goes to pet products—often an entire aisle. Petsmart, a chain store, sells over 12,000 pet-related items. Veterinarians offer cancer treatment, cataract removal, and root canals for pets. Kidney dialysis for a pet can cost $55,000 per year. In the next chapter, we'll discuss some limitations of market economies and introduce government.

endofchaptermaterial

- **Summary**
- **Questions for Review**
- **Problems and Exercises**
- **Experiential Exercises**

- **Wall Street Journal Exercise**
- **Graphing Workshop: Apply It Exercises**

Take the Post-Test to assess your overall understanding of the key ideas in this chapter. The Post-Test provides a comprehensive selection of exam-style questions addressing the main topics and concepts of the chapter. At the completion of each Post-Test, you will receive a score and instructive feedback on how you answered each question, and a direct link to the part of the chapter addressed in the question. Take the Post-Test as often as you need to—a record of your progress for each attempt is kept for you to revisit and gauge your improvement. And each Post-Test is randomly generated, so every attempt is new.

Post-Test

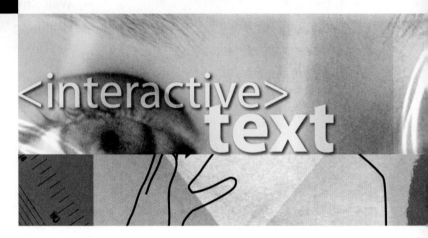

Economic Decision Makers

If we live in the age of specialization, then why haven't specialists taken over all production—that is, why do most of us still do our own laundry and perform dozens of other tasks for ourselves? In what sense has production moved from the household to the firm and then back to the household? If the "invisible hand" of competitive markets is such an efficient allocator of resources, why does government get into the act? Answers to these and other questions are addressed in this chapter, which examines the four economic decision makers: households, firms, governments, and the rest of the world.

To develop a better feel for how the economy works, you must become more acquainted with these key players in the economy. You already know more about them than you may realize. You grew up in a household. You have dealt with firms all your life, from Subway to Sony. You know a lot about governments, from taxes to public schools. And you have a growing awareness of the rest of the world, from foreign travel to the World Wide Web.

In this chapter, you will draw on your abundant personal experience with economic decision makers to consider their structure, organization, and objectives. Topics discussed in this chapter include:

- Evolution of the household
- Evolution of the firm
- Household production versus firm production

- Government spending and taxation
- International trade and finance
- Trade restrictions

<interactive>exercise

ECONDEBATE ONLINE: GOVERNMENT AND THE ECONOMY

<interactive>update

- **ECONDATA ONLINE: GOVERNMENT AND THE ECONOMY**
- **ECONLINKS ONLINE: ECONOMICS WEB LINKS**
- **ECONNEWS ONLINE: GOVERNMENT AND THE ECONOMY**

THE HOUSEHOLD

Households play the starring role in a market economy. Their demand for goods and services determines what gets produced. And their supplies of labor, capital, land, and entrepreneurial ability produce that output. As demanders of goods and services and suppliers of resources, households make all kinds of choices, such as what to buy, how much to save, where to live, and where to work. Although a household usually consists of several individuals, we will view each household as acting like a single decision maker.

The Evolution of the Household

In earlier times, when the economy was primarily agricultural, a farm household was largely self-sufficient. Individual family members specialized in specific farm tasks—making furniture, sewing clothes, tending livestock, and so on. These early households produced what they consumed and consumed what they produced. With the introduction of new seed varieties, fertilizers, and laborsaving machinery, farm productivity increased sharply. Fewer farmers were needed to grow enough food to feed a nation. Simultaneously, the growth of urban factories increased the demand for factory labor. As a result, many people moved from farms to cities, where they became far less self-sufficient.

Households have evolved in other ways. For example, in 1950, only about 15 percent of married women with children under 18 years old were in the labor force. Since then, higher levels of education among married women and a growing demand for labor increased women's earnings, which raised their opportunity cost of working in the home. This rising opportunity cost likely contributed to growing labor force participation.[1] Today more than half of married women with young children are in the labor force.

The rise of two-earner households has affected the family as an economic unit. Less production occurs in the home, and more goods and services are demanded from the market. For example, child-care services and fast-food restaurants have displaced some household production. Most people eat at least one meal a day away from home. The rise in two-earner families has reduced the advantages of specialization within the household—a central feature of the farm family, where each family member specialized in particular tasks. Nonetheless, some production still occurs in the home, as we'll explore later.

Households Maximize Utility

There are more than 100 million U.S. households. All those who live under one roof are considered part of the same household. What exactly do households attempt to accomplish in making decisions? Economists assume that people attempt to maximize their level of satisfaction, sense of well-being, or overall welfare. For the sake of brevity, we can say that households attempt to maximize **utility.** Households, like other economic decision makers, are viewed as rational, meaning that they try to act in their best interests and do not deliberately make choices that are likely to make them worse off. Utility maximization depends on each household's subjective goals, not on some objective standard. For example, some households maintain neat homes with well-groomed lawns; others pay little attention to their homes and use their lawns as junkyards.

---

[1]Professor Claudia Goldin, an economic historian from Harvard, argues that an increase in wages, the growth of white-collar jobs, and the decline in the average workweek increased the percentage of women in the workforce. See Goldin's *Understanding the Gender Gap: An Economic History of American Women* (New York: Oxford University Press, 1990).

Chapter 4 Economic Decision Makers

55

Households as Resource Suppliers

Households use their limited resources—labor, capital, land, and entrepreneurial ability—in an attempt to satisfy their unlimited wants. They can use these resources to produce goods and services in their homes. For example, they can prepare meals, mow the lawn, and fix that leaky faucet. They can also sell these resources in the resource market and use the income to buy goods and services in the product market. The most valuable resource sold by most households is labor.

Panel (a) of Exhibit 1 shows the sources of personal income received by U.S. households in 2000, when personal income totaled about $8 trillion. As you can see, 64 percent, or nearly two-thirds, of personal income came from wages, salaries, and other labor income. A distant second was interest earnings, at 13 percent of personal income, followed by proprietors' income and transfer payments (to be discussed shortly), tied at 8 percent. *Proprietors* are people who work for themselves rather than for employers; farmers, plumbers, and doctors are often self-employed. Only 5 percent of personal income comes from dividends, and only 2 percent comes from rental income. *Nearly two-thirds of personal income in the United States comes from labor earnings rather than from the ownership of other resources such as capital or land.*

Because of a poor education, disability, discrimination, time demands of caring for small children, or bad luck, some households have few resources that are valued in the market. Society has made the political decision that individuals in such circumstances should receive short-term public assistance. Consequently, the government gives some households **transfer payments,** which are outright grants. *Cash transfers* are monetary payments, such as welfare benefits, Social Security, unemployment compensation, and disability benefits. *In-kind* transfers provide for specific goods and services, such as food stamps, Medicare, and Medicaid.

Households as Demanders of Goods and Services

What happens to personal income once it comes into the household? Most goes to personal consumption, which sorts into three broad spending categories: (1) *durable goods*—that is, goods expected to last three or more years—such as automobiles and refrigerators; (2) *nondurable goods,* such as food, clothing, and gasoline; and (3) *services,* such as haircuts, plane trips, and medical care. As you can see from panel (b) of Exhibit 1, durable goods in 2000 made up 10 percent of U.S. personal income; nondurables, 24 percent; and services, 47 percent. Taxes

EXHIBIT 1

Where U.S. Personal Income Comes From and Where It Goes

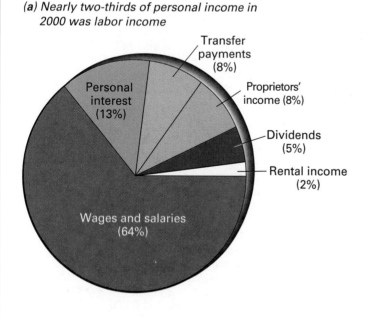

(a) *Nearly two-thirds of personal income in 2000 was labor income*

Transfer payments (8%)
Personal interest (13%)
Proprietors' income (8%)
Dividends (5%)
Rental income (2%)
Wages and salaries (64%)

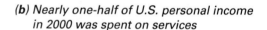
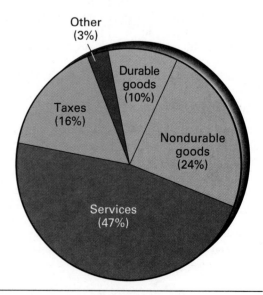

(b) *Nearly one-half of U.S. personal income in 2000 was spent on services*

Other (3%)
Durable goods (10%)
Taxes (16%)
Nondurable goods (24%)
Services (47%)

Source: Based on figures from the *Economic Report of the President*, January 2001, Tables B-1 and B-30. For the latest figures, go to http://w3.access.gpo.gov/eop/.

accounted for 16 percent, and all other categories, including savings, made up 3 percent. So nearly half of all personal income was spent on services—the fastest growing sector, since many services, such as child care and meals, are shifting from home production to market production.

THE FIRM

Members of households once built their own homes, made their own clothes and furniture, grew their own food, and amused themselves. Over time, however, the efficiency arising from comparative advantage resulted in a greater specialization among resource suppliers. In this section, we take a look at firms, beginning with their evolution.

The Evolution of the Firm

Specialization and comparative advantage explain why households are no longer self-sufficient. But why is a firm the natural result? For example, rather than make a woolen sweater from scratch, couldn't a consumer take advantage of specialization by negotiating with someone who produced the wool, another who spun the wool into yarn, and a third who knit the yarn into a sweater? Here's the problem with that model: If the consumer had to visit each of these specialists and strike an agreement, the resulting *transaction costs* could easily erase the gains from specialization. Instead of visiting and bargaining with each specialist, the consumer can pay someone to do the bargaining—an entrepreneur, who hires all the resources necessary to make the sweater. *An entrepreneur, by contracting for the construction of many sweaters rather than just one, is able to reduce the transaction costs per sweater.*

For about 200 years, profit-seeking entrepreneurs relied on "putting out" raw material, like wool and cotton, to rural households that turned it into finished products, like woolen goods made from yarn. The system developed in the British Isles, where workers' cottages served as tiny factories. This approach, which came to be known as the *cottage industry system,* still exists in some parts of the world. You might think of this system as halfway between household self-sufficiency and the modern firm.

As the British economy expanded in the 18th century, entrepreneurs began organizing the various stages of production under one roof. Technological developments, such as waterpower and later steam power, increased the productivity of each worker and contributed to the shift of employment from rural areas to urban factories. *Work, therefore, became organized in large, centrally powered factories that (1) promoted a more efficient division of labor, (2) allowed for the direct supervision of production, (3) reduced transportation costs, and (4) facilitated the use of machines far bigger than anything that had been used in the home.* The development of large-scale factory production, known as the **Industrial Revolution,** began in Great Britain around 1750 and spread to the rest of Europe, North America, and Australia.

Production, then, evolved from self-sufficient rural households to the cottage industry system, where specialized production occurred in the household, to the current system of handling most production under one roof. Today, entrepreneurs combine resources in firms such as factories, mills, offices, stores, and restaurants. **Firms** are economic units formed by profit-seeking entrepreneurs who combine labor, capital, and land to produce goods and services. Just as we assume that households attempt to maximize utility, we assume that firms attempt to *maximize profit.* Profit, the entrepreneur's reward, equals revenue minus the cost of production.

Why Does Household Production Still Exist?

Why are some activities, such as cooking and cleaning, still undertaken primarily by households, not by firms? Why hasn't all production shifted to firms? *If a household's opportunity cost of performing a task is below the market price for the task, then the household usually performs that task.* Those with a lower opportunity cost of time will do more for themselves. For example, janitors typically mow their own lawns; physicians do not. Let's look at some reasons for household production.

No Skills or Specialized Resources Are Required. Some activities require so few skills or specialized resources that householders find it cheaper to do the jobs themselves. Sweeping the floor requires only a broom and time so is usually performed by household members. Sanding a wooden floor, however, involves costly machinery and special skills, so this service is usually purchased in the market. Similarly, although you wouldn't hire someone to brush your teeth, dental work is another matter. *Households usually perform tasks that demand neither special skills nor specialized machinery.*

Household Production Avoids Taxes. Governments tax income, sales, and other market transactions. Suppose you are trying to decide whether to paint your home or hire a painter. If the income tax rate is one-third, a painter who requires $2,000 net after taxes to do the job must charge you \$3,000 to net \$2,000 after paying \$1,000 in taxes. And you must earn \$4,500 before taxes to have \$3,000 after taxes to pay the painter. Thus, you must earn \$4,500 so that the painter can net \$2,000 after taxes. If you paint the house yourself, no taxes are collected. *The tax-free nature of do-it-yourself activity favors household production over market purchases.*

Household Production Reduces Transaction Costs. Getting estimates, hiring a contractor, negotiating terms, and monitoring job performance all take time and require information. Doing the job yourself reduces these *transaction costs.* Household production also allows for more personal control over the final product than is usually available through the market. For example, some people prefer home-cooked meals to restaurant food, because home-cooked meals can be tailored to individual tastes.

Technological Advances Increase Household Productivity. Technological breakthroughs are not confined to market production. Vacuum cleaners, clothes washers and dryers, dishwashers, microwave ovens, and other modern appliances reduce the time and often the skill required to perform household tasks. Also, new technologies such as VCRs, DVD/CD players, cable TV, and computer games produce home entertainment. Indeed, microchip-based technologies have shifted some production from the firm back to the household, as discussed in the following case study.

CASESTUDY | The Electronic Cottage

● *The Information Economy*

The Industrial Revolution shifted production from rural cottages to large urban factories. But the **Information Revolution** spawned by the invention of the microchip is decentralizing the acquisition, analysis, and transmission of information. These days, someone who claims to work at a home office is usually referring not to a corporate headquarters but to a spare bedroom. According to a recent survey, in the last decade, the number of telecommuters increased from 4 million to 24 million. Increasing connectivity through PCs and the Internet is pushing the trend along with worsening traffic in major cities. Nearly half the white-collar workforce at AT&T works at home at least part of the time.

From home, people can write a document with coworkers scattered throughout the world and then discuss the project online in real time or have a videoconference (McDonald's saves millions in travel costs by videoconferencing). An entire industry has sprung up to serve those who work at home, with magazines, newsletters, Web pages, even national conferences. Software allows thousands of employees to share electronic files. When Accenture moved its headquarters from Boston to a suburb, the company got rid of 120 tons of paper, replacing it with a huge online database accessible anytime from anywhere in the world.

In fact, an office need not even be in a specific place. With chip-based technology, some people now work in a *virtual office,* which has no permanent location. With cellular phones and other handheld devices people can conduct business on the road—literally, "deals on wheels." Accountants at Ernst & Young spend most of their time in the field. When returning to company headquarters, they call a few hours ahead to reserve an office. Some companies have no particular location. During its first two years, Valent Software's employees were sprinkled across the country (the chief executive in Massachusetts, the president in Utah, some engineers in Ohio, and the rest elsewhere).

Chip technology is decentralizing the world of work, shifting it from a central place either back to the household or to no place in particular. More generally, electronic commerce has reduced the transaction costs of making a product, whether it's a market report authored jointly by researchers from around the world or a new computer system assembled from parts ordered over the Internet.

<interactive>**exercise**

• eACTIVITY: THE ELECTRONIC COTTAGE
• READING IT RIGHT: WALL STREET JOURNAL EXERCISE

Sources: Jonathan Glater, "Telecommuting's Big Experiment," *New York Times,* 9 May 2001; Scott Rice, "The Online Commute," *New York Times,* 2 September 2000; and Dagmar Aalund, "Some Rules for Managing Your Home Office," *Wall Street Journal,* 1 June 2001. For a discussion of the virtual office, go to http://www.office.com/.

Types of Firms

There are about 25 million for-profit businesses in the United States. Two-thirds of these are small retail businesses, small service operations, part-time home-based businesses, and small farms. Each year more than a million new businesses start up and almost as many fail. Entrepreneurs organize a firm in one of three ways: as a sole proprietorship, as a partnership, or as a corporation.

Sole Proprietorships. The simplest form of business organization is the **sole proprietorship,** a single-owner firm. Examples are self-employed plumbers, farmers, and dentists. To organize a sole proprietorship, the proprietor simply opens for business by, for example, taking out a classified ad announcing availability for plumbing, or whatever. The owner is in complete control. But he or she faces *unlimited liability* and could lose everything, including a home and other assets, as a result of debts or claims against the business. Also, since the sole proprietor has no partners or other financial backers, raising enough money to get the business going can be challenging. One final disadvantage is that a sole proprietorship usually goes out of business when the the proprietor dies. Still, a sole proprietorship is the most common type of business, accounting most recently for 73 percent of all U.S. businesses. Nonetheless, because this type of firm is typically small, proprietorships generate a tiny portion of all U.S. business sales—only 5 percent.

Partnerships. A more complicated form of business organization is the **partnership,** which involves two or more individuals who agree to contribute resources to the business in return for a share of the profit or loss. Law, accounting, and medical partnerships typify this business form. Partners have strength in numbers and often find it easier than sole proprietors to raise sufficient funds to get the business going. But the partners may not always agree. Also, each partner usually faces unlimited liability for any debts or claims against the partnership, so one partner could lose everything because of another's carelessness. Finally, the death or departure of one partner can disrupt the firm's continuity and prompt a complete reorganization. The partnership is the least common form of U.S. business, making up only 7 percent of all firms and 7 percent of all business sales.

Corporations. By far the most influential form of business organization is the **corporation.** A corporation is a legal entity established through articles of incorporation. The owners of a corporation are issued shares of stock entitling them to corporate profits in proportion to their stock ownership. A major advantage of the corporate form is that many investors—hundreds, thousands, even millions—can pool their money, so incorporating represents the easiest way to amass large sums of money to finance the firm. Also, stockholders have *limited liability,* meaning their liability for any loss is limited to the value of their stock. A final advantage of this form of organization is that the corporation has a life apart from those of its owners. The corporation continues to exist even if ownership changes hands, and it can be taxed and sued as if it were a person.

The corporate form has some disadvantages as well. A stockholder's ability to influence corporate policy is limited to voting for a board of directors, which oversees the operation of the firm. Each share of stock usually carries with it one vote; the typical stockholder of a large corporation owns only a tiny fraction of the shares and thus has little say. Whereas the income from sole proprietorships and partnerships is taxed only once, corporate income is taxed twice: first as corporate profits and second as stockholder income, either as corporate dividends or as realized capital gains. A *realized capital gain* is any increase in the market value of a share that occurs between the time the share is purchased and the time it is sold.

A hybrid type of corporation has evolved to take advantage of the limited liability feature of the corporate structure while reducing the impact of double taxation. The *S corporation* provides owners with limited liability, but profits are taxed only once—as income on each shareholder's personal income tax return. To qualify as an S corporation, a firm must have no more than 75 stockholders and must have no foreign or corporate stockholders.

Corporations make up only 20 percent of all U.S. businesses, but because they tend to be much larger than the other two business forms, they account for 88 percent of all business sales. Exhibit 2 shows, by type of U.S. firm, the percentage of firms and the percentage of total sales. *The sole proprietorship is the most important form in terms of total number of firms, but the corporation is the most important in terms of total sales.*

Nonprofit Institutions

To this point we have considered firms that maximize profit. Some institutions, such as museums, ballet companies, nonprofit hospitals, the Red Cross, the Salvation Army, churches, synagogues, mosques, and perhaps the college you attend, are private organizations that do not

EXHIBIT 2

Number and Sales of Each Type of Firm

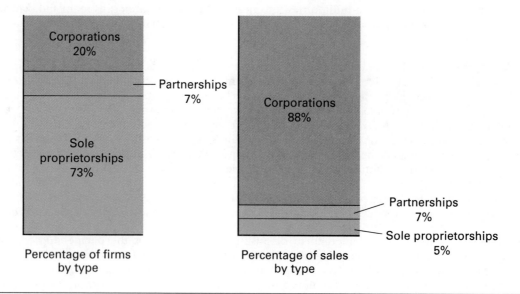

Corporations
20%

Partnerships
7%

Sole
proprietorships
73%

Corporations
88%

Partnerships
7%

Sole proprietorships
5%

Percentage of firms
by type

Percentage of sales
by type

Source: U.S. Census Bureau, *Statistical Abstract of the United States: 2001,* http://www.census.gov/prod/statistical-abstract-us.html.

have profit as an explicit objective. Yet even nonprofit institutions must somehow pay for the resources they employ. Revenue sources typically include some combination of voluntary contributions and service charges, such as college tuition and hospital bills. Although there are millions of nonprofit institutions, when we use the term *firms* in this book, we will be referring to for-profit firms.

THE GOVERNMENT

You might think that production by firms and households could satisfy all consumer demands. Why must yet another economic decision maker get into the act?

<interactive>video

CNN VIDEO: "A MATTER OF PRIORITIES"

The Role of Government

Sometimes the unrestrained operation of markets yields undesirable results. Too many of some goods and too few of other goods may be produced. In this section, we discuss the sources of **market failure** and how society's overall welfare could at times be improved through government intervention.

Establishing and Enforcing the Rules of the Game. Market efficiency depends on people like you using your resources to maximize your utility. But what if you were repeatedly robbed of your paycheck on your way home from work? Or what if, after you worked two weeks in a new job, your employer called you a sucker and said you wouldn't get paid? Why bother working? The system of private markets would break down if you could not safeguard your private property or if you could not enforce contracts. Governments play a role in *safeguarding private property* through police protection and in *enforcing contracts* through a judicial system. More generally, governments try to make sure that market participants play fairly and abide by the "rules of the game." These rules are established through laws and through the customs and conventions of the marketplace.

Promoting Competition. Although the "invisible hand" of competition usually promotes an efficient allocation of resources, some firms try to avoid competition through *collusion,* which is an agreement among firms to divide the market or to fix prices. Or an individual firm may try to eliminate the competition by using unfair business practices. For example, to drive out local competitors, a large firm may temporarily sell at a price below its cost. *Government antitrust laws try to promote competition by prohibiting collusion and other anticompetitive practices.*

Regulating Natural Monopolies. Competition usually keeps the product price lower than it is when the product is sold by a **monopoly,** a sole supplier to the market. In rare instances, however, a monopoly can produce and sell the product for less than could several competing firms. For example, electricity is delivered more efficiently by a single firm that wires the community than by competing firms stringing their own wires. When it is cheaper for one firm to serve the market than for two or more firms to do so, that firm is called a **natural monopoly.** Since a natural monopoly faces no competition, it maximizes profit by charging a higher price than is optimal from society's point of view. Therefore, the government usually regulates the natural monopoly, forcing it to lower its price.

Providing Public Goods. So far in this book, we have been talking about private goods, which have two important features. First, private goods are rival in consumption, meaning that the amount consumed by one person is unavailable for others to consume. For example, when you and some friends share a pizza, each slice they eat is one less available for you. Second, the supplier of a private good can easily exclude those who fail to pay. Only paying customers get pizza. Thus, private goods are said to be *exclusive.* In contrast, **public goods,** such as reducing terrorism, providing national defense, and administering a system of justice, are *nonrival* in consumption. One person's benefit from the good does not diminish the amount available to others. What's more, once produced, public goods are available to all. Suppliers cannot easily prevent consumption by those who fail to pay. For example, reducing terrorism is *nonexclusive.* It benefits all in the community, regardless of who pays for it and who doesn't. Because public goods are *nonrival* and *nonexclusive,* private firms cannot sell them profitably. The government, however, has the authority to collect taxes for public goods.

Dealing with Externalities. Market prices reflect the *private* costs and benefits of producers and consumers. But sometimes production or consumption imposes costs or benefits on third parties—on those who are neither suppliers nor demanders in a market transaction. For example, a paper mill fouls the air breathed by nearby residents, but the price of paper, as determined in the private market, fails to reflect such costs. Since these pollution costs are outside, or *external* to, the market activity, they are called *externalities.* An **externality** is a cost or a benefit that falls on a third party. A *negative externality* imposes an external cost, such as factory pollution or auto emissions. A *positive externality* confers an external benefit, such as driving carefully or beautifying your property.

Because market prices do not reflect externalities, governments often use taxes, subsidies, and regulations to discourage negative externalities and encourage positive externalities. For example, because education generates positive externalities (educated people can read road signs and are less likely to resort to violent crime for income), governments try to encourage education with free public schools, subsidized higher education, and requirements to stay in school until a minimum age is reached.

A More Equal Distribution of Income. As mentioned earlier, some people, because of poor education, mental or physical disabilities, or perhaps the need to care for small children, may be unable to support themselves and their families. Since resource markets do not guarantee even a minimum level of income, transfer payments reflect society's attempt to provide a basic standard of living to all households. Nearly all citizens agree that government should redistribute income to the poor (note the normative nature of this statement). Differences of opinion arise in deciding just how much should be redistributed, what form it should take, who should receive benefits, and how long benefits should continue.

Full Employment, Price Stability, and Economic Growth. Perhaps the most important responsibility of government is fostering a healthy economy, which benefits just about everyone. The government—through its ability to tax, to spend, and to control the money supply—attempts to promote full employment, price stability, and an adequate rate of growth in the economy. Pursuing these objectives through taxing and spending is called **fiscal policy;** pursuing them through regulating the money supply is called **monetary policy.** Macroeconomics examines both policies.

NETBOOKMARK: THE ANNUAL ECONOMIC REPORT OF THE PRESIDENT

Government's Structure and Objectives

The United States has a *federal system* of government, meaning that responsibilities are shared across levels of government. State governments grant some powers to local governments and surrender some powers to the national, or federal, government. As the system has evolved, the federal government has assumed primary responsibility for national security and the stability of the economy. State governments fund public higher education, prisons and, with aid from the federal government, highways and welfare. Local governments fund primary and secondary education, plus police and fire protection. Here are some distinguishing features of government.

Difficulty in Defining Government Objectives. We assume that households try to maximize utility and firms try to maximize profit, but what about governments—or, more specifically, what about government decision makers? What do they try to maximize? One problem is that our federal system consists of many governments—more than 87,000 separate jurisdictions in all. What's more, because the federal government relies on offsetting, or countervailing, powers among the *executive, legislative,* and *judicial* branches, government does not act as a single, consistent decision maker. Even within the federal executive branch, there are so many agencies and bureaus that at times they seem to work at cross-purposes. For example, at the same time as the U.S. Surgeon General requires health warnings on cigarettes, the U.S. Department of Agriculture subsidizes tobacco farmers. Given this thicket of jurisdictions, branches, and bureaus, one useful theory of government behavior is that elected officials try to maximize their number of votes in the next election. So we can assume that elected officials try to *maximize votes.* In this theory, vote maximization guides the decisions of elected officials who, in turn, control government employees.

Voluntary Exchange Versus Coercion. Market exchange relies on the voluntary behavior of buyers and sellers. Don't like tofu? No problem—don't buy any. But in political markets, the situation is different. Any voting rule except unanimous consent will involve some government coercion. Public choices are enforced by the police power of the state. Those who fail to pay their taxes could go to jail, even though they may object to some programs those taxes support.

No Market Prices. Another distinguishing feature of governments is that the selling price of public output is usually either zero or some amount below its cost. If you are now paying in-state tuition at a public college or university, your tuition probably covers only about half the full cost of providing your education. Since the revenue side of the government budget is usually separate from the expenditure side, there is no necessary link between the cost and benefit of a public program. In the private sector, however, marginal benefits are at least as great as marginal costs; otherwise, market exchange would not occur.

The Size and Growth of Government

One way to track the impact of government over time is by measuring government outlays relative to the U.S. *gross domestic product,* or *GDP,* which is the total value of all final goods and services produced in the United States. In 1929, the year the Great Depression began, government outlays, mostly by state and local governments, totaled about 10 percent of GDP. At that time, the federal government played a minor role. In fact, during the nation's first 150 years, federal outlays, except during times of war, never exceeded 3 percent relative to GDP.

The Great Depression, World War II, and a change in macroeconomic thinking boosted the role of government in the economy to a peak of 35 percent of GDP in 1992. By 2000, government outlays settled back to 29 percent of GDP, with 18 percent by the federal government and 11 percent by state and local governments. In comparison, government outlays relative to GDP in 2000 were 38 percent in Japan, the United Kingdom, and Canada; 43 percent in Germany; 47 percent in Italy; and 51 percent in France. Government outlays by the 24 largest industrial economies averaged 36 percent of GDP in 2000, down from 40 percent in 1992.[2] Thus, government outlays in the United States represent a relatively smaller share of GDP compared to other advanced economies. But both here and in other advanced economies, outlays have shrunk relative to GDP since 1992.

Let's look briefly at the composition of federal outlays. Since 1960, defense spending has declined from over half of federal outlays to less than one-fifth by 2000, as shown in Exhibit 3. Redistribution—Social Security, Medicare, and welfare programs—is the mirror image of defense spending, jumping from only about one-fifth of federal outlays in 1960 to nearly half by 2000.

[2]The Organization of Economic Cooperation and Development, *OECD Economic Outlook* 68 (December 2000): Annex Table 28.

EXHIBIT 3

Redistribution Has Grown and Defense Has Declined as Share of Federal
Outlays Since 1960

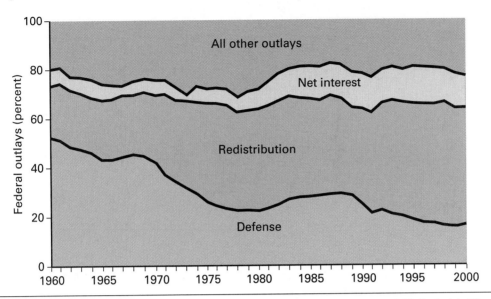

Source: Computed based on figures from the *Economic Report of the President,* January 2001, Table B-80. For the latest figures, go to http://w3.access.gpo.gov/eop.

ASK THE INSTRUCTOR: HOW BIG IS GOVERNMENT AND WHAT ARE ITS MAJOR FUNCTIONS?

Sources of Government Revenue

Taxes provide the bulk of revenue at all levels of government. The federal government relies primarily on the individual income tax, state governments rely on income and sales taxes, and local governments rely on the property tax. In addition to taxes, other revenue sources include user charges, such as highway tolls, and borrowing. Some states also sell stuff, such as lottery tickets and liquor, to raise money.

Exhibit 4 focuses on the composition of federal revenue since 1960. The share made up by the individual income tax has remained relatively constant, ranging from a low of 42 percent in the mid-1960s to a high of 50 percent in 2000. The share from payroll taxes more than doubled from 15 percent in 1960 to 34 percent in 2000. *Payroll taxes* are deducted from paychecks to support Social Security and medical care for the elderly. Corporate income taxes and revenue from other sources, such as excise (sales) taxes and user charges, have declined as a share of the total since 1960.

Tax Principles and Tax Incidence

The structure of a tax is often justified on the basis of one of two general principles. First, a tax could relate to the individual's ability to pay, so those with a greater ability pay more taxes. Income or property taxes often rely on this **ability-to-pay tax principle.** Alternatively, the **benefits-received tax principle** relates taxes to the benefits taxpayers receive from the government activity funded by the tax. For example, the tax on gasoline funds highway construction and maintenance, thereby linking tax payment to road use, since the more people drive, the more gas tax they pay.

Tax incidence indicates who actually bears the burden of the tax. One way to evaluate tax incidence is by measuring the tax as a percentage of income. Under **proportional taxation,** taxpayers at all income levels pay the same percentage of their income in taxes. A proportional income tax is also called a flat tax, since the tax as a percentage of income remains constant, or flat, as income increases. Under **progressive taxation,** the percentage of income paid in taxes increases as income increases.

EXHIBIT 4

Payroll Taxes Have Grown as a Share of Federal Revenue Since 1960

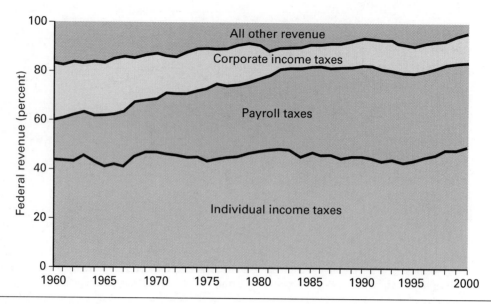

Source: Computed based on figures from the *Economic Report of the President,* January 2001, Tables B-81 and B-84. For the latest figures, go to http://w3.access.gpo.gov/eop.

The **marginal tax rate** indicates the percentage of each additional dollar of income that goes to taxes. Because high marginal rates reduce the after-tax return from working or investing, they can reduce people's incentives to work and invest. When recent cuts in U.S. federal personal income tax rates are fully implemented in 2006, the six marginal rates will range from 10 to 35 percent, down from a range of 15 to 39.6 percent in 2000. The top 10 percent of tax filers, based on income, paid 68 percent of all income taxes collected in 2000 (after the rate cuts, the share paid by the top 10 percent is projected to increase). So the U.S. income tax is progressive, and high-income filers pay the overwhelming share of the total.

Finally, under **regressive taxation,** the percentage of income paid in taxes decreases as income increases, so the marginal tax rate declines as income increases. Most U.S. *payroll taxes* are regressive, because they impose a flat rate up to a certain level of income, above which the marginal rate drops to zero. For example, Social Security taxes were levied on the first $80,400 of workers' income in 2001. Half the 12.4 percent tax is paid by employers and half by employees (the self-employed pay the entire amount). But the 2.9 percent Medicare tax is proportional, because it applies to all labor earnings. For example, Julia Roberts pays $435,000 just in Medicare taxes on the $15 million she earns per movie.

This discussion of revenue sources brings to a close, for now, our examination of the role of government in the U.S. economy. Government has a pervasive influence on the economy, and its role is discussed throughout the book.

THE REST OF THE WORLD

So far, we have focused on institutions within the United States—that is, on *domestic* households, firms, and governments. This initial focus was appropriate because our primary objective has been to understand the workings of the U.S. economy, by far the largest national economy in the world. But the rest of the world affects what U.S. households consume and what U.S. firms produce. For example, Japan and South Korea supply U.S. markets with autos, electronic equipment, and other manufactured goods, thereby affecting U.S. prices, wages, and profits. Likewise, political unrest in the Persian Gulf can drive up the price of oil.

Foreign decision makers, therefore, have a significant effect on the U.S. economy—on what we consume and what we produce. The *rest of the world* consists of the households, firms, and governments in more than 200 sovereign countries throughout the world.

<interactive>update

ECONNEWS ONLINE: CHIQUITA GOING BANANAS OVER QUOTAS

<interactive>exercise

ECONDEBATE ONLINE: DOES THE U.S. ECONOMY BENEFIT FROM FOREIGN TRADE?

International Trade

In Chapter 2, you learned about comparative advantage and the gains from specialization. These gains explain why householders stopped trying to do everything for themselves and began to specialize. International trade arises for the same reasons. *International trade occurs because the opportunity cost of producing specific goods differs across countries.* Americans import raw materials like crude oil, diamonds, and coffee beans and finished goods like cameras, DVD players, and automobiles. U.S. producers export sophisticated products like computer hardware and software, aircraft, and movies, as well as agricultural products like wheat and corn.

International trade between the United States and the rest of the world has increased in recent decades. In 1970, U.S. exports of goods and services amounted to only 6 percent of the gross domestic product. That figure has since more than doubled to 14 percent. Chief destinations for U.S. exports in order of importance are Canada, Japan, Mexico, Great Britain, Germany, France, South Korea, and Taiwan.

The **merchandise trade balance** equals the value of exported goods minus the value of imported goods. Goods in this case are distinguished from services, which show up in another trade account. For the last two decades, the United States has experienced a merchandise trade deficit, meaning that the value of goods imported into the U.S. has exceeded the value of U.S. goods exported. Just as a household must cover its spending, so too must a nation. The deficit in our merchandise trade balance must be offset by a surplus in one or more of the other *balance-of-payments* accounts. A nation's **balance of payments** is the record of all economic transactions between its residents and the residents of the rest of the world.

Exchange Rates

The lack of a common currency complicates trade between countries. How many U.S. dollars buy a Porsche? An American buyer cares only about the dollar cost; the German carmaker cares only about the euros received (the new common currency of 12 European countries). To facilitate trade when two currencies are involved, a market for foreign exchange has developed. **Foreign exchange** is foreign currency needed to carry out international transactions. The supply and demand for foreign exchange come together in *foreign exchange markets* to determine the equilibrium exchange rate. The *exchange rate* measures the price of one currency in terms of another. For example, the exchange rate between the euro and the dollar might indicate that one euro exchanges for $0.90. At that exchange rate, a Porsche selling for 100,000 euros costs $90,000. The exchange rate affects the prices of imports and exports and thus helps shape the flow of foreign trade. The greater the demand for a particular foreign currency or the smaller the supply, the higher its exchange rate—that is, the more dollars it costs.

Trade Restrictions

Although there are clear gains from international specialization and exchange, nearly all nations restrict trade to some extent. These restrictions can take the form of (1) **tariffs,** which are taxes on imports; (2) **quotas,** which are legal limits on the quantity of a particular good that can be imported; and (3) other restrictions, such as the voluntary agreement by Japanese automobile manufacturers to limit their exports to the United States.

If specialization according to comparative advantage is so beneficial, why do most countries restrict trade? Restrictions benefit certain domestic producers that lobby their governments for these benefits. For example, U.S. textile manufacturers have sought and received from Congress protective legislation that restricts textile imports, thereby raising U.S. textile prices. These higher prices harm domestic consumers, but consumers are usually unaware of this harm. Trade restrictions interfere with the free flow of products across borders and tend to hurt the overall economy. International trade in the auto industry is discussed in the following case study.

CASE**STUDY**	Wheels of Fortune
	● *The World of Business*

The U.S. auto industry is huge, with annual sales exceeding $275 billion a year, an amount exceeding the gross domestic product of 90 percent of the world's economies. There are over 200 million motor vehicles in the United States alone, nearly one for each person. In the decade following World War II, imports accounted for only 0.4 percent of U.S. auto sales. In 1973, however, the suddenly powerful Organization of Petroleum Exporting Countries (OPEC) more than tripled oil prices. In response, Americans scrambled for more fuel-efficient automobiles, which at the time were sold primarily by foreign manufacturers, especially the Japanese. As a result, imports jumped to 21 percent of U.S. auto sales by 1980.

In the early 1980s, at the urging of the so-called Big Three automakers (General Motors, Ford, and Chrysler), the Reagan administration persuaded Japanese producers to adopt "voluntary" quotas limiting the number of Japanese automobiles they exported to the United States. The quotas, or supply restrictions, drove up the price of Japanese imports. U.S. auto producers used this as an opportunity to raise their own prices. Experts estimate that the so-called protection from foreign competition cost U.S. consumers over $15 billion.

The quotas had two effects on Japanese producers. First, faced with a strict limit on the number of cars they could export to the United States, they began shipping more upscale models instead of subcompacts. Second, the quotas encouraged Japanese firms to establish manufacturing plants in the United States. Making autos here also reduced problems caused by fluctuations in the value of the yen relative to the dollar. Japanese-owned auto plants in the U.S. now account for more than one-quarter of car production in the United States. Two German automakers, Mercedes-Benz (now DaimlerChrysler) and BMW, also built plants here.

Imports still make up about one-quarter of U.S. car sales, with Japan accounting for most of that. Imports include cars produced abroad by foreign firms but sold under the names of U.S. firms. U.S. automakers also produce around the world. In fact, Ford is the largest automaker in Australia, Great Britain, Mexico, and Argentina.

In China, India, and Latin America, the potential car market is enormous. Here's something to think about: There are more people in China under 26 years of age than the combined population of the United States, Japan, Germany, the United Kingdom, and Canada. Automobile production in China jumped from 23,500 in 1988 to more than 2 million in 2000, and plans call for boosting production to 3.2 million by 2005. Because Chinese tariffs double the price of imported vehicles, only about 100,000 vehicles were imported in 2000. As a condition for entry into the World Trade Organization, a group that streamlines world trade, China must cut its auto tariffs to 25 percent by 2006.

<interactive>exercise

eACTIVITY: WHEELS OF FORTUNE

Sources: Keith Bradsher, "G.M. Offers Deep Discounts on Some of Its Big Moneymakers," *New York Times,* 16 May 2001; Owen Brown, "Chinese Govt. Targets 3.2 Million Car Annual Output by 2005," Dow Jones Newswire, 27 June 2001; Scott Miller, "Luxury-Car Makers Squeeze Out Some Mass Market Competition, *Wall Street Journal,* 3 October 2000; and Walter Adams and James Brock, "Automobiles," in *The Structure of American Industry,* 9th ed. (New York: Prentice-Hall, 1995), 65–92. For the latest in the auto industry, go to http://www.autocentral.com/.

CONCLUSION

In this chapter, we examined the four economic decision makers: households, firms, governments, and the rest of the world. Domestic households are by far the most important, for they, along with foreign households, supply the resources and demand the goods and services produced. In recent years, the U.S. economy has come to depend more on the rest of the world as a market for U.S. goods and as a source of products.

endofchaptermaterial

- **Summary**
- **Questions for Review**
- **Problems and Exercises**

- **Experiential Exercises**
- **Wall Street Journal Exercise**

Take the Post-Test to assess your overall understanding of the key ideas in this chapter. The Post-Test provides a comprehensive selection of exam-style questions addressing the main topics and concepts of the chapter. At the completion of each Post-Test, you will receive a score and instructive feedback on how you answered each question, and a direct link to the part of the chapter addressed in the question. Take the Post-Test as often as you need to—a record of your progress for each attempt is kept for you to revisit and gauge your improvement. And each Post-Test is randomly generated, so every attempt is new.

Post-Test

5

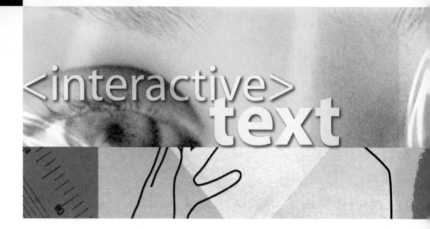

Elasticity of Demand and Supply

Why did visits to Microsoft's online magazine, *Slate,* drop 95 percent when the access charge increased from zero to $20 a year? Why do higher cigarette taxes cut smoking by teenagers more than by other age groups? Why did total online usage explode when AOL switched from an hourly charge to a flat monthly fee? Why does a good harvest often spell trouble for farmers? Answers to these and other questions are explored in this chapter, which takes a closer look at demand and supply.

As you learned in Chapter 1, macroeconomics concentrates on aggregate markets—on the big picture. But the big picture is a mosaic pieced together from individual decisions made by households, firms, governments, and the rest of the world. To understand how a market economy works, we must take a closer look at these individual decisions, especially at the role played by prices. In a market economy, prices inform producers and consumers about the relative scarcity of products and resources.

A downward-sloping demand curve and an upward-sloping supply curve combine to form a powerful analytical tool. But to use this tool, you must learn more about demand and supply curves. The more you know, the better you can predict the effects of a change in the price on quantity demanded and quantity supplied. Decision makers are willing to pay dearly for such knowledge. For example, Taco Bell would like to know what happens to sales if taco prices decline. Governments would like to know how higher cigarette taxes affect teenage smoking. Colleges would like to know how tuition hikes affect enrollments. And subway officials would like to know how fare cuts affect ridership. To answer such questions, we must learn how responsive consumers and producers are to price changes. *Elasticity* measures *responsiveness*. Topics discussed in this chapter include:

- Price elasticity of demand
- Determinants of price elasticity
- Price elasticity and total revenue
- Price elasticity of supply
- Income elasticity of demand
- Cross-price elasticity of demand

<interactive>exercise

ECONDEBATE ONLINE: UTILITY AND CONSUMER CHOICE

<interactive>update

`1000110111C`

- **ECONDATA ONLINE: UTILITY AND CONSUMER CHOICE**
- **ECONLINKS ONLINE: ECONOMICS WEB LINKS**
- **ECONNEWS ONLINE: UTILITY AND CONSUMER CHOICE**

PRICE ELASTICITY OF DEMAND

To fill more seats just before a recent Thanksgiving weekend, Delta Airlines cut fares up to 50 percent. Was this a good idea for Delta? A firm's success or failure often depends on how much it knows about the demand for its product. For Delta's total revenue to increase, the gain in ticket sales would have to more than make up for the decline in ticket prices. Likewise, the operators of Taco Bell would like to know what happens to sales if taco prices drop, say, from $1.10 to $0.90. The law of demand says a lower price increases quantity demanded, but by how much? How sensitive is quantity demanded to a change in price? After all, if quantity demanded increases enough, a price cut might be a profitable move for Taco Bell.

Calculating Price Elasticity of Demand

Let's get more specific about how sensitive changes in quantity demanded are to changes in price. Take a look at the demand curve in Exhibit 1. At the initial price of $1.10 per taco, consumers demand 95,000 per day. If the price drops to $0.90, quantity demanded increases by 10,000 to 105,000. Is such a response in quantity demanded a little or a lot? The *price elasticity of demand* measures in a standardized way how responsive consumers are to the price change. *Elasticity* is another word for *responsiveness*. In simplest terms, the **price elasticity of demand** measures the percentage change in quantity demanded divided by the percentage change in price, or:

$$\text{Price elasticity of demand} = \frac{\text{Percentage change in quantity demanded}}{\text{Percentage change in price}}$$

So what's the price elasticity of demand when the price of tacos falls from $1.10 to $0.90—that is, what's the price elasticity of demand between points *a* and *b* in Exhibit 1? For price elasticity to be a clear and useful measure, we should come up with the same result between points *a* and *b* as we get between points *b* and *a*. To ensure that consistency, we must take the average of the initial price and the new price and use that as the base in computing the percentage change in price. For example, in Exhibit 1, the base used to calculate the percentage change in price is the average of $1.10 and $0.90, which is $1.00. The percentage change in price is therefore the change in price, −$0.20, divided by $1.00, which works out to be −20 percent.

The same holds for changes in quantity demanded. In Exhibit 1, the base used for computing the percentage change in quantity demanded is the average of 95,000 and 105,000, which is 100,000. So the percentage increase in quantity demanded is the change in quantity

EXHIBIT 1 |

Demand Curve for Tacos

If the price of tacos drops from $1.10 to $0.90, the quantity demanded increases from 95,000 to 105,000.

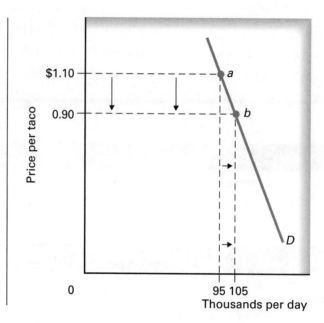

demanded, 10,000, divided by 100,000, which works out to be 10 percent. So the resulting price elasticity of demand between points *a* and *b* is the percentage increase in quantity demanded, 10 percent, divided by the percentage decrease in price, −20 percent, which works out to be −0.5 (=10%/−20%).

Let's generalize the price elasticity formula. If the price drops from p to p', other things constant, the quantity demanded increases from q to q'. The change in price can be represented as Δp and the change in quantity as Δq. The **formula** for calculating the price elasticity of demand, E_D, between the two points is the percentage change in quantity demanded divided by the percentage change in price, or:

$$E_D = \frac{\Delta q}{(q + q')/2} \div \frac{\Delta p}{(p + p')/2}$$

Again, because the average quantity and average price are used as the bases for computing percentage change, the same elasticity results whether going from the higher price to the lower price or the other way around.

Elasticity expresses a relationship between two amounts: the percentage change in quantity demanded and the percentage change in price. Since the focus is on the percentage change, we need not be concerned with how output or price is measured. For example, suppose the good in question is apples. It makes no difference in the elasticity formula whether we measure apples in pounds, bushels, or even tons. All that matters is the percentage change in quantity demanded. Nor does it matter whether we measure price in U.S. dollars, Mexican pesos, French francs, or Zambian kwacha. All that matters is the percentage change in price.

Finally, the law of demand states that price and quantity demanded are inversely related, so the change in price and the change in quantity demanded move in opposite directions. In the elasticity formula, the numerator and the denominator have opposite signs, leaving the price elasticity of demand with a negative sign. Since constantly referring to elasticity as a negative number gets old fast, from here on we will discuss the price elasticity of demand as an absolute value, or as a positive number. For example, the absolute value of the elasticity measured in Exhibit 1 is 0.5. Still, from time to time, you will be reminded that we are discussing absolute values.

<interactive>video

ASK THE INSTRUCTOR: IS PRICE ELASTICITY OF DEMAND THE SAME THING AS SLOPE?

Categories of Price Elasticity of Demand

As you will see, the price elasticity of demand usually varies along a given demand curve. The price elasticity of demand can be divided into three general categories, depending on how responsive quantity demanded is to a change in price. If the percentage change in quantity demanded is smaller than the percentage change in price, the resulting price elasticity has an absolute value between 0 and 1.0. That portion of the demand curve is said to be **inelastic,** meaning that quantity demanded is relatively *unresponsive* to a change in price. For example, the elasticity derived in Exhibit 1 between points *a* and *b* is 0.5, so that portion of the demand curve is inelastic. If the percentage change in quantity demanded just equals the percentage change in price, the resulting price elasticity has an absolute value of 1.0, and that portion of a demand curve has **unit-elastic demand.** Finally, if the percentage change in quantity demanded exceeds the percentage change in price, the resulting price elasticity has an absolute value exceeding 1.0, and that portion of a demand curve is said to be **elastic.** In summary, *the price elasticity of demand is inelastic if its absolute value is between 0 and 1.0, unit elastic if equal to 1.0, and elastic if greater than 1.0.*

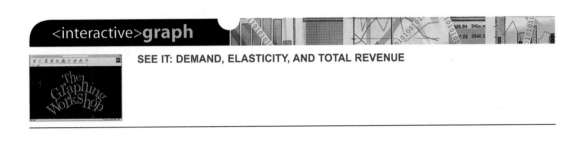

SEE IT: DEMAND, ELASTICITY, AND TOTAL REVENUE

ECONNEWS ONLINE: GOVERNMENT AND CIGARETTE MANUFACTURERS BUTT HEADS

Elasticity and Total Revenue

Knowledge of price elasticity is especially valuable to producers, because it indicates the effect of a price change on total revenue. **Total revenue** (*TR*) is the price (*p*) multiplied by the quantity demanded (*q*) at that price, or $TR = p \times q$. What happens to total revenue when price decreases? Well, a lower price means producers get less for each unit sold, which tends to decrease total revenue. But, according to the law of demand, a lower price increases quantity demanded, which tends to increase total revenue. The overall impact of a lower price on total revenue depends on the net result of these opposite effects. *If the positive effect of greater quantity demanded more than offsets the negative effect of a lower price, then total revenue will rise.* More specifically, if demand is *elastic,* the percentage increase in quantity demanded exceeds the percentage decrease in price, so total revenue increases. If demand is *unit elastic,* the percentage increase in quantity demanded just equals the percentage decrease in price, so total revenue remains unchanged. Finally, if demand is *inelastic,* the percentage increase in quantity demanded is more than offset by the percentage decrease in price, so total revenue decreases.

Price Elasticity and the Linear Demand Curve

A look at elasticity along a particular type of demand curve, the linear demand curve, will tie together the ideas examined so far. A **linear demand curve** is simply a straight-line demand curve, as in panel (a) of Exhibit 2. Panel (b) shows the total revenue generated by each price-quantity combination along the demand curve in panel (a). Recall that total revenue equals price times quantity.

Since the demand curve is linear, its slope is constant, so a given decrease in price always causes the same unit increase in quantity demanded. For example, along the demand curve in Exhibit 2, a $10 drop in price always increases quantity demanded by 100 units. But the price elasticity of demand is larger on the higher-price end of the demand curve than on the lower-price end. Here's why. Consider a movement from point *a* to point *b* on the upper end of the demand curve in Exhibit 2. The 100-unit increase in quantity demanded is a percentage

EXHIBIT 2

Demand, Price Elasticity, and Total Revenue

Where demand is elastic in panel (a), total revenue in panel (b) increases following a price decrease. Total revenue attains its maximum value at the level of output where demand is unit elastic. Where demand is inelastic, further decreases in price cause total revenue to fall.

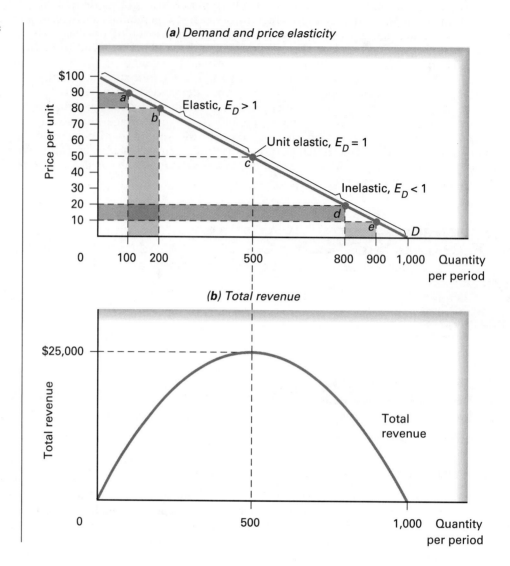

(a) Demand and price elasticity

Elastic, $E_D > 1$

Unit elastic, $E_D = 1$

Inelastic, $E_D < 1$

(b) Total revenue

Total revenue

change of 100/150, or 67 percent. The $10 price drop is a percentage change of 10/85, or 12 percent. Therefore, the price elasticity of demand between points *a* and *b* is 67%/12%, which equals 5.6. Between points *d* and *e* on the lower end, however, the 100-unit quantity increase is a percentage change of 100/850, or only 12 percent, and the $10 price decrease is a percentage change of 10/15, or 67 percent. The price elasticity of demand is 12%/67%, or 0.2. In other words, *if the demand curve is linear, consumers are more responsive to a given price change when the initial price is high than when it's low.*

Demand becomes less elastic as we move down the curve. At a point halfway down the linear demand curve in Exhibit 2, the elasticity equals 1.0. *This halfway point divides a linear demand curve into an elastic upper half and an inelastic lower half.* You can observe a clear relationship between the elasticity of demand in panel (a) and total revenue in panel (b). Notice that where demand is elastic, a decrease in price increases total revenue because the gain in revenue from selling more units [represented by the large blue rectangle in panel (a)] exceeds the loss in revenue from selling at the lower price (the small red rectangle). But where demand is inelastic, a price decrease reduces total revenue because the gain in revenue from selling more units (the small blue rectangle) is less than the loss in revenue from selling at the lower price (the large red rectangle). And where demand is unit elastic, the gain and loss of revenue exactly cancel each other out, so total revenue at that point remains constant [thus, total revenue "peaks" in panel (b)].

To review, total revenue increases as the price declines until the midpoint of the linear demand curve is reached, where total revenue peaks. In Exhibit 2, total revenue peaks at

$25,000 when quantity demanded equals 500 units. To the right of the midpoint of the demand curve, total revenue declines as the price falls. More generally, regardless of whether the demand curve is a straight line or a curve, there is a consistent relationship between the price elasticity of demand and total revenue: *A price decline increases total revenue if demand is elastic, decreases total revenue if demand is inelastic, and has no effect on total revenue if demand is unit elastic.* Finally, note that a downward-sloping linear demand curve has a constant slope but a varying elasticity, so *the slope of a demand curve is not the same as the price elasticity of demand.*

NETBOOKMARK: AIR TRAFFIC FORECASTS FOR THE UNITED KINGDOM

SEE IT: DEMAND, ELASTICITY, AND TOTAL REVENUE

Constant-Elasticity Demand Curves

Again, price elasticity measures the responsiveness of consumers to a change in price. This responsiveness varies along a linear demand curve unless the demand curve is horizontal or vertical, as in panels (a) and (b) of Exhibit 3. These two demand curves, along with the special demand curve in panel (c), are called *constant-elasticity demand curves* because the elasticity does not change along the curves.

Perfectly Elastic Demand Curve. The horizontal demand curve in panel (a) indicates that consumers will demand all that is offered for sale at the given price *p* (the quantity actually demanded will depend on the amount supplied at that price). If the price rises above *p*, however, quantity demanded drops to zero. This is a **perfectly elastic demand curve,** and its elasticity value is infinity, a number too large to be defined. You may think this is an odd sort of demand curve: Consumers, as a result of a small increase in price, go from demanding as much as is supplied to demanding none. Consumers are so sensitive to price changes that they do not tolerate any price increase. As you will see in a later chapter, this reflects the demand for the output of any individual producer when many producers sell identical products. The shape of the demand curve for a firm's product is an important element in the pricing and output decision.

Perfectly Inelastic Demand Curve. Along the vertical demand curve in panel (b) of Exhibit 3, quantity demanded does not vary when the price changes. This demand curve expresses consumer sentiment when "price is no object." For example, if you were extremely rich and needed insulin injections to survive, price would be no object. No matter how high the price, you would continue to demand whatever it takes. And if the price of insulin should drop, you would not increase your quantity demanded. Since the percentage change in quantity demanded is zero for any given percentage change in price, the numerical value of the price elasticity is zero. A vertical demand curve is called a **perfectly inelastic demand curve** because price changes do not affect quantity demanded.

Unit-Elastic Demand Curve. Panel (c) in Exhibit 3 presents a demand curve that is unit elastic everywhere. Along a **unit-elastic demand curve,** any percentage change in price results in an identical and offsetting percentage change in quantity demanded. Because percentage changes in price and in quantity are equal and offsetting, total revenue remains constant for every price-quantity combination along the curve. For example, when the price falls from $10 to $6, the quantity demanded increases from 60 to 100 units. The pink shaded rectangle shows the loss in total revenue because units are sold at the lower price; the blue shaded rectangle shows the gain in total revenue because more units are sold when the price drops. Because the demand curve is unit elastic, the revenue gained from selling more units just equals the revenue lost from lowering the price on all units, so total revenue is unchanged at $600. A demand curve that is unit elastic everywhere would actually be quite rare.

EXHIBIT 3

Three Constant-Elasticity Demand Curves

Along the perfectly elastic (horizontal) demand curve of panel (a), consumers will purchase all that is offered for sale at price *p*. Along the perfectly inelastic (vertical) demand curve of panel (b), consumers will purchase quantity *Q* regardless of price. Along the unit-elastic demand curve of panel (c), total revenue is the same for every price-quantity combination.

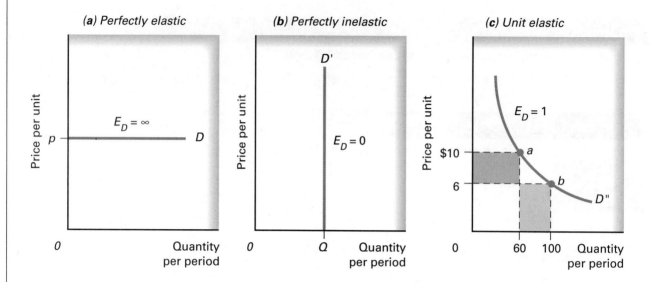

Each demand curve in Exhibit 3 is called a **constant-elasticity demand curve** because the elasticity is the same all along the curve. In contrast, the downward-sloping linear demand curve examined earlier had a different elasticity value at each point along the curve. Exhibit 4 lists the absolute values for the five categories of price elasticity we have discussed, summarizing the effects of a 10 percent price increase on quantity demanded and on total revenue. Give this exhibit some thought now, and see if you can draw a demand curve for each category of elasticity.

DETERMINANTS OF THE PRICE ELASTICITY OF DEMAND

So far we have explored the technical properties of demand elasticity and discussed why price elasticity varies along a downward-sloping demand curve. But we have not yet considered why price elasticities of demand are different for different goods. Several characteristics influence the price elasticity of demand for a good.

EXHIBIT 4

Summary of Price Elasticity of Demand

Effects of a 10 Percent Increase in Price

Absolute Value of Price Elasticity	Type of Demand	What Happens to Quantity Demanded	What Happens to Total Revenue
$E_D = 0$	Perfectly inelastic	No change	Increases by 10 percent
$0 < E_D < 1$	Inelastic	Drops by less than 10 percent	Increases by less than 10 percent
$E_D = 1$	Unit elastic	Drops by 10 percent	No change
$1 < E_D < \infty$	Elastic	Drops by more than 10 percent	Decreases
$E_D = \infty$	Perfectly elastic	Drops to 0	Drops to 0

Availability of Substitutes

As we saw in Chapter 3, your particular wants can be satisfied in a variety of ways. A rise in the price of pizza makes other foods relatively cheaper. If close substitutes are available, an increase in the price of pizza will prompt some consumers to shift to the substitutes. But if nothing else satisfies like pizza, the quantity of pizza demanded will not decline as much. *The greater the availability of substitutes for a good and the more similar the substitutes are to the original, the greater the good's price elasticity of demand.*

The number and similarity of substitutes depend on how we define the good. *The more broadly we define a good, the fewer substitutes there are and the less elastic the demand.* For example, the demand for shoes is less elastic than the demand for running shoes because there are few substitutes for shoes but several substitutes for running shoes, such as sneakers, tennis shoes, cross-trainers, and so on. The demand for running shoes, however, is less elastic than the demand for Nike running shoes because the consumer has more substitutes for the Nike brand, including Reebok, New Balance, Fila, and so on. Finally, the demand for Nike running shoes is less elastic than the demand for a specific model of Nikes, because Nike has dozens of models.

Certain goods—many prescription drugs, for instance—have no close substitutes. The demand for such goods tends to be less elastic than for goods with close substitutes, such as Bayer aspirin. Much advertising is aimed at establishing in the consumer's mind the uniqueness of a particular product—an effort to convince consumers "to accept no substitutes." Why might a firm want to make the demand for its product less elastic?

As an example of the impact of substitutes on price elasticity, consider the pattern of commercial breaks during network TV movies. When the movie begins, viewers have several substitutes for it, including other shows and perhaps movies on other networks. To keep viewers from switching channels, the first movie segment is longer than usual, perhaps 20 or 25 minutes before a commercial break. But once viewers get interested in the movie, shows on other channels are no longer close substitutes, so broadcasters inject commercials with greater frequency without fear of losing many viewers.

Proportion of the Consumer's Budget Spent on the Good

Recall that a higher price reduces quantity demanded in part because a higher price reduces the real spending power of consumer income. A demand curve reflects both the *willingness* and *ability* to purchase a good at alternative prices. Because spending on some goods represents a large share of the consumer's budget, a change in the price of such a good has a substantial impact on the amount consumers are *able* to purchase. An increase in the price of housing, for example, reduces consumers' ability to purchase housing. The income effect of a higher price reduces the quantity demanded. In contrast, the income effect of an increase in the price of, say, paper towels is trivial because paper towels represent such a tiny share of any budget. *The more important the item is as a share of the consumer's budget, other things constant, the greater is the income effect of a change in price, so the more price elastic is the demand for the item.* Hence the quantity of housing demanded is more responsive to a given percentage change in price than is the quantity of paper towels demanded.

A Matter of Time

Consumers can substitute lower-priced goods for higher-priced goods, but finding substitutes usually takes time. Suppose your college announces a significant increase in room and board fees, effective immediately. Some students will move off campus as soon as they can; others will wait until the next school year. Over time, fewer students may apply for admission, and more incoming students will choose off-campus housing. *The longer the adjustment period, the greater the consumers' ability to substitute away from relatively higher-priced products toward lower-priced substitutes. Thus, the longer the period of adjustment, the more responsive the change in quantity demanded is to a given change in price.* Here's another example: Between 1973 and 1974, the OPEC cartel raised the price of oil sharply. The result was a 45 percent increase in the price of gasoline, but the quantity demanded decreased only 8 percent. As more time passed, however, people purchased smaller cars and made greater use of public transportation. Because the price of oil used to generate electricity and to heat homes increased as well, people bought more energy-efficient appliances and added more insulation to their homes. Again, the change in the amount of oil demanded was greater as consumers adjusted to the price hike.

Exhibit 5 demonstrates how demand becomes more elastic over time. Given an initial price of \$1.00, let D_w be the demand curve one week after a price change; D_m, one month after; and D_y, one year after. Suppose the price increases to \$1.25. The more time consumers have to respond to the price increase, the greater the reduction in quantity demanded. The demand

EXHIBIT 5

Demand Becomes More Elastic over Time

D_w is the demand curve one week after a price increase from $1.00 to $1.25. Along this curve, quantity demanded per day falls from 100 to 95. One month after the price increase, quantity demanded has fallen to 75 along D_m. One year after the price increase, quantity demanded has fallen to 50 along D_y. At any given price, D_y is more elastic than D_m, which is more elastic than D_w.

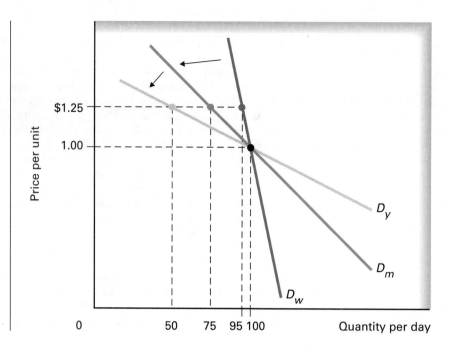

curve D_w shows that one week after the price increase, the quantity demanded has not declined much—in this case, from 100 to 95 per day. The demand curve D_m indicates a reduction to 75 per day after one month, and demand curve D_y shows a reduction to 50 per day after one year. Notice that among these demand curves and over the range starting from the point where the demand curves intersect, the flatter the demand curve, the more price elastic the demand. Here, elasticity appears to be linked to the slope because we begin from the same point—the same price-quantity combination.

Elasticity Estimates

Let's look at some estimates of the price elasticity of demand for particular goods and services. As we have noted, the substitution of lower-priced goods for a good whose price has just increased often takes time. Thus, when estimating price elasticity, economists often distinguish between a period during which consumers have little time to adjust—let's call it the *short run*—and a period during which consumers can more fully adjust to a price change—let's call it the *long run*. Exhibit 6 provides some short-run and long-run price elasticity estimates for selected products.

READING IT RIGHT: WALL STREET JOURNAL EXERCISE

The price elasticity of demand is greater in the long run because consumers have more time to adjust. For example, if the price of electricity rose today, consumers in the short run might cut back a bit in their use of electrical appliances, and those in homes with electric heat might lower the thermostat in winter. Over time, however, consumers would switch to more energy-efficient appliances and might convert from electric heat to oil or natural gas. So the demand for electricity is more elastic in the long run than in the short run, as shown in Exhibit 6. In fact, in every instance where values for both the short run and the long run are listed, the long run is more elastic than the short run. Notice also that the long-run price elasticity of demand for Chevrolets exceeds that for automobiles in general. There are many more substitutes for

EXHIBIT 6

Selected Price Elasticities of Demand (absolute values)

Product	Short Run	Long Run
Cigarettes (among adults)	—	0.4
Electricity (residential)	0.1	1.9
Air travel	0.1	2.4
Medical care and hospitalization	0.3	0.9
Gasoline	0.4	1.5
Milk	0.4	—
Fish (cod)	0.5	—
Wine	0.7	1.2
Movies	0.9	3.7
Natural gas (residential)	1.4	2.1
Automobiles	1.9	2.2
Chevrolets	—	4.0

Sources: F. Chaloupka, "Rational Addictive Behavior and Cigarette Smoking," *Journal of Political Economy* (August 1991); Hsaing-tai Cheng and Oral Capps, Jr., "Demand for Fish," *American Journal of Agricultural Economics* (August 1998); J. Johnson et al., "Short-Run and Long-Run Elasticities for Canadian Consumption of Alcoholic Beverages," *Review of Economics and Statistics* (February 1992); R. Archibald and R. Gillingham, "The Review of the Short-Run Consumer Demand for Gasoline Using Household Survey Data," *Review of Economics and Statistics* 62 (November 1980); J. Griffin, *Energy Conservation in the OECD, 1980–2000* (Cambridge, Mass.: Balinger, 1979); H. Houthakker and L. Taylor, *Consumer Demand in the United States: Analysis and Projections,* 2nd ed. (Cambridge, Mass.: Harvard University Press, 1970); and G. Lakshmanan and W. Anderson, "Residential Energy Demand in the United States," *Regional Science and Urban Economics* 10 (August 1980).

Chevrolets than for automobiles in general. There are no close substitutes for cigarettes, even in the long run, so the demand for cigarettes among adults is price inelastic. Such elasticity measures are of more than just academic interest, as discussed in the following case study.

CASE**STUDY**	Deterring Young Smokers
	● *Public Policy*

As the U.S. Surgeon General warns on each pack of cigarettes, smoking can be hazardous to your health. Researchers estimate that smoking causes more than 400,000 deaths a year in the United States—nearly 10 times the total from traffic accidents. Lung cancer is now the top cancer killer among women. A federal study found that cigarette smoking cost the U.S. economy at least $130 billion in 1998—more than was spent on public higher education that year.

Health-related issues, including depression and the addictive nature of cigarettes, have created a growing public policy concern about smoking, especially smoking by teenagers, which jumped by one-third during the 1990s. A federal study of 16,000 U.S. high school students found cigarette smoking rose from 27.5 percent of those surveyed in 1991 to 36.4 percent in 1997. Among black youths, the rate nearly doubled from 12.6 percent to 22.7 percent. Reasons behind these jumps include stable prices for cigarettes (prices didn't increase between 1992 and 1997), more glamorization of smoking in movies and television (for example, in the hit movie of the decade, *Titanic,* the two young, attractive leading characters smoked cigarettes), and advertising (such as Joe Camel) aimed at young people.

One way to reduce smoking is to raise the price of cigarettes through higher cigarette taxes. Researchers estimate the price elasticity of demand for cigarettes among young smokers to be about 1.3, so a 10 percent increase in the price of cigarettes would reduce smoking by 13 percent. As shown in Exhibit 6, among adult smokers, the estimated elasticity was only 0.4, or only about one-third that for young smokers.

Why are teenagers more sensitive to price changes than adults? First, recall that one of the factors affecting price elasticity of demand is the importance of the item in the consumer's budget. The share of income that a young smoker spends on cigarettes usually exceeds the share for adult smokers. Second, peer pressure is much more influential in a young person's decision to smoke than in an adult's decision to continue smoking (if anything, adults face negative peer pressure). The effects of a higher price get multiplied among young smokers because a higher price reduces smoking by peers. With fewer peers smoking, there is less pressure to smoke. And third, since smoking is addictive, young people who are not yet hooked are more sensitive to price increases than are adult smokers, who are already hooked.

If a price elasticity of 1.3 remains constant over the relevant range of price changes, a price increase of $1.80 per pack would reduce smoking among young people by 60 percent. To be fully effective, the price increase must be introduced quickly, not, as was proposed in Congress, phased in over five years. The experience from other countries supports the effectiveness of higher prices. For example, a large tax increase on cigarettes in Canada during the 1980s cut youth smoking by two-thirds.

Another approach has been to try to change consumer tastes through the Surgeon General's warning. The Canadian government has proposed putting pictures of cancerous tongues and lips on cigarette packs and publicizing the link between smoking and male impotence (so much for the Marlboro man). In California, a combination of higher cigarette taxes and an ambitious awareness program has contributed to a 5 percent decline in lung cancer among women there, even as it rose 13 percent in the rest of the country.

In a 1998 U.S. court settlement, tobacco companies agreed not to target young smokers in their marketing (Joe Camel was retired). A federal study reported a slight decline in teenage smoking, dropping from 36.4 percent of those surveyed in 1997 to 34.8 percent in 1999.

<interactive>exercise

eACTIVITY: DETERRING YOUNG SMOKERS

Sources: "Study Suggests Smoking May Cause Teenager Depression," Dow Jones Newswire, 2 October 2000; Lauran Neergaard, "Tobacco Claims More Women as Victims," *Hartford Courant,* 28 March 2001; "Prepared Statement of Frank J. Chaloupka, Ph.D., Before the Senate Judiciary Committee," Federal News Service, 29 October 1997. For more background on the tobacco settlement, go to http://www.pbs.org/wgbh/pages/frontline/ shows/settlement/.

PRICE ELASTICITY OF SUPPLY

Prices are signals to both sides of the market about the relative scarcity of products. High prices discourage consumption but encourage production. The price elasticity of demand measures how responsive consumers are to a price change. Likewise, the **price elasticity of supply** measures how responsive producers are to a price change. This elasticity is calculated in the same way as price elasticity of demand. In simplest terms, the price elasticity of supply equals the percentage change in quantity supplied divided by the percentage change in price. Since the higher price usually results in an increased quantity supplied, the percentage change in price and the percentage change in quantity supplied move in the same direction, so the price elasticity of supply is usually a positive number.

Exhibit 7 depicts a typical upward-sloping supply curve. As you can see, if the price increases from p to p', the quantity supplied increases from q to q'. Price and quantity supplied move in the same direction. Let's look at the elasticity formula for the supply curve. The price elasticity of supply, E_S, is:

$$E_S = \frac{\Delta q}{(q + q')/2} \div \frac{\Delta p}{(p + p')/2}$$

where Δq is the change in quantity supplied and Δp is the change in price. This is the same formula used to compute the price elasticity of demand except that q here is quantity supplied, not quantity demanded.

Categories of Supply Elasticity

The terminology for supply elasticity is the same as for demand elasticity: If supply elasticity is less than 1.0, supply is **inelastic;** if it equals 1.0, supply is **unit elastic;** and if it exceeds 1.0, supply is **elastic.** There are also some special values of supply elasticity to consider.

EXHIBIT 7

Price Elasticity of Supply

If the price increases from *p* to *p'*, the quantity supplied increases from *q* to *q'*. Price and quantity supplied move in the same direction, so the price elasticity of supply is a positive number.

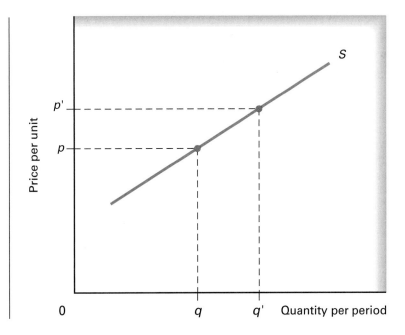

Perfectly Elastic Supply Curve.

At one extreme is the horizontal supply curve, such as supply curve *S* in panel (a) of Exhibit 8. In this case, producers will supply none of the good at a price below *p* but will supply any amount at price *p* (the quantity actually supplied at price *p* will depend on the amount demanded at that price). Because a tiny increase from a price just below *p* to a price of *p* results in an unlimited quantity supplied, this is a **perfectly elastic supply curve,** which has a numerical value of infinity. As individual consumers, we typically face perfectly elastic supply curves. When we go to the supermarket, we usually can buy as much as we want at the prevailing price but none at a lower price. This is not to say that all consumers together could buy an unlimited amount at the prevailing price. (Recall the fallacy of composition from Chapter 1.)

Perfectly Inelastic Supply Curve.

The most unresponsive relationship is where there is no change in the quantity supplied regardless of the price, as shown by the vertical supply curve *S'* in panel (b) of Exhibit 8. Because the percentage change in quantity supplied is zero, regardless of the change in price, the price elasticity of supply is zero. This is a **perfectly inelastic supply curve.** Any good in fixed supply, such as Picasso paintings, 1990 Dom Perignon champagne, or Cadillacs once owned by Elvis Presley, has a perfectly inelastic supply curve.

Unit-Elastic Supply Curve.

Any supply curve that is a straight line from the origin—such as *S''* in panel (c) of Exhibit 8—is a **unit-elastic supply curve.** This means that a percentage change in price will always generate an identical percentage change in quantity supplied. For example, along *S''* a doubling of the price results in a doubling of the quantity supplied. Note that unit elasticity is based not on the slope of the line but on the fact that the linear supply curve emanates from the origin.

Determinants of Supply Elasticity

The elasticity of supply indicates how responsive producers are to a change in price. Their responsiveness depends on how easy it is to alter output when the price changes. If the cost of supplying additional units rises sharply as output expands, then a higher price will elicit little increase in quantity supplied, so supply will tend to be inelastic. But if the marginal cost rises slowly as output expands, the lure of a higher price will prompt a large increase in output. In this case, supply will be more elastic.

EXHIBIT 8

Three Constant-Elasticity Supply Curves

Supply curve *S* in panel (a) is perfectly elastic (horizontal). Along *S*, firms will supply any amount of output demanded at price *p*. Supply curve *S'* is perfectly inelastic (vertical). *S'* shows that the quantity supplied is independent of the price. In panel (c), *S"*, a straight line from the origin, is a unit-elastic supply curve. Any percentage change in price results in the same percentage change in quantity supplied.

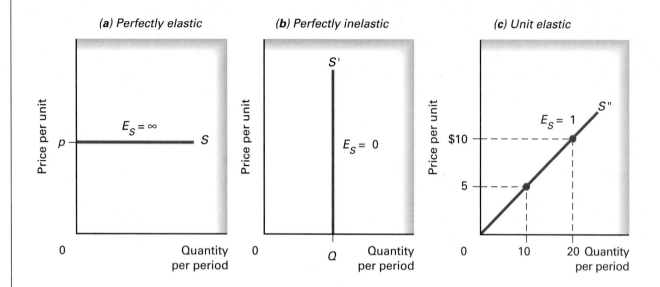

One determinant of supply elasticity is the length of the adjustment period under consideration. Just as demand becomes more elastic over time as consumers adjust to price changes, supply also becomes more elastic over time as producers adjust to price changes. The longer the time period under consideration, the more able producers are to adjust to changes in relative prices. Exhibit 9 presents a different supply curve for each of three periods. S_w is the supply curve when the period of adjustment is a week. As you can see, a higher price will not elicit much of a response in quantity supplied because firms have little time to adjust. This supply curve is inelastic if the price increases from $1.00 to $1.25.

S_m is the supply curve when the adjustment period under consideration is a month. Firms have a greater ability to vary output in a month than they do in a week. Thus, supply is more elastic when the adjustment period is a month than when it's a week. Supply is even more elastic when the adjustment period is a year, as is shown by S_y. So a given price increase elicits a greater quantity supplied as the adjustment period lengthens. For example, if the price of oil increases, oil producers in the short run can try to pump more from existing wells, but in the long run, a higher price stimulates more exploration. Research confirms the positive link between the price elasticity of supply and the length of the adjustment period. *The elasticity of supply is typically greater the longer the period of adjustment is.*

The ease of increasing quantity supplied in response to a higher price differs across industries. The response time will be slower for producers of electricity, oil, and timber (where expansion may take years) than for window washing, lawn maintenance, and hot-dog vending (where expansion may take only days).

OTHER ELASTICITY MEASURES

Price elasticities of demand and supply are frequently used in economic analysis, but two other elasticity measures also provide useful information.

ECONNEWS ONLINE: HAPPY HOLIDAYS FOR RETAILERS

EXHIBIT 9

Market Supply Becomes More Elastic over Time

The supply curve one week after a price increase, S_w, is less elastic, at a given price, than the curve one month later, S_m, which is less elastic than the curve one year later, S_y. Given a price increase from $1.00 to $1.25, quantity supplied per day increases to 110 units after one week, to 140 units after one month, and to 200 units after one year.

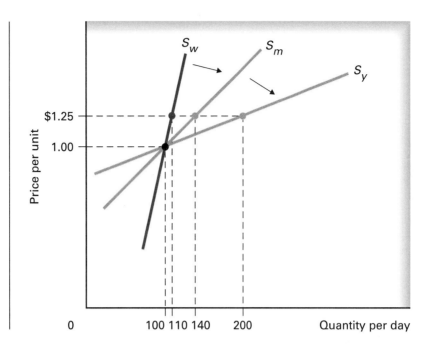

<interactive>**video**

CNN VIDEO: "CONSUMERS CREAMED BY HIGH MILK PRICES"

<interactive>**update**

ECONNEWS ONLINE: DRINK SUPPLIERS TRY TO KEEP SPIRITS UP

Income Elasticity of Demand

What happens to the demand for new cars, fresh vegetables, or computer software if consumers' money income increases by, say, 10 percent? The answer is of great interest to producers because it helps them predict the effect of changing income on quantity sold and on total revenue. The **income elasticity of demand** measures how responsive demand is to a change in income. Specifically, *the income elasticity of demand measures the percentage change in demand divided by the percentage change in income that caused it.*

As noted in Chapter 3, the demand for some products, such as used furniture and used clothing, actually declines, or shifts leftward, as income increases. Thus, the income elasticity of demand for such products is negative. Goods with income elasticities less than zero are called *inferior goods.* The demand for most goods increases, or shifts rightward, as income increases. These are called *normal goods* and have income elasticities greater than zero.

Let's take a closer look at normal goods. Suppose demand increases as income increases but by a smaller percentage than income increases. In such cases, the income elasticity is greater than zero but less than 1. For example, people buy more food as their incomes rise, but the percentage increase in demand is less than the percentage increase in income. Normal goods with income elasticities less than 1 are called *income inelastic. Necessities* such as food, housing, and clothing often have income elasticities less than 1.

Goods with income elasticity greater than 1 are called *income elastic. Luxuries,* such as luxury cars, vintage wine, and meals at fancy restaurants, have income elasticities greater than 1. For

EXHIBIT 10

Selected Income Elasticities of Demand

Product	Income Elasticity	Product	Income Elasticity
Private education	2.46	Physicians' services	0.75
Automobiles	2.45	Coca-Cola	0.68
Wine	2.19	Beef	0.62
Owner-occupied housing	1.49	Food	0.51
Furniture	1.48	Coffee	0.51
Dental service	1.42	Cigarettes	0.50
Restaurant meals	1.40	Gasoline and oil	0.48
Shoes	1.10	Rental housing	0.43
Chicken	1.06	Beer	0.27
Spirits ("hard" liquor)	1.02	Pork	0.18
Clothing	0.92	Flour	−0.36

Sources: F. Gasmi et al., "Econometric Analysis of Collusive Behavior in a Soft-Drink Market," *Journal of Economics and Management Strategy* (Summer 1992); J. Johnson et al., "Short-Run and Long-Run Elasticities for Canadian Consumption of Alcoholic Beverages," *Review of Economics and Statistics* (February 1992); H. Houthakker and L. Taylor, *Consumer Demand in the United States: Analyses and Projections,* 2nd ed. (Cambridge, Mass.: Harvard University Press, 1970); C. Huang et al., "The Demand for Coffee in the United States, 1963–77," *Quarterly Review of Economics and Business* (Summer 1980); and G. Brester and M. Wohlgenant, "Estimating Interrelated Demands for Meats Using New Measures for Ground and Table Cut Beef," *American Journal of Agricultrual Economics* (November 1991).

example, during 1990 and 1991, the U.S. economy experienced a recession, meaning that national income declined. As a result, the demand for meals at fancy restaurants decreased, and some went out of business. During the same period, the demand for basic food such as bread, sugar, and cheese changed very little. Incidentally, the terms *inferior goods, necessities,* and *luxuries* are not meant to imply a value judgment about the merit of particular goods; these terms are simply convenient ways of classifying economic behavior.

Exhibit 10 presents some income elasticity estimates for various goods and services. The figures indicate, for example, that as income increases, consumers spend proportionately more on restaurant meals, owner-occupied housing, and wine. Spending on food, rental housing, and beer also increases as income increases, but less than proportionately. So as income rises, the demand for restaurant meals increases more in percentage terms than does the demand for food, the demand for owner-occupied housing increases more in percentage terms than does the demand for rental housing, and the demand for wine increases more in percentage terms than does the demand for beer. Flour has negative income elasticity, indicating that the demand for flour declines as income increases.

As we have seen, the demand for food is income inelastic. The demand for food also tends to be price inelastic. This combination of income and price inelasticity creates special problems in agricultural markets, as discussed in the following case study.

CASE**STUDY**	The Market for Food and "The Farm Problem"
	● *Public Policy*

Despite decades of federal support and billions of tax dollars spent on various farm-assistance programs, the number of American farmers continues its long decline. Farm employment dropped by more than two-thirds from 10 million in 1950 to about 3 million today. The demise of the family farm can be traced to the price and income elasticities of demand for farm products and to technological breakthroughs that increased production.

Many of the forces that determine farm production are beyond a farmer's control. Temperature, rainfall, crop pests, and other natural forces affect crop size and quality. For example, weather in 1995 offered favorable growing conditions, and crop production increased 16 percent. Such swings in production create special problems for farmers because the demand for most farm crops, such as milk, eggs, corn, potatoes, oats, sugar, and beef, is price inelastic.

The effect of inelastic demand on farm revenue is illustrated in Exhibit 11. Suppose that in a normal year, farmers supply 10 billion bushels of grain at a market price of $5 a bushel. Annual farm revenue, which is price times quantity, totals $50 billion in our example. What if more favorable weather boosts grain production to 11 billion bushels, an increase of 10 percent? Because demand is price inelastic, the average price in our example must fall by more than 10 percent to, say, $4 per bushel to sell the additional billion bushels. Thus, the 10 percent increase in farm production gets sold only if the price drops by 20 percent.

Because, in percentage terms, the drop in price exceeds the increase in quantity demanded, total revenue declines from $50 billion to $44 billion. So total revenue drops by over 10 percent, despite the 10 percent increase in production. *Since demand is price inelastic, an increase in output reduces total revenue.* Of course, for farmers, the upside of inelastic demand is that a lower-than-normal crop results in a higher total revenue. For example, because of the drought of 1988, corn prices rose by more than 50 percent and farm income jumped. So weather-generated changes in farm production create year-to-year swings in farm revenue.

Problems created by fluctuations in farm revenue are compounded in the long run by the *income inelasticity* of demand for grain and, more generally, for food. As household incomes grow over time, spending on food may increase because consumers substitute prepared foods and restaurant meals for home cooking. But this switch has little effect on the total demand for farm products. Thus, as the economy grows over time and incomes rise, the demand for farm products tends to increase but by less than the increase in income. This is reflected by the modest increase in demand from D to D' in Exhibit 12.

Because of technological improvements in production, however, the supply of farm products has increased sharply. Farm output per hour of labor is about *eight times* greater now than in 1950 because of such developments as more sophisticated machines, better fertilizers, and healthier seed strains. For example, farmers in the Mississippi Delta using new strains of pest-resistant plants have cut insecticide applications from seven per season to one or none. Exhibit 12 shows a big increase in the supply of grain from S to S'. Since the increase in supply exceeds the increase in demand, the price of grain declines. And because the demand for grain is price inelastic, the percentage drop in price exceeds the percentage increase in output. The combined effect in our example is lower total revenue. In fact, net income (adjusted for inflation) to all U.S. farmers is now only half what it was in the early 1950s.

EXHIBIT 11

The Demand for Grain

The demand for grain tends to be price inelastic. As the market price falls, total revenue also falls.

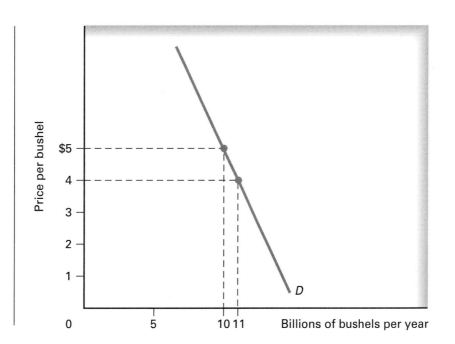

EXHIBIT 12|

The Effect of Increases in Supply and Demand on Farm Revenue

Over time, technological advances in farming have sharply increased the supply of grain. In addition, increases in household income over time have increased the demand for farm products. But because increases in the supply of grain have exceeded increases in demand, the combined effect has been a drop in the market price and a fall in total farm revenue.

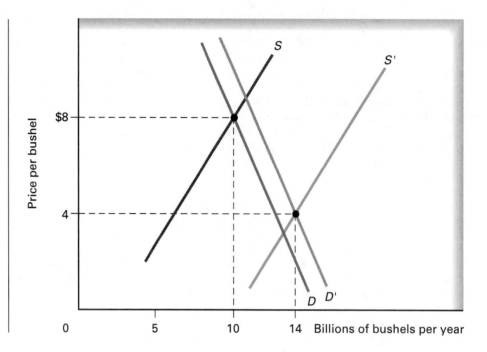

Another wild card in the farm-revenue equation is unstable foreign demand. Foreign demand for U.S. crops depends on foreign production and prices, on the exchange rate between the dollar and foreign currencies, and on public policy with regard to foreign trade. Some U.S. agricultural exports face foreign tariffs of 100 percent or more. Thus, many of the forces that shape the market for farm products are beyond the farmer's control. And demand that is both price inelastic and income inelastic means that greater farm output may lower total revenue.

<interactive>exercise

eACTIVITY: THE MARKET FOR FOOD AND "THE FARM PROBLEM"

Sources: Nicholas Kalaitzandonakes, "Biotechnology and Competitiveness," chap. 18 in *Competition in Agriculture: The United States in the World Market,* edited by W. Amponsah, et al. (Binghamton, NY: Haworth Press, 2000); Bruce L. Gardner, "Changing Economic Perspective on the Farm Problem," *Journal of Economic Literature* 30 (March 1992): 62–105; and *Economic Report of the President,* January 2001, Tables B–97 to B–101, at http://w3.access.gpo.gov/eop/. For current economic research at the U.S. Department of Agriculture, go to http://www.ers.usda.gov/.

Cross-Price Elasticity of Demand

Since a firm often produces an entire line of products, it has a special interest in how a change in the price of one product will affect the demand for another. For example, the Coca-Cola Company needs to know how changing the price of Cherry Coke will affect sales of Classic Coke. The company also needs to know the relationship between the price of Coke and the demand for Pepsi and vice versa. The responsiveness of the demand for one good to changes in the price of another good is called the **cross-price elasticity of demand.** It is defined as the percentage change in the demand of one good divided by the percentage change in the price of another good. Its numerical value can be positive, negative, or zero, depending on whether the two goods in question are substitutes, complements, or unrelated, respectively.

Substitutes. If an increase in the price of one good leads to an increase in the demand for another good, their cross-price elasticity is positive and the two goods are *substitutes.* For example, an increase in the price of Coke, other things constant, shifts the demand for Pepsi rightward, so the two are substitutes. The cross-price elasticity between Coke and Pepsi is estimated to be about 0.7, indicating that a 10 percent increase in the price of one will increase the demand for the other by 7 percent.[1]

Complements. If an increase in the price of one good leads to a decrease in the demand for another, their cross-price elasticity is negative and the goods are *complements*. For example, an increase in the price of gasoline, other things constant, shifts the demand for tires leftward because people drive less and replace their tires less frequently. Gasoline and tires have a negative cross-price elasticity and are complements.

In summary: *The cross-price elasticity of demand is positive for substitutes and negative for complements.* Most pairs of goods selected at random are *unrelated,* so the value of their cross-price elasticity is zero.

CONCLUSION

Because this chapter has been more quantitative than earlier ones have, you may have gotten overwhelmed by the mechanics and overlooked the intuitive appeal and neat simplicity of elasticity. *Elasticity measures the willingness and ability of buyers and sellers to alter their behavior in response to changes in their economic circumstances.* Firms try to estimate the price elasticity of demand for their products. Governments also have an ongoing interest in various elasticities. For example, state governments want to know the effect of an increase in the sales tax on total tax receipts, and local governments want to know how an increase in income will affect the demand for real estate and thus the revenue generated by a property tax. International groups are interested in elasticities; for example, the Organization of Petroleum Exporting Countries (OPEC) is concerned about the price elasticity of demand for oil—in the short run and in the long run. Since a corporation often produces an entire line of products, it also has a special interest in certain cross-price elasticities. Some corporate economists estimate elasticities for a living.

The appendix to this chapter shows how price elasticities of demand and supply shed light on the incidence of a tax.

endofchaptermaterial

- **Summary**
- **Questions for Review**
- **Problems and Exercises**

- **Experiential Exercises**
- **Wall Street Journal Exercise**
- **Appendix Questions**

[1] F. Gasmi, J. Laffont, and Q. Vuong, "Econometric Analysis of Collusive Behavior in a Soft-Drink Market," *Journal of Economics and Management Strategy* (Summer 1992).

Take the Post-Test to assess your overall understanding of the key ideas in this chapter. The Post-Test provides a comprehensive selection of exam-style questions addressing the main topics and concepts of the chapter. At the completion of each Post-Test, you will receive a score and instructive feedback on how you answered each question, and a direct link to the part of the chapter addressed in the question. Take the Post-Test as often as you need to—a record of your progress for each attempt is kept for you to revisit and gauge your improvement. And each Post-Test is randomly generated, so every attempt is new.

Post-Test

APPENDIX

PRICE ELASTICITY AND TAX INCIDENCE

A contributing factor to the Revolutionary War was a British tax on tea imported by the American Colonies. The tea tax led to the Boston Tea Party, where colonists dumped tea leaves into Boston Harbor. There was confusion about who would actually pay such a tax: would it be paid by tea suppliers, tea demanders, or both? As you will see, tax incidence—that is, who ultimately pays a tax—depends on the price elasticities of demand and supply.

DEMAND ELASTICITY AND TAX INCIDENCE

Panel (a) of Exhibit 13 depicts the market for tea leaves, with demand D and supply S. Before the tax is imposed, the intersection of demand and supply yields a market price of $1.00 per ounce and a market quantity of 10 million ounces per day. Now suppose a tax of $0.20 is imposed on each ounce sold. Recall that the supply curve represents the amount that producers are willing and able to supply at each price. Since the government now gets $0.20 for each ounce sold, that amount must be added to the original supply curve to get a supply curve that includes the tax. Thus, the shift in the supply curve from S to S_t reflects the decrease in supply resulting from the tax. *The effect of a tax on tea is to decrease the supply by the amount of the tax.* The demand curve remains the same because nothing happened to demand; only the quantity demanded changes.

The result of the tax in panel (a) is to raise the equilibrium price from $1.00 to $1.15 and to decrease the equilibrium quantity from 10 million to 9 million ounces. As a result of the tax,

---

EXHIBIT 13

Tea Leaf Market: Effects of Different Demand Elasticities on Sales Tax Incidence

The imposition of a $0.20-per-ounce tax shifts the supply curve leftward from S to S_t. In panel (a), with less elastic demand, the market price rises from $1.00 to $1.15 per ounce and the quantity demanded and supplied falls from 10 million ounces to 9 million. In panel (b), with more elastic demand, the same tax leads to an increase in price from $1.00 to $1.05 per ounce; the quantity demanded and supplied falls from 10 million ounces to 7 million. The more elastic the demand, the more the tax is paid by producers in the form of a lower net-of-tax receipt.

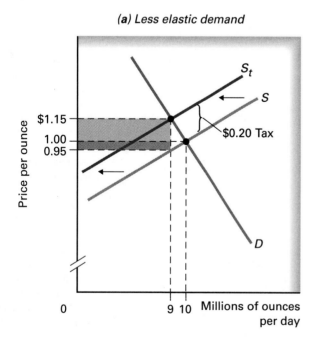

(a) Less elastic demand

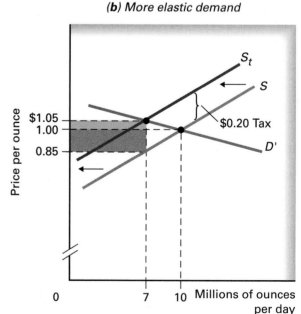

(b) More elastic demand

consumers pay $1.15, or $0.15 more per ounce, and producers receive $0.95 after the tax, or $0.05 less per ounce. Thus, consumers pay $0.15 of the $0.20 tax as a higher price, and producers pay $0.05 as a lower receipt.

The shaded area of panel (a) shows the total tax collected, which equals the tax per ounce of $0.20 times the 9 million ounces sold, for a total of $1.8 million in tax revenue per day. You can see that the original price line at $1 divides the shaded area into two portions—an upper portion showing the tax paid by consumers through a higher price and a lower portion showing the tax paid by producers through a lower net-of-tax receipt.

The same situation is depicted in panel (b) of Exhibit 13, except that demand is more elastic than in the left panel. Consumers in panel (b) cut their quantity demanded more sharply in response to a price change, so producers cannot as easily pass the tax along as a higher price. The tax increases the price by $0.05, to $1.05, and the net-of-tax receipt to suppliers declines by $0.15 to $0.85. Total tax revenue equals $0.20 per ounce times 7 million ounces sold, or $1.4 million per day. Again, the upper rectangle of the shaded area shows the portion of the tax paid by consumers through a higher price, and the lower rectangle shows the portion paid by producers through a lower net-of-tax receipt. The tax is the difference between the amount consumers pay and the amount producers receive.

More generally, as long as the supply curve slopes upward, *the more price elastic the demand, the more tax producers pay as a lower net-of-tax receipt and the less consumers bear as a higher price.* Also notice that the amount sold decreases more in panel (b) than in panel (a): Other things constant, the total tax revenue declines more when demand is more elastic. Because tax revenue falls as the price elasticity of demand increases, governments around the world tend to tax products with inelastic demand, such as cigarettes, liquor, gasoline, gambling, coffee, and tea.

<interactive>graph

TRY IT: TAX INCIDENCE IN THE CIGARETTE MARKET

SUPPLY ELASTICITY AND TAX INCIDENCE

The effect of the elasticity of supply on tax incidence is shown in Exhibit 14. The same demand curve appears in both panels, but the supply curve is more elastic in panel (a). Again we begin with an equilibrium price of $1.00 per ounce and an equilibrium quantity of 10 million ounces of tea leaves per day. Once the sales tax of $0.20 per ounce is imposed, supply decreases in both panels to reflect the tax. Notice that in panel (a), the price rises to $1.15, or $0.15 above the pretax price of $1.00, while in panel (b), the price increases by only $0.05. Thus, more of the tax is passed on to consumers in panel (a), where supply is more elastic. The more readily suppliers can cut production in response to a newly imposed tax, the more of the tax consumers will pay. More generally, as long as the demand curve slopes downward, *the more elastic the supply, the less tax producers pay as a lower net-of-tax receipt and the more consumers bear as a higher price.*

We conclude that *the less elastic the demand and the more elastic the supply, the greater the share of the tax paid by consumers.* You can think of a sales tax as a hot potato. The side of the market that's more nimble (that is, more price elastic) in adjusting to a price increase is more able to stick the other side of the market with most of the tax.

EXHIBIT 14

Tax on Tea Leaf Market: Effects of Different Supply Elasticities on Sales Tax Incidence

The imposition of a $0.20-per-ounce tax shifts leftward both the more elastic supply curve of panel (a) and the less elastic curve of panel (b). In panel (a), the market price rises from $1.00 per ounce to $1.15; in panel (b), the price rises to $1.05 per ounce. Thus, the more elastic the supply, the more the tax is paid by consumers.

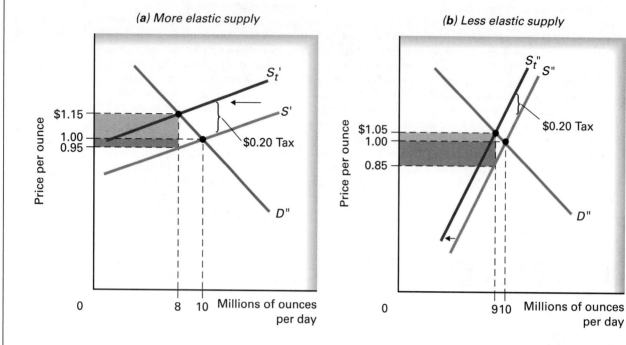

CHAPTER 6

Consumer Choice and Demand

Why are newspapers sold in vending machines that allow you to take more than one copy? How much do you eat when you can eat all you want? Why don't restaurants allow doggie bags with their all-you-can-eat specials? What's a cure for spring fever? Why is water cheaper than diamonds even though water is essential to life and diamonds are mere baubles? To answer these and other questions, we take a closer look at consumer demand, a key building block in economics.

You have already learned two reasons why demand curves slope downward. The first is the *substitution effect* of a price change. When the price of a good falls, consumers substitute that now-cheaper good for other goods. The second is the *income effect* of a price change. When the price of a good falls, consumers' real incomes increase, increasing their ability to buy more.

Demand is so important that we must know more about it. In this chapter, we develop the law of demand based on the satisfaction derived from consumption. As usual, we assume that consumer choice in a world of scarcity is motivated by the desire to maximize utility, or satisfaction. The point of this chapter is not to tell you how to maximize utility—that comes naturally. But understanding the theory behind our behavior helps us understand the implications of that behavior, making predictions more accurate. Topics discussed in this chapter include:

Pre-Test

Take the Pre-Test to assess your initial knowledge of the key ideas in this chapter. The Pre-Test provides exam-style questions addressing the main topics and concepts of the chapter. At the completion of each Pre-Test, you will receive a score and instructive feedback on how you answered each question, and a direct link to the part of the chapter addressed in the question. Take the Pre-Test as often as you need to—a record of your progress for each attempt is kept for you to revisit and gauge your improvement.

- Total and marginal utility
- Law of diminishing marginal utility
- Measuring utility
- Utility-maximizing condition
- Consumer surplus
- Role of time in demand
- Money price and time price of goods

‹interactive›exercise

ECONDEBATE ONLINE: UTILITY AND CONSUMER CHOICE

‹interactive›update

- ECONDATA ONLINE: UTILITY AND CONSUMER CHOICE
- ECONLINKS ONLINE: ECONOMICS WEB LINKS
- ECONNEWS ONLINE: UTILITY AND CONSUMER CHOICE

UTILITY ANALYSIS

Suppose you and a friend dine out together. After dinner, your friend asks how you liked your meal. You wouldn't say, "I liked mine twice as much as you liked yours." Nor would you say, "It deserves a rating of 86 on the U.S. Consumer Satisfaction Index." The utility, or satisfaction, you derive from that meal cannot be compared with another person's experience, nor can you measure your utility objectively. But you might say, "I liked it better than my last meal here." More generally, you can say whether one of your experiences was more satisfying than another. Even if you say nothing, we can draw inferences by observing your behavior. For example, we can conclude that you like apples more than oranges if, when the two are priced the same, you always buy apples.

Tastes and Preferences

As was mentioned in Chapter 4, *utility* is the sense of pleasure, or satisfaction, that comes from consumption. Utility is subjective. The utility you derive from consuming a particular good depends on your **tastes,** which are your preferences for different goods and services—your likes and dislikes in consumption. Some goods are extremely appealing to you and others are not. You may not understand, for example, why someone would pay good money for sharks' fin soup, calves' brains, polka music, or martial arts movies. Why are nearly all baby carriages sold in the United States navy blue, whereas they are yellow in Italy and chartreuse in Germany? And why do Australians favor chicken-flavored potato chips and chicken-flavored salt?

Economists actually have little to say about the origin of tastes or why tastes differ across individuals, across households, across regions, and across countries. *Economists assume simply that tastes are given and are relatively stable—that is, different people may have different tastes, but an individual's tastes are not constantly in flux.* To be sure, tastes for some products do change over time. Here are two examples: (1) during the last decade, hiking and work boots replaced running shoes as everyday footwear among college students, and (2) Americans began consuming leaner cuts of beef after a 1982 report linked the fat in red meat to a greater risk of cancer. Still, economists believe tastes are stable enough to allow us to examine relationships such as that between price and quantity demanded. If tastes were not relatively stable, then we could not reasonably make the other-things-constant assumption in demand analysis. We could not even draw a demand curve.

The Law of Diminishing Marginal Utility

Suppose it's a hot summer day and you are extremely thirsty after jogging four miles. You pour yourself an eight-ounce glass of ice water. That first glass is wonderful, and it puts a serious dent in your thirst; the next one is not quite as wonderful, but it is still pretty good; the third one is just fair; and the fourth glass you barely finish. Let's talk about the *utility,* or satisfaction, you get from consuming water.

We want to distinguish between total utility and marginal utility. **Total utility** is the total satisfaction you derive from consumption. For example, total utility is the total satisfaction you get from consuming four glasses of water. **Marginal utility** is the change in total utility resulting from a one-unit change in consumption of a good. For example, the marginal utility of a third glass of water is the change in total utility resulting from consuming that third glass of water.

Your experience with water reflects a law of utility analysis: the **law of diminishing marginal utility.** This law states that the more of a good an individual consumes per period, other things constant, the smaller the increase in total utility from additional consumption—that is, the smaller the marginal utility of each additional unit consumed. The marginal utility you derive from each additional glass of water declines as your consumption increases. You enjoy the first glass a lot, but each additional glass provides less and less marginal utility. If forced to drink a fifth glass, you wouldn't enjoy it; your marginal utility would be negative. Diminishing marginal utility is a feature of all consumption. A second foot-long Subway sandwich at one meal, for most people, would provide little or no marginal utility. You might still enjoy a second movie on Friday night, but a third would probably be too much to take. Marginal utility does not always decline right away or very quickly, but it eventually declines. For example, you might eat a lot of potato chips before the marginal utility of additional chips begins to fall.

After a long winter, that first warm day of spring is something special and is the cause of "spring fever." The fever is "cured" by many warm days like the first. By the time August rolls around, most people attach much less marginal utility to yet another warm day. For some goods, the drop in marginal utility with additional consumption is more pronounced. A second copy of the same daily newspaper would likely provide you with no marginal utility (in fact, the design of newspaper vending machines relies on the fact that you will not want to take more than one).[1] Likewise, a second viewing of the same movie at one sitting usually yields no additional utility. More generally, the expression "Been there, done that" conveys the idea that, for many activities, things start to get old after the first time. Restaurants depend on the law of diminishing marginal utility when they hold all-you-can-eat specials—and no doggie bags, since the deal is all you can eat now, not now and for the next two weeks.

<interactive>video

ASK THE INSTRUCTOR: HOW IS WEIGHT GAIN RELATED TO THE LAW OF DIMINISHING MARGINAL UTILITY?

MEASURING UTILITY

So far, our descriptions of utility have used such words as *wonderful, good,* and *fair.* We cannot push the analysis very far with such subjective language. If we want to predict behavior based on changes in the economic environment, we must develop a consistent way of viewing utility.

Units of Utility

Let's go back to the water example. Although there really is no objective way of measuring utility, if pressed, you might be more specific about how much you enjoyed each glass of water. For example, you might say the second glass was half as good as the first, the third was half as good as the second, the fourth was half as good as the third, and you passed up a fifth glass because you expected no positive utility. To get a handle on this description of your satisfaction, let's assign arbitrary numbers to the amount of utility from each quantity consumed, so the pattern of numbers reflects your expressed satisfaction. Let's say the first glass of water provides you with 40 units of utility, the second glass with 20, the third with 10, and the fourth with 5. A fifth glass, if you were forced to drink it, would yield negative utility, in this case, say, −2 units of utility. *Developing numerical values for utility allows us to be more specific about the utility derived from consumption.* If it would help, you could think of units of utility more playfully as thrills, kicks, or jollies—as in, getting your kicks from consumption.

---

[1]Marshall Jevons, *The Fatal Equilibrium* (Cambridge, MA: MIT Press, 1985).

By attaching a numerical measure to utility, we can compare the total utility a particular consumer gets from different goods as well as the marginal utility that same consumer gets from additional consumption. Thus, we can employ units of utility to evaluate a consumer's preferences for additional units of a good or even additional units of different goods. Note, however, that we should not try to compare units of utility across consumers. *Each person has a uniquely subjective utility scale.*

The first column of Exhibit 1 lists possible quantities of water you might consume after running four miles on a hot day. The second column presents the total utility derived from that

EXHIBIT 1

Utility You Derive from Water After Jogging Four Miles

Units of Water Consumed (8-ounce glasses)	Total Utility	Marginal Utility
0	0	—
1	40	40
2	60	20
3	70	10
4	75	5
5	73	−2

EXHIBIT 2

Total Utility and Marginal Utility You Derive from Water After Jogging Four Miles

Total utility, shown in panel (a), increases with each of the first four glasses of water consumed but by smaller and smaller amounts. The fifth glass causes total utility to fall, implying that marginal utility is negative, as shown in panel (b).

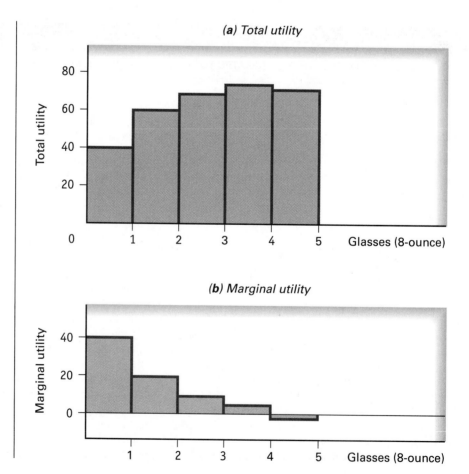

(a) Total utility

(b) Marginal utility

EXHIBIT 3

Total and Marginal Utilities from Pizza and Video Rentals

Pizza				Video Rental			
(1) Consumed per Week	(2) Total Utility	(3) Marginal Utility	(4) Marginal Utility per Dollar if p = $8	(5) Consumed per Week	(6) Total Utility	(7) Marginal Utility	(8) Marginal Utility per Dollar if p = $4
0	0	—	—	0	0	—	—
1	56	56	7	1	40	40	10
2	88	32	4	2	68	28	7
3	**112**	**24**	**3**	3	88	20	5
4	130	18	2¼	**4**	**100**	**12**	**3**
5	142	12	1½	5	108	8	2
6	150	8	1	6	114	6	1½

consumption, and the third column shows the marginal utility of each additional glass of water consumed. Recall that marginal utility is the change in total utility that results from consuming an additional unit of the good. You can see from the second column that total utility increases with each of the first four glasses but by smaller and smaller amounts. The third column shows that the first glass of water yields 40 units of utility, the second glass yields an additional 20 units, and so on. Marginal utility declines after the first glass of water, becoming negative with the fifth glass. At any level of consumption, marginal utilities sum to total utility. Total utility is graphed in panel (a) of Exhibit 2. Again, because of diminishing marginal utility, each glass adds less to total utility, so total utility increases for the first four glasses but at a decreasing rate. Marginal utility appears in panel (b).

Utility Maximization in a World Without Scarcity

Economists assume that your purpose for drinking water, as with all consumption, is to *maximize your total utility*. So how much water do you consume? If the price of water is zero, you drink water as long as each additional glass increases total utility; so you consume four glasses of water. *If a good is free, you increase consumption as long as additional units provide positive marginal utility.*

Let's extend the analysis of utility to discuss the consumption of two goods—pizza and video rentals. We will continue to translate the satisfaction you receive from consumption into units of utility. Given your tastes and preferences, suppose your total utility and marginal utility from consumption are as presented in Exhibit 3. The first four columns apply to pizza and the second four to video rentals. Please spend a little time right now becoming familiar with each column.

Notice from columns (3) and (7) that both goods exhibit diminishing marginal utility. Given this set of preferences, how much of each good would you consume per week? At a zero price, you would increase consumption as long as you derive positive marginal utility from additional units of each good. Thus, you would consume at least the first six pizzas and first six videos because both generate positive marginal utility at that level of consumption. Did you ever go to a party where the food and drinks were free to you? How much did you eat and drink? You ate and drank until you didn't want any more—that is, until the marginal utility of each good consumed fell to zero.

Utility Maximization in a World of Scarcity

Alas, scarcity is our lot, so we should focus on how a consumer chooses when goods are not free. Suppose the price of a pizza is $8, the rental price of a video is $4, and your after-tax income from a part-time job is $40 per week. You still want to maximize utility, but now it is subject to the conditions that your income is limited and prices are greater than zero. Under these conditions, *the utility you receive from different goods relative to their prices determines how you allocate your income.* In the real world, consumption depends on tastes (as reflected by the marginal utilities), prices, and your income.

How do you allocate income between the two goods to maximize utility? Suppose you start off with some combination of pizzas and videos. If you can increase your utility by reallocating expenditures, you will do so, and you will continue to make adjustments as long as you can increase your utility. There may be some trial and error at first, but by learning from your mistakes, you move toward the utility-maximizing position. When no further utility-increasing moves are possible, you have settled on the combination that maximizes your utility, given your tastes, prices, and your income—*you have arrived at the equilibrium combination.* Once you achieve utility-maximizing equilibrium, you will maintain this consumption pattern unless there is a change in your tastes, your income, or the prices you face.

To get the process rolling, suppose you start off spending your entire budget of $40 on pizza, purchasing five pizzas a week, which yields a total of 142 units of utility. You soon realize that if you buy one less pizza, you free up enough money to rent two movies. Would total utility increase? Sure. You give up 12 units of utility, the marginal utility of the fifth pizza, to get 68 units of utility from the first two videos. Total utility thereby increases from 142 to 198. Then you notice that if you reduce purchases to three pizzas, you give up 18 units of utility from the fourth pizza but gain a total of 32 units of utility from the third and fourth videos. This is another utility-increasing move.

Further reductions in pizza, however, would reduce your total utility because you would give up 24 units of utility from the third pizza but gain only 14 from the fifth and sixth videos. Thus, by trial and error, you find that the utility-maximizing equilibrium combination is three pizzas and four videos per week, for a total utility of 212. This involves an outlay of $24 on pizza and $16 on videos. *You are in equilibrium when consuming this combination because any affordable change would reduce your total utility.* Note that you demand fewer pizzas and videos now than when their price was zero.

Utility-Maximizing Conditions

As you can see from the previous example, once equilibrium has been achieved, any change in your consumption bundle will decrease utility. *Once a consumer is in equilibrium, there is no way to increase utility by reallocating the budget.* But we can say more: *In equilibrium, the last dollar spent on each good yields the same marginal utility.* Let's see how this works. Column (4) shows the marginal utility of pizza divided by its price of $8. Column (8) shows the marginal utility of video rentals divided by its price of $4. You can see that the equilibrium choice of three pizzas and four video rentals exhausts the $40 budget and yields 3 more units of utility for the last dollar spent on each good. **Consumer equilibrium** is achieved when the budget is completely spent and the last dollar spent on each good yields the same utility, or when the marginal utility of pizza divided by its price equals the marginal utility of video rental divided by its price. In short, the consumer gets the same bang per last buck spent on each good. This equality can be expressed as:

$$\frac{MU_p}{p_p} = \frac{MU_v}{p_v}$$

where MU_p is the marginal utility of pizza, p_p is the price of pizza, MU_v is the marginal utility of video rentals, and p_v is the price of renting videos. Although we have considered only two goods, the logic of utility maximization applies to any number of goods. The consumer will reallocate spending until the last dollar spent on each product yields the same marginal utility.

In equilibrium, higher-priced goods must yield more marginal utility than lower-priced goods—enough additional utility to compensate for their higher price. Since a pizza costs twice as much as a video rental, the marginal utility of the final pizza purchased must, in equilibrium, be twice that of the final video rented. Indeed, the marginal utility of the third pizza, 24, is twice that of the fourth video, 12. Economists do not claim that you consciously equate the ratios of marginal utility to price, but they do claim that you act as if you had made such calculations. *Thus, you decide how much of each good to purchase by considering your preferences, market prices, and your income.*

So *consumers maximize utility by equalizing the marginal utility per dollar of expenditure across goods.* This equality resolved what had been an economic puzzle, as discussed in the following case study.

● *Bringing Theory to Life*

Centuries ago, economists puzzled over the price of diamonds relative to the price of water. Diamonds are mere baubles—certainly not a necessity of life in any sense. Water is essential to life and has a huge number of uses. Yet diamonds are expensive, while water is cheap. For example, the $10,000 spent on a one-carat diamond could instead buy about 10,000 bottles of water or about 5 million gallons of municipally supplied water (which typically sells for about 20 cents per 100 gallons). However measured, diamonds are extremely expensive relative to water. For the price of a one-carat diamond, you could buy enough water to last a lifetime.

How can the price of something as useful as water be so much lower than something of such limited use as diamonds? In 1776, Adam Smith discussed what has come to be called the *diamonds-water paradox.* Because water is essential to life, the total utility derived from water greatly exceeds the total utility derived from diamonds. Yet the market value of a good is based not on its total utility but on what consumers are willing and able to pay for an additional unit of the good—that is, on its marginal utility. Since water is so abundant in nature, we consume water to the point where the marginal utility of the last gallon purchased is relatively low. Since diamonds are relatively scarce in nature, the marginal utility of the last diamond purchased is relatively high. Thus, water is cheap and diamonds expensive. As Ben Franklin said "We will only know the worth of water when the well is dry."

Speaking of water, in the past decade, sales of bottled water gushed 150 percent—faster than any other beverage category—creating a $5 billion industry in the United States. Annual consumption of bottled water increased from 5 gallons to 12 gallons per capita. The United States offers the world's largest market for bottled water—importing water from places such as Italy, France, Sweden, Wales, and even Fiji. "Water bars" in Boston, New York, and Los Angeles offer bottled water as the main attraction.

Why would consumers pay a premium for bottled water when they can drink tap water for virtually nothing? First, many people do not view the two as good substitutes. Some have concerns about the safety of tap water, and they consider bottled water a healthy alternative (in a recent Gallup Poll, about half those surveyed said they won't drink water straight from the tap). Second, even those who drink tap water find bottled water a convenient option away from home.

According to the theory of utility maximization, people who buy bottled water apparently feel the additional benefit offsets the additional cost. Bottled-water sales are expected to grow and represent the top threat to the soft-drink industry. But if you can't fight 'em, join 'em: Pepsi's Aquafina is the top-selling U.S. brand of bottled water, and Coke also launched its own brand, Dasani.

eACTIVITY: WATER, WATER, EVERYWHERE

Sources: Corby Kummer, "What's In the Water?" *New York Times Magazine,* 30 August 1998; Betsy McKay, "Consumers' Appetite for Soda Is Going Flat," *Wall Street Journal,* 19 September 2000; and "Lax Laws Raise Tap Water Risks," *USA Today,* 21 October 1998. The Definitive Bottled Water Site is http://www.bottledwaterweb.com/ and the International Bottled Water Association site is http://www.bottledwater.org/.

The Law of Demand and Marginal Utility

The purpose of utility analysis is to provide information about quantity demanded. How does the previous analysis relate to your demand for pizza? It yields a single point on your demand curve for pizza: At a price of $8, you demand three pizzas per week. This point is based on a given income of $40 per week, a given rental price of $4 per video, and your tastes reflected by the utility tables in Exhibit 3. This single point, in itself, offers no inkling about the shape of your demand curve. To generate another point, let's see what happens to quantity demanded if the price of pizza changes, while keeping other things constant (such as tastes, income, and the price of video rentals). Suppose the price of a pizza drops from $8 to $6.

Exhibit 4 is the same as Exhibit 3, except the price per pizza has been reduced from $8 to $6. Your original choice was three pizzas and four video rentals. At that combination and with

EXHIBIT 4

Total and Marginal Utilities from Pizza and Video Rentals After the Price of Pizza Decreases from $8 to $6 Each

	Pizza				Video Rental			
(1) Consumed per Week	(2) Total Utility	(3) Marginal Utility	(4) Marginal Utility per Dollar if p = $6	(5) Consumed per Week	(6) Total Utility	(7) Marginal Utility	(8) Marginal Utility per Dollar if p = $4
0	0	—	—	0	0	—	—
1	56	56	9⅓	1	40	40	10
2	88	32	5⅓	2	68	28	7
3	112	24	4	3	88	20	5
4	**130**	**18**	**3**	**4**	**100**	**12**	**3**
5	142	12	2	5	108	8	2
6	150	8	1⅓	6	114	6	1½

the price of pizza now $6, the marginal utility per dollar expended on the third pizza is 4, but the marginal utility per dollar on the fourth video remains at 3. The marginal utilities of the last dollar spent on each good are no longer equal. What's more, if you maintained the original combination, you would be spending only $18 on pizza, leaving $6 unspent. So you could still buy your original combination but have $6 left over (this, incidentally, shows the income effect of a lower price of pizza). You can increase your utility by consuming a different bundle. Take a moment now to see if you can figure out what that new equilibrium bundle should be.

In light of your utility schedules in Exhibit 4, you would increase your consumption to four pizzas per week. This increase exhausts your budget and equates the marginal utilities of the last dollar expended on each good. Your video rentals remain the same (although they could have changed due to the income effect of the price change). But as your consumption increases to four pizzas, the marginal utility of the fourth pizza, 18, divided by the price of $6 yields 3 units of utility per dollar of expenditure, which is the same as for the fourth video. You are in equilibrium once again. Your total utility increases by the 18 units you derive from the fourth pizza. Thus, you are clearly better off as a result of the price decrease.

We now have a second point on your demand curve for pizza—if the price of pizza is $6, your quantity demanded is four pizzas. The two points are presented as *a* and *b* in Exhibit 5. We could continue to change the price of pizza and thereby generate additional points on the demand curve, but you can get some idea of the demand curve's downward slope from these two points. The shape of the demand curve for pizza conforms to our expectations based on the law of demand: Price and quantity demanded are inversely related. (Try to estimate your price elasticity of demand between points *a* and *b*. Hint: What does your total spending on pizza tell you?)

We have gone to some length to see how you (or any consumer) maximize utility. Given prices and your income, your tastes and preferences naturally guide you to the most preferred bundle. You are not even conscious of your behavior. The urge to maximize utility is like the force of gravity—both work whether or not you understand them. Even animals seem to behave in a way that appears consistent with the law of demand. Wolves, for example, exhibit no territorial concerns when game is plentiful. But when game becomes scarce, wolves carefully mark their territory and defend it against interlopers. Thus, wolves appear to value game more when it is relatively scarce.

Now that you have some idea of utility, let's consider an application of utility analysis.

Consumer Surplus

In our earlier example, total utility increased when the price of pizza fell from $8 to $6. In this section, we take a closer look at how consumers benefit from a lower price. Suppose your demand for foot-long Subway sandwiches is as shown in Exhibit 6. Recall that in constructing

EXHIBIT 5

Demand for Pizza Generated from Marginal Utility

At a price of $8 per pizza, the consumer is in equilibrium when consuming three pizzas (point *a*). Marginal utility per dollar is the same for all goods consumed. If the price falls to $6, the consumer will increase consumption to four pizzas (point *b*). Points *a* and *b* are two points on this consumer's demand curve for pizza.

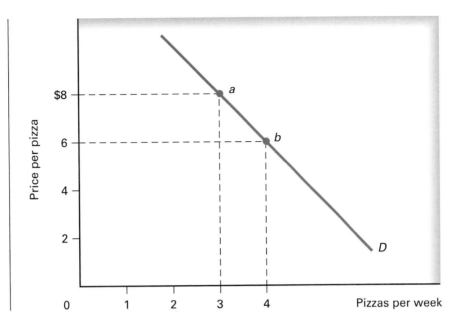

EXHIBIT 6

Consumer Surplus from Subway Sandwiches

At a given quantity of Subway sandwiches, the height of the demand curve shows the value of the last one purchased. The area under the demand curve up to a specific quantity shows the total value the consumer places on that quantity. At a price of $4, the consumer purchases four Subways. The first one is valued at $7, the second at $6, the third at $5, and the fourth at $4. The consumer values four at $22. Since the consumer pays $4 per Subway, all four can be obtained for $16. The difference between what the consumer would have been willing to pay ($22) and what the consumer actually pays ($16) is called consumer surplus. When the price is $4, the consumer surplus is represented by the dark shaded area under the demand curve above $4. When the price of Subways falls to $3, consumer surplus increases by $4, as reflected by the lighter shaded area.

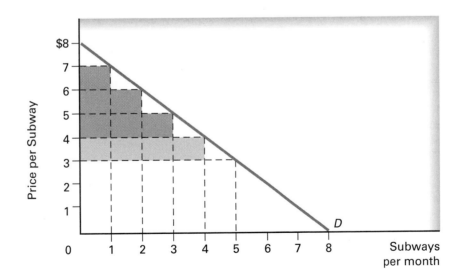

an individual's demand curve, we hold tastes, income, and the prices of related goods constant; only the price varies.

At a price of $8 or above, you find that the marginal utility of other goods that you could buy for $8 to be higher than the marginal utility of a Subway. Consequently, you buy no Subways. At a price of $7, you are willing and able to buy one per month, so the marginal utility of that first Subway exceeds the marginal utility you expected from spending that $7 on your best alternative—say, a movie ticket. A price of $6 prompts you to buy two Subways a month. The second is worth at least $6 to you. At a price of $5, you buy three Subways, and at $4, you buy four. *In each case, the value to you of the last Subway purchased must at least equal the price; otherwise, you wouldn't buy it.* Along the demand curve, therefore, the price reflects your **marginal valuation** of the good, or the dollar value of the marginal utility derived from consuming each additional unit.

Notice that if the price is $4, you can purchase each of the four Subways for that price, even though you would have been willing to pay more than $4 for each of the first three Subways. The first sandwich provides marginal utility that you valued at $7; the second you valued at $6; and the third you valued at $5. In fact, if you had to, you would have been willing to pay $7 for the first, $6 for the second, and $5 for the third. The dollar value of the total utility of the first four sandwiches is $7 + $6 + $5 + $4 = $22. But when the price is $4, you get all four for $16. Thus, a price of $4 confers a **consumer surplus,** or a consumer bonus, equal to the difference between the maximum amount you would have been willing to pay ($22) rather than go without Subways altogether and what you actually paid ($16). When the price is $4, your consumer surplus is $6, as shown by the six darker shaded blocks in Exhibit 6. Consumer surplus equals the value of the total utility you receive from consuming the sandwiches minus your total spending on them. An approximation of consumer surplus is the area under the demand curve but above the price.

If the price falls to $3, you purchase five Subways a month. Apparently, you feel that the marginal utility you receive from the fifth one is worth at least $3. The lower price means that you get to buy all five for $3 each, even though all but the fifth are worth more to you than $3. Your consumer surplus when the price is $3 is the value of the total utility conferred by the first five, which is $7 + $6 + $5 + $4 + $3 = $25, minus your cost, which is $3 × 5 = $15. Thus, your consumer surplus totals $25 − $15 = $10, as indicated by both the dark and the light shaded blocks in Exhibit 6. So if the price declines to $3, your consumer surplus increases by $4, as reflected by the four lighter-shaded blocks in Exhibit 6. You can see how consumers benefit from lower prices.

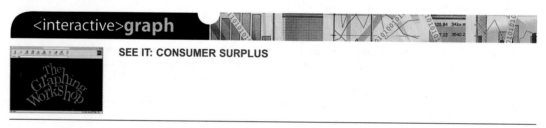

<interactive>graph

SEE IT: CONSUMER SURPLUS

Market Demand and Consumer Surplus

Let's talk more generally now about the market demand for a good, assuming the market consists of you and two other consumers. *The market demand curve is simply the horizontal sum of the individual demand curves for all consumers in the market.* Exhibit 7 shows how the demand curves for three consumers in the market for Subway sandwiches are summed horizontally to yield the market demand. At a price of $4, for example, you demand four Subways per month, Brittany demands two, and Chris demands none. The market demand at a price of $4 is therefore six sandwiches. At a price of $2, you demand six per month, Brittany four, and Chris two, for a market demand of 12. *The market demand curve shows the total quantity demanded per period by all consumers at various prices.*

The idea of consumer surplus can be used to examine market demand as well as individual demand. *At a given price, consumer surplus for the market is the difference between the amount consumers are willing to pay for that quantity and the total amount they do pay.*

Instead of just three consumers in the market, suppose there are many. Exhibit 8 presents market demand for a good when there are millions of consumers. If the price is $2 per unit, each person adjusts his or her quantity demanded until the marginal valuation of the last unit purchased equals $2. But each consumer gets to buy all other units for $2 each as well. In Exhibit 8, the dark shading, bounded above by the demand curve and below by the price of $2, depicts the consumer surplus when the price is $2. The light shading shows the increase in consumer surplus if the price drops to $1. Notice that if this good were given away, the consumer surplus would not be significantly greater than when the price is $1.

Consumer surplus is the net benefit consumers get from market exchange. It can be used to measure economic welfare and to compare the effects of different market structures, different tax structures, and different public expenditure programs, such as medical care, as discussed in the following case study.

EXHIBIT 7

Summing Individual Demands to Derive the Market Demand for Subway Sandwiches

At a price of $4 per Subway, you demand 4 per month, Brittany demands 2, and Chris demands none. Total market demand at a price of $4 is $4 + 2 + 0 = 6$ Subways per month. At a lower price of $2, you demand 6, Brittany demands 4, and Chris demands 2. Market demand at a price of $2 is 12 Subways. The market demand curve D is the horizontal sum of individual demand curves d_Y, d_B, and d_C.

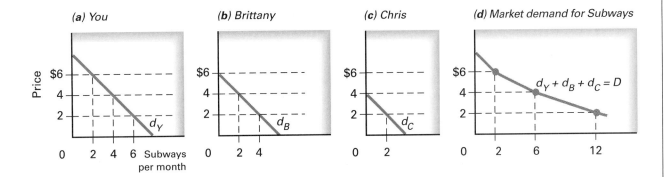

EXHIBIT 8

Market Demand and Consumer Surplus

Consumer surplus at a price of $2 is shown by the darker area. If the price falls to $1, consumer surplus increases to include the lighter area.

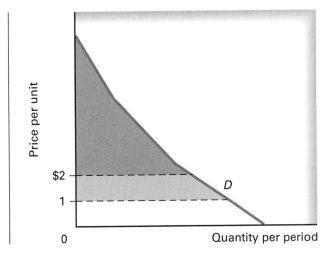

<interactive>**exercise**

READING IT RIGHT: WALL STREET JOURNAL EXERCISE

| CASE**STUDY** | The Marginal Value of Free Medical Care |

● *Public Policy*

Certain Americans, such as the elderly and those on welfare, are provided government-subsidized medical care. State and federal taxpayers spent over $420 billion in 2000 to provide medical care to 75 million Medicare and Medicaid recipients, for an average annual cost of about $5,600 per beneficiary. The dollar cost to most beneficiaries of these programs was usually little or nothing. The problem with giving something away is that beneficiaries consume it to the point where their marginal benefit from the final unit is zero, although the marginal cost to taxpayers can be substantial.

This is not to say that beneficiaries derive no benefit from free medical care. Although they may attach little or no value to marginal units, they likely derive a large consumer surplus from the other units they consume. For example, suppose that Exhibit 8 represents the demand for medical care by Medicaid beneficiaries. Since the price to them is zero, they consume up to the point where the demand curve intersects the horizontal axis, so their consumer surplus is the entire area under the demand curve.

But the cost to taxpayers of providing that final unit of medical care may be $100 or more. One way to reduce the total cost to taxpayers of such programs without significantly harming beneficiaries is to charge a small price—say, $1 per physician visit. Beneficiaries would eliminate visits they value less than $1. This would yield significant savings to taxpayers but would still leave beneficiaries with adequate health care and a substantial consumer surplus (measured in Exhibit 8 as the area under the demand curve but above the $1 price). As a case in point, one Medicaid experiment in California required some beneficiaries to pay $1 per visit for their first two office visits per month (after two visits, the price of additional visits reverted to zero). A cost of at most $2 per month would not impose much of a burden on recipients. A control group continued to receive completely free medical care. The $1 charge reduced office visits by 8 percent compared to the control group.

Medical care, like other goods and services, is also sensitive to the time component of the cost (a topic discussed in the next section). For example, a 10 percent increase in the average travel time required to visit a free outpatient clinic reduced visits by 10 percent. Similarly, when the relocation of a free clinic at one college campus increased students' walking time by 10 minutes, student visits dropped 40 percent.

These findings do not mean that certain groups do not deserve low-cost medical care. The point is that when something is free, people consume it until the marginal valuation is zero. Even a modest money cost or time cost reduces consumption yet leaves beneficiaries with a substantial consumer surplus. Another problem with giving something away is that beneficiaries are less vigilant about getting honest value. With hundreds of millions of claims to process each year, Medicare and Medicaid must rely on provider honesty, but only 9 of 50 states evaluate health-care providers in any comprehensive way. This increases the possibility of fraud and abuse by health-care providers. According to a study by the U.S. General Accounting Office, about $1 in $7 spent on Medicare is wasted because of padded bills, fake claims, and other activities that would be less tolerated if beneficiaries were paying their own bills. For example, in one case, the government was billed for round-the-clock cardiac monitoring when the patient was in fact monitored only 30 minutes a month. And experts say that at least 10 percent of Medicaid payments are wasted on fraud and abuse. Such abuse by health-care providers translates into a waste of at least $40 billion per year in federal health programs, or more than $500 per year for each person in the program.

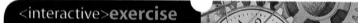

eACTIVITY: THE MARGINAL VALUE OF FREE MEDICAL CARE

Sources: "Medicare Improper Payments," U.S. General Accounting Office Report T-AIMD/OSI-00-251 (12 July 2000); "Medicaid: HCFA and States Could Work Together to Better Insure the Integrity of Providers," U.S. General Accounting Office Report GAO-T-HEHS-00-159 (18 July 2000); Paul Gertler and Jacques van der Gaag, *The Willingness to Pay for Medical Care* (Baltimore, MD: Johns Hopkins University Press, 1990); and Steven Rhoads, "Marginalism," in *The Fortune Encyclopedia of Economics,* edited by D. R. Henderson (New York: Warner Books, 1993), pp. 31–33. For more on Medicare and Medicaid, go to the U.S. Health Care Financing Administration site at http://www.hcfa.gov/.

THE ROLE OF TIME IN DEMAND

Because consumption does not occur instantaneously, time also plays an important role in demand analysis. Consumption takes time and, as Ben Franklin said, time is money—time has a positive value for most people. Consequently, the cost of consumption has two components: the *money price* of the good and the *time price* of the good. Goods are demanded because of the benefits they offer. Thus, you may be willing to pay more for medicine that works more quickly. Similarly, it is not the microwave oven, personal computer, or airline trip that you value but the benefits they provide. Other things constant, the good that provides the same benefit in less time is preferred. That's why we are willing to pay more for seedless grapes, seedless oranges, and seedless watermelon.

Your willingness to pay a premium for time-saving goods and services depends on the opportunity cost of your time. Differences in the value of time among consumers help explain differences in the consumption patterns observed in the economy. For example, a retired couple has more leisure time than a working couple and may clip coupons and search the newspapers for bargains, sometimes going from store to store for particular grocery items on sale that week. The working couple will usually ignore the coupons and sales and will eat out more often or purchase more items at convenience stores, where they pay extra for the "convenience." The retired couple will be more inclined to drive across the country on vacation, whereas the working couple will fly to a vacation destination.

Just inside the gates at Disneyland, Disney World, and Universal Studios are signs posting the waiting times of each attraction and ride. At that point, the dollar cost of admission has already been paid, so the marginal dollar cost of each ride and attraction is zero. The waiting times offer a menu of the marginal *time costs* of each ride or attraction. Incidentally, people who are willing to pay up to $55 an hour at Disney World and $60 an hour at Disneyland (plus the price of admission) can take VIP tours that bypass the lines.[2] How much would you pay to avoid the lines?

Differences in the opportunity cost of time among consumers shape consumption patterns and add another dimension to our analysis of demand.

<interactive>example

NETBOOKMARK: UNIVERSAL STUDIOS ORLANDO

CONCLUSION

We have developed a utility-based analysis of consumer choice, focusing on the utility, or satisfaction, that consumers receive from consumption. In observing consumer behavior, we assume that, for a particular individual, utility can be measured in some systematic way, even though different consumers' utility levels cannot be compared. Our ultimate objective is to predict how consumer choice is affected by such variables as a change in price. We judge a theory not by the realism of its assumptions but by the accuracy of its predictions. Based on this criterion, the theory of consumer choice presented in this chapter has proven to be quite useful.

Again, to maximize utility, consumers need not understand the material presented in this chapter. Economists assume that rational consumers seek to maximize utility naturally and instinctively. In this chapter, we simply tried to analyze that process. A more general approach to consumer choice and utility analysis, an approach that does not require a specific measure of utility, is developed in the appendix to this chapter.

endofchaptermaterial

- **Summary**
- **Questions for Review**
- **Problems and Exercises**
- **Experiential Exercises**

- **Wall Street Journal Exercise**
- **Appendix Questions**
- **Graphing Workshop: Apply It Exercises**

[2]Nancy Keates, "Tourists Learn How to Mouse Around Disney's Long Lines," *Wall Street Journal,* 27 March 1998.

Take the Post-Test to assess your overall understanding of the key ideas in this chapter. The Post-Test provides a comprehensive selection of exam-style questions addressing the main topics and concepts of the chapter. At the completion of each Post-Test, you will receive a score and instructive feedback on how you answered each question, and a direct link to the part of the chapter addressed in the question. Take the Post-Test as often as you need to—a record of your progress for each attempt is kept for you to revisit and gauge your improvement. And each Post-Test is randomly generated, so every attempt is new.

INDIFFERENCE CURVES AND UTILITY MAXIMIZATION

The approach used in the main part of the chapter, marginal utility analysis, requires some numerical measure of utility to determine the optimal consumption combinations. Economists have developed another, more general, approach to utility and consumer behavior, one that does not require that numbers be attached to specific levels of utility. All this new approach requires is that consumers be able to rank their preferences for various combinations of goods. For example, the consumer should be able to say whether combination A is preferred to combination B, combination B is preferred to combination A, or both combinations are equally preferred. This approach is more general and more flexible than the one developed in the body of the chapter. We begin by examining consumer preferences.

CONSUMER PREFERENCES

Indifference curve analysis is an approach to the study of consumer behavior that does not require a numerical measure of utility. An **indifference curve** shows all combinations of goods that provide the consumer with the same satisfaction, or the same utility. Thus, the consumer finds all combinations on a curve equally preferred. Since each alternative bundle of goods yields the same level of utility, the consumer is *indifferent* about which combination is actually consumed. We can best understand the use of indifference curves through the following example.

In reality, consumers choose from among thousands of goods and services, but to keep the analysis manageable, suppose there are only two goods available: pizzas and video rentals. In Exhibit 9, the horizontal axis measures the number of pizzas you purchase per week, and the vertical axis measures the number of videos you rent per week. Point *a*, for example, shows the consumption bundle consisting of one pizza and eight video rentals. Suppose you are given a choice of the combination at point *a* or some other combination. The question is: Holding your total utility constant, how many video rentals would you be willing to give up to get a second pizza? As you can see, in moving from point *a* to point *b*, you are willing to give up four

EXHIBIT 9

An Indifference Curve

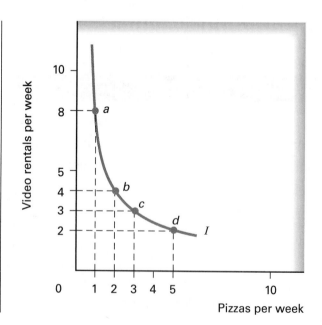

An indifference curve shows all combinations of two goods that provide a consumer with the same total utility. Points *a* through *d* depict four such combinations. Indifference curves have negative slopes and are convex to the origin.

videos to get a second pizza. Total utility is the same at points *a* and *b*. The marginal utility of that additional pizza per week is just sufficient to compensate you for the utility lost from decreasing your videos by four movies per week. Thus, at point *b*, you are eating two pizzas and watching four movies a week, and you are indifferent about variations between this combination and the one represented by point a because total utility is the same at both points.

In moving from point *b* to point *c*, again total utility is constant; you are now willing to give up only one video for another pizza. At point *c*, your consumption bundle consists of three pizzas and three videos. Once at point *c*, you are willing to give up another video only if you get two more pizzas in return. Combination *d*, therefore, consists of five pizzas and two videos.

Points *a*, *b*, *c*, and *d* can be connected to form indifference curve *I*, which represents possible combinations of pizza and video rentals that would keep you at the same level of total utility. Since points on the curve offer the same total utility, you are indifferent about which you choose—hence the name *indifference curve*. Note that we don't know, nor do we need to know, the value you attach to the utility reflected by the indifference curve—that is, there is no particular number attached to the total utility along *I*. *Combinations of goods along an indifference curve reflect some constant, though unspecified, level of total utility.*

For you to remain indifferent about consumption combinations, the increase in your utility from eating more pizza must just offset the decrease in your utility from watching fewer videos. Thus, along an indifference curve, there is an inverse relationship between the quantity of one good consumed and the quantity of another consumed. Because of this inverse relationship, *indifference curves slope downward.*

Indifference curves are also *convex to the origin*, which means they are bowed inward toward the origin. The curve gets flatter as you move down it. Here's why. Your willingness to substitute pizza for videos depends on how much of each is in your current consumption bundle. At combination *a*, for example, you watch eight videos and eat only one pizza, so there are many videos relative to pizza. Because movies are relatively abundant in your consumption bundle, you are willing to give up four movies to get another pizza. Once you reach point *b*, your pizza consumption has doubled, so you are not quite so willing to give up movies to get a third pizza. In fact, you will forgo only one video to get one more pizza. This moves you from point *b* to point *c*.

The **marginal rate of substitution,** or **MRS,** between pizza and video rentals indicates the number of videos that you are willing to give up to get one more pizza, neither gaining nor losing utility in the process. Because the MRS measures your willingness to trade videos for pizza, it depends on the amount of each good you are consuming at the time. Mathematically, the MRS is equal to the absolute value of the slope of the indifference curve. Recall that the slope of any line is the vertical change between two points on the line divided by the corresponding horizontal change. For example, in moving from combination *a* to combination *b* in Exhibit 9, you are willing to give up four videos to get one more pizza; the slope between those two points equals -4, so the MRS is 4. In the move from *b* to *c*, the slope is -1, so the MRS is 1. And from *c* to *d*, the slope is $-\frac{1}{2}$, so the MRS is $\frac{1}{2}$.

The **law of diminishing marginal rate of substitution** says that as your consumption of pizza increases, the number of videos that you are willing to give up to get another pizza declines. This law applies to most pairs of goods. Because your marginal rate of substitution of videos for pizza declines as your pizza consumption increases, the indifference curve has a diminishing slope, meaning that it is convex when viewed from the origin. As you move down the indifference curve, your pizza consumption increases, so the marginal utility of additional pizza decreases. Conversely, the number of movies you rent decreases, so the marginal utility of movies increases. Thus, in moving down the indifference curve, you require more pizza to offset the loss of each video.

We have focused on a single indifference curve, which indicates some constant but unspecified level of utility. We can use the same approach to generate a series of indifference curves, called an **indifference map.** An indifference map is a graphical representation of a consumer's tastes. Each curve in the map reflects a different level of utility. Part of such a map is shown in Exhibit 10, where indifference curves for a particular consumer, in this case you, are labeled I_1, I_2, I_3, and I_4. Each consumer has a unique indifference map based on his or her preferences.

Because both goods yield marginal utility, you, the consumer, prefer more of each, rather than less. Curves farther from the origin represent greater consumption levels and, therefore, higher levels of total utility. The total utility level along I_2 is higher than that along I_1. I_3 reflects a higher level of utility than I_2, and so on. We can show this best by drawing a line from the origin and following it to higher indifference curves. Such a line has been included in Exhibit 10. By following that line to higher and higher indifference curves, you can see that the combination on each successive indifference curve reflects greater amounts of *both* goods. Because you value both goods, the greater amounts of each good reflected on higher indifference curves represent higher levels of utility.

EXHIBIT 10|

An Indifference Map

Indifference curves I_1 through I_4 are four examples from a consumer's indifference map. Indifference curves farther from the origin depict higher levels of utility. A line intersects each higher indifference curve, reflecting more of both goods.

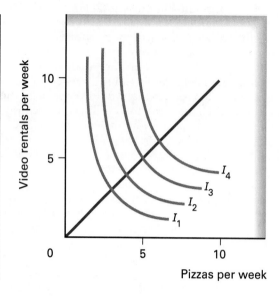

Indifference curves in a consumer's indifference map do not intersect. Exhibit 11 shows why. If indifference curves did cross, as at point i, then every point on indifference curve I and every point on curve I' would have to reflect the same level of utility as at point i. But because point k in Exhibit 11 is a combination with more pizza and more videos than point j, it must represent a higher level of utility. This contradiction means that indifference curves cannot intersect.

Let's summarize the properties of indifference curves:

1. A particular indifference curve reflects a constant level of utility, so the consumer is indifferent about all consumption combinations along a given curve. They are equally attractive.
2. If total utility is to remain constant, an increase in the consumption of one good must be offset by a decrease in the consumption of the other good, so each indifference curve slopes downward.
3. Because of the law of diminishing marginal rate of substitution, indifference curves bow in toward the origin.

EXHIBIT 11|

Indifference Curves Do Not Intersect

If indifference curves crossed, as at point i, then every point on indifference curve I and every point on curve I' would have to reflect the same level of utility as at point i. But point k is a combination with more pizza and more videos than point j, so k must represent a higher level of utility. This contradiction means that indifference curves cannot intersect.

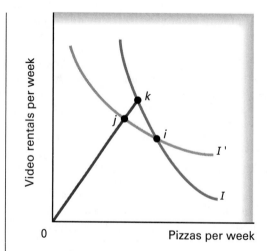

4. Higher indifference curves represent higher levels of utility.
5. Indifference curves do not intersect.

An indifference map is really a graphical representation of a consumer's tastes for the two goods. Given a consumer's indifference map, how much of each good will be consumed? To determine that, we must consider the relative prices of the goods and the consumer's income. In the next section, we will focus on the consumer's budget.

ASK THE INSTRUCTOR: ARE DEMAND CURVES AND INDIFFERENCE CURVES THE SAME?

THE BUDGET LINE

The **budget line** depicts all possible combinations of video rentals and pizzas, given the prices and your budget. Suppose videos rent for $4, pizza sells for $8, and your budget is $40 per week. If you spend the entire $40 on videos, you can afford 10 videos per week. Alternatively, if you spend the entire $40 on pizzas, you can afford 5 per week. In Exhibit 12, your budget line meets the vertical axis at 10 video rentals and meets the horizontal axis at 5 pizzas. We connect the intercepts to form the budget line. You can purchase any combination on your budget line, or your budget constraint. You might think of the budget line as your *consumption possibilities frontier.*

Let's find the slope of the budget line. At the point where the budget line meets the vertical axis, the maximum number of videos you can rent equals your income (I) divided by the video rental price (p_v), or I/p_v. At the point where the budget line meets the horizontal axis, the maximum quantity of pizzas that you can purchase equals your income divided by the price of a pizza (p_p), or I/p_p. The slope of the budget line between the vertical intercept in Exhibit 12 and the horizontal intercept equals the vertical change, or $-I/p_v$, divided by the horizontal change, or I/p_p:

$$\text{Slope of budget line} = \frac{I/p_v}{I/p_p} = -\frac{p_p}{p_v}$$

In our example it is $-\$8/\$4$, which equals -2. The slope of the budget line indicates what it costs you in terms of forgone video rentals to get another pizza. You must give up two videos

---

EXHIBIT 12

A Budget Line

The budget line shows all combinations of pizza and videos that can be consumed at fixed prices with a given amount of income. If all income is spent on videos, 10 can be consumed. If all income is spent on pizzas, 5 can be consumed. Points between the vertical intercept and the horizontal intercept represent combinations of some pizza and some videos. The slope of the budget line is −2, illustrating that the cost of 1 pizza is 2 videos.

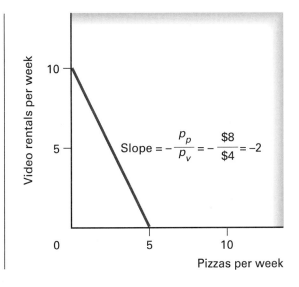

for each additional pizza. *Note that the income term cancels out, so the slope of a budget line depends only on relative prices, not on the level of income.*

The indifference curve indicates what you are *willing* to buy. The budget line shows what you are *able* to buy. We must therefore bring together the indifference curve and the budget line to find out what quantities of each good you are both *willing* and *able* to buy.

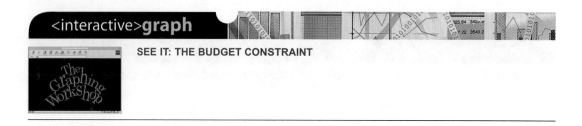

CONSUMER EQUILIBRIUM AT THE TANGENCY

As always, the objective of consumption is to maximize utility. We know that indifference curves farther from the origin represent higher levels of utility. You, as a utility-maximizing consumer, will select a combination along the budget line in Exhibit 13 that lies on the highest attainable indifference curve. Given prices and income, you maximize utility at the combination of pizza and videos depicted by point e in Exhibit 13, where indifference curve I_2 just touches, or *is tangent to,* your budget line. At point e, you buy three pizzas at \$8 each and rent four videos at \$4 each, exhausting your budget of \$40 per week. Other attainable combinations along the budget line reflect lower levels of utility. For example, point a is on the budget line, making it a combination you are *able* to purchase, but a is on a lower indifference curve, I_1. Other "better" indifference curves, such as I_3, lie completely above the budget line and are thus unattainable.

Since you maximize your utility at point e, that combination is an equilibrium outcome. Note that the indifference curve is tangent to the budget line at the equilibrium point, and at the point of tangency, the slope of a curve equals the slope of a line drawn tangent to that curve. At point e, the slope of the indifference curve equals the slope of the budget line. Recall that the absolute value of the slope of the indifference curve is your marginal rate of substitution, and the absolute value of the slope of the budget line equals the price ratio. In equilibrium, therefore, your marginal rate of substitution between videos and pizza, MRS, must equal the ratio of the price of pizza to the price of video rentals:

EXHIBIT 13

Utility Maximization

The consumer's utility is maximized at point e, where indifference curve I_2 is just tangent to the budget line.

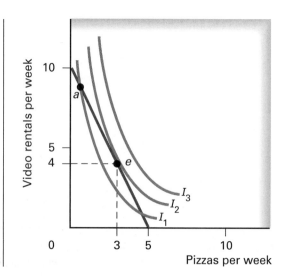

$$\text{MRS} = \frac{p_p}{p_v}$$

The marginal rate of substitution of pizza for video rentals can also be found from the marginal utilities of pizza and videos presented in the chapter. Exhibit 3 indicated that, at the consumer equilibrium, the marginal utility you derived from the third pizza was 24 and the marginal utility you derived by the fourth video was 12. Since the marginal utility of pizza (MU_p) is 24 and the marginal utility of videos (MU_v) is 12, in moving to that equilibrium, you were willing to give up two videos to get one more pizza. Thus, the marginal rate of substitution of pizza for videos equals the ratio of pizza's marginal utility (MU_p) to video's marginal utility (MU_v), or

$$\text{MRS} = \frac{MU_p}{MU_v}$$

In fact, the absolute value of the slope of the indifference curve equals MU_p/MU_v. Since the absolute value of the slope of the budget line equals p_p/p_v, the equilibrium condition for the indifference curve approach can be written as

$$\frac{MU_p}{p_p} = \frac{MU_v}{p_v}$$

This equation is the same equilibrium condition for utility maximization presented in the chapter using marginal utility analysis. The equality says that in equilibrium—that is, when the consumer maximizes utility—the last dollar spent on each good yields the same marginal utility. If this equality does not hold, the consumer can increase utility by adjusting consumption until the equality occurs.

EFFECTS OF A CHANGE IN PRICE

What happens to your equilibrium consumption when there is a change in price? The answer can be found by deriving the demand curve. We begin at point *e*, our initial equilibrium, in panel (a) of Exhibit 14. At point *e*, you eat 3 pizzas and watch 4 videos per week. Suppose that the price of pizzas falls from $8 to $6 per unit, other things constant. The price drop means that if the entire budget were devoted to pizza, you could purchase 6.67 pizzas (= $40/$6). Your money income remains at $40 per week, but your real income has increased because of the lower pizza price. Since the rental price of videos has not changed, however, 10 remains the maximum number you can rent. Thus the budget line's vertical intercept remains fixed at 10 videos, but the lower end of the budget line shifts to the right from 5 to 6.67.

After the price of pizza changes, the new equilibrium occurs at *e"*, where pizza purchases increase from 3 to 4 and, as it happens, video rentals remains at 4. Thus, price and the quantity of pizza demanded are inversely related. The demand curve in panel (b) of Exhibit 14 shows how price and quantity demanded are related. Specifically, if the price of pizza falls from $8 per unit to $6 per unit, other things constant, your quantity demanded increases from 3 to 4. Since you are on a higher indifference curve at *e"*, you are clearly better off after the price reduction (your consumer surplus has increased).

TRY IT: PRICE CHANGE AND THE BUDGET LINE

INCOME AND SUBSTITUTION EFFECTS

The law of demand was initially explained in terms of an income effect and a substitution effect. You now have the analytical tools to examine these two effects more precisely. Suppose the price of a pizza falls from $8 to $4, other things constant. You can now purchase a maximum of 10 pizzas with a budget of $40 per week. As shown in Exhibit 15, the budget-line intercept rotates out from 5 to 10 pizzas. After the price change, the quantity of pizzas demanded increases from 3 to 5. The increase in utility shows how you benefit from the price decrease.

EXHIBIT 14

Effect of a Drop in the Price of Pizza

A reduction in the price of pizza rotates the budget line rightward in panel (a). The consumer is back in equilibrium at point e" along the new budget line. Panel (b) shows that a drop in the price of pizza from $8 per unit to $6 leads to an increase in quantity demanded from 3 to 4. Price and quantity demanded are inversely related.

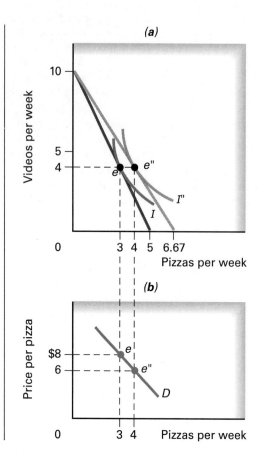

EXHIBIT 15

Substitution and Income Effects of a Drop in the Price of Pizza from $8 to $4 Each

A reduction in the price of pizza moves the consumer from point e to point e*. This movement can be decomposed into a substitution effect and an income effect. The substitution effect (from e to e') reflects a reaction to a change in relative prices along the original indifference curve. The income effect (from e' to e*) moves the consumer to a higher indifference curve at the new relative price ratio.

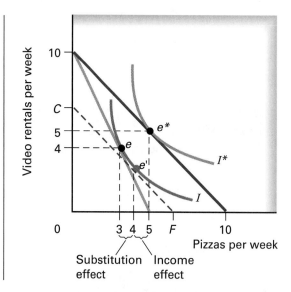

The increase in the quantity of pizzas demanded can be broken down into the substitution effect and the income effect of a price change. When the price of pizza falls, the change in the ratio of the price of pizza to the price of video rentals shows up through the change in the slope of the budget line. To derive the substitution effect, let's assume that you must maintain the same level of utility after the price change as before. In other words, let's suppose your utility level has not yet changed, but the relative prices you face have changed. We want to learn how you would adjust to the price change. A new budget line reflecting just the change in relative prices, not a change in utility, is shown by the dashed line, *CF*, in Exhibit 15. Given the new set of relative prices, you would increase the quantity of pizza demanded to the point on indifference curve *I* where the indifference curve is just tangent to the dashed budget line. That tangency keeps utility at the initial level but reflects the new set of relative prices. Thus, we adjust your budget line to correspond to the new relative prices, but we adjust your income level so that your utility remains unchanged.

You move down along indifference curve *I* to point *e'*, renting fewer videos but buying more pizza. These changes in quantity demanded reflect the *substitution effect* of lower pizza prices. The substitution effect always increases the quantity demanded of the good whose price has dropped. Since consumption bundle *e'* represents the same level of utility as consumption bundle *e*, you are neither better off nor worse off at point *e'*.

But at point *e'*, you have not spent your full budget. The drop in the price of pizza has increased the quantity of pizza you can buy, as shown by the expanded budget line that runs from 10 video rentals to 10 pizzas. Your *real income* has increased because of the lower price of pizza. As a result, you are able to attain point *e** on indifference curve *I**. At this point, you buy 5 pizzas and rent 5 videos. Because prices are held constant during the move from *e'* to *e**, the change in consumption is due solely to a change in real income. Thus, the change in the quantity demanded from 4 to 5 pizzas reflects the *income effect* of the lower pizza price.

We can now distinguish between the substitution effect and the income effect of a drop in the price of pizza. The substitution effect is shown by the move from point *e* to point *e'* in response to a change in the relative price of pizza, with your utility held constant along *I*. The income effect is shown by the move from *e'* to *e** in response to an increase in your real income, with relative prices held constant.

The overall effect of a change in the price of pizza is the sum of the substitution effect and the income effect. In our example, the substitution effect accounts for a one-unit increase in the quantity of pizza demanded, as does the income effect. Thus, the income and substitution effects combine to increase the quantity of pizza demanded by two units when the price falls from $8 to $4. The income effect is not always positive. For inferior goods, the income effect is negative; so as the price falls, the income effect can cause consumption to fall, offsetting part or even all the substitution effect. Incidentally, notice that as a result of the increase in your real income, video rentals increase as well—from four to five rentals per week in our example, though it will not always be the case that the income effect is positive.

TRY IT: INCOME CHANGE AND THE BUDGET LINE

ECONNEWS ONLINE: SALES SLUMP

CONCLUSION

Indifference curve analysis does not require us to attach numerical values to particular levels of utility, as marginal utility theory does. The results of indifference curve analysis confirm the conclusions drawn from our simpler models. Indifference curves provide a logical way of viewing consumer choice, but consumers need not be aware of this approach to make rational choices. The purpose of the analysis in this chapter is to predict consumer behavior—not to advise consumers how to maximize utility.

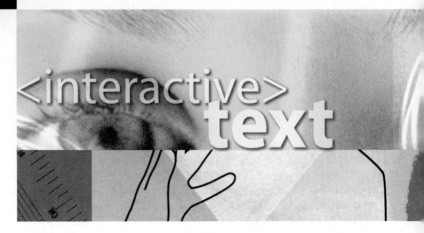

CHAPTER 7

Production and Cost in the Firm

Why is fast food is so fast? How do too many cooks spoil the broth? Why do movie theaters have so many screens? Why don't they add even more? If you go into business for yourself, how much must you earn just to break even? Why might your grade average fall even though you improved from the previous term? Answers to these and other questions are discovered in this chapter, which introduces production and cost in the firm.

The previous chapter explored the consumer behavior shaping the demand curve. This chapter examines the producer behavior shaping the supply curve. We will discuss a firm's production and cost of operation as a prelude to our analysis of supply. In the previous chapter, you were asked to think like a consumer, or demander. In this chapter, you must think like a producer, or supplier. You may feel more natural as a consumer (after all, you *are* one), but you know more about producers than you may realize. You have been around them all your life— Wal-Mart, Blockbuster, Dunkin' Donuts, 7-Eleven, Exxon, Barnes & Noble, McDonald's, Pizza Hut, Kinko's, Ford, The Gap, and hundreds more. So you already have some idea how businesses operate. They all have the same objective—they try to maximize profit, which is revenue minus cost. This chapter introduces the cost side of the profit equation. Topics discussed include:

- Explicit and implicit costs
- Economic and normal profit
- Increasing and diminishing returns
- Short-run costs
- Long-run costs
- Economies and diseconomies of scale

Take the Pre-Test to assess your initial knowledge of the key ideas in this chapter. The Pre-Test provides exam-style questions addressing the main topics and concepts of the chapter. At the completion of each Pre-Test, you will receive a score and instructive feedback on how you answered each question, and a direct link to the part of the chapter addressed in the question. Take the Pre-Test as often as you need to—a record of your progress for each attempt is kept for you to revisit and gauge your improvement.

\<interactive\>exercise

- ECONDEBATE ONLINE: SCARCITY, CHOICE, AND OPPORTUNITY COST
- ECONDEBATE ONLINE: SUPPLY AND DEMAND

\<interactive\>update

- ECONDATA ONLINE: SCARCITY, CHOICE, AND OPPORTUNITY COST
- ECONDATA ONLINE: SUPPLY AND DEMAND
- ECONLINKS ONLINE: ECONOMICS WEB LINKS
- ECONNEWS ONLINE: SCARCITY, CHOICE, AND OPPORTUNITY COST
- ECONNEWS ONLINE: SUPPLY AND DEMAND

COST AND PROFIT

With demand, we assume that consumers try to maximize utility, a goal that motivates their behavior. With supply, we assume that producers try to maximize *profit,* and this goal motivates their behavior. Firms transform resources into products to earn a profit. Over time, firms that survive and grow are those that are the more profitable. Unprofitable firms eventually fail. Each year, millions of new firms enter the marketplace and almost as many leave. The firm's decision makers must choose what goods and services to produce and what resources to employ. They must make plans while confronting uncertainty about consumer demand, resource availability, and the intentions of other firms in the market. *The lure of profit is so strong, however, that eager entrepreneurs are always ready to pursue their dreams.*

Explicit and Implicit Costs

To hire a resource, a firm must pay at least the resource's *opportunity cost*—that is, at least what the resource could earn in its best alternative use. For most resources, a cash payment approximates the opportunity cost. For example, the $3 per pound that Domino's Pizza pays for cheese must at least equal the cheese producer's opportunity cost of supplying it. Some firms (or firm owners) own their resources, so they make no direct cash payments. For example, a firm pays no rent to operate in a company-owned building. Similarly, small-business owners usually don't pay themselves an hourly wage. Yet these resources are not free. *Whether hired in resource markets or owned by the firm, all resources have an opportunity cost.* Company-owned buildings can be rented or sold; small-business owners can find other jobs.

A firm's **explicit costs** are its actual cash payments for resources: wages, rent, interest, insurance, taxes, and the like. In addition to these direct cash outlays, or explicit costs, the firm also incurs **implicit costs,** which are the opportunity costs of using resources owned by the firm or provided by the firm's owners. Examples include the use of a company-owned building, use of company funds, or the time of the firm's owners. Like explicit costs, implicit costs are opportunity costs. But unlike explicit costs, implicit costs require no cash payment and no entry in the firm's *accounting statement,* which records its revenues, explicit costs, and accounting profit.

Alternative Measures of Profit

An example may help clarify the distinction between explicit and implicit costs. Wanda Wheeler earns $50,000 a year as an aeronautical engineer with Skyhigh Aircraft. On her way home from work one day, she gets an idea for a rounder, more friction-resistant airplane wheel. She decides to quit her job and start a business, which she calls Wheeler Dealer. To buy the necessary machines and equipment, she withdraws $20,000 from her savings account, where it had been earning interest of $1,000 a year. She hires an assistant and starts producing the wheel using the spare bay in her condominium's parking garage that she had been renting to a neighbor for $100 a month.

Sales are slow at first—people keep telling her she is just trying to reinvent the wheel—but her wheel eventually gets rolling. When Wanda and her accountant examine the firm's performance after the first year, they are quite pleased. As you can see in the top portion of Exhibit 1, company revenue in 2001 was $105,000. After paying her assistant and the cost of materials and equipment, the firm shows an accounting profit of $64,000. **Accounting profit** equals total revenue minus explicit costs. This is the profit used by accountants to determine a firm's taxable income.

But accounting profit ignores the opportunity cost of Wanda's own resources used in the firm. First is the opportunity cost of her time. Remember, she quit a $50,000-a-year job to work full time on her business, thereby forgoing that salary. Second is the $1,000 annual interest she passes up by funding the operation with her own savings. And third, by using the spare bay in the garage for the business, she forgoes $1,200 per year in rental income. The forgone salary, interest, and rental income are implicit costs because she no longer earns income generated from their best alternative uses.

Economic profit equals total revenue minus all costs, both implicit and explicit; *economic profit takes into account the opportunity cost of all resources used in production.* In Exhibit 1, accounting profit of $64,000 less implicit costs of $52,200 equals economic profit of $11,800. What would happen to the accounting statement if Wanda decided to pay herself a salary of $50,000 per year? Explicit costs would increase by $50,000, and implicit costs would decrease by $50,000 (because her salary is no longer forgone). Thus, accounting profit would decrease by $50,000, but economic profit would not change because it reflects both implicit and explicit costs.

There is one other profit measure to consider: the accounting profit required to induce the firm's owners to employ their resources in the firm. The accounting profit just sufficient to ensure that *all* resources used by the firm earn their opportunity cost is called a **normal profit.** Wanda's firm earns a normal profit when her accounting profit equals her implicit costs—the sum of the salary she gave up at her regular job ($50,000), the interest she gave up by using her own savings ($1,000), and the rent she gave up on her garage ($1,200). Thus, if the accounting profit is $52,200 per year—the opportunity cost of resources Wanda supplies to the firm—the company is said to earn a normal profit. *Any accounting profit in excess of a normal profit is economic profit.* If accounting profit is large enough, it can be divided into normal profit and economic profit. The $64,000 in accounting profit earned by Wanda's firm consists of (1) a normal profit of $52,200, which covers her implicit costs—the opportunity cost of resources she supplies the firm, and (2) an economic profit of $11,800, which is over and above what these resources, including Wanda's time, could earn in their best alternative use.

As long as economic profit is positive, Wanda is better off running her own firm than working for Skyhigh Aircraft. If total revenue had been only $50,000, accounting profit of only $9,000 would cover less than one-fifth of her salary, to say nothing of her forgone rent and interest. Since Wanda would not have covered her implicit costs, she would not be earning even a normal profit and would be better off back in her old job.

To understand profit maximization, you must develop a feel for both revenue and cost. In this chapter, you will begin learning about the cost of production, starting with the relationship between inputs and outputs.

EXHIBIT 1

Accounts of Wheeler Dealer, 2001

Total revenue		$105,000
Less explicit costs:		
Assistant's salary	−21,000	
Material and equipment	−20,000	
Equals accounting profit		$64,000
Less implicit costs:		
Wanda's forgone salary	−$50,000	
Forgone interest on savings	−1,000	
Forgone garage rental	−1,200	
Equals economic profit		$11,800

<interactive>video

ASK THE INSTRUCTOR: WHY DO ECONOMISTS AND ACCOUNTANTS DISAGREE?

PRODUCTION IN THE SHORT RUN

We shift now from a discussion of profit to a discussion of how firms operate. Suppose a new McDonald's has just opened in your neighborhood and business is booming far beyond expectations. The manager responds to the unexpected demand by quickly hiring more workers. But cars are still backed up into the street waiting for a parking space. The solution is to add a drive-through window, but such an expansion takes time.

Fixed and Variable Resources

Some resources, such as labor, are called **variable resources** because they can be varied quickly to change the output rate. But adjustments in some other resources take more time. Resources that cannot be altered easily—the size of the building, for example—are called **fixed resources.** When considering the time required to change the quantity of resources employed, economists distinguish between the short run and the long run. In the **short run,** at least one resource is fixed. In the **long run,** no resource is fixed.

Output can be changed in the short run by adjusting variable resources, but the size, or *scale,* of the firm is fixed in the short run. In the long run, all resources can be varied. The length of the long run differs from industry to industry because the nature of production differs. For example, the size of a McDonald's outlet can be increased more quickly than the size of an auto plant can. Thus, the long run for that McDonald's is shorter than the long run for an automaker.

The Law of Diminishing Marginal Returns

Let's focus on the short-run link between resource use and the rate of output by considering a hypothetical moving company called Smoother Mover. Suppose the company's fixed resources are already in place and consist of a warehouse, a moving van, and moving equipment. In this example, labor is the only variable resource.

Exhibit 2 relates the amount of labor employed to the amount of output produced. Labor is measured in worker-days, which is one worker for one day, and output is measured in tons

EXHIBIT 2

The Short-Run Relationship Between Units of Labor and Tons of Furniture Moved

Units of the Variable Resource (worker-days)	Total Product (tons moved per day)	Marginal Product (tons moved per day)
0	0	—
1	2	2
2	5	3
3	9	4
4	12	3
5	14	2
6	15	1
7	15	0
8	14	–1

of furniture moved per day. The first column shows the amount of labor employed, which ranges from 0 to 8 worker-days. The second column shows the tons of furniture moved, or the **total product,** at each level of employment. The relationship between the amount of resources employed and total product is called the firm's **production function.** The third column shows the **marginal product** of each worker—that is, the amount by which the total product changes with each additional unit of labor, assuming all other resources remain unchanged. Spend a little time acquainting yourself with each column.

Increasing Marginal Returns. Without labor, nothing gets moved, so total product is 0. If one worker is hired, that worker must do all the driving, packing, crating, and moving. Some of the larger items, such as couches and major appliances, cannot easily be moved by a single worker. Still, in our example one worker manages to move 2 tons of furniture per day. When a second worker is hired, some division of labor occurs, and two can move the big stuff more easily, so production more than doubles to 5 tons per day. The marginal product of the second worker is 3 tons per day. Adding a third worker allows for a finer division of labor, which contributes to increased output. For example, one worker can specialize in packing fragile items while the other two do the heavy lifting. The total product of three workers is 9 tons per day, 4 tons more than with two workers. Because the marginal product increases, the firm experiences **increasing marginal returns** from labor as each of the first three workers is hired.

Diminishing Marginal Returns. Hiring a fourth worker adds to the total product but not as much as added by a third. Hiring still more workers increases total product by successively smaller amounts, so the marginal product in Exhibit 2 declines after three workers. With four workers, the **law of diminishing marginal returns** takes hold. This law states that as more of a variable resource is combined with a given amount of a fixed resource, marginal product eventually declines. *The law of diminishing marginal returns is the most important feature of production in the short run.*

As additional units of labor are added, total product may eventually decline. For example, when Smoother Mover hires eight workers, the working area becomes so crowded that workers get in each other's way. Transporting so many people to and from moving sites cuts into production because workers take up valuable space in the moving van. As a result, the eighth worker actually subtracts from total output, yielding a negative marginal product. Likewise, a McDonald's outlet can hire only so many workers before congestion and confusion in the work area cut total product ("too many cooks spoil the broth").

ASK THE INSTRUCTOR: WHY CAN'T WE FEED THE WORLD FROM A FLOWER POT?

The Total and Marginal Product Curves

Exhibit 3 illustrates the relationship between total product and marginal product, using data from Exhibit 2. Note that because of increasing marginal returns, marginal product in panel (b) increases with each of the first three workers. With marginal product increasing, total product in panel (a) increases at an increasing rate (although this is hard to see in Exhibit 3). But once decreasing marginal returns set in, which begins with the fourth worker, marginal product declines. Total product continues to increase but at a decreasing rate. As long as marginal product is positive, total product increases. At the output rate where marginal product turns negative, total product starts to fall. Exhibit 3 summarizes all this by sorting production into three ranges: (1) increasing marginal returns, (2) diminishing but positive marginal returns, and (3) negative marginal returns. These ranges for marginal product correspond with total product that (1) increases at an increasing rate, (2) increases at a decreasing rate, and (3) declines.

NETBOOKMARK: LABOR COSTS, BUREAU OF LABOR STATISTICS

EXHIBIT 3

The Total and Marginal Product of Labor

When marginal product is rising, total product is increasing by increasing amounts. When marginal product is decreasing but still positive, total product is increasing by decreasing amounts. When marginal product equals 0, total product is at a maximum. Finally, when marginal product is negative, total product is falling.

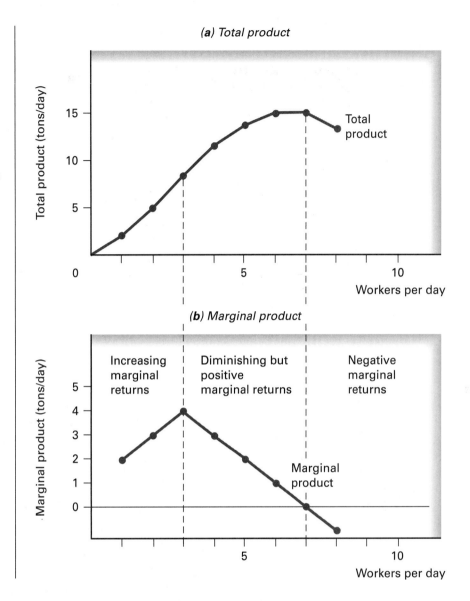

<interactive>**graph**

- **SEE IT: PRODUCTION IN THE SHORT RUN**
- **TRY IT: IDENTIFYING MARGINAL PRODUCT FROM THE TOTAL PRODUCT CURVE**

COSTS IN THE SHORT RUN

Now that we have examined the relationship between the amount of resources used and the rate of output, let's consider how the cost of production varies as output varies. There are two kinds of costs in the short run: fixed and variable. Fixed cost pays for fixed resources and variable cost pays for variable resources. A firm must pay a **fixed cost** even if no output is produced. Even if Smoother Mover hires no labor and moves no furniture, it incurs costs for property taxes, insurance, vehicle registration, plus any opportunity costs for warehouse and equipment. By definition, fixed cost is just that: fixed—it does not vary with output in the short run. Suppose the firm's *fixed cost* amounts to $200 per day.

Variable cost, as the name implies, is the cost of variable resources—in this case, labor. When no labor is employed, output is 0, as is variable cost. As more labor is employed, output increases, as does variable cost. Variable cost depends on the amount of labor employed and the wage. If the firm can hire labor at $100 per worker-day, *variable cost* equals $100 times the number of workers hired.

<interactive>**video**

ASK THE INSTRUCTOR: WHAT DO WE MEAN BY FIXED VERSUS VARIABLE COSTS?

Total Cost and Marginal Cost in the Short Run

Exhibit 4 offers cost data for Smoother Mover. The table lists the daily cost of production associated with alternative rates of output. Column (1) shows possible rates of output in the short run, measured in tons of furniture moved per day.

Total Cost. Column (2) indicates the fixed cost (*FC*) at each rate of output. Note that fixed cost remains constant at $200 per day regardless of output. Column (3) shows the amount of labor needed to produce each rate of output based on the productivity figures reported in the previous two exhibits. For example, moving 2 tons a day requires one worker, 5 tons requires two workers, and so on. Only the first six units of labor are listed; units beyond that add nothing to total product. Column (4) lists variable cost (*VC*) per day, which equals $100 times the number of workers employed. For example, the variable cost of moving 9 tons of furniture per day is $300 because this output requires three workers. Column (5) lists the **total cost** (*TC*) of each rate of output, which is the sum of fixed cost and variable cost: $TC = FC + VC$. As you can see, when output is zero, variable cost is zero, so total cost consists entirely of the fixed cost of $200. Incidentally, since total cost is the opportunity cost of all resources used by the firm, total cost includes a normal profit but not an economic profit. Think about that.

Marginal Cost. Of special interest to the firm is how total cost changes as output changes. In particular, what is the marginal cost of producing another unit? The **marginal cost** (*MC*) of production listed in column (6) of Exhibit 4 is simply the change in total cost divided by the change in output, or $MC = \Delta TC/\Delta q$, where Δ means "change in." For example, increasing output from 0 to 2 tons increases total cost by $100 (= $300 − $200). The marginal cost of each of the first 2 tons is the change in total cost, $100, divided by the change in output, 2 tons, or $100/2, which equals $50. The marginal cost of each of the next 3 tons is $100/3, or $33.33.

Notice in column (6) that marginal cost first decreases and then increases. *Changes in marginal cost reflect changes in the marginal productivity of the variable resource employed.* Recall from

EXHIBIT 4

Short-Run Cost Data for Smoother Mover

(1) Tons Moved per day (*q*)	(2) Fixed Cost (*FC*)	(3) Workers per day	(4) Variable Cost (*VC*)	(5) Total Cost (*TC = FC + VC*)	(6) Marginal Cost $\left(MC = \frac{\Delta TC}{\Delta q} \right)$
0	$200	0	$ 0	$200	—
2	200	1	100	300	$ 50.00
5	200	2	200	400	33.33
9	200	3	300	500	25.00
12	200	4	400	600	33.33
14	200	5	500	700	50.00
15	200	6	600	800	100.00

Exhibit 2 that the first three workers show increasing marginal returns, with each worker producing more than the last. This greater productivity of labor results in a falling marginal cost for the first 9 tons moved. Beginning with the fourth worker, however, the firm experiences diminishing marginal returns from labor, so the marginal cost of output increases. *When the firm experiences increasing marginal returns, the marginal cost of output decreases; when the firm experiences diminishing marginal returns, the marginal cost of output increases.* Thus, marginal cost in Exhibit 4 first falls and then rises, because marginal returns first increase and then diminish.

Total and Marginal Cost Curves. Exhibit 5 draws cost curves for the data in Exhibit 4. Since fixed cost does not vary with output, the fixed cost curve is a horizontal line at the $200 level in panel (a). Variable cost is zero when output is zero, so the *variable cost curve* starts from the origin. For reasons that we will get to soon, variable cost increases slowly at first and then increases sharply. The *total cost curve* sums the variable cost curve and the fixed cost curve. Because a constant fixed cost is added to variable cost, the total cost curve is just the variable cost curve shifted vertically by the amount of fixed cost.

In panel (b) of Exhibit 5, marginal cost declines until the ninth unit of output and then increases, reflecting labor's increasing and then diminishing marginal returns. There is a

EXHIBIT 5

Total and Marginal Cost Curves for Smoother Mover

In panel (a), fixed cost is constant at all levels of output. Variable cost starts from the origin and increases slowly at first as output increases. When the variable resource generates diminishing marginal returns, variable cost begins to increase more rapidly. Total cost is the vertical sum of fixed cost and variable cost. In panel (b), marginal cost first declines, reflecting increasing marginal returns, and then increases, reflecting diminishing marginal returns.

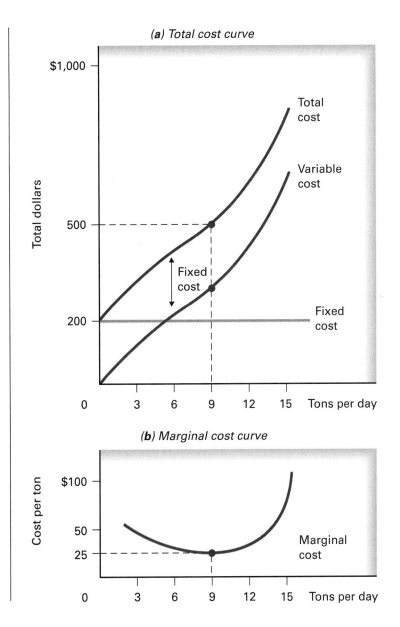

geometric relationship between the two graphs because the change in total cost resulting from a one-unit change in production equals the marginal cost. With each successive unit of output, total cost increases by the marginal cost of that unit. Thus, *the slope of the total cost curve at each rate of output equals the marginal cost at that rate of output.* The total cost curve can be divided into two sections, based on what happens to marginal cost:

1. Because of increasing marginal returns from labor, marginal cost at first declines, so total cost initially increases by successively smaller amounts and the total cost curve becomes flatter.
2. Because of diminishing marginal returns from labor, marginal cost starts increasing after the ninth unit of output, leading to a steeper total cost curve.

Notice that the total cost curve has a backward S shape, the result of combining the two sections discussed above.

Keep in mind that economic analysis is marginal analysis. Marginal cost is the key to economic decisions made by firms. A firm operating in the short run has no control over its fixed cost, but, by varying output, the firm alters its variable cost and thus its total cost. *Marginal cost indicates how much total cost will increase if one more unit is produced or how much total cost will drop if production declines by one unit.*

Average Cost in the Short Run

Although total cost and marginal cost are of the greatest analytical interest, the average cost per unit of output is also useful. There are average cost measures corresponding to variable cost and total cost. These average costs appear in columns (5) and (6) of Exhibit 6. Column (5) lists **average variable cost,** or *AVC,* which equals variable cost divided by output, or $AVC = VC/q$. The final column lists **average total cost,** or *ATC,* which equals total cost divided by output, or $ATC = TC/q$. Both average variable cost and average total cost first decline as output expands and then increase.

The Relationship Between Marginal Cost and Average Cost

To understand the relationship between marginal cost and average cost, let's begin with an analogy of college grades. Think about how your grades each term affect your cumulative grade point average (GPA). Suppose you do well your first term, starting your college career with a 3.4 GPA. Your grades for the second term drop to a 2.8 average, reducing your GPA to 3.1. You slip again in the third term to a 2.2 average, lowering your GPA to 2.8. Your fourth-term grades improve a bit to a 2.4 average, but your GPA continues to slide to 2.7. In the fifth term, your grades improve to a 2.7 average, leaving your GPA unchanged at 2.7. And in the sixth term, you get a 3.3 average, boosting your GPA to 2.8. Notice that when your average term grade is below your GPA grade, your GPA falls. When your average term grade improves,

EXHIBIT 6

Short-Run Cost Data for Smoother Mover

(1) Tons Moved per day (q)	(2) Variable Cost (VC)	(3) Total Cost (TC = FC + VC)	(4) Marginal Cost (MC = ΔTC/Δq)	(5) Average Variable Cost (AVC = VC/q)	(6) Average Total Cost (ATC = TC/q)
0	$ 0	$200	$ 0	—	∞
2	100	300	50.00	$50.00	$150.00
5	200	400	33.33	40.00	80.00
9	300	500	25.00	33.33	55.55
12	400	600	33.33	33.33	50.00
14	500	700	50.00	35.71	50.00
15	600	800	100.00	40.00	53.33

your GPA does not improve until your average term grade exceeds your GPA. After the first term, your average term grade first pulls your GPA down and then pulls it up.

Let's now take a look at the relationship between marginal cost and average cost. In Exhibit 6, marginal cost has the same relationship to average cost as your term grades have to your GPA. You can observe this marginal-average relationship in columns (4) and (5). Because of increasing marginal returns from the first three workers, the marginal cost falls for the first 9 tons of furniture moved. Where marginal cost is below average cost, marginal cost pulls down average cost. Marginal cost and average cost are equal when output equals 12 tons, and marginal cost exceeds average cost when output exceeds 12 tons, so marginal cost pulls up average cost.

Exhibit 7 shows the same marginal cost curve first presented in Exhibit 5, along with average cost curves based on data in Exhibit 6. At low rates of output, marginal cost declines as output expands because of increasing marginal returns from labor. As long as marginal cost is below average cost, average cost falls as output expands. At higher rates of output, marginal cost increases because of diminishing marginal returns from labor. Where marginal cost exceeds average cost, marginal cost pulls up the average. The fact that marginal cost first pulls average cost down and then pulls it up explains why each average cost curve has a U shape. The shapes of the average variable cost curve and the average total cost curve are determined by the shape of the marginal cost curve, so each is shaped by increasing and diminishing marginal returns.

Notice also that the rising marginal cost curve intersects both the average variable cost curve and the average total cost curve where these average curves are at their minimum. This occurs because the marginal pulls down the average where the marginal is below the average and pulls up the average where the marginal is above the average. One more thing: The distance between the average variable cost curve and the average total cost curve is *average fixed cost,* which gets smaller as the rate of output increases. (Why does average fixed cost get smaller?)

ECONNEWS ONLINE: SAWMILLS ARE ALL A-BUZZ ABOUT NEW SAWS

EXHIBIT 7 |

Average and Marginal Cost Curves for Smoother Mover

Average variable cost and average total cost drop, reach low points, and then rise; overall, they take on U shapes. When marginal cost is below average variable cost, average variable cost is falling. When marginal cost equals average variable cost, average variable cost is at its minimum value. When marginal cost is above average variable cost, average variable cost is increasing. The same relationship holds between marginal cost and average total cost.

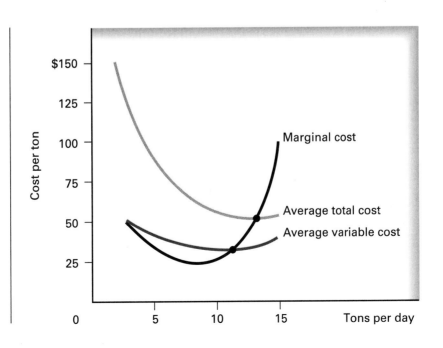

TRY IT: UNDERSTANDING THE RELATIONSHIP BETWEEN AVERAGE TOTAL COST (ATC) AND MARGINAL COST (MC)

A Summary of Short-Run Cost Curves

The law of diminishing marginal returns determines the shapes of short-run cost curves. The shape of the marginal product curve discussed earlier in the chapter determines the shape of the marginal cost curve. And the shape of the marginal product curve is determined by the law of diminishing marginal returns, which is the relationship between the variable resource and output. Thus, the marginal cost curve ultimately depends on how much each unit of the variable resource, in this case labor, produces. When the marginal product of labor increases, the marginal cost of output must fall. Once diminishing marginal returns set in, the marginal cost of output must rise. Thus, marginal cost first falls and then rises. And the marginal cost curve dictates the shapes of the average variable cost and average total cost curves. When marginal cost is less than average cost, average cost declines; when marginal cost is above average cost, average cost increases. Got it? If not, please reread this paragraph.

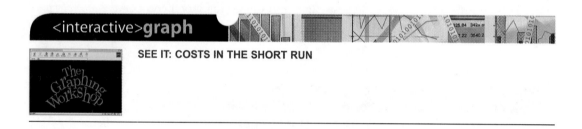

SEE IT: COSTS IN THE SHORT RUN

COSTS IN THE LONG RUN

So far, our analysis has focused on how costs vary as the rate of output expands in the short run for a firm of a given size. In the long run, all inputs that are under the firm's control can be varied, so there is no fixed cost. The long run is not just a succession of short runs. The long run is best thought of as a *planning horizon.* In the long run, the choice of input combinations is flexible, but that flexibility is available only to firms that have not yet acted on their plans. Firms plan for the long run, but they produce in the short run. Once the size of the plant has been selected and the concrete has been poured, the firm has fixed costs and is operating in the short run. We turn now to long-run costs.

The Long-Run Average Cost Curve

Suppose that, because of the special nature of technology in the industry, a firm must choose among only three possible sizes: small, medium, and large. Exhibit 8 presents this simple case. The short-run average total cost curves for the three plant sizes are *SS'*, *MM'*, and *LL'*. Which size of plant should the firm build to minimize the average cost of production? The appropriate size, or *scale,* for the plant depends on how much the firm thinks it will produce. For example, if q is the desired rate of output in the long run, the average cost per unit will be lowest with a small plant. If the desired output rate is q', the medium plant size ensures the lowest average cost.

More generally, for any output less than q_a, average cost is lowest when the plant is small. For output rates between q_a and q_b, average cost is lowest for the plant of medium size. And for output rates that exceed q_b, average cost is lowest when the plant is large. The **long-run average cost curve,** sometimes called the firm's *planning curve,* connects portions of the three short-run average cost curves that are lowest for each output rate. In Exhibit 8, that curve consists of the line segments connecting *S, a, b,* and *L'*.

Now suppose there are many possible plant sizes. Exhibit 9 presents a sample of short-run average total cost curves shown in *blue.* The long-run average cost curve, shown in *red,* is formed by connecting the points on the various short-run average cost curves that represent

EXHIBIT 8

Short-Run Average Total Cost Curves Form the Long-Run Average Cost Curve, or Planning Curve

Curves *SS'*, *MM'*, and *LL'* show short-run average total costs for small, medium, and large plants, respectively. For output less than q_a, average cost is lowest when the plant is small. Between q_a and q_o, cost is lowest with a medium-size plant. If output exceeds q_b, the large plant is best. The long-run average-cost curve is *SabL'*.

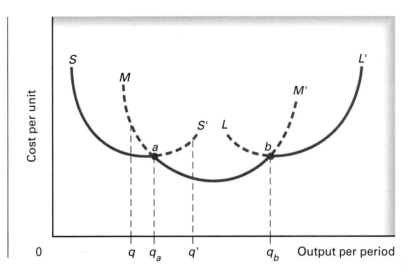

EXHIBIT 9

Many Short-Run Average Total Cost Curves Form a Firm's Long-Run Average Cost Curve, or Planning Curve

With many possible plant sizes, the long-run average cost curve is the envelope of portions of the short-run average cost curves. Each short-run curve is tangent to the long-run average cost curve. Each point of tangency represents the least-cost way of producing a particular level of output.

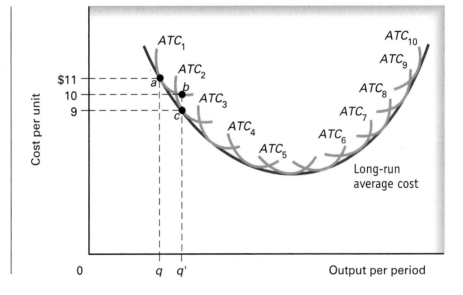

the lowest per-unit cost for each rate of output. Each of the short-run average cost curves is tangent to the long-run average cost curve, or *planning curve*. If we could display enough short-run cost curves, we would have a different plant size for each rate of output. *These points of tangency represent the least-cost way of producing each particular rate of output, given the technology and resource prices.* For example, the short-run average total cost curve ATC_1 is tangent to the long-run average cost curve at point *a*, indicating that the least-cost way of producing output rate *q* is with the plant size associated with ATC_1. No other size plant would produce *q* at as low an average cost per unit. Note, however, that other output rates along ATC_1 have a lower average cost of production. In fact, for output rate *q'* at point *b*, the average cost per unit is only $10, compared to an average cost per unit of $11 for producing *q* at point *a*. Point *b* depicts the lowest average cost along ATC_1. So while the point of tangency reflects the least-cost way of producing a particular rate of output, that tangency point does not reflect the minimum average cost for this particular plant size.

If the firm decides to produce q', which size plant should it choose to minimize the average cost of production? Output rate q' could be produced at point b, which represents the minimum average cost along ATC_1. But average cost is lower with a larger plant. With the plant size associated with ATC_2, the average cost of producing q' would be minimized at $9 per unit at point c. *Each point of tangency between a short-run average cost curve and the long-run average cost curve represents the least-cost way of producing that particular rate of output.*

Economies of Scale

Like short-run average cost curves, the long-run average cost curve is U-shaped. Recall that the shape of the short-run average total cost curve is determined primarily by increasing and diminishing marginal returns. A different principle shapes the long-run cost curve. If a firm experiences **economies of scale,** long-run average cost falls as output expands. Consider some sources of economies of scale. *A larger size often allows for larger, more specialized machines and greater specialization of labor.* For example, compare the household-size kitchen of a small restaurant with the kitchen at a McDonald's. At low rates of output, say 20 meals a day, the smaller kitchen produces meals at a lower average cost than does McDonald's. But if production in the smaller kitchen increases beyond, say, 100 meals per day, a kitchen on the scale of McDonald's would produce at a lower average cost. Thus, because of economies of scale, the long-run average cost for a restaurant may fall as size increases.

A larger scale of operation allows a firm to use larger, more efficient machines and allows workers a greater degree of specialization. Production techniques such as the assembly line can be introduced only if the rate of output is great enough. Typically, as the scale of firm increases, capital substitutes for labor and complex machines substitute for simpler machines. As an extreme example of capital substituting for labor, some Japanese auto factories are completely automated and operate in the dark.

READING IT RIGHT: WALL STREET JOURNAL EXERCISE

<interactive>video

CNN VIDEO: "ECONOMIC HEALTH OF HMOs POOR"

<interactive>update

ECONNEWS ONLINE: ROYAL AHOLD ADDS TO ITS GROCERY LIST

Diseconomies of Scale

Often another force, called **diseconomies of scale,** eventually takes over as a firm expands, increasing long-run average cost as output expands. As the amount and variety of resources employed increase, so does the *task of coordinating all these inputs.* As the workforce grows, additional layers of management are needed to monitor production. In the thicket of bureaucracy that develops, communications may get mangled. Top executives have more difficulty keeping in touch with the factory floor because information is distorted as it passes up or down the chain of command. Indeed, in very large organizations, rumors may become a primary source of information, reducing the efficiency of the organization and increasing average cost. For example, IBM undertook a massive restructuring program because the firm was experiencing diseconomies of scale, particularly in management. IBM's solution was to decentralize into six smaller decision-making groups. To reduce diseconomies of scale, some big corporations have spun off parts of their operation to form new corporations. For example, Hewlett-Packard created Agilent Technologies, and AT&T created Lucent Technologies.

Note that *diseconomies of scale result from a larger firm size, whereas diminishing marginal returns result from using more variable resources in a firm of a given size.*

In the long run, a firm can vary the inputs under its control. Some inputs, however, are not under the firm's control, and the inability to vary these inputs may be a source of diseconomies of scale. Let's look at economies and diseconomies of scale at movie theaters in the following case study.

CASE**STUDY**	At the Movies
	● *The World of Business*

Movie theaters experience both economies and diseconomies of scale. A theater with one screen needs someone to sell tickets, someone to sell popcorn (concession stand sales, incidentally, account for well over half the profit at most theaters), and someone to operate the projector. If another screen is added, the same staff can perform these tasks for both screens. Thus, the ticket seller becomes more productive by selling tickets to both movies. Furthermore, construction costs per screen are reduced because only one lobby and one set of rest rooms are required. The theater can run bigger, more noticeable newspaper ads and can spread the cost over more films. These are the reasons why we see theater owners adding more and more screens at the same location; they are taking advantage of economies of scale. From 1990 to 2000, the number of screens in the United States grew faster than the number of theaters, so the average number of screens per theater increased. Europe experienced similar growth.

But why stop at, say, 10 or even 20 screens per theater? Why not 50 screens, particularly in thickly populated urban areas with sufficient demand for such a high rate of output? One problem with expanding the number of screens is that the public roads leading to the theater are a resource the theater cannot control. The congestion around the theater grows with the number of screens at that location. Also, the supply of popular films may not be sufficiently large to fill so many screens.

Finally, time itself is a resource that the firm cannot easily control. Only certain hours are popular with moviegoers. Scheduling becomes more difficult because the manager must space out starting and ending times to avoid the congestion that occurs when too many customers come and go at the same time. No more additional "prime time" can be created. Thus theater owners lack control over such inputs as the size of public roads, the supply of films, and the amount of "prime time" in the day, and this lack of control may contribute to an increase in the long-run average cost as output expands, or to diseconomies of scale.

<interactive>exercise

eACTIVITY: AT THE MOVIES

Sources: Joahn Tagliabue, "Now Playing Europe: Invasion of Multiplex," *New York Times,* 27 January 2000; Bruce Orwall and Gregory Zuckerman, "After Joining the Megaplex Frenzy, Regal Gets the Box-Office Blues," *Wall Street Journal,* 27 September 2000; Kenneth Gosselin, "State's Cinema Building Boom Fading to Black," *Hartford Courant,* 26 October 2000; and U.S. Census Bureau, *Statistical Abstract of the United States: 2000,* at http://www.census.gov/prod/www/statistical-abstract-us.html.

It is possible for average cost to neither increase nor decrease with changes in firm size. If neither economies of scale nor diseconomies of scale are apparent over some range of output, a firm experiences **constant long-run average cost.** Perhaps economies and diseconomies of scale exist simultaneously in the firm but have offsetting effects.

Exhibit 10 presents a firm's long-run average cost curve, which is divided into segments reflecting economies of scale, constant long-run average costs, and diseconomies of scale. The rate of production must reach quantity *A* for the firm to achieve the **minimum efficient scale,** which is the lowest rate of output at which long-run average cost is at a minimum. From output rate *A* to rate *B*, average cost is constant. Beyond output rate *B*, diseconomies of scale increase long-run average cost.

EXHIBIT 10

A Firm's Long-Run Average Cost Curve

Up to output level *A*, the long-run average cost curve has a negative slope; the firm is experiencing economies of scale. Output level *A* is the minimum efficient scale—the lowest rate of output at which the firm takes full advantage of economies of scale. Between *A* and *B*, the average cost is constant. Beyond output level *B*, the long-run average cost curve has a positive slope, reflecting diseconomies of scale.

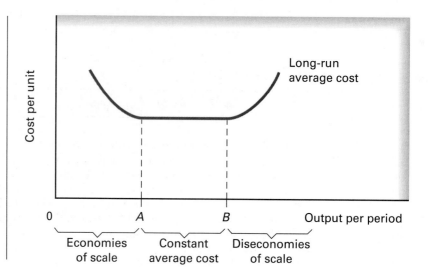

Economies and Diseconomies of Scale at the Firm Level

Our discussion so far has referred to a particular plant—a movie theater or a restaurant, for example. But a firm could also be a collection of plants, such as the hundreds of Wal-Marts or the thousands of McDonald's restaurants. More generally, we can distinguish between economies and diseconomies of scale at the *plant level*—that is, at a particular location—and at the *firm level*, where the firm is a collection of plants. We explore issues of multi-plant scale economies and diseconomies in the following case study.

CASE**STUDY**	Billions and Billions of Burgers
	● *The World of Business*

McDonald's experiences economies of scale at the plant, or restaurant, level because of its specialization of labor and machines, but it also benefits from economies of scale at the firm level. Experience gained from decades of selling hamburgers can be shared with new managers through centralized training programs. Costly research and more efficient production techniques can be shared across thousands of locations. For example, McDonald's took three years to decide on the exact temperature of the holding cabinets for its hamburger patties and took seven years to develop Chicken McNuggets. What's more, the cost of advertising and promoting McDonald's through sponsorship of world events such as the Olympics can be spread across the more than 13,000 U.S. locations and the more than 10,000 locations in 110 foreign countries.

Some diseconomies may also arise in such large-scale operations. The fact that the menu must be reasonably uniform across thousands of locations means that if customers in some parts of the country or the world do not like a product, it may not get on the menu, even though it might be popular elsewhere. Another problem with a uniform menu is that the ingredients must be available around the world and cannot be subject to droughts or sharp swings in price. For example, one chain decided not to top its burgers with bacon strips because the price of bacon fluctuates too much.

Because McDonald's has moved aggressively overseas (10 percent of the beef sold in Japan is in McDonald's hamburgers, and McDonald's is the third largest corporate employer in Brazil), planning has grown increasingly complex. For example, McDonald's is kosher in Israel and closes five times a day for Muslim prayer in Saudi Arabia. In Russia, McDonald's had to develop sources for beef, potatoes, lettuce, and other ingredients and had to train farmers how to grow products to specifications.

Change comes slowly in large firms, but it does come. In 1997, McDonald's reorganized its U.S. operation into five regions, allowing managers in each region more leeway in pricing and promotion. McDonald's has also become more flexible by putting mini-restaurants in airports, gas stations, and Wal-Marts. These so-called satellite restaurants recently accounted for half of the company's new U.S. openings. This greater flexibility in product and pricing across regions and in restaurant structure is an effort by McDonald's to address diseconomies of scale.

<interactive>exercise

eACTIVITY: BILLIONS AND BILLIONS OF BURGERS

Sources: Miriam Jordan, "McDonald's Strikes Sparks with Fast Growth in Brazil," *Wall Street Journal,* 4 October 2000; Bernard Stalmer, "McDonald's Pushes to Get Its Money's Worth on Olympic Tie," *New York Times,* 5 September 2000; Thomas L. Friedman, *The Lexus and the Olive Tree: Understanding Globalization* (New York: Farrar, Straus and Giroux, 1999); James L. Watson, ed., *Golden Arches East: McDonald's in East Asia* (Palo Alto, CA: Stanford University Press, 1998); and McDonald's Web site at http://www.mcdonalds.com/.

CONCLUSION

By considering the relationship between production and cost, we have developed the foundations for a theory of firm behavior. Despite what may appear to be a tangle of short-run and long-run cost curves, *only two relationships between resources and output underlie all the curves. In the short run, it is increasing and diminishing returns from the variable resource. In the long run, it is economies and diseconomies of scale.* If you understand the sources of these two phenomena, you have grasped the central ideas of the chapter. Our examination of the relationship between resource use and the amount produced in both the short run and the long run will help us derive an upward-sloping supply curve in the next chapter. The appendix of the chapter develops a more sophisticated approach to production and cost.

<interactive>update

ECONNEWS ONLINE: STEELING FOR RECESSION AND COMPETITION

endofchaptermaterial

- **Summary**
- **Questions for Review**
- **Problems and Exercises**
- **Experiential Exercises**

- **Wall Street Journal Exercise**
- **Graphing Workshop: Apply It Exercises**
- **Appendix Questions**

Take the Post-Test to assess your overall understanding of the key ideas in this chapter. The Post-Test provides a comprehensive selection of exam-style questions addressing the main topics and concepts of the chapter. At the completion of each Post-Test, you will receive a score and instructive feedback on how you answered each question, and a direct link to the part of the chapter addressed in the question. Take the Post-Test as often as you need to—a record of your progress for each attempt is kept for you to revisit and gauge your improvement. And each Post-Test is randomly generated, so every attempt is new.

Post-Test

A CLOSER LOOK AT PRODUCTION AND COSTS

This appendix develops a model for determining how a profit-maximizing firm will combine resources to produce a particular amount of output. The quantity of output that can be produced with a given amount of resources depends on the existing *state of technology*, which is the prevailing knowledge of how resources can be combined. Therefore, let's begin by considering the technological possibilities available to the firm.

THE PRODUCTION FUNCTION AND EFFICIENCY

The ways in which resources can be combined to produce output are summarized by a firm's production function. The *production function* identifies the maximum quantities of a particular good or service that can be produced per time period with various combinations of resources, for a given level of technology. The production function can be presented as an equation, a graph, or a table.

The production function summarized in Exhibit 11 reflects, for a hypothetical firm, the output resulting from particular combinations of resources. This firm uses only two resources: capital and labor. The amount of capital used is listed in the first column of the table, and the amount of labor employed is listed across the top. For example, if 1 unit of capital is combined with 7 units of labor, the firm can produce 290 units of output per month. The firm produces the maximum possible output given the combination of resources used; that same output could not be produced with fewer resources. Because the production function combines resources efficiently, 290 units is the most that can be produced with 7 units of labor and 1 unit of capital. Thus we say that production is **technologically efficient.**

We can examine the effects of adding labor to an existing amount of capital by starting with any level of capital and reading across the table. For example, when the firm uses 1 unit of capital and 1 unit of labor, it produces 40 units of output per month. If the amount of labor increases by 1 unit and the amount of capital remains constant, output increases to 90 units, so the marginal product of labor is 50 units. If the amount of labor employed increases from 2 to 3 units, other things constant, output goes to 150 units, yielding a marginal product of 60 units. By reading across the table, you will discover that the marginal product of labor first rises, showing increasing marginal returns from labor, and then declines, showing diminishing marginal returns. Similarly, by holding the amount of labor constant and following down the column, you will find that the marginal product of capital also reflects first increasing marginal returns and then diminishing marginal returns.

ISOQUANTS

Notice from the tabular presentation of the production function in Exhibit 11 that different combinations of resources yield the same rate of output. For example, several combinations of labor and capital yield 290 units of output per month (try to find all four combinations). Some of the information provided in Exhibit 11 can be presented more clearly in graphical form. In Exhibit 12, labor is measured along the horizontal axis and capital along the vertical axis. Combinations that yield 290 units of output are presented in Exhibit 12 as points *a*, *b*, *c*, and *d*. These points can be connected to form an *isoquant*, Q_1, a curve that shows the possible combinations of the two resources that produce 290 units of output per month. Likewise, Q_2 shows combinations of inputs that yield 415 units of output, and Q_3, 475 units of output. (The isoquant colors match those of the corresponding entries in the production function table in Exhibit 11.)

An **isoquant,** such as Q_1 in Exhibit 12, is a curve that shows all the technologically efficient combinations of two resources, such as labor and capital, that produce a certain rate of out-

EXHIBIT 11

A Firm's Production Function Using Labor and Capital: Production per Month

Units of Capital Employed per month	Units of Labor Employed per Month						
	1	2	3	4	5	6	7
1	40	90	150	200	240	270	290
2	90	140	200	250	290	315	335
3	150	195	260	310	345	370	390
4	200	250	310	350	385	415	440
5	240	290	345	385	420	450	475
6	270	320	375	415	450	475	495
7	290	330	390	435	470	495	510

put. *Iso* is from the Greek word meaning "equal," and *quant* is short for "quantity"; so *isoquant* means "equal quantity." Along a particular isoquant, such as Q_1, the rate of output produced remains constant—in this case, 290 units per month—but the combination of resources varies. To produce a particular rate of output, the firm can use resource combinations ranging from much capital and little labor to little capital and much labor. For example, a paving contractor can put in a new driveway with 10 workers using shovels, wheelbarrows, and hand rollers; the same job can also be done with only 2 workers, a road grader, and a paving machine. A charity car wash is labor intensive, involving many workers per car, plus buckets, sponges, and hose. In contrast, a professional car wash is fully automated, requiring only one worker to turn on the machine and collect the money. An isoquant depicts alternative combinations of resources that produce the same rate of output. Although we have included only three isoquants in Exhibit 12, there is a different isoquant for every quantity of output listed in Exhibit 11. Indeed, there is a different isoquant for every output rate the firm could possibly produce. Let's consider some properties of isoquants:

1. **Isoquants farther from the origin represent greater output rates.**
2. **Isoquants have negative slopes** because along a given isoquant, the quantity of labor employed inversely relates to the quantity of capital employed.

EXHIBIT 12

A Firm's Isoquants

Isoquant Q_1 shows all technologically efficient combinations of labor and capital that can be used to produce 290 units of output. Isoquant Q_2 is drawn for 415 units, and Q_3 for 475 units. Each isoquant has a negative slope and is convex to the origin.

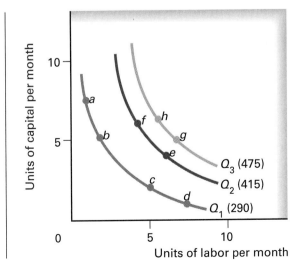

3. **Isoquants do not intersect** because each isoquant refers to a specific rate of output. An intersection would indicate that the same combination of resources could, with equal efficiency, produce two different amounts of output.
4. **Isoquants are usually convex to the origin,** which means that any isoquant becomes flatter as you move down along the curve.

The slope of an isoquant measures the ability of additional units of one resource—in this case, labor—to substitute in production for another—in this case, capital. As noted already, the isoquant has a negative slope. The absolute value of the slope of the isoquant is the **marginal rate of technical substitution,** or **MRTS,** between two resources. The MRTS is the rate at which labor substitutes for capital without affecting output. When much capital and little labor are used, the marginal productivity of labor is relatively great and the marginal productivity of capital relatively small, so one unit of labor will substitute for a relatively large amount of capital. For example, in moving from point *a* to *b* along isoquant Q_1 in Exhibit 12, one unit of labor substitutes for two units of capital, so the MRTS between points *a* and *b* equals 2. But as more labor and less capital are employed, the marginal product of labor declines and the marginal product of capital increases, so it takes more labor to make up for a one-unit reduction in capital. For example, in moving from point *c* to point *d,* two units of labor substitute for one unit of capital; thus, the MRTS between points *c* and *d* equals ½.

The extent to which one input substitutes for another, as measured by the marginal rate of technical substitution, is directly linked to the marginal productivity of each input. For example, between points *a* and *b,* one unit of labor replaces two units of capital, yet output remains constant. So labor's marginal product, MP_L—that is, the additional output resulting from an additional unit of labor—must be twice as large as capital's marginal product, MP_C. In fact, *anywhere along the isoquant, the marginal rate of technical substitution of labor for capital equals the marginal product of labor divided by the marginal product of capital, which also equals the absolute value of the slope of the isoquant,* or:

$$|\text{Slope of isoquant}| = \text{MRTS} = MP_L / MP_C$$

where the vertical lines on either side of "Slope of isoquant" mean the absolute value. For example, the slope between points *a* and *b* equals -2 and has an absolute value of 2, which equals both the marginal rate of substitution of labor for capital and the ratio of marginal productivities. Between points *b* and *c,* three units of labor substitute for three units of capital, while output is constant at 290. Thus, the slope between *b* and *c* is $-3/3$, for an absolute value of 1. Note that the absolute value of the isoquant's slope declines as we move down the curve because larger increases in labor are required to offset each one-unit decline in capital. Put another way, as less capital is employed, its marginal product increases, and as more labor is employed, its marginal product decreases.

If labor and capital were perfect substitutes in production, the rate at which labor substituted for capital would remain fixed along the isoquant, so the isoquant would be a downward-sloping straight line. Since most resources are *not* perfect substitutes, however, the rate at which one substitutes for another changes along an isoquant. As we move down along an isoquant, more labor is required to offset each one-unit decline in capital, so the isoquant becomes flatter and is convex to the origin.

Let's summarize the properties of isoquants.

1. Isoquants farther from the origin represent higher rates of output.
2. Isoquants slope downward.
3. Isoquants never intersect.
4. Isoquants are bowed toward the origin.

ISOCOST LINES

Isoquants graphically illustrate a firm's production function for all quantities of output the firm could possibly produce. We turn now to the question of what combination of resources to employ to minimize the cost of producing a given rate of output. The answer, as we'll see, depends on the cost of resources.

Suppose a unit of labor costs the firm $1,500 per month, and a unit of capital costs $2,500 per month. The total cost (TC) of production is

$$TC = (w \times L) + (r \times C)$$
$$= \$1,500L + \$2,500C$$

where *w* is the monthly wage rate, *L* is the quantity of labor employed, *r* is the monthly cost of capital, and *C* is the quantity of capital employed. An **isocost line** identifies all combinations of capital and labor the firm can hire for a given total cost. Again, *iso* is Greek for "equal," so an isocost line is a line representing resource combinations of equal cost. In Exhibit 13, for example, the line $TC = \$15,000$ identifies all combinations of labor and capital that cost the firm a total of $15,000 per month. The entire $15,000 could pay for either 6 units of capital or 10 units of labor per month. Or the firm could employ any other combination of resources along the isocost line.

Recall that the slope of any line is the vertical change between two points on the line divided by the corresponding horizontal change. At the point where the isocost line meets the vertical axis, the quantity of capital that can be purchased equals the total cost divided by the monthly cost of a unit of capital, or TC/r. At the point where the isocost line meets the horizontal axis, the quantity of labor that can be hired equals the firm's total cost divided by the monthly wage, or TC/w. The slope of any isocost line in Exhibit 13 can be calculated by considering a movement from the vertical intercept to the horizontal intercept. That is, we divide the vertical change $(-TC/r)$ by the horizontal change (TC/w), as follows:

$$\text{Slope of isocost line} = -\frac{TC/r}{TC/w} = -\frac{w}{r}$$

The slope of the isocost line is the negative of the price of labor divided by the price of capital, or $-w/r$, which indicates the relative prices of the inputs. In our example, the absolute value of the slope of the isocost line equals w/r, or

$$
\begin{aligned}
|\text{Slope of isocost line}| &= w/r \\
&= \$1,500/\$2,500 \\
&= 0.6
\end{aligned}
$$

The monthly wage is 0.6, or six-tenths, of the monthly cost of a unit of capital, so hiring one more unit of labor, without incurring any additional cost, implies that the firm must employ 0.6 fewer units of capital.

A firm is not confined to a particular isocost line. This is why Exhibit 13 includes three of them, each corresponding to a different total budget. In fact, there is a different isocost line for every possible budget. *These isocost lines are parallel because each reflects the same relative resource price.* Resource prices in our example are assumed to be constant regardless of the amount of each resource the firm employs.

<interactive>**update**

- **ECONNEWS ONLINE: PRECISION PLOWING**
- **ECONNEWS ONLINE: OPTIMIZING OPERATIONS**

EXHIBIT 13

A Firm's Isocost Lines

Each isocost line shows combinations of labor and capital that can be purchased for a fixed amount of total cost. The slope of each is equal to the negative of the wage rate divided by the monthly cost of capital. Higher levels of cost are represented by isocost lines farther from the origin.

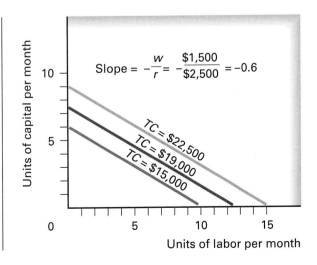

THE CHOICE OF INPUT COMBINATIONS

Exhibit 14 brings together the isoquants and the isocost lines. Suppose the firm has decided to produce 415 units of output and wants to minimize the cost of doing so. The firm could select point *f*, where 6 units of capital combine with 4 units of labor to produce 415 units. This combination, however, would cost $21,000 at prevailing prices. Since the profit-maximizing firm wants to produce its chosen output at the minimum cost, it tries to find the isocost line closest to the origin that still touches the isoquant. From a point of tangency, any movement in either direction along an isoquant results in a higher cost. *So a tangency between the isocost line and the isoquant shows the minimum cost required to produce a given output.*

Look at what's going on at the point of tangency. At point *e* in Exhibit 14, the isoquant and the isocost line have the same slope. As mentioned already, the absolute value of the slope of an isoquant equals the *marginal rate of technical substitution* between labor and capital, and the absolute value of the slope of the isocost line equals the *ratio of the input prices.* So when a firm produces output in the least costly way, the marginal rate of technical substitution must equal the ratio of the resource prices, or:

$$\text{MRTS} = w/r = 1{,}500/2{,}500 = 0.6$$

This equality shows that the firm adjusts resource use so that the rate at which one input can be substituted for another in production—that is, the marginal rate of technical substitution—equals the rate at which one resource can be exchanged for another in resource markets, which is w/r. If this equality does not hold, the firm could adjust its input mix to produce the same output for a lower cost.

THE EXPANSION PATH

Imagine a set of isoquants representing each possible rate of output. Given the relative cost of resources, we could then draw isocost lines to determine the optimal combination of resources for producing each rate of output. The points of tangency in Exhibit 15 show the least-cost input combinations for producing several output rates. For example, output rate Q_2 can be produced most cheaply using *C* units of capital and *L* units of labor. The line formed by connecting these tangency points is the firm's **expansion path.** The expansion path need not be a straight line, although it will generally slope upward, indicating that the firm will expand the use of both resources in the long run as output increases. Note that we have assumed that the prices of inputs remain constant as the firm varies output along the expansion path, so the isocost lines at the points of tangency are parallel—that is, they have the same slope.

The expansion path indicates the lowest long-run total cost for each rate of output. For example, the firm can produce output rate Q_2 for TC_2, output rate Q_3 for TC_3, and so on. Similarly, the firm's long-run average cost curve indicates, at each rate of output, the total cost divided by the rate of output. The firm's expansion path and the firm's long-run average cost

EXHIBIT 14

A Firm's Optimal Combinations of Inputs

At point *e*, isoquant Q_2 is tangent to the isocost line. The optimal combination of inputs is 6 units of labor and 4 units of capital. The maximum output that can be produced for $19,000 is 415 units. Alternatively, point *e* determines the minimum-cost way of producing 415 units of output.

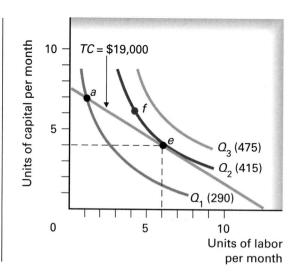

EXHIBIT 15

A Firm's Expansion Path

The points of tangency between isoquants and isocost lines each show the least expensive way of producing a particular level of output. Connecting these tangency points gives the firm's expansion path.

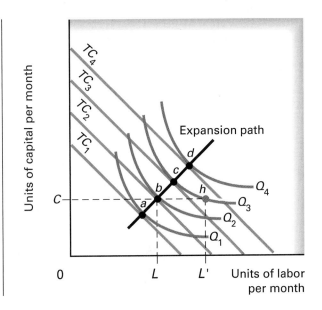

curve represent alternative ways of portraying costs in the long run, given resource prices and technology.

We can use Exhibit 15 to distinguish between short-run and long-run adjustments in output. Let's begin with the firm producing Q_2 at point b, which requires C units of capital and L units of labor. Now suppose that in the short run, the firm wants to increase output to Q_3. Since capital is fixed in the short run, the only way to produce Q_3 is by increasing the quantity of labor employed to L', which requires moving to point h in Exhibit 15. Point h is not the cheapest way to produce Q_3 in the long run because it is not a tangency point. In the long run, capital usage is variable, and if the firm wishes to produce Q_3, it should minimize total cost by adjusting from point h to point c.

One final point: If the relative prices of resources change, the least-cost resource combination will also change, so the firm's expansion path will change. For example, if the price of labor increases, capital becomes cheaper relative to labor. The efficient production of any given rate of output will therefore call for less labor and more capital. With the cost of labor higher, the firm's total cost for each rate of output rises. Such a cost increase would also be reflected by an upward shift in the average total cost curve.

SUMMARY

A firm's *production function* specifies the relationship between resource use and output, given prevailing technology. An *isoquant* is a curve that illustrates the possible combinations of resources that will produce a particular rate of output. An *isocost* line presents the combinations of resources the firm can employ, given resource prices and the firm's total budget. For a given rate of output—that is, for a given isoquant—the firm minimizes total cost by choosing the lowest isocost line that just touches, or is tangent to, the isoquant. The least-cost combination of resources depends on the productivity of resources and their relative cost. Economists believe that although firm owners may not understand the material in this appendix, they must act as if they do to maximize profit.

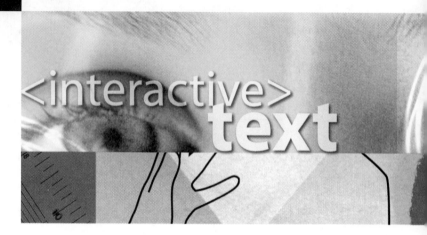

CHAPTER 8

Perfect Competition

What does a bushel of wheat have in common with an ounce of gold? Why might a firm continue to operate even though it's losing money? Why do some firms fail to earn an economic profit? In what sense can it be said that the more competitive the industry, the less individual firms compete with each other? And what's so perfect about perfect competition? To answer these and other questions, we examine our first market structure—perfect competition.

The previous chapter developed cost curves for an individual firm in both the short run and the long run. In light of these costs, how much should a firm produce and what price should it charge? To discover the firm's profit-maximizing output and price, we revisit an old friend—demand. Demand and production costs, or supply, together guide the firm to maximum economic profit. In the next few chapters, we will examine how firms respond to their economic environments in deciding what to supply, in what quantities, and at what price. No matter what the market structure, we assume that firms try to maximize profit. Topics discussed in this chapter include:

- Market structure
- Price takers
- Marginal revenue

- Golden rule of profit maximization
- Loss minimization
- Firm and industry short-run supply curves

132

- Industry long-run supply curve
- Competition and efficiency
- Producer surplus
- Gains from exchange

Pre-Test

Take the Pre-Test to assess your initial knowledge of the key ideas in this chapter. The Pre-Test provides exam-style questions addressing the main topics and concepts of the chapter. At the completion of each Pre-Test, you will receive a score and instructive feedback on how you answered each question, and a direct link to the part of the chapter addressed in the question. Take the Pre-Test as often as you need to—a record of your progress for each attempt is kept for you to revisit and gauge your improvement.

\<interactive\>exercise

ECONDEBATE ONLINE: SUPPLY AND DEMAND

\<interactive\>update

- ECONDATA ONLINE: PERFECT COMPETITION
- ECONDATA ONLINE: SUPPLY AND DEMAND
- ECONLINKS ONLINE: ECONOMICS WEB LINKS
- ECONNEWS ONLINE: PERFECT COMPETITION
- ECONNEWS ONLINE: SUPPLY AND DEMAND

AN INTRODUCTION TO PERFECT COMPETITION

First, a few words about terminology. An industry consists of all firms that supply output to a particular market, such as the auto market, the shoe market, or the wheat market. The terms *industry* and *market* are used interchangeably throughout this chapter. Many of the firm's decisions depend on the structure of the market in which it operates. **Market structure** describes the important features of a market, such as the number of suppliers (are there many or few?), the product's degree of uniformity (do firms in the market supply identical products, or are there differences across firms?), the ease of entry into the market (can new firms enter easily, or are they blocked by natural or artificial barriers?), and the forms of competition among firms (do firms compete only through prices, or are advertising and product differences common as well?). The various features will become clearer as we examine each type of market structure in the next few chapters.

Perfectly Competitive Market Structure

We begin with **perfect competition,** in some ways the most basic of market structures. A *perfectly competitive* market is characterized by (1) many buyers and sellers—so many that each buys or sells only a tiny fraction of the total amount exchanged in the market; (2) firms that sell a standardized, or *homogeneous,* product, such as bushels of wheat or ounces of gold; (3) buyers and sellers that are fully informed about the price and availability of all resources and products; and (4) firms and resources that are freely mobile—that is, over time they can easily enter or leave the industry without facing obstacles like patents, licenses, high capital costs, or ignorance about available technology.

If these conditions are present in a market, individual participants have no control over the price. Price is determined by market supply and demand. A perfectly competitive firm is called a **price taker** because that firm must "take," or accept, the market price—as in "take it or leave it." Once the market establishes the price, each firm is free to produce whatever quantity maximizes profit. *A perfectly competitive firm is so small relative to the size of the market that the firm's choice about how much to produce has no perceptible effect on the market price.*

Examples of perfectly competitive markets include those for most agricultural products, such as wheat, corn, and livestock; markets for basic commodities, such as gold, silver, and copper; and markets for foreign exchange, such as for yen, euros, and pesos. Again, there are so many buyers and sellers that the actions of any one cannot influence the market price. For example, about 150,000 farmers in the United States raise hogs, and tens of millions of U.S. households buy pork products.

The model of perfect competition allows us to make a number of predictions that hold up well when compared to the real world. Perfect competition is also an important benchmark for evaluating the efficiency of other types of markets. Let's look at demand under perfect competition.

Demand under Perfect Competition

Suppose the market in question is the world market for wheat and the firm in question is a wheat farm. In the world market for wheat, there are tens of thousands of farms, so any one supplies only a tiny fraction of market output. For example, the thousands of wheat farmers in Kansas together produce less than 3 percent of the world's supply of wheat. In Exhibit 1, the market price of wheat of $5 per bushel is determined in panel (a) by the intersection of the market demand curve *D* and the market supply curve *S*. Once the market price is established, any farmer can sell all he or she wants at that market price.

Each farm is so small relative to the market that each has no impact on the market price; each farmer is a *price taker.* Because all farmers produce an identical product—bushels of wheat, in this case—anyone who charges more than the market price cannot sell any wheat. For example, if a farmer charged $5.25 per bushel, buyers would simply turn to other suppliers. Of course, any farmer is free to charge less than the market price, but why do that when all wheat can be sold at the market price? Farmers aren't stupid (or if they are, they don't last long). *The demand curve facing an individual farmer is, therefore, a horizontal line drawn at the market price.* In our example, the demand curve facing an individual farmer, identified as *d* in panel (b), is drawn at the market price of $5 per bushel. Thus, each farmer faces a horizontal, or a *perfectly elastic,* demand curve.

It has been said, "In perfect competition there is no competition." Ironically, two neighboring wheat farmers in perfect competition are not really rivals. They both can sell as much wheat as they want to at the market price. The amount one sells has no effect on the market price or on the amount the other can sell.

EXHIBIT 1

Market Equilibrium and a Firm's Demand Curve in Perfect Competition

In panel (a), the market price of $5 is determined by the intersection of the market demand and supply curves. The individual perfectly competitive firm can sell any amount at that price. The demand curve facing the perfectly competitive firm is horizontal at the market price, as shown by demand curve *d* in panel (b).

(a) Market equilibrium

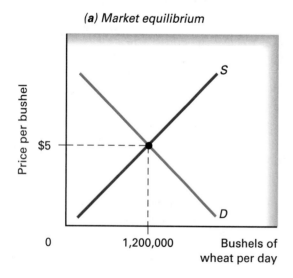

(b) Firm's demand

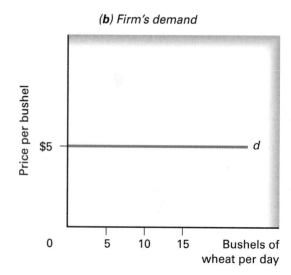

SHORT-RUN PROFIT MAXIMIZATION

Each firm tries to maximize economic profit. Firms that ignore this strategy don't survive. Economic profit equals total revenue minus total opportunity cost, including both explicit and implicit costs. Implicit cost, you will recall, is the opportunity cost of resources owned by the firm and includes a normal profit; economic profit is any profit above normal profit. How do firms maximize profit? You have already learned that the perfectly competitive firm has no control over price. What the firm does control is the amount produced, the rate of output. The question the wheat farmer asks boils down to: *How much should I produce to earn the most profit?*

Total Revenue Minus Total Cost

The firm maximizes economic profit by finding the rate of output at which total revenue exceeds total cost by the greatest amount. The firm's total revenue is simply its output times the price per unit. Column (1) in Exhibit 2 shows an individual farmer's output possibilities measured in bushels of wheat per day. Column (2) shows the market price per bushel of $5, a price that does not vary as that farmer's output changes. Column (3) shows total revenue, which is output times price, or column (1) times column (2). And column (4) shows the total cost of production. Total cost already includes a normal profit, so total cost includes all opportunity costs. Although the exhibit does not distinguish between fixed and variable costs, fixed cost must equal $15 per day, since total cost is $15 when output is zero. The fact that this farm incurs a fixed cost indicates that at least one resource must be fixed, so the farm must be operating in the short run.

Total revenue in column (3) minus total cost in column (4) yields the farmer's economic profit or economic loss in column (7). As you can see, total revenue exceeds total cost when between 7 and 14 bushels per day are produced, so the farm earns an *economic profit* at those output rates. Economic profit is maximized at $12 per day when the farm produces 12 bushels of wheat per day (the $12 and 12 bushels combination is just a coincidence).

EXHIBIT 2

Short-Run Costs and Revenues for a Perfectly Competitive Firm

(1) Bushels of Wheat per day (q)	(2) Marginal Revenue (Price) (p)	(3) Total Revenue $(TR = q \times p)$	(4) Total Cost (TC)	(5) Marginal Cost $\left(MC = \dfrac{\Delta TC}{\Delta q}\right)$	(6) Average Total Cost $\left(ATC = \dfrac{TC}{q}\right)$	(7) Economic Profit or Loss = $TR - TC$
0	——	$ 0	$15.00	——	∞	−$15.00
1	$5	5	19.75	$4.75	$19.75	−14.75
2	5	10	23.50	3.75	11.75	−13.50
3	5	15	26.50	3.00	8.83	−11.50
4	5	20	29.00	2.50	7.25	−9.00
5	5	25	31.00	2.00	6.20	−6.00
6	5	30	32.50	1.50	5.42	−2.50
7	5	35	33.75	1.25	4.82	1.25
8	5	40	35.25	1.50	4.41	4.75
9	5	45	37.25	2.00	4.14	7.75
10	5	50	40.00	2.75	4.00	10.00
11	5	55	43.25	3.25	3.93	11.75
12	**5**	**60**	**48.00**	**4.75**	**4.00**	**12.00**
13	5	65	54.50	6.50	4.19	10.50
14	5	70	64.00	9.50	4.57	6.00
15	5	75	77.50	13.50	5.17	−2.50
16	5	80	96.00	18.50	6.00	−16.00

These results are graphed in panel (a) of Exhibit 3, which shows the total revenue and total cost curves. As output increases by 1 bushel, total revenue increases by $5, so the farm's total revenue curve is a straight line emanating from the origin, with a slope of 5. The short-run total cost curve has the backward S shape introduced in the previous chapter, showing first increasing and then diminishing marginal returns from the variable resource. Total cost always increases as more output is produced.

Comparing total revenue and total cost is one way to find the profit-maximizing output. At rates of output less than 7 bushels and greater than 14 bushels, total cost exceeds total revenue, resulting in an economic loss, which is measured by the vertical distance between the two curves. Total revenue exceeds total cost between 7 and 14 bushels per day, so the farmer earns an economic profit. *Profit is maximized at the rate of output where total revenue exceeds total cost by the greatest amount.* We already know that profit is greatest when 12 bushels are produced per day.

EXHIBIT 3

Short-Run Profit Maximization

In panel (a), the total revenue curve for a competitive firm is a straight line with a slope equal to the market price of $5. Total cost increases with output, first at a decreasing rate and then at an increasing rate. Profit is maximized at 12 bushels of wheat per day, where total revenue exceeds total cost by the greatest amount. In panel (b), marginal revenue is a horizontal line at the market price of $5. Profit is maximized at 12 bushels of wheat per day, where the marginal cost equals marginal revenue (point e). Profit per day is output (12 bushels) multiplied by the difference between price ($5) and average total cost ($4), as shown by the shaded rectangle.

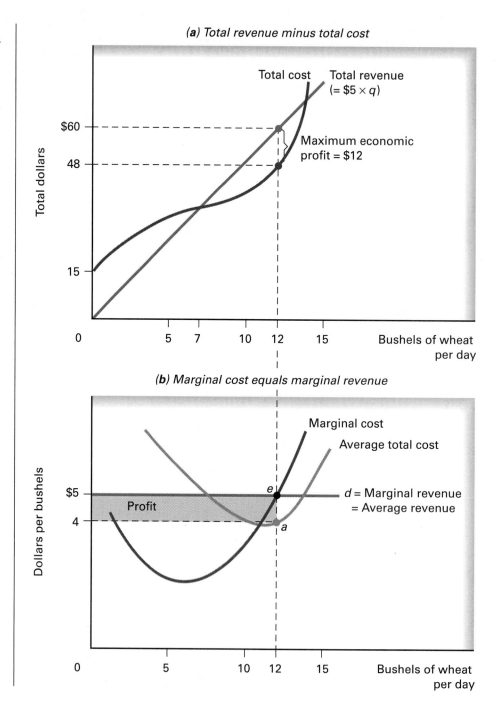

(a) Total revenue minus total cost

(b) Marginal cost equals marginal revenue

\<interactive\>**graph**

SEE IT: FIRM AND MARKET IN PERFECT COMPETITION (SHORT-RUN PROFIT MAXIMIZATION)

Marginal Revenue Equals Marginal Cost in Equilibrium

Another way to find the profit-maximizing rate of output is to focus on marginal revenue and marginal cost. **Marginal revenue,** or *MR*, is the change in total revenue from selling another unit of output. In perfect competition, each firm is a price taker, so selling one more unit increases total revenue by the market price. Thus, *in perfect competition, marginal revenue is the market price.* In this example, marginal revenue, the revenue from selling one more bushel of wheat, is $5. The first two columns of Exhibit 2 present the farm's marginal revenue for each bushel of wheat. In the previous chapter, you learned that *marginal cost* is the change in total cost resulting from producing another unit of output. Column (5) of Exhibit 2 presents the farm's marginal cost for each bushel of wheat. Marginal cost first declines, reflecting increasing marginal returns in the short run as more of the variable resource is employed. Marginal cost then increases, reflecting diminishing marginal returns from the variable resource.

The firm will increase quantity supplied as long as each additional unit adds more to total revenue than to total cost—that is, as long as marginal revenue exceeds marginal cost. Comparing columns (2) and (5) in Exhibit 2, we see that marginal revenue exceeds marginal cost for each of the first 12 bushels of wheat. The marginal cost of bushel 13, however, is $6.50, compared with its marginal revenue of $5. Therefore, producing bushel 13 would reduce economic profit by $1.50. The farmer, as a profit maximizer, will limit output to 12 bushels per day. More generally, a firm will expand output as long as marginal revenue exceeds marginal cost and will stop expanding before marginal cost exceeds marginal revenue. A shorthand expression for this approach is the **golden rule of profit maximization,** which says that a profit-maximizing firm produces where *marginal revenue equals marginal cost.*

Economic Profit in the Short Run

Per-unit revenue and cost data from Exhibit 2 are graphed in panel (b) of Exhibit 3. Since marginal revenue in perfect competition equals the market price, the marginal revenue curve is a horizontal line at the market price of $5, which is also the perfectly competitive firm's demand curve. At any point along the demand curve, marginal revenue is the price. Because the perfectly competitive firm can sell any quantity for the same price per unit, marginal revenue is also **average revenue,** or *AR*, which equals the total revenue divided by quantity, or $AR = TR/q$. Regardless of the rate of output, therefore, the following equality holds along a perfectly competitive firm's demand curve:

$$\text{Market price} = \text{Marginal revenue} = \text{Average revenue}$$

The marginal cost curve intersects the marginal revenue curve at point *e*, where output is about 12 bushels per day. At lower rates of output, marginal revenue exceeds marginal cost, so the farm could increase profit by expanding output. At higher rates of output, marginal cost exceeds marginal revenue, so the farm could increase profit by reducing output. Profit itself appears as the shaded rectangle. The height of that rectangle, *ae*, equals the price (or average revenue) of $5 minus the average total cost of $4. Thus, price minus average total cost yields an average profit of $1 per bushel. Profit per day, $12, equals the average profit per bushel, $1 (denoted by *ae*), times the 12 bushels produced.

Note that with the total cost and total revenue curves, we measure economic profit by the vertical *distance* between the two curves, as shown in panel (a). But with per-unit curves, we measure economic profit by an *area*—that is, by multiplying the average profit of $1 per bushel times the 12 bushels sold, as shown in panel (b).

<interactive>graph

- **SEE IT: FIRM AND MARKET IN PERFECT COMPETITION (SHORT-RUN PROFIT MAXIMIZATION)**
- **TRY IT: IDENTIFYING SHORT RUN PROFIT FOR A PERFECTLY COMPETITIVE FIRM**

MINIMIZING SHORT-RUN LOSSES

An individual firm in perfect competition has no control over the market price. Sometimes the price may be so low that no rate of output will yield an economic profit. Faced with losses at all rates of output, the firm can either continue to produce at a loss or temporarily shut down. But even if the firm shuts down, it cannot, *in the short run,* go out of business or produce something else. The short run is by definition a period too short to allow existing firms to leave or new firms to enter this industry. In a sense, firms are trapped in their industry in the short run.

Fixed Cost and Minimizing Losses

Your instincts probably tell you that, rather than produce at a loss, the firm should shut down. It's not that simple. Keep in mind that the firm has two types of costs in the short run: fixed costs, such as property taxes and fire insurance, which must be paid in the short run even if the firm produces nothing, and variable costs, such as labor, which depend on the rate of output. A firm that shuts down in the short run must still pay its fixed costs. But, by producing, a firm's revenue may more than cover variable costs. *A firm will produce if revenue generated exceeds the variable cost of production;* after all, revenue in excess of variable costs pays a portion of fixed costs.

Let's look at the same cost data presented in Exhibit 2, but now suppose the market price has fallen from $5 to $3 per bushel of wheat. This new situation is presented in Exhibit 4. Because of the lower price, total revenue is lower at all rates of output and economic profit has disappeared. Column (8) indicates that each quantity results in a loss. If the firm produces nothing, its loss is the fixed cost of $15 per day. But, by producing between 6 and 12 bushels per day, the firm cuts its loss to less than $15 per day. From column (8), you can see that the firm's loss is minimized at $10 per day when 10 bushels are produced. Compared with zero output, producing 10 bushels increases total cost by only $25 but increases total revenue by $30. The net gain of $5 can cover a portion of the firm's fixed cost.

Panel (a) of Exhibit 5 presents the firm's total cost and total revenue curves from data in Exhibit 4. The total cost curve remains the same as shown in Exhibit 3. The drop in price from $5 to $3 per unit changes the slope of the total revenue curve from 5 to 3, so the curve is now flatter than in Exhibit 3. Notice that the total revenue curve now lies below the total cost curve at all output rates. The vertical distance between the two curves measures the loss at each rate of output. If the farmer produces nothing, the loss is the fixed cost of $15 per day. The vertical distance between the two curves is minimized at an output rate of about 10 bushels, where the loss is $10 per day.

Marginal Revenue Equals Marginal Cost

Again, we get the same result using marginal analysis. The per-unit data from Exhibit 4 are presented in panel (b) of Exhibit 5. *The firm will produce rather than shut down if marginal revenue equals marginal cost at a rate of output where the price equals or exceeds average variable cost.* The marginal revenue and marginal cost curves intersect at point *e,* where the output rate is about 10 bushels per day and the price of $3 exceeds the average variable cost per bushel of $2.50.

Because the price of $3 per bushel exceeds average variable cost, the farmer is able to cover variable cost and a portion of fixed cost. Specifically, $2.50 of the price pays the average variable cost, and $0.50 covers a portion of the average fixed cost of $1.50 (average fixed cost is average total cost of $4.00 minus average variable cost of $2.50). This still leaves a loss of $1 per bushel, which when multiplied by 10 bushels yields an economic loss of $10 per day, identified in panel (b) by the shaded rectangle. (Why is the farmer in the short run better off operating at a loss rather than shutting down?)

Shutting Down in the Short Run

As long as the loss that results from producing is less than the shutdown loss, the farmer will remain open for business in the short run. You may have read or heard about firms that report a loss; most firms reporting a loss continue to operate. In fact, many new firms lose money in

EXHIBIT 4

Minimizing Short-Run Losses

(1) Bushels of Wheat per day (q)	(2) Marginal Revenue (Price) (p)	(3) Total Revenue (TR = q × p)	(4) Total Cost (TC)	(5) Marginal Cost $\left(MC = \frac{\Delta TC}{\Delta q}\right)$	(6) Average Total Cost $\left(ATC = \frac{TC}{q}\right)$	(7) Average Variable Cost $\left(AVC = \frac{VC}{q}\right)$	(8) Economic Profit or Loss = TR − TC
0	——	$ 0	$15.00	——	∞	——	−$15.00
1	$3	3	19.75	$4.75	$19.75	$4.75	−16.75
2	3	6	23.50	3.75	11.75	4.25	−17.50
3	3	9	26.50	3.00	8.83	3.83	−17.50
4	3	12	29.00	2.50	7.25	3.50	−17.00
5	3	15	31.00	2.00	6.20	3.20	−16.00
6	3	18	32.50	1.50	5.42	2.92	−14.50
7	3	21	33.75	1.25	4.82	2.68	−12.75
8	3	24	35.25	1.50	4.41	2.53	−11.25
9	3	27	37.25	2.00	4.14	2.47	−10.25
10	**3**	**30**	**40.00**	**2.75**	**4.00**	**2.50**	**−10.00**
11	3	33	43.25	3.25	3.93	2.57	−10.25
12	3	36	48.00	4.75	4.00	2.75	−12.00
13	3	39	54.50	6.50	4.19	3.04	−15.50
14	3	42	64.00	9.50	4.57	3.50	−22.00
15	3	45	77.50	13.50	5.17	4.17	−32.50
16	3	48	96.00	18.50	6.00	5.06	−48.00

the first few years (for example, the upstart TV network UPN lost $1 billion during its first five years[1]). But *if the average variable cost of production exceeds the price at all rates of output, the firm will shut down.* After all, why produce if doing so only increases the short-run loss? For example, suppose the price of wheat falls to $2 per bushel. As you can see from column (7) of Exhibit 4, average variable cost exceeds $2 at all rates of output. By shutting down, the farmer pays only fixed cost, not fixed cost plus a portion of variable cost.

From column (7) of Exhibit 4, you can also see that the lowest price at which the farmer would cover average variable cost is $2.47 per bushel, which is the average variable cost when output is 9 bushels per day. At this price, the farmer is indifferent about producing or shutting down, since either way the loss is the $15 per day in fixed cost. Any price above $2.47 allows the farmer, by producing, to cover some portion of fixed cost.

Note that shutting down is not the same as going out of business. In the short run, even a firm that shuts down keeps its productive capacity intact—paying the rent, fire insurance, and property taxes, keeping water pipes from freezing in the winter, and so on. For example, Dairy Queen closes for the winter, a business that serves the college community closes when school is not in session, or an auto plant responds to slack demand by temporarily halting production (as expressed in the headline "DaimlerChrysler Will Idle Three Plants in North America as

[1]Joe Flint, "Will Viacom's Big Bet on 'Buffy' Become UPN's Savior or Slayer," *Wall Street Journal,* 12 July 2001.

EXHIBIT 5

Minimizing Short-Run Losses

Since total cost always exceeds total revenue in panel (a), the firm suffers a loss at every rate of output. The loss is minimized where the rate of output is 10 bushels per day. Panel (b) shows that marginal cost equals marginal revenue at point e. The loss is equal to output (10) multiplied by the difference between average total cost ($4) and price ($3). Since price exceeds average variable cost ($2.50), the firm is better off continuing to produce in the short run.

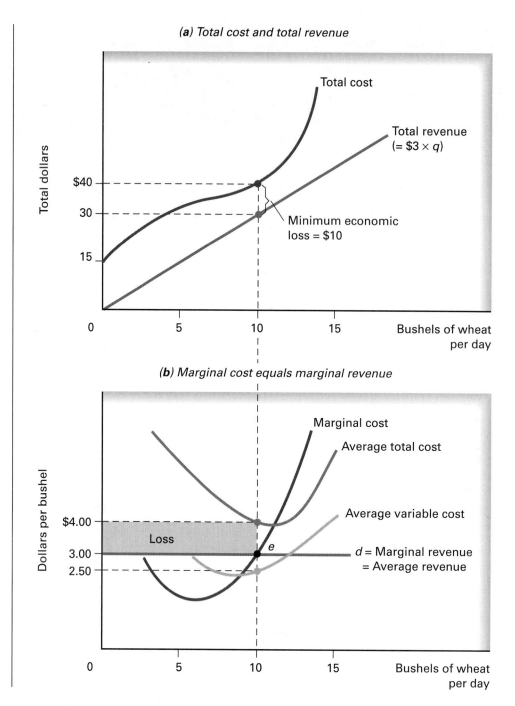

(a) Total cost and total revenue

Total cost

Total revenue (= $3 × q)

Total dollars

$40

30

15

Minimum economic loss = $10

0   5   10   15   Bushels of wheat per day

(b) Marginal cost equals marginal revenue

Marginal cost

Average total cost

Average variable cost

Dollars per bushel

$4.00

Loss

3.00

2.50

e

d = Marginal revenue = Average revenue

0   5   10   15   Bushels of wheat per day

Inventories Pile Up"[2]). These firms do not escape fixed cost by shutting down, since fixed cost by definition is not affected by changes in output. If demand increases enough, the firm will resume operation. If market conditions look grim and are not expected to improve, the firm may decide to leave the market, but that's a long-run decision. The short run is defined as a period during which some resources and some costs are fixed, so a firm cannot escape those costs in the short run, no matter what it does. *Fixed cost is sunk cost in the short run, no matter what decision the firm makes.*

[2]*Wall Street Journal*, 22 November 2000.

THE FIRM AND INDUSTRY SHORT-RUN SUPPLY CURVES

If average variable cost exceeds price at all output rates, the firm will shut down in the short run. But if price exceeds average variable cost, the firm will produce the quantity at which marginal revenue equals marginal cost. As we'll see, a firm will vary output as the market price changes. The effects of various prices on the firm's output decision are summarized in Exhibit 6. Points 1, 2, 3, 4, and 5 identify where the marginal cost curve intersects various marginal revenue, or demand, curves.

At a price as low as p_1, the firm will shut down rather than produce at point 1 because that price is below average variable cost at all output rates; so the loss-minimizing output rate at price p_1 is zero, as identified by q_1. At price p_2, the firm will be indifferent about producing q_2 or shutting down; either way the loss will equal fixed cost because the price just covers average variable cost. Point 2 is called the *shutdown point*. If the price is p_3, the firm will produce q_3 to minimize its loss (see if you can identify the loss in the diagram when the price is p_3). At p_4, the firm will produce q_4 to earn just a normal profit, since price equals average total cost. Point 4 is called the *break-even point*. If the price rises to p_5, the firm will earn a short-run economic profit by producing q_5 (see if you can identify economic profit in the diagram when the price is p_5).

The Short-Run Firm Supply Curve

As long as the price covers average variable cost, the firm will supply the quantity resulting from the intersection of its upward-sloping marginal cost curve and its marginal revenue, or demand, curve. Thus, that portion of the firm's marginal cost curve that intersects and rises above the lowest point on its average variable cost curve becomes the **short-run firm supply curve.** In Exhibit 6, the short-run supply curve is the upward-sloping portion of the marginal cost curve, beginning at point 2, the shutdown point. The solid portion of the short-run supply curve indicates the quantity the firm is willing and able to supply in the short run at each alternative price. The quantity supplied when the price is p_2 or higher is determined by the intersection of the firm's marginal cost curve and its demand, or marginal revenue, curve. At prices below p_2, the firm shuts down in the short run.

EXHIBIT 6

Summary of Short-Run Output Decisions

At price p_1, the firm produces nothing because p_1 is less than the firm's average variable cost. At price p_2, the firm is indifferent about shutting down or producing q_2 units of output, because in either case, the firm suffers a loss equal to its fixed cost. At p_3, it produces q_3 units and suffers a loss that is less than its fixed cost. At p_4, the firm produces q_4 and just breaks even because p_4 equals average total cost. Finally, at p_5, the firm produces q_5 and earns an economic profit. The firm's short-run supply curve is that portion of its marginal cost curve at or rising above the minimum point of average variable cost (point 2).

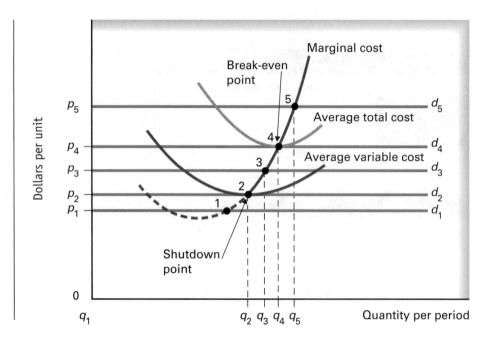

The Short-Run Industry Supply Curve

Exhibit 7 presents examples of how supply curves for three firms with identical marginal cost curves can be summed *horizontally* to form the short-run industry supply curve (in perfectly competitive markets, there will be many more firms). The **short-run industry supply curve** is the horizontal sum of all firms' short-run supply curves. At a price below p, no output is supplied. At price p, each of the three firms supplies 10 units, for a market supply of 30 units. At p', which is above p, each firm supplies 20 units, so the market supply is 60 units.

EXHIBIT 7

Aggregating Individual Supply to Form Market Supply

At price p, each firm supplies 10 units of output. Total market supply is 30 units. In general, the market supply curve in panel (d) is the horizontal summation of the individual firm supply curves s_A, s_B, and s_C.

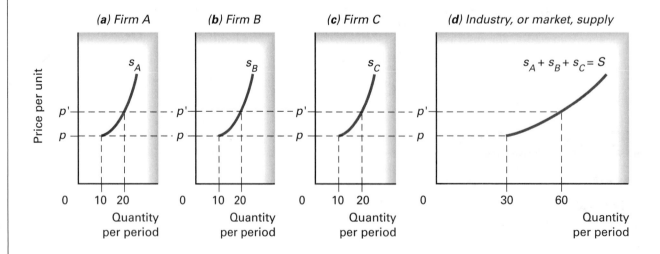

Firm Supply and Market Equilibrium

Exhibit 8 shows the relationship between the short-run profit-maximizing output of the individual firm and market equilibrium price and quantity. Suppose there are 100,000 identical wheat farmers in this industry. Their individual supply curves (represented by the portions of the marginal cost curve at or rising above the average variable cost) are summed horizontally to yield the market, or industry, supply curve. The market supply curve appears in panel (b), in which the market price of $5 per bushel is determined. At that market price, each farmer produces 12 bushels per day, as shown in panel (a), for a total quantity supplied of 1,200,000 bushels per day, as shown in panel (b). Each farmer in the short run earns an economic profit of $12 per day, represented by the shaded rectangle in panel (a).

In summary: *A perfectly competitive firm selects the short-run output rate that maximizes profit or minimizes loss. When confronting a loss, a firm either produces an output that minimizes that loss or shuts down temporarily.*

Given the conditions for perfect competition, the market will converge toward the equilibrium price and quantity. But how is that equilibrium actually reached? In the real world, markets operate based on customs and conventions, which vary across markets. For example, the rules acceptable on the New York Stock Exchange are not the same as those followed in the market for fresh fish. The following case study discusses one mechanism for reaching equilibrium—an auction.

SEE IT: FIRM AND MARKET IN PERFECT COMPETITION (SHORT-RUN PROFIT MAXIMIZATION)

EXHIBIT 8

Relationship Between Short-Run Profit Maximization and Market Equilibrium

The market supply curve S in panel (b) is the horizontal sum of the supply curves of all firms in the industry. The intersection of S with the market demand curve D determines the market price, $5. That price, in turn, determines the height of the perfectly elastic demand curve facing the individual firm in panel (a). That firm produces 12 bushels per day (where marginal cost equals marginal revenue of $5) and earns an economic profit of $1 per bushel, or $12 in total per day.

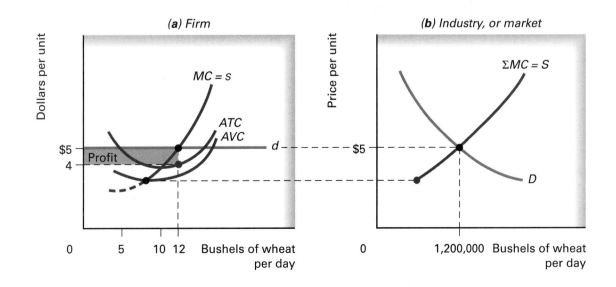

Five days a week, in a huge building 10 miles outside Amsterdam, some 2,500 buyers gather to participate in Flower Auction Holland, the largest auction of its kind in the world. Over 14 million flowers from 5,600 growers around the globe are auctioned off each day in the world's largest commercial building, spread across the equivalent of 100 football fields. Flowers are grouped and auctioned off by type—long-stemmed roses, tulips, and so on. Hundreds of buyers are seated in theater settings with their fingers on buttons. Once the flowers are presented, a clock-like instrument starts ticking off descending prices until a buyer stops it by pushing a button. The winning bidder gets to choose how many and which items to take. The clock starts again until another buyer stops it, and so on, until all flowers are sold. Buyers can also bid from remote locations. Flower auctions occur swiftly—on average a transaction occurs every four seconds.

This is an example of a *Dutch auction,* which starts at a high price and works down. Dutch auctions are more common when there are multiple lots of similar, though not identical, items to be sold, such as flowers in Amsterdam, tobacco in Canada, and fish in seaports around the world. Because there is some difference among the products for sale in a given market—for example, some flower lots are in better condition than others—this is not quite perfect competition, since perfectly competitive markets sell identical products.

More common than the Dutch auction is the *English open outcry auction,* where bidding opens at a low price and moves up until only one buyer remains. Products sold this way include stocks, bonds, wine, art, antiques, and livestock. For example, on commodity markets, such as the Chicago Board of Trade, market prices for homogeneous commodities like wheat, gold, and coffee beans are continuously determined in the trading pits using variations of an open outcry auction.

The birth of the Internet has breathed new life into auctions. Web sites such as eBay, Ubid, Yahoo! and hundreds more hold online auctions for old maps, used computers, wine, airline tickets, antiques, military memorabilia, comic books, paperweights—you name it. The largest online auction site, eBay, offers 2,000 categories in a forum that mimics a live auction. A listing on eBay is exposed to a potential audience of more than 20 million people in at least 100 countries. Internet auctions allow specialized sellers to reach a world of customers.

Computers are taking over markets in other ways. In New York, Chicago, Philadelphia, London, and Frankfurt, hand-waving traders in what seem like mosh pits are gradually being replaced by electronic trading. The Nasdaq was the world's first virtual stock market. There is no Nasdaq trading floor as with the New York Stock Exchange. On the Matif, the French futures exchange, after electronic trading was added as an option to the open-outcry system, electronic trading dominated within a matter of months. Computers reduce the transaction costs of reaching a mutually agreeable price.

<interactive>exercise

eACTIVITY: AUCTION MARKETS

Sources: Steve Frank, "Ebay's Stock Charges Ahead," *Wall Street Journal,* 8 July 2001; Michelle Slatalla, "At a Virtual Garage Sale, It Frequently Pays to Wait," *New York Times,* 2 November 2000; "The Heyday of the Auction," *Economist,* 24 July 1999. Flower Auction Holland's online address is http://www.bvh.nl/html/en/home.htm/; eBay's is http://www.ebay.com/; Nasdaq's is http://nasdaq.com/; and the French trading exchange, Matif, has a Web site at http://www.matif.fr/.

PERFECT COMPETITION IN THE LONG RUN

In the short run, the quantity of variable resources can change, but other resources, which mostly determine firm size, are fixed. In the long run, however, firms have time to enter and exit and to adjust their size—that is, to adjust the scale of their operations. In the long run, there is no distinction between fixed and variable costs because all resources under the firm's control are variable.

Short-run economic profit will, in the long run, encourage new firms to enter the market and may prompt existing firms to expand their scale of operations. Economic profit will attract resources from industries where firms earn only normal profit or perhaps suffer losses. This expansion in the number and size of firms will shift the industry supply curve rightward in the long run, driving down the price. New firms will continue to enter a profitable industry and existing firms will continue to increase in size as long as economic profit is greater than zero. Entry and expansion will stop only when the resulting increase in supply cuts the price to where economic profit disappears. *Short-run economic profit attracts new entrants in the long run and may cause existing firms to expand; market supply thereby increases, driving down the market price until economic profit is erased.*

On the other hand, a short-run loss will, in the long run, force some firms to leave the industry or to reduce their scale of operation. In the long run, departures and reductions in scale shift market supply to the left, thereby increasing the market price until remaining firms just break even—that is, earn just a normal profit.

NETBOOKMARK: ONLINE AUCTIONS

Zero Economic Profit in the Long Run

In the long run, firms in perfect competition earn just a normal profit, which means zero economic profit. Exhibit 9 shows one firm and the market in long-run equilibrium. In the long run, market supply adjusts as firms enter or leave or change their size; *this process continues until the market supply curve intersects the market demand curve at a price that corresponds to the lowest point on each firm's long-run average cost curve, or LRAC curve.* A higher price would generate economic profit in the short run and would thus attract new entrants in the long run. In the case of wheat farming, economic profit attracts new wheat farmers and may encourage existing wheat farmers to expand their scale of operation. A lower price would create a loss in the short run, causing some farmers in the long run to scale back their wheat production or give up wheat farming altogether.

In the long run, perfect competition cuts economic profit to zero. Because the long run is a period during which all resources under a firm's control can be varied and because the firm tries to maximize profit, *a firm in the long run will adjust its scale of operation until its average cost of production is minimized.* A firm that fails to minimize cost will not survive in the long run. At point *e* in panel (a) of Exhibit 9, the firm is in equilibrium, producing *q* units and earning just a normal profit. At point *e*, price, marginal cost, short-run average total cost, and long-run average cost are all equal. No firm in the market has any reason to change its output rate, and no outside firm has any incentive to enter this industry, because firms in the market are earning normal, but not economic, profit.

ASK THE INSTRUCTOR: DO COMPETITIVE FIRMS EARN ECONOMIC PROFIT IN THE LONG RUN?

TRY IT: IDENTIFYING LONG RUN ECONOMIC PROFIT FOR A PERFECTLY COMPETITIVE FIRM

The Long-Run Adjustment to a Change in Demand

To explore the long-run adjustment process, let's consider how a firm and an industry respond to an increase in market demand. Suppose that the costs facing each individual firm do not depend on the number of firms in the industry (this assumption will be explained soon).

Effects of an Increase in Demand. Exhibit 10 shows a perfectly competitive firm and industry in long-run equilibrium, with the market supply curve intersecting the market demand curve at point a in panel (b). The market-clearing price is p, and the market quantity is Q_a. The firm, shown in panel (a), supplies q units at that market price, earning a normal profit in long-run equilibrium. This representative firm produces at a level where price, or marginal revenue,

EXHIBIT 9

Long-Run Equilibrium for a Firm and the Industry

In long-run equilibrium, the firm produces q units of output per period and earns a normal profit. At point e, price, marginal cost, short-run average total cost, and long-run average cost are all equal. There is no reason for new firms to enter or for existing firms to leave the market. Thus, the market supply curve S in panel (b) does not shift. As long as the market demand D is stable, the industry will continue to produce a total of Q units of output at price p.

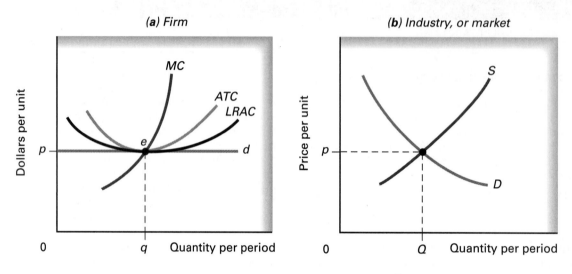

EXHIBIT 10

Long-Run Adjustment to an Increase in Demand

An increase in market demand from D to D' in panel (b) moves the short-run equilibrium point from a to b. Output rises to Q_b, and price increases to p'. The rise in market price causes the demand curve facing the firm to rise from d to d' in panel (a). The firm responds by increasing output to q' and earns an economic profit, identified by the shaded rectangle. With existing firms earning economic profit, new firms enter the industry in the long run. Market supply shifts right to S' in panel (b). Output rises further, to Q_c, and price falls back to p. In panel (a), the firm's demand curve shifts back to d, eliminating economic profit. The short-run adjustment is from point a to point b in panel (b), but the long-run adjustment is from point a to point c.

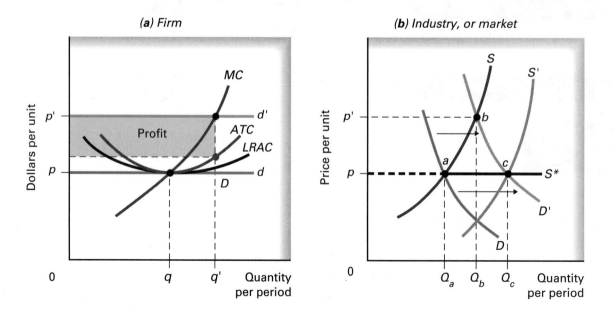

equals marginal cost, short-run average total cost, and long-run average cost. (Remember, a normal profit is included in the firm's average total cost curve.)

Now suppose market demand increases, as reflected by a shift to the right in the market demand curve, from D to D', causing the market price to increase in the short run to p'. Each firm responds to the higher price by expanding output along its short-run supply, or marginal cost, curve until the quantity supplied increases to q', shown in panel (a) of Exhibit 10. At that rate of output, the firm's marginal cost curve intersects the new marginal revenue curve, which is also the firm's new demand curve, d'. Because all firms expand production, industry output increases to Q_b, where the change in industry output is the sum of the changes of all the individual firms in the industry. Note that in the short run, each firm is earning an economic profit, shown by the shaded rectangle.

In the long run, economic profit attracts new firms. Their entry adds additional supply to the market, shifting the market supply curve to the right, which causes the market price to fall. Firms continue to enter as long as they can earn economic profit. The market supply curve eventually shifts to S', where it intersects D' at point c, returning the price to its initial equilibrium level, p. The decline in the market price has dropped the demand curve facing the individual firm from d' back down to d. As a result, each firm reduces output from q' back to q, and once again, each earns just a normal profit. Notice that although industry output increases from Q_a to Q_c, each firm's output returns to q. In this case, the additional output comes from new firms attracted to the industry rather than from greater output by existing firms, because an existing firm could not expand without increasing its long-run average cost.

New firms are attracted to the industry by short-run economic profits arising from the increase in demand. The resulting increase in market supply, however, forces the price down until economic profit disappears. In panel (b) of Exhibit 10, the short-run adjustment to increased demand is from point a to point b; the long-run adjustment moves to point c.

Effects of a Decrease in Demand. Next, let's consider the effect of a decrease in demand on the long-run market adjustment process. The initial long-run equilibrium situation in Exhibit 11 is the same as in Exhibit 10. Market demand and supply curves intersect at point a in panel (b), yielding the equilibrium price p and an equilibrium quantity Q_a. As shown in panel (a), the firm earns a normal profit in the long run by producing output rate q, where price, or marginal revenue, equals marginal cost, short-run average total cost, and long-run average cost.

Now suppose that the demand for this product declines, as reflected by a leftward shift of the market demand curve, from D back to D''. In the short run, this decline in demand reduces

EXHIBIT 11

Long-Run Adjustment to a Decrease in Demand

A decrease in demand to D'' in panel (b) disturbs the long-run equilibrium at point a. The price is driven down to p'' in the short run; output falls to Q_f. In panel (a), the firm's demand curve shifts down to d''. Each firm reduces its output to q'' and suffers a loss. As firms leave the industry in the long run, the market supply curve shifts left to S''. Market price rises to p as output falls further to Q_g. At price p, the remaining firms once again earn zero economic profit. Thus, the short-run adjustment is from point a to point f in panel (b); the long-run adjustment is from point a to point g.

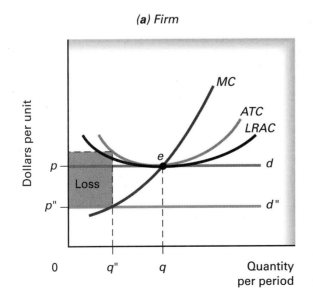

(a) Firm

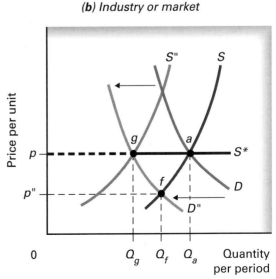

(b) Industry or market

the market price to p''. As a result, the demand curve facing each individual firm drops from d to d''. Each firm responds in the short run by cutting its output to q'', where marginal cost equals the now-lower marginal revenue, or price. Market output falls to Q_f. Since the lower market price is below short-run average total cost, each firm operates at a loss. This loss is shown by the shaded rectangle (here, the price must still be above the average variable cost, since the firm's short-run supply curve, *MC*, is defined as that portion of the firm's marginal cost curve at or above its average variable cost curve).

A short-run loss, if it continues, will in the long run force some firms out of this business. As firms leave, market supply decreases, so the price increases. Firms continue to leave until the market supply curve decreases to S'', where it intersects D'' at point g. Market output has fallen to Q_g, and price has returned to p. With the price back up to p, the remaining firms once again earn a normal profit. When the dust settles, each remaining firm produces q, the initial equilibrium quantity. But, because some firms have left the industry, market output has fallen from Q_a to Q_g. Again, note that the adjustment involves the departure of firms from the industry rather than a reduction in the scale of firms, as a reduction in scale would increase each firm's long-run average cost.

ECONNEWS ONLINE: WINN-DIXIE LOSES DIXIE

SEE IT: LONG-RUN ADJUSTMENT TO AN INCREASE IN DEMAND

THE LONG-RUN INDUSTRY SUPPLY CURVE

Thus far, we have looked at a firm's and industry's response to changes in demand, distinguishing between a short-run adjustment and a long-run adjustment. In the short run, a firm alters quantity supplied by moving up or down its marginal cost curves (that portion at or above average variable cost) until marginal cost equals marginal revenue, or price. If price is too low to cover minimum average variable cost, a firm shuts down in the short run. An economic profit or loss will, in the long run, prompt some firms to enter or leave the industry or to adjust firm size until the resulting equilibrium price provides remaining firms with a normal profit.

In Exhibits 10 and 11, we began with an initial long-run equilibrium point; then, in response to a shift of demand, we found two more long-run equilibrium points. In each case, the price remained the same in the long run, but industry output increased in Exhibit 10 and decreased in Exhibit 11. Connecting these long-run equilibrium points yields the *long-run industry supply curve*, labeled *S** in Exhibits 10 and 11. The **long-run industry supply curve** shows the relationship between price and quantity supplied once firms fully adjust to any short-term economic profit or loss resulting from a shift of demand.

Constant-Cost Industries

The industry we have studied thus far is called a **constant-cost industry** because each firm's long-run average cost curve does not shift up or down as industry output changes. Resource prices and other production costs remain constant in the long run as industry output increases or decreases. In a constant-cost industry, each firm's per-unit production costs are independent of the number of firms in the industry, so a firm's long-run average cost curve remains constant in the long run as firms enter or leave the industry. *The long-run supply curve for a constant-cost industry is horizontal,* as is depicted in Exhibits 10 and 11.

A constant-cost industry uses such a small portion of the resources available that increasing industry output does not bid up resource prices. For example, output in the pencil industry can expand without bidding up the prices of wood, graphite, and rubber because the pencil industry uses such a small share of the market supply of these resources.

Increasing-Cost Industries

The firms in some industries encounter higher average costs as industry output expands in the long run. Firms in these **increasing-cost industries** find that expanding output bids up the prices of some resources or otherwise increases per-unit production costs, and these higher production costs shift each firm's cost curves upward. For example, an industry-wide expansion of oil production could bid up the price of drilling equipment and the wages of petroleum engineers and geologists, raising per-unit production costs for each firm. Likewise, more housing construction could bid up what developers must pay for carpenters, land, lumber, and other building materials.

To illustrate the equilibrium adjustment process for an increasing-cost industry, we begin again in long-run equilibrium in Exhibit 12, with the firm shown in panel (a) and the industry in panel (b). Market demand curve D intersects short-run market supply curve S at equilibrium point a to yield market price p_a and market quantity Q_a. When the price is p_a, the demand (and marginal revenue) curve facing each firm is d_a. The firm produces the rate of output at which marginal revenue equals marginal cost, shown by intersection point a. At the firm's equilibrium rate of output, q, average total cost is at a minimum, so average total cost equals the price and the firm earns no economic profit in this long-run equilibrium.

Suppose an increase in the demand for this product shifts the market demand curve to the right from D to D'. The new demand curve intersects the short-run market supply curve S at point b, yielding the short-run equilibrium price p_b and market quantity Q_b. With an increase in the equilibrium price, each firm's demand curve shifts from d_a up to d_b. The new short-run equilibrium occurs at point b in panel (a), where the marginal cost curve intersects the new demand curve, which is also the marginal revenue curve. Each firm produces output q_b. In the short run, each firm earns an economic profit equal to q_b times the difference between price p_b and the average total cost at that rate of output. So far, the sequence of events is the same as for a constant-cost industry.

Economic profit attracts new entrants like bears to honey. Because this is an increasing-cost industry, new entrants' increase the demand for resources, driving up the cost of production

EXHIBIT 12 |

An Increasing-Cost Industry

An increase in demand to D' in panel (b) disturbs the initial equilibrium at point a. A short-run equilibrium is established at point b, where D' intersects the short-run market supply curve S. At the higher price p_b, the firm's demand curve shifts up to d_b, and its output increases to q_b in panel (a). At point b, the firm is earning an economic profit. New firms enter to try to capture some of the profits. As they do so, input prices are bid up, so each firm's marginal and average cost curves rise. The intersection of the new market supply curve, S', with D' determines the market price, p_c. At p_c, individual firms are earning zero economic profit. Point c is a point of long-run equilibrium. By connecting long-run equilibrium points a and c in panel (b), we obtain the upward-sloping long-run market supply curve S^* for this increasing-cost industry.

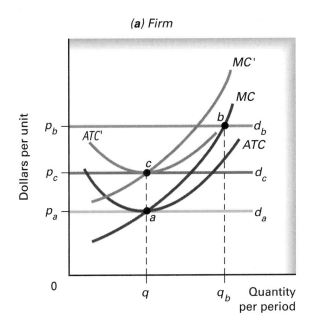

(a) Firm

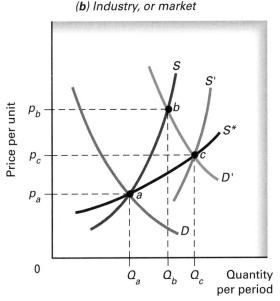

(b) Industry, or market

and raising each firm's marginal and average cost curves. In panel (a) of Exhibit 12, *MC* and *ATC* shift up to *MC'* and *ATC'*. (We assume for simplicity that new average cost curves are vertical shifts of the initial ones, so the minimum efficient plant size remains the same.)

The entry of new firms also shifts the short-run industry supply curve to the right in panel (b), thus reducing the market price. *New firms enter the industry until the combination of a higher production cost and a lower price squeezes economic profit to zero.* This long-run equilibrium occurs when the entry of new firms has shifted the short-run industry supply curve out to *S'*, which lowers the price until it equals the minimum on each firm's new average total cost curve. The market price does not fall back to the initial equilibrium level because each firm's average total cost curve has shifted up with the expansion of industry output. The intersection of the new short-run market supply curve, *S'*, and the new market demand curve, *D'*, determines the new long-run market equilibrium point, *c*. Points *a* and *c* in panel (b) are on the upward-sloping long-run supply curve, *S**, for this increasing-cost industry.

In constant-cost industries, each firm's costs depend simply on the scale of its plant and its rate of output. For firms in increasing-cost industries, costs depend also on the number of firms in the market. By bidding up the price of resources, long-run expansion in an increasing-cost industry increases each firm's marginal and average costs. The long-run supply curve slopes upward, like *S** in Exhibit 12.

To review: Firms in perfect competition can earn an economic profit, a normal profit, or an economic loss in the short run. But in the long run, the entry or exit of firms and adjustments in firm scale drive economic profit to zero, so firms earn only a normal profit. This is true whether the industry in question exhibits constant costs or increasing costs in the long run. Notice that, regardless of the nature of costs in the industry, the market supply curve is less elastic in the short run than in the long run. In the long run, firms can adjust all their resources, so they are better able to respond to changes in price. One final point: Firms in an industry could theoretically experience a lower average cost as output expands in the long run, and thus have a downward-sloping long-run industry supply curve. But such a possibility is considered so rare that we have not examined it.

As mentioned at the outset, perfect competition serves as a useful benchmark for evaluating the efficiency of markets. Let's examine the qualities of perfect competition that make it so useful.

SEE IT: LONG-RUN ADJUSTMENT TO AN INCREASING-COST INDUSTRY

ECONNEWS ONLINE: IT'S HARD TO KEEP ON TRUCKING

PERFECT COMPETITION AND EFFICIENCY

How does perfect competition stack up as an efficient allocator of resources? Two concepts of efficiency are used to judge market performance. The first, called *productive efficiency,* refers to producing output at the least possible cost. The second, called *allocative efficiency,* refers to producing the output that consumers value the most. Perfect competition guarantees both productive efficiency and allocative efficiency in the long run.

TRY IT: UNDERSTANDING ALLOCATIVE EFFICIENCY

Productive Efficiency: Making Stuff Right

Productive efficiency occurs when the firm produces at the minimum point on its long-run average cost curve, so the market price equals the minimum average total cost. The entry and exit of firms and any adjustment in the scale of each firm ensure that each firm produces at the minimum point on its long-run average cost curve. Firms that do not reach minimum long-run average cost must, to avoid continued losses, either adjust their size or leave the industry. Thus, *perfect competition produces output at the least possible cost per unit in the long run.*

Allocative Efficiency: Making the Right Stuff

Just because *production* occurs at the least possible cost does not mean that the *allocation* of resources is the most efficient one possible. The goods being produced may not be the ones consumers most prefer. This situation is akin to that of the airline pilot who informs passengers that there's good news and bad news: "The good news is that we're making record time. The bad news is that we're lost!" Likewise, firms may be producing goods efficiently but producing the wrong goods—that is, making stuff right but making the wrong stuff.

Allocative efficiency occurs when firms produce the output that is most valued by consumers. How do we know that perfect competition guarantees allocative efficiency? The answer lies with the market demand and supply curves. You'll recall that the demand curve reflects the marginal value that consumers attach to each unit, so the market price is the amount of money people are willing and able to pay for the final unit they consume. We also know that, in both the short run and the long run, the equilibrium price in perfect competition equals the marginal cost of supplying the last unit sold. Marginal cost measures the opportunity cost of all resources employed by the firm to produce that last unit sold. Thus, the supply and demand curves intersect at the combination of price and quantity at which *the marginal value, or the marginal benefit that consumers attach to the final unit purchased, just equals the opportunity cost of the resources employed to produce that unit.*

As long as marginal benefit equals marginal cost, the last unit produced is valued as much as, or more than, any other good that could have been produced using those same resources. There is no way to reallocate resources to increase the total value of output. Thus, there is no way to reallocate resources to increase the total utility or total benefit consumers reap from production. *When the marginal benefit that consumers derive from a good equals the marginal cost of producing that good, that market is said to be allocatively efficient.* Firms not only are making stuff right, they are making the right stuff.

What's So Perfect About Perfect Competition?

If the marginal cost to firms of supplying a good just equals the marginal benefit to consumers, does this mean that market exchange confers no net benefits to participants? No. Market exchange usually benefits both consumers and producers. Recall that consumers enjoy a surplus from market exchange because the maximum amount they would be willing to pay for each unit of the good exceeds the amount they actually do pay. Exhibit 13 depicts a market in short-run equilibrium. The *consumer surplus* in this exhibit is represented by blue shading, which is the area below the demand curve but above the market-clearing price of $10.

Producers in the short run also usually derive a net benefit, or a surplus, from market exchange, because the amount they receive for their output exceeds the minimum amount they would require to supply that amount in the short run. Recall that the short-run market supply curve is the sum of that portion of each firm's marginal cost curve at or above the minimum point on its average variable cost curve. Point *m* in Exhibit 13 is the minimum point on the market supply curve; it indicates that at a price of $5, firms are willing to supply 100,000 units. At prices below $5, quantity supplied is zero because firms could not cover variable costs and would shut down. At point *m*, firms in this industry gain no net benefit from production in the short run, because the total industry revenue derived from selling 100,000 units at $5 each just covers the variable cost of producing that amount.

If the price increases to $6, firms increase their quantity supplied until their marginal cost equals $6. Market output increases from 100,000 to 120,000 units, and total revenue increases from $500,000 to $720,000. Part of the increased revenue covers the higher marginal cost of production. But the balance of the increased revenue is a bonus to producers, who would have been willing to supply the first 100,000 units for only $5 each. If the price is $6, they get to sell these 100,000 units for $6 each rather than $5 each. Producer surplus at a price of $6 is the shaded area between $5 and $6.

In the short run, **producer surplus** is the total revenue producers are paid minus their variable cost of production. In Exhibit 13, the market-clearing price is $10 per unit, and producer

EXHIBIT 13|

Consumer Surplus and Producer Surplus for a Competitive Market in the Short Run

Consumer surplus is represented by the area above the market-clearing price of $10 per unit and below the demand curve; it is shown as a blue triangle. Producer surplus is represented by the area above the short-run market supply curve and below the market-clearing price of $10 per unit; it is shown by the gold shading. At a price of $5 per unit, there is no producer surplus. At a price of $6 per unit, producer surplus is the shaded area between $5 and $6.

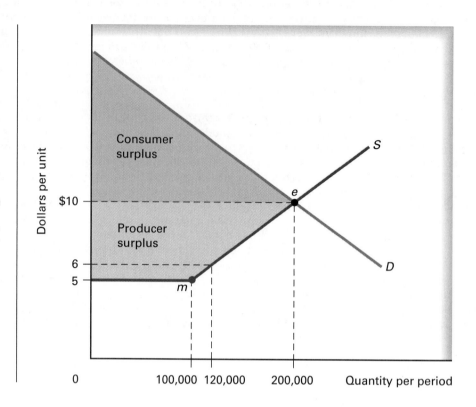

surplus is depicted by the gold-shaded area under the price but above the market supply curve. That area represents the market price minus the marginal cost of each unit produced.

The combination of consumer surplus and producer surplus shows the gains from voluntary exchange. Productive and allocative efficiency in the short run occurs at equilibrium point *e*, which also is the combination of price and quantity that maximizes the sum of consumer surplus and producer surplus. Even though marginal cost equals marginal benefit in equilibrium, both consumers and producers usually derive a surplus, or a bonus, from market exchange.

Note that producer surplus is not the same as economic profit. Any price that exceeds average variable cost will result in a short-run producer surplus, even though that price could result in a short-run economic loss. The definition of producer surplus ignores fixed cost, because fixed cost is irrelevant to the firm's short-run production decision. Fixed cost is *sunk* in the short run since the firm must pay it whether or not production occurs. Only variable cost matters. For each firm, the marginal cost is the increase in variable cost as output increases, and the sum of the marginal costs for all units is the variable cost.

The gains from market exchange have been examined in an experimental setting, as discussed in the following case study.

CASE**STUDY**	Experimental Economics
	● *The Information Economy*

Economists have limited opportunities to carry out the kind of controlled experiments available in the physical and biological sciences. But about four decades ago, Professor Vernon Smith, now at the University of Arizona, began some experiments to see how quickly and efficiently a group of test subjects could achieve market equilibrium. His original experiment involved 22 students, 11 of whom were designated as "buyers" and 11 as "sellers." Each buyer was given a card indicating the value of purchasing one unit of a hypothetical commodity; these values ranged from $3.25 down to $0.75, forming a downward-sloping demand curve. Each seller was given a card indicating the cost of supplying one unit of that commodity; these costs ranged from $0.75 up to $3.25, forming an upward-sloping supply curve. Each buyer and seller knew only what was on his or her own card.

To provide market incentives, participants were told they would receive a cash bonus at the end of the experiment based on the difference between their value (for buyers) or their cost (for sellers) and the price they negotiated in the market. As a way of trading, Smith employed a system in which any buyer or seller could announce a bid or an offer to the entire group— a system called a *double-continuous auction*—based on rules similar to those governing stock markets and commodity exchanges. A transaction occurred whenever any buyer accepted an offer to sell or when any seller accepted an offer to buy. *Smith found that the price quickly converged to the market-clearing level,* which in his experiment was $2.00.

Economists have since performed thousands of experiments to test the properties of markets. These experiments show that under most circumstances, markets are extremely efficient in moving goods from the lowest-cost producers to the consumers who place the highest value on the goods. This movement maximizes the sum of consumer and producer surplus and thus maximizes social welfare. One surprising finding is how few participants are required to establish a market price. Market experiments sometimes use only four buyers and four sellers, each capable of trading several units. Some experiments use only two sellers, yet the competitive equilibrium model performs quite well under double-continuous auction rules.

Incidentally, most U.S. retail markets, such as supermarkets and department stores, use *posted-offer pricing*—that is, the price is marked, not negotiated. Experiments show that posted pricing does not adjust to changing market conditions as quickly as does a double-continuous auction. Despite their slow response times, posted prices may be the choice for large, relatively stable markets, because posted prices involve low transaction costs—that is, buyer and seller don't have to haggle over the price each time a transaction occurs. In contrast, double-continuous-auction pricing involves high transaction costs and, in the case of stock and commodity markets, requires thousands of people in full-time negotiations to maintain prices at their equilibrium levels (although, as discussed in the previous case study, the Internet has reduced the transaction costs of establishing prices through double-continuous auctions).

Experiments have provided empirical support for economic theory and have yielded insights about how market rules affect market outcomes. They have also helped shape markets that did not exist before, such as the market for pollution rights or for broadcast spectrum rights—markets to be discussed in later chapters. Experiments also offer a safe and inexpensive way for people in emerging market economies to learn how markets work. What's more, the rapid development of online auctions has opened up a world of data for experimentalists.

Experimental economics is now a hot area for research and industry. For example, the number of papers published in the field jumped from fewer than 20 per year in the 1970s to 232 in 1999. Most of the top U.S. business schools have hired experimental economists. And some top corporations, such as Hewlett-Packard and IBM, have opened experimental-economics labs.

<interactive>exercise

eACTIVITY: EXPERIMENTAL ECONOMICS

Sources: Vernon Smith, "Experimental Methods in Economics," *The New Palgrave Dictionary of Economics,* Vol. 2, edited by J. Eatwell et al. (Hampshire, England: Stockton Press, 1987), 241–249; T. C. Bergstrom and J. H. Miller, *Experiments with Economic Principles* (New York: McGraw-Hill, 1997); and Joel Rosenblatt, "Moving Past Rats: More Economists Study Behavior in Online Experiments," *Wall Street Journal,* 2 October 2000. The University of Arizona's economic science laboratory Web address is http://www.econlab.arizona.edu/.

CONCLUSION

Let's review the assumptions of a perfectly competitive market and see how each relates to ideas developed in this chapter. *First,* there are many buyers and many sellers. This assumption ensures that no individual buyer or seller can influence the price (although recent experiments show that the large-number assumption may be stronger than necessary). *Second,* firms produce a homogeneous product. If consumers could distinguish between the products of different suppliers, they might prefer one firm's product even at a higher price, so different producers could sell at different prices. In that case, not every firm would be a price taker—that is, each firm's demand curve would no longer be horizontal. *Third,* all market participants have full information about all prices and all production processes. Otherwise, some producers could charge more than the market price, and some uninformed consumers would pay that higher price. Also, through ignorance, some firms might select outdated technology or fail to recognize opportunities for short-run economic profits. *Fourth,* all resources are mobile in the long run, with no obstacles preventing new firms from entering profitable markets. Otherwise, some firms could earn economic profit in the long run.

Perfect competition is not the market structure most commonly observed in the real world. The markets for agricultural products, commodities such as gold and silver, and foreign exchange come close to being perfect. But even if not a single example of perfect competition could be found, the model would still serve as a useful tool for analyzing market behavior. As you will see in the next two chapters, perfect competition provides a valuable benchmark for evaluating the efficiency of other market structures.

endofchaptermaterial

- **Summary**
- **Questions for Review**
- **Problems and Exercises**
- **Experiential Exercises**

- **Wall Street Journal Exercises**
- **Graphing Workshop: Apply It Exercises**

Take the Post-Test to assess your overall understanding of the key ideas in this chapter. The Post-Test provides a comprehensive selection of exam-style questions addressing the main topics and concepts of the chapter. At the completion of each Post-Test, you will receive a score and instructive feedback on how you answered each question, and a direct link to the part of the chapter addressed in the question. Take the Post-Test as often as you need to—a record of your progress for each attempt is kept for you to revisit and gauge your improvement. And each Post-Test is randomly generated, so every attempt is new.

Post-Test

CHAPTER 9

Monopoly

How can a firm monopolize a market? Why aren't most markets monopolized? Why don't most monopolies last? Why don't monopolies charge the highest price possible? Why do some firms offer discounts to students, senior citizens, and other groups? Why do airlines charge less if you stay over Saturday night? These and other questions are answered in this chapter, which examines monopoly.

Monopoly is from the Greek, meaning "one seller." In some parts of the United States, monopolists sell electricity, cable TV service, and local phone service. Monopolists also sell postage stamps, hot dogs at sports arenas, some patented products, and other goods and services with no close substitutes. You have probably heard about the evils of monopoly. You may have even played the board game *Monopoly* on a rainy day. Now we will sort out fact from fiction.

Like perfect competition, pure monopoly is not as common as other market structures. But by understanding monopoly, you will grow more familiar with the market structures that lie between the two extremes of perfect competition and pure monopoly. In this chapter, we examine the sources of monopoly power, how a monopolist maximizes profit, differences in efficiency between monopoly and perfect competition, and why a monopolist often charges different prices for the same product. Topics discussed in this chapter include:

- Barriers to entry
- Price elasticity and marginal revenue
- Profit maximization in the short run and the long run

Take the Pre-Test to assess your initial knowledge of the key ideas in this chapter. The Pre-Test provides exam-style questions addressing the main topics and concepts of the chapter. At the completion of each Pre-Test, you will receive a score and instructive feedback on how you answered each question, and a direct link to the part of the chapter addressed in the question. Take the Pre-Test as often as you need to—a record of your progress for each attempt is kept for you to revisit and gauge your improvement.

- Monopoly and resource allocation
- Welfare cost of monopoly
- Price discrimination
- The monopolist's dream

<interactive>exercise

ECONDEBATE ONLINE: MONOPOLY

<interactive>update

- **ECONDATA ONLINE: MONOPOLY**
- **ECONLINKS ONLINE: ECONOMICS WEB LINKS**
- **ECONNEWS ONLINE: MONOPOLY**

BARRIERS TO ENTRY

As noted in Chapter 4, a *monopoly* is the sole supplier of a product with no close substitutes. Why do some markets come to be dominated by a single supplier? Perhaps the most important reason is that a monopolized market is characterized by *barriers to entry;* new firms cannot profitably enter that market. **Barriers to entry** are restrictions on the entry of new firms into an industry. Let's examine three types of entry barriers: legal restrictions, economies of scale, and the monopolist's control of an essential resource.

Legal Restrictions

One way to prevent new firms from entering a market is to make entry illegal. Patents, licenses, and other legal restrictions imposed by the government provide some producers with legal protection against competition.

Patents and Invention Incentives. In the United States, a **patent** awards an inventor the exclusive right to produce a good or service for 20 years. Originally enacted in 1790, patent laws encourage inventors to invest the time and money required to discover and develop new products and processes. If others could simply copy successful products, inventors would be less willing to incur the up-front costs of invention. Patents also provide the stimulus to turn inventions into marketable products, a process called **innovation.**

<interactive>example

NETBOOKMARK: U.S. PATENT AND TRADEMARK OFFICE

Licenses and Other Entry Restrictions. Governments often confer monopoly status by awarding a single firm the exclusive right to supply a particular good or service. Federal licenses give certain firms the right to broadcast radio and TV signals. State licenses are required to provide services such as medical care, haircuts, and legal assistance. A license may not grant a monopoly, but it often confers the ability to charge a price above the competitive level; thus, a license can serve as an effective barrier to new firms. Governments confer monopoly rights to sell hot dogs at civic auditoriums, collect garbage, provide bus and taxi service, and supply services ranging from electricity to cable TV. The government itself may claim the right to provide certain products by outlawing competitors. For example, many states are monopoly sellers of liquor and lottery tickets, and the U.S. Postal Service has the exclusive right to deliver first-class mail.

Economies of Scale

A monopoly sometimes emerges naturally when a firm experiences *economies of scale*, as reflected by the downward-sloping, long-run average cost curve shown in Exhibit 1. A single firm can sometimes supply market demand at a lower average cost per unit than could two or more firms operating at smaller rates of output. Put another way, market demand is not great enough to permit more than one firm to achieve sufficient economies of scale. Thus, a single firm will emerge from the competitive process as the sole seller in the market. For example, even though the production of electricity has grown more competitive, the *transmission* of electricity still exhibits economies of scale. Once wires are run throughout a community, the marginal cost of linking additional households to the power grid is relatively small. Consequently, the average cost declines as more and more households are wired into the system.

A monopoly that emerges from the nature of costs is called a *natural monopoly*, to distinguish it from the artificial monopolies created by government patents, licenses, and other legal barriers to entry. A new entrant cannot sell enough output to experience the economies of scale enjoyed by an established natural monopolist, so entry into the market is naturally blocked. We will have more to say about the regulation of natural monopolies in a later chapter, where we examine government regulation of markets.

Control of Essential Resources

Sometimes the source of monopoly power is a firm's control over some nonreproducible resource critical to production. Here are four examples: Professional sports leagues try to block the formation of competing leagues by signing the best athletes to long-term contracts and by seeking the exclusive use of sports stadiums and arenas. Alcoa was the sole U.S. maker of aluminum from the late 19th century until World War II; its monopoly power initially stemmed from production patents that expired in 1909, but for the next three decades, it

EXHIBIT 1

Economies of Scale as a Barrier to Entry

A monopoly sometimes emerges naturally when a firm experiences economies of scale as reflected by a downward-sloping, long-run average cost curve. An individual firm can satisfy market demand at a lower average cost per unit than could two or more firms operating at smaller rates of output.

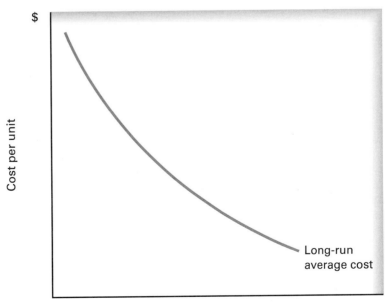

controlled the supply of bauxite, the key raw material. China is a monopoly supplier of pandas to the world's zoos. The zoo in Washington, D.C., for example, rents its pair from China for $1 million a year. As a way of controlling the panda supply, China stipulates that any offspring from the Washington pair becomes China's property.[1] Finally, since the 1930s, the world's diamond trade has been controlled primarily by De Beers Consolidated Mines, which mines diamonds and also buys most of the world's supply of rough diamonds, as discussed in the following case study.

\<interactive\>exercise

ECONDEBATE ONLINE: IS MICROSOFT A MONOPOLY?

CASE**STUDY** | Is a Diamond Forever?

● *The World of Business*

In 1866, a child walking along the Orange River in South Africa picked up an interesting-looking pebble that turned out to be a 21-carat diamond. That discovery on a farm owned by Johannes De Beers sparked the development of the largest diamond mine in history. De Beers Consolidated Mines eventually expanded from mining diamonds to buying rough diamonds mined elsewhere. Ever since the Great Depression caused a price slump in diamonds, De Beers has tried to maintain a worldwide monopoly by controlling the world supply of rough diamonds.

The company has kept prices high by carefully limiting supply and by promoting market demand through advertising. De Beers spends $170 million a year convincing people that diamonds are scarce, valuable, and perfect reflections of love. One promotional coup was to persuade the producers of *Baywatch,* a TV show watched around the world, to devote an entire episode to a story of a diamond engagement ring. The story played up the company line that the ring should cost two months' salary.

De Beers limits supply by trying to control the quantity of rough diamonds. The company invites 125 wholesalers to London, where they are offered a box of uncut diamonds for a set price—no negotiating. If the box is rejected, the buyer may not be invited back next time. In restricting competition in the market for rough diamonds, De Beers violates U.S. antitrust laws (De Beers executives would be arrested if they traveled to America). But there are no laws prohibiting U.S. wholesalers from buying from De Beers, so U.S. diamond sales account for nearly half the world's total.

It might surprise you that diamonds are not especially rare gems, either in nature or in jewelry stores. Nearly all jewelry stores offer more diamonds for sale than any other gem. Diamonds may be the most common natural gemstone. Jewelers are willing to hold large inventories because they are confident that De Beers will keep prices from plummeting tomorrow. De Beers' slogan, "A diamond is forever," sends several messages, including (1) a diamond lasts forever, and so should love; (2) diamonds should remain in the family and not be sold; and (3) diamonds retain their value. This slogan is aimed at increasing the demand for diamonds and at keeping secondhand diamonds, which are good substitutes for newly cut diamonds, off the market, where they could otherwise increase supply and drive down the price.

But De Beers has recently lost control of some rough diamond supplies. Russian miners have apparently been selling half their diamonds to independent dealers. Australia's Argyle mine, the world's largest, stopped selling to De Beers in 1996. And a huge Canadian mine began operations in 1998, but De Beers is guaranteed only about one-third of its output. As a result of all this erosion, De Beers' control over the world's uncut diamond supply slipped from nearly 90 percent in the mid-1980s to 63 percent in 2000. Worse still, newly developed synthetic diamonds with the same atomic structure as natural diamonds are starting to appear on the market.

A monopoly that relies on the control of a key resource, as De Beers does, loses its power once that control slips away. In a reversal of policy, De Beers now says it will abandon efforts to control the world diamond supply and will instead become the "supplier of choice" by

[1]Francis Clines, "Capital Exults Over Pandas," *New York Times,* 7 December 2000.

promoting the De Beers brand of diamonds. In an effort to distinguish between its diamonds and those of other producers, De Beers is test-marketing diamonds that are etched with the company name and an individual security number. Whether this branding effort will work remains to be seen.

<interactive>exercise

eACTIVITY: IS A DIAMOND FOREVER?

Sources: Neil Behrmann and Robert Block, "De Beers Said It Will Abandon Its Monopoly of Diamond Supply," *Wall Street Journal,* 13 July 2000; Paul Meller, "De Beers Wins and Loses Before Regulators in Europe," *New York Times,* 26 July 2001; "The New Enforcers," *Economist,* 7 October 2000; Joel Bagole, "Canada's Yellowknife Becomes a Diamond Town in the Rough," *Wall Street Journal,* 5 July 2001; Vito Racanelli, "Diamonds.com?" *Barrons,* 7 February 2000; and the De Beers home page at http://www.adiamondisforever.com/.

Local monopolies are more common than national or international monopolies. In rural areas, monopolies may include the only grocery store, movie theater, or restaurant for miles around. These are natural monopolies for products sold in local markets. But long-lasting monopolies are rare because, as we will see, a profitable monopoly attracts competitors. Also, over time, technological change tends to break down barriers to entry. For example, the development of wireless transmission of long-distance telephone calls created competitors to AT&T. Wireless transmission will soon erase the monopoly held by local cable TV providers and even local phone service. Likewise, fax machines, e-mail, the Internet, and firms such as FedEx now compete with the U.S. Postal Service's monopoly on first-class mail, as we will see in a later case study.

REVENUE FOR THE MONOPOLIST

Because a monopoly, by definition, supplies the entire market, the demand for goods or services produced by a monopolist is also the market demand. The demand curve for the monopolist's output therefore slopes downward, reflecting the law of demand—price and quantity demanded are inversely related. Let's look at demand and marginal revenue.

<interactive>video

CNN VIDEO: "MOBILE PHONE NUMBERS NOW MOBILE"

Demand, Average Revenue, and Marginal Revenue

Suppose De Beers controls the entire diamond market. Exhibit 2 shows the demand curve for 1-carat diamonds. De Beers, for example, can sell three diamonds a day at $7,000 each. That price-quantity combination yields total revenue of $21,000 (= 3 × $7,000). Total revenue divided by quantity is the *average revenue per diamond,* which also is $7,000. Thus, the monopolist's price equals the average revenue per unit. To sell a fourth diamond, De Beers must drop the price to $6,750. Total revenue for four diamonds is $27,000 (= 4 × $6,750) and average revenue is $6,750. All along the demand curve, price equals average revenue. Therefore, *the demand curve is also the monopolist's average revenue curve,* just as the perfectly competitive firm's demand curve is that firm's average revenue curve.

What's the monopolist's marginal revenue from selling a fourth diamond? When De Beers drops the price from $7,000 to $6,750, total revenue goes from $21,000 to $27,000. Thus, *marginal revenue*—the change in total revenue from selling one more diamond—is $6,000, which is less than price, or average revenue, of $6,750. *For a monopolist, marginal revenue is less than price, or average revenue.* Recall that for a perfectly competitive firm, marginal revenue equals the price, or average revenue, since that firm can sell all it wants to at the market price.

EXHIBIT 2

A Monopolist's Gain and Loss in Total Revenue from Selling One More Unit

If De Beers increases production from 3 to 4 diamonds per day, the gain in revenue from the fourth diamond is $6,750. But the monopolist loses $750 from selling the first 3 diamonds for $6,750 each instead of $7,000. Marginal revenue from the fourth diamond equals the gain minus the loss, or $6,750 − $750 = $6,000. Thus, the marginal revenue of $6,000 is less than the price of $6,750.

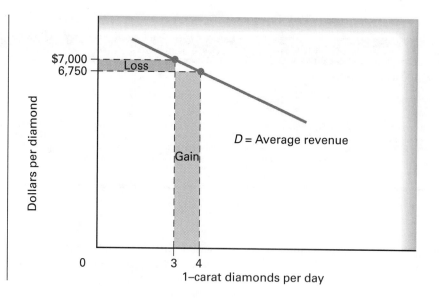

The Gains and Loss from Selling One More Unit

A closer look at Exhibit 2 reveals why a monopolist's marginal revenue is less than the price. By selling another diamond, De Beers gains the revenue from that sale. For example, De Beers gets $6,750 from the fourth diamond, as shown by the blue-shaded vertical rectangle marked "Gain." But to sell that fourth unit, De Beers must sell all four diamonds for $6,750 each. Thus, to sell a fourth diamond, De Beers must sacrifice $250 on each of the first three diamonds, which could have been sold for $7,000 each. This loss in revenue from the first three units totals $750 (= 3 × $250) and is identified in Exhibit 2 by the pink-shaded horizontal rectangle marked "Loss." The net change in total revenue from selling the fourth diamond—that is, the marginal revenue from the fourth diamond—equals the *gain* minus the *loss,* which equals $6,750 minus $750, or $6,000. So marginal revenue equals the gain minus the loss, or the price minus the revenue forgone by selling all units for a lower price. Since a monopolist's marginal revenue equals the price minus the loss, you can see why the price exceeds marginal revenue.

Incidentally, this analysis assumes that all units of the good are sold at the market price; for example, when the price is $6,750, each of the four diamonds is sold for that price. Although this is usually true, later in the chapter you will learn how some monopolists can charge different customers different prices.

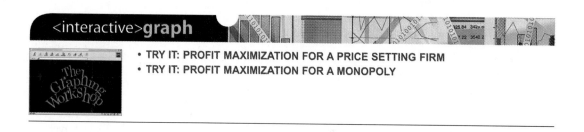

<interactive>**graph**

- TRY IT: PROFIT MAXIMIZATION FOR A PRICE SETTING FIRM
- TRY IT: PROFIT MAXIMIZATION FOR A MONOPOLY

Revenue Schedules

Let's flesh out more fully the revenue schedules behind the demand curve of Exhibit 2. Column (1) of Exhibit 3 lists the quantity of diamonds demanded per day, and column (2) lists the corresponding price, or average revenue. The two columns together are the demand schedule facing De Beers for 1-carat diamonds. The monopolist's *total revenue,* which equals

EXHIBIT 3

Revenue for De Beers, a Monopolist

(1) 1-Carat diamonds per day (*Q*)	(2) Price (average revenue) (*p*)	(3) Total Revenue (*TR = Q × p*)	(4) Marginal Revenue (*MC = ΔTR/ΔQ*)
0	$7,750	0	——
1	7,500	$ 7,500	$7,500
2	7,250	14,500	7,000
3	7,000	21,000	6,500
4	6,750	27,000	6,000
5	6,500	32,500	5,500
6	6,250	37,500	5,000
7	6,000	42,000	4,500
8	5,750	46,000	4,000
9	5,500	49,500	3,500
10	5,250	52,500	3,000
11	5,000	55,000	2,500
12	4,750	57,000	2,000
13	4,500	58,500	1,500
14	4,250	59,500	1,000
15	4,000	60,000	500
16	3,750	60,000	0
17	3,500	59,500	−500

price times quantity, appears in column (3). As De Beers expands output, total revenue increases until quantity reaches 15 diamonds, when total revenue tops out.

Marginal revenue, the change in total revenue from selling one more diamond, appears in column (4). Note that for all units of output except the first, marginal revenue is less than price, and the gap between the two widens as the price declines. As the price declines, the gap between price and marginal revenue widens because the *loss* from selling all diamonds at this lower price increases (because quantity increases).

Revenue Curves

The data in Exhibit 3 are graphed in Exhibit 4, which shows the demand and marginal revenue curves in panel (a) and the total revenue curve in panel (b). Recall that total revenue equals price times quantity. Note that the marginal revenue curve is below the demand curve and that total revenue is at a maximum when marginal revenue reaches zero. Take a minute to study these relationships—they are important.

Again, at any level of sales, price equals average revenue, so the demand curve is also the monopolist's average revenue curve. In Chapter 5 you learned that the price elasticity for a straight-line demand curve decreases as you move down the curve. When demand is elastic—

EXHIBIT 4

Monopoly Demand and Marginal Total Revenue

Where demand is price elastic, marginal revenue is positive, so total revenue increases as the price falls. Where demand is price inelastic, marginal revenue is negative, so total revenue decreases as the price falls. Where demand is unit elastic, marginal revenue is zero, so total revenue is at a maximum, neither increasing nor decreasing.

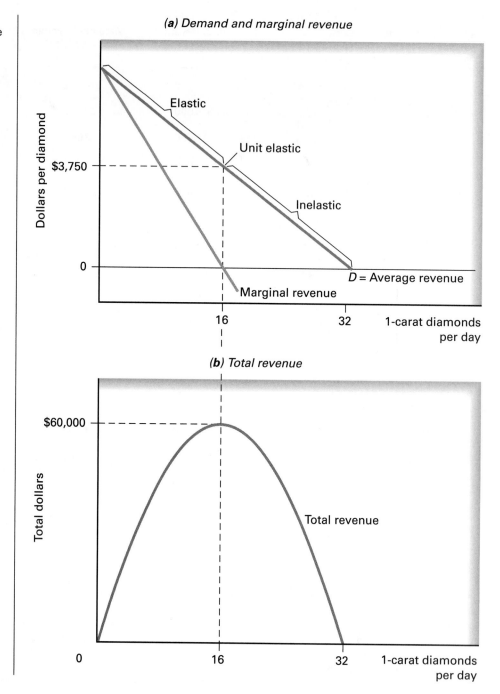

(a) Demand and marginal revenue

Elastic

Unit elastic

Inelastic

$3,750

0

Dollars per diamond

16   32   1-carat diamonds per day

D = Average revenue

Marginal revenue

(b) Total revenue

$60,000

Total dollars

Total revenue

0   16   32   1-carat diamonds per day

that is, when the percentage increase in quantity demanded more than offsets the percentage decrease in price—a decrease in price increases total revenue. Therefore, *where demand is elastic, marginal revenue is positive, and total revenue increases as price falls.* On the other hand, where demand is inelastic—that is, where the percentage increase in quantity demanded is less than the percentage decrease in price—a decrease in price reduces total revenue. In other words, the loss in revenue from selling all diamonds for the lower price overwhelms the gain in revenue from selling more diamonds. Therefore, *where demand is inelastic, marginal revenue is negative, and total revenue decreases as the price falls.*

From Exhibit 4, you can see that marginal revenue turns negative if the price drops below $3,750, indicating inelastic demand below that price. A profit-maximizing monopolist would never willingly expand output to where demand is inelastic because doing so would reduce total revenue. Also note that demand is unit elastic at the price of $3,750. At that price, marginal revenue is zero and total revenue reaches a maximum.

<interactive>graph

SEE IT: MONOPOLY BEHAVIOR IN THE SHORT-RUN

The Graphing Workshop

THE FIRM'S COSTS AND PROFIT MAXIMIZATION

In the case of perfect competition, each firm's choice is confined to *quantity* because the market already determines the price. The perfect competitor is a *price taker*. The monopolist, however, can choose either the price or the quantity, but choosing one determines the other. Because the monopolist can select the price that maximizes profit, we say the monopolist is a *price maker*. More generally, any firm that has some control over what price to charge is a **price maker.**

Profit Maximization

Exhibit 5 repeats the revenue data from Exhibits 3 and 4 and also includes short-run cost data reflecting costs similar to those already introduced in the two previous chapters. Take some time now to become familiar with this table. Then ask yourself, which price-quantity combination should De Beers select to maximize profit? As was the case with perfect competition, the monopolist can approach profit maximization in two ways—the total approach and the marginal approach.

Total Revenue Minus Total Cost. The profit-maximizing monopolist employs the same decision rule as the competitive firm. *The monopolist produces the quantity at which total revenue exceeds total cost by the greatest amount.* Economic profit appears in column (8) of Exhibit 5. As you can see, the maximum profit is $12,500 per day, which occurs when output is 10 diamonds per day and the price is $5,250 per diamond. At that rate of output, total revenue is $52,500 and total cost is $40,000.

Marginal Revenue Equals Marginal Cost. De Beers, as a profit-maximizing monopolist, increases output as long as selling additional diamonds adds more to total revenue than to total cost. So De Beers expands output as long as marginal revenue, shown in column (4) of Exhibit 5, exceeds marginal cost, shown in column (6). But De Beers will stop short of where marginal cost exceeds marginal revenue. Again, profit is maximized at $12,500 when output is 10 diamonds per day. For the 10th diamond, marginal revenue is $3,000 and marginal cost is $2,750. As you can see, if output exceeds 10 diamonds per day, marginal cost exceeds marginal revenue. An 11th diamond's marginal cost of $3,250 exceeds its marginal revenue of $2,500. For simplicity, we say that *the profit-maximizing output occurs where marginal revenue equals marginal cost,* which, you will recall, is the golden rule of profit maximization.

Graphical Solution. The cost and revenue data in Exhibit 5 are graphed in Exhibit 6, with per-unit cost and revenue curves in panel (a) and total cost and revenue curves in panel (b). The intersection of the two marginal curves at point *e* in panel (a) indicates that profit is maximized when 10 diamonds are sold. At that rate of output, we move up to the demand curve to find the profit-maximizing price of $5,250. The average total cost of $4,000 is identified by point *b*. The average profit per diamond equals the price of $5,250 minus the average total cost of $4,000. Economic profit is the average profit per unit of $1,250 multiplied by the 10 units sold, for a total profit of $12,500 per day, as identified by the shaded rectangle. *So the profit-maximizing rate of output is found where the rising marginal cost curve intersects the marginal revenue curve.*

In panel (b), the firm's profit or loss is measured by the vertical distance between the total revenue and total cost curves. De Beers will expand output as long as the increase in total revenue from selling one more diamond exceeds the increase in total cost. *The profit-maximizing firm will produce the rate of output where total revenue exceeds total cost by the greatest amount.* Again, profit is maximized where De Beers produces 10 diamonds per day. Note again that in panel

EXHIBIT 5

Short-Run Costs and Revenue for a Monopolist

(1) Diamonds per day (Q)	(2) Price (p)	(3) Total Revenue (TR = Q × p)	(4) Marginal Revenue (MR = ΔTR/ΔQ)	(5) Total Cost (TC)	(6) Marginal Cost (MC = ΔTC/ΔQ)	(7) Average Total Cost (ATC = TC/Q)	(8) Total Profit or Loss = TR − TC
0	$7,750	0	⎯	$15,000	⎯	⎯	−$15,000
1	7,500	$7,500	$7,500	19,750	$4,750	$19,750	−12,250
2	7,250	14,500	7,000	23,500	3,750	11,750	−9,000
3	7,000	21,000	6,500	26,500	3,000	8,830	−5,500
4	6,750	27,000	6,000	29,000	2,500	7,750	−2,000
5	6,500	32,500	5,500	31,000	2,000	6,200	1,500
6	6,250	37,500	5,000	32,500	1,500	5,420	5,000
7	6,000	42,000	4,500	33,750	1,250	4,820	8,250
8	5,750	46,000	4,000	35,250	1,500	4,410	10,750
9	5,500	49,500	3,500	37,250	2,000	4,140	12,250
10	**5,250**	**52,500**	**3,000**	**40,000**	**2,750**	**4,000**	**12,500**
11	5,000	55,000	2,500	43,250	3,250	3,930	11,750
12	4,750	57,000	2,000	48,000	4,750	4,000	9,000
13	4,500	58,500	1,500	54,500	6,500	4,190	4,000
14	4,250	59,500	1,000	64,000	9,500	4,570	−4,500
15	4,000	60,000	500	77,500	13,500	5,170	−17,500
16	3,750	60,000	0	96,000	18,500	6,000	−36,000
17	3,500	59,500	−500	121,000	25,000	7,120	−61,500

(b), total profit is measured by the *vertical distance* between the two total curves, and in panel (a), total profit is measure by the shaded *area* formed by multiplying average profit per unit by the number of units.

One common myth about monopolies is that they will charge as high a price as possible. But the monopolist is interested in maximizing profit, not price. The monopolist's price is limited by consumer demand. De Beers, for example, could charge $7,500 but would sell only one diamond at that price and would lose money. Indeed, De Beers could charge $7,750 or more but would sell no diamonds. So charging the highest possible price is not consistent with maximizing profit.

SEE IT: PROFIT MAXIMIZATION

EXHIBIT 6

Monopoly Costs and Revenue

The monopolist produces 10 diamonds per day and charges a price of $5,250. Total profit, shown by the blue rectangle in panel (a), is $12,500, the profit per unit multiplied by the number of units sold. In panel (b), profit is maximized where total revenue exceeds total cost by the greatest amount, which occurs at an output rate of 10 diamonds per day. Profit is total revenue ($52,500) minus total cost ($40,000), or $12,500.

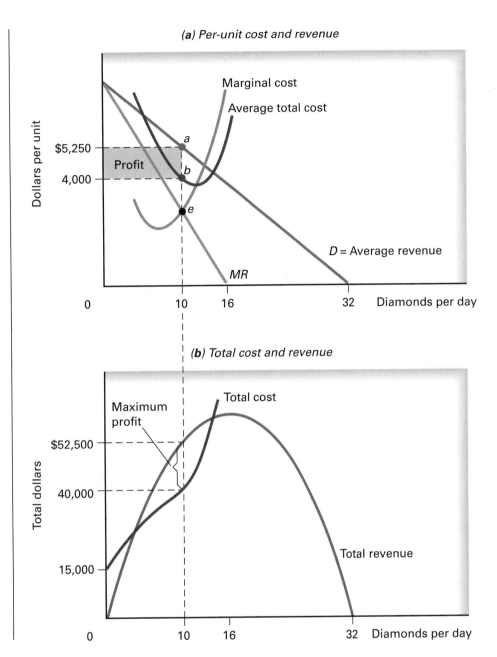

(a) Per-unit cost and revenue

(b) Total cost and revenue

Short-Run Losses and the Shutdown Decision

A monopolist is not assured of profit. Although a monopolist is the sole producer of a good with no close substitutes, the demand for that good may not be great enough to generate economic profit in either the short run or the long run. After all, many new products are protected from direct competition by patents, yet most patented products fail to attract enough buyers to survive. And even a monopolist that is initially profitable may eventually suffer losses because of rising costs, falling demand, or market entry of similar products. For example, Coleco, the original mass producer of Cabbage Patch dolls, went bankrupt after that craze died down. And Cuisinart, the company that introduced the food processor in the early 1980s, soon faced many imitators and filed for bankruptcy before the end of the decade (though the name lives on). In the short run, the loss-minimizing monopolist, like the loss-minimizing perfect competitor, must decide whether to produce or to shut down. *If the price covers average variable cost, the firm will produce. If not, the firm will shut down, at least in the short run.*

Exhibit 7 brings average variable cost back into the picture. Recall from Chapter 7 that average variable cost and average fixed cost sum to average total cost. Loss minimization occurs in Exhibit 7 at point *e*, where the marginal revenue curve intersects the marginal cost curve. At the equilibrium rate of output, *Q*, price *p* is found on the demand curve at point *b*. That price exceeds average variable cost, at point *c*, but is below average total cost, at point *a*. Since price covers average variable cost and makes some contribution to average fixed cost, this monopolist loses less by producing *Q* than by shutting down. The average loss per unit, measured by *ab*, is average total cost minus average revenue, or price. The loss, identified by the shaded rectangle, is the average loss per unit, *ab*, times the quantity sold, *Q*. The firm will shut down if the average variable cost curve is above the demand curve, or average revenue curve, at all output rates.

Recall that a perfectly competitive firm's supply curve is that portion of the marginal cost curve at or above the average variable cost curve. The intersection of a monopolist's marginal revenue and marginal cost curves identifies the profit-maximizing (or loss-minimizing) quantity, but the price is found up on the demand curve. Since the equilibrium quantity can be found along a monopolist's marginal cost curve, but the equilibrium price appears on the demand curve, there is no curve that shows both price and quantity supplied. Since there is no curve that reflects combinations of price and quantity supplied, *there is no monopolist supply curve.*

<interactive>**update**

- **ECONNEWS ONLINE: EUROPEAN AIRLINES: TOO MANY FOR THEIR OWN GOOD?**
- **ECONNEWS ONLINE: CRANBERRY GIANT MADE TO LOOK LIKE A TURKEY**

Long-Run Profit Maximization

For perfectly competitive firms, the distinction between the short run and the long run is important because entry and exit of firms can occur in the long run, erasing any economic profit or loss. For the monopolist, the distinction is less important. *If a monopoly is insulated from competition by high barriers that block new entry, economic profit can persist in the long run.*

EXHIBIT 7

The Monopolist Minimizes Losses in the Short Run

Marginal cost equals marginal revenue at point *e*. At quantity *Q*, price *p* (at point *b*) is less than average total cost (at point *a*), so the monopolist is suffering a loss. The monopolist will continue to produce in the short run because price is greater than average variable cost (at point *c*).

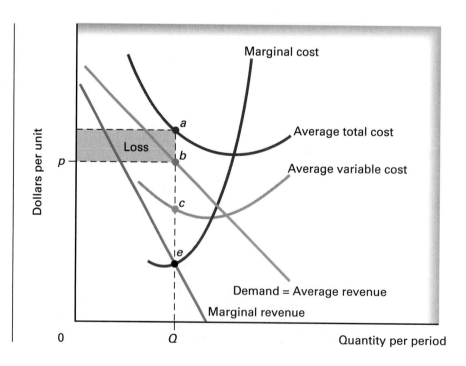

Yet short-run profit is no guarantee of long-run profit. For example, suppose that monopoly power rests on a patent. Patents last only a specified time and even while a product is under patent, the monopolist often must defend the patent in court (patent litigation has increased by more than half in the last decade). A monopolist that earns economic profit in the short run may find that profit can be increased in the long run by adjusting the scale of the firm. A monopolist that suffers a loss in the short run may be able to eliminate that loss in the long run by adjusting to a more efficient size or by trying to increase demand through advertising (most start-up firms lose money initially). A monopolist unable to erase a loss in the long run will exit the market.

CNN VIDEO: "JUDGE OFFERS WINDOWS INTO MICROSOFT'S OPERATING SYSTEM"

MONOPOLY AND THE ALLOCATION OF RESOURCES

If monopolists are no greedier than perfect competitors (since both maximize profit), if monopolists do not charge the highest possible price, and if monopolists are not guaranteed a profit, then what's the problem with monopoly? To get a handle on the problem, let's compare monopoly with the benchmark established in the previous chapter—perfect competition.

Price and Output Under Perfect Competition

Let's begin with the long-run equilibrium price and output for a perfectly competitive market. Suppose the long-run market supply curve in perfect competition is horizontal, as shown by S_c in Exhibit 8. Since this is a constant-cost industry, the horizontal long-run supply curve also shows marginal cost and average total cost at each rate of output. Equilibrium occurs at point c, where market demand and market supply intersect to yield price p_c and quantity Q_c. Remember, the demand curve reflects the marginal benefit of each unit purchased. In competitive equilibrium, the marginal benefit equals the marginal cost to society of producing the final unit sold. As noted in the previous chapter, when the marginal benefit that consumers derive from a good equals the marginal cost of producing that good, that market is said to be allocatively efficient. There is no way of reallocating resources to increase the total value of output. Because consumers are able to purchase Q_c units at price p_c, they enjoy a net benefit from consumption, or a consumer surplus, measured by the entire shaded triangle, acp_c.

EXHIBIT 8

Perfect Competition and Monopoly

A perfectly competitive industry would produce output Q_c, determined at the intersection of market demand curve D and supply curve S_c. The price would be p_c. A monopoly that could produce output at the same minimum average cost would produce output Q_m, determined at point b, where marginal cost and marginal revenue intersect. It would charge price p_m. Thus, output is lower and price is higher under monopoly than under perfect competition.

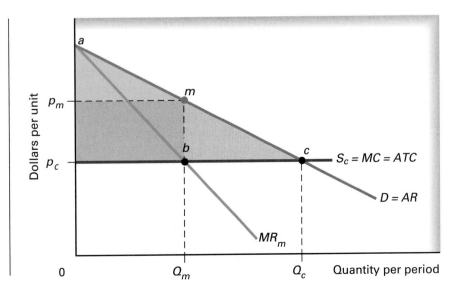

Price and Output Under Monopoly

When there is only one firm in the industry, the industry demand curve becomes the monopolist's demand curve, so the price the monopolist charges determines how much gets sold. Because the monopolist's demand curve slopes downward, the marginal revenue curve also slopes downward and is beneath the demand curve, as is indicated by MR_m in Exhibit 8. Suppose the monopolist can produce at the same constant cost in the long run as can the competitive industry. The monopolist maximizes profit by equating marginal revenue with marginal cost, which occurs at point b, yielding equilibrium price p_m and output Q_m. Again, the price shows the consumers' marginal benefit at that output rate. This marginal benefit, identified at point m, exceeds the monopolist's marginal cost, identified at point b. Because the marginal benefit consumers attach to additional units exceeds the marginal cost of producing those additional units, society would be better off if output were expanded beyond Q_m. The monopolist restricts output below the level that maximizes social welfare. But consumers still benefit even though the monopolist restricts output; consumer surplus is shown by the smaller triangle, amp_m.

Allocative and Distributive Effects

Consider the allocative and distributive effects of monopoly versus perfect competition. In Exhibit 8, consumer surplus under perfect competition was the large triangle, acp_c. Under monopoly, consumer surplus shrinks to the smaller triangle amp_m, which in this example is only one-fourth as large. The monopolist earns economic profit equal to the shaded rectangle. By comparing the situation under monopoly with that under perfect competition, you can see that the monopolist's economic profit comes entirely from what was consumer surplus under perfect competition. Because the profit rectangle reflects a transfer from consumer surplus to monopoly profit, this amount is not lost to society and so is not considered a welfare loss from monopoly.

Notice, however, that consumer surplus has been reduced by more than the profit rectangle. Consumers have also lost the triangle mcb, which was part of the consumer surplus under perfect competition. The mcb triangle is called the **deadweight loss of monopoly** because it is a loss to consumers but a gain to nobody. This loss results from the *allocative inefficiency arising from the higher price and reduced output of monopoly*. Again, society would be better off if output exceeded the monopolist's profit-maximizing rate, because the marginal benefit of additional output exceeds its marginal cost. Under monopoly, the price, or marginal benefit, always exceeds marginal cost. Empirical estimates of the annual deadweight loss of monopoly in the United States range from about 1 percent to about 5 percent of national income. Applied to national income data for 2000, these estimates imply a deadweight loss of about $320 to $1,600 per capita.

PROBLEMS ESTIMATING THE WELFARE COST OF MONOPOLY

The actual cost of monopoly could differ from the welfare loss described in the previous section.

Why the Welfare Loss of Monopoly Might Be Lower

If economies of scale are extensive enough, a monopolist might be able to produce output at a lower cost per unit than could competitive firms. Therefore, the price, or at least the cost of production, could be lower under monopoly than under competition. The welfare loss shown in Exhibit 8 may also overstate the true cost of monopoly because monopolists might, in response to public scrutiny and political pressure, keep prices below what the market could bear. Although monopolists would like to earn as great an economic profit as possible, they realize that if the public outcry over high prices and high profits grows loud enough, some sort of government intervention could reduce or even erase profits. For example, the prices and profits of drug companies, which individually are monopoly producers of patented medicines, come under scrutiny from time to time by federal legislators who want to regulate drug prices. Drug firms might try to avoid such treatment by keeping prices below the level that would maximize economic profit. Finally, a monopolist might keep the price below the profit-maximizing level to avoid attracting new competitors. For example, some observers claim that Alcoa, when it was the only U.S. producer of aluminum, kept prices low enough to discourage new entry.

ASK THE INSTRUCTOR: WHY DO PROFESSIONS TRY TO LIMIT ENTRY?

Why the Welfare Loss of Monopoly Might Be Higher

Another line of thought suggests that the welfare loss of monopoly might, in fact, be greater than shown in our simple diagram. *If resources must be devoted to securing and maintaining a monopoly position, monopolies may involve more of a welfare loss than simple models suggest.* For example, radio and TV broadcasting rights confer on the recipient the exclusive right to use a particular band of the scarce broadcast spectrum. In the past, these rights have been given away by government agencies to the applicants deemed most deserving. Because these rights are so valuable, numerous applicants spend millions on lawyers' fees, lobbying expenses, and other costs associated with making themselves appear the most deserving. The efforts devoted to securing and maintaining a monopoly position are largely a social waste because they use up scarce resources but add not one unit to output. Activities undertaken by individuals or firms to influence public policy in a way that will directly or indirectly redistribute income to them are referred to as **rent seeking.**

The monopolist, insulated from the rigors of competition in the marketplace, might also grow fat and lazy—and become inefficient. Because some monopolies could still earn an economic profit even if output were not produced at the least possible cost, corporate executives might waste resources in creating a more comfortable life for themselves. Long lunches, afternoon golf, plush offices, corporate jets, and extensive employee benefits might make company life more enjoyable, but these additional expenses also increase the average cost of production.

Monopolists have also been criticized for being slow to adopt the latest production techniques, being reluctant to develop new products, and generally lacking innovativeness. Because monopolists are largely insulated from the rigors of competition, they might take it easy. It's been said "The best of all monopoly profits is a quiet life."

The following case study discusses the performance of one of the nation's oldest monopolies, the U.S. Postal Service.

CASE**STUDY**	The Mail Monopoly
	● *Public Policy*

The U.S. Post Office was granted a monopoly in 1775 and has operated under federal protection ever since. In 1971, Congress converted the Post Office Department into a semi-independent agency called the U.S. Postal Service, or USPS, with revenue exceeding $65 billion in 2000. USPS pays no taxes and is exempt from local zoning laws. It has a legal monopoly in delivering regular, first-class letters; it also has the exclusive right to use the space inside mailboxes. About 800,000 USPS employees handle more than half a billion pieces of mail a day—over 40 percent of the world's total.

The USPS monopoly has suffered in recent years because of growing costs and competition from new technologies. The price of a first-class stamp climbed from 6 cents in 1970 to 34 cents by 2001, for a growth rate double that of overall inflation and quadruple the increase in telephone rates, one possible substitute for first-class mail. The United Parcel Service (UPS) is more mechanized and more containerized than the USPS and thus has lower costs and less breakage. The USPS has tried to emulate UPS but with only limited success. Postal employees are paid more on average than those at UPS or other private-sector delivery services, such as FedEx. New technologies such as fax machines and e-mail also compete with USPS (e-mail messages now greatly outnumber first-class letters).

Since its monopoly applies only to regular first-class mail, USPS has lost huge chunks of other business to private firms offering lower rates and better service. For example, UPS and others have taken away 95 percent of fourth-class mail—parcel post business. When the Postal Service recently raised third-class ("junk" mail) rates, businesses substituted other forms of advertising, including cable TV and telemarketing. Even USPS's first-class monopoly is being threatened, since FedEx and others have captured 90 percent of the overnight mail business. Thus, USPS is losing business because of competition from overnight mail and from new technologies. In 2001, the USPS lost more than $2 billion, a loss compounded by the anthrax scare.

But USPS is fighting back, trying to leverage its monopoly power while increasing efficiency. On the electronic front, USPS now offers online postage purchases, online bill-paying service, and secure online document transmission service. In 2001, USPS hired FedEx for air transport of priority mail, express mail, and first-class mail. USPS, in turn, has begun providing local delivery service—the so-called "last mile"—for several major shippers including DHL, Emery, and FedEx. And USPS is selling advertising space on its trucks, buildings, and other surfaces.

For example, Visa bought ad space on 20 million Priority Mail envelopes. Despite these efforts, changing technology and competition are eroding USPS's government-granted monopoly.

Not all economists believe that monopolies, especially private monopolies, manage their resources with any less vigilance than perfect competitors do. Some argue that because monopolists are protected from rivals, they are in a good position to capture the fruits of any innovation and therefore will be more innovative than competitive firms are. Others believe that if a private monopolist strays from the path of profit maximization, the value of the firm's stock will drop. This lower stock price provides an incentive for someone to buy a controlling share of the firm's stock, shape up the operation, and watch profits—as well as the value of the firm's stock—grow. This market for corporate control is said to guide monopolists along the path of efficient production.

PRICE DISCRIMINATION

In the model developed so far, a monopolist, to sell more output, must lower the price for all output sold. In reality, a monopolist can sometimes increase economic profit by charging higher prices to consumers who value the product more. This practice of charging different prices to different consumers when the price differences are not justified by differences in cost is called **price discrimination.** For example, children, students, and senior citizens often pay lower admission prices to ball games, movies, plays, and other events. Firms offer certain groups reduced prices because doing so enhances profits. Let's see how and why.

Conditions for Price Discrimination

To practice price discrimination, a firm must meet certain conditions. First, the demand curve for the firm's product must slope downward, indicating that the firm is a price maker—the producer has some market power, some control over the price. Second, there must be at least two groups of consumers for the product, each with a different price elasticity of demand. Third, the producer must be able, at little cost, to charge each group a different price for essentially the same product. Finally, the producer must be able to prevent those who pay the lower price from reselling the product to those who pay the higher price.

A Model of Price Discrimination

Exhibit 9 shows the effects of price discrimination. Consumers are divided into two groups with different demands. *At a given price,* the price elasticity of demand in panel (b) is greater than that in panel (a). Think of panel (b) as reflecting the demand of college students, senior citizens, or some other group more sensitive to the price. For simplicity, we assume that the firm produces at a constant long-run average and marginal cost of $1. *This firm maximizes profit by finding the price in each market that equates marginal revenue with marginal cost.* As a result, consumers with a lower price elasticity pay $3, and those with a higher price elasticity pay $1.50. Profit maximization results in charging a lower price to the group with the more elastic demand. Despite the price difference, the firm collects the same marginal revenue from the last unit sold to each group. This firm increases profit by charging different prices to the two groups.

Note that charging both groups $3 would eliminate any profit from that right-hand group of consumers, who would be priced out of the market. Charging both groups $1.50 would lead to negative marginal revenue from the left-hand group, which would reduce profit. No single price could generate the profit achieved by price discrimination.

EXHIBIT 9

Price Discrimination with Two Groups of Consumers

A monopolist that faces two groups of consumers with different demand elasticities may be able to practice price discrimination. With marginal cost the same in both markets, the firm sells 400 units to the high-marginal-value consumers in panel (a) and charges them a price of $3 per unit. It sells 500 units to the low-marginal-value consumers in panel (b) and charges them a price of $1.50.

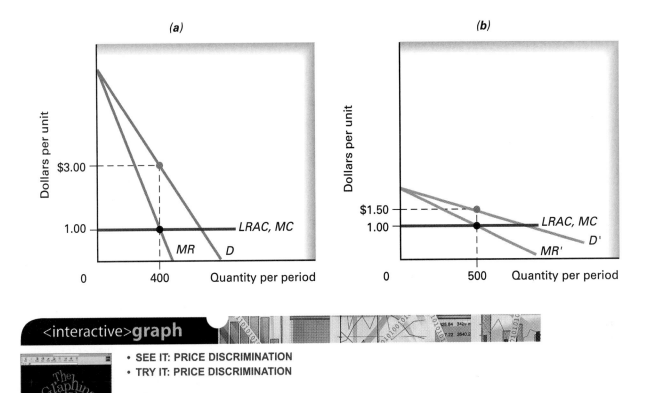

<interactive>graph

- SEE IT: PRICE DISCRIMINATION
- TRY IT: PRICE DISCRIMINATION

Examples of Price Discrimination

Let's look at some examples of price discrimination. Because businesspeople face unpredictable yet urgent demands for travel and communication, and because their employers pay such expenses, businesspeople are less sensitive to price than are householders. In other words, businesspeople have a less elastic demand for business travel and long-distance phone use than do householders, so airlines and telephone services try to maximize profits by charging business customers higher rates than residential customers.

But how do firms distinguish between groups of customers? Telephone companies are able to sort out their customers by charging different rates based on the time of day. Long-distance rates are often higher during normal *business* hours than during evenings and weekends, when householders, who have a higher price elasticity of demand, make social calls. Airlines distinguish between business and household customers based on the terms under which tickets are purchased. Householders plan their trips well in advance and often spend the weekend. But business travel is more unpredictable, more urgent, and seldom involves a weekend stay. The airlines sort out the two groups by limiting discount fares to travelers who buy tickets well in advance and who stay over Saturday night. Airlines also charge more for those who fly business class rather than coach class.

Here's another example of price discrimination: IBM wanted to charge business users of its laser printer more than home users. To distinguish between the two groups, IBM decided to slow down the home printer to 5 pages a minute (versus 10 for the business model). To do this, they added an extra chip that inserted pauses between pages.[2] Thus, IBM could sell the home model for less than the business model without cutting into sales of its business model.

---

[2]Carl Shapiro and Hal Varian, *Information Rules: A Strategic Guide to the Network Economy* (Boston: Harvard Business School Press, 1999), 59.

Here's a final example. Major amusement parks, such as Disney World and Universal Studios, distinguish between local residents and out-of-towners when it comes to the price of admission. Out-of-towners typically spend a substantial amount on airlines and lodging just to be there, so they are less sensitive to the admission price than are local residents. The problem is how to charge a lower price to locals. The parks do this by making discount coupons available at local businesses, such as dry cleaners, which tourists seldom visit.

Perfect Price Discrimination: The Monopolist's Dream

The demand curve shows the marginal value of each unit consumed, which is also the maximum amount consumers would pay for each unit. If the monopolist could charge a different price for each unit sold—a price reflected by the height of the demand curve—the firm's marginal revenue from selling one more unit would equal the price of that unit. Thus, the demand curve would become the firm's marginal revenue curve. A **perfectly discriminating monopolist** charges a different price for each unit of the good.

In Exhibit 10, again for simplicity, the monopolist is assumed to produce at a constant average and marginal cost in the long run. A perfectly discriminating monopolist, like any producer, would maximize profit by producing the quantity at which marginal revenue equals marginal cost. Since the demand curve is now the marginal revenue curve, the profit-maximizing output occurs at the point where the demand, or marginal revenue, curve intersects the marginal cost curve, identified at point e in Exhibit 10. Price discrimination is a way of increasing profit. The area of the shaded triangle *aec* defines the perfectly discriminating monopolist's economic profit.

By charging a different price for each unit of output, the perfectly discriminating monopolist is able to convert every dollar of consumer surplus into economic profit. Although this may seem unfair to consumers, perfect price discrimination gets high marks based on allocative efficiency. Because such a monopolist does not have to lower the price to all customers when output expands, there is no reason to restrict output. In fact, because this is a constant-cost industry, Q is the same quantity produced in perfect competition (though in perfect competition, the triangle aec would be consumer surplus instead of economic profit). As in the perfectly competitive outcome, the marginal benefit of the final unit of output produced just equals its marginal cost. And although perfect price discrimination yields no consumer surplus, the total benefits consumers derive just equal the total amount they pay for the good. Note also that because the monopolist does not restrict output, there is no deadweight loss triangle. Thus, perfect price discrimination enhances social welfare when compared with monopoly output in the absence of price discrimination. But the monopolist reaps all net gains from production, while consumers just break even on the deal because their total cost equals their total benefit.

EXHIBIT 10

Perfect Price Discrimination

If a monopolist can charge a different price for each unit sold, it may be able to practice perfect price discrimination. By setting the price of each unit equal to the maximum amount consumers are willing to pay for that unit (shown by the height of the demand curve), the monopolist can achieve a profit equal to the area of the shaded triangle. Consumer surplus is zero.

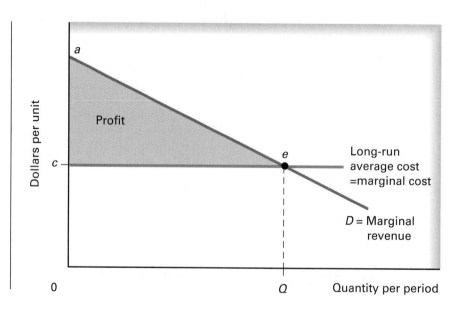

<interactive>**exercise**

READING IT RIGHT: WALL STREET JOURNAL EXERCISE

<interactive>**update**

ECONNEWS ONLINE: PRESCRIPTION DRUG IMPORT LAWS PROVE ADDICTIVE FOR PRODUCERS

CONCLUSION

Pure monopoly, like perfect competition, is not that common. Perhaps the best examples are firms producing patented items with unique characteristics, such as certain prescription drugs. Some firms may have monopoly power in the short run, but the lure of economic profit encourages rivals to hurdle seemingly high entry barriers. Changing technology also works against monopoly in the long run. The railroad monopoly was erased by the interstate highway system. AT&T's monopoly on long-distance phone service crumbled as microwave technology replaced copper wire. The U.S. Postal Service's monopoly on first-class mail is being eroded by overnight delivery, fax machines, and e-mail. And cable TV may soon lose its local monopoly to technological breakthroughs in fiber-optics technology, wireless communications, and the Internet.

Although perfect competition and pure monopoly are relatively rare, our examination of them yields a framework that will help us view market structures that lie between the two extremes. As we will see, many firms have some degree of monopoly power—that is, they face downward-sloping demand curves. In the next chapter, we will consider two market structures that lie in the gray region between perfect competition and monopoly.

endofchaptermaterial

- **Summary**
- **Questions for Review**
- **Problems and Exercises**
- **Experiential Exercises**

- **Wall Street Journal Exercises**
- **Graphing Workshop: Apply It Exercises**

Take the Post-Test to assess your overall understanding of the key ideas in this chapter. The Post-Test provides a comprehensive selection of exam-style questions addressing the main topics and concepts of the chapter. At the completion of each Post-Test, you will receive a score and instructive feedback on how you answered each question, and a direct link to the part of the chapter addressed in the question. Take the Post-Test as often as you need to—a record of your progress for each attempt is kept for you to revisit and gauge your improvement. And each Post-Test is randomly generated, so every attempt is new.

Post-Test

CHAPTER 10

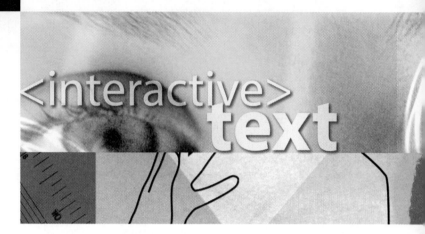

Monopolistic Competition and Oligopoly

Why are some panty hose sold in egg-shaped cartons? Why are some shampoos sold only in salons? Why do some pizza makers deliver? Why do airlines sometimes engage in airfare warfare? Why was the oil cartel, OPEC, created, and why has it met with only spotty success? Why is there a witness protection program? To answer these and other questions, we turn in this chapter to the vast gray area that lies between perfect competition and monopoly.

Perfect competition and pure monopoly are extreme market structures. Under perfect competition, many suppliers offer an identical product to a market where firms in the long run can enter or leave with ease. A monopoly sells a product with no close substitutes in a market where natural and artificial barriers keep out would-be competitors. These polar market structures are logically appealing and offer a useful description of some industries observed in the economy.

But most firms operate in markets that are not well described by either model. Some firms are in markets that have many sellers producing goods that vary slightly, such as the many radio stations that vie for your attention or the convenience stores that abound. Other firms are in markets consisting of a small number of sellers that in some cases produce homogeneous goods (such as the markets for oil, steel, and aluminum) and in other cases produce differentiated goods (such as the markets for automobiles, breakfast cereals, and cigarettes). In this chapter, we examine the two additional market structures that together include the majority of firms in the economy. Topics discussed in this chapter include:

174

PHOTO: © IMAGE 100

- Monopolistic competition
- Oligopoly
- Product differentiation
- Collusion
- Excess capacity
- Prisoner's dilemma

<interactive>exercise

ECONDEBATE ONLINE: MONOPOLISTIC COMPETITION AND OLIGOPOLY

<interactive>update

- ECONLINKS ONLINE: ECONOMICS WEB LINKS
- ECONNEWS ONLINE: MONOPOLISTIC COMPETITION AND OLIGOPOLY

<interactive>video

ASK THE INSTRUCTOR: WHAT ARE THE DIFFERENCES AMONG THE FOUR MARKET STRUCTURES?

MONOPOLISTIC COMPETITION

During the 1920s and 1930s, economists began formulating models to fit between perfect competition and pure monopoly. Two models of *monopolistic competition* were developed independently. In 1933 at Harvard University, Edward Chamberlin published *The Theory of Monopolistic Competition*. Across the Atlantic that same year, Cambridge University's Joan Robinson published *The Economics of Imperfect Competition*. Although the theories differed, their underlying principles were similar. We will discuss Chamberlin's approach.

Characteristics of Monopolistic Competition

As the expression **monopolistic competition** suggests, this market structure contains elements of both monopoly and competition. Chamberlin used the term to describe a market in which many producers offer products that are close substitutes but are not viewed as identical by consumers. Because the products of different suppliers differ slightly—for example, some convenience stores are closer to you than others—the demand curve for each is not horizontal but rather slopes downward. Each supplier has some power over the price it can charge. Thus, the firms that populate this market are not *price takers,* as they would be under perfect competition, but are *price makers.*

Because barriers to entry are low, firms in monopolistic competition can, in the long run, enter or leave the market with ease. Consequently, there are enough sellers that they can behave competitively. There are also enough sellers that each tends to get lost in the crowd. For example, in a large metropolitan area, an individual restaurant, gas station, drugstore, video store, dry cleaner, or convenience store tends to act *independently*. In other market structures, there may be only two or three sellers in each market, so they keep an eye on one another; they act *interdependently*. You will understand the significance of this distinction later in the chapter.

Product Differentiation

In perfect competition, the product is homogeneous, such as a bushel of wheat or an ounce of gold. In monopolistic competition, the product differs among sellers, as with the difference between a Big Mac and a Whopper or between one rock radio station and another. Sellers differentiate their products in four basic ways.

Physical Differences. The most obvious way products differ is in their physical appearance and their qualities. Product differentiation is seemingly endless: size, weight, color, taste, texture, and so on. Shampoos, for example, differ in color, scent, thickness, lathering ability, and

bottle design. Particular brands aim at consumers with dandruff and those with normal, dry, or oily hair. Packaging is also designed to make a product stand out in a crowded field, such as panty hose in a plastic eggshell (L'Eggs®) and instant soup in a cup (Cup O' Soup®).

Location. The number and variety of locations where a product is available are other means of differentiation. Some products seem to be available everywhere, including the Internet; finding other products requires some search and travel. If you live in a metropolitan area, you are no doubt accustomed to the large number of convenience stores that populate the region. Each wants to be closest to you when you need that gallon of milk or bag of Doritos—thus, the proliferation of stores. As the name says, these mini grocery stores are selling *convenience*. Their prices are higher and selections more limited than those of regular grocery stores, but they are likely to be nearer customers, don't have long lines, and stay open late.

Services. Products also differ in terms of their accompanying services. For example, some pizza sellers, like Domino's, and some booksellers, like Amazon.com, deliver; others do not. Some retailers offer product demonstrations by a well-trained staff; others are mostly self-service. Some products include online support and toll-free numbers; others provide no help. Some offer money-back guarantees; others say "no returns."

Product Image. A final way products differ is in the image the producer tries to foster in the consumer's mind. For example, suppliers of footwear, clothing, watches, and cosmetics often pay for endorsements from athletes, models, and other celebrities. Some producers try to demonstrate high quality based on where products are sold, such as shampoo sold only in beauty salons. Some products tout their all-natural ingredients, such as Ben & Jerry's ice cream and Tom's of Maine toothpaste, or appeal to environmental concerns by focusing on recycled packaging, such as the Starbucks coffee cup insulating sleeve "made from 60% post-consumer recycled fiber."

NETBOOKMARK: U.S. PATENT AND TRADEMARK OFFICE

Short-Run Profit Maximization or Loss Minimization

Because each monopolistic competitor offers a product that differs somewhat from what others supply, each has some control over the price. This *market power* means that each firm's demand curve slopes downward. Since many firms are selling close substitutes, any firm that raises its price can expect to lose some customers, but not all, to rivals. By way of comparison, a price hike would cost a monopolist a few customers but would cost a perfect competitor *all* customers. Therefore, a monopolistic competitor faces a demand curve that tends to be more elastic than a monopolist's but less elastic than a perfect competitor's.

Recall that the availability of substitutes for a given product affects its price elasticity of demand. The price elasticity of the monopolistic competitor's demand depends on (1) the number of rival firms that produce similar products and (2) the firm's ability to differentiate its product from those of its rivals. *A firm's demand curve will be more elastic the more competing firms there are and the less differentiated its product is.*

Marginal Revenue Equals Marginal Cost. From our study of monopoly, we know that the downward-sloping demand curve means the marginal revenue curve also slopes downward and lies beneath the demand curve. Exhibit 1 depicts demand and marginal revenue curves for a monopolistic competitor. The exhibit also presents per-unit cost curves. In the short run, a firm that can at least cover its variable cost will increase output as long as marginal revenue exceeds marginal cost. A monopolistic competitor maximizes profit in the short run just as a monopolist does: *the profit-maximizing quantity occurs where marginal revenue equals marginal cost; the profit-maximizing price for that quantity is found on the demand curve.* Exhibit 1 shows the price and quantity combinations that, in panel (a), maximize short-run profit and, in panel (b), minimize short-run loss. In each panel, the marginal cost and marginal revenue curves intersect at point *e*, yielding equilibrium output *q*, equilibrium price *p*, and average total cost *c*. Demand and marginal revenue are the same in both panels, but average cost is higher in the right panel.

Maximizing Profit or Minimizing Loss in the Short Run. Recall that the short run is a period too brief to allow firms to enter or leave the market. The demand and cost conditions shown in panel (a) of Exhibit 1 indicate that this firm will earn economic profit in the short run. At the firm's

EXHIBIT 1 |

The Firm in Monopolistic Competition in the Short Run

The monopolistically competitive firm produces the level of output at which marginal cost equals marginal revenue (point e) and charges the price indicated by point b on the downward-sloping demand curve. In panel (a), the firm produces q units, sells them at price p, and earns a short-run economic profit equal to $(p - c)$ multiplied by q, shown by the blue rectangle. In panel (b), the average total cost exceeds the price at the optimal level of output. Thus, the firm suffers a short-run loss equal to $(c - p)$ multiplied by q, represented by the red rectangle.

(a)

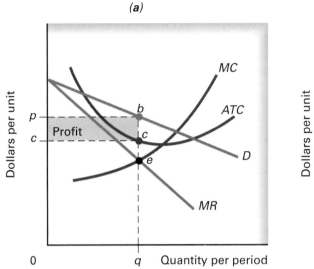

(b)

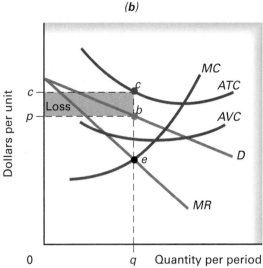

profit-maximizing quantity, average total cost, measured as c on the vertical axis, is below the price, p. Price minus average total cost is the firm's profit per unit, which, when multiplied by the quantity, is economic profit, shown by the blue-shaded rectangle. Again, the profit-maximizing quantity is found where marginal revenue equals marginal cost; price is found up on the demand curve at that quantity. Thus, a monopolistic competitor, like a monopolist, has no supply curve—that is, *there is no curve that uniquely relates price and quantity supplied.*

The monopolistic competitor, like other firms, is not assured of economic profit. The firm's demand curve is the same in both panels, but the average total cost curve is higher in panel (b). Because the firm's average total cost curve lies entirely above the demand curve, all quantities result in losses. In such a situation, the firm must decide whether to shut down temporarily. The rule here is the same as with perfect competition and monopoly: As long as the price covers average variable cost, the firm should produce in the short run. The firm should shut down if no price covers average variable cost. Recall that shutting down is not the same as going out of business; the halt in production may be only temporary. But firms that expect economic losses to persist will leave the industry in the long run.

Short-run profit maximization in monopolistic competition is quite similar to that under monopoly. But the stories differ in the long run, as we'll see next.

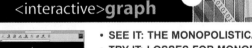

- **SEE IT: THE MONOPOLISTICALLY COMPETITIVE FIRM IN THE SHORT-RUN**
- **TRY IT: LOSSES FOR MONOPOLISTICALLY COMPETITIVE FIRM**

- **ECONNEWS ONLINE: RESTAURANTS OR MACHINES? THE VIABILITY OF VENDING VENTURES**
- **ECONNEWS ONLINE: PRODUCT PROFUSION AND PACKAGING**

Zero Economic Profit in the Long Run

Low barriers to entry in monopolistic competition mean that short-run economic profit will attract new entrants in the long run. New entrants offer products that are similar to those offered by existing firms, so they draw some customers away from existing firms, thereby reducing the demand facing each firm. Furthermore, each firm's demand curve becomes more elastic because there are now more substitutes for each firm's product. Entry will continue in the long run until the demand facing each firm falls enough to erase economic profit. So short-run economic profit attracts new entry in the long run; this entry will continue until economic profit is erased. *Because of the ease of entry, monopolistically competitive firms earn zero economic profit in the long run.*

If they continue to suffer short-run losses, some monopolistic competitors will leave the industry in the long run, redirecting their resources to activities expected to earn at least a normal profit. As firms leave, their customers will switch to the remaining firms, increasing the demand for each remaining firm's product and making that demand curve less elastic (because each firm now has fewer competitors). Firms will continue to leave in the long run until the remaining firms have enough customers to earn normal profit but not economic profit.

Exhibit 2 shows long-run equilibrium for a typical monopolistic competitor. In the long run, entry and exit will shift each firm's demand curve until economic profit disappears—that is, until the price equals average total cost. This long-run outcome is shown in Exhibit 2, where the marginal revenue curve intersects the marginal cost curve at point *a*. At the equilibrium quantity, *q*, the average total cost curve is tangent to the demand curve at point *b*. Since average total cost equals the price, the firm earns no economic profit. At all other rates of output, the firm's average total cost is above the demand curve, so the firm would lose money with any other quantity.

Thus, if entry is easy, short-run economic profit will draw new entrants into the industry in the long run. The demand curve facing each monopolistic competitor shifts left and becomes more elastic until economic profit disappears and firms earn only a normal profit. A short-run economic loss will prompt some firms to leave the industry in the long run. The demand curve facing each remaining firm shifts right and becomes less elastic until the loss disappears and remaining firms earn just a normal profit.

In summary: *Monopolistic competition is like pure monopoly in that both types of firms are price makers—that is, they face downward-sloping demand curves. Monopolistic competition is like perfect competition in that easy entry and exit eliminate economic profit or economic loss in the long run.*

One way to understand how firm entry erases short-run economic profit is to consider the evolution of an industry, as is discussed in the following case study.

EXHIBIT 2

Long-Run Equilibrium in Monopolistic Competition

If existing firms are earning economic profits, new firms will enter the industry. The entry of firms reduces the demand facing each firm. In the long run, demand is reduced until marginal revenue equals marginal cost (point *a*) and the demand curve is tangent to the average total cost curve (point *b*). Profit is zero at output *q*. With zero economic profit, no new firms enter, so the industry is in long-run equilibrium.

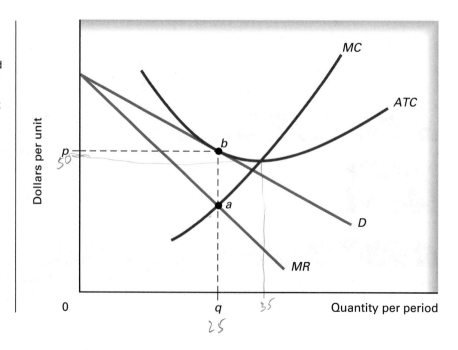

● *The World of Business*

The videocassette recorder, or VCR, has become standard equipment in the typical American home, with 9 of 10 households owning at least one. The introduction of the VCRs fueled demand for videotape rentals. The initial surge in demand was boosted by rentals of older movies that consumers had missed at theaters. The first wave of outlets charged about $5 per day, required security deposits, and imposed membership fees of up to $100. In the late 1970s and early 1980s, most rental stores faced no competition and most earned short-run economic profit.

But this profit attracted competitors. Since entry was relatively easy, many new rental stores opened for business. Other types of stores—convenience stores, grocery stores, bookstores, even drugstores—also began renting videos. Between 1982 and 1987, the number of video outlets quadrupled. The growth rate of outlets exceeded the growth rate of VCRs. And once consumers caught up with the backlog of older movies, demand focused primarily on new releases.

Thus, the supply of rental outlets increased faster than the demand. Worse was yet to come for video stores in the 1990s, when cable television's hundreds of channels and pay-per-view options plus direct sales of movie videos to consumers became substitutes for video rentals. The greater supply of rentals along with the increased availability of substitutes had the predictable effect on market prices. Rental rates crashed to as little as $0.99, and membership fees and tape deposits disappeared. Rental stores that could not survive folded. In fact, so many failed that a market developed to buy and resell their tape inventories.

The video rental business grew hardly at all during most of the last decade. The "shakeout" in the industry is still going on—video rental revenue declined industry-wide in 2000. Rental stores have tried to diversify by renting DVDs and video games, but many will fail. As the market evolves, one large firm, Blockbuster, has grown to more than 5,000 U.S. stores, accounting for 35 percent of the U.S. market in 2000, four times the share of second-ranked Hollywood Video. Blockbuster is transforming the tape rental industry from monopolistic competition to *oligopoly,* a market structure to be examined later in the chapter. But Blockbuster faces its own growing pains, including an "excess inventory" of tapes and a failed effort to sell books, magazines, and snacks at its rental stores.

VCRs and even DVD players could go the way of eight-track tapes and record players if newer technologies, such as on-demand movies delivered by broadband cable, catch on. With a remote control and a digital cable box, customers can rent, rewind, pause, and replay new release movies, all without leaving the couch. Blockbuster is trying to get into the broadband business, but success there could make videotapes and DVDs obsolete. With an average inventory of over 12,000 tapes and DVDs per store, Blockbuster would be stuck with more than 60 million nationwide. To survive in this new era, Blockbuster is also collaborating with Radio Shack to sell consumer electronics in some of its video stores. Such is the dynamic nature of market evolution—out with the old, in with the new, in a competitive process that has been aptly called "creative destruction."

<interactive>exercise

eACTIVITY: FAST FORWARD

Sources: Chris Gaither, "DVD's Shine Despite Tough Market for Electronics," *New York Times,* 23 July 2001; Martin Peers, "Blockbuster Tests Postvideo Future, Looks to Consumer-Electronics Sales, *Wall Street Journal,* 18 June 2001; and Sue Zeidler, "Universal Signs Video-On-Demand Deal," Reuters, 20 July 2001. Blockbuster's home page is http://www.blockbuster.com/.

Monopolistic Competition and Perfect Competition Compared

How does monopolistic competition compare with perfect competition in terms of efficiency? In the long run, neither can earn economic profit, so what's the difference? The difference appears in the different demand curves facing individual firms in each of the two market structures. Exhibit 3 presents the long-run equilibrium price and quantity for a typical firm in each market structure, assuming the two firms have identical cost curves. In each case, the marginal

EXHIBIT 3

Perfect Competition Versus Monopolistic Competition

The perfectly competitive firm of panel (a) faces a demand curve that is horizontal at market price p. Long-run equilibrium occurs at output q, where the demand curve is tangent to the average total cost curve at its lowest point. The monopolistically competitive firm of panel (b) is in long-run equilibrium at output q', where demand is tangent to average total cost. However, since the demand curve slopes downward, the tangency does not occur at the minimum point of average total cost. Thus, the monopolistically competitive firm produces less output at a higher price than does a perfectly competitive firm facing the same cost conditions.

(a) Perfect competition   **(b)** Monopolistic competition

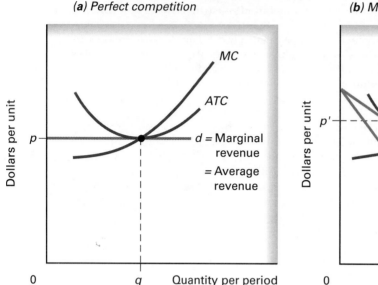
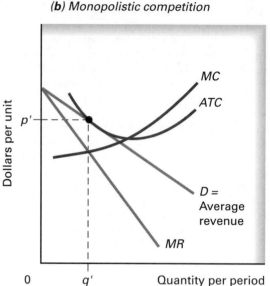

cost curve intersects the marginal revenue curve at the quantity where the average total cost curve is tangent to the firm's demand curve.

A perfect competitor's demand curve is a horizontal line drawn at the market price, as shown in panel (a). This demand curve is tangent to the lowest point of the long-run average total cost curve. Thus, a perfect competitor produces at the lowest possible average cost in the long run. In panel (b), a monopolistic competitor faces a downward-sloping demand curve because its product differs somewhat from those of other producers. In the long run, the monopolistic competitor fails to reach the lowest possible average cost. Thus, the price and average cost under monopolistic competition, identified as p' in panel (b), exceed the price and average cost under perfect competition, identified as p in panel (a). *If firms have the same cost curves, the monopolistic competitor produces less and charges more than the perfect competitor does.*

Firms in monopolistic competition are said to have **excess capacity** because production is short of the rate that would achieve the lowest average cost. Excess capacity means that each producer could easily produce more and in the process lower the average cost. *The marginal value of increased output would exceed its marginal cost, so greater output would increase economic welfare.* Such excess capacity exists with gas stations, drugstores, convenience stores, restaurants, motels, bookstores, flower shops, and firms in other monopolistic competitive industries. A good example is the funeral business. Industry analysts argue that the nation's 22,000 funeral directors could efficiently handle 4 million funerals a year, but only about 2.3 million people die. So the industry operates at less than 60 percent of capacity, resulting in a higher average cost per funeral because valuable resources remain idle much of the time.

There is another difference between perfect competition and monopolistic competition that does not show up in Exhibit 3. Although the cost curves drawn in each panel of the exhibit are identical, firms in monopolistic competition in fact spend more on advertising and other promotional expenses to differentiate their products than do firms in perfect competition. These higher costs shift up their average cost curves.

Some economists have argued that monopolistic competition results in too many suppliers and in product differentiation that is often artificial. The counter-argument is that consumers are willing to pay a higher price for greater selection. According to this latter view, consumers benefit from the wider choice among gas stations, restaurants, convenience stores, clothing stores, video stores, drugstores, textbooks, hiking boots, and many other goods and services. For example, what if half of the restaurants in your area were to close just so the remaining ones could eliminate excess capacity? Some consumers, including you, might be disappointed if their favorite or most convenient restaurant went out of business.

AN INTRODUCTION TO OLIGOPOLY

Perfect competitors and monopolistic competitors are so numerous in their respective markets that an action by any one of them has little or no effect on the behavior of others in the market. Another important market structure between perfect competition and monopoly is *oligopoly,* a Greek word meaning "few sellers." When you think of "big business," you are thinking of **oligopoly,** a market dominated by just a few firms. Perhaps three or four firms account for more than half the market output. Many industries, including steel, automobiles, oil, breakfast cereals, and tobacco, are *oligopolistic.* Because an oligopoly has only a few firms, each must consider the effect of its own actions on competitors' behavior. Oligopolists are therefore *interdependent.*

<interactive>video

CNN VIDEO: "CONSUMERS CREAMED BY HIGH MILK PRICES"

Varieties of Oligopoly

In some oligopolistic industries, such as steel and oil, the product is homogeneous across producers—an ingot of steel or a barrel of oil. In other industries, such as automobiles and breakfast cereal, the product is differentiated across producers—Ford versus Toyota or General Food's Wheaties versus Kellogg's Corn Flakes. The more homogeneous the products, the greater the interdependence among the few dominant firms in the industry. For example, because steel ingots are essentially identical, steel producers are quite sensitive to each other's pricing policies. A small rise in one producer's price will send customers to rivals. But in markets where the product is differentiated, such as the auto industry, producers are not quite as sensitive about each other's policies. As with monopolistic competitors, oligopolists differentiate their products through (1) physical qualities, (2) sales locations, (3) services provided with the product, and (4) the image of the product established in the consumer's mind.

Because of interdependence among firms in an industry, the behavior of any particular firm is difficult to analyze. *Each firm knows that any changes in its product quality, price, output, or advertising policy may prompt a reaction from its rivals. And each firm may react if another firm alters any of these features.* Monopolistic competition is like a golf tournament, in which each player is striving for a personal best; oligopoly is more like a tennis match, where each player's actions depend on how and where the opponent hits the ball.

Why have some industries evolved into an oligopolistic market structure, dominated by only a few firms, whereas other industries have not? Although the reasons are not always clear, *an oligopoly can often be traced to some form of barrier to entry, such as economies of scale, legal restrictions, brand names built up by years of advertising, or control over an essential resource.* In the previous chapter, we examined barriers to entry as they applied to monopoly. The same principles apply to oligopoly. In the following case study, we consider some barriers to entry in the airline industry.

CASE**STUDY**	The Unfriendly Skies
	● *The World of Business*

At one time, airline routes were straight lines from one city to another. Now they radiate like the spokes of a wagon wheel from a "hub" city. From 29 hub airports across the country, the airlines send out planes along the spokes to about 400 commercial airports and then quickly bring them back to the hubs. Major airlines dominate hub airports. For example, United Airlines accounts for half the passengers at Dallas–Fort Worth airport. A new airline trying to enter the industry must secure a hub airport as well as landing slots at crowded airports around the country—not an easy task since all the viable hubs are taken and landing slots are scarce. Hubs and landing slots create the first barrier to entry in the airline industry. Research shows that ticket prices at airports dominated by a single airline are higher than ticket prices at more competitive airports.

A second barrier to entry is frequent-flyer mileage programs. The biggest airlines fly more national and international routes, so they offer greater opportunities both to accumulate frequent-flyer miles and to use the mileage for free flights. Thus, the biggest airlines have the most attractive programs. Until recently, another barrier to entry was the computerized reservation systems used by travel agents, but these systems are now available to all airlines. And Internet sites allow individuals to buy tickets online. Orbitz, a site formed by major airlines, claims to have the lowest fares and the widest selection ("scan more than two billion possibilities").

Seven airlines dominate the U.S. market, the largest in the world: United, American, Delta, Northwest, Southwest, Continental, and US Airways together handle over four-fifths of all passenger service. The dominance of U.S. carriers is enhanced by federal regulations that prevent foreigners from owning U.S. airlines and block foreign airlines from offering connecting service between U.S. cities.

Thus, scarce hubs and gates, frequent-flier programs, and regulations against foreign competition create barriers to entry in the airline industry.

<interactive>exercise

eACTIVITY: THE UNFRIENDLY SKIES

Sources: Martha Brannigan, "Congress's Removal of 'Slots' Opens a Flood of New York Airports Gates," *Wall Street Journal,* 4 December 2000; "Air Travel, Air Trouble," *Economist,* 7 July 2001; Rafer Guzman and Jane Costello, "Weather, La Guardia Flight Reductions Lift Airlines' On-Time Arrival Records," *Wall Street Journal,* 20 July 2001; and Steven Morrison and Clifford Winston, *The Evolution of the Airline Industry* (Washington, D.C.: Brookings Institution, 1995). The travel site formed by the world's major airlines is http://www.orbitz.com/.

Economies of Scale

Perhaps the most significant barrier to entry is economies of scale. Recall that the minimum efficient scale is the lowest rate of output at which the firm takes full advantage of economies of scale. If a firm's minimum efficient scale is relatively large compared to industry output, then only one or a few firms are needed to produce the total output demanded in the market. For example, research shows that an automobile plant of minimum efficient scale could make enough cars to supply nearly 10 percent of the U.S. market. If there were 100 auto plants, each would supply such a tiny portion of the market that the average cost per car would be higher than if only 10 plants manufacture autos. In the automobile industry, economies of scale create a barrier to entry. To compete with existing producers, a new entrant must sell enough automobiles to reach a competitive scale of operation. Exhibit 4 presents the long-run average cost curve for a typical firm in the industry. If a new entrant sells only S cars, the average cost per unit, c_a, far exceeds the average cost, c_b, of a manufacturer that sells enough cars to reach the minimum efficient size, M. If autos sell for a price less than c_a, a potential entrant can expect to lose money, and this prospect will discourage entry. For example, John Delorean tried to break into the auto industry in the early 1980s with a modern design featured in the movie *Back to the Future.* But his plant built only 8,583 Deloreans before the company folded.

The High Cost of Entry

Potential entrants into oligopolistic industries may face another problem. The total investment needed to reach the minimum efficient size is often gigantic. A new auto plant or new semiconductor plant can cost over $1 billion. The average cost of developing and testing a new drug exceeds $300 million. Advertising a new product enough to compete with established brands may also require enormous outlays.

High start-up costs and established brand names can create substantial barriers to entry, especially since the fortunes of a new product are so uncertain. In fact, 8 out of 10 new consumer products don't survive. An unsuccessful attempt at securing a place in the market could result in crippling losses for upstart firms. The prospect of such losses turns away many potential entrants. Most new products come from existing firms, which can better withstand the possible losses. For example, Colgate-Palmolive spent $100 million introducing Total toothpaste, as did McDonald's in its failed attempt to sell the Arch Deluxe. And Unilever lost $160 million when its new detergent, Power, failed to catch on.

EXHIBIT 4

Economies of Scale as a Barrier to Entry

At point *b*, an existing firm can produce *M* automobiles at an average cost of c_b. A new entrant that can hope to sell only *S* automobiles will incur a much higher average cost of c_a at point *a*. If cars sell for less than c_a, the new entrant will suffer a loss. In this case, economies of scale serve as a barrier to entry, protecting the existing firms from new competitors.

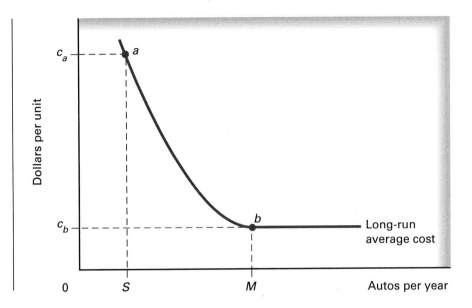

In perfect competition, all firms sell identical products. There is no incentive to advertise or to promote a particular product since consumers know that all products are the same. Moreover, producers can already sell all they want at the prevailing market price, so why advertise? In oligopoly, however, firms often spend millions and sometimes billions trying to differentiate their products. Some of these expenditures have the beneficial effects of providing valuable information to consumers and offering them a wider array of products. But some forms of product differentiation are of little value. Slogans such as "Generation Next" or "Always Cola-Cola" convey little information, yet Pepsi and Coke spend huge sums on such messages (Coke spent nearly $2 billion on advertising in 2000).

Product differentiation expenditures create barriers to entry. Oligopolies compete with existing rivals and try to block new entry by offering a variety of models or products. For example, a few cereal makers offer more than a dozen products each, and seven of the top-selling cereals are from Kellogg.[1] Multiple products from the same brand dominate shelf space and crowd out new entrants. Worse still, supermarkets charge a "stocking fee" for shelf space needed to give the new product a chance. With the proliferation of products from the same small group of producers, retail shelf space grows scarce, blocking out potential competitors and serving as another barrier to entry. Entrenched producers may flood the market with new products in part to crowd out any new entrants. One study of 25,500 new products introduced one year found only 7 percent offered new or added benefits.[2]

MODELS OF OLIGOPOLY

Because oligopolists are interdependent, analyzing their behavior is complicated. We should not expect any one model or one approach to explain oligopoly behavior completely. At one extreme, the firms in the industry may try to coordinate their behavior so they act collectively as a single monopolist, forming a cartel, such as the Organization of Petroleum Exporting Countries (OPEC). At the other extreme, oligopolists may compete so fiercely that price fights erupt, such as those that occur among airlines, cigarettes, computer chips, and long-distance phone service.

Many theories have been developed to explain oligopoly behavior. We will study three of the better-known approaches: collusion, price leadership, and game theory. As you will see, each approach has some relevance in explaining observed behavior, although none is entirely

[1]Rankings are for 1997 sales according to the Food Marketing Policy Center at the University of Connecticut.
[2]The study was carried out by Market Intelligence Service and was reported in "Market Makers," *The Economist,* 14 March 1998.

satisfactory as a general theory of oligopoly. Thus, *there is no general theory of oligopoly but rather a set of theories, each based on the diversity of observed behavior in an interdependent market.*

Collusion and Cartels

In an oligopolistic market, there are few firms so they may try to *collude,* or agree on a price to decrease competition and increase profit. **Collusion** is an agreement among firms in the industry to divide the market and fix the price. A **cartel** is a group of firms that agree to collude so they can act as a single monopolist and earn monopoly profits. Colluding firms, compared with competing firms, usually produce less, charge higher prices, and block the entry of new firms. Cartels are more likely when the good supplied is homogeneous, like oil or steel. A cartel provides benefits to member firms—greater certainty about the behavior of "competitors," and an organized effort to block new entry—that result in increased profit. Consumers suffer from the higher prices, and potential entrants suffer from being denied the chance to compete.

Collusion and cartels are illegal in the United States, but other countries are more tolerant. Some countries even promote cartels, as with the 11 member-nations of OPEC. But if OPEC ever met in the United States, its members could be arrested for price fixing. Cartels can operate worldwide (even though they are outlawed in some countries) because there are no international laws against them. Still, monopoly profit can be so tempting that some U.S. firms break the law. For example, top executives at Archer Daniels Midland were convicted in 1998 of conspiring with four Asian competitors to rig the $650 million world market for lysine, an amino acid used in animal feed.

Suppose all firms in an industry establish a cartel. The market demand curve, *D*, appears in Exhibit 5. What price will maximize the cartel's profit, and how will production be allocated among participating firms? The first task of the cartel is to determine its marginal cost of production. Since the cartel acts as if it were a single monopoly operating many plants, the marginal cost curve in Exhibit 5 is the horizontal sum of the marginal cost curves of all firms in the cartel. The cartel's marginal cost curve intersects the market's marginal revenue curve to determine the price and output that maximize the cartel's profit. This intersection yields price *p*, industry output *Q*, and marginal cost of production *c*. Again, the profit-maximizing quantity is found where marginal revenue equals marginal cost; price is found on the demand curve at that quantity. Thus, firms in this oligopoly, like a monopolist and monopolistic competitors, have no supply curve—that is, *there is no curve that uniquely relates price and quantity supplied.*

So far, so good. To maximize cartel profit, output *Q* must be allocated among cartel members so that each firm's marginal cost equals *c*. Any other allocation would lower cartel profit. Thus, *for cartel profit to be maximized, output must be allocated so that the marginal cost for the final unit produced by each firm is identical.* Let's look at why this is easier said than done.

EXHIBIT 5

Cartel as a Monopolist

A cartel acts like a monopolist. Here, *D* is the market demand curve, *MR* the associated marginal revenue curve, and *MC* the horizontal sum of the marginal cost curves of cartel members. Cartel profits are maximized when the industry produces quantity *Q* and charges price *p*.

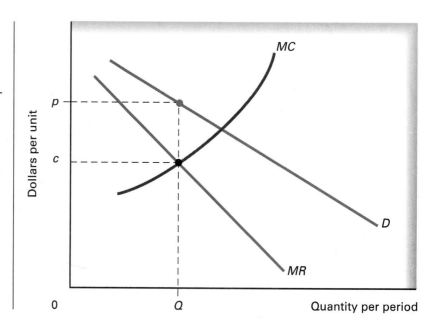

Differences in Cost. If all firms have identical cost curves, output and profit are easily allocated across firms (each firm produces the same quantity), but if costs differ, as they usually do, problems arise. The greater the differences in average cost curves across firms, the greater will be the differences in economic profits among firms. If cartel members try to equalize each firm's total profit, a high-cost firm would need to sell more than would a low-cost firm. But this allocation scheme violates the cartel's profit-maximizing condition of finding the output for each firm that results in identical marginal costs across firms. Thus, *if average cost curves differ across firms, the output allocation that maximizes cartel profit will yield unequal profit across cartel members.* If the cartel allocates less output to high-cost firms than they want, these firms could drop out of the cartel, thereby undermining it. Usually, the allocation of output is the result of haggling among cartel members. Firms that are more influential or more adept at bargaining get a larger share of output. Allocation schemes are sometimes based on geography or on the historical division of output among firms. OPEC, for example, allocates output among member-countries in proportion to their share of estimated oil reserves.

Number of Firms in the Cartel. The more firms in the industry, the more difficult it is to negotiate an acceptable allocation of output among them. Consensus becomes harder to achieve as the number of firms grows. And the more firms in the industry, the greater the chances are that one or more will become dissatisfied with the cartel and break with the agreement.

New Entry into the Industry. If a cartel cannot block the entry of new firms into the industry, new entry will eventually force prices down, squeezing economic profit and undermining the cartel. The profit of the cartel attracts entry, entry increases market supply, and increased supply forces the price down. A cartel's continued success therefore depends on barriers that block the entry of new firms.

Cheating. Perhaps the biggest obstacle to keeping the cartel running smoothly is the powerful temptation to cheat on the agreement. By offering a price slightly below the established price, a firm can usually increase its sales and economic profit. Because oligopolists usually operate with excess capacity, some cheat on the established price. Even if cartel members keep an eagle eye on each firm's price, one firm can increase sales by offering extra services, secret rebates, or other concessions. The incentive to cut prices is particularly strong when industry sales are in a slump. Typically, when production is low, so is the marginal cost of producing more output. Cartels collapse if cheating becomes widespread.

In summary: *Establishing and maintaining an effective cartel will be more difficult if (1) the product is differentiated among firms, (2) costs differ among firms, (3) there are many suppliers in the industry, (4) entry barriers are low, or (5) cheating on the agreement becomes widespread.* The problems of establishing and maintaining a cartel are reflected in the spotty history of OPEC. In 1985, the average price of oil reached $34 a barrel. After falling below that level for 15 years, the price reached that level again briefly in 2000. Many of the 11 OPEC members are poor countries that rely on oil as a major source of revenue, so they argue over the price and their market share. OPEC members also cheat on the cartel.

Like other cartels, OPEC has also experienced difficulty with new entrants. The high prices resulting from OPEC's early success back in the 1970s attracted new oil suppliers from the North Sea, Mexico, and elsewhere. Sixty percent of the world's oil supply now comes from non-OPEC countries. Most observers doubt that OPEC will ever regain its former power. Efforts to cartelize the world supply of a number of products, including bauxite, copper, and coffee, have failed so far.

<interactive>exercise

READING IT RIGHT: WALL STREET JOURNAL EXERCISE

<interactive>update

- **ECONNEWS ONLINE: AIRLINE CARTEL CRITICIZED: BEING UNITED IS UN-AMERICAN**
- **ECONNEWS ONLINE: COFFEE CARTEL**

CNN VIDEO: "CONSUMERS CREAMED BY HIGH MILK PRICES"

Price Leadership

An informal, or *tacit,* type of collusion occurs in industries that contain **price leaders,** who set the price for the rest of the industry. A dominant firm or a few firms establish the market price, and other firms in the industry follow that lead, thereby avoiding price competition. The price leader also initiates any change in the price, and others follow.

The steel industry was an example of the price-leadership form of oligopoly. Typically, U.S. Steel, the largest firm in the industry, would set the price for various products, and other firms would follow. Public pressure on U.S. Steel not to raise its price shifted the price-leadership role onto smaller producers, resulting in a rotation of leadership among firms. Although the rotating price leadership did reduce price conformity among firms in the industry, particularly during the 1970s, prices in the steel industry were still higher than they would have been without price leadership.

Like other forms of collusion, price leadership is subject to a variety of obstacles. First, the practice usually violates U.S. antitrust laws. Second, the greater the product differentiation among sellers, the less effective price leadership will be as a means of collusion. Third, there is no guarantee that other firms will follow the leader. If other firms in the industry do not follow a price increase, the leading firm must either roll back prices or risk losing sales to lower-priced competitors. Fourth, as with formal cartels, some firms will try to cheat on the agreement by cutting the price to increase sales and profits. And finally, unless there are barriers to entry, a profitable price will attract entrants into the market, which could destabilize the price-leadership agreement.

Game Theory

How will firms act when they recognize their interdependence but either cannot or do not collude? Because oligopoly involves interdependence among a few firms, we can think of interacting firms as players in a game. **Game theory** examines oligopolistic behavior as a series of strategic moves and countermoves among rival firms. It analyzes the behavior of decision makers, or players, whose choices affect one another. Game theory is not really a separate model of oligopoly but a general approach—an approach that can focus on each player's incentives to cooperate or not.

To get some feel for game theory, let's work through the **prisoner's dilemma,** the most widely examined game. The game originally considered a situation in which two thieves, let's call them Ben and Jerry, are caught near the crime scene and brought to police headquarters, where they are interrogated in separate rooms. The police believe the two are guilty but can't prove it, so they need a confession. Each thief faces a choice of confessing, thereby "squealing" on the other, or "clamming up," thereby denying any knowledge of the crime. If Ben confesses, turning state's evidence, then he is granted immunity from prosecution and goes free, while Jerry is put away for 10 years. If both clam up, each gets only a 1-year sentence on a technicality. If both confess, each gets 5 years.

What will Ben and Jerry do? The answer depends on the assumptions about their behavior—that is, what *strategy* each pursues. A **strategy** reflects a player's game plan. In this game, each player tries to save his own skin—each tries to minimize his time in jail, regardless of what happens to the other (there is no honor among thieves). Exhibit 6 shows the *payoff matrix* for the game. A **payoff matrix** is a table listing the rewards (or, in this case, the penalties) that Ben and Jerry can expect based on the strategy each pursues.

Each prisoner pursues one of two strategies—either confessing or clamming up. Ben's strategies are shown down the left margin and Jerry's across the top. The numbers in the matrix indicate the prison sentence in years for each based on the corresponding strategies. The number in red shows Ben's sentence in years and the number in blue shows Jerry's sentence. Take a moment now to see how the matrix works. Be sure to notice that the sentence each player receives depends upon the strategy he chooses *but* it also depends on the strategy the other player chooses.

What strategies are rational assuming that each player tries to minimize jail time? Put yourself in Ben's shoes. You know that Jerry, who is being questioned in another room, will either confess or clam up. Suppose Jerry confesses; the left column of Exhibit 6 shows the penalties.

EXHIBIT 6

The Prisoner's Dilemma Payoff Matrix (years in jail)

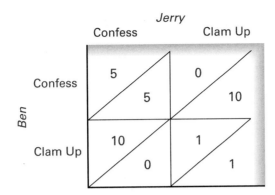

If you confess too, you both get 5 years in jail, but if you deny involvement, you get 10 years and Jerry "walks." Thus, if you think Jerry will confess, you should too.

If Jerry clams up, the right-hand column shows the two possible outcomes. If you confess, you do no time, but if you clam up too, you each get 1 year in jail. Thus, if you think Jerry will clam up, you are better off confessing. In short, whatever Jerry does, Ben is better off confessing. The same incentives hold for Jerry. He is better off confessing, regardless of what Ben does. So each has an incentive to confess and both get 5 years in jail. This is called the **dominant-strategy equilibrium** of the game because each player's strategy does not depend on what the other player does.

But notice that if each thief could just hang tough and clam up, both would be better off. After all, if both confess, each gets 5 years, but if both clam up, the police can't prove otherwise, so each gets only 1 year in jail. If each could trust the other to clam up, they both would be better off. But there is no way for the two to communicate or coordinate their actions. That's why organized crime discourages turning state's evidence by threatening to kill any "squealer"—thus, the government created the witness protection program.

Price-Setting Game. The prisoner's dilemma applies to a broad range of economic phenomena such as pricing policy and advertising strategy. For example, consider the market for gasoline in a rural community with only two gas stations, Texaco and Exxon. Here we focus on an oligopoly consisting of two sellers, or a **duopoly.** Suppose customers are indifferent about the two brands and consider only the price. Each station sets its daily price early in the morning before knowing the price set by the other. To keep it simple, suppose only two prices are possible—a low price and a high price. If both charge the low price, they split the market and each earns a profit of $500 per day. If both charge the high price, they also split the market, but profit jumps to $700 each. If one charges the high price but the other the low one, the low-price station gets most of the business, earning a profit of $1,000, leaving the high-price station with only $200.

Exhibit 7 shows the matrix of these payoffs, with Texaco's strategy down the left margin and Exxon's across the top. Texaco's profit appears in red, and Exxon's in blue. Given this payoff matrix, what price would each charge to maximize profit? Suppose you are running the Texaco station and are trying to decide what price to charge. If Exxon charges the low price, you earn $500 charging the low price but only $200 charging the high price. So your payoff is greater charging the low price. If instead Exxon charges the high price, you earn $1,000 charging the low price and $700 charging the high price. Again, you earn more charging the low price. Exxon faces the same incentives. Thus, each charges the low price, regardless of what the other does, so each earns $500 a day.

In this prisoner's dilemma, each charges the low price, earning $500 a day, although each would earn $700 charging the high price. Think of yourself as a member of the oil cartel discussed earlier, where the cartel determines the price and sets production quotas for each member. If you think other firms in the cartel will stick with their quotas, you can increase your profit by cutting your price and increasing quantity. If you think the other firms will cheat and overproduce, then you should too—otherwise, you will get your clock cleaned by those cheaters. Either way, your incentive as a cartel member is to cheat on the quota. All members

EXHIBIT 7

Price-Setting Game Payoff Matrix (profit per day)

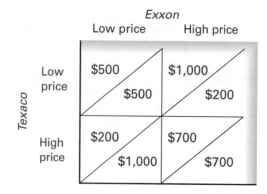

Exxon

	Low price	High price
Low price	$500 / $500	$1,000 / $200
High price	$200 / $1,000	$700 / $700

Texaco

have an incentive to cheat, although all would earn more by sticking with the agreement that maximizes joint profit.

This incentive to cut prices suggests why price wars sometimes break out among oligopolists. For example, in the summer of 1997, automakers aggressively matched and exceeded one another's price cuts, leaving cars more affordable relative to consumers' average income than they had been in the previous decade.[3] And just before a Thanksgiving weekend, a price war erupted in airfares. American Airlines first announced holiday discounts. Delta responded with cuts of up to 50 percent. Within hours, American, United, and other major carriers said they would match Delta's reductions. So go sporadic price wars.

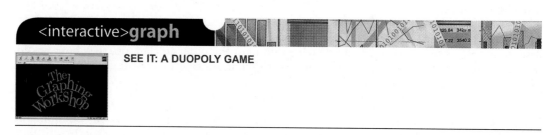

<interactive>**graph**

SEE IT: A DUOPOLY GAME

Cola War Game. As a final example of a prisoner's dilemma, consider the marketing strategies of Coke and Pepsi. Suppose each is putting together its promotional budget, not knowing the other's plans. The choice boils down to adopting either a moderate promotional budget or a big budget that involves multiple Super Bowl ads, showy in-store displays, and other efforts aimed mostly at attracting customers from the other brand. If each adopts a big budget, their costly efforts for the most part cancel each other out and keep each company's profit to $2 billion a year. If each adopts a moderate promotional budget, the money saved boosts profit for each to $3 billion a year. And if one adopts a big budget but the other does not, the heavy promoter captures a bigger market share and earns $4 billion, while the other loses market share and earns only $1 billion. What to do, what to do?

Exhibit 8 shows the payoff matrix for the two strategies, with Pepsi's budget choices listed down the left margin and Coke's across the top. In each cell of the matrix, Pepsi's profit appears in red, and Coke's in blue. Let's look at Pepsi's decision. If Coke adopts a big promotional budget, Pepsi earns $2 billion by doing the same but only $1 billion by adopting a moderate budget. Thus, if Coke adopts a big budget, so should Pepsi. If Coke adopts a moderate budget, Pepsi earns $4 billion with a big budget and $3 billion with a moderate one. Again, Pepsi earns more with a big budget. Coke faces the same incentives, so both adopt big budgets, earning $2 billion each in profit, even though both would have earned $3 billion with a moderate budget.

One-Shot Versus Repeated Games. The outcome of a game often depends on whether it is a *one-shot game* or a *repeated game*. The classic prisoner's dilemma is a one-shot game. If the game is going to be played just once, the strategy of confessing makes you better off regardless of what

[3]Keith Bradsher, "Price War Leaves Cars Positively Affordable," *New York Times,* 3 July 1997.

EXHIBIT 8

Cola War Game Payoff Matrix (annual profit in billions)

	Coke	
	Big budget	Moderate budget
Pepsi Big budget	$2 / $2	$4 / $1
Moderate budget	$1 / $4	$3 / $3

the other player does. If the game is played only once, your choice won't influence the other player's behavior.

But if the same players repeat the prisoner's dilemma, as would likely occur with the price-setting game, the cola war game, or the OPEC cartel, other possibilities unfold. In a repeated-game setting, each player has a chance to establish a reputation for cooperation and thereby can encourage the other player to do the same. After all, the cooperative solution—whether that involves clamming up, maintaining a high price, or adopting a moderate promotional budget—makes both players better off than if both fail to cooperate.

Experiments have shown that the strategy with the highest payoff in repeated games turns out to be the simplest—**tit-for-tat.** You begin by cooperating in the first round of play. On every round thereafter, you cooperate if the other player cooperated in the previous round, and you cheat if your opponent cheated in the previous round. In short, in any given round, you do whatever your opponent did in the previous round. The tit-for-tat strategy offers an immediate punishment for cheating and an immediate reward for cooperation. A player cooperates with the cartel now to encourage greater cooperation in the future. Some cartels seem to employ tit-for-tat strategies.

Our discussion has given you some idea of game theory by focusing on the prisoner's dilemma. Other games can be more complicated and involve more strategic interaction.

Each approach we have considered helps explain certain phenomena observed in oligopolistic markets. Because firms are interdependent, oligopoly gives rise to all kinds of behavior and many approaches. The *cartel,* or *collusion,* model shows why oligopolists might want to cooperate to determine market price and output; that model also explains why cartels are hard to establish and maintain. The *price-leadership* model explains why and how firms may act in unison in setting prices without actually establishing a formal cartel. Finally, *game theory,* expressed here by the prisoner's dilemma, shows how difficult a cooperative solution might be even though players benefit from cooperation. Game theory is more of an approach than a distinct model.

Comparison of Oligopoly and Perfect Competition

As we have seen, each oligopoly approach explains a piece of the oligopoly puzzle. Each has limitations, however, and none provides a full picture of oligopoly behavior. Since there is no typical, or representative, model of oligopoly, "the" oligopoly model cannot be compared with the competitive model. We might, however, imagine an experiment in which we took the many firms that populate a competitive industry and, through a series of giant mergers, combined them to form, say, four firms. We would thereby transform the industry from perfect competition to oligopoly. How would the behavior of firms in this industry differ before and after the massive merger?

Price Is Usually Higher Under Oligopoly. With fewer competitors after the merger, remaining firms would become more interdependent. Oligopoly models presented in this chapter suggest that firms may try to coordinate their pricing policies. *If oligopolists engaged in some sort of implicit or explicit collusion, industry output would be smaller and the price would be higher than under perfect competition.* Even if oligopolists did not collude but simply operated with excess capacity, the price would be higher and the quantity lower with oligopoly than with perfect competition. The price could become temporarily lower under oligopoly compared to perfect competition only if a lively price war broke out among oligopolists. In general, oligopolists' behavior will depend on whether there are barriers to entry. The lower the barriers to entry into the oligopoly, the more oligopolists will act like perfect competitors.

Higher Profits Under Oligopoly. In the long run, easy entry prevents perfect competitors from earning more than a normal profit. With oligopoly, however, there may be barriers to entry, such as economies of scale or brand names, that allow firms in the industry to earn long-run economic profit. Such barriers could be insurmountable for a new entrant. Therefore, *if there are barriers to entry into the oligopoly, we should expect profit in the long run to be higher under oligopoly than under perfect competition.* Profit rates do in fact appear to be higher in industries where a few firms account for a high proportion of industry sales. Some economists view these higher profit rates as troubling evidence of market power. But not all economists share this view. Some note that the largest firms in oligopolistic industries tend to earn the highest rate of profit. Thus, the higher profit rates observed in oligopolistic industries do not necessarily stem from market power per se. Rather, these higher profit rates stem from the greater efficiency arising from economies of scale in these large firms.[4] Many of these issues will be examined later, when we explore the government's role in regulating markets.

CONCLUSION

This chapter moved us from the extremes of perfect competition and pure monopoly to the gray area inhabited by most firms. Firms in monopolistic competition and in oligopoly face a downward-sloping demand curve for their products. In choosing the profit-maximizing price-quantity combination, a monopolistically competitive firm is not concerned much about the effects of this choice on the behavior of competitors. There are so many firms in the market that each tends to get lost in the crowd. But oligopolistic firms are interdependent, so they must consider the effects their pricing and output decisions will have on other firms. This interdependence complicates the analysis of oligopoly, supporting several possible approaches, three of which were discussed in this chapter.

The analytical results derived in this chapter are not as neat as those derived for the polar cases of perfect competition and pure monopoly, but we can still point to general conclusions, using perfect competition as a benchmark. In the long run, perfect competitors operate at minimum average cost, while the other types of firms usually operate with some excess capacity. Therefore, given identical cost curves, monopolistic competitors and oligopolists tend to charge higher prices than perfect competitors, especially in the long run. In the long run, monopolistic competitors, like perfect competitors, earn only a normal profit because entry barriers are low. But oligopolists can earn economic profit in the long run if new entry is somehow restricted. In a later chapter, we will examine government policies aimed at making industries more competitive. *Regardless of the market structure, however, profit maximization prompts firms to produce where marginal revenue equals marginal cost.*

Take the Post-Test to assess your overall understanding of the key ideas in this chapter. The Post-Test provides a comprehensive selection of exam-style questions addressing the main topics and concepts of the chapter. At the completion of each Post-Test, you will receive a score and instructive feedback on how you answered each question, and a direct link to the part of the chapter addressed in the question. Take the Post-Test as often as you need to—a record of your progress for each attempt is kept for you to revisit and gauge your improvement. And each Post-Test is randomly generated, so every attempt is new.

endofchaptermaterial

- **Summary**
- **Questions for Review**
- **Problems and Exercises**
- **Experiential Exercises**

- **Wall Street Journal Exercises**
- **Graphing Workshop: Apply It Exercises**

[4]Harold Demsetz, "Industry Structure, Market Rivalry, and Public Policy," *Journal of Law and Economics* 16 (April 1973): 1–10.

CHAPTER 11

Resource Markets

Why do surgeons earn twice as much as general practitioners? Why do truck drivers in the United States earn at least 20 times more than rickshaw drivers in India? Why do Super Bowl ads cost 15 times more than the prime-time average? Why does prime Iowa corn acreage cost more than scrubland in the Texas panhandle? Why are buildings taller in downtown Chicago than in the suburbs? To answer these and other questions, we turn to the demand and supply of resources.

You say you've been through the demand-and-supply drill already? True. But earlier we focused on the product market—that is, the market for final goods and services. Goods and services, however, are produced by resources—labor, capital, land, and entrepreneurial ability. Demand and supply in resource markets determine the price and quantity of resources. And the distribution of resource ownership determines the distribution of income throughout the economy.

Because your earnings depend on the market value of your resources, you should find resource markets particularly relevant. Certainly one factor in your career decision will be the expected income associated with alternative careers. The next three chapters will examine how demand and supply interact to establish market prices for various resources. Topics discussed in this chapter include:

- Demand and supply
  of resources

- Opportunity cost and
  economic rent

- Marginal revenue product
- Marginal resource cost
- Shifts in resource demand

ECONDEBATE ONLINE: LABOR MARKETS

- **ECONDATA ONLINE: RESOURCE MARKETS**
- **ECONDATA ONLINE: LABOR MARKETS**
- **ECONLINKS ONLINE: ECONOMICS WEB LINKS**
- **ECONNEWS ONLINE: RESOURCE MARKETS**
- **ECONNEWS ONLINE: LABOR MARKETS**

THE ONCE-OVER

Just to prove you already know a lot more about resource markets than you may think, try answering the questions that come up in the following examples of resource demand and supply.

Resource Demand

Let's begin with the demand for labor. The manager of Wal-Mart estimates that hiring another sales clerk would increase total cost by $400 per week but would increase total revenue by $500 per week. Should an additional sales clerk be hired? Sure, since Wal-Mart's profit would increase by $100 per week. *As long as the additional revenue from employing another worker exceeds the additional cost, the firm should hire that worker.*

What about capital? Suppose that you operate a lawn service during the summer, earning an average of $40 per lawn. You mow about 15 lawns a week, for total revenue of $600. You are thinking of upgrading to a larger, faster mower called the Lawn Monster, which would cost you an extra $400 per week. The bigger mower would cut your time per lawn in half, enabling you to mow 30 lawns per week, so your total revenue would double to $1,200. Should you make the switch? Since the additional revenue of $600 exceeds the additional cost of $400, you should move up to the Monster.

What about land? A neighbor offers Farmer Jones the opportunity to lease 100 acres of farmland. Jones figures that farming the extra land would cost $70 per acre but would yield $60 per acre in additional revenue. Should Jones lease the extra land? What do you think? Since the additional cost of farming that land would exceed the additional revenue, the answer is no.

These examples show that *a producer demands an additional unit of a resource as long as its marginal revenue exceeds its marginal cost.*

Resource Supply

You likely also understand the economic logic behind resource supply. Suppose you are trying to decide between two jobs that are identical except that one pays more than the other. Is there any question which job to take? If the working conditions are equally attractive, you would choose the higher-paying job. Now consider your choice between two jobs that pay the same. One job has normal nine-to-five hours, but the other starts at 5:00 A.M., an hour when your body tends to reject conscious activity. Which would you choose? You would select the job more in accord with your natural body rhythms.

Resource owners will supply their resources to the highest-paying alternative, other things assumed constant. Since other things are not always equal, resource owners must be paid more to supply their resources to certain uses. In the case of labor, the worker's utility depends on both monetary and nonmonetary aspects of the job. People must be paid more to work in jobs that are dirty, dangerous, dull, exhausting, illegal, low status, have no future, and involve inconvenient hours than to work in jobs that are clean, safe, interesting, energizing, legal, high status, have bright prospects, and involve convenient hours.

<interactive>example

NETBOOKMARK: *FORTUNE* MAGAZINE: 100 BEST EMPLOYERS

THE DEMAND AND SUPPLY OF RESOURCES

In the market for goods and services—that is, in the product market—households are the demanders and firms are suppliers. Households demand the goods and services that maximize utility, and firms supply the goods and services that maximize profit. In the resource market, roles are reversed: Firms are demanders and households are suppliers. Firms demand resources to maximize profit, and households supply resources to maximize utility. *Any differences between the profit-maximizing goals of firms and the utility-maximizing goals of households are reconciled through voluntary exchange in markets.*

Exhibit 1 presents the market for a particular resource—in this case, carpenters. As you can see, the demand curve slopes downward and the supply curve slopes upward. *Like the demand and supply for final goods and services, the demand and supply for resources depend on the willingness and ability of buyers and sellers to participate in market exchange.* This market will converge to the equilibrium wage rate, or the market price, for this type of labor.

The Market Demand for Resources

Why do firms employ resources? Resources are used to produce goods and services, which firms try to sell for a profit. A firm values not the resource itself but the resource's ability to produce goods and services. Because the value of any resource depends on the value of what it produces, the demand for a resource is said to be a **derived demand**—derived from the demand for the final product. For example, a carpenter's pay derives from the demand for the carpenter's output, such as a cabinet or a new deck; a professional baseball player's pay derives from the demand for ballgames; a truck driver's pay derives from the demand for transporting goods. The derived nature of resource demand helps explain why professional baseball players usually earn more than professional hockey players, why brain surgeons earn more

EXHIBIT 1

Resource Market for Carpenters

The intersection of the upward-sloping supply curve of carpenters with the downward-sloping demand curve determines the equilibrium wage rate, *W,* and the level of employment, *E.*

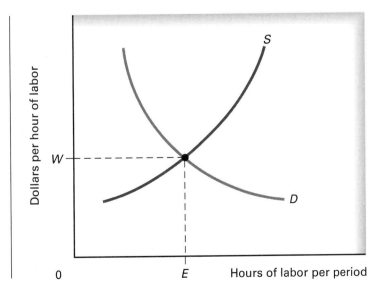

than tree surgeons, why drivers of big rigs earn more than drivers of delivery vans, and why a 30-second TV ad during the Super Bowl costs much more than one during a typical game.

The market demand for a particular resource is the sum of demands for that resource in all its different uses. For example, the market demand for carpenters adds together the demands for carpenters in residential and commercial construction, remodeling, cabinetmaking, and so on. Similarly, the market demand for the resource, timber, sums the demand for timber as lumber, railway ties, firewood, furniture, pencils, toothpicks, paper products, and so on. The demand curve for a resource, like the demand curves for the goods produced by that resource, slopes downward, as depicted in Exhibit 1.

`As the price of a resource falls, producers are more willing and able to employ that resource. Consider first the producer's greater *willingness* to hire resources as the resource price falls. In developing the demand curve for a particular resource, we assume the prices of other resources remain constant. So if the price of a particular resource falls, it becomes relatively cheaper compared with other resources the firm could use to produce the same output. Firms therefore are more willing to hire this resource rather than hire other, now relatively more costly, resources. Thus, we observe *substitution in production*—carpenters for masons, coal for oil, security alarms for security guards, and backhoes for grave diggers, as the relative prices of carpenters, coal, security alarms, and backhoes fall.

A lower price for a resource also increases a producer's *ability* to hire that resource. For example, if the wage for carpenters falls, home builders can hire more carpenters for the same total cost. The lower resource price means the firm is *more able* to buy the resource.

The Market Supply of Resources

The market supply curve for a resource sums all the individual supply curves for that resource. Resource suppliers tend to be both more *willing* and more *able* to supply the resource as its price increases, so the market supply curve slopes upward, as in Exhibit 1. Resource suppliers are more *willing* because a higher resource price, other things constant, means more goods and services can be purchased with the earnings from each unit of the resource supplied.

Resource prices are signals about the rewards for supplying resources to alternative activities. A high resource price tells the resource owner, "The market really values your resource and is willing to pay you well for what you supply." Higher prices will draw resources from lower-valued uses, including leisure. For example, as the wage rate for carpenters increases, the quantity of labor supplied will increase; some carpenters will give up leisure to work more hours.

The second reason a resource supply curve slopes upward is that resource owners are *able* to supply more of the resource at a higher price. For example, a higher carpenter's wage means more apprentices can undergo extensive training to become carpenters. The higher wage *enables* resource suppliers to increase their quantity supplied. Similarly, a higher timber price enables loggers to harvest trees in more remote regions, and a higher oil price enables drillers to explore in more inaccessible parts of the world.

Temporary and Permanent Resource Price Differences

Resource owners have a strong interest in selling their resources where they are most valued. *Resources tend to flow to their highest-valued use.* If, for example, carpenters can earn more by building homes than by making furniture, they will shift into home building until wages in the two activities are equal. Because resource owners seek the highest pay, *other things constant*, the prices paid for identical resources should tend toward equality.

For example, suppose carpenters who build homes are paid $25 per hour, which is $5 more than that earned by carpenters who make furniture. This difference is shown in Exhibit 2 by an initial wage of $25 per hour in panel (a) and a wage of $20 per hour in panel (b). This difference will encourage some carpenters to move from furniture making to home building, decreasing the wage in home building and increasing the wage in furniture making. Carpenters will move into home building until wages equalize. In Exhibit 2, supply shifts leftward for furniture making and rightward for home building until the wage is $24 in both markets. Note that 2,000 hours of labor per day move from furniture making to home building. *As long as the nonmonetary benefits of supplying resources to alternative uses are identical and as long as resources are freely mobile, resources will adjust across uses until they are paid the same rate.*

Sometimes earnings appear to differ between seemingly similar resources. For example, corporate economists on average earn more than academic economists, and land in the city costs more than land in the country. As you will now see, these differences also reflect the workings of demand and supply.

EXHIBIT 2

Market for Carpenters in Alternative Uses: Home Building and Furniture Making

Suppose the wage offered carpenters is $25 per hour in home building but only $20 per hour in furniture making. As a result of the wage differential, some carpenters will shift from furniture making to home building and continue to shift until the wage offered carpenters is identical in both uses. In panel (b), the reduction in the supply of carpenters to furniture making increases the equilibrium wage from $20 per hour to $24 per hour. In panel (a), the increase in the supply of carpenters to home building decreases the equilibrium wage from $25 per hour to $24 per hour. A total of 2,000 carpenter hours per day are shifted from furniture making to home building.

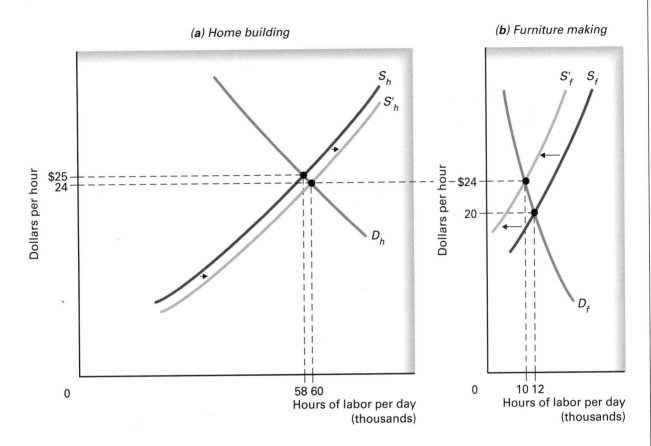

(a) Home building

(b) Furniture making

Temporary Differences in Resource Prices. Resource prices sometimes differ temporarily across markets because adjustment takes time. For example, sometimes wage differences occur among workers who appear equally qualified. As you have seen, however, a difference between the prices of similar resources prompts resource owners and firms to make adjustments that drive resource prices toward equality, as with the carpenters in Exhibit 2. The process may take years, but when resource markets are free to adjust, price differences trigger the reallocation of resources, which equalizes payments for similar resources.

Permanent Differences in Resource Prices. Not all resource price differences cause reallocation of resources. For example, land along New York's Fifth Avenue sells for as much as $36,000 a *square yard!* For that amount, you could buy several acres in Upstate New York. Yet such a difference does not prompt Upstate landowners to supply their land to New York City—obviously that's impossible. Likewise, the price of farmland varies widely, reflecting differences in the land's productivity and location. Such differences do not trigger actions that result in price equality. Similarly, certain wage differentials stem in part from the different costs of acquiring the education and training required to perform particular tasks. This difference explains why brain surgeons earn more than tree surgeons, why ophthalmologists earn more than optometrists, and why airline pilots earn more than truck drivers.

Other earning differentials reflect differences in the nonmonetary aspects of similar jobs. For example, other things constant, most people require higher pay to work in a grimy factory than in a pleasant office. Similarly, academic economists earn less than corporate economists, in part because academic economists typically have more freedom in their daily schedules, their attire, their choices of research topics, and even in their public statements.

Temporary price differences are temporary because they spark the movement of resources away from lower-paid uses and toward higher-paid uses. Permanent price differences cause no such reallocations. Permanent price differences are explained by *a lack of resource mobility* (rural land versus urban land), *differences in the inherent quality of the resource* (scrubland versus fertile land), *differences in the time and money involved in developing the necessary skills* (file clerk versus certified public accountant), and *differences in nonmonetary aspects of the job* (prison guard at San Quentin versus lifeguard at Malibu Beach).

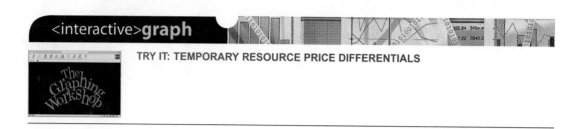

<interactive>graph

TRY IT: TEMPORARY RESOURCE PRICE DIFFERENTIALS

Opportunity Cost and Economic Rent

Shaquille O'Neal reportedly earned over $35 million in 2000, nearly half from product endorsements. But he would probably have been willing to play basketball and to endorse products for less. The question is, how much less? What is his best alternative? Suppose his best alternative is to devote his energy full time to becoming a rap artist, something he now pursues in his spare time. Suppose, as a full-time rap artist, he could earn $1 million per year, including endorsements. And suppose, aside from the pay gap, he's indifferent about rap and basketball, so the nonmonetary aspects of the two jobs balance out. Thus, he must be paid at least $1 million to remain a basketball player. This $1 million represents his opportunity cost. *Opportunity cost is what that resource could earn in its best alternative use.*

The amount O'Neal earns in excess of his opportunity cost is called *economic rent.* **Economic rent** is that portion of a resource's total earnings that is not necessary to keep the resource in its present use; it is, as the saying goes, "pure gravy." In O'Neal's case, economic rent is $35 million minus $1 million, or $34 million. Economic rent is a form of producer surplus earned by resource suppliers. The *division* of earnings between opportunity cost and economic rent depends on the resource owner's elasticity of supply. *In general, the less elastic the resource supply, the greater the economic rent as a proportion of total earnings.* To develop a feel for the difference between opportunity cost and economic rent, let's go over three cases.

Case A: All Earnings Are Economic Rent. If the supply of a resource to a particular market is perfectly inelastic, that resource has no alternative use. Thus, there is no opportunity cost, and all earnings are economic rent. For example, scrubland in the high plains of Montana has no use other than for grazing cattle. The supply of this grazing land is depicted by the red vertical line in panel (a) of Exhibit 3, which indicates that the 10 million acres have no alternative use. Since supply is fixed, the amount paid to rent this land for grazing has no effect on the quantity supplied. The land's opportunity cost is zero, so all earnings are economic rent, shown by the blue-shaded area. Here, *fixed supply determines the equilibrium quantity of the resource, but demand determines the equilibrium price.*

Case B: All Earnings Are Opportunity Costs. At the other extreme is the case in which a resource can earn as much in its best alternative use as in its present use. This situation is illustrated by the perfectly elastic supply curve in panel (b) of Exhibit 3, which shows the market for janitors in the local school system. Here, janitors earn $10 an hour to supply 1,000 hours of labor per day. If the school system paid less than $10 per hour, janitors would find jobs elsewhere, perhaps in nearby factories, where the wage is $10 per hour. The janitors earn their opportunity costs. In this case, *the horizontal supply curve determines the equilibrium wage, but demand determines the equilibrium quantity.*

Case C: Earnings Include Both Economic Rent and Opportunity Costs. If the supply curve slopes upward, most resource suppliers earn economic rent in addition to their opportunity cost. For example, if the market wage for unskilled work in your college community increases from $5 to $10 per hour, the quantity of labor supplied would increase, as would the economic rent earned by resource suppliers. This situation occurs in panel (c) of Exhibit 3, where the pink shading identifies opportunity costs and the blue shading, economic rent. If the wage

EXHIBIT 3

Opportunity Cost and Economic Rent

In panel (a), the resource supply curve is vertical, indicating that the resource has no alternative use. The price is demand determined, and all earnings are in the form of economic rent. In panel (b), the supply curve is horizontal, indicating that the resource can also earn $10 in its best alternative use. Employment is demand determined, and all earnings are opportunity costs. Panel (c) shows an upward-sloping supply curve. At the equilibrium wage of $10, resource earnings are partly opportunity costs and partly economic rent. Both supply and demand determine the equilibrium price and quantity.

(**a**) *All resource returns are economic rent*

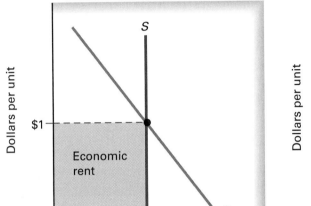

(**b**) *All resource returns are opportunity costs*

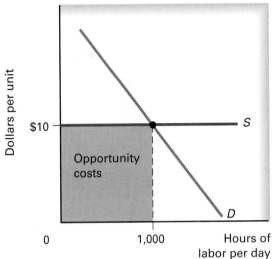

(**c**) *Resource returns are divided between economic rent and opportunity cost*

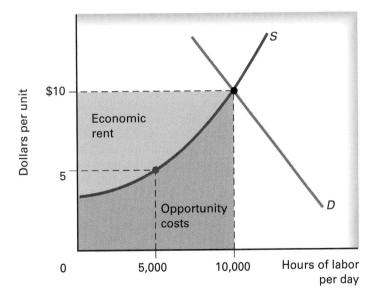

increases from $5 to $10 per hour, the quantity supplied per day will increase by 5,000 hours. For those resource suppliers who had been offering their services at a wage of $5 per hour, the difference between $5 and $10 is economic rent. These workers did not require the higher wage to supply their services, but they certainly are not going to turn it down. *In the case of an upward-sloping supply curve and a downward-sloping demand curve, both demand and supply determine equilibrium price and quantity.*

Note that specialized resources tend to earn a higher proportion of economic rent than do resources with many alternative uses. Thus, Shaquille O'Neal earns a greater *proportion* of his income as economic rent than does the janitor who cleans the Los Angeles Lakers' locker room. O'Neal would take a huge pay cut if he didn't play professional basketball, but the Lakers' janitor could probably find another semiskilled job that would pay nearly as much.

To review: Given a resource demand curve that slopes downward, when the resource supply curve is vertical (perfectly inelastic), all earnings are economic rent; when that supply curve is horizontal (perfectly elastic), all earnings are opportunity cost; and when that supply curve slopes upward (an elasticity greater than zero but less than infinity), earnings divide between economic rent and opportunity cost. Remember, *the opportunity cost of a resource is what that resource could earn in its best alternative use. Economic rent is earnings in excess of opportunity cost.*

This completes our introduction to resource supply. In the balance of this chapter, we take a closer look at the demand for resources. The determinants of the demand for a resource are largely the same whether we are talking about labor, capital, or land. The supply of different resources, however, has certain peculiarities depending on the resource, so the supply of resources will be taken up in the next two chapters.

SEE IT: OPPORTUNITY COST AND ECONOMIC RENT

ECONNEWS ONLINE: TRADE CENTER DISASTER LEAVES BUSINESSES HOMELESS

A CLOSER LOOK AT RESOURCE DEMAND

Although production usually involves many resources, we will cut the analysis down to size by focusing on a single resource, assuming that the quantities of other resources employed remain constant. As usual, we will assume that firms try to maximize profit and households try to maximize utility.

The Firm's Demand for a Resource

You may recall that when the firm's costs were first introduced, we considered a moving company, where labor was the only variable resource in the short run. By varying the amount of labor employed, we examined the relationship between the quantity of labor and the amount of furniture moved per day. We use the same approach in Exhibit 4, where all but one of the firm's inputs remain constant. Column (1) in the table lists possible employment levels of the variable resource, here measured as workers per day. Column (2) lists the total output, or total product, and column (3) lists the marginal product. The *marginal product* of labor is the change in total product from employing one more unit of labor.

When one worker is employed, total product is 10 units and so is the marginal product. The marginal product of adding the second worker is 9 units. As the firm hires more workers, the marginal product of labor declines, reflecting the law of diminishing marginal returns. Notice in this example that diminishing marginal returns set in immediately—that is, right after the first worker.

Although labor is the variable resource here, we could examine the marginal product of any resource. For example, we could consider how many lawns could be cut per week by varying the quantity of capital employed. We might start off with very little capital—imagine cutting grass with a pair of scissors—and then move up to a push mower, a power mower, and the Lawn Monster. By holding labor constant and varying the quantity of capital employed, we could compute the marginal product of capital. Likewise, we could compute the marginal product of land by examining crop production for varying amounts of land, holding other inputs constant.

Marginal Revenue Product

The important question is, what happens to the firm's *revenue* when additional workers are hired? The first three columns of Exhibit 4 show output as the firm hires more workers. The *marginal revenue product* of labor indicates how much total revenue changes as more labor is

EXHIBIT 4

Marginal Revenue Product When a Firm Sells as a Price Taker

(1) Workers per day	(2) Total Product	(3) Marginal Product	(4) Product Price	(5) Total Revenue (5) = (2) × (4)	(6) Marginal Revenue Product (6) = (3) × (4)
0	0	—	$20	$ 0	—
1	10	10	20	200	$200
2	19	9	20	380	180
3	27	8	20	540	160
4	34	7	20	680	140
5	40	6	20	800	120
6	45	5	20	900	100
7	49	4	20	980	80
8	52	3	20	1040	60
9	54	2	20	1080	40
10	55	1	20	1100	20
11	55	0	20	1100	0
12	53	−2	20	1060	−40

employed, other things constant. The **marginal revenue product** of any resource is the change in the firm's total revenue resulting from employing an additional unit of the resource, other things constant. You could think of the marginal revenue product as the firm's "marginal benefit" from hiring one more unit of the resource. A resource's marginal revenue product depends on how much additional output the resource produces and the price at which output is sold.

Selling Output as a Price Taker. The calculation of marginal revenue product is simplest when the firm sells output in a perfectly competitive market, which is the assumption underlying Exhibit 4. Since an individual firm in perfect competition can sell as much as it wants at the market price, a perfectly competitive firm is a *price taker.* That firm must accept, or "take," the market price for its product. The marginal revenue product, listed in column (6), is the change in total revenue that results from changing input usage by one unit. For the perfectly competitive firm, the marginal revenue product is simply the marginal product of the resource multiplied by the product price of $20. Notice that because of diminishing returns, the marginal revenue product falls steadily as the firm employs additional units of the resource.

Selling Output as a Price Maker. If the firm has some market power in the product market—that is, some ability to set the price—the demand curve for that firm's output slopes downward. To sell more output, the firm must lower its price. The firm, consequently, must search for the price that maximizes profit. Such a firm is called a *price maker.* Exhibit 5 reproduces the first two columns of Exhibit 4. Column (3) shows the price at which that total output can be sold. Total output multiplied by the price yields the firm's total revenue, which appears in column (4).

The marginal revenue product of labor, which is the change in total revenue resulting from a 1-unit change in the quantity of labor employed, appears in column (5). For example, the first worker produced 10 units per day, which sell for $40 each, yielding total revenue of $400. Hiring the second worker adds 9 more units to the total product, but to sell 9 more units, the firm must lower the price of all units from $40 to $35.20. Total revenue increases to $668.80, which means the marginal revenue product from hiring a second worker is $268.80.

EXHIBIT 5

The Marginal Revenue Product When a Firm Sells as a Price Maker

(1) Workers per day	(2) Total Product	(3) Product Price	(4) Total Revenue (4) = (2) × (3)	(5) Marginal Revenue Product
0	0	—	—	—
1	10	$40.00	$400.00	$400.00
2	19	35.20	668.80	268.80
3	27	31.40	847.80	179.00
4	34	27.80	945.20	97.40
5	40	25.00	1000.00	54.80
6	45	22.50	1012.50	12.50
7	49	20.50	1004.50	−8.00
8	52	19.00	988.00	−16.50
9	54	18.00	972.00	−16.00
10	55	17.50	962.50	−9.50
11	55	17.50	962.50	0.00

Again, *the marginal revenue product is the additional revenue that results from employing each additional worker.* The profit-maximizing firm should be willing and able to pay as much as the marginal revenue product for an additional unit of the resource; thus, *the marginal revenue product curve can be thought of as the firm's demand curve for that resource.* You could think of the marginal revenue product curve as the marginal benefit to the firm of hiring each additional unit of the resource.

To review: Whether a firm is a price taker or a price maker, the marginal revenue product of a resource is the change in total revenue resulting from a one-unit change in that resource, other things constant. The marginal revenue product curve of a resource is the demand curve for that resource—it shows the most a firm would be willing and able to pay for each successive unit of the resource. *For a price taker, the marginal revenue product curve slopes downward only because of diminishing marginal returns. For a price maker, the marginal revenue product curve slopes downward both because of diminishing marginal returns and because additional output can be sold only if the price falls.* For both price takers and price makers, the marginal revenue product is the change in total revenue resulting from hiring an additional unit of the resource.

<interactive>update
ECONNEWS ONLINE: TIGER KING OF APPEARANCE FEES AND PRIZE MONEY

<interactive>video
ASK THE INSTRUCTOR: HOW WOULD A ZERO-RADIUS LAWN MOWER AFFECT YOUR PRODUCTIVITY?

Marginal Resource Cost

Given the firm's marginal revenue product, can we determine how much labor the firm should employ to maximize profit? Not yet, because we must also know how much labor costs the firm. Specifically, what is the **marginal resource cost**—that is, what is the additional cost to the firm of employing one more unit of labor? The typical firm hires such a tiny fraction of the available resource that its employment decision has no effect on the market price of the resource. Thus, each firm usually faces a given market price for the resource and decides only on how much to hire at that price.

For example, panel (a) of Exhibit 6 shows the market for factory workers, measured as workers per day. The intersection of market demand and supply determines the market wage of $100 dollars per day. Panel (b) shows the situation for the firm. The market wage becomes the marginal resource cost of labor to the firm regardless of how many workers that firm employs. The *marginal resource cost* curve is shown by the horizontal line drawn at the $100 level in panel (b); this is the labor supply curve to the firm. Panel (b) also shows the marginal revenue product curve, or resource demand curve, based on the schedule presented in Exhibit 4, where the firm was a price taker. The marginal revenue product curve indicates the additional revenue the firm receives as a result of employing each additional unit of labor.

Given a marginal resource cost of $100 per worker per day, how much labor will the firm employ to maximize profit? *The firm will hire more labor as long as doing so adds more to revenue than to cost—that is, as long as the marginal revenue product exceeds the marginal resource cost. The firm will stop hiring labor only when the two are equal.* If marginal resource cost is a constant $100 per worker, the firm will hire six workers per day because the marginal revenue product from hiring a sixth worker equals $100. Thus, the firm hires additional resources up to the level at which

$$\text{Marginal revenue product (MRP)} = \text{Marginal resource cost (MRC)}$$

This equality holds for all resources employed, whether the firm sells output as a price taker or as a price maker. Profit maximization occurs where labor's marginal revenue product equals the market wage (assuming the supply of labor to the firm is perfectly elastic). Based on data presented so far, we can't yet determine the firm's actual profit because we don't yet know the firm's other costs. We do know, however, that in Exhibit 6, a seventh worker would add $100 to cost but would add less than that to revenue, so hiring a seventh worker would reduce the firm's profit (or increase its loss).

EXHIBIT 6

Market Equilibrium for a Resource and the Firm's Employment Decision

Market demand and supply determine the equilibrium price and quantity. Given the market price of the resource, the individual firm employs as much as it wants at that price, so the market price is the firm's marginal resource cost. The firm's demand curve for the resource is based on that resource's marginal revenue product. The firm maximizes profit by hiring up to the point where the marginal revenue product equals the marginal resource cost.

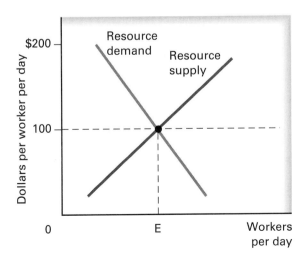

(a) Market

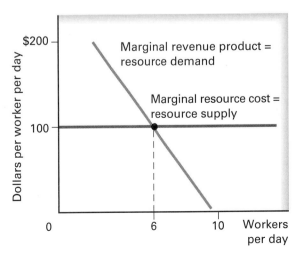

(b) Firm

Whether the firm sells output as a price taker or as a price maker, the profit-maximizing level of employment occurs where the marginal revenue product of labor equals its marginal resource cost. Similarly, profit-maximizing employment of other resources, such as land and capital, occurs where their respective marginal revenue products equal their marginal resource costs. Each resource must "pull its own weight"—it must yield additional revenue that at least equals the additional cost.

In an earlier chapter, we developed a rule for determining the profit-maximizing level of output. Maximum profit (or minimum loss) occurs where the marginal revenue from *output* equals its marginal cost. Likewise, maximum profit (or minimum loss) occurs at the resource level where the marginal revenue from an *input* equals its marginal resource cost. Although the first rule focuses on output and the second on input, the two approaches are equivalent ways of deriving the same principle of profit maximization. For example, in Exhibit 6, the firm maximizes profit by hiring six workers when the wage is $100 per day. Details of production from Exhibit 4 indicate that a sixth worker adds five units to output, which sell for $20 each, yielding labor's marginal revenue product of $100. The marginal revenue of that output is the change in total revenue from selling another unit of output, which is $20. The marginal cost of that output is the change in total cost, $100, divided by the change in output, five units; so the marginal cost of output is $100/5, or $20. Thus, *in equilibrium, the marginal revenue of output equals its marginal cost.*

Now that you have some idea of how to derive the demand for a resource, let's discuss what could shift resource demand.

<interactive>update

- ECONNEWS ONLINE: THE RISE AND FALL OF ECONOMISTS
- ECONNEWS ONLINE: BRITISH EMPLOYERS CAST A NET FOR SOCIAL WORKERS

<interactive>video

CNN VIDEO: "UNITED KINGDOM BUTCHER'S SHOPS CHOP EMPLOYEES"

Shifts in the Demand for Resources

As we have seen, a resource's marginal revenue product consists of two components: the resource's marginal product and the price at which that product is sold. Two factors can change a resource's marginal product: a change in the amount of other resources employed and a change in technology. One factor can change the price of the product: a change in demand for the product. Let's first consider changes that could affect marginal product, then changes that could affect demand for the product.

Change in the Price of Other Resources. Although our analysis so far has focused on a single input, in reality the marginal product of any resource depends on the quantity and quality of other resources used in production. Sometimes resources are *substitutes*. For example, coal substitutes for oil in generating electricity. And automatic teller machines substitute for tellers in handling bank transactions. If two resources are **substitutes,** an increase in the price of one increases the demand for the other. An increase in the price of oil increases the demand for coal, and an increase in the wage of tellers increases the demand for ATMs.

Sometimes resources are *complements*—trucks and truck drivers, for example. If two resources are **complements,** a decrease in the price of one leads to an increase in the demand for the other. If the price of tractor-trailers decreases, the quantity demanded increases, which increases the demand for truck drivers. More generally, any increase in the quantity and quality of a complementary resource, such as trucks, boosts the marginal productivity of the resource in question, such as truck drivers, and so increases the demand for that resource. A bigger and better truck makes the driver more productive. Part of the reason a truck driver in the United States earns much more than a rickshaw driver in India is the truck.

Changes in Technology. *Technological improvements can boost the productivity of some resources but can make others obsolete.* The development of computer-controlled machines increased the demand for computer-trained machinists but decreased the demand for machinists without computer skills. The development of synthetic fibers, such as rayon and Orlon, increased the demand for acrylics and polyesters but reduced the demand for natural fibers, such as cotton and wool.

Breakthroughs in fiber-optic and satellite communication increased the demand for fiberglass and satellites and reduced the demand for copper wire.

Computer programs are changing job prospects in fields such as law, medicine, accounting, and computer programming. For example, the software WillMaker has written more wills than any lawyer alive. In medicine, software called Iliad can, in response to a series of questions, help diagnose 1,200 diseases and 5,600 disease manifestations. In accounting, programs like TurboTax and Quicken reduce the demand for CPAs. And in computer programming, Web page construction is now as easy as other forms of desktop publishing with programs like Fusion, Texture, and FrontPage. As software and hardware get cheaper, better, and more accessible, the demand for some professional skills will decline.

Changes in the Demand for the Final Product. Because the demand for a resource is derived from the demand for the final output, any change in the demand for output affects resource demand. For example, an increase in the demand for automobiles increases their market price and thereby increases the marginal revenue product of autoworkers. Let's look at the derived demand for architects in the following case study.

\<interactive\>**graph**

- TRY IT: DEMAND AND SUPPLY OF LABOR IN THE NATIONAL BASKETBALL ASSOCIATION (NBA)
- TRY IT: THE BANK TELLER AND THE AUTOMATED TELLER

CASE**STUDY**	The Derived Demand for Architects
	● *The World of Business*

The big drop in real estate prices, particularly for commercial buildings, that occurred in the late 1980s and early 1990s cut demand for new construction, thus reducing the demand for resources used in construction, such as builders and architects. Look at what happened to the demand for architects. In New York City, the number of classified ads for architectural positions declined from 5,000 in 1987 to 500 in 1991. Similar drops occurred in other major cities. Employment at one national architectural firm shrank from 1,600 to 700 between 1988 and 1992.

Among entry-level architects, job losses were compounded by improving technology. Drafting jobs long represented the traditional entry-level positions for new architects, but computer-assisted design (CAD) software coupled with cheaper and more powerful computers reduced the demand for new architects. Programs such as Auto-Architect and 3D Manager help configure all aspects of a structure and create plans that can be manipulated in three-dimensional space, something impossible with traditional drawings. Design software such as Home Design 3D and 3D Home Architect help amateurs as well as professionals and offer accompanying Web sites and online help. Whereas construction-grade blueprints drafted by an architect cost about $550 a set, do-it-yourself CDs sell for $40 to $70. Thus, software substitutes for entry-level architectural positions.

The declining demand for architects had a predictable effect on the demand for higher education, which itself is a derived demand. Enrollment in undergraduate architecture classes declined as entry-level positions disappeared. Enrollment in graduate courses, however, remained relatively stable. Apparently, many out-of-work architects decided to pursue graduate study, since the poor job market reduced their opportunity cost of time.

The exception that proves the rule about derived demand is that those architectural firms that specialize in the health-care industry flourished as health care became the fastest-growing sector of the economy.

\<interactive\>**exercise**

eACTIVITY: THE DERIVED DEMAND FOR ARCHITECTS

Sources: Tracie Rozhou, "At Hospitals, Construction Is Regaining Its Health," *New York Times,* 7 July 1997; D. W. Dunlap, "Recession Is Ravaging Architects' Firms," *New York Times,* 17 May 1992; Leslie Miller, "Net Might Free Architects from Reality," *USA Today,* 23 November 1999; Steven Ross, "Will Amateur CAD Put Residential Architects Out of Business?" *Architectural Record* (April 1994); and http://www3.autodesk.com/. The employment outlook for architects can be found at http://stats.bls.gov/oco/ocos038.htm.

In summary: The demand for a resource depends on its marginal revenue product, which is the change in total revenue resulting from employing one more unit of the resource. Any change that increases a resource's marginal revenue product will increase resource demand.

The Optimal Use of More Than One Resource

As long as the marginal revenue product exceeds the marginal resource cost, the firm can increase profit or reduce a loss by employing more of a resource. Again, the firm will increase resource use until the marginal revenue product just equals the marginal resource cost. This holds for each resource employed. Profit-maximizing employers will hire each resource up to the point at which the last unit hired adds as much to revenue as it does to cost.

The beginning of the chapter asked why buildings at the center of Chicago are taller than those farther from the center. Land and capital, to a large extent, substitute in the production of building space. Since land is more expensive at the center of the city, builders there substitute additional capital for land, building up instead of out. Hence, buildings are taller when they are closer to the center of the city and are tallest in cities where land is most expensive. Buildings in Chicago and New York City are taller than those in Salt Lake City and Tucson, for example.

The high price of land in metropolitan areas has other implications for the efficient employment of resources. For example, on New York City sidewalks, as in many large cities, vending carts specialize in everything from hot dogs to ice cream. Why are there about 4,100 licensed pushcarts in New York City? Consider the resources used to supply hot dogs: land, labor, capital, entrepreneurial ability, plus intermediate goods such as hot dogs, buns, and other ingredients. Which of these do you suppose is most expensive in New York City? Retail space along Madison Avenue rents for an average of $550 a year per square foot. Since operating a hot dog cart requires about four square yards, it could cost as much as $20,000 a year to rent the required commercial space. Aside from the necessary public permits, however, space on the public sidewalk is free to vendors. Profit-maximizing street vendors substitute public sidewalk space, which is free to them, for costly commercial space.

Government policy can affect resource allocation in other ways, as discussed in this closing case study.

CASE**STUDY**	The McMinimum Wage
	● *Public Policy*

In March 2000, Congress sent to the president a measure to increase the minimum wage by $1.00 to $6.15 over two years; the legislation was vetoed because it was tied to a tax cut for businesses. Ever since a federal minimum wage of 25 cents was established in 1938, economists have debated the benefits and costs of the law. The federal law initially covered only 43 percent of the workforce—primarily workers in large firms involved in interstate commerce. Over the years, the minimum wage has been raised and the coverage has been broadened; by 2000, coverage doubled to about 86 percent of the workforce (groups still not covered include domestic workers and those in small retail establishments and small restaurants).

When the 2000 legislation was vetoed, about 7 percent of the workforce earned between $5.15 and $6.15 an hour and thus could be affected by an increase. This group included mostly young workers, the majority working part time, primarily in service and sales occupations. For example, while 8 of 10 working teenagers earned less than a dollar above the minimum wage, fewer than 1 in 10 workers in their mid-40s earned that little. Ten states and the District of Columbia have a higher minimum wage than the federal level. And about 60 municipalities across the country have adopted so-called living-wage laws that exceed federal and state minimums. For example, Santa Monica, California's, living wage exceeds $10 an hour. (By way of comparison, the minimum wage in Mexico is less than $5 *a day*.)

Advocates of minimum-wage legislation argue that an appropriately applied minimum wage can increase the income of the poorest workers at little or no cost to overall employment. Critics argue that a minimum wage set above the market-clearing level causes employers either to cut nonwage compensation or to scale back employment.

There have been over 40 U.S. studies published since 1970 examining the effect of changes in the minimum wage on employment. A few found a small positive effect of the minimum wage on employment, but most found either no effect or a negative effect, particularly among teenage workers. One reason an increase in the minimum wage may not always have the expected negative effect on total employment is that employers often react to a wage increase by substituting part-time jobs for full-time jobs, by substituting more-qualified minimum-wage workers (such as college students) for less-qualified workers (such as high school dropouts), and by adjusting some nonwage features of the job to reduce costs or increase worker productivity.

Here are some of the nonwage job components that an employer could alter in response to a higher minimum wage: the convenience of work hours, expected work effort, on-the-job training, time allowed for meals and breaks, wage premiums for night shifts and weekends, vacation days, paid holidays, sick leave policy, health-care benefits, tolerance for tardiness, parking provisions, air conditioning, dress code, and so on. For example, William Alpert of the University of Connecticut found that restaurants responded to a higher minimum wage by reducing expenditures on fringe benefits, particularly vacation time and shift premiums.

Of most concern to economists is a possible reduction in on-the-job training of young workers, especially those with little education. A higher minimum wage also raises the opportunity cost of staying in school. According to one study, an increase in the minimum wage encouraged some 16- to 19-year-olds to quit school and look for work, though many failed to find jobs. And those who had already left school were more likely to become unemployed because of a higher minimum wage. Thus, an increase in the minimum wage may have the unintended consequence of cutting school enrollment.

Robert Whaples of Wake Forest University surveyed 193 labor economists and found that 87 percent believed "a minimum wage increases unemployment among young and unskilled workers." Minimum-wage increases, however, have broad public support. According to one recent poll, the highest support, 81 percent, came from those aged 18 to 29, the group most likely to be affected by a hike in the minimum wage. The typical college student has a part-time job that pays the minimum wage or close to it. An increase in the minimum wage would benefit college students more than high school dropouts. The unemployment rate is typically twice as high for high school dropouts as for college students.

\<interactive\>exercise

- eACTIVITY: THE McMINIMUM WAGE
- READING IT RIGHT: WALL STREET JOURNAL EXERCISE
- ECONDEBATE ONLINE: DOES AN INCREASE IN THE MINIMUM WAGE RESULT IN A HIGHER UNEMPLOYMENT RATE?

Sources: Michael Wartzman, "How the Minimum Wage Lost Its Status as a Tool of Social Progress in the U.S.," *Wall Street Journal,* 19 July 2001; Robert Whaples, "Is There Consensus Among American Labor Economists? Survey Results of Forty Propositions," *Journal of Labor Research* 27 (Fall 1996): 725–734; "Review Symposium: Myth and Measurement: The New Economics of the Minimum Wage," *Industrial and Labor Relations Review* 48 (July 1995): 827–849; William Alpert, *The Minimum Wage in the Restaurant Industry* (New York: Praeger, 1986); and William Carrington and Bruce Fallick, "Do Some Workers Have Minimum Wage Careers?" *Monthly Labor Review* (May 2001): 7–26, which can also be found online at http://www.bls.gov/opub/mlr/mlrhome.htm.

CONCLUSION

The framework we have developed focuses on the marginal analysis of resource use to determine equilibrium price and quantity. The firm uses each resource until the marginal revenue product of that resource equals its marginal cost. The objective of profit maximization ensures that to produce any given level of output, firms will employ the least-cost combination of resources and thereby will use the economy's resources most efficiently. Although our focus has been on the marginal productivity of each resource, we should keep in mind that resources combine to produce output, so the marginal productivity of a particular resource depends in part on what other resources are employed.

endofchaptermaterial

- **Summary**
- **Questions for Review**
- **Problems and Exercises**
- **Experiential Exercises**
- **Wall Street Journal Exercise**

Take the Post-Test to assess your overall understanding of the key ideas in this chapter. The Post-Test provides a comprehensive selection of exam-style questions addressing the main topics and concepts of the chapter. At the completion of each Post-Test, you will receive a score and instructive feedback on how you answered each question, and a direct link to the part of the chapter addressed in the question. Take the Post-Test as often as you need to—a record of your progress for each attempt is kept for you to revisit and gauge your improvement. And each Post-Test is randomly generated, so every attempt is new.

Post-Test

12

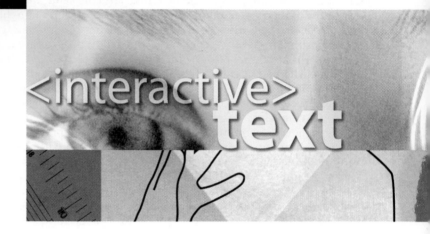

Labor Markets and Labor Unions

How do you divide your time between work and leisure? Why do some people work *less* when the wage increases? For example, why do unknown rock groups spend hours playing for peanuts, while famous bands play much less for much more? What factors, other than the wage, affect your labor supply? And what determines the wage structure in the economy? You don't need a course in economics to figure out why corporate presidents earn more than file clerks, or why heart surgeons earn more than registered nurses. But why do lawyers earn more than accountants and schoolteachers earn more than truck drivers? You can be sure of one thing: demand and supply play a central role in the wage structure. In this chapter, we dig deeper into wage determination.

You have already examined the demand for resources. Demand depends on a resource's marginal productivity. In the first half of this chapter, we focus on the supply of labor and then bring demand and supply together to arrive at the market wage. In the latter part of the chapter, we consider the role that labor unions play in labor markets. We examine the economic effects of unions and review recent trends in union membership. Topics discussed in this chapter include:

- Theory of time allocation
- Backward-bending supply curve for labor
- Nonwage factors in labor supply
- Why wages differ

- Unions and collective bargaining
- Union wages and employment
- Recent trends in union membership

Pre-Test

Take the Pre-Test to assess your initial knowledge of the key ideas in this chapter. The Pre-Test provides exam-style questions addressing the main topics and concepts of the chapter. At the completion of each Pre-Test, you will receive a score and instructive feedback on how you answered each question, and a direct link to the part of the chapter addressed in the question. Take the Pre-Test as often as you need to—a record of your progress for each attempt is kept for you to revisit and gauge your improvement.

<interactive>exercise

ECONDEBATE ONLINE: LABOR MARKETS

<interactive>update

- ECONDATA ONLINE: LABOR MARKETS
- ECONLINKS ONLINE: ECONOMICS WEB LINKS
- ECONNEWS ONLINE: LABOR MARKETS

LABOR SUPPLY

As a resource supplier, you have a labor supply curve for each of the many possible uses of your labor. To some markets, your quantity supplied is zero over the realistic range of wages. The qualifier "over the realistic range" is added because, for a high enough wage (say, $1 million per hour), you might supply labor to just about *any* activity. In most labor markets, your quantity supplied may be zero either because you are *willing* but *unable* to perform the job (airline pilot, professional golfer, novelist) or because you are *able* but *unwilling* to do so (soldier of fortune, prison guard, P.E. instructor).

So you have as many supply curves as there are labor markets, just as you have as many demand curves as there are markets for goods and services. Your labor supply to each market depends, among other things, on your abilities, your taste for the job in question, and the opportunity cost of your time. Your supply to a particular labor market assumes that wages in other markets are constant, just as your demand for a particular product assumes that other prices are constant.

Labor Supply and Utility Maximization

Recall the definition of economics: *the study of how people use their scarce resources in an attempt to satisfy their unlimited wants*. That is, individuals attempt to use their scarce resources to maximize their utility. Two sources of utility are of special interest to us in this chapter: the consumption of goods and services and the enjoyment of leisure. The utility derived from consuming goods and services is obvious and serves as the foundation for consumer demand. Another valuable source of utility is leisure—time spent relaxing, sleeping, eating, and in recreational activities. Leisure is a normal good that, like other goods, is subject to the law of diminishing marginal utility. Thus, the more leisure time you have, the less you value an additional hour of it. Sometimes you may have so much leisure that you "have time on your hands" and are "just killing time." As that sage of the comic page Garfield the cat once lamented, "Spare time would be more fun if I had less to spare." Or as Shakespeare wrote, "If all the year were playing holidays, to sport would be as tedious as to work." Leisure's diminishing marginal utility explains why some of the so-called idle rich grow bored in their idleness.

Three Uses of Time. Some of you are at a point in your careers when you have few resources other than time. Time is the raw material of life. You can use your time in three ways. First, you can undertake **market work**—selling your time in the labor market in return for income. When you supply labor, you usually surrender control of your time to the employer in return for a wage. Second, you can undertake **nonmarket work**—using time to produce your own goods and services. Nonmarket work includes the time you spend doing your laundry, making a sandwich, or cleaning up after yourself. Nonmarket work also includes the time spent acquiring skills and education to enhance your productivity. Although studying and attending class may provide little immediate payoff, you are betting that the knowledge and perspective so gained will enrich your future. Third, you can spend time as **leisure**—using your time in non-work pursuits.

Work and Utility. Unless you are one of the fortunate few, work is not a pure source of utility, as it often generates some boredom, discomfort, and aggravation. In short, time spent working can be "a real pain," a source of *disutility*—the opposite of utility. And work is subject to increasing marginal disutility—the more you work, the greater the marginal disutility of working another hour. You work nonetheless, because your earnings buy goods and services. You expect the utility from these products to more than offset the disutility of work. Thus, the *net utility of work*—the utility of the consumption made possible through work minus the disutility of the work itself—usually makes some amount of work an attractive use of your time. In the case of market work, your income buys goods and services. In the case of nonmarket work, either you produce goods and services directly, as in making yourself a tuna sandwich, or you invest your time in education with an expectation of higher future earnings and higher future consumption. The additional utility you expect from the tuna sandwich and higher future consumption possibilities resulting from education are the marginal benefits of nonmarket work.

Utility Maximization. Within the limits of a 24-hour day, seven days a week, you balance your time among market work, nonmarket work, and leisure to maximize utility. As a rational consumer, *you attempt to maximize utility by allocating your time so that the expected marginal utility of the last unit of time spent in each activity is identical.* Thus, in the course of a week or a month, the expected marginal utility of the last hour of leisure equals the expected net marginal utility of the last hour of market work, which equals the expected net marginal utility of the last hour of non-market work. In the case of time devoted to acquiring more human capital, you must consider the marginal utility expected from the future increase in earnings that will result from your enhanced productivity.

Perhaps at this point you are saying, "Wait a minute. I don't know what you're talking about. I don't allocate my time like that. I just sort of bump along, doing what feels good." Economists do not claim that you are even aware of making these marginal calculations. But as a rational decision maker, you allocate your scarce time trying to satisfy your unlimited wants, or trying to maximize utility. And utility maximization, or "doing what feels good," implies that you act *as if* you allocated your time to derive the same expected net marginal utility from the last unit of time spent in each alternative use.

You probably have settled into a rough plan for meals, work, entertainment, study, sleep, and so on—a plan that fits your overall objectives and seems reasonable. This plan is probably in constant flux as you make expected and unexpected adjustments in your use of time. For example, last weekend you may have failed to crack a book, despite good intentions. This morning you may have slept later than you planned because you were up late last night. Over a week or a month, however, your use of time is roughly in line with an allocation that maximizes utility as you perceive it at the time. Put another way, if you could change your use of time to increase your utility, you would do so. Nobody's stopping you! You may emphasize immediate gratification over long-term goals, but that's your choice and you bear the consequences. *This time-allocation process ensures that at the margin, the expected net utilities from the last unit of time spent in each activity are equal.*

Because information is costly and because the future is uncertain, you sometimes make mistakes; you don't always get what you expect. Some mistakes are minor, such as going to a movie that turns out to be a waste of time. But other mistakes can be costly. For example, you may now be studying for a field that will grow crowded by the time you graduate, or you may be acquiring skills that will be made obsolete by new software.

Implications. The theory of time allocation described thus far has several implications for individual choice. First, consider the choices of market work, nonmarket work, and leisure. The higher your market wage, other things constant, the higher your opportunity cost of leisure and nonmarket work. For example, individuals with a high market wage will spend less time on nonmarket work, other things constant. Surgeons are less likely to mow their lawns than are butchers. And among those earning the same market wage, people who are handy around the house and are good cooks—á la Martha Stewart—will do more for themselves. Conversely, those who are all thumbs around the house and have trouble boiling water will hire more household services and eat out more frequently.

By the same logic, the higher the expected earnings right out of high school, other things constant, the higher the opportunity cost of attending college. Most young, successful movie stars do not attend college. Some, such as Tom Cruise, are high school dropouts. And the most promising athletes "turn pro" right after high school or before completing college. Top players who never attended college include Ken Griffey Jr. and Mark McGwire in baseball, Kobe Bryant and Kevin Garnett in basketball, Mario Lemieux and Wayne Gretzky in hockey, as well as most top tennis players. But the vast majority of people, including female basketball stars, do not face such a high opportunity cost of higher education. As one poor soul explained, "Since my wife left me, my kids joined a cult, my job is history, and my dog died, I think now might be a good time to go back for my MBA."

Wages and Individual Labor Supply

To breathe life into the time-allocation problem, consider your choices for the summer. If you can afford to, you can take the summer off, spending it entirely on leisure, perhaps as a fitting reward for a rough academic year. Or you can supply your time to market work. Or you can undertake nonmarket work, such as cleaning the garage or attending summer school. As a rational decision maker, you will select the combination of leisure, market work, and nonmarket work that you expect will maximize your utility. And the optimal combination is likely to involve allocating some time to each activity. For example, even if you work during the summer, you might still consider taking one or two summer courses.

Suppose the only summer job available is some form of unskilled labor, such as working in a fast-food restaurant or for the municipal parks department. For simplicity, let's assume that you view all such jobs as equally attractive (or unattractive) in terms of their nonmonetary aspects, such as working conditions, working hours, and so on. (These nonmonetary aspects are discussed in the next section.) If there is no difference among these unskilled jobs, the most important question for you in deciding how much market labor to supply is: What is the market wage?

Suppose the wage is $6 per hour. Rather than working at a wage that low, you might decide to work around the house, attend summer school full time, take a really long nap, travel across the country to find yourself, or perhaps do some combination of these. In any case, you supply no market labor at such a low wage. The market wage must rise to $7 before you supply any market labor. Suppose at a wage of $7, you supply 20 hours per week, perhaps taking fewer summer courses and shorter naps.

As the wage increases, your opportunity cost of time spent in other activities rises, so you substitute market work for other uses of your time. You decide to work 30 hours per week at a wage of $8 per hour, 40 hours at $9, 48 hours at $10, and 55 hours at $11. At a wage of $12 you go to 60 hours per week; you are starting to earn serious money—$720 a week.

If the wage hits $13 per hour, you decide to cut back to 58 hours per week. Despite the cutback, your pay rises to $754 a week, which is more than when the wage was $12. Finally, if the wage hits $14, you cut back to 55 per week and earn $770. To explain why you may eventually reduce the quantity of labor supplied, let's consider the impact of wage increases on your allocation of time.

Substitution and Income Effects. An increase in the wage affects your choice between market work and other uses of your time in two ways. First, a higher wage provides you with an incentive to work more, since each hour of work now buys more goods and services. As the wage increases, the opportunity cost of other uses of your time, such as leisure, also increases. Thus, as the wage increases, you substitute market work for other activities; this is the **substitution effect of a wage increase.** But a higher wage means a higher income for the same number of hours, and a higher income means that you demand more of all normal goods. Since leisure is a normal good, a higher income increases your demand for leisure, thereby reducing your allocation of time to market work. This **income effect of a wage** increase tends to reduce the quantity of labor supplied to market work.

As the wage rate increases, the substitution effect causes you to supply more time to market work; but the income effect causes you to demand more leisure and, thus, to supply less time to market work. In our example, the substitution effect exceeds the income effect for wage rates up to $12 per hour, resulting in a greater quantity of market labor supplied as the wage increases. When the wage reaches $13, however, the income effect exceeds the substitution effect, causing a net reduction in the quantity of labor supplied to market work.

Backward-Bending Labor Supply Curve. The labor supply curve just described appears in Exhibit 1. As you can see, this individual supply curve slopes upward until a wage of $12 per hour is reached; then it bends backward. The **backward-bending supply curve** gets its shape because the income effect of a higher wage eventually dominates the substitution effect, reducing the quantity of labor supplied as the wage increases. We see evidence of a backward-bending supply curve particularly among high-wage individuals, who reduce their work and consume more leisure as their wage increases. For example, entertainers typically perform less as they become more successful. Unknown musicians will play for hours at a time for hardly any money; famous musicians can play much less but get paid much more. The income effect of rising real wages helps explain the decline in the U.S. workweek from an average of 60 hours in 1900 to less than 40 hours today.

Flexibility of Hours Worked. The model we have been discussing assumes that workers have some control over the number of hours they work. Opportunities for part-time work and overtime allow workers to put together their preferred quantity of hours (for instance, working 20 hours a week at Subway and 15 hours at the college bookstore). Workers also have some control over the timing and length of their vacations. More generally, individuals can control how long they stay in school, when and to what extent they enter the workforce, and when they retire. Thus, they actually have more control over the number of hours worked than you might think if you focused simply on the benchmark of, say, 40 hours per week.

Nonwage Determinants of Labor Supply

The supply of labor to a particular market depends on a variety of factors other than the wage, just as the demand for a particular good depends on factors other than the price. As we have already seen, the supply of labor to a particular market depends on wages in other labor markets. So what are the nonwage factors that shape a college student's labor supply for the summer?

EXHIBIT 1

Individual Labor Supply Curve for Market Work

When the substitution effect of a wage increase outweighs the income effect, the quantity of labor supplied increases with the wage rate. Above some wage (here, $12 per hour), the income effect dominates. Above that wage, the supply curve bends backward; further increases in the wage rate reduce the quantity of labor supplied.

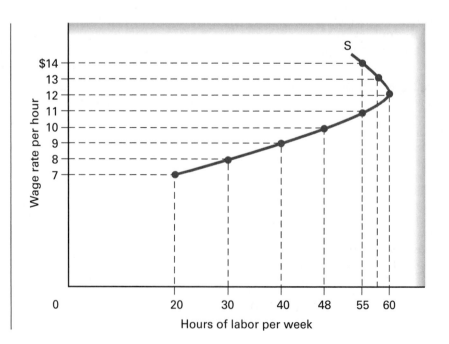

Other Sources of Income. Although some jobs are rewarding in a variety of nonmonetary ways, the main reason people work is to earn money to buy goods and services. Thus, the willingness to supply time to a labor market depends on income from other sources, including prior savings, borrowing, family support, and scholarships. A student who receives a generous scholarship, for example, may feel less pressure to earn a summer income. More generally, wealthy people have less incentive to work. For example, a multimillion-dollar lottery winner is likely to quit working after hitting the jackpot.

Nonmonetary Factors. Labor is a special kind of resource. Unlike capital and land, which can be supplied regardless of the whereabouts of the resource owner, the supplier of labor must be in the same place that the work is performed. Because the individual must be physically present to supply labor, such *nonmonetary factors* as the difficulty of the job, the quality of the work environment, and the status of the position have important effects on the labor supply. For example, deckhands on fishing boats in the winter waters of the Bering Sea off Alaska earn over $3,000 for five days' work, but the temperature seldom gets above zero and daily shifts allow only three hours for sleep.

Consider the different working conditions you might encounter. If you are a college student, a library job that allows you to study much of the time is more attractive than a job that affords no study time. Some jobs have flexible hours; others have rigid schedules. Is the workplace air-conditioned, or do you have to sweat it out? The more attractive the working conditions, the more labor you will supply to that particular market, other things constant. Finally, some jobs convey more status than others. For example, the president of the United States earns only about one-tenth the average pay of top corporate heads, but there is no shortage of candidates. Similarly, U.S. Supreme Court appointments typically take a huge pay cut to accept the job.

The Value of Job Experience. All else equal, you are more inclined to take a job that provides valuable experience. Serving as the assistant treasurer for a local business provides better job experience and looks better on a résumé than serving mystery meat at the college cafeteria. Some people are willing to accept relatively low wages now because of the promise of higher wages later. For example, new lawyers are eager to fill clerkships for judges, though the pay is low and the hours long, because these positions offer experience and contacts valued by future employers. Likewise, athletes who play in the minor leagues do so because they hope the experience they gain will move them up to the major leagues. Thus, *the more a job enhances future earning possibilities, the greater the supply of labor to that occupation, other things constant.* Because of the greater supply of labor to such positions, other things constant, the pay is usually lower than for similar jobs that impart less valuable experience.

Taste for Work. Just as the tastes for goods and services differ among consumers, the tastes for work also differ among labor suppliers. Some people prefer physical labor and would hate a desk job. Some become surgeons; others can't stand the sight of blood. Some become airline pilots; others are afraid to fly. Many struggling writers, artists, actors, and dancers could earn more elsewhere, but apparently the satisfaction of the creative process and the chance, albeit slim, of hitting it big more than offset the low pay (for example, members of the Screen Actors Guild earn less than $15,000 a year on average). Some people have such strong preferences for certain jobs that they work for free, such as auxiliary police officers or volunteer firefighters. Teenagers seem to prefer certain types of employers. Jobs at Starbucks and Gap, for example, rank above jobs at McDonald's and Burger King.[1]

As with the taste for goods and services, economists do not attempt to explain the origin of taste for work. They simply argue that your tastes are relatively stable and you supply more labor to jobs you like. Voluntary sorting based on tastes allocates workers among different jobs in a way that tends to minimize the disutility of work. This is not to say that everyone will end up in his or her most preferred occupation. The transaction costs of acquiring job information and of changing jobs may prevent some matchups that might otherwise seem desirable. But in the long run, people tend to find jobs that suit them. We are not likely to find tour directors who hate to travel, zookeepers who are allergic to animals, or garage mechanics who hate getting their hands dirty.

Market Supply of Labor

In the previous section, we considered those factors, both monetary and nonmonetary, that influence individual labor supply. *The supply of labor to a particular market is the horizontal sum of all the individual supply curves.* The horizontal sum is found by adding the quantities supplied

---

[1]Dirk Johnson, "For Teenagers, Fast Food Is a Snack, Not a Job," *New York Times,* 8 January 2001.

by each worker at each particular wage. If an individual supply curve of labor bends backward, does this mean that the market supply curve for labor also bends backward? Not necessarily. Since different individuals have different opportunity costs and different tastes for work, the bend in the supply curve occurs at different wages for different individuals. And, for some individuals, the labor supply curve may not bend backward over the realistic range of wages. Exhibit 2 shows how just three individual labor supply curves sum to yield a market supply curve that slopes upward.

<interactive>update

ECONNEWS ONLINE: ENERGIZED CEOs: THEY KEEP GOING AND GOING

Why Wages Differ

Just as both blades of scissors contribute equally to cutting cloth, both demand and supply determine the market wage. Therefore, wage differences across markets trace to differences in labor demand, in labor supply, or in both. In the previous chapter, we discussed the elements that influence the demand for resources and examined labor in particular. In brief, *a profit-maximizing firm hires labor up to the point where labor's marginal revenue product equals its marginal resource cost*—that is, where the last unit employed earns the firm just enough to cover its cost (MRP = MRC). Because we have already discussed what affects the demand for labor—namely, labor's marginal revenue product—let's focus more on labor supply.

Differences in Training, Education, Age, and Experience. Some jobs pay more because they require a long and expensive training period. Costly training reduces market supply because fewer individuals are willing to incur the time and expense required. But extensive training increases the productivity of labor, thereby increasing demand for the skills. Reduced supply and increased demand both have a positive effect on the market wage. Certified public accountants earn more than file clerks because the extensive training of CPAs limits the supply to this field and because this training increases the productivity of CPAs compared to file clerks.

Exhibit 3 shows how education and experience affect earnings based on education and age. Age groups are indicated on the horizontal axis and average annual earnings on the vertical axis. Figures are for full-time, year-round male workers in 1999. The lines are labeled to reflect the highest level of education achieved and range from "Less Than Ninth Grade" (bottom line) to a "Doctoral Degree" (top line). The relationship between income and education is clear. At every age, those with more education earn more. For example, among the 45-to-54 age group, those with doctorates earn four times more on average than those with less than a

EXHIBIT 2

Deriving the Market Labor Supply Curve

The individual labor supply curve in panel (a) bends backward. The market supply curve, however, still slopes upward over the relevant range of wage rates.

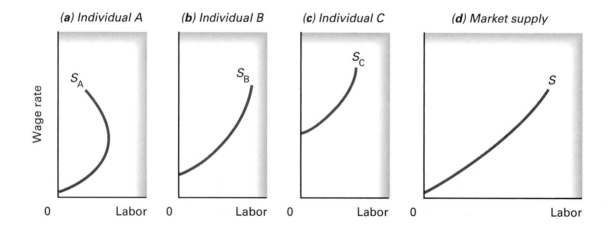

EXHIBIT 3

Age, Wage, and Education

For every age group, the more education a worker has, the more money he or she can earn.

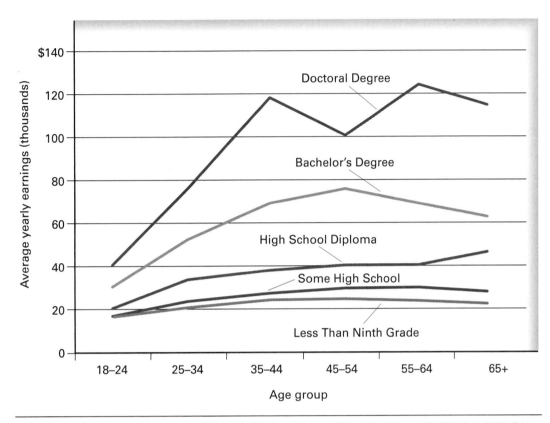

Source: U.S. Census Bureau, *Money Income in the United States 1999,* Current Population Report P60–209 (Sept. 2000), Table 9, at http://www.census.gov/hhes/www/income.html. Note: Average earnings for full-time, year-round male workers.

ninth-grade education. Age itself also has an important effect on income. Earnings tend to increase as workers acquire job experience and get promoted. The pay boost with experience is greater for more-educated workers. Differences in earnings reflect the normal workings of resource markets, whereby workers are rewarded according to their marginal productivity.

Differences in Ability. Because they are more able and talented, some individuals earn more than others with the same training and education. For example, two lawyers may have identical educations, but one earns more because of differences in underlying ability. Most executives have extensive training and business experience, but only a few become chief executives of large corporations. In major-league sports, some players earn up to 60 times more than others. From lawyers to executives to professional athletes, pay differences often reflect differing abilities. The following case study examines why the premium awarded greater ability has grown in the last two decades.

CASE**STUDY**	Winner-Take-All Labor Markets
	● *The World of Business*

Each year *Forbes* magazine reports on the multimillion-dollar earnings of top entertainers and professional athletes. Entertainment and sports have come to be called "winner-take-all" labor markets because a few key people critical to the overall success of an enterprise are richly rewarded. For example, the credits at the end of a movie list the dozens of people directly involved in the production. Hundreds, sometimes thousands, more are employed behind the scenes. Despite a huge cast and crew, the difference between a movie's financial success and its failure depends primarily on the performance of just a few people in crucial roles—the lead actors, the director, and the screenwriter. The same happens in sports. Although thousands of players compete each year in professional tennis, the value of television time, ticket sales, and endorsements is based on the drawing power of just the top players. In professional golf, attendance and TV ratings are significantly higher for tournaments in which Tiger Woods is in the running. Thus, top performers generate a high marginal revenue product.

But high marginal productivity alone is not enough. To be paid the value of their marginal product, there must be an open competition for the talents of the top people. Competition for top performers bids up their pay to extremely high levels, such as the $20 million per movie garnered by top stars—more than 1,000 times the average annual earnings of Screen Actors Guild members. In professional sports, before the free-agency rule was introduced (which allows players to go to the highest bidder), top players could not move on their own from team to team. They were, in a sense, trapped with the team that drafted them and, consequently, earned only a fraction of today's pay, despite their huge economic value to a team.

Relatively high pay in entertainment and sports is not new. What is new is the proliferation of winner-take-all pay structures to other markets in the United States. The "star" treatment has spread to such fields as management, law, banking, finance, even academia. Consider, for example, what has happened to the pay of top U.S. executives in the last quarter century. In 1974, the chief executive officers (CEOs) of the 200 largest U.S. corporations earned on average about 35 times more than the average U.S. production worker. By 1999, average pay for this top group had increased to over 150 times the average production worker's pay. Comparable multiples that year were only 13 in Germany and 11 in Japan. Why the big jump?

Robert Frank and Philip Cook argue in their book *The Winner-Take-All Society* that the relatively higher pay for top U.S. performers resulted from three developments. First, breakthroughs in communications, production, and transportation allowed talented people to serve wider markets, thereby enhancing their marginal product. For example, a well-run U.S. company supplying a valued product can now sell that product around the world. Second, greater market freedom has enhanced competition for the top performers, so these top people earn closer to their marginal productivity. For example, in the 1970s, U.S. businesses usually selected their CEOs from company ranks, promoting mainly from within (a practice still alive today in Germany and Japan). Because other firms were not trying to bid away the most talented executives, companies were able to retain them for just a fraction of the pay that now prevails in a more competitive market. Today top executives are drawn from outside the firm—even outside the industry and the country. This wider competition for the top people has ratcheted up the top pay. A final reason cited by Frank and Cook is that large salaries have become more socially acceptable in the United States than they once were. High salaries are still frowned upon in some countries.

\<interactive\>exercise

eACTIVITY: WINNER-TAKE-ALL LABOR MARKETS

Sources: Stefan Fatsis, "Thanks to Tiger's Roar, PGA Tour Signs Record TV Deal Through 2007," *Wall Street Journal,* 17 July 2001; "Executive Pay," *Economist,* 30 September 2000; Robert H. Frank and Philip J. Cook, *The Winner-Take-All Society* (New York: Free Press, 1995); Barbara Whitaker, "Producers and Actors Reach Accord," *New York Times,* 5 July 2001; and *Economic Report of the President,* January 2001, at http://w3.access.gpo.gov/eop/.

Differences in Risk. Research indicates that jobs with a higher probability of injury or death, such as coal mining, pay more, other things constant. As another example, Russians working at the partially disabled nuclear power plant Chernobyl earned in 2000 a wage that was 10 times the national average.[2] Workers also earn more, other things constant, in seasonal jobs such as construction, where the risks of unemployment are greater.

Geographic Differences. People have a strong incentive to sell their resources in the market where they earn the most, other things constant. For example, place kickers come from around the world for the attractive salaries available in the National Football League. Likewise, because physicians earn more in the United States than elsewhere, thousands of foreign-trained physicians migrate here each year. The flow of labor is not all one way: Some Ameri-

[2]Matthew Brzezinski, "The Silver Lining in Chernobyl's Cloud," *New York Times,* 3 September 2000.

cans seek their fortune abroad, with basketball players going to Europe and baseball players going to Japan. Workers often face migration hurdles if they seek higher pay in another country. Any reduction in these hurdles would reduce wage differentials across countries.

CNN VIDEO: "FRENCH DESERT FRANCE FOR UNITED KINGDOM"

Job Discrimination. Sometimes individuals earn different wages because of racial or gender discrimination in the job market. Although such discrimination is illegal, history shows that certain groups—including blacks, Hispanics, and women—have systematically earned less than others of apparently equal ability.

ECONDEBATE ONLINE: DOES A GENDER WAGE GAP STILL EXIST?

Union Membership. Other things equal, members of organized labor tend to earn more than nonmembers. The balance of this chapter discusses the effects of unions on the market for labor.

- SEE IT: WAGE DIFFERENTIALS
- TRY IT: THE MAKING OF A SHORTAGE IN THE LABOR MARKET FOR PUBLIC EMPLOYEES

- ASK THE INSTRUCTOR: WHY DO LANGUAGE TEACHERS EARN LESS?
- ASK THE INSTRUCTOR: SHOULD YOU HAVE GONE TO COLLEGE?
- ASK THE INSTRUCTOR: WHAT WOULD HAPPEN IF EVERYONE WERE PAID THE SAME?

<interactive>update

- ECONNEWS ONLINE: TEACHER TRAUMA
- ECONNEWS ONLINE: TEACHERS WORK FOR PEANUTS, NOT APPLES

UNIONS AND COLLECTIVE BARGAINING

Few aspects of the labor market make the news more often than the activities of labor unions. Labor negotiations, strikes, picket lines, confrontations between workers and employers—all fit neatly into TV's "action news" format. Despite media attention, only about one in seven U.S. workers belongs to a labor union and the overwhelming share of union agreements are reached without a strike. Let's examine the tools that unions employ to seek higher pay for their members.

Types of Unions

A **labor union** is a group of workers who join together to improve their terms of employment. Labor unions in the United States date back to the early days of national independence, when employees in various crafts—such as carpenters, shoemakers, and printers—formed local groups to seek higher wages and shorter hours. Membership to a **craft union** was confined to people with a particular skill, or craft. Craft unions eventually formed their own national organization, the *American Federation of Labor (AFL)*. The AFL, founded in 1886 under the direction of Samuel Gompers, was not a union itself but rather an organization of national unions, each retaining its autonomy.

By the beginning of World War I, the AFL, still under Gompers, was viewed as the voice of labor. The Clayton Act of 1914 exempted labor unions from antitrust laws, meaning that *unions at competing companies could legally join forces in an attempt to raise wages.* Unions were also tax exempt. Membership jumped during World War I but dropped in half between 1920 and 1933, as the government retreated from its support of union efforts.

The *Congress of Industrial Organizations (CIO)* was formed in 1935 to serve as a national organization of unions in mass-production industries, such as cars and steel. Whereas the AFL organized workers in particular crafts, such as plumbers and carpenters, the CIO consisted of unions whose membership embraced all workers in a particular industry. These **industrial unions** included unskilled, semiskilled, and skilled workers in an industry, such as all autoworkers and all steelworkers.

Collective Bargaining

Collective bargaining is the process by which representatives of union and management negotiate a mutually agreeable contract specifying wages, employee benefits, and working conditions. Once a tentative agreement is reached, union representatives present it to the membership for a vote. If the agreement is rejected, the union can strike or continue negotiations.

Mediation and Arbitration. If negotiations stall and the public interest is involved, government officials may ask an independent mediator to step in. A **mediator** is an impartial observer who listens to both sides separately and then suggests how each side could adjust its position to resolve differences. If a resolution appears possible, the mediator brings the parties together to work out a contract. The mediator has no power to impose a settlement on the parties.

In certain critical sectors, such as police and fire protection, where a strike could harm the public interest, an impasse in negotiations is sometimes settled through **binding arbitration,** whereby a neutral third party evaluates both sides of the dispute and issues a ruling that the parties must accept. Some disputes skip the mediation and arbitration steps and go directly from impasse to strike.

The Strike

A major source of union power in the bargaining relationship is the threat of a **strike,** which is a union's attempt to withhold labor from the firm. The purpose of a strike is to stop production, forcing the firm to accept the union's position. But strikes can also impose significant costs on union members, who forgo pay and benefits during the strike and risk losing their jobs. Union funds and other sources, such as unemployment benefits in some states, may provide support during a strike, but the typical striker's income falls substantially. The threat of a strike hangs over labor negotiations and can encourage an accord. *Although neither party usually wants a strike, both sides, rather than concede on key points, typically act as if they could and would endure a strike.*

Unions usually picket the targeted employer to prevent or discourage so-called strikebreakers, or "scabs," from crossing the picket lines to work. But the firm, by hiring temporary workers and nonstriking union workers can sometimes continue production.

UNION WAGES AND EMPLOYMENT

Union members, like everyone else, have unlimited wants, but no union can regularly get everything it desires. Because resources are scarce, choices must be made. A menu of union desires includes higher wages, more benefits, greater job security, better working conditions, and so on. To keep the analysis manageable, let's focus on a single objective, higher wages, and consider three ways unions might increase wages: (1) by forming an inclusive, or industrial, union; (2) by forming an exclusive, or craft, union; and (3) by increasing the demand for union labor.

Inclusive, or Industrial, Unions

With the *inclusive*, or *industrial*, approach, the union tries to negotiate an industry-wide wage for each class of labor. The market demand and supply for a particular type of labor are labeled *D* and *S* in panel (a) of Exhibit 4. In the absence of a union, the equilibrium wage is *W* and the equilibrium employment level is *E*. At the market wage, each individual employer faces a horizontal, or perfectly elastic, supply of labor, as depicted by *s* in panel (b) of Exhibit 4. Thus, each firm can hire as much labor as it wants at the market wage of *W*. The firm hires up to the point where labor's marginal revenue product equals its marginal resource cost, resulting in quantity *e* in panel (b). As we saw earlier, in equilibrium, each worker is paid a wage just equal to the marginal revenue product.

Now suppose that the union is able to negotiate a wage above the market-clearing wage. Specifically, suppose the wage negotiated is *W'* in panel (a) of Exhibit 4, meaning that no labor will be supplied at a lower wage, but any amount demanded up to the quantity identified at point *a* will be supplied at the wage floor. In effect, the supply of union labor is perfectly elastic at the union wage out to point *a*. If more than *E''* workers are demanded, however, the wage floor no longer applies; the relevant part of the labor supply curve becomes the upward-sloping portion, *aS*. For an industry facing a wage floor of *W'*, the entire labor supply curve is *W'aS*, which has a kink where the wage floor joins the upward-sloping portion of the original supply curve.

Once this wage floor is established, each firm faces a horizontal supply curve of labor at the collectively bargained wage, *W'*. Since the wage is now higher, the quantity of labor demanded by each employer declines, as reflected by the reduction in employment from *e* to *e'* in panel (b). Consequently, the higher wage leads to a reduction in total employment; the quantity demanded by the industry drops from *E* to *E'* in panel (a).

EXHIBIT 4

Effect of a Union's Wage Floor

In panel (a), the equilibrium wage rate in the abskence of a labor union is *W*. At that wage, the individual firm of panel (b) hires labor up to the point where the marginal revenue product equals *W*. Each firm hires quantity *e;* total employment is *E*. If a union can negotiate a wage *W'* above the equilibrium level, the supply curve facing the firm shifts up to *s'*. The firm hires fewer workers, *e'*, and total employment falls to *E'*. At wage *W'* there is an excess quantity of labor supplied equal to *E'' − E'*.

(a) Industry

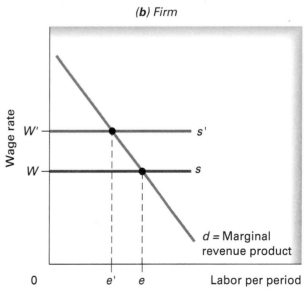

(b) Firm

At wage W' the amount of labor workers would like to supply, E'', exceeds the amount demanded, E'. In the absence of a union, this excess quantity of labor supplied would cause unemployed workers to lower their asking wage. But union members agree *collectively* to a wage, so individual workers cannot offer to work for less, nor can employers offer to hire them at a lower wage. Because the number of union members willing and able to work exceeds the number of jobs available, the union must somehow ration available jobs, such as awarding jobs based on worker seniority or connections within the union. *With the inclusive, or industrial, union, which negotiates with the entire industry, the wage rate is higher and total employment lower than they would be in the absence of a union.*

Those who cannot find union employment will look for jobs in the nonunion sector. *This increased supply of labor in the nonunion sector drives down the nonunion wage.* So wages are relatively higher in the union sector: first, because unions bargain for a wage that exceeds the market-clearing wage, and second, because those unable to find employment in the union sector crowd into the nonunion sector. A survey of more than 200 studies concluded that unions increased members' wages by an average of about 15 percent above the wages of similarly skilled nonunion workers.[3] Unions are more successful at raising wages in less-competitive industries. For example, unions have little impact on the wages in the garment and textile industries, which are competitive, but have greater impact on the wages in the auto, steel, mining, and transportation industries, which historically have been less competitive. Competitive firms cannot easily pass along higher union wages as higher product prices. New firms can enter a competitive industry, pay nonunion wages, and sell the product for less.

Exclusive, or Craft, Unions

One way to increase wages while avoiding an excess quantity of labor supplied is for the union to somehow reduce the supply of labor, shown as a leftward shift in panel (a) of Exhibit 5. Successful supply restrictions of this type require that the union first limit its membership and second force all employers in the industry to hire only union members. The union can restrict membership with high initiation fees, long apprenticeship periods, difficult qualification exams, restrictive licensing requirements, and other devices aimed at slowing down or discouraging new membership. But even if unions can restrict membership, they have difficulty requiring all firms in the industry to hire only union workers.

Whereas wage setting is more typical of the industrial unions, restricting supply is more typical of the craft unions, such as unions of carpenters, plumbers, and bricklayers. Professional groups—doctors, lawyers, and accountants, for instance—also impose entry restrictions through education and examination standards. These restrictions, usually defended on the grounds that they protect the public, are often little more than self-serving attempts to increase wages by restricting labor supply.

Increasing Demand for Union Labor

A third way to increase the wage is to increase the demand for union labor by somehow shifting the labor demand curve outward as from D to D'' in panel (b) of Exhibit 5. This approach is an attractive alternative *because it increases both the wage rate and employment,* so there is no need to ration jobs among union members. Here are some ways unions try to increase the demand for union labor.

Increase Demand for Union-Made Goods. The demand for union labor may be increased through a direct appeal to consumers to buy only union-made products. Because the demand for labor is a derived demand, increasing the demand for union-made products increases the demand for union labor.

Restrict Supply of Nonunion-Made Goods. Another way to increase the demand for union labor is to restrict the supply of products that compete with union-made products. Again, this approach relies on the derived nature of labor demand. The United Auto Workers (UAW), for example, supports restrictions on imported cars. Fewer imported cars means greater demand for cars produced by U.S. workers, who are mostly union members.

Increase Productivity of Union Labor. Some observers claim that the efficiency with which unions structure and monitor the labor-management relationship increases the demand for union labor. According to this theory, unions increase worker productivity by minimizing conflicts, resolving differences, and at times even straightening out workers who are goofing off. In the

[3]H. Gregg Lewis, *Union Relative Wage Effects: A Survey* (Chicago: University of Chicago Press, 1986).

EXHIBIT 5

Effect of Reducing Supply or Increasing Labor Demand

If a union can restrict labor supply to an industry, the supply curve shifts to the left from S to S', as in panel (a). The wage rate rises from W to W', but at the cost of a reduction in employment from E to E'. In panel (b), an increase in labor demand from D to D'' raises both the wage and the level of employment.

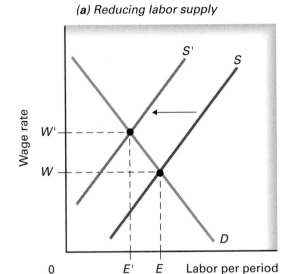

(a) Reducing labor supply

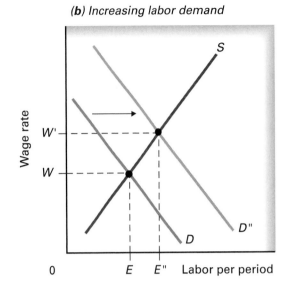

(b) Increasing labor demand

absence of a union, a dissatisfied worker may simply look for another job, causing job turnover. Turnover is costly to the firm because the departing worker leaves with company-specific, on-the-job training. With a union, however, workers usually can file complaints through grievance and arbitration channels, and the negotiated responses they receive may reduce their urge to leave the firm. Quit rates are in fact significantly lower among union workers (although this could be due to the higher pay). If unions increase the productivity of workers in this way, the demand for union labor will increase.

Featherbedding. Still another way unions try to increase the demand for union labor is by **featherbedding,** which is an attempt to ensure that more union labor is hired than producers would prefer. For example, union rules require that each Broadway theater have a permanent "house" carpenter, electrician, and property manager. Once the show run begins, these workers appear only on payday. (Changing a light bulb for the play *The Iceman Cometh* required a three-person crew, each earning $43.36 an hour.[4]) The box office must be staffed by three people. The musicians' union requires that from 9 to 22 musicians be employed at each theater staging a musical, even if the show calls for just a piano player.

Featherbedding does not create a true increase in demand, in the sense of shifting the demand curve to the right. Instead, it forces firms to hire more labor than they really want or need, thus moving the firm to a point to the right of its true labor demand curve. The union tries to limit a firm to an all-or-none choice: Either hire the number of workers the union requires, or a strike will halt production. Thus, with featherbedding, *the union attempts to dictate not only the wage but also the quantity that must be hired at that wage, thereby moving employers to the right of their labor demand curve.*

To review: We have examined three ways in which unions can try to raise members' wages: (1) by negotiating a wage floor above the equilibrium wage for the industry and somehow rationing the limited jobs among union members, (2) by restricting the supply of labor, and (3) by increasing the demand for union labor. Unions try to increase the demand for union labor in several ways: (1) through a direct public appeal to buy only union-made products, (2) by restricting the supply of products made by nonunion labor, (3) by reducing labor turnover and thereby increasing marginal productivity, and (4) through featherbedding, which forces employers to hire more union workers than they would prefer.

[4]Jesse McKinley, "$100 a Ticket? Here's Why," *New York Times,* 8 April 1999.

Recent Trends in Union Membership

In 1955, about one-third of wage and salary workers in the United States belonged to unions. Union membership as a fraction of the workforce has since declined; now only one in seven belongs to a union. Government workers, who account for just one in six U.S. workers, make up nearly half of all union members. A typical union member is a schoolteacher. Compared with other industrialized countries, the United States ranks relatively low in the extent of unionization, though rates abroad are also declining.

The bar graph in Exhibit 6 indicates U.S. union membership rates by age and gender in 2000. The rates for men, shown by the green bars, are higher than the rates for women, in part because men are employed more in manufacturing and women more in the service sector, where union membership historically has been lower. The highest membership rates are for middle-aged males. Although the exhibit does not show it, blacks have a higher union membership rate than whites (17 percent versus 13 percent), in part because blacks are more often employed by government and by heavy industries such as autos and steel, where union representation is higher. Union membership among those of Hispanic origin, who can be of any race, averaged only 11 percent.

Union membership rates also vary greatly across states. Rates in 2000 were 16 percent or more in the industrial states of the North and 8 percent or less in the South. New York had the highest rate in 2000 at 26 percent; North Carolina had the lowest at 4 percent.

The decline in union membership is due partly to structural changes in the U.S. economy. Unions have long been more important in the industrial sector than in the service sector. But employment in the industrial sector, which includes manufacturing, mining, and construction,

EXHIBIT 6

Unionization Rates

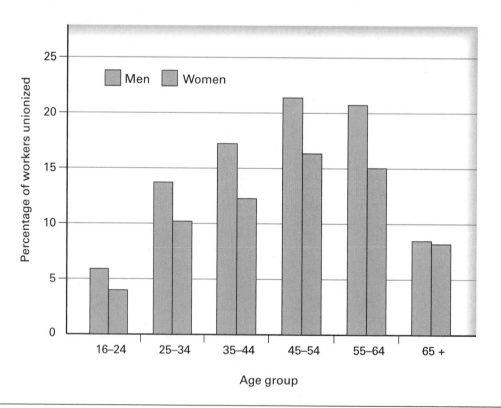

Source: U.S. Bureau of Labor Statistics, "Union Members in 2000," 18 January 2001. For latest figures go to http://www.stats.bls.gov/newsrels.htm. Note: Figures for union membership as a percentage of U.S. wage and salary workers.

has declined in recent decades as a share of all jobs. Another factor in the decline of the union movement is a growth in market competition, particularly from imports. Increased competition from nonunion employers, both foreign and domestic, has reduced the ability of unionized firms to pass on higher labor costs as higher prices. And fewer union members mean fewer voters who belong to unions, so unions have lost political clout.

Finally, the near disappearance of the strike has also reduced union power. During the 1970s, there were about 300 strikes a year in the United States involving 1,000 or more workers. Such strikes averaged just 36 a year during the 1990s. Many recent strikes ended badly for union workers; companies such as Caterpillar, Phelps Dodge Copper, Continental Airlines, and Hormel Foods hired replacement workers. Union members have become less inclined to strike because of the increased willingness of employers to hire strikebreakers and the increased willingness of workers—both union and nonunion—to cross picket lines. Strikes also cut company profits, which hurts workers who share in profits and dampens the incentive to strike. For example, a strike against General Motors in 1998 cut each worker's average profit share that year to just $200 from more than $6,000 the year before. Since the strike and the threat of a strike have become less important, this has diminished the power of unions.

The final case study examines why unions have achieved only limited success in organizing the fastest growing job sector—that for information technology workers.

| CASE**STUDY** | Unionizing Information Technology Workers |

● *The Information Economy*

Despite the demise of many online ventures, information technology (IT) workers still make up the fastest growing sector of the labor force. The U.S. Bureau of Labor Statistics predicts that job growth in computer and data processing will exceed that of most other industries during the next decade. Since labor unions want to grow, why don't they focus on the fastest growing sector? Well, unions have tried to organize IT workers, but this group poses some special challenges. To succeed, a union must convince workers that a union can make a difference. But most employers make every effort to hire and retain IT workers, including hiring bonuses, health insurance, good retirement plans, stock options, free wireless phone service, laptops, flextime, and a more relaxed work environment. Such working conditions do not offer fertile ground for organized labor.

Another problem for labor organizers is that, compared to traditional union members, such as blue-collar and government workers, IT workers tend to be younger and comprise a motley crew of regular workers, telecommuters, part-timers, temporary workers, freelancers, and a growing number of foreigners on short-term work visas. Unions have a hard time even communicating with such a fragmented, independent bunch.

Finally, IT firms are more dynamic than traditional labor strongholds, such as autos, steel, and the public school system. By the time a union has targeted an IT firm for organizing, that firm may have already moved, merged with another firm, or folded.

The only union with a significant presence among IT workers is the Communications Workers of America (CWA), which began decades ago with the then stodgy phone monopoly, AT&T. The breakup of that monopoly in the early 1980s coupled with breakthroughs such as cable and wireless transmission turned telecommunications into a hot, high-tech industry. Thus CWA was in the right place at the right time. But the union has had difficulty moving into other IT industries. For example, since 1996 it has tried to organize Microsoft's 40,000 workers but has signed up only about 250, mostly temporary workers. At Silicon Valley firms such as Intel and Hewlett-Packard, unions have successfully organized janitors but not high-tech workers. Worse yet for CWA, traditional telephone systems are gradually being replaced by networks using Internet-based technology sold by companies with no union members, such as Cisco. To keep from falling too far behind, CWA has even hired Cisco to help retrain some CWA members.

In summary: Good pay, attractive perks, and bright job prospects, not to mention an independent streak, make trying to organize IT workers like trying to herd cats.

<interactive>**exercise**

eACTIVITY: UNIONIZING INFORMATION TECHNOLOGY WORKERS

Sources: John Miano, "Do High-Tech Firms Really Need Imported Workers?" *USA Today,* 21 September 2000; Scott Thurm, "Cisco Systems Helps to Train Union Workers in Web's Ways," *Wall Street Journal,* 3 July 2001; Mark Boslet, "Lighting the Labor Fuse," *The Standard.com,* 20 August 2000; Steven Greenhouse, "Amazon Fights Union Activity," *New York Times,* 29 November 2000; Keith Ervin, "Microsoft Temps Group Joins Union," *Seattle Times,* 4 June 1999; and the CWA Web site at http://www.cwa-union.org/.

Finally, some observers argue that unions have been in decline because employers have discouraged organizing efforts. Although federal law bars employers from firing or penalizing workers for supporting a union, a federal study estimates that employers punished or fired over 125,000 workers between 1992 and 1997 for trying to establish a union.[5] This seems like a lot, but it works out to be only about one in a thousand workers during the six-year period. Others say that unions have failed to grow not so much because of what employers do but because of the larger forces in the economy already discussed—growing global competition, the shift from manufacturing to services, the increased reluctance to strike, and the growth of the high-tech sector. The union movement got a small lift in November 2000 when a federal body recognized the right of graduate assistants and research assistants at New York University to join unions. That could be the foot in the door to a fresh supply of union members.

CONCLUSION

The first half of this chapter focused on the supply of labor and explained why wages differ both across occupations and among individuals within an occupation. The interaction of labor demand and supply determines wage rates and the level of employment. The second half of the chapter explored the effect of unions on the labor market. At one time unions dominated some key industries. But as global competition intensifies, employers have a harder time passing higher union labor costs along to consumers. Both in the United States and in other industrial economies, union members represent a dwindling segment of the labor force.

<interactive>**update**

1000110111C

ECONNEWS ONLINE: AD AGENCIES' PROBLEMS MULTIPLY AS WORKERS ARE TAKEN AWAY AND ACTORS WON'T ACT

Take the Post-Test to assess your overall understanding of the key ideas in this chapter. The Post-Test provides a comprehensive selection of exam-style questions addressing the main topics and concepts of the chapter. At the completion of each Post-Test, you will receive a score and instructive feedback on how you answered each question, and a direct link to the part of the chapter addressed in the question. Take the Post-Test as often as you need to—a record of your progress for each attempt is kept for you to revisit and gauge your improvement. And each Post-Test is randomly generated, so every attempt is new.

endofchaptermaterial

- **Summary**
- **Questions for Review**
- **Problems and Exercises**
- **Experiential Exercises**
- **Wall Street Journal Exercises**

[5]The study by the National Labor Relations Board is discussed in Steven Greenhouse, "Report Faults Laws for Slowing Growth of Unions," *New York Times,* 24 October 2000.

Post-Test

CHAPTER 13

Capital, Interest, and Corporate Finance

Why can first-run movie theaters charge more than other theaters? Why do you burn your mouth eating pizza? What's seed money, and why can't Farmer Jones grow anything without it? Why are state lottery jackpots worth much less than the advertised millions? What's the big deal with pirated software? These and other questions are answered in this chapter, which concerns capital and investment.

So far, our discussion of resources has focused primarily on labor markets. This emphasis is appropriate because labor claims most resource income—more than two-thirds of the total. The rewards to labor, however, depend in part on the amount and quality of the other resources employed, particularly capital. A farmer plowing a field with a tractor is more productive than one scraping the soil with a stick. In this chapter, you will examine the role of capital in production—its cost and its expected return. You will learn about optimal employment of capital and how firms finance their investments.

First a note of caution. Earlier we distinguished between opportunity cost (the payment necessary to attract a resource to a particular use) and economic rent (a payment in excess of opportunity cost). Often economists refer to the return on land as rent, because land is typically thought to be in fixed supply; and the return on a resource in fixed supply consists entirely of economic rent. Describing the earnings on land as rent is quite

Take the Pre-Test to assess your initial knowledge of the key ideas in this chapter. The Pre-Test provides exam-style questions addressing the main topics and concepts of the chapter. At the completion of each Pre-Test, you will receive a score and instructive feedback on how you answered each question, and a direct link to the part of the chapter addressed in the question. Take the Pre-Test as often as you need to—a record of your progress for each attempt is kept for you to revisit and gauge your improvement.

appropriate, but land as a resource does not receive special treatment in this book. Topics discussed in this chapter include:

- Production, saving, and time
- Consumption, saving, and time
- Optimal investment
- Loanable funds market
- Present value and discounting
- Corporate finance
- Stocks, bonds, and retained earnings

<interactive>exercise

- ECONDEBATE ONLINE: MONEY AND THE FINANCIAL SYSTEM
- ECONDEBATE ONLINE: SUPPLY AND DEMAND

<interactive>update

- ECONDATA ONLINE: MONEY AND THE FINANCIAL SYSTEM
- ECONDATA ONLINE: SUPPLY AND DEMAND
- ECONLINKS ONLINE: ECONOMICS WEB LINKS
- ECONNEWS ONLINE: MONEY AND THE FINANCIAL SYSTEM
- ECONNEWS ONLINE: SUPPLY AND DEMAND

THE ROLE OF TIME IN PRODUCTION AND CONSUMPTION

Time plays an important role in both production and consumption. In this section, we first consider the effect of time on the production decision and show why firms are willing to pay to borrow household savings. Next we consider time in the consumption decision and show why households must be rewarded to save, or for deferring present consumption. Then, bringing together the desires of borrowers and of savers, we find the market interest rate.

Production, Saving, and Time

Suppose Jones is a primitive farmer in a simple economy. Isolated from any neighbors or markets, he literally scratches out a living on a plot of land, using only crude sticks. While a crop is growing, none of it is available for current consumption. Since production takes time, Jones must rely on food saved from prior production while the new crop comes in. The longer the growing season, the more Jones must save. Thus, even in this simple example, it is clear that *production cannot occur without prior saving.*

Suppose that with his current resources, consisting of land, labor, seed corn, fertilizer, and some crude sticks, Jones grows about 200 bushels of corn a year. He soon realizes that if he had a plow—a type of investment good, or capital—his productivity would increase. Making a plow in such a primitive setting, however, is time consuming and would keep him away from the fields for a year. Thus, the plow has an opportunity cost of 200 bushels of corn. Jones would be unable to sustain such a temporary drop in production unless he has saved enough from previous harvests.

The question is, should he invest his time in the plow? The answer depends on the costs and benefits of the plow. We already know that its opportunity cost is 200 bushels—the forgone output. The benefit depends on how much the plow will increase crop production and how long it will last. Jones figures that the plow will boost the annual yield by 50 bushels and will last his lifetime. In making the investment decision, he compares current costs to future benefits. Suppose he decides that adding 50 more bushels a year outweighs the one-time cost of 200 bushels sacrificed to make the plow.

In making the plow, Jones engages in *roundabout production.* Rather than working the soil with his crude sticks, the farmer produces capital to increase his future productivity. An increased amount of roundabout production in an economy means that more capital accumulates, so more goods can be produced in the future. Advanced industrial economies are characterized by much roundabout production and thus abundant capital accumulation.

You can see why production cannot occur without prior saving. *Production requires saving because both direct and roundabout production require time—time during which goods and services are not available from current production.* Now let's modernize the example by introducing the ability to borrow. Many farmers visit the bank each spring to borrow enough "seed money" to get by until their crops come in. Likewise, other businesses often borrow at least a portion of the start-up funds needed to get going. Thus, in a modern economy, producers need not rely exclusively on their own prior saving. Banks and other financial institutions serve as *intermediaries* between savers and borrowers. As you will see toward the end of the chapter, financial markets for trading stocks and bonds also help channel savings to producers. Let's take a look at the incentive to save.

Consumption, Saving, and Time

Did you ever burn the roof of your mouth by biting into a slice of pizza that hadn't sufficiently cooled? Have you done this more than once? Why do you persist in such self-mutilation? You persist because that bite of pizza is worth more to you now than the same bite two minutes from now. In fact, you are willing to risk burning your mouth rather than wait until the pizza has lost its destructive properties. In a small way, this phenomenon reflects the fact that you and other consumers value *present* consumption more than *future* consumption. You and other consumers are said to have a **positive rate of time preference.**

Because you value present consumption more than future consumption, you are willing to pay more to consume now rather than wait. And prices often reflect this greater willingness to pay. Consider the movies. You pay more at a first-run theater than at other theaters. If you are patient, you can wait for the video. The same is true for books. By waiting for the paperback, you can save more than half the price of the hardback. Photo developers, dry cleaners, fast-food restaurants, convenience stores, cable news networks, and other suppliers tout the speed of their services, knowing that consumers prefer earlier availability.

Thus, *impatience* is one explanation for a positive rate of time preference. Another is *uncertainty.* If you wait, something might prevent you from consuming the good. A T-shirt slogan captures this point best: "Life is uncertain. Eat dessert first."

Because present consumption is valued more than future consumption, households must be rewarded to postpone consumption—savers must be rewarded. Saving equals income minus consumption. By saving a portion of their incomes in financial institutions such as banks, households forgo present consumption for a greater ability to consume in the future. Interest is the reward offered households for forgoing present consumption. The **interest rate** is the annual interest as a percentage of the amount saved. For example, if the interest rate is 5 percent, the interest paid is $5 per year for each $100 saved. The higher the interest rate, other things constant, the more consumers are rewarded for saving, so the more willing they are to save. You will learn more about this later in the chapter.

Optimal Investment

In a market economy characterized by specialization and exchange, Farmer Jones no longer needs to produce his own capital, nor must he rely on his own saving. He can purchase capital using borrowed funds. Suppose he wants to buy some farm equipment and he estimates its expected productivity. Column (1) in panel (a) of Exhibit 1 identifies six pieces of farm machinery that Jones has ranked from most to least productive. The total product of the farm equipment is listed in column (2), and the marginal product of each piece is listed in column (3). Note that other resources are assumed to be constant (in this case, the farmer's labor, land, seeds, and fertilizer).

With just his crude sticks, Jones can grow 200 bushels of corn per year. He figures that a tractor-tiller would increase production to 1,200 bushels. Thus the tractor-tiller would yield a marginal product of 1,000 bushels per year. The addition of a combine would increase total output to 2,000 bushels, thus yielding a marginal product of 800 bushels. Note that in this example, diminishing marginal returns to capital set in immediately. Marginal product continues to decrease as more capital is added, dropping to zero for a post-hole digger, for which Jones has no use.

Suppose Jones sells corn in a perfectly competitive market, so he can sell all he wants at the market price of $4 a bushel. This price is multiplied by the marginal product from column (3) to yield capital's *marginal revenue product* listed in column (4). Since Jones is a price taker,

EXHIBIT 1

Marginal Rate of Return on Investment in Farm Equipment

The marginal rate of return, shown in the last column, equals the marginal revenue product of each additional piece of farm equipment divided by its marginal resource cost. The marginal rate of return curve in the lower portion of the exhibit consists of line segments showing the relationship between the market rate of interest and the amount invested in farm equipment. This curve is the demand for investment.

(a)

(1) Farm Equipment	(2) Total Product (bushels)	(3) Marginal Product (bushels)	(4) Marginal Revenue Product (4) = (3) × $4	(5) Marginal Resource Cost	(6) Marginal Rate of Return (6) = (4)/(5)
No equipment	200	—	—	—	—
Tractor-tiller	1,200	1,000	$4,000	$10,000	40%
Combine	2,000	800	3,200	10,000	32
Irrigator	2,600	600	2,400	10,000	24
Harrow	3,000	400	1,600	10,000	16
Crop sprayer	3,200	200	800	10,000	8
Post-hole digger	3,200	0	0	10,000	0

(b)

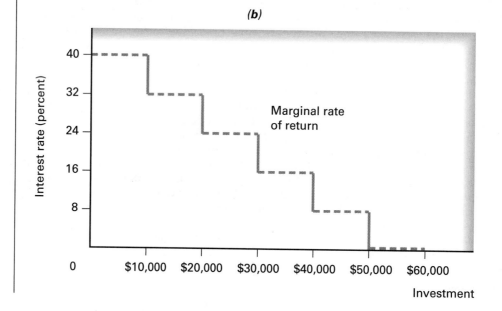

the marginal revenue product of machinery is its marginal product times the price, or the change in total revenue resulting from adding another piece of farm equipment.

For simplicity, let's say that each piece of farm equipment costs $10,000. Thus, the marginal resource cost is $10,000, as listed in column (5). Suppose also that the equipment is so durable that it lasts indefinitely, that operating expenses are negligible, and that the price of corn is expected to remain at $4 per bushel in the future. This farm equipment will increase revenue not only in the first year but every year into the future. The optimal investment solution requires Jones to take *time* into account. He can't simply equate marginal resource cost with marginal revenue product, because the marginal cost is an outlay this year, whereas the marginal product is an annual amount this year and each year in the future. As we will see, *markets bridge time with the interest rate.*

Jones must decide how much to invest. His first task is to compute the *marginal rate of return* he would earn each year by investing in farm machinery. The **marginal rate of return on investment** is capital's marginal revenue product as a percentage of its marginal resource cost. For example, the tractor-tiller yields a marginal revenue product of $4,000 per year and has a marginal resource cost of $10,000. The rate of return Jones could earn on this investment is

$4,000/\$10,000$, or 40 percent per year. Therefore, this investment yields a *marginal rate of return* of 40 percent per year, as shown in column (6). The combine yields a marginal revenue product of \$3,200 per year and has a marginal cost of \$10,000, so its marginal rate of return equals $\$3,200/\$10,000$, or 32 percent per year. Dividing the marginal revenue product of capital in column (4) by the marginal resource cost of that capital in column (5) yields the marginal rate of return in column (6) for each piece of equipment.

Given the marginal rate of return, how much should Jones invest to maximize profit? Suppose he borrows the money, paying the *market interest rate*. Jones will buy more capital as long as its marginal rate of return exceeds the market interest rate. He will stop before capital's marginal rate of return falls below the market rate of interest. For example, if the market interest rate is 20 percent, Jones will invest \$30,000 in three pieces of equipment. The marginal rate of return on the final item purchased, an irrigator, is 24 percent. Investing another \$10,000 to buy a harrow would yield a marginal return of only 16 percent, a rate below his cost of borrowing. At a market interest rate of 10 percent, Jones would invest in the harrow as well. An interest rate of 6 percent would lead Jones to also invest in the crop sprayer.

Farmer Jones should increase his investment as long as the marginal rate of return on that investment exceeds the market rate of interest. The marginal rate of return is the marginal benefit of the investment, and the market interest rate is the marginal cost, so Jones is simply maximizing profit (or minimizing loss) by investing until marginal benefit equals the marginal cost. The data in column (6) are depicted in panel (b) of Exhibit 1 as a step-like curve, where the solid lines reflect the amount Jones will invest at each interest rate. For example, if the market interest rate is between 32 percent and 40 percent, Jones should invest in the tractor-tiller. Because the marginal rate of return shows how much should be invested at each interest rate, this step-like curve represents the farmer's *demand for investment*. This is a derived demand, based on each additional piece of equipment's marginal productivity. The curve steps down to reflect the diminishing marginal productivity of capital.

Would the example change if Jones did not need to borrow? Not as long as he can save at the market interest rate. For example, suppose Jones has saved \$50,000 earning an interest rate of 10 percent per year. In that case, Jones should invest \$40,000 in capital, with the last piece purchased, the harrow, earning a marginal return of 16 percent. The 10 percent interest Jones earns on his remaining savings of \$10,000 exceeds the 8 percent he could earn by investing that amount in the crop sprayer. Thus, as long as he can borrow and save at the same interest rate, Jones ends up with the same equipment whether he borrows funds or draws upon his own savings. *Whether Jones borrows the money or uses savings on hand, the market interest rate represents his opportunity cost of investing.*

Let's review the steps Jones used to determine the optimal amount of investment. First, compute the marginal revenue product of capital. Next, divide the marginal revenue product by the marginal resource cost to determine the marginal rate of return. The marginal rate of return curve becomes a firm's demand curve for investment—that is, it shows the amount a firm is willing and able to invest at each interest rate. The market interest rate is the opportunity cost of investing either borrowed funds or savings, and can be thought of as the supply of investment funds to the firm. A firm should invest more as long as the marginal rate of return on capital exceeds the market rate of interest.

We have now discussed investing in physical capital. Let's turn to a less tangible form of capital, intellectual property, in the following case study.

- SEE IT: THE DEMAND FOR INVESTMENT
- TRY IT: THE EFFECT OF A CHANGE IN PRODUCT DEMAND ON INVESTMENT DEMAND

ECONDEBATE ONLINE: IS A COLLEGE EDUCATION A GOOD INVESTMENT?

CASE**STUDY**	The Value of a Good Idea—Intellectual Property
	● *The Informaion Economy*

One potentially valuable capital asset is information, or so-called *intellectual property*. But the market for information is unusual. On the demand side, consumers are uncertain about the value of information until they acquire it. But they can't acquire it until they pay for it. So there is a circularity problem. There is also a problem on the supply side. Information is costly to produce, but it can be transmitted at low cost. For example, the first copy of a new software program may cost millions to produce, but each additional copy can be streamed over the Internet for virtually nothing.

Because of these demand and supply problems, producers of information may have difficulty getting paid for their product. As soon as the producer sells information, that first customer becomes a potential supplier of that information. (Do you use any pirated software?) The original producer has difficulty controlling distribution of the product.

To address these problems, laws grant property rights to the creators of new ideas and new inventions. Originators are thereby better able to appropriate the value of their creations. The *patent system* establishes property rights to inventions and other technical advances. The *copyright system* confers property rights to original expressions of an author, artist, composer, or programmer. And the *trademark system* establishes property rights in unique commercial marks and symbols, such as McDonald's arches or Nike's swoosh.

Granting property rights is one thing; enforcing them is quite another. Much of the software, music CDs, and movie videos sold around the world, particularly in China, are pirated editions of products developed in the United States. In fact, some movies are available on the black market as videos before they appear in U.S. theaters. U.S. companies spend half their total anticounterfeiting budgets trying to stop violations in China. Enforcement of property rights is costly, which diminishes the incentive to create new products and new ideas.

Each new generation of technology offers new ways of communicating ideas and thus calls for new ways to help protect those ideas. For example, copyright laws originally applied only to writing but now extend to pictures, computer software, and a growing list of items including the circuitry design of a computer chip. But the Internet may pose the biggest challenge yet to copyright protection, since someone can download the contents of a site and derive commercial benefit from that material. For example, Web sites such as Napster facilitate online swapping of digital-music files. The ability to exchange files online now extends to movies and other forms of intellectual property. Some digital gurus argue that the ease of duplicating data on the Internet dooms copyright protection. They say that anything that can be reduced to bits can be copied. The courts are currently sorting out these issues.

The Internet has created pressure to come up with new ways to sell intellectual property. For example, horror writer Stephen King began publishing a serial novel on the Internet in June 2000. Under an honor system, he asked readers to voluntarily pay him $1 for each chapter downloaded. He agreed to keep adding chapters as long at least 75 percent of readers complied: "If you pay, the story rolls. If you don't, the story folds." The venture started out strong, but five months later, downloads of new chapters dropped to only a third of their initial level and the percentage of paying readers dropped to less than half. King announced in November 2000 that he would suspend further installments.

Intellectual property is a capital asset that fuels the information economy. How society nurtures incentives to create new ideas and new inventions will affect capital accumulation and economic growth around the globe.

The Market for Loanable Funds

You earlier learned why producers are willing to pay interest to borrow money: *Money provides a command over resources that makes roundabout production possible.* The simple principles developed for Farmer Jones can be generalized to other producers. The major demanders of loans are firms that borrow to invest in physical capital, such as machines, trucks, and buildings, and in intellectual capital, such as patents, copyrights, and trademarks. At any time, a firm has a variety of investment opportunities. The firm ranks its opportunities from highest to lowest, based on the expected marginal rates of return. The firm will increase its investment until the expected marginal rate of return just equals the market interest rate. With other inputs held constant, as they were on the farm, the demand curve for investment slopes downward.

But firms are not the only demanders of loans. As we have seen, households value present consumption more than future consumption; they are often willing to pay extra to consume now rather than later. One way to ensure that goods and services are available now is to borrow for present consumption. Some people borrow also to invest in their human capital. Home mortgages, car loans, credit-card purchases, and college loans are examples of household borrowing. The household's demand curve for loans, like the firm's, slopes downward, reflecting consumers' greater willingness and ability to borrow at lower interest rates, other things constant. The government sector and the rest of the world are also demanders of loans.

Banks are willing to pay interest on consumer savings because the banks can, in turn, lend these savings to those who need credit, such as farmers, home buyers, college students, and entrepreneurs looking to start a new business. Banks play the role of *financial intermediaries* in what is known as the market for loanable funds. The **loanable funds market** brings together savers, or suppliers of loanable funds, and borrowers, or demanders of loanable funds, to determine the market rate of interest.

The higher the interest rate, other things constant, the greater the reward for saving. As people save more, the quantity of loanable funds increases. The **supply of loanable funds** curve shows the positive relationship between the market interest rate and the quantity of savings supplied, other things constant, as reflected by the usual upward-sloping supply curve shown as *S* in Exhibit 2.

For the economy as a whole, if the amount of other resources and the level of technology are fixed, diminishing marginal productivity causes the marginal rate of return curve, which is the demand curve for investment, to slope downward. The **demand for loanable funds** curve is based on the expected marginal rate of return these borrowed funds yield when invested in capital. Each firm has a downward-sloping demand curve for loanable funds, reflecting a declining marginal rate of return on investment. With some qualifications, the demand for loanable funds by each firm can be summed horizontally to yield the demand for loanable funds by all firms, shown as *D* in Exhibit 2. Factors assumed constant along this demand curve include the prices of other resources, the level of technology, and the tax laws.

The demand and supply for loanable funds together, as in Exhibit 2, determine the market interest rate. In this case, the equilibrium interest rate of 8 percent is the only one that exactly matches the wishes of borrowers and savers. The equilibrium quantity of loanable funds is $100 billion per year. Any change in the demand or supply for loanable funds will change the market interest rate. For example, a major technological breakthrough that increases the productivity of capital will increase its marginal rate of return and shift the demand curve for loanable funds rightward, as shown in the movement from *D* to *D'*. Such an increase in the demand for loanable funds would raise the equilibrium interest rate to 9 percent and increase the quantity of loanable funds to $115 billion per year.

Why Interest Rates Differ

So far, we have been talking about *the* market rate of interest, implying that only one interest rate prevails in the loanable funds market. At any particular time, however, a range of interest rates coexist in the economy. For example, there are different interest rates on home mortgages, car loans, student loans, and credit cards, as well as the so-called *prime rate*—the rate offered the most trustworthy corporate borrowers. Let's see why interest rates differ.

Risk. Some borrowers are more likely than others to default on their loans. Differences in default risk get reflected in differences in the interest rate. Lenders are less willing to lend to more risky borrowers, so the interest rate charged on these loans rises. For example, the

EXHIBIT 2

Market for Loanable Funds

Because of the declining marginal rate of return on capital, the quantity of loanable funds demanded is inversely related to the rate of interest. The equilibrium rate of interest, 8 percent, is determined at the intersection of the demand and supply curves for loans. An increase in the demand for loans from *D* to *D'* leads to an increase in the equilibrium rate of interest from 8 percent to 9 percent.

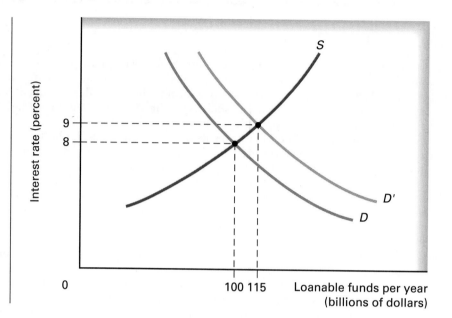

interest rate charged on a car loan is higher than on a home mortgage because a car offers worse collateral than a home. A car depreciates faster and can be driven away.

Duration of the Loan. The future is uncertain, and the further into the future a loan is to be repaid, the more uncertain that repayment becomes. Thus, as the duration of a loan increases, lenders become less willing to supply funds and require a higher interest rate to compensate for the greater risk. The **term structure of interest rates** is the relationship between the duration of a loan and the interest rate charged. The interest rate usually increases with the duration of the loan.

Cost of Administration. The costs of executing the loan agreement, monitoring the loan, and collecting payments are called the *administration costs* of the loan. These costs, as a proportion of the total amount of the loan, decrease as the size of the loan increases. For example, the cost of administering a $100,000 loan will be less than 10 times the cost of administering a $10,000 loan. Consequently, that portion of the interest charge reflecting the cost of administering the loan becomes smaller as the size of the loan increases, thus reducing the interest rate for larger loans.

Tax Treatment. Differences in the tax treatment of different types of loans will also affect the interest rate charged. For example, the interest earned on loans to state and local governments is not subject to federal income taxes. Because lenders focus on their after-tax rate of interest, state and local governments can pay a lower interest rate than other borrowers pay.

\<interactive\>**video**

ASK THE INSTRUCTOR: WHY DO INTEREST RATES VARY?

PRESENT VALUE AND DISCOUNTING

Because present consumption is valued more than future consumption, present and future consumption cannot be directly compared. A way of standardizing the discussion is to measure all consumption in terms of its present value. **Present value** is the current value of a payment or payments that will be received in the future. For example, how much would you pay now for the right to receive $100 one year from now? Put another way, what is the *present value* to you of receiving $100 one year from now?

SEE IT: COMPUTING PRESENT VALUES

Present Value of Payment One Year Hence

Suppose the market interest rate is 10 percent, so you can either lend or borrow at that rate. One way to determine how much you would pay for the opportunity to receive $100 one year from now is to ask how much you would have to save now, at the market interest rate, to end up with $100 one year from now. Here's the problem we are trying to solve: What amount of money, if saved at a rate of 10 percent, will accumulate to $100 one year from now? We can calculate the answer with a simple formula. We can say:

$$\text{Present value} \times 1.10 = \$100$$

or:

$$\text{Present value} = \frac{\$100}{1.10} = \$90.91$$

Thus, if the interest rate is 10 percent, $90.91 is the present value of receiving $100 one year from now; it is the most you would be willing to pay today to receive $100 one year from now. Rather than pay more than $90.91, you could simply deposit your $90.91 at the market interest rate and end up with $100 a year from now (ignoring any taxes). The procedure of dividing the future payment by 1 plus the prevailing interest rate to express it in today's dollars is called **discounting.**

The present value of $100 to be received one year from now depends on the interest rate. The more that present consumption is preferred to future consumption, the higher the interest rate that must be offered savers to defer consumption. *The higher the interest rate, the more the future payment is discounted and the lower its present value.* Put another way, the higher the interest rate, the less you need to save now to yield a given amount in the future. For example, if the interest rate is 15 percent, the present value of receiving $100 one year from now is $100/1.15, which equals $86.96.

Conversely, the less present consumption is preferred to future consumption, the less savers need to be paid to defer consumption and lower the interest rate. The lower the interest rate, the less the future income is discounted and the greater its present value. A lower interest rate means that you must save more now to yield a given amount in the future. As a general rule, the present value of receiving an amount one year from now is:

$$\text{Present value} = \frac{\text{Amount received one year from now}}{1 + \text{interest rate}}$$

For example, when the interest rate is 5 percent, the present value of receiving $100 one year from now is:

$$\text{Present value} = \frac{\$100}{1 + 0.05} = \frac{\$100}{1.05} = \$95.24$$

Present Value for Payments in Later Years

Now consider the present value of receiving $100 two years from now. What amount of money, if deposited at the market interest rate of 5 percent, would yield $100 two years from now? At the end of the first year, the value would be the present value times 1.05, which would then earn the market interest rate during the second year. At the end of the second year, the deposit would have accumulated to the present value times 1.05 times 1.05. Thus, we have the equation:

$$\text{Present value} \times 1.05 \times 1.05 = \text{Present value} \times (1.05)^2 = \$100$$

Solving for the present value yields:

$$\text{Present value} = \frac{\$100}{(1.05)^2} = \frac{\$100}{1.1025} = \$90.70$$

If the $100 were to be received three years from now, we would discount the payment over three years:

$$\text{Present value} = \frac{\$100}{(1.05)^3} = \$86.38$$

If the interest rate is i, the present value formula of a payment of M dollars t years from now is:

$$\text{Present value} = \frac{M}{(1 + i)^t}$$

Because $(1 + i)$ is greater than 1, the more times it is multiplied by itself (as determined by t), the bigger the denominator and the smaller the present value. Thus, *the present value of a given payment will be smaller the further into the future that payment is to be received.*

Present Value of an Income Stream

The previous method is used to compute the present value of a single sum to be paid at some point in the future. Most investments, however, yield a stream of income over time. In cases where the income is received over a period of years, the present value of each receipt can be computed individually and the results summed to yield the present value of the entire income stream. For example, the present value of receiving $100 next year and $150 the year after is simply the present value of the first year's receipt plus the present value of the second year's receipt. If the interest rate is 5 percent:

$$\text{Present value} = \frac{\$100}{1.05} + \frac{\$150}{(1.05)^2} = \$231.29$$

Present Value of an Annuity

A given sum of money received each year for a specified number of years is called an **annuity.** Such an income stream is called a *perpetuity* if it continues indefinitely into the future, as it would in our earlier example of the productivity gain stemming from the purchase of indestructible farm machinery. The present value of receiving a certain amount forever seems like it should be a very large sum indeed. But because future income is valued less the more distant into the future it is to be received, the present value of receiving a particular amount forever is not much more than that of receiving it for, say, 20 years.

To determine the present value of receiving $100 a year forever, we need only ask how much money must be deposited in a savings account to yield $100 in interest each year. If the interest rate is 10 percent, a deposit of $1,000 will earn $100 per year. Thus, the present value of receiving $100 a year indefinitely when the interest rate is 10 percent is $1,000. More generally, the present value of receiving a sum forever equals the amount received each year divided by the interest rate.

The concept of present value is useful in making investment decisions. Farmer Jones, by investing $10,000 in the crop sprayer, expected to earn $800 more per year. So his marginal rate of return was 8 percent. At a market interest rate of 8 percent, the present value of a cash flow of $800 per year discounted at that rate would be $800/0.08, which equals $10,000. Thus, *Jones was willing to invest capital until, at the margin, his investment yielded a cash stream with a present value just equal to the marginal cost of the investment.*

What about your decision to invest in human capital—to go to college? A chart in the previous chapter showed that those with at least a college degree earned more than twice as much as those with just a high school education. We could compute the present value of each level of education by discounting earnings based on that level of education, then summing total earnings over your working life. Even without carrying out those calculations, we can say with reasonable certainty that the present value of at least a college education will be more than twice that of just a high school education. You also learned way back in Chapter 1 that some college majors earn more than others. For example, based on a survey of people 35 to 44 years old with a college degree as their highest degree, males who majored in economics had median earnings 55 percent higher than those who majored in philosophy. Among females, that advantage was 91 percent for the same majors. If such an advantage prevailed throughout all working years, the present value of a degree in economics would be 55 percent higher than the present value of a degree in philosophy for males and 91 percent higher for females.

To develop a hands-on appreciation for present value and discounting, let's size up the payoff from state lotteries.

● *Bringing Theory to Life*

Since 1963, when New Hampshire introduced the first modern state-run lottery, 37 states and the District of Columbia have followed suit, generating profits of over $12 billion a year. Publicity photos usually show the winner receiving an oversized check. But winners usually get paid in annual installments, and the present value of the prize is much less than the advertised millions. For example, a million-dollar prizewinner usually gets $50,000 a year for 20 years. To put this in perspective, keep in mind that at an interest rate of 10 percent, the $50,000 received in the 20th year has a present value of only $7,432. If today you deposited $7,432 in an account earning 10 percent interest, you would wind up with $50,000 in 20 years (if we ignore taxes).

If the interest rate is 10 percent, the present value of a $50,000 annuity for the next 20 years is $425,700. Thus the present value of actual payments is less than half of the promised million, which is why lottery officials pay in installments (the multistate Powerball lottery pays out over 25 years, so it's worth even less). Incidentally, we might consider the present value of receiving $50,000 a year forever. Using the formula for an annuity discussed earlier, the present value with an interest rate of 10 percent is $50,000/0.10 = $500,000. Since the present value of receiving $50,000 for 20 years is $425,700, continuing the $50,000 annual payment *forever* adds only $74,300 to the present value. This shows the dramatic effect of discounting.

In some states, lottery winners are allowed to sell their jackpots. Winners typically receive only 40 cents on the dollar for the 20-year annuity. So a million-dollar pot, if sold by the winner, would fetch only $400,000. At tax rates prevailing in 2001, federal income taxes on $400,000 for a single tax filer amount to at least $140,000. State and local income taxes could subtract another $40,000. All told, because of time and taxes, the much-touted million could shrink to about $220,000 in after-tax income—only a fraction of the advertised million.

Among all the forms of legal gambling, the payout is the smallest for state lotteries—only $0.55 of every dollar wagered on average. Still, lotteries are apparently attractive, especially to the 5 percent of the population who buy half of all the lottery tickets sold.

<interactive>exercise

eACTIVITY: THE MILLION-DOLLAR LOTTERY?

<interactive>video

ASK THE INSTRUCTOR: WHAT IS THE ACTUAL VALUE OF LOTTERY WINNINGS?

Sources: Nicholas Thompson, "Snake Eyes: Even Education Cannot Save State Lotteries," *Washington Monthly* (December 1999); Adam Wolfson, "Life Is a Gamble," *Wall Street Journal*, 14 August 1998; "S.C. Legislature Approves Bill to Create State Lottery," *USA Today*, 20 June 2001; and an index of lottery sites found at http://www.state.wv.us/lottery/links.htm.

This discussion of present value and discounting concludes our treatment of capital and interest. We now have the tools to consider how firms, especially corporations, are financed.

CORPORATE FINANCE

During the Industrial Revolution, labor-saving machinery made large-scale production more profitable, but building huge factories filled with heavy machinery required substantial investments. The corporate structure became the easiest way to finance such investments, and by 1920, corporations accounted for most employment and output in the U.S. economy.

Way back in Chapter 4, you learned about the pros and cons of the corporate form of business organization, but thus far little has been said about corporate finance. As was noted in Chapter 4, a corporation is a legal entity, distinct from its shareholders. The corporation may own property, earn a profit, sue or be sued, and incur debt. Stockholders, the owners of the corporation, are liable only to the extent of their investment in the firm. Use of the abbreviation Inc. or Corp. in the company name serves as a warning to potential creditors that stockholders will not accept personal liability for the debts the company incurs.

<interactive>**example**

NETBOOKMARK: *WALL STREET WEEK* NEWSLETTER AND THE MOTLEY FOOL

Corporate Stock and Retained Earnings

Corporations acquire funds for investment in three ways: by issuing stock, by retaining some of their profits, and by borrowing. Corporations *issue and sell stock* to raise money for operations and for new plants and equipment. Suppose you have developed a recipe for a hot, spicy chili that your friends have convinced you will be a best-seller. You start a company called Six-Alarm Chili. As the founder, you are that firm's entrepreneur. An **entrepreneur** is a profit-seeking decision maker who organizes an enterprise and assumes the risk of operation. An entrepreneur pays resource owners for the opportunity to use their resources in the firm. The entrepreneur need not actually manage the firm's resources as long as he or she has the power to hire and fire the manager—that is, as long as the entrepreneur controls the manager.

Your company meets with early success, but you find that to remain competitive, you need to grow. To get the funds needed for growth, you decide to incorporate the business. The newly incorporated company issues 1,000,000 shares of stock. You take 100,000 shares yourself as your *owner's equity* in the corporation. The rest are sold to the public for $10 per share, which raises $9 million for the company. You, in effect, paid for your shares with the "sweat equity" required to found the company and get it rolling. The initial sale of stock to the public is called an **initial public offering,** or **IPO.** A *share* of **corporate stock** represents a claim on the net income and assets of a corporation, as well as the right to vote on corporate directors and on other important matters. A person who buys 1 percent of the 1,000,000 shares issued thereby owns 1 percent of the corporation, is entitled to 1 percent of any profit, and gets to cast 1 percent of the votes.

Corporations must pay corporate income taxes on any profit. After-tax profit is either paid as **dividends** to shareholders or reinvested in the corporation. Reinvested profit, or **retained earnings,** allows the firm to finance expansion. Stockholders expect dividends, but the corporation is not required to pay dividends. Once shares are issued, their price tends to fluctuate directly with the firm's profit prospects. People buy stock because of the dividends and because they hope the value of the stock will appreciate, or increase, in the future.

<interactive>**graph**

TRY IT: THE EFFECT OF CHANGES IN A FIRM'S PRODUCT MARKET ON ITS STOCK PRICE

Corporate Bonds

Again, your corporation can acquire funds by issuing stock, by retaining earnings, or by borrowing. To borrow money, the corporation can go to a bank for a loan or it can issue and sell bonds. A **bond** is the corporation's promise to pay back the holder a fixed sum of money on the designated *maturity date* plus make interest payments until that date. For example, a corporation might sell for $1,000 a bond that promises to make an annual interest payment of, say, $100 and to repay the $1,000 at the end of 20 years.

The payment stream for bonds is more predictable than that for stocks. Unless this corporation goes bankrupt, it is obliged to pay bondholders the promised amounts. In contrast, stockholders are last in line when resource holders get paid, so bondholders get paid before stockholders. Investors usually consider bonds less risky than stocks, although bonds involve some risk as well.

Securities Exchanges

Once stocks and bonds have been issued and sold, owners of these securities are free to resell them on *security exchanges*. In the United States, there are seven security exchanges registered with the *Securities and Exchange Commission (SEC)*, the federal body that regulates securities markets. The two largest are the New York Stock Exchange, which trades the securities of over 3,300 major companies, and the Nasdaq, which trades over 4,600 companies, many of them technology firms. Nearly all the securities traded each day are *secondhand securities* in the sense that they have already been issued by the corporation. So the bulk of daily transactions do not finance firms in need of investment funds. Most money goes from a securities buyer to a securities seller. *Institutional investors,* such as banks, insurance companies, and mutual funds, account for over half the trading volume on major exchanges. By providing a *secondary market* for securities, exchanges enhance the *liquidity* of these securities—that is, the exchanges make the securities more readily sold for cash and thus more attractive to investors.

The secondary markets for stocks also determine the current market value of the corporation. The market value of a firm at any given time can be found by multiplying the share price by the number of shares outstanding. The share price reflects the present value of the discounted stream of expected profit. Just to give you some idea, General Electric, the top-valued U.S. firm, had a market value of about $370 billion in October 2001. The market value of all firms on U.S. exchanges totaled about $15 trillion.

Securities prices give the firm's management some indication of the wisdom of raising investment funds through retained earnings, new stock issues, or new bond issues. The greater a corporation's expected profit, other things constant, the higher the value of shares on the stock market and the lower the interest rate that would have to be paid on new bond issues. *Thus, securities markets allocate funds more readily to successful firms than to firms in financial difficulty.* Some firms may be in such poor shape that they cannot sell new securities. Securities markets usually promote the survival of the fittest by allocating investment funds to those firms that seem able to make the most profitable use of those funds.

CONCLUSION

This chapter introduced you to capital, interest, and corporate finance. Capital is a more complicated resource than this chapter has conveyed. For example, the demand curve for investment is a moving target, not the stable relationship drawn in Exhibit 1. An accurate depiction of the investment demand curve calls for knowledge of the marginal product of capital and the price of output in the future. But capital's marginal productivity changes with breakthroughs in technology and with changes in the employment of other resources. And the future price of the product can also vary widely. Consider, for example, the dilemma of a firm contemplating an investment in oil drilling rigs in recent years, when the price of crude oil fluctuated between $10 and $36 per barrel, as it has since 1998.

One final point: When economists talk about investing, they have in mind purchases of new capital, such as new machines and new buildings. When the media talk about investing, they usually mean buying stocks and bonds. To an economist, Farmer Jones is investing only when he buys new farm machinery, not when he buys stocks and bonds.

endofchaptermaterial

- **Summary**
- **Questions for Review**
- **Problems and Exercises**
- **Experiential Exercises**

- **Wall Street Journal Exercise**
- **Graphing Workshop: Apply It Exercises**

Take the Post-Test to assess your overall understanding of the key ideas in this chapter. The Post-Test provides a comprehensive selection of exam-style questions addressing the main topics and concepts of the chapter. At the completion of each Post-Test, you will receive a score and instructive feedback on how you answered each question, and a direct link to the part of the chapter addressed in the question. Take the Post-Test as often as you need to—a record of your progress for each attempt is kept for you to revisit and gauge your improvement. And each Post-Test is randomly generated, so every attempt is new.

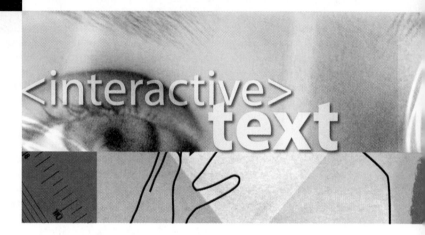

14

Transaction Costs, Imperfect Information, and Market Behavior

General Motors offers car loans and issues credit cards, so why don't some banks make automobiles? Why do some firms, such as Domino's Pizza, specialize in a single product, while other firms, such as General Electric, produce hundreds of different products? Why stop at hundreds? Why not thousands? In fact, why isn't there a giant firm that makes everything? Why is proper spelling important on your résumé? Why is buying a used car so dicey? Why do some winners of online auctions end up losers? Answers to these and other seemingly unrelated questions are addressed in this chapter, which digs deeper into some assumptions about firms, households, and the availability of market information.

In the first half of this chapter, we will step inside the firm to reconsider some simplifying assumptions about how firms work. We ask: Why do firms exist? How do they decide what to produce themselves and what inputs to buy from other firms? Why do some firms produce a wide range of products? These steps toward realism move us beyond the simple depiction of the firm employed to this point. In the second half of this chapter, we challenge some simplifying assumptions about the information available to market participants. We ask: How does missing information affect the behavior of market participants and shape market outcomes? Overall, this chapter should help you develop a more realistic view of market behavior. Topics discussed in this chapter include:

- Transaction costs
- Vertical integration
- Economies of scope
- Optimal search

- Winner's curse
- Asymmetric information
- Adverse selection
- Principal-agent problem
- Moral hazard
- Signaling and screening

Pre-Test

Take the Pre-Test to assess your initial knowledge of the key ideas in this chapter. The Pre-Test provides exam-style questions addressing the main topics and concepts of the chapter. At the completion of each Pre-Test, you will receive a score and instructive feedback on how you answered each question, and a direct link to the part of the chapter addressed in the question. Take the Pre-Test as often as you need to—a record of your progress for each attempt is kept for you to revisit and gauge your improvement.

RATIONALE FOR THE FIRM AND ITS SCOPE OF OPERATION

The competitive model assumes that all participants in the market know everything they need to about the price and availability of all inputs, outputs, and production processes. Perfect competition assumes that the firm is headed by a brilliant decision maker with a computerlike ability to calculate all the relevant marginal productivities. This individual knows everything necessary to solve complex production and pricing problems.

The irony is that if the marginal products of all inputs could be measured easily and if prices for all inputs could be determined without cost, there would be little reason for production to take place in firms. In a world characterized by perfect competition, perfect information, constant returns to scale, and costless exchange, the consumer could bypass the firm to deal directly with resource suppliers, purchasing inputs in the appropriate amounts. Someone who wanted a table could buy timber, have it milled, contract with a carpenter, contract with a painter, and end up with a finished product. The consumer could carry out transactions directly with each resource supplier.

The Firm Reduces Transaction Costs

So why is production carried out within firms? More than 60 years ago, in a classic article entitled "The Nature of the Firm," Nobel Prize winner Ronald Coase asked the fundamental question, "Why do firms exist?"[1] Why do people organize in the hierarchical structure of the firm and coordinate their decisions through a manager rather than simply rely on market exchange? His answer would not surprise today's students of economics: *Organizing activities through the hierarchy of the firm is often more efficient than market exchange because production requires the coordination of many transactions among many resource owners. The firm is the favored means of production when the transaction costs involved in using the price system exceed the costs of organizing those same activities through direct managerial controls within a firm.*

Consider again the example of purchasing a table by contracting directly with all the different resource suppliers, from the grower of timber to the painter who applied the varnish. Using resource markets directly involves (1) the cost of determining what inputs are needed and how they should be combined and (2) the cost of negotiating an agreement with each resource owner for each specific contribution to production *over and above* the direct costs of the timber, nails, machinery, paint, and labor required to make the table. Where inputs are easily identified, measured, priced, and hired, production can be carried out through a price-guided "do it yourself" approach using the market. For example, getting your house painted is a relatively simple task: You can buy the paint and brushes and hire painters by the hour. In this case, you become your own painting contractor, hiring inputs in the market and combining them to do the job.

[1]*Economica* 4 (November 1937): 386–405.

Where the costs of identifying the appropriate inputs and negotiating for each specific contribution are high, the consumer minimizes transaction costs by purchasing the finished product from a firm. For example, although some people serve as their own painting contractor, fewer do so when building a house; most hire a building contractor. *The more complicated the task, the greater the ability to economize on transaction costs through specialization and centralized control.* For example, attempting to buy a car by contracting with the hundreds of resource suppliers required to assemble one would be time consuming, costly, and impossible for most people. What type of skilled labor should be hired and at what wages? How much steel, aluminum, plastic, glass, paint, and other materials should be purchased? How should the resources be combined and in what proportions? Anyone without detailed knowledge of auto production couldn't do it. That's why consumers buy assembled cars rather than contract separately with each resource supplier.

At the margin, there will be some activities that could go either way, with some consumers using firms and some hiring resources directly in the markets. The choice will depend on each consumer's skill and opportunity cost of time. For example, some people may not want to be troubled with hiring all the inputs to get their house painted; instead, they will simply contract with a firm to do the entire job for an agreed-upon price—they will hire a painting contractor. As you will see later in the chapter, however, hiring a contractor may give rise to other problems of quality control.

The Boundaries of the Firm

So far, the chapter has explained why firms exist: *Firms minimize both the transaction costs and the production costs of economic activity.* The next question is: What are the efficient boundaries of the firm? The theory of the firm described in earlier chapters is largely silent on questions concerning the boundaries of the firm—that is, on the appropriate degree of vertical integration. **Vertical integration** is the expansion of a firm into stages of production earlier or later than those in which it has specialized. For example, a steel company may decide (1) to integrate backward by mining its own iron ore or even mining the coal used to smelt iron ore (for example, U.S. Steel owns coal mines) or (2) to integrate forward by forming raw steel into various components. A large manufacturer employs an amazing variety of production processes, but on average about half of the cost of production goes to purchasing inputs from other firms. For example, General Motors and Ford each spends over $80 billion a year on parts, materials, and services obtained from over 30,000 suppliers. The combined total exceeds the annual output of most countries of the world.

How does the firm determine which activities to undertake and which to purchase from other firms? Should IBM manufacture its own computer chips or buy them from another firm? The answer depends on a comparison of the benefits and costs of internal production versus market purchases. The point bears repeating: *Internal production and markets are alternative ways of organizing transactions.* The choice will depend on which form of organization is a more efficient way of carrying out the transaction in question. Keep in mind that market prices coordinate transactions *between* firms, whereas managers coordinate activities *within* firms. The market coordinates resources by harmonizing the independent plans of separate decision makers, but a firm coordinates resources through the conscious direction of the manager.

The usual assumption is that transactions will be organized by market exchange unless markets pose problems. Market exchange allows each firm to benefit from specialization and comparative advantage. For example, IBM can specialize in making computers and buy from chip makers what they produce. But sometimes the input is not standardized or the exact performance requirements are hard to specify. For example, suppose one firm wants another firm to supply research and development services. The uncertainty involved in such a nonspecific service makes it difficult to write, execute, and enforce a purchase agreement covering all possible contingencies that could arise. What if the R&D supplier, in the course of fulfilling the agreement, makes a valuable discovery for an application in a different field? Who has the right to that new application—the firm that paid for the R&D service or the firm that supplied it? And who determines if the field is different? Since incomplete contracts create potentially troublesome situations, conducting research and development *within the firm* often involves a lower transaction cost than purchasing it in the market.

At this point, it might be useful to discuss specific criteria the firm considers when deciding whether to purchase a particular input from the market, thereby benefiting from another producer's comparative advantage, or to produce that input internally.

Bounded Rationality of the Manager. To direct and coordinate activity in a conscious way in the firm, a manager must understand how all the pieces of the puzzle fit together. As the firm takes on more and more activities, however, the manager starts losing track of details, so the quality of managerial decisions suffers. The more tasks the firm takes on, the longer the lines of communication between the manager and the production workers who must implement the decision. One constraint on vertical integration is the manager's **bounded rationality,** which limits the amount of information a manager can comprehend about the firm's operation. As the firm takes on additional functions, coordination and communication become more difficult. The firm can experience diseconomies similar to those it experiences when it expands output beyond the efficient scale of production. The solution is for the firm to reduce its functions to those it does best. Such cutbacks occurred when automakers increased the proportion of parts they purchased from other firms.

Minimum Efficient Scale. As noted when firm costs were first discussed, the *minimum efficient scale* is the minimum level of output at which economies of scale have been fully exploited. For example, suppose that minimum efficient scale in the production of personal computers is achieved when output reaches 1 million per year, as shown by the long-run average cost curve in panel (a) of Exhibit 1. Suppose this output rate turns out to be the amount the firm needs to produce to maximize profit. Because the computer chip is an important component in the personal computer, should the PC maker integrate backward into chip production? What if the minimum efficient scale in chip production is not achieved until production reaches 5 million

EXHIBIT 1

Minimum Efficient Scale and Vertical Integration

The computer manufacturer in panel (a) is producing at the minimum efficient scale of 1,000,000 units per period. That level of production requires 1,000,000 computer chips. If the manufacturer produced its own chips, the cost would be much higher than if it purchased them from a chip manufacturer operating on a much larger scale. As panel (b) shows, at 1,000,000 chips, economies of scale in chip production are far from exhausted.

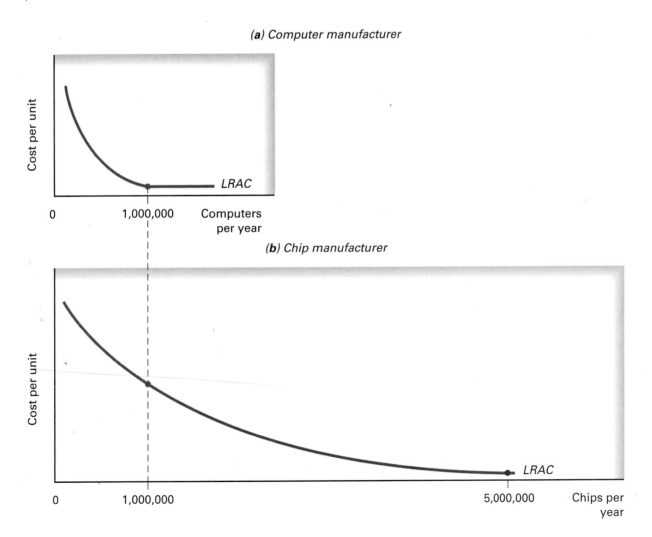

(a) Computer manufacturer

(b) Chip manufacturer

chips per year? A PC manufacturer that requires only one chip per PC needs only 20 percent of the chips produced at the minimum efficient scale. As you can see in panel (b) of Exhibit 1, if only 1 million chips were produced, the cost per chip would be high relative to the cost that could be achieved at minimum efficient scale in chip production. The PC manufacturer therefore minimizes production costs by buying chips from a chip maker of optimal size. More generally, *other things constant, a firm should buy an input if the market price is below what it would cost the firm to make.*

Easily Observable Quality. If an input is well defined and its quality is easily determined at the time of purchase, that input is more likely to be purchased in the market than produced internally, other things constant. For example, a flourmill will typically buy wheat in the market rather than grow its own, as the quality of the wheat can be easily assessed upon inspection. In contrast, the quality of certain inputs can be determined only as they are produced. Firms whose reputations depend on the operation of a key component are likely to produce the component, especially if the quality of that component varies widely across producers over time and cannot be easily observed by inspection. For example, suppose that the manufacturer of a sensitive measuring instrument requires a crucial gauge, the quality of which can be observed only as the gauge is assembled. If the firm produces the gauge itself, it can closely monitor quality.

Producers sometimes integrate backward so they can offer consumers a guarantee about the quality of the components or ingredients in a product. For example, Frank Perdue can talk about the health and quality of his chickens because his company raises its own. Kentucky Fried Chicken, however, does not discuss the family background of its chickens because the company makes no claim about raising them. Instead, KFC ads focus on the secret ingredients used to fry the chicken and the fact that, by specializing in chicken, the company does a better job than other fast-food franchises that sell many different items.

Number of Suppliers. A firm wants an uninterrupted source of component parts. When there are many interchangeable suppliers of a particular input, a firm is more likely to purchase that input in the market than to produce it internally, other things constant. Not only does the existence of many suppliers ensure a dependable source of components, but also competition among these suppliers keeps the price down. But if the resource market is so unstable that the firm cannot rely on a consistent supply of components, the firm may produce the item to insulate itself from the vagaries of that market.

To review: If a firm relies on market purchases of inputs rather than on vertical integration, it can benefit from the specialization and comparative advantage of individual suppliers. Other things constant, the firm is more likely to buy a component part rather than produce it if (1) the item can be purchased for less than it could be if produced by the firm, (2) the item is well defined and its quality easily observable, and (3) there are many suppliers. These issues are discussed in the following case study.

CASESTUDY | The Trend Toward Outsourcing

● *The Information Economy*

Outsourcing occurs when a firm buys products, such as auto parts, or services, such as data processing, from outside suppliers. A firm relies on the division of labor and the law of comparative advantage to focus on what it does best, while depending on other firms to supply component parts, payroll services, data processing, Web sites, building security, and other inputs that are beyond that firm's "core competency." Firms, particularly manufacturing firms, have long purchased some components from other firms, but the outsourcing movement extended these purchases to a broader range of products and activities that typically had been produced internally. Japanese firms pioneered outsourcing to reduce production costs and enhance quality. In the United States, outsourcing blossomed in manufacturing during the 1980s and spread to virtually every industry.

For example, faced with outdated computer hardware and software, Bethlehem Steel executives realized they could no longer hire and retain enough information technology (IT) workers to keep up with the changes in such a dynamic field. So Bethlehem outsourced its IT system. Even Microsoft outsources some software development. DuPont, which produces hundreds of products from chemicals to carpeting, outsources responsibility for shipping all imports and exports. Dell Computer, the world's largest online, phone, and mail-order seller of personal computers, turns over shipping to an outside firm. And a growing number of computer makers are outsourcing computer assembly. The head of Handspring has never visited the Mexican plant that manufactures the palm-size organizer, noting that "Our value-added is in product design, product development, marketing, and branding."

Alcatel, a telephone equipment maker, plans to sell off more than 100 of its 120 manufacturing plants. The move allows Alcatel to adjust production up or down more quickly without having to worry about hiring or laying off workers. Outsourcing, in effect, turns some fixed costs into variable costs.

Perhaps the poster-child of outsourcing is TopsyTail. Just about everything the company does—design, production, marketing, forecasting, packaging, and distribution—is outsourced to subcontractors. With just a few employees, the company has grossed $100 million so far selling its simple hair-styling gadgets. The founder says the company could not have grown so fast any other way.

The boom in outsourcing has benefited firms that supply what other firms no longer do for themselves. IBM's major business has shifted from selling hardware and software to servicing firms that have outsourced their information technology needs. Firms in India have sprung up to offer IT services to major U.S. corporations, often supplying them over the Internet. Many U.S. corporations have also outsourced customer-service call centers to India.

What are the limits to outsourcing? One cost of outsourcing can be a loss of control. For example, when Compaq Computer outsourced some laptop production to a Japanese manufacturer, problems mushroomed in design, cost, and quality. Compaq now has a management team that oversees outsourced activities. Some companies fear that outsourcing can weaken customer ties. For example, several automakers had to recall 8 million vehicles because of faulty seat belts from a Japanese supplier. Customers blamed the auto companies for the recall, not the subcontractor.

Recently, there has been a modest return to in-house production. For example, because of better software and cheaper computers, some firms are now "insourcing" data processing activities once supplied by other firms. Insourcing reduces the number of times that records must be handled, improving data quality and reducing errors. DaimlerChrysler considered outsourcing its data processing, but its own division was the low bidder. Because computer software has made Harley-Davidson more efficient, the company now makes more of its own motorcycle parts. By taking back or keeping key production steps in house, some managers think they can respond more flexibly to custom orders and changing market conditions.

\<interactive\>exercise

- eACTIVITY: THE TREND TOWARD OUTSOURCING
- READING IT RIGHT: WALL STREET JOURNAL EXERCISE

Sources: Lisa DiCarlo, "IBM for Hire," *Forbes,* 31 October 2000; Julia King, "Farming Out Everything: TopsyTail Focus," *Computerworld,* 23 March 1998; Kevin Delaney, "Alcatel Plans to Shed the Bulk of Its Manufacturing Operations," *Wall Street Journal,* 27 June 2001; Beth Duff-Brown, "Services—By Way of Bangalore," *Hartford Courant,* 12 July 2001; "Sri Lankan Software Firm Wins Microsoft Deal," *Reuters,* 18 October 2000; Beth Ellyn Rosenthal, "Fast Growth in Hard Times, *Outsourcing Journal* (July 2001) at http://www.outsourcing-journal.com/issues/jul2001/ headlines.html; and the Outsourcing Institute at http://www.outsourcing.com/.

Economies of Scope

So far we have considered issues affecting the optimal degree of vertical integration in producing a particular product. Even with outsourcing, the focus is on how best to produce a particular product, such as an automobile or a computer. But some firms branch into product lines that do not have a vertical relationship. **Economies of scope** exist when it is cheaper to combine two or more product lines in one firm than to produce them in separate firms. For example, General Electric produces hundreds of different products ranging from light bulbs to jet engines to NBC-TV. By spreading outlays for research and development and marketing over different products ("We bring good things to life"), GE can minimize those costs. Ford Motor Company owns Hertz Rent-A-Car. Travelers Insurance and Citibank merged to offer consumers a smorgasbord of financial services. Or consider economies of scope on the farm. A farmer often grows a variety of crops and raises different farm animals—animals that recycle damaged crops and food scraps into useful fertilizer. With economies of *scale,* the average cost per unit of output falls as the *scale* of the firm increases; *with economies of scope, average costs*

per unit fall as the scope of the firm increases—that is, as the firm produces more types of products. The cost of some fixed resources, such as specialized knowledge, can be spread across product lines.

Some combinations don't work out. For example, in 1994, Quaker Oats paid $1.7 billion for the Snapple drink business. After Snapple sales dropped, Quaker sold its Snapple division in 1997 for $300 million, or less than one-fifth the purchase price. Likewise, AT&T bought NCR, which provides hardware and software for customer transactions, for $7.5 billion in 1991 and, after spending another $2 billion trying to make the marriage work, sold NCR in 1997 for $3.4 billion—taking a $6.1 billion haircut on the deal. Some mergers of firms in different business lines don't yield the expected economies of scope.

Our focus has been on why firms exist, why they often integrate vertically, why they outsource, and why they sometimes produce a whole range of products. These steps toward realism move us beyond the simple picture of the firm we created earlier. The rest of the chapter challenges some simplifying assumptions about the amount of information available to market participants.

MARKET BEHAVIOR WITH IMPERFECT INFORMATION

For the most part, our analysis of market behavior has assumed that market participants have full information about products and resources. For consumers, full information involves knowledge about a product's price, quality, and availability. For firms, full information includes knowledge about the marginal productivity of various resources, about the appropriate technology for combining them, and about the demand for the firm's product. In reality, *reliable information is costly for both consumers and producers.* What's more, in some markets, one side of a transaction has more information than does the other side. This section examines the impact of less-than-perfect information on market behavior.

NETBOOKMARK: NATIONAL ASSOCIATION OF REALTORS®

Optimal Search with Imperfect Information

Suppose you want to buy a new computer. You need information about the quality and features of each model and the prices at various retail outlets, mail-order firms, and online sites. To learn more about your choices, you may talk with experts, read promotional brochures and computer publications, and visit the Web. Once you narrow your choice to one or two models, you may shop by going from store to store or by letting your fingers do the walking through the *Yellow Pages,* computer catalogs, Internet search engines, newspaper ads, and the like. Searching for the lowest price for a particular model involves a cost, primarily the opportunity cost of your time. This cost will obviously vary from individual to individual and from item to item. Some people actually enjoy shopping, but this "shop 'til you drop" attitude does not necessarily carry over to all items. *For most of us, the process of gathering consumer information can be considered nonmarket work.*

Marginal Cost of Search. In your quest for product information, you gather the easy and obvious information first. You may check on the price and availability at the few computer stores at the mall. But as your search widens, the *marginal cost* of acquiring additional information increases, both because you may have to travel greater distances to check prices and services and because the opportunity cost of your time increases as you spend more time acquiring information. Consequently, the marginal cost curve for additional information slopes upward, as is shown in Exhibit 2. Note that a certain amount of information, I_f, is common knowledge and is freely available.

Marginal Benefit of Search. The *marginal benefit* from acquiring additional information is better quality for a given price or a lower price for a given quality. The marginal benefit is relatively large at first, but as you gather more information and grow more acquainted with the market, additional information yields less and less additional benefit. For example, the likelihood of uncovering valuable information, such as an attractive feature or a lower price, at the second store visited is greater than the likelihood of finding this information at the twentieth store visited. Thus, the marginal benefit curve for additional information slopes downward, as is shown in Exhibit 2.

EXHIBIT 2

Optimal Search with Imperfect Information

When information is not free, additional information is acquired as long as its marginal benefit exceeds its marginal cost. Equilibrium, or optimal search, occurs where marginal benefit equals marginal cost.

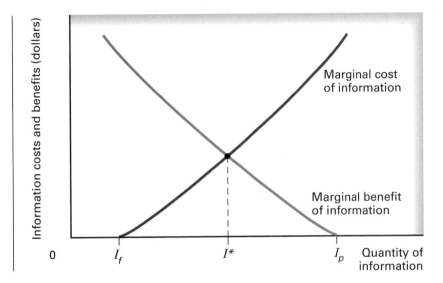

Optimal Search. Market participants will continue to gather information as long as the marginal benefit of additional information exceeds its marginal cost. *Optimal search occurs when the marginal benefit just equals the marginal cost,* which in Exhibit 2 occurs where the two marginal curves intersect. Notice that at search levels exceeding the equilibrium amount, the marginal benefit of additional information is still positive, but it's below the marginal cost. Notice also that at some point the value of additional information reaches zero, as identified by I_p on the horizontal axis. This level of information could be identified as *perfect information.* The high marginal cost of acquiring I_p, however, makes it impractical to become perfectly informed. Thus, firms and consumers, by gathering the optimal amount of information, I^*, have less-than-perfect information about the price, availability, and quality of products and resources.

Implications. The search model we have described was developed by George Stigler, winner of the Nobel Prize in 1982. Four decades ago, he showed that the price of a product can differ among sellers because some consumers are unaware of lower prices offered by some sellers.[2] Thus, *search costs result in price dispersion, or different prices, for the same product.* Some sellers call attention to price dispersions by claiming to have the lowest prices around and by promising to match any competitor's price (Gateway Computers does this). *Search costs also lead to quality differences across sellers, even for identically priced products, because consumers find it too costly to shop for the highest quality product.*

There are other implications of Stigler's search model. The more expensive the commodity, the greater the price dispersion in dollar terms. Thus, the more expensive the item, the greater the incentive to shop around. You are more likely to shop around for a car than for a comb. Also, as the consumer's wage increases, so does the opportunity cost of time. This increases the marginal cost of acquiring additional information, resulting in less searching and more price dispersion. On the other hand, any change in technology that lowers the marginal cost of information will reduce the marginal cost of additional information, resulting in more information and less price dispersion. For example, some Internet sites, like mySimon.com, identify the lowest prices for sellers of books, airfares, automobiles, computers, and dozens of other products. And some Internet sellers, like buy.com, maintain the lowest prices on the Web as a way of attracting customers undertaking such searches.

The Winner's Curse

In 1996, the federal government auctioned off leases to valuable space on the scarce radio spectrum. The space was to be used for newly invented personal communications services, such as cellular telephones, portable fax machines, and wireless computer networks. The bidding

[2]George Stigler, "The Economics of Information," *Journal of Political Economy* (June 1961): 213–225.

was carried out in the face of much uncertainty about future competition in the industry, the potential size of the market, and future technological change. Thus, bidders had little experience with the potential value of such leases. At the time, 89 companies made winning bids totaling $10.2 billion for 493 licenses. But by 1998, it became clear that many of the winning bidders couldn't pay, and dozens of licenses were tied up in bankruptcy proceedings.[3] The auction eventually raised only half the amount of the winning bids. In auctions for products of uncertain value, such as wireless communications licenses and drilling rights in the Gulf of Mexico, why do many "winners" end up losers?

The actual value of space on the radio spectrum was unknown and could only be estimated. For example, suppose the average bid was $10 million, with some higher and others lower. Suppose also that the winning bid was $20 million. The winning bid was not the average bid, which may have been the most reliable estimate of the true value, but the highest bid, which was the most optimistic estimate. Winners of such bids are said to experience the **winner's curse** because they often lose money after winning the bid, the price of being overly optimistic.

The winner's curse applies to all cases of bidding in which the true value is unknown at the outset. For example, movie companies often bid up the price of screenplays to what many argue are unrealistic levels. Likewise, publishers get into bidding wars over book manuscripts and even book proposals that are little more than titles. Team owners bid for free agents and often overpay. CBS lost money on the 1998 Winter Olympics. And NBC may have overbid by offering $2.3 billion for the rights to broadcast the Olympics in 2002, 2006, and 2008; at the time of the bid, Olympic cities had not even been selected. Online auctions, like eBay, often sell items of unknown value. With perfect information about market value, potential buyers would never bid more than that market value. But when competitive bidding is coupled with imperfect information, the winning bidder often ends up a loser.

ASYMMETRIC INFORMATION IN PRODUCT MARKETS

We have considered the effects of costly information and limited information on market behavior. But the issue becomes more complicated when one side of the market has more reliable information than the other side does, a situation in which there is **asymmetric information.** This section examines several examples of asymmetric information in the product market and the effect on market efficiency.

There are two types of information that a market participant may want but lack. First, one side of the market may know more about *characteristics* of the product for sale than the other side knows. For example, the seller of a used car knows more about that car's record of reliability than the buyer does. Likewise, the buyer of a health insurance policy knows more about his or her general health than does the insurance company. When one side of the market knows more than the other side about important product characteristics, the asymmetric information problem involves **hidden characteristics.**

A second type of problem occurs when one side of a transaction can pursue an *action* that affects the other side but that cannot be observed by the other side. For example, the mechanic you hire to check out that strange engine noise may undertake unneeded repairs, charging three hours' work for a job that should have taken only 10 minutes. Whenever one side of an economic relationship can take a relevant action that the other side cannot observe, the situation is described as one of **hidden actions.**

Hidden Characteristics: Adverse Selection

One type of hidden-characteristic problem occurs when the seller knows more about the quality of the product than the buyer does, as with the market for used cars. The seller of a used car normally has abundant personal experience with important *characteristics* of that car: accidents, breakdowns, gas mileage, maintenance, performance in bad weather, and so on. A prospective buyer can only guess at these based on the car's appearance and perhaps a test drive. The buyer cannot really know how good the car is without driving it for several months under varying traffic and weather conditions.

To simplify the problem, suppose there are only two types of used cars for sale: good ones and bad ones, or "lemons." Suppose that a buyer who is certain about a car's type would be willing to pay $10,000 for a good used car but only $4,000 for a lemon. Again, only the seller knows which type is for sale. A buyer who believes that half the used cars on the market are good ones and half are lemons would be willing to pay, say, $7,000 for a car of unknown type (the average perceived value of cars on the market). Would $7,000 be the equilibrium price of used cars?

[3]Scott Ritter, "FCC Says Several Bidders to Return Wireless Licenses," *Wall Street Journal,* 18 June 1998.

So far, the analysis has ignored the actions of potential sellers, who know which type of car they have. Since sellers of good cars can get only $7,000 for cars they know to be worth $10,000 on average, many will choose to keep their cars or will sell them to friends or relatives. But sellers of lemons will find $7,000 an attractive price because they know their cars are worth only $4,000 on average. As a result, the proportion of good cars on the market will fall and the proportion of lemons will rise, reducing the average value of used cars on the market.

As buyers come to realize that the mix has shifted toward lemons, they will reduce what they are willing to pay for cars of unknown quality. As the market price of used cars falls, potential sellers of good cars become even more reluctant to sell at such a low price, so the proportion of lemons increases, leading to still lower prices. The process could continue until there are very few good cars sold on the open market. More generally, *when sellers have better information about a product's quality than buyers do, lower-quality products tend to dominate the market.*

When those on the informed side of the market self-select in a way that harms the uninformed side of the market, the problem is one of **adverse selection.** In our example, car sellers, the informed side, self-select—that is, they decide whether or not to offer their cars for sale—in a way that increases the percentage of lemons for sale. Because of adverse selection, car buyers, the uninformed side of the market, end up trading primarily with owners of lemons—exactly the group buyers don't want to deal with.

Hidden Actions: The Principal-Agent Problem

In this age of specialization, there are many tasks we do not perform for ourselves because others do them better and because others have a lower opportunity cost of time. Suppose your objective is to get your car repaired, but you can't do it yourself. The mechanic you hire may have other objectives, such as maximizing on-the-job leisure or maximizing the garage's profit. But the mechanic's actions are hidden from you. Although your car may have only a loose electrical wire, the mechanic could inflate the bill by charging you for "repairs" not really needed or not performed. This asymmetric information problem occurs because one side of a transaction can pursue *hidden actions* that affect the other side. When buyers have difficulty monitoring and evaluating the quality of goods or services purchased, some suppliers may substitute poor-quality resources or exercise less diligence in providing the service.

The problem that arises from hidden actions is called the **principal-agent problem,** which describes a relationship in which one party, known as the **principal,** contracts with another party, known as the **agent,** in the expectation that the agent will act on behalf of the principal. *The problem arises when the goals of the agent are incompatible with those of the principal and when the agent can pursue hidden actions.* You could confront a principal-agent problem when you deal with a doctor, lawyer, auto mechanic, or stock broker, to name a few. Any employer-employee relationship could potentially be a source of a principal-agent problem. Again, the problem arises because the agent's objectives are not the same as the principal's *and* because the agent's actions are hidden. Not all principal-agent relationships pose a problem. For example, when you hire someone to mow your lawn or cut your hair, there are no hidden actions and you can judge the results.

Asymmetric Information in Insurance Markets

Asymmetric information also creates problems in insurance markets. For example, from an insurer's point of view, ideal candidates for health insurance are those who lead long, healthy lives and then die peacefully in their sleep. But many people are poor risks for health insurers because of hidden characteristics (bad genes) or hidden actions (smoking and drinking excessively, getting exercise only on trips to the refrigerator, and thinking a seven-course meal consists of beef jerky and a six-pack of beer). In the insurance market, it is the buyers, not the sellers, who have more information about the characteristics and actions that predict their likely need for insurance in the future.

If the insurance company has no way of distinguishing among applicants, it must charge those who are good health risks the same as those who are poor ones. This price is attractive to poor health risks but will seem too high to good health risks, some of whom will choose not to buy insurance. As the number of healthy people who don't buy health insurance increases, the insured group becomes less healthy on average, so rates must rise, making insurance even less attractive to healthy people. Because of adverse selection, insurance buyers tend to be less healthy than the population as a whole. Adverse selection has been used as an argument for national health insurance.

The insurance problem is compounded by the fact that once people buy insurance, their behavior may change in a way that increases the probability that a claim will be made. For example, those with health insurance may take less care of their health, and those with theft insurance may take less care of insured valuables. This incentive problem is referred to as *moral hazard.* **Moral hazard** occurs when an individual's behavior changes in a way that increases the likelihood of an unfavorable outcome.

More generally, *moral hazard is a principal-agent problem since it occurs when those on one side of a transaction have an incentive to shirk their responsibilities because the other side is unable to observe them.* The responsibility could be to repair a car, maintain health, or safeguard valuables. Both the mechanic and the policy buyer may take advantage of the ignorant party. In the car-repair example, the mechanic is the agent; in the insurance example, the policy buyer is the principal. Thus, moral hazard arises when someone can undertake hidden action; this could be either the agent or the principal, depending on the circumstances.

ECONDEBATE ONLINE: SHOULD U.S. FINANCIAL MARKETS BE DEREGULATED?

ASK THE INSTRUCTOR: HOW DOES "ADVERSE SELECTION" AFFECT MARKETS?

Coping with Asymmetric Information

There are ways of reducing the consequences of asymmetric information. An incentive structure or an information-revealing system can be developed to reduce the problems associated with the lopsided availability of information. For example, some states have passed "lemon laws" that offer compensation to buyers of new or used cars that turn out to be lemons. Used-car dealers also usually offer warranties to reduce the buyer's risk of getting stuck with a lemon. Most auto-repair garages provide written estimates before a job is done, and some return the defective parts to the customer as evidence that the repair was necessary and was carried out. Consumers often get multiple estimates for major expenditures.

Health insurance companies deal with adverse selection and moral hazard in a variety of ways. Most require applicants to take a physical exam and to answer questions about their medical histories. An insurer often covers all those in a group, such as all company employees, not just those who would otherwise self-select, thus avoiding the problem of adverse selection. Insurers reduce moral hazard by making the policyholder pay, say, the first $250 of a claim as a "deductible" or by requiring the policyholder to co-pay a certain percentage of a claim. Also, if more claims are filed on a policy, the premiums go up and the policy may be canceled.

ASK THE INSTRUCTOR: WHY DOES ASYMMETRIC INFORMATION CREATE PROBLEMS?

ECONDEBATE ONLINE: IS THERE A NEED FOR HEALTH-CARE REFORM?

ASYMMETRIC INFORMATION IN LABOR MARKETS

Our market analysis for particular kinds of labor typically assumed that workers are identical. In equilibrium, each worker in a particular labor market is assumed to be paid the same wage, a wage that is equal to the marginal revenue product of the last unit of labor hired. But what if ability differs across workers? Differences in ability present no particular problem as long as these differences can be readily observed by the employer. If the productivity of each worker is easily quantified through a measure such as the quantity of oranges picked, the number of garments sewed, or the number of cars sold, that measure itself can and does serve as the basis for pay. And such per-unit incentives seem to affect output. For example, when the British National Health Service changed the way dentists were paid from "contact hours" with patients to the number of cavities filled, dentists found more cavities and filled them in only a third of the time they took under the contact-hour pay scheme.[4]

But because production often takes place through the coordinated efforts of several workers, the employer may not be able to attribute specific outputs to each particular worker. Since information about each worker's marginal productivity is hard to come by, employers usually pay workers by the hour rather than try to keep track of each worker's contribution to total output. Sometimes the pay is some combination of an hourly rate and incentive pay linked to a measure of productivity. For example, a sales representative typically receives a base salary plus a commission tied to the amount sold. At times, the task of evaluating performance is left to the consumer rather than to the firm. Workers who provide personal services, such as waiters and waitresses, barbers and beauticians, pizza deliverers, and bellhops, are paid partly in tips. These services are by definition "personal," so customers are usually in the best position to judge the quality and timeliness of service and to tip accordingly.

Adverse Selection in Labor Markets

Adverse selection occurs in the labor market when labor suppliers have better information about their own productivities than do employers, because a worker's ability is not easily observed prior to employment. Before being hired, a worker's true abilities—motivation, work habits, skills, ability to get along with others, and the like—are, to a large extent, *hidden characteristics.*

Suppose an employer wants to hire a program coordinator for a new project, a job that calls for imagination, organizational skills, and the ability to work independently. The employer would like to attract the most qualified person in the market, but the qualities demanded are not directly observable. The employer offers the market wage for such a position. Individual workers are able to evaluate this wage in light of their own abilities and opportunities. Talented people will find that wage to be below their marginal productivities and will be less inclined to apply for the job. Less-talented individuals, however, will find that the offered wage exceeds their marginal productivities, so they will be more likely to seek the position. Because of adverse selection, the employer ends up with a pool of applicants of below-average ability.

In a labor market with hidden characteristics, employers might be better off offering a higher wage. The higher the wage, the more attractive the job is to more-qualified workers. Paying a higher wage also encourages workers not to goof off or otherwise do anything that would risk losing an attractive job. So paying a high wage gets at the problem of hidden actions by workers. Paying a higher wage to attract and retain more-productive workers is called paying **efficiency wages.**

Signaling and Screening

The person on the side of the market with hidden characteristics and hidden actions has an incentive to say the right thing. For example, a job applicant might say, "Hire me because I am hardworking, reliable, prompt, highly motivated, and just an all-around great employee." Or a producer might say, "At Ford, quality is job one." But such direct claims appear self-serving and thus are not necessarily believable. To cut through this fog, both sides of the market have an incentive to develop credible ways of communicating reliable information about qualifications.

Therefore, adverse selection may give rise to **signaling,** which is the attempt by the informed side of the market to communicate information that the other side would find valuable. Consider signaling in the job market. Because the true requirements for many jobs are qualities that are unobservable on a résumé or in an interview, job applicants offer evidence of the unobservable features by relying on proxy measures, such as years of education, college grades, and letters of recommendation. A proxy measure is called a *signal,* which is an observable indicator of some hidden characteristic. A signal is sent by the informed side of the market to the uninformed side and will serve as a useful way of sorting out applicants as long as less-qualified applicants have more difficulty sending the signal.

To identify the best workers, employers try to *screen* applicants. **Screening** is the attempt by the uninformed side of the market to uncover the relevant but hidden characteristics of the informed party. An initial screen might check each résumé for spelling and typographical errors. Although not important in themselves, such errors suggest a lack of attention to detail—attention to detail that could prove important on the job. The uninformed party must detect signals that less-productive individuals will have more difficulty sending. A signal that

[4]John Pencavel, "Piecework and On-the-Job Screening," Working Paper, Stanford University, June 1975.

can be sent with equal ease or difficulty by all workers, regardless of their productivity, does not provide a useful way of screening applicants. But if, for example, more-productive workers find it easier to graduate from college than do less-productive workers, a college degree is a measure worth using to screen workers. In this case, education may be valuable, not so much because of its effects on a worker's productivity per se, but simply because it enables employers to distinguish among types of workers. Indeed, there is empirical evidence that the actual pay increase, the marginal pay, resulting from a fourth year of college that results in a college degree is several times that from a third year of college, a finding consistent with the screening theory of education.

To summarize: Because the potential productivity of job applicants cannot be measured directly, an employer must rely on some proxy to screen applicants. The most valuable proxy is one that best reflects future productivity. The problems of adverse selection, signaling, and screening are discussed in the following case study of McDonald's choosing franchisees.

CASE**STUDY** | The Reputation of a Big Mac

● *The World of Business*

McDonald's has over 15,000 restaurants in more than 115 countries and is opening another 500 each year. The secret to their success is that the more than 40 million customers served around the world each day can count on product consistency whether they buy a Big Mac in Anchorage, Moscow, or Singapore. McDonald's has grown because it has attracted competent and reliable franchise owners and has provided these owners with appropriate incentives and constraints to offer a product of consistent quality.

To avoid adverse selection, McDonald's seldom advertises for franchisees but still averages more than 10 applicants for each new restaurant. Even to be granted an interview, applicants must show substantial financial resources and adequate business experience. Those who pass an initial screening must come up with a security deposit and complete the 12- to 18-month training program. McDonald's Hamburger University trains thousands each year (offering simultaneous translations in more than 27 different languages). During this training period, the applicant is paid nothing, not even expenses. Some who complete the training are rejected for a franchise. Once the restaurant opens, a franchisee must work full-time in its daily operation.

Franchisees make a huge investment of time and money. Forty percent of the $400,000 to $675,000 cost of a new restaurant must come from the franchisee's own savings, not from borrowed funds. Thus, the franchisee has a clear financial stake in the success of the operation. The fact that the potential franchisee has saved so much also signals a level of financial competence. Because each franchisee gets a large share of the restaurant's profit, there is a strong incentive to operate efficiently. As a further incentive, successful owners may get additional restaurants.

If all goes well, the franchise is valid for 20 years and renewable after that, but it can be canceled *at any time* if the restaurant fails the company's standards of quality, pricing, cleanliness, hours of operation, and so on. Thus, the franchisee is bound to the company by highly specific investments of money and time, such as the time required to learn McDonald's operating system. The loss of a franchise would represent a huge financial blow. In selecting and monitoring franchisees, McDonald's has successfully addressed problems stemming from hidden characteristics and hidden actions.

Through its franchise policies, McDonald's is trying to protect its most important asset—the reputation of its brand name. To leverage that brand name around the world, the company is experimenting with other products such as McDonald's ketchup in Germany, Golden Arch Hotels in Switzerland, and McCafé coffee bars in Portugal, Austria, and Hong Kong.

<interactive>exercise

eACTIVITY: THE REPUTATION OF A BIG MAC

Source: Margaret Studer and Jennifer Ordonez, "McDonald's Plans to Open Two Hotels in Switzerland," *Wall Street Journal,* 17 November 2000; "Big Mac's New Tack," *Worldlink,* May/June 1999; D. L. Noren, "The Economics of the Golden Arches," *American Economist* (Fall 1990); Dana Canedy, "McDonald's Alters System for Kitchens," *New York Times,* 27 March 1998; and McDonald's home page at http://www.mcdonalds.com/.

CONCLUSION

The firm has evolved through a natural selection process as the form of organization that minimizes both transaction and production costs. According to this type of natural selection, forms of organization that are most efficient will be selected by the economic system for survival. Attributes that yield an economic profit will thrive, and those that do not will fall away. The form of organization selected may not be optimal in the sense that it cannot be improved, but it will be the most efficient of those that have been tried. If there is a way to organize production that is more efficient than the traditional firm, some entrepreneur will stumble on it one day and will be rewarded with greater profit. Thus, the improvement may not be the result of any conscious design. Once a more efficient way of organizing production is uncovered, others will imitate it.

Problems created by asymmetric information are not reflected in the simple account of how markets work. In conventional demand-and-supply analysis, trades occur in impersonal markets, and the buyer has no special concern about who is on the selling side. But with asymmetric information, the mix and characteristics of the other side of the market become important. When the problem of adverse selection is severe enough, some markets may cease to function. Market participants try to overcome the limitations of asymmetric information by signaling, screening, and trying to be quite explicit and transparent about the terms of the transaction.

endofchaptermaterial

- **Summary**
- **Questions for Review**
- **Problems and Exercises**
- **Experiential Exercises**
- **Wall Street Journal Exercises**

Take the Post-Test to assess your overall understanding of the key ideas in this chapter. The Post-Test provides a comprehensive selection of exam-style questions addressing the main topics and concepts of the chapter. At the completion of each Post-Test, you will receive a score and instructive feedback on how you answered each question, and a direct link to the part of the chapter addressed in the question. Take the Post-Test as often as you need to—a record of your progress for each attempt is kept for you to revisit and gauge your improvement. And each Post-Test is randomly generated, so every attempt is new.

Economic Regulation and Antitrust Activity

If the "invisible hand" of competition yields such desirable results for the economy, why does the government need to regulate business? When is monopoly good for the economy and when is it harmful? Who benefits most when government tries to regulate monopoly? Why did the government haul Microsoft into court? Is the U.S. economy more competitive now than it used to be? Answers to these and other questions are addressed in this chapter, which discusses government regulation of business.

It has been said that businesspeople praise competition but love monopoly. They praise competition because it harnesses the diverse and often conflicting objectives of various market participants and channels them into the efficient production of goods and services. And competition does this as if by "an invisible hand." Business-people love monopoly because it provides the surest path to economic profit in the long run—and, after all, profit is the name of the game. The fruits of monopoly are so tempting that a firm sometimes tries to eliminate competitors or conspire with them. As Adam Smith remarked more than 200 years ago, "People of the same trade seldom meet together, even for merriment or diversion, but the conversation ends in a conspiracy against the public, or in some contrivance to raise prices."

The tendency of firms to seek monopolistic advantage is understandable, but monopoly often harms the economy. Public policy can play a role by promoting competition in those markets where competition seems desirable and by reducing the harmful consequences of monopoly in those markets where the output can be most efficiently produced by one or a few firms. Topics discussed in this chapter include:

- Regulating natural monopolies
- Theories of economic regulation
- Deregulation
- Antitrust activity
- Per se illegality
- Rule of reason
- Merger movements
- Competitive trends

<interactive>exercise

- ECONDEBATE ONLINE: MARKET FAILURE, REGULATION, AND PUBLIC CHOICE
- ECONDEBATE ONLINE: GOVERNMENT AND THE ECONOMY

<interactive>update

- ECONDATA ONLINE: MARKET FAILURE, REGULATION, AND PUBLIC CHOICE
- ECONDATA ONLINE: GOVERNMENT AND THE ECONOMY
- ECONLINKS ONLINE: ECONOMICS WEB LINKS
- ECONNEWS ONLINE: MARKET FAILURE, REGULATION, AND PUBLIC CHOICE
- ECONNEWS ONLINE: GOVERNMENT AND THE ECONOMY

BUSINESS BEHAVIOR, PUBLIC POLICY, AND GOVERNMENT REGULATION

You'll recall that a monopolist supplies a product with no close substitutes, so a monopolist can charge a higher price than would prevail with more competition. When a few firms account for most of the sales in a market, those firms are sometimes able to coordinate their actions, either explicitly or implicitly, to act like a monopolist. The ability of a firm to raise its price without losing all its sales to rivals is called **market power.** Any firm facing a downward-sloping demand curve has some control over the price and thus some market power. The presumption is that a monopoly, or a group of firms acting as a monopoly, restricts output to charge a higher price than competing firms would charge. With output restricted, the marginal benefit of the final unit produced exceeds its marginal cost, so expanding output would increase social welfare. By failing to expand output to the point where marginal benefit equals marginal cost, firms with market power produce too little of the good than would be socially optimal.

Other distortions have also been associated with monopolies. For example, some critics argue that because a monopoly is insulated from competition, it is not as innovative as aggressive competitors would be. Worse still, because of their size and economic importance, monopolies may exert disproportionate influence on the political system, which they use to protect and enhance their monopoly power.

There are three kinds of government policies designed to alter or control firm behavior: social regulation, economic regulation, and antitrust activity. **Social regulation** consists of government measures designed to improve health and safety, such as control over unsafe working conditions and dangerous products. Social regulation can have economic consequences, but we will not discuss social regulation in this chapter. **Economic regulation** controls price, output, the entry of new firms, and the quality of service *in industries in which monopoly appears inevitable or even desirable.* The regulation of *natural monopolies,* such as local electricity transmission, local phone service, or a city subway system, is an example of economic regulation. Several other industries, such as land and air transportation, have also been regulated in the past. Various regulatory bodies at the federal, state, and local levels carry out economic regulation.

Antitrust activity attempts to prohibit firm behavior that tries to monopolize, or cartelize, markets in which competition is desirable. Antitrust activity is pursued in the courts by government attorneys and by individual firms that charge other firms with violating antitrust laws.

Both economic regulation and antitrust activity will be examined in this chapter. Let's turn first to economic regulation—specifically, the regulation of natural monopolies.

REGULATING NATURAL MONOPOLIES

Because of economies of scale, natural monopolies have a long-run average cost curve that slopes downward over the entire range of market demand. This means that the lowest average cost is achieved when one firm serves the entire market. A subway system is a natural monopoly. If two competing subway systems dug parallel routes throughout a city, the average cost per trip would be higher than if a single system provided this service.

SEE IT: REGULATING NATURAL MONOPOLY

Unregulated Profit Maximization

Exhibit 1 shows the demand and cost conditions for a natural monopoly, in this case a metropolitan subway system. A natural monopoly usually faces huge capital costs, such as those associated with digging a subway system, laying tracks for a railroad, launching a satellite into orbit, building a natural gas pipeline, or wiring a city for electricity, phone service, or cable TV. Because of the heavy capital outlays, average cost falls as output increases, so the average cost curve slopes downward over a broad range of output. In this situation, average cost is lowest when a single firm supplies the market.

A monopolist, if unregulated, will choose the price-quantity combination that maximizes profit. In Exhibit 1, the monopolist—in this case, the operator of a subway system—maximizes profit by producing where marginal revenue equals marginal cost, which occurs with 50 million riders per month paying $4 per trip. The monopolist will reap the profit identified by the blue-shaded rectangle. The *abc* triangle, which is below the demand curve and above the $4 price, measures consumer surplus. The problem with letting the monopolist maximize profit is that the resulting price-output combination is inefficient in terms of social welfare. Consumers pay a price that far exceeds the marginal cost of providing the service. The marginal value of additional output exceeds its marginal cost, so economic welfare will increase if output expands.

To repeat, an unregulated monopolist will maximize profit. Even a government-run monopoly may choose to maximize profit, as with state lotteries, state liquor stores, or concession stands at the civic center. So one option for government is to allow the monopolist to maximize profit. But government can increase social welfare by forcing the monopolist to expand output and lower price. To do this, government can either operate the monopoly itself, as with most urban transit systems, or *regulate* a privately owned monopoly, as it does with some urban transit systems, local phone services, and electricity transmission. Government-owned and government-regulated monopolies are called *public utilities*. Here we focus on government regulation, though the issues discussed are similar if the government chooses to own and operate the monopoly.

Setting Price Equal to Marginal Cost

Many facets of a natural monopoly have been regulated, but the price-output combination captures the most attention. Suppose government regulators require the monopolist to produce the level of output that is allocatively efficient—that is, where the price, which is the marginal benefit to consumers, equals marginal cost. This price-output combination is depicted in Exhibit 1 as point *e*, where the demand curve, or the marginal benefit curve, intersects the marginal cost curve, yielding a price of $0.50 per trip and quantity of 105 million trips per month. Since this price is much lower than the $4 charged under profit maximization, consumers will clearly prefer this price to the profit-maximizing one. Consumer surplus, a measure of consumers' net gain from riding the subway, increases from triangle *abc* with profit maximization to triangle *aef* with regulated efficiency.

EXHIBIT 1

Regulating a Natural Monopoly

With a natural monopoly, the long-run average cost curve slopes downward at its point of intersection with the demand curve. The unregulated firm produces where marginal revenue equals marginal cost, in this case, 50 million trips per month at a price of $4.00 per trip. This outcome is inefficient because price, or marginal benefit, exceeds marginal cost. To achieve the efficient level of output, government could regulate the monopolist's price. At $0.50 per trip, the subway would sell 105 million trips per month, which would be an efficient outcome. But at that price, the subway would lose money and require a subsidy to keep going. As an alternative, regulators could require the subway to charge $1.50 per trip. The subway would sell 90 million trips per month and would break even (since price equals average cost). Although the subway would earn a normal profit, social welfare could still be increased by expanding output as long as the price, or marginal benefit, exceeds marginal cost.

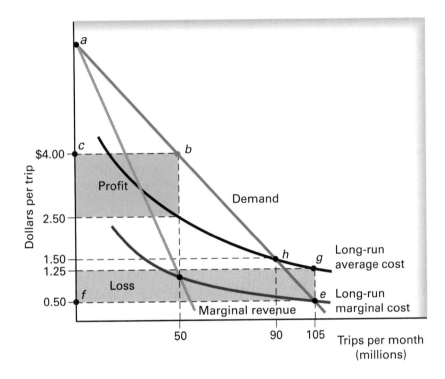

Notice, however, that the monopolist now has a problem. The average cost of supplying 105 million trips per month is $1.25, identified by point *g* on the average cost curve. This is more than double the regulated price of $0.50. Rather than earning a profit, the monopolist suffers a loss—in this case, $0.75 per rider, for a total loss of about $80 million a month, identified by the pink-shaded rectangle. *Forcing a natural monopolist to produce where price, or marginal benefit, equals marginal cost may result in an economic loss.* In the long run, the monopolist would go out of business rather than continue suffering such a loss.

Subsidizing the Natural Monopolist

How can regulators encourage the monopolist to stay in business yet produce at a level where price equals marginal cost? The government can compensate the monopolist for the loss—*subsidize* the firm so it earns a normal profit. Bus and subway fares are typically set below the average cost of providing the service, with the difference covered by a government subsidy. For example, the Washington, D.C., Metro subway system gets over $200 million per year in federal subsidies; Amtrak also receives substantial federal subsidies to cover ongoing losses (Amtrak lost nearly $1 billion in 2000). One drawback with the subsidy solution is that, to provide the subsidy, the government must raise taxes or forgo public spending in some other area. Thus, the subsidy has an opportunity cost.

Setting Price Equal to Average Cost

Although some public utilities are subsidized, most are not. Instead, regulators try to set a price that will provide the monopolist with a "fair return." Recall that the average cost curve includes a normal profit. Thus, *setting price equal to average cost* provides a normal, or "fair," profit for the monopolist. In Exhibit 1, the demand curve intersects the average cost curve at point *h*, yielding a price of $1.50 and a quantity of 90 million trips a month. This price-output combination will allow the monopolist to stay in business without a subsidy.

Setting price equal to average total cost enhances economic welfare compared to the unregulated situation, but the monopolist would prefer to earn an economic profit. If given no other choice, however, the monopolist will continue to operate with a normal profit, since that is what could be earned if the monopolist's resources were redirected to their most profitable alternative. But note that the marginal benefit to consumers of the 90 millionth trip, exceeds the marginal cost. Therefore, lowering the price to expand output beyond 90 million trips per month would increase social welfare.

The Regulatory Dilemma

Setting price equal to marginal cost yields the *socially optimal* allocation of resources because *the consumers' marginal benefit from the last unit sold equals the marginal cost of producing that last unit.* In our example, setting the price per trip at $0.50 equates marginal benefit and marginal cost, but the monopolist will face recurring losses unless a subsidy is provided. These losses disappear if price is set equal to average cost, which in our example is $1.50. The higher price ensures a normal profit, but the output of 90 million trips per month falls 15 million short of the socially optimal level. Thus the dilemma facing the regulator is whether to set price equal to marginal cost, which is socially optimal but requires a subsidy, or to set a break-even price even though output falls short of the socially optimal level. There is no right answer. Compared with the unregulated profit-maximizing price of $4, both regulatory options reduce the price, increase output, increase consumer surplus, eliminate economic profit, and increase social welfare.

Although Exhibit 1 lays out the options neatly, regulators usually face a fuzzier picture of things. Demand and cost curves can only be estimated, and the regulated firm may not always be completely forthcoming about this information. For example, a utility may overstate its costs so it can charge a higher price and earn more than a normal profit.

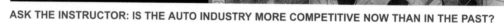

<interactive>update

ECONNEWS ONLINE: PEAK POWER PRICES

<interactive>video

ASK THE INSTRUCTOR: IS THE AUTO INDUSTRY MORE COMPETITIVE NOW THAN IN THE PAST?

ALTERNATIVE THEORIES OF ECONOMIC REGULATION

Why do governments regulate certain markets? Why not let market forces allocate resources? There are two views of government regulation. The first view has been implicit in the discussion so far—namely, economic regulation is in the *public interest*. Economic regulation promotes social welfare by controlling the price and output when one or just a few firms serve a market. A second view is that economic regulation is not in the public interest but is in the *special interest* of producers. According to this view, *well-organized producer groups expect to profit from economic regulation and can persuade public officials to impose restrictions that existing producers find attractive, such as limiting entry into the industry or preventing competition among existing firms.* Individual producers have more to gain or to lose from regulation than do individual consumers. Producers typically are also better organized and more focused than consumers and are therefore better able to bring about regulations that favor them.

Producers' Special Interest in Economic Regulation

To understand how and why producer interests could influence public regulation, think back to the last time you had your hair cut. Most states regulate the training and licensing of hair professionals. If any new regulation affecting the profession is proposed, such as longer training requirements, who do you suppose has more interest in the outcome of that legislation, you or those who cut hair for a living? *Producers have a strong interest in matters that affect their livelihood, so they play a disproportionately large role in trying to influence such legislation.* If there are public hearings on haircut regulations, the industry will provide self-serving testimony, while consumers will largely ignore the whole thing.

As a consumer, you do not specialize in getting haircuts. You purchase haircuts, hardware, soft drinks, software, underwear, and thousands of other goods and services. You have no *special interest* in haircut legislation. Some critics argue that because of this asymmetry between the interests of producers and consumers, business regulations often favor producer interests rather than consumer interests. Well-organized producer groups, as squeaky wheels in the legislative machinery, get the most grease in the form of favorable regulations.

Legislation favoring producer groups is usually introduced under the guise of advancing consumer interests. Producer groups may argue that unbridled competition in their industry would hurt consumers. For example, the alleged problem of "cutthroat" competition among taxi drivers has led to regulations that eliminate price competition and restrict the number of taxis in most large metropolitan areas. As a result, taxis are more expensive and harder to find. Or regulation may appear under the guise of quality control, such as keeping unlicensed "quacks" from certain professions. But these supply restrictions mostly reduce competition in the profession and increase the price.

The special-interest theory may be valid even when the initial intent of the legislation was in the consumer interest. Over time, the regulatory machinery may begin acting more in accord with the special interests of producers. Producers' political power and strong stake in the regulatory outcome lead them, in effect, to "capture" the regulating agency and prevail upon it to serve producers. This **capture theory of regulation** was best explained by George Stigler, the Nobel Prize winner mentioned in the previous chapter, who argued that "as a general rule, regulation is acquired by the industry and is designed and operated for its benefit."[1]

Perhaps it would be useful at this point to discuss in some detail the direction that economic regulation and, more recently, deregulation has taken in a particular industry—airlines.

<interactive>update

- **ECONNEWS ONLINE: AIRLINES OF PREY PROTECTED BY GOVERNMENT INACTION**
- **ECONNEWS ONLINE: THAT'S THE WAY COKE BOTTLERS LIKE IT, AH-HA**

CASESTUDY | Airline Regulation and Deregulation

● *Public Policy*

The Civil Aeronautics Board (CAB), established in 1938, once tightly regulated the U.S. interstate airline business. Any potential entrant interested in serving an interstate route had to persuade the CAB that the route needed another airline, a task that proved impossible. During the 40 years prior to deregulation, potential entrants submitted more than 150 applications for long-distance routes, *but not a single new interstate airline was allowed.* The CAB also forced strict compliance with regulated prices. A request to lower prices on any route would result in a rate hearing, during which both the CAB and competitors scrutinized the request. In effect, the CAB had created a cartel that fixed prices among the 10 existing major airlines and blocked new entry. This was a perfect example of the capture theory of regulation.

Although the CAB prohibited price competition in the industry, *nonprice competition flourished.* Airlines competed based on the frequency of flights, the quality of meals, the width of the seats, even the friendliness of the staff. For example, American Airlines put pianos in its jumbo jet lounges. United Airlines countered with wine tastings and guitars. Such competition increased operating costs until firms earned only a normal rate of return. Thus, *airfares set above competitive levels coupled with entry restrictions were no guarantee of economic profit as long as airlines were free to compete in other ways, such as in the frequency of flights.*

The CAB had no regulatory power over airlines that flew only *intrastate* routes—flights between Los Angeles and San Francisco, for instance. The record shows that fares on intrastate

[1]George Stigler, "The Theory of Economic Regulation," *Bell Journal of Economics and Management Science* (Spring 1971): 3.

airlines were only half those on identical routes flown by regulated airlines. So regulated airlines cost consumers much more.

Airline Deregulation. In 1978, despite opposition from the existing airlines and labor unions, Congress passed the Airline Deregulation Act, which allowed price competition and new entry. By 2000, airfares in inflation-adjusted dollars averaged 27 percent below regulated prices. The airlines could afford to lower fares because they became more productive by filling a greater percentage of seats. Passenger miles flown nearly tripled. The net benefits of deregulation now exceed $20 billion a year, or about $75 per U.S. resident. The hub-and-spoke system developed under deregulation also allowed airlines to route planes more efficiently. Airline routes used to be straight lines from one city to another. Now they radiate like the spokes of a wagon wheel from a "hub" city. From 29 hub airports across the country, airlines send out planes along the spokes to 400 commercial airports and then quickly bring them back to the hubs.

Regulation had insulated the industry from price competition, allowing labor unions to demand and get higher wages than they could in a more competitive setting. The Air Line Pilots Association, the union that represented pilots for all the major airlines prior to deregulation, had been able to negotiate extremely attractive pay for its members, averaging six figures annually for less than two weeks a month (many pilots had so much free time that they pursued second careers). Just how attractive a pilot's position was became apparent after deregulation. America West, a nonunion airline that sprouted from deregulation, paid its pilots only $32,000 a year and required them to work 40 hours a week, performing other duties when they were not flying. Yet the company received more than 4,000 applications for its 29 pilot openings.

Critics of deregulation were concerned that the government would lose control over the quality and safety of airline service. Despite the demise of the CAB, however, the Federal Aviation Administration still regulates the safety and quality of air service. And the Department of Transportation can stop any unfair trade practice. Research indicates that between 1979 and 1990, accident rates declined by anywhere from 10 to 45 percent, depending on the specific measure used. Also, lower fares encouraged more people to fly rather than drive, thereby saving thousands of lives that would have been lost driving (per passenger mile, flying is about 20 times safer than driving).

Another concern with deregulation was that small communities would no longer be served. This has not been a problem; commuter airlines have replaced major airlines in servicing small communities. Because of the hub-and-spoke system, the number of scheduled departures from small cities and rural communities has actually increased more than one-third. The latest development in air travel is the regional jet that bypasses the hub-and-spoke system to fly 40 to 70 passengers from, say, Hartford, Connecticut, to Rochester, New York. The demand for air travel has increased enough to make this point-to-point service profitable. This new wave of air travel promises to connect hundreds of city pairs, but will impose more strain on airport capacity, the Achilles' heel of the deregulated industry.

Airport Capacity Has Restricted Competition. Despite the overall success of deregulation, competitive trends in the airline industry in recent years raise some troubling questions. Although airline traffic has more than doubled since deregulation, the air traffic control system has not expanded, and only one new airport, in Denver, has opened. Airports and the air traffic control system are owned and operated by government agencies. Congress funds these agencies, but the entire system tends to be unresponsive to an increase in demand (revenue from an airline ticket tax goes elsewhere). Thus, *the government did not follow up deregulation with an expansion of airport capacity.* Departure gates, landing rights, and hub airports became the scarce resources in the industry, and airlines unable to secure such facilities at major airports went out of business.

Some argue that the major airlines have not pushed for an expansion of airport facilities because additional capacity could encourage new entry and increase competition. The market share of the five largest airlines climbed from 63 percent before deregulation to about 70 percent in 2000, and most key airports came to be dominated by one or two airlines. For example, United and American control 82 percent of the landing slots at Chicago's O'Hare Airport, up from 66 percent in 1986. American and Delta control 83 percent of the slots at New York's Kennedy Airport, up from 43 percent in 1986. Increased concentration at certain hubs gives airlines market power to raise prices; ticket prices are higher for trips involving concentrated hubs than are prices at more-competitive airports.

On a positive note, federal regulators in recent years have blocked mergers that were judged as reducing competition. For example, the proposed merger of United Airlines and US Airways was scuttled (the two airlines carried more than half the passengers in 20 of the nation's busiest routes). Another bright spot on the competitive front has been the success of low-cost, no-frills carriers such as Southwest Airlines, which forces down fares wherever they fly.

Despite concerns about recent anticompetitive trends in the industry, deregulation on the whole has been quite beneficial for consumers. Few are calling for re-regulation of the industry.

eACTIVITY: AIRLINE REGULATION AND DEREGULATION

Sources: Steven Morrison and Clifford Winston, *The Evolution of the Airline Industry* (Washington, D.C.: Brookings Institution, 1995); "The Airline Industry: Grounded Again," *Economist,* 7 July 2001; Scott McCartney et al., "UAL, American Plan Asset Swap, Raising Consolidation Worries," *Wall Street Journal,* 9 January 2001; Laurence Zuckerman, "White House to Press Airlines on Consolidation," *New York Times,* 16 January 2001; and http://flyaow.com/, with links to nearly 500 airlines worldwide.

The course of regulation and deregulation raises some interesting questions about the true objective of regulation. Recall the competing views of regulation: one holds that regulation is in the public, or consumer, interest; the other holds that regulation is in the special, or producer, interest. In the airline industry, regulation appeared more in accord with producer interests, and producer groups fought deregulation, which benefited consumers.

This concludes our discussion of economic regulation, which tries to reduce the harmful consequences of monopolistic behavior in those markets where the output can be most efficiently produced by one or a few firms. We now turn to antitrust activity, which tries to promote competition in those markets where competition seems desirable.

ANTITRUST LAW AND ENFORCEMENT

Although competition typically ensures the most efficient use of the nation's resources, an individual firm would prefer to operate as a monopoly. If left alone, a firm might try to create a monopolistic environment by driving competitors out of business, by merging with competitors, or by colluding with competitors. In the United States, *antitrust policy* is an attempt to curb these anticompetitive tendencies by (1) promoting the sort of market structure that will lead to greater competition and (2) reducing anticompetitive behavior. *Antitrust laws attempt to promote socially desirable market performance.*

NETBOOKMARK: OWEN GRADUATE SCHOOL OF MANAGEMENT AT VANDERBILT UNIVERSITY: ANTITRUST ISSUES

ASK THE INSTRUCTOR: WHICH ANTITRUST CASES HAVE RECEIVED A LOT OF ATTENTION?

Origins of Antitrust Policy

Economic developments in the last half of the 19th century created a political climate supportive of antitrust legislation. Perhaps the two most important were (1) technological breakthroughs that led to more extensive use of capital and a larger optimal plant size in manufacturing and (2) lower transportation costs as railroad coverage increased from 9,000 miles of track in 1850 to 167,000 miles by 1890. *Economies of scale and cheaper transportation costs extended the geographical size of markets.* So firms grew larger and reached markets over a broader geographical area.

Declines in the national economy in 1873 and in 1883, however, caused panics among these large manufacturers, which, because of their heavy fixed costs, required large-scale production. Their defensive reaction was to lower prices in an attempt to stimulate sales. Price wars erupted among firms, creating economic turmoil. Firms desperately sought ways to stabilize their markets. One solution was for competing firms to form a *trust* by transferring their voting stock to a single board of trustees, which would vote in the interest of the entire industry group. Early trusts were formed in the sugar, tobacco, and oil industries. Although the impact of these early trusts is still a matter of debate today, they allegedly pursued anticompetitive practices to develop and maintain a monopoly advantage. Gradually the word *trust* came to represent any firm or group of firms that tried to monopolize a market.

These practices provoked widespread criticism and earned the creators of trusts the derisive title of "robber barons." Public sentiment lay on the side of the smaller competitors. Farmers, especially, resented the higher prices of manufactured goods, which resulted from the trusts' activities, particularly since farm prices were declining through the latter part of the 19th century because of more efficient farming techniques. At the time, agriculture accounted for 40 percent of the U.S. workforce and thus had political clout. Eighteen states, primarily agricultural, enacted *antitrust* laws in the 1880s, prohibiting the formation of trusts. But these laws were largely ineffective because the trusts could simply move across state lines to avoid them.

Sherman Antitrust Act of 1890. In the presidential election of 1888, the major political parties put antitrust planks in their platforms. This consensus culminated in the passage of the **Sherman Antitrust Act of 1890,** the first national legislation in the world against monopoly. The law prohibited the creation of trusts, restraint of trade, and monopolization, although it failed to define what constituted such activities. Its vague language hampered its enforcement.

Clayton Act of 1914. Ambiguous language in the Sherman Act allowed much anticompetitive activity to slip by. The **Clayton Act of 1914** was passed to outlaw certain practices not prohibited by the Sherman Act and to help government stop a monopoly before it developed. For example, the Clayton Act prohibits price discrimination when this practice tends to create a monopoly. You'll recall that *price discrimination* is charging different customers different prices for the same good. The act also prohibits *tying contracts* and *exclusive dealing* if they substantially lessen competition. **Tying contracts** require the buyer of one good to purchase another good as well. For example, a seller of a patented machine might require customers to purchase other supplies from the seller as part of the deal. **Exclusive dealing** occurs when a producer will sell a product only if the buyer agrees not to buy from other manufacturers. For example, a manufacturer might sell computer chips to a computer maker only if the computer maker agrees not to buy any chips elsewhere. Another prohibition of the act is **interlocking directorates,** whereby the same individual serves on the boards of directors of competing firms. Finally, merger through the acquisition of the stock of a competing firm is outlawed if the merger would substantially lessen competition. More on mergers later.

Federal Trade Commission Act of 1914. The **Federal Trade Commission (FTC) Act of 1914** established a federal body to help enforce antitrust laws. The commission consists of five full-time commissioners appointed by the president for seven-year terms and assisted by a staff of mostly economists and lawyers.

The Sherman, Clayton, and FTC acts provided the antitrust framework, a framework that has been clarified and embellished by subsequent amendments and court decisions. A loophole in the Clayton Act was closed in 1950 with the passage of the *Celler-Kefauver Anti-Merger Act,* which prevents one firm from buying the *assets* of another firm if the effect is to reduce competition. This law can block both **horizontal mergers,** or the merging of firms that produce the same product, such as Coke and Pepsi, and **vertical mergers,** or the merging of firms where one supplies inputs to the other or demands output from the other, such as Microsoft and Dell.

<interactive>exercise

ECONDEBATE ONLINE: SHOULD THE ANTITRUST EXEMPTION FOR BASEBALL BE ELIMINATED?

Antitrust Law Enforcement

Any law's effectiveness depends on the vigor and vigilance of enforcement. The pattern of antitrust enforcement goes something like this. Either the Antitrust Division of the U.S. Justice Department or the FTC charges a firm or group of firms with breaking the law. These federal agencies are often acting on a complaint by a customer or a competitor. At that point, those charged with the wrongdoing may be able, without admitting guilt, to sign a **consent decree,** whereby they agree not to continue doing what they had been charged with. If the accused contests the charges, evidence from both sides is presented in a court trial, and a judge renders a decision. Certain decisions may be appealed all the way to the Supreme Court, and in such cases the courts may render new interpretations of existing laws.

Per Se Illegality and the Rule of Reason

The courts have interpreted antitrust laws in essentially two ways. One set of practices has been declared **per se illegal**—that is, illegal regardless of the economic rationale or consequences. For example, under the Sherman Act, all formal agreements among competing firms to fix prices, restrict output, or otherwise restrain competition are viewed as per se illegal. For the defendant to be found guilty under a per se rule, the government need only show that the offending practice took place; thus, the government need only examine the firm's *behavior.*

Another set of practices falls under the **rule of reason.** Here the courts engage in a broader inquiry into the facts surrounding the particular offense—namely, the reasons why the offending practice was adopted and its effect on competition. The rule of reason was first set forth in 1911, when the Supreme Court held that Standard Oil had illegally monopolized the petroleum refining industry. Standard Oil allegedly had come to dominate 90 percent of the market by acquiring more than 120 former rivals and by practicing **predatory pricing** to drive remaining rivals out of business—for example, by temporarily selling below marginal cost or dropping the price only in certain markets. In finding Standard Oil guilty, the Court focused on both the company's *behavior* and the *market structure* that resulted from that behavior. Based on this approach, the Court found that the company had behaved *unreasonably* and ruled that the monopoly should be broken up.

But in 1920, the rule of reason led the Supreme Court to find U.S. Steel not guilty of monopolization. In that case, the Court ruled that not every contract or combination in restraint of trade was illegal; only those that "unreasonably" restrained trade violated antitrust laws. The Court said that *mere size was not an offense.* Although U.S. Steel clearly possessed market power, the company was not in violation of antitrust laws because, in the Court's view, U.S. Steel had not unreasonably used that power. The Court switched positions in 1945, ruling that although Alcoa's conduct might be reasonable and legal, its mere possession of market power—Alcoa controlled 90 percent of the aluminum ingot market—violated antitrust laws. Here the Court was using *market structure* rather than firm *behavior* as the test of legality.

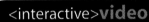

<interactive>video

CNN VIDEO: "JUDGE OFFERS WINDOWS INTO MICROSOFT'S OPERATING SYSTEM"

Mergers and Public Policy

Some firms have pursued rapid growth by merging with other firms. Much of what the Antitrust Division in the U.S. Justice Department and the FTC's Bureau of Competition do is approve or deny proposed mergers and acquisitions. In determining possible harmful effects that a merger might have on competition, one important consideration is its impact on the share of sales accounted for by the largest firms in the industry. If a few firms account for a relatively large share of sales, the industry is said to be *concentrated.* As a measure of sales concentration, the Justice Department uses the **Herfindahl index,** which is found by squaring the percentage of market share of each firm in the market and then summing those squares. For example, if the industry consists of 100 firms of equal size, the Herfindahl index is 100 [= 100 $\times$ $(1)^2$]. If the industry is a pure monopoly, its index is 10,000 [= $(100)^2$], the largest possible value. The more firms there are in the industry and the more equal their size, the smaller the Herfindahl index. This index gives greater weight to firms with larger market shares, as can be seen for the three examples presented in Exhibit 2. Each industry has 44 firms, but, for ease of exposition, only the market share of the top four firms differs across industries. Note that the index for Industry III is nearly triple that for each of the two other industries. Take a minute now to work through the logic of the exhibit.

The Justice Department's guidelines also sort all mergers into two categories: *horizontal mergers,* which involve firms in the same market, and *nonhorizontal mergers,* which include all other types of mergers. Of greatest interest for antitrust purposes are horizontal mergers, such as a merger between competing oil companies like Mobil and Exxon. The Justice Department generally challenges any merger in an industry that meets two conditions: (1) the postmerger Herfindahl index exceeds 1,800 and (2) the merger increases the index by more than 100 points. Mergers in an industry that would have a postmerger index of less than 1,000 are seldom challenged. Other factors, such as the ease of entry into the market and gains in efficiency, are considered for intermediate cases.

EXHIBIT 2

Computation of the Herfindahl Index Based on Market Share in Three Industries

	Industry I		Industry II		Industry III	
Firm	Market Share (percent)	Market Share Squared	Market Share (percent)	Market Share Squared	Market Share (percent)	Market Share Squared
A	23	529	15	225	57	3,249
B	18	324	15	225	1	1
C	13	169	15	225	1	1
D	6	36	15	225	1	1
Remaining 40 firms (at 1 percent each)	1 each	40	1 each	40	1 each	40
Herfindahl Index		1,098		940		3,292

Merger Movements

There have been four merger waves in this country over the last century, as outlined in Exhibit 3. Between 1887 and 1904 some of today's largest firms, including U.S. Steel and Standard Oil, were formed. Mergers during this first wave tended to be horizontal. For example, the firm that is today U.S. Steel was created in 1901 through a billion-dollar merger that involved dozens of individual steel producers and two-thirds of the industry's production capacity. This wave of mergers was a reaction to technological progress in transportation, communication, and manufacturing. Simply put, it became easier and cheaper to run a corporation that stretched across the nation, so firms merged to achieve national size. The merger wave cooled with the severe national recession of 1904 and with the early stirrings of antitrust laws. During

EXHIBIT 3

Merger Waves in the Past Century

Wave	Years	Dominant Type of Merger	Examples	Stimulus
First	1887–1904	Horizontal	U.S. Steel, Standard Oil	Span national markets
Second	1916–1929	Vertical	Copper refiners with fabricators	Stock market boom
Third	1948–1969	Conglomerate	Litton Industries	Diversification
Fourth	1982–present	Horizontal and vertical	Banking, telecommunications, health services, insurance	Span national and global markets, stock market boom

this first wave, similar merger trends occurred in Canada, Great Britain, and elsewhere, creating dominant firms, some of which still exist.

Because antitrust laws began to restrain horizontal mergers, vertical mergers became more common during the second merger wave, which occurred between 1916 and 1929. A vertical merger is the merger of one firm with a firm that either supplies its inputs or demands its outputs—the merger of firms at different stages of the production process. For example, a copper refiner merges with a copper fabricator. The stock market boom of the 1920s fueled this second wave, but the stock market crash stopped it cold in 1929.

The Great Depression and World War II cooled merger activity for two decades, but the third merger wave got under way after the war. More than 200 of the 1,000 largest firms in 1950 had disappeared by the early 1960s as a result of the third merger wave, which occurred between 1948 and 1969. In that span, many large firms were absorbed by other, usually larger, firms. The third merger wave culminated in the peak activity of 1964 to 1969, when **conglomerate mergers,** which join firms in different industries, accounted for four-fifths of all mergers. For example, Litton Industries combined firms that made calculators, appliances, electrical equipment, and machine tools. Merging firms were looking to diversify their product mix and perhaps achieve some *economies of scope*—meaning, to reduce average costs by producing a variety of goods.

The fourth merger wave, which is still under way, began in 1982, the onset of the "deal decade." This wave involves both horizontal and vertical mergers. Some large conglomerate mergers of the 1960s were dissolved in the 1980s as the core firm sold off unrelated operations. About one-third of mergers in the 1980s resulted from *hostile takeovers,* where one firm would buy control of another against the wishes of the target firm's management. Hostile takeovers dwindled to less than one-tenth of mergers during the 1990s.

Merger activity gained momentum during the latter half of the 1990s, with the dollar value of each new merger topping the previous record. Most mergers during this period were financed by the exchange of corporate stock and were spurred on by a booming stock market (like the mergers of the 1920s). A surging stock market reduced the cost of funding mergers through stock swaps, as one firm exchanged its shares for shares of the other firm. The end of the Cold War stabilized world markets and expanded capitalism around the world. Companies merged to achieve a stronger competitive position in global markets. The largest mergers in history were proposed during the late 1990s, with the biggest action in banking, radio and television, insurance, telecommunications, and health services. One big deal, for example, was the $103 billion merger in 2001 of AOL and Time Warner.

In recent years, there have been fewer objections to mergers on antitrust grounds either from academics or regulatory officials. The government shifted from rules that restrict big mergers to a more flexible approach that allows big companies to merge. For example, the government approved Boeing's $15 billion acquisition of McDonnell Douglas, the commercial aircraft manufacturer, because the airlines said it made no difference to them whether or not the two combined. Boeing still competes with Airbus, the European rival, in the world market for aircraft. As one Justice Department official put it, "We have very flexible guidelines. Bigness in and of itself doesn't tell me much. I want to know about the market, the players and what competition exists to judge."[2] The chairman of the FTC said, "the mergers we see these days make more sense" than earlier mergers.[3] He also said, "I do not believe that size alone is a basis to challenge a merger transaction."[4] Regulators ultimately challenged only two percent of all mergers proposed during the 1990s, though just the threat of a legal challenge has deterred countless potentially anticompetitive mergers and acquisitions.

One industry in which mergers seem to be reducing competition is local phone service. In 1996, Congress enacted a law designed to reduce the monopoly power of local phone companies by allowing long-distance carriers, cable operators, and other telecommunications providers to enter the local market. But rather than enhancing competition, the 1996 act spawned a wave of mergers among local providers as they raced to span the country. This seems to be one area where efforts to introduce more competition backfired.

COMPETITIVE TRENDS IN THE U.S. ECONOMY

For years, there has been concern about the sheer size of some firms because of the real or potential power they might exercise in both the economic and political arenas. One way to measure the power of the largest corporations is to calculate the share of the nation's corporate

[2]As quoted by Leslie Wayne in "Wave of Mergers Recasts the Face of Business," *New York Times,* 19 January 1998.
[3]As quoted by John R. Wilke in "Greenspan Questions Governments Antitrust-Enforcement Campaigns," *Wall Street Journal,* 17 June 1998.
[4]As quoted by Leslie Wayne in "Wave of Mergers Recasts the Face of Business," *New York Times,* 19 January 1998.

assets controlled by the 100 largest firms. The largest 100 manufacturers now control about half of all production assets in the United States, up from a 40 percent share after World War II. We should recognize, however, that size alone is not synonymous with market power. A very big firm, such as a large oil company, may face stiff competition from other very big oil companies both foreign and domestic; on the other hand, the only movie theater in an isolated community may be able to raise its price with less concern about competition.

Market Competition over Time

More important than the size of the largest firms in the nation is the market structure in each industry. Various studies have examined the level of competition by industry and changes in competition over the years. All have used some measure of market share, such as the Herfindahl index, as a point of departure, sometimes supplementing these measures with data from each industry. Among the most comprehensive of these is the research of William G. Shepherd of the University of Massachusetts, who relied on many sources to determine the competitiveness of each industry in the U.S. economy.[5]

Shepherd sorted industries into four groups: (1) pure monopoly, in which a single firm controlled the entire market and was able to block entry; (2) dominant firm, in which a single firm had more than half the market share and had no close rival; (3) tight oligopoly, in which the top four firms supplied more than 60 percent of market output, with stable market shares and evidence of cooperation; and (4) effective competition, in which firms in the industry exhibited low concentration, low entry barriers, and little or no collusion.

Exhibit 4 presents Shepherd's breakdown of U.S. industries into the four categories for the years 1939, 1958, and 1988. The table shows a modest trend toward increased competition between 1939 and 1958, with the share of those industries rated as "effectively competitive" growing from 52 percent to 56 percent of all industries. Between 1958 and 1988, however, there was a sharp rise in competitiveness in the economy, with the share of effectively competitive industries jumping from 56 percent to 77 percent.

EXHIBIT 4

Competitive Trends in the U.S. Economy

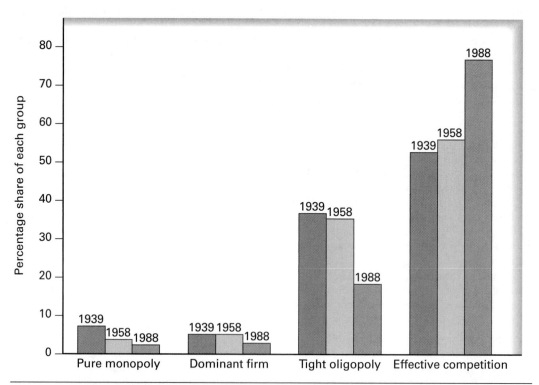

Sources: W. G. Shepherd, "Causes of Increased Competition in the U.S. Economy, 1939–1980," *Review of Economics and Statistics* 64 (November 1982); and W. G. Shepherd, *The Economics of Industrial Organization,* 3rd ed. (Englewood Cliffs, NJ: Prentice Hall, 1990), 15.

[5]William G. Shepherd, "Causes of Increased Competition in the U.S. Economy, 1939–1980," *Review of Economics and Statistics* 64 (November 1982); and William G. Shepherd, *The Economics of Industrial Organization,* 3rd ed. (Englewood Cliffs, NJ: Prentice Hall, 1990), 15.

According to Shepherd, the growth in competition from 1958 to 1988 can be traced to three main sources: *competition from imports, deregulation, and antitrust activity*. Foreign imports between 1958 and 1988 increased competition in 13 major industries, including autos, tires, and steel. According to Shepherd, the growth in imports accounted for one-sixth of the overall increase in competition. Imports were attractive to consumers because of their superior quality and lower price. Finding themselves at a cost and technological disadvantage, U.S. producers initially sought protection from foreign competitors through trade barriers, such as quotas and tariffs.

Shepherd argues that deregulation accounted for one-fifth of the increase in competition. Trucking, airlines, securities trading, banking, and telecommunications were among the industries deregulated between 1958 and 1988. We have already discussed some of the effects of deregulation in airlines, particularly in reducing barriers to entry and in eliminating uniform pricing schedules. With regard to telecommunications, in 1982, AT&T was forced to sell 22 companies that provided most of the country's local phone service. Since 1984, AT&T's share of the long-distance market declined from 88 percent to less than 50 percent today. This enhanced competition reduced long-distance rates. But, as noted earlier, local service providers have started to join forces again.

Although it is difficult to attribute an increase in competition to specific antitrust cases, Shepherd credits antitrust activity with two-fifths of the growth in competition between 1958 and 1988. To summarize: According to Shepherd, the three primary reasons for increased competition were international trade, deregulation, and antitrust activity. One-sixth of the growth in competition between 1958 and 1988 came from imports, one-fifth from deregulation, and two-fifths, the largest share, from antitrust activity. In light of the important role that Shepherd accords antitrust, let's look at the most significant antitrust case in the last decade.

CASESTUDY | Microsoft on Trial

● *Public Policy*

Microsoft released its long-awaited Windows 98 operating system in June 1998 under a cloud. The U.S. Justice Department and 20 state attorneys general had filed lawsuits a month earlier alleging that Microsoft engaged in a pattern of predatory conduct to protect its operating-system monopoly and to extend that monopoly into Internet software. At the time, Windows software was used on 90 percent of the nation's desktop computers. The plaintiffs charged that Microsoft's integration of its browser, Internet Explorer, into Windows 98 was not, as the company claimed, solely to make life easier for customers but was aimed at boosting Explorer's market share. Dominance in browser software is important because controlling the gateway to the Internet is a big step in directing traffic and commerce there. Government officials wanted Microsoft customers to be free to choose a browser. Microsoft disputed the charges and said the government was interfering with its right to create new products that benefit consumers.

Prior to any judicial ruling on the suit, Microsoft's choices were (1) to separate its Internet browser from Windows 98, a task the company claimed would take "months if not years"; (2) to ship its major rival's browser, Netscape, as well as its own browser with Windows 98—a task Bill Gates likened to "requiring Coke to include three cans of Pepsi in every six-pack it sells"; or (3) to ship Windows 98 with Microsoft's browser bundled in the software. Microsoft chose the third alternative, which involved some risk because the practice could ultimately be deemed illegal.

The trial began in October 1998. The government argued that Microsoft engaged in predatory practices aimed at winning the browser war and harming competitors (the company's behavior would be considered illegal only if Microsoft was found to possess monopoly power). The government, by focusing on Microsoft's anticompetitive *behavior*, was using a rule-of-reason approach. Microsoft, for its part, characterized itself as an aggressive but legal player in a fiercely competitive industry. Microsoft's lawyers said that the company would not have gained such a huge market share if it failed to improve quality and value with each new version. They argued that the high market share "does not begin to reflect the intense competitive dynamic in the software industry." Even such a market share, they said, is "susceptible to rapid deterioration should the market leader fail to innovate at a rapid and competitive pace."

Bill Gates did not testify live but was questioned by government lawyers during a videotaped deposition, parts of which were shown during the trial to support the government's case. Presiding Judge Thomas Penfield Jackson said, "I think it is evident to every spectator that, for whatever reasons, in many respects, Mr. Gates has not been particularly responsive to his deposition."

After 78 days of testimony and months of deliberation, Judge Jackson ruled that Microsoft maintained a monopoly in operating-system software by anti-competitive means and attempted to monopolize the Web browser market by unlawfully "tying" Internet Explorer with Windows. He called Microsoft "an untrustworthy monopoly that refuses to abandon illegal business practices that crush competitors and harm consumers." As a remedy, he proposed restricting Microsoft's business practices and dividing the firm into a Windows-based operating-system company and an applications-software company.

Microsoft appealed the decision to the U.S. Court of Appeals, arguing that it did not hold a monopoly, it had not engaged in anticompetitive practices, and Judge Jackson showed bias in his ruling. In June 2001, the appeals court upheld unanimously the finding that Microsoft violated antitrust laws and acted illegally in maintaining a monopoly in its operating system. But they also found that Judge Jackson had engaged in "serious judicial misconduct" in making derogatory comments about Microsoft to the media, so a new judge should decide on the punishment.

Even before a final decision was rendered, Microsoft said it would change its licensing agreements with personal computer manufacturers, allowing them to add software from other manufacturers to the Windows operating system as long as Microsoft's products also appear. Microsoft now says, "Our philosophy is that users should get to choose." In September 2001, the Justice Department announced it would not seek a breakup of Microsoft, but would ask the court for a series of tough restrictions.

In November 2001, Microsoft reached a settlement with the Justice Department and with most of the state attorneys general. The settlement, which still had to be approved by a federal judge, gives personal-computer makers greater freedom to install non-Microsoft software on new machines and to remove access to competing Microsoft features, such as Internet browsers. It also bans retaliation against companies that take advantage of these freedoms, prohibits exclusive contracts, and requires Microsoft to disclose design information to hardware and software makers so they can build competing products that will run smoothly with Windows. The states that did not settle with Microsoft continued to press their case in the courts.

\<interactive\>exercise

- **eACTIVITY: MICROSOFT ON TRIAL**
- **READING IT RIGHT: WALL STREET JOURNAL EXERCISE**

Sources: James Grimaldi, "Judge Orders Microsoft Split in 2," *Washington Post,* 8 June 2000; Ted Bridis, "Microsoft Ruling Sets High Standard for Proving Antitrust-Law Violations," *Wall Street Journal,* 2 July 2001; Paul Krugman, "The Smell Test," *New York Times,* 1 July 2001; John Wilke et al., "Ruling Sends Case to Lower Court, Denounces Judge Jackson's Findings," *Wall Street Journal,* 29 June 2001; John Wilke and Ted Bridis, "Justice Department Says It Won't Seek Court-Ordered Breakup of Microsoft," *Wall Street Journal,* 7 September 2001; "Microsoft Announces Concessions on Licensing Deals with PC Makers," *Wall Street Journal,* 11 July 2001; Steven Levy, "Shooting with Live Ammo," *Newsweek,* 13 August 2001; and a Web site that discusses the case, http://www.msnbc.com/news/ COMJUSTICEVSMS_Front.asp.

Recent Competitive Trends

Shepherd's analysis of competition extended only to 1988. What has been the trend in competition since then? Growing world trade has increased competition in the U.S. economy. For example, the share of the U.S. market controlled by the three major automakers fell from 80 percent in 1970 to 60 percent by 2000. And federal action to deregulate international phone service should force down the average price of international phone calls from $0.88 a minute in 1997 to under $0.20 a minute by 2002.

Other major markets are also growing more competitive in part as a result of *technological change,* a factor not identified by Shepherd as a main cause of increased competition. In the last two decades, the prime-time audience share of the three major television networks (NBC, CBS, and ABC) dropped from 91 percent to 46 percent as satellite and cable technology delivered many more networks. Despite Microsoft's dominance in operating systems, the packaged software market for personal computers barely existed in 1980 but has flourished in a technology-rich environment now populated by more than 8,000 producers. And the Internet has opened possibilities for greater competition in a number of industries, from online stock trading to all manner of electronic commerce.

But some deregulation has hit bumps in the road. Airlines are now more concentrated than they were before deregulation, although plane service is still cheaper and safer than during the era of regulation. The bankruptcy of many savings institutions during the 1980s was blamed in part on deregulation. California is experiencing growing pains from its partial deregulation of the electric industry. And the recent federal efforts to promote competition in local phone service seem to have backfired, as local providers merge with other local providers across the country. Despite these setbacks, the trend toward deregulation continues to increase competition, both here and abroad.

Problems with Antitrust Legislation

Despite the publicity and hoopla surrounding the Microsoft antitrust case (there was even a thinly disguised movie about Microsoft called *Antitrust)*, there is growing doubt about the economic value of some of the lengthy antitrust cases pursued in the past. A case against Exxon, for example, was in the courts for 17 years before the company was cleared of charges in 1992. Another case began in 1969 when IBM, with nearly 70 percent of domestic sales of electronic data-processing equipment, was accused of monopolizing that market. IBM responded that its large market share was based on its innovative products and on its economies of scale. The trial began in 1975, the government took nearly three years to present its case, and litigation dragged on for four more years. In the meantime, many other computer manufacturers emerged both in this country and abroad to challenge IBM's dominance. In 1982, the government dropped the case, noting that the threat of monopoly had diminished enough that the case was "without merit."

Too Much Emphasis on the Competitive Model. Joseph Schumpeter argued half a century ago that competition should be viewed as a dynamic process, one of "creative destruction." Firms are continually in flux—introducing new products, phasing out old ones, trying to compete for the consumer's dollar in a variety of ways. In light of this, antitrust policy should not necessarily be aimed at increasing the *number* of firms in each industry. In some cases, firms will grow large because they are more efficient than rivals at offering what consumers want. Accordingly, firm size should not be the primary concern. Moreover, as noted in the chapter on perfect competition, economists have shown through market experiments that most of the desirable properties of perfect competition can be achieved with a relatively small number of firms.[6] For example, the two leading chip makers, Intel and Advanced Micro Devices, have been locked in a price war for years, as each fights for market share.

Abuse of Antitrust. Parties that can show injury from firms that have violated antitrust laws can sue the offending company and recover three times the amount of the damages sustained. These so-called *treble damage* suits increased after World War II. More than 1,000 suits are filed each year. Courts have been relatively generous to those claiming to have been wronged. But studies show that such suits can be used to intimidate an aggressive competitor or to convert a contract dispute between, say, a firm and a supplier into treble damage payoffs. The result can have a chilling effect on competition. Many economists now believe that the anticompetitive costs from this abuse of treble damage suits may exceed any competitive benefits of these laws.

Growing Importance of International Markets. Finally, a standard approach to measuring the market power of a firm is its share of the market. With the growth of international trade, however, the local or even national market share becomes less relevant. General Motors may dominate U.S. auto manufacturing, accounting for half of national sales by U.S. firms. But when auto sales by Japanese and European producers are included, GM's share of the U.S. auto market falls to only 28 percent. GM's share of world production has declined steadily since the mid-1950s. *Where markets are open to foreign competition, antitrust enforcement that focuses on domestic producers makes less economic sense.*

CONCLUSION

Competition has been growing in recent decades because of changing technology, greater international trade, industry deregulation, and antitrust activity. The current merger movement could diminish competition, but the jury is still out on that question. Federal Reserve Chairman Alan Greenspan, testifying before Congress about antitrust policy, expressed skepticism about some antitrust intervention, arguing that changes in market conditions and technologies tend to undermine monopolies over time. He called for "a higher degree of humility

---

[6]See, for example, Vernon Smith, "Markets as Economizers of Information: Experimental Examinations of the 'Hayek Hypothesis,'" *Economic Inquiry* 20 (1982); and Douglas Davis and Charles Holt, *Experimental Economics* (Princeton, NJ: Princeton University Press, 1993).

when enforcers make . . . projections" about the lasting effects of monopoly power. But, at the same hearing, Joel Klein, then the antitrust chief for the Justice Department, said "we reject categorically the notion that markets will self-correct and we should sit back and watch."[7] So goes the public policy debate.

endofchaptermaterial

- **Summary**
- **Questions for Review**
- **Problems and Exercises**

- **Experiential Exercises**
- **Wall Street Journal Exercise**

Take the Post-Test to assess your overall understanding of the key ideas in this chapter. The Post-Test provides a comprehensive selection of exam-style questions addressing the main topics and concepts of the chapter. At the completion of each Post-Test, you will receive a score and instructive feedback on how you answered each question, and a direct link to the part of the chapter addressed in the question. Take the Post-Test as often as you need to—a record of your progress for each attempt is kept for you to revisit and gauge your improvement. And each Post-Test is randomly generated, so every attempt is new.

[7]As quoted in John R. Wilke, "Greenspan Questions Government's Antitrust-Enforcement Campaigns," *Wall Street Journal,* 17 June 1998.

16

Public Goods and Public Choice

How do public goods differ from private goods? Why do most people remain largely ignorant about what's happening in the public sector? Why is voter turnout so low? Why do politicians cater to special interests? Why are elected officials more likely than challengers to support campaign spending limits? Answers to these and related questions are discussed in this chapter, which focuses on the public sector—both the rationale for public goods and public choices about those goods.

The effects of government are all around us. Stitched into the clothes you put on this morning are government-required labels providing washing instructions. The prices of the milk and sugar you put on your Cheerios are propped up by government. The condition of the vehicle in which you rode to campus is regulated by the government, as are its speed and the sobriety of the driver. Your education is being subsidized by the public sector in a variety of ways. Government has a pervasive influence on all aspects of your life and on the economy. Yes, government is big business. Every year, the federal government alone spends more than $1,800,000,000,000— that is, $1.8 *trillion*—including more than $1 million on paper clips. State and local governments tax and spend another $1 trillion on their own.

The role of government has been discussed throughout this book. For the most part, we assumed that government makes optimal adjustments to the shortcomings of the private sector; that is, when confronted with market failure, government adopts and implements the appropriate program to address the problem. But there are limits to government's effectiveness, just as there are limits to the market's effectiveness. In this chapter, we look at the pros and cons of government activity. We begin with public goods, discuss the decision-making process, and then examine the limitations of that process. Topics discussed in this chapter include:

- Private versus public goods
- Representative democracy
- Rational ignorance
- Special-interest legislation
- Rent seeking
- Underground economy
- Bureaucratic behavior
- Private versus public production

\<interactive\>exercise

- ECONDEBATE ONLINE: MARKET FAILURE, REGULATION, AND PUBLIC CHOICE
- ECONDEBATE ONLINE: GOVERNMENT AND THE ECONOMY

\<interactive\>update

- ECONDATA ONLINE: MARKET FAILURE, REGULATION, AND PUBLIC CHOICE
- ECONDATA ONLINE: GOVERNMENT AND THE ECONOMY
- ECONLINKS ONLINE: ECONOMICS WEB LINKS
- ECONNEWS ONLINE: MARKET FAILURE, REGULATION, AND PUBLIC CHOICE
- ECONNEWS ONLINE: GOVERNMENT AND THE ECONOMY

\<interactive\>example

NETBOOKMARK: THE CATO INSTITUTE, THE HERITAGE FOUNDATION, AND NOBEL LAUREATE IN ECONOMICS, JAMES BUCHANAN'S INTERVIEW WITH *THE REGION*.

PUBLIC GOODS

Throughout most of this book, we have been talking about *private goods*. Private goods have two important features. First, they are *rival* in consumption, meaning that the amount consumed by one person is unavailable for others to consume. For example, when you and friends share a pizza, each slice others eat is one less available for you (which is why you usually eat a little faster when sharing). A second key feature of private goods is that suppliers can easily *exclude* those who don't pay. Only paying customers get pizzas. Thus private goods are said to be *rival* and *exclusive*.

Private Goods, Public Goods, and in Between

In contrast to private goods, public goods, such as national defense, the national weather service, the Center for Disease Control, or a neighborhood mosquito-control program, are *non-rival* in consumption. One person's consumption does not diminish the amount available to others. Once produced, such goods are available to all in equal amount; the marginal cost of providing the good to an additional consumer is zero. But once a public good is produced, suppliers cannot easily deny it to those who fail to pay. For example, if a firm sprays a community for mosquitoes, all households benefit. The firm can't exclude those households that failed to pay. Thus, the mosquito spraying is *nonexclusive*—it is available to all households, regardless of who pays and who doesn't. Some people figure, "I can enjoy the benefits without paying, so why bother paying?" For-profit producers find it difficult or impossible to charge people for nonexclusive goods.

In short, public goods are both *nonrival* and *nonexclusive*. Once produced, public goods are available for all to consume, regardless of who pays and who doesn't. As a consequence, for-profit firms cannot profitably sell public goods. There are no vending machines for public goods. In this case of market failure, government comes to the rescue by providing public goods and paying for them through enforced taxation. Sometimes nonprofit agencies also provide public goods, funding them through contributions and other revenue sources.

But the economy consists of more than just private and public goods. Some goods are *nonrival* but *exclusive*. For example, additional households can watch a TV show without affecting the TV reception of other viewers. It's not as if there is a limited amount of TV signal to go around. Television signals are nonrival in consumption. Yet the program's producers, should they choose to, could require cable boxes and charge each household for the show, as with cable TV, so the TV signal is exclusive. A good that is nonrival but exclusive is called a **quasi-public good.**

Along the same lines, short of the point of congestion, additional people can benefit from a golf course, swimming pool, rock concert, or bridge crossing without diminishing the benefit to other users. These goods, when not congested, are nonrival. Yet producers can, with relative ease, exclude those who don't pay the greens fee, pool admission, ticket price, or bridge toll. These uncongested goods are both nonrival and exclusive and are therefore quasi-public goods. If congestion sets in, however, these goods become rival—space is scarce on a backed-up golf course, in a crowded swimming pool, at a jam-packed rock concert, or on a traffic-laden bridge. Once congestion sets in, these quasi-public goods become private goods—both rival and exclusive.

Some other goods are *rival* but *nonexclusive*. The fish in the ocean are rival in that every fish caught is not available for others to catch; the same goes for migratory game, like wild ducks. But ocean fish and migratory game are nonexclusive in that it would be costly or impossible for a private firm to prevent access to these goods. A good that is rival but nonexclusive is called an **open-access good** because it would be difficult and costly to prevent individuals from consuming the good. Problems that arise with open-access goods will be examined in the next chapter.

Exhibit 1 offers a matrix that sorts out the four types of goods discussed. Across the top, goods are either *rival* or *nonrival*, and along the left margin, goods are either *exclusive* or *nonexclusive*. Private goods are usually provided by the private sector. Quasi-public goods are sometimes provided by government, as with a municipal golf course, and sometimes provided by the private sector, as with a private golf course. Open-access goods are usually regulated by government, as you will see in the next chapter. And public goods are usually provided by government.

EXHIBIT 1

Categories of Private and Public Goods

	Rival	Nonrival
Exclusive	1. Private Goods —Pizza —Crowded swimming pool	2. Quasi-Public Goods —Cable TV —Uncrowded swimming pool
Nonexclusive	3. Open-Access Goods —Ocean fish —Migratory birds	4. Public Goods —National defense —Mosquito control

Optimal Provision of Public Goods

Because private goods are rival in consumption, the market demand for a private good is the sum of the quantities demanded by each consumer. For example, the market quantity of pizza demanded when the price is $10 is the quantity demanded by Alan plus the quantity demanded by Maria plus the quantity demanded by all other consumers in the market. The market demand curve for a private good is the *horizontal* sum of individual demand curves, an idea developed back in Exhibit 7 of Chapter 6. The efficient quantity of a private good occurs where the market demand curve intersects the market supply curve.

But a public good is nonrival in consumption, so that good, once produced, is available to all consumers in an identical amount. For example, the market demand for a given level of mosquito control reflects the marginal benefit that Alan gets from that amount of the good plus the marginal benefit that Maria gets from that amount plus the marginal benefit that all others in the community get from that amount of the good. Therefore, the market demand curve for a public good is the *vertical* sum of each consumer's demand for the public good. To arrive at the efficient level of the public good, we find where the market demand curve intersects the marginal cost curve—that is, where the sum of the marginal valuations equals the marginal cost.

Suppose the public good in question is mosquito control in a neighborhood, which, for simplicity, consists of only two houses, one headed by Alan and the other by Maria. Alan spends a lot of time in the yard and thus values a mosquito-free environment more than does Maria, who spends more time away from home. Their demand curves are shown in Exhibit 2 as D_a and D_m, reflecting the marginal benefits that Alan and Maria enjoy at each rate of output. Quantity is measured here as hours of mosquito spraying per week.

For example, when the town sprays two hours a week, Maria values the second hour at $5 and Alan values it at $10. To derive the sum of the marginal benefits for the neighborhood, we simply add each resident's marginal benefit to get $15, as identified by point *e*. By vertically summing marginal valuations at each rate of output, we derive the neighborhood demand curve, *D*, for mosquito spraying.

How much mosquito spraying should the government provide? Suppose the marginal cost of spraying is a constant $15 an hour, as shown in Exhibit 2. The efficient level of output is

EXHIBIT 2

Market for Public Goods

Because public goods, once produced, are available to all in identical amounts, the demand for a public good is the vertical sum of each individual's demand. Thus, the market demand for mosquito spraying is the vertical sum of Maria's demand, D_m, and Alan's demand, D_a. The efficient level of provision is found where the marginal cost of mosquito spraying equals its marginal benefit. This occurs where the marginal cost curve intersects the market demand curve, *D*, resulting in point *e*.

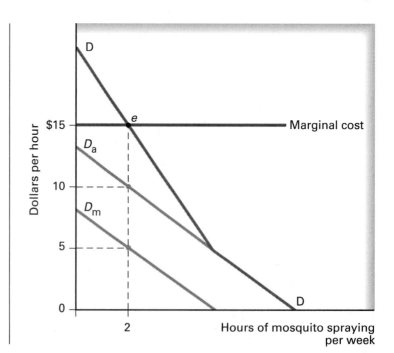

found where the marginal benefit to the neighborhood equals the marginal cost, which occurs where the neighborhood demand curve intersects the marginal cost curve. In our example, these curves intersect where quantity is two hours per week.

The government pays for the mosquito spray through taxes, user fees, or some combination of the two. The efficient approach would be to impose a tax on each resident equal to his or her marginal valuation. Simple enough, but there are at least two problems with this. First, once people realize their taxes are based on how much the government thinks they value the good, people tend to understate their true valuation. Why admit you really value the good if, as a result, you get smacked with a higher tax bill? So taxpayers are reluctant to offer information about their true valuation of public goods. This creates the **free-rider problem,** which occurs because people try to benefit from the public good without paying for it. For example, they can enjoy the benefits of mosquito abatement whether or not they pay. But even if the government had accurate information about marginal valuations, some households earn much more than others and thus have a greater ability to pay taxes. In our example, Alan values mosquito control more because he spends more time in the yard than Maria does. What if Alan is around more because he couldn't find a job? Should his taxes be double those of Maria, who, say, has a high-paying job? Thus, taxing people according to their marginal valuations of the public good may be efficient, but it may not be considered fair, or equitable, if the ability to pay differs.

Once the public good is produced, only that output is available. Since only one amount is produced, each individual's consumption is limited to that particular quantity. In contrast, with private goods, each consumer is free to purchase any quantity he or she prefers. Thus, public goods are more complicated than private goods in terms of what goods should be provided, in what quantities, and who should pay. These decisions are thrashed out through public choices, which we examine in the balance of this chapter.

SEE IT: OPTIMAL PROVISION FOR A PUBLIC GOOD

PUBLIC CHOICE IN A REPRESENTATIVE DEMOCRACY

Government decisions about the provision of public goods and the collection of tax revenues are *public choices*. In a democracy, public choices usually require approval by a majority of voters. As it turns out, we can frequently explain the choice of the electorate with majority rule by focusing on the preferences of the median voter. The *median voter* is the one whose preferences lie in the middle of the set of all voters' preferences. For example, if the issue is the size of the government budget, half the voters prefer a larger budget and half prefer a smaller one.

ASK THE INSTRUCTOR: WHY DO WE KEEP THE INCOME TAX IF IT IS SO UNPOPULAR?

Median Voter Model

The **median voter model** predicts that under certain conditions, the preference of the median, or middle, voter will dominate other choices. Here is the logic behind the model. Suppose you and two roommates have just moved into an apartment, and the three of you must decide on furnishings. You all agree to share the common costs equally and to let majority rule prevail. The issue at hand is whether to buy a TV and, if so, of what size. But you each have a different preference. Your studious roommate considers a TV an annoying distraction and would rather go without; otherwise, the smaller the TV, the better. Your other roommate, a real TV fan, prefers a 48-inch screen but would settle for a smaller size rather than go without. Although you are by no means a TV addict, you enjoy watching TV as a relief from the rigors of academe;

a 27-inch screen is your first choice, but you prefer the 48-inch screen to none at all. What to do, what to do?

You all agree to make the decision by voting on two alternatives at a time, then pairing the winner against the remaining alternative until one dominates the others. When the 27-inch set is paired with the no-TV option, the 27-inch set wins by getting both your vote and the TV fan's vote. When the 27-inch screen is then paired with the 48-inch screen, the 27-inch screen wins again, this time because your studious roommate sides with you rather than voting for the super screen.

Majority voting in effect delegates the public choice to the person whose preference is the median for the group. You, as the median voter in this case, can have your way. If you had preferred a 13-inch or 36-inch screen, you could have received majority support for either. Similarly, *the median voter in an electorate often determines public choices. Political candidates try to get elected by appealing to the median voter.* This is one reason why candidates often seem so much alike. Note that under majority rule, only the median voter gets his or her way. Other voters are required to go along with what the median voter wants. Thus, other voters usually end up paying for what they consider to be either too much or too little of the public good, and this is another welfare cost of public goods.

People vote directly on issues at New England town meetings and on the occasional referendum, but direct democracy is not the most common means of public choice. When you consider the thousands of public choices made on behalf of individual voters, it becomes clear that direct democracy through referenda would be unwieldy and impractical. Rather than make decisions by direct referenda, voters elect *representatives,* who, at least in theory, make public choices that reflect their constituents' views. Under certain conditions, the resulting public choices reflect the preferences of the median voter. Some complications of making public choices through representative democracy will be explored next.

Special Interest and Rational Ignorance

We assume that consumers maximize utility and firms maximize profit, but what about governments? As noted in Chapter 4, there is no common agreement about what governments maximize or, more precisely, what elected officials maximize, if anything. One theory that parallels the rational self-interest assumption employed in private choices is that elected officials attempt to *maximize their political support.*

It is possible that elected representatives will cater to special interests rather than serve the interests of the majority. The problem arises because of the asymmetry between special interests and the public interest, an idea introduced in the previous chapter. Consider only one of the thousands of decisions that are made each year by elected representatives: funding an obscure federal program that subsidizes U.S. wool production. Under the wool-subsidy program, the federal government guarantees that a floor price is paid to sheep farmers for each pound of wool they produce, a subsidy that costs taxpayers over $75 million per year. During deliberations to renew the program, the only person to testify before Congress was a representative of the National Wool Growers Association, who claimed that the subsidy was vital to the nation's economic welfare. Why didn't a single taxpayer challenge the subsidy? Why were sheep farmers able to pull the wool over taxpayers' eyes?

Households consume so many different public and private goods and services that they have neither the time nor the incentive to understand the effects of public choices on every product. What's more, voters realize that each of them has only a tiny possibility of influencing the outcome of public choices. And even if an individual voter is somehow able to affect the outcome, the impact on that voter is likely to be small. For example, if a taxpayer could successfully stage a grassroots campaign to eliminate the wool subsidy, the taxpayer would save, on average, less than $0.60 per year in federal income taxes (based on about 130 million individual tax filings in 2001). Therefore, unless voters have a special interest in the legislation, they adopt a stance of **rational ignorance,** which means that they remain largely oblivious to the costs and benefits of the thousands of proposals considered by elected officials. The cost to the typical voter of acquiring and acting on such information is usually greater than any expected benefit.

In contrast, consumers have more incentive to gather and act on information about decisions they make in private markets because they benefit directly from such information. *Because information and the time required to acquire and digest it are scarce, consumers concentrate on private choices rather than public choices. The payoff in making wise private choices is usually more immediate, more direct, and more substantial.* For example, a consumer in the market for a new car has an incentive to examine the performance records of different models, test-drive a few, and check prices at dealerships and on the Internet. That same individual has less incentive to examine the performance records of candidates for public office because that single voter has virtually no chance of deciding the election. What's more, candidates aim to please the median voter, so they often take positions that are similar anyway.

Distribution of Costs and Benefits

Let's turn now to a different topic—how the costs and benefits of public choices are spread across the population. The benefits of particular legislation may be conferred on only a small group or on much of the population, depending on the issue. Likewise, the costs imposed by a particular legislative measure may be distributed either narrowly or widely over the population. The possible combinations of benefits and costs yield four categories of distributions: (1) widespread benefits and widespread costs, (2) concentrated benefits and widespread costs, (3) widespread benefits and concentrated costs, and (4) concentrated costs and concentrated benefits.

Traditional public-goods legislation, such as for national defense or a system of justice, have widespread benefits and widespread costs—nearly everyone benefits and nearly everyone pays. Traditional public-goods legislation usually has a positive impact on the economy because total benefits exceed total costs.

With **special-interest legislation,** benefits are concentrated but costs widespread. For example, as you'll see shortly, price supports for dairy products benefit dairy farmers with higher prices. The program's costs are spread across nearly all consumers and taxpayers. Legislation that caters to special interests usually harms the economy, on net, because total costs often exceed total benefits.

Populist legislation involves widespread benefits but concentrated costs. Populist legislation usually has a tough time getting approved because the widespread group that benefits typically remains rationally ignorant of the proposed legislation, so these voters provide little political support. But the concentrated group getting whacked will object strenuously. Tort-reform legislation, for example, would benefit the economy as a whole by limiting product liability lawsuits, reducing insurance costs, and bringing some goods to the market that, because of liability suits, have all but disappeared, such as personal aircraft. But trial lawyers, the group most harmed by such limits, have successfully blocked reforms for years. Because the small group that bears the cost is savvy about the impact of the proposed legislation but those who reap the benefits remain rationally ignorant, populist legislation has little chance of approval, unless elected officials can somehow get the issue on the voter's radar screen. It's been said, "It's not easy to interest the public in the public interest."

Finally, **competing-interest legislation** involves both concentrated benefits and concentrated costs, such as legislation affecting the relative market position of Microsoft versus AOL, or legislation affecting the power of labor unions in their dealings with employers.

Exhibit 3 arrays the four categories of distributions. Across the top, benefits of legislation are either *widespread* or *concentrated,* and along the left margin, costs are either *widespread* or

EXHIBIT 3

Categories of Legislation Based on the Distribution of Costs and Benefits

Distribution of Benefits

		Widespread	Concentrated
Distribution of Costs	**Widespread**	1. Traditional Public Goods —National defense	2. Special Interest —Farm subsidies
	Concentrated	3. Populist —Tort reform	4. Competing Interest —Labor union issues

concentrated. Box 1 shows *traditional public-goods legislation,* with both widespread benefits and costs, such as national defense. Box 2 shows *special-interest legislation,* with concentrated benefits but widespread costs, such as farm subsidies. Box 3 shows *populist legislation,* with widespread benefits but concentrated costs, such as tort reform. And Box 4 shows *competing-interest legislation,* with both concentrated benefits and costs, such as labor union issues.

The following case study considers a special-interest program—milk price supports.

<interactive>update

ECONNEWS ONLINE: TORTILLA TROUBLES

CASE**STUDY**	Farm Subsidies
	● *Public Policy*

The Agricultural Marketing Agreement Act became law in 1937 to prevent what was viewed as "ruinous competition" among farmers. In the years since, the government-run introduced a variety of policies to set floor prices for a wide range of farm products. Until the federal government began scaling back farm subsidies in 1996, direct costs exceeded $10 billion a year for dozens of agricultural products. Direct support programs for milk, sugar, and some other products still persist, and federal aid has averaged more than $7 billion a year since 1998.

In much of the country, milk prices are the most heavily regulated of farm products. Explaining the intricacies of the price support program for milk takes up three volumes of the *Code of Federal Regulations,* and administering the regulations employs 650 people at the U.S. Department of Agriculture—more than oversee the entire federal budget in the Office of Management and Budget. These rules cost consumers at least $1.7 billion a year, according to Agriculture Department studies.

Let's see how price supports work in the dairy industry, using a hypothetical example. Exhibit 4 depicts a simplified view of the market for milk. Suppose that, in the absence of government intervention, the market price of milk would average $1.50 per gallon and the equilibrium quantity would average 100 million gallons per month. In long-run equilibrium, dairy

EXHIBIT 4

Effects of Milk Price Supports

In the absence of government intervention, the market price of milk is $1.50 per gallon, and 100 million gallons are sold per month. If Congress establishes a floor price of $2.50 per gallon, then the quantity supplied will increase and the quantity demanded will decrease. To maintain the higher price, the government must buy the excess quantity at $2.50 per gallon.

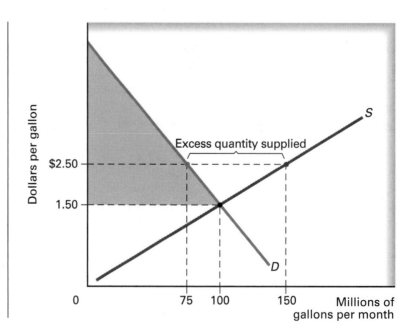

farmers would earn a normal rate of return in this competitive industry. Consumers as a group would capture the consumer surplus shown by the blue-shaded area. Recall that consumer surplus is the difference between the most that consumers would have been willing to pay and the amount they actually pay.

But suppose dairy farmers persuade Congress that the market price is too low, so legislation establishes a price floor for milk of, say, $2.50 per gallon. The higher price floor provides farmers with an incentive to increase the quantity supplied to 150 million gallons per month. In response to the higher price, however, consumers reduce their quantity demanded to 75 million gallons. To make the higher price stick, the government must buy the 75 million gallons of "surplus" milk generated by the floor price or somehow get dairy farmers to restrict their output to 75 million gallons per month. For example, the government could pay dairy farmers not to produce or could buy cows from farmers to reduce production (as was done in the 1980s).

Consumers end up paying dearly to subsidize farmers. First, the price increases by $1 per gallon. Second, consumers, as taxpayers, must pay for the surplus milk or otherwise pay farmers not to produce that milk. And third, if the government buys the surplus, taxpayers must then pay for storage. So consumers pay $2.50 per gallon for milk they buy on the market, another $2.50 for each gallon the government buys, plus, say, an extra $0.50 per gallon to convert surplus milk into powder and to store it. Instead of paying just $1.50 for a gallon of milk, the free-market price, the typical consumer-taxpayer in effect pays $5.50 (=$2.50 + $2.50 + $0.50), or nearly four times as much, for each gallon actually consumed.

How do farmers make out? Each receives an extra $1 per gallon in additional revenue compared to the free-market price. As farmers increase their output, however, the marginal cost of production increases; at the margin, the higher price just offsets the higher production costs. The subsidy increases the value of specialized resources, such as cows and grazing land, and farmers who own these resources when the subsidy program is approved will benefit. Farmers who purchase them after the subsidy is operating earn only a normal rate of return on their investment. So with free entry into the dairy industry, farmers earn just a normal rate of return in the long run, despite the billions spent on farm subsidies.

If the extra $1 per gallon that farmers receive for milk were pure profit, farm profits would increase by $150 million per month. But consumer-taxpayer costs increase by $300 million per month ($75 million for the higher price of each of the 75 million gallons consumers purchase, plus $187.5 million in higher taxes to pay for the 75 million surplus gallons purchased by the government, plus $37.5 million to store the 75 million surplus gallons). Thus, costs to consumer-taxpayers are double the farmers' maximum possible gain of $150 million. The government subsidy therefore has a negative impact on the economy, as the losses outweigh the gains of this special-interest legislation. This does not mean nobody gains—those who own specialized resources gain when the subsidy is first introduced. But once the price of farm resources increases, new farmers must pay more to get in a position to reap the subsidies. Ironically, subsidies aimed at preserving the family farm raise the costs to a young person entering the industry.

The dairy industry is supported in other ways. Some state programs ensure even higher prices. Other laws promote the consumption of dairy products. For example, laws in many states prohibit restaurants from serving margarine instead of butter unless the customer specifically requests it. Margarine has faced a long history of discrimination dating back a century.

The profound long-run problem for dairy farmers is that technological breakthroughs, such as genetically engineered hormones that stimulate milk production, have made farmers far more productive. Yet, despite the widely advertised "Got milk?" and milk-mustache campaigns, milk consumption remains flat. The combination of increased supply and stagnant demand creates excess quantity supplied.

Everyone would be better off if the government made a direct payment to dairy farmers, a payment not tied to milk production or the price. But even if one could work out a system for paying dairy farmers, such a transparent payoff could attract the public's attention and be doomed.

‹interactive›exercise

eACTIVITY: FARM SUBSIDIES

Sources: Bruce L. Gardner, "Changing Economic Perspectives on the Farm Problem," *Journal of Economic Literature* 30 (March 1992): 62–101; Ken Bailey and Jose Gamboa, "A Regional Economic Analysis of Dairy Compacts," University of Missouri (January

1999); "Proposed Bill Sets Up Milk Price Minimums," *Milwaukee Journal Sentinel*, 3 August 2000; "The OPEC of Milk," *Wall Street Journal*, 20 June 2001; Philip Shenon, "Senate Passes Farm Measure Supported by President," *New York Times*, 4 August 2001; and the U.S. Department of Agriculture's marketing service site for dairy products at http://www.ams.usda.gov/dairy/index.htm.

Rent Seeking

An important feature of representative democracy is the incentive and political power it offers participants to employ legislation that increases their wealth, either through direct transfers or through favorable public expenditures and regulations. Special-interest groups, such as dairy farmers and trial lawyers, try to persuade elected officials to approve measures that provide the special interest with some market advantage or some outright transfer or subsidy. Such benefits are sometimes called *rents*. The term in this context means that the government transfer or subsidy constitutes a payment to the resource owner that exceeds the earnings necessary to call forth that resource—*a payment exceeding opportunity cost.* The activity that interest groups undertake to elicit these special favors from government is called *rent seeking*, a term already introduced.

<interactive>exercise

READING IT RIGHT: WALL STREET JOURNAL EXERCISE

The government frequently bestows some special advantage on a producer or group of producers, and abundant resources are expended to secure these rights. For example, *political action committees,* known more popularly as *PACs,* contribute millions to congressional campaigns. More than 4,000 PACs try to shape federal legislation; the top contributors recently included the tobacco lobby and the American Trial Lawyers Association. Tobacco interests would like to influence cigarette legislation, and lawyers fear tort reforms that would limit liability lawsuits.

To the extent that special-interest groups engage in rent seeking, they shift resources from productive endeavors that create output and income to activities that focus more on transferring income to their special interests. *Resources employed to persuade government to redistribute income and wealth are unproductive because they do nothing to increase output and usually end up reducing it.* Often many firms compete for the same government advantage, thereby wasting still more resources. If the advantage conferred by government on some special-interest group requires higher income taxes, the net return individuals expect from working and investing will fall, so they may work less and invest less. If this happens, productive activity declines.

As a firm's profitability becomes more and more dependent on decisions made in Washington, resources are diverted from productive activity to rent seeking, or lobbying efforts, to gain special advantage. One firm may thrive because it secured some special government advantage at a critical time; another firm may fail because its managers were more concerned with productive efficiency than with rent seeking.

Special-interest groups have little incentive to make the economy more efficient. In fact, they will usually support legislation that transfers wealth to them even if the economy's overall efficiency declines. For example, suppose that the American Trial Lawyers Association is able to revise product liability laws in a way that boosts lawyers' annual incomes by a total of $1 billion, or about $1,900 for each lawyer in private practice. Suppose, too, that this measure drives up insurance premiums, raising the total cost of production by, say, $2 billion per year. Lawyers themselves will have to bear part of this higher cost, but since they account for only about 1 percent of the spending in the economy, they will bear only about 1 percent of the $2 billion in higher costs, or a total of $20 million, which amounts to about $40 per lawyer per year. Thus, the legislation is a good deal for lawyers because their annual incomes grow about $1,900 each but their costs increase only about $40 each, resulting in the net average gain of $1,860 per lawyer.

Think of the economy's output in a particular period as depicted by a pie. The pie represents the total value of goods and services produced. In answering the what, how, and for whom questions introduced in Chapter 2, policy makers have three alternatives: (1) they can introduce changes that increase the size of the pie (that is, positive-sum changes); (2) they can decide simply to carve up the existing pie differently (redistribute income); or (3) they can start fighting over how the pie is carved up, causing some of it to end up on the floor (negative-sum changes). Much special-interest legislation leads to a net reduction in social welfare. For example, some of the nation's best minds are occupied with devising schemes to avoid taxes or divert income to favored groups at the expense of market efficiency.

There are hundreds of special-interest groups representing farmers, physicians, lawyers, teachers, manufacturers, barbers, and so on. One way special interests try to gain access to the political process is through campaign contributions. The elusive issue of campaign finance reform is discussed in the following case study.

CASESTUDY | Campaign Finance Reform

● *Public Policy*

Critics of the current campaign finance system have argued that American politics is awash in special-interest money. Most Americans seem to agree. Two-thirds of those surveyed in a recent poll said they support public financing of campaigns if this eliminates funding from large private donations and organized interest groups. Since the 1970s, presidential campaigns have been in part publicly funded, but not congressional races (the Bush and Gore campaigns each received $67.6 million during the 2000 presidential election).

Senators John McCain and Russ Feingold have proposed a ban on so-called soft-money contributions to national parties. *Soft money* allows parties to raise unlimited amounts from individuals, corporations, and labor unions and to spend it freely on party-building activities, such as get-out-the-vote efforts, but not on direct support for candidates. *Hard money* is the cash parties raise under rules that limit individual contributions and require public disclosure of donors. Individual contributions to candidates have been limited to $1,000 per person since 1974; in today's dollars, that's less than one-third the 1974 value. The McCain-Feingold measure has not garnered the 60 votes in the Senate needed to break a filibuster. In the House, a similar bill did not get enough votes in 2001.

Even if passed, the measure would face legal obstacles. The Supreme Court has declared unconstitutional any effort that would prevent individual citizens from spending their own money on issue advocacy, so long as the ads did not support a particular candidate (such as "Will McEachern for President—Where there's a Will, there's a way"). According to the Constitution, "Congress shall make no law . . . abridging freedom of speech." The Supreme Court ruled that "dollars are not stuffed in ballot boxes. . . . The mediating factor that turns money into votes is speech . . . . Advocacy cannot be proscribed because it's effective."

Limits on special-interest contributions may help reduce their influence in the political process, but such limits would heighten the current advantage of incumbency. About 95 percent of congressional incumbents are reelected. Observers claim that this results from the unfair advantages that incumbents have in the electoral process, especially because of taxpayer-funded staff and free mailing privileges (campaign literature masquerading as official communications).

Limits on campaign spending would magnify the advantages of incumbency by reducing a challenger's ability to appeal directly to voters. Some liberal *and* conservative thinkers agree that the supply of political money should be increased, not decreased. As Curtis Gans, director of the Committee for the Study of the American Electorate argues, "The overwhelming body of scholarly research . . . indicates that low spending limits will undermine political competition by enhancing the existing advantages of incumbency." *Money matters more to challengers than to incumbents* since the public knows less about challengers than about incumbents. Challengers must be able to spend enough to get their message out. One study found a positive relationship between spending by challengers and their election success but found no relationship between spending by incumbents and their reelection success. So a limit on spending favors incumbents.

According to Common Cause, national party groups took in a total of $441 million in soft money for the 2000 election, with $225 million raised by Republicans and $216 million by Democrats. That money was used to fund presidential and congressional races across the country. Nearly half a billion dollars sounds like a lot, but Coke spent nearly five times that on advertising in 2000.

The point is that legislation often has unintended consequences. Efforts to limit campaign spending may or may not reduce the influence of special-interest groups, but a limit would reduce a challenger's ability to reach the voters and thereby increase the advantage of incumbency, thus reducing political competition.

<interactive>exercise

eACTIVITY: CAMPAIGN FINANCE REFORM

Sources: Stanley Brubaker, "The Limits of Campaign Spending Limits," *Public Interest* (Fall 1998): 33–54; Carey Goldberg, "Publicly Paid Elections Put to Test in 3 States," *New York Times,* 19 November 2000; Alison Mitchell, "Blacks and Hispanics in House Balk at Campaign Finance Bill," *New York Times,* 9 May 2001; Robert Zausner, "Both Parties on a 'Soft Money' Spending Spree," *Philadelphia Inquirer,* 2 November 2000; Bradley Smith, "Free Speech Costs Money," *Wall Street Journal,* 29 March 2001; "The Costliest Race Ends," *Forbes,* 7 November 2000; the Federal Election Commission at http://www.fec.gov/; and Common Cause at http://www.commoncause.org.

The Underground Economy

A government subsidy promotes production, as we saw in the case study on milk price supports. Conversely, a tax discourages production. Perhaps it would be more accurate to say that when government taxes productive activity, less production gets *reported.* If you ever worked as a waitress or waiter, did you faithfully report all your tips to the Internal Revenue Service? To the extent that you didn't, your income became part of the underground economy. The **underground economy** is a term used for all market activity that goes unreported to the government either to avoid taxes or because the activity itself is illegal. Income arising in the underground economy ranges from unreported tips to the earnings of drug dealers.

The introduction of a tax on productive activity has two effects. First, resource owners may supply less of the taxed resource because the after-tax wage declines. Second, to evade taxes, some people will shift from the formal, reported economy to an underground, "off the books" economy. Thus, when the government taxes market exchange or the income it generates, less market activity gets reported.

We should distinguish between tax *avoidance* and tax *evasion.* Tax avoidance is a *legal* attempt to arrange one's economic affairs to pay the least tax possible, such as buying municipal bonds because they yield tax-free interest. Tax evasion, on the other hand, is *illegal;* it takes the form of either failing to file a tax return or filing a fraudulent return by understating income or overstating deductions. Research around the world indicates that the underground economy grows more when (1) government regulations increase, (2) the tax rate increases, and (3) government corruption is more widespread.[1]

The U.S. Commerce Department estimates that official figures capture only 90 percent of U.S. income. An Internal Revenue Service survey estimates that only 87 percent of taxable income gets reported on tax returns. These studies suggest an underground economy of between $700 billion and $900 billion in 2001.

Those who pursue rent-seeking activity and those involved in the underground economy view government from opposite sides. Rent seekers want government to become actively involved in transferring wealth to them, but those in the underground economy want to avoid government contact. *Subsidies and other advantages bestowed by government draw some groups closer to government; taxes drive others underground.*

BUREAUCRACY AND REPRESENTATIVE DEMOCRACY

Elected representatives approve legislation, but the task of implementing that legislation is typically left to **bureaus,** which are government departments and agencies whose activities are financed by appropriations from legislative bodies.

Ownership and Funding of Bureaus

We can get a better feel for government bureaus by comparing them to corporations. Ownership of a corporation is based on the shares owned by stockholders. Stockholders share any profit or loss arising from the firm's operations; stockholders also get to vote on important corporate matters based on the number of shares owned. Ownership in a corporation is *transferable:* the shares can be bought and sold in the stock market. Taxpayers are in a sense the "owners" of government bureaus in the jurisdiction in which they live. If the bureau earns a "profit," taxes may decline; if the bureau operates at a "loss," as most do, this loss must be covered by taxes. Each taxpayer has just one vote, regardless of the taxes he or she pays. Ownership in the bureau is surrendered only if the taxpayer dies or moves out of the jurisdiction; ownership is not transferable—it cannot be bought or sold directly.

Whereas firms receive their revenue when customers voluntarily purchase their products, bureaus are typically financed by a budget appropriation from the legislature. Most of this budget comes from taxpayers. Some bureaus earn revenue through user charges, such as

[1]For a summary of these studies, see Simon Johnson et al., "Regulatory Discretion and the Unofficial Economy," *American Economic Review* 88 (May 1998): 387–392.

admission fees to state parks or tuition at state colleges, but supplementary funds for these activities often come from budget appropriations. Because of these differences in the forms of ownership and in the sources of revenue, bureaus have different incentives than do for-profit firms, so they are likely to behave differently.

Ownership and Organizational Behavior

A central assumption of economics is that people behave rationally and respond to economic incentives. The more tightly compensation is linked to individual incentives, the more people will behave in accordance with those incentives. If a letter carrier's pay is based on customer satisfaction, the carrier will make a greater effort to deliver mail promptly and intact.

A private firm receives a steady stream of consumer feedback. If the price is too high or too low to clear the market, surpluses or shortages will become obvious. Not only is consumer feedback abundant, but the firm's owners have a profit incentive to act on that information to satisfy consumer wants. The promise of profits also creates incentives to produce output at minimum cost. Thus, the firm's owners stand to gain from any improvement in customer satisfaction or any reduction in cost.

Since public goods and services are not sold in markets, government bureaus receive less consumer feedback and have less incentive to act on any feedback they do receive. There are usually no prices and no obvious shortages or surpluses. For example, how would you know whether there was a shortage or a surplus of police protection in your community? (Would gangs of police officers hanging around Dunkin' Donuts indicate a surplus?) Not only do bureaus receive less consumer feedback than firms do, they also have less incentive to act on the information available. Because any "profit" or "loss" arising in the bureau is spread among all taxpayers, and because there is no transferability of ownership, bureaus have less incentive to satisfy customers or to produce their output using the least-cost combination of resources. (Laws prevent bureaucrats from taking home any "profit.")

Some pressure for customer satisfaction and cost minimization may be communicated by voters to their elected representatives and thereby to the bureaus. But this discipline is not very precise, particularly since any gains or losses in efficiency are diffused among all taxpayers. For example, suppose that you are one of a million taxpayers in a city and you learn that by having Kinko's do all public copying, the city could save $1 million a year. If, through letters to the editor and calls to local officials, you convince the city to adopt this cost-saving measure, you would save yourself about a dollar a year in taxes.

Voters can leave a jurisdiction if they believe government is inefficient. This mechanism, whereby people "vote with their feet," does promote some efficiency and consumer satisfaction at the state and local levels, but it's rather crude. Moreover, voters dissatisfied with the biggest spender, the federal government, cannot easily vote with their feet.

Because of differences between public and private organizations—in the owners' ability both to transfer ownership and to appropriate profits—we expect bureaus to be less concerned with satisfying consumer demand and with minimizing costs than private firms are. A variety of empirical studies compare costs for products that are provided by both public bureaus and private firms, such as garbage collection. Of those studies that show a difference, a few find public bureaus to be more efficient, but the majority find private firms to be more efficient.

Bureaucratic Objectives

Assuming that bureaus are not simply at the beck and call of the legislature—that is, assuming that bureaucrats have some autonomy—what sort of objectives will *they* pursue? The traditional view is that bureaucrats are "public servants," who try to serve the public as best they can. No doubt many public employees do just that, but is this a realistic assumption for bureaucrats more generally? Why should we assume self-sacrificing behavior by public-sector employees when we make no such assumption about private-sector employees?

One widely discussed theory of bureaucratic behavior claims that bureaus try to *maximize the bureau's budget,* for along with a bigger budget come size, prestige, amenities, staff, and pay—all features that are valued by bureaucrats.[2] According to this view, bureaus are monopoly suppliers of their output to the legislature. Rather than charge a price per unit, bureaus offer the legislature the entire amount as a package deal in return for the requested appropriation. The legislature has only limited ability to dig into the budget and cut particular items. If the legislature does try to cut the bureau's budget, the bureau will threaten to make those cuts as painful to the legislature and constituents as possible. For example, if city officials attempt to reduce the school budget, school bureaucrats, rather than increase teaching loads, may threaten to

---

[2]William A. Niskanen Jr., in *Bureaucracy and Representative Government* (New York: Aldine-Atherton, 1971).

eliminate kindergarten, abolish the high school football team, or cut textbook purchases. If such threats force the legislature to back off, the government budget turns out to be larger than most taxpayers would prefer. *Budget maximization results in a larger budget than that desired by the median voter.* The key to this argument is that bureaus are monopoly suppliers. If taxpayers have alternatives in the private sector, the monopoly power of the bureau is diminished.

Private Versus Public Production

Simply because some goods and services are financed by the government does not mean that they must be produced by the government. Elected officials may contract directly with private firms to produce public output. For example, a city council may contract with a firm to handle garbage collection for the city. Profit-making firms now provide everything from fire protection to prisons in certain jurisdictions. Elected officials may also use some combination of bureaus and firms to produce the desired output. For example, the Pentagon, a giant bureau, hires and trains military personnel, yet contracts with private firms to develop and produce various weapon systems. State governments typically hire private contractors to build roads but employ state workers to maintain them. The mix of firms and bureaus varies over time and across jurisdictions, but the trend is toward increased *privatization,* or production by the private sector, of government goods and services.

When governments produce public goods and services, they are using the *internal organization of the government*—the bureaucracy—to supply the product. When governments contract with private firms to produce public goods and services, they are using *the market* to supply the product. Legislators might prefer dealing with bureaus rather than with firms for two reasons. First, in situations where it is difficult to specify a contract that clearly spells out all the possible contingencies, the internal organization of the bureau may be more responsive to the legislature's concerns than the manager of a firm would be. Second, bureaus provide legislators with opportunities to reward friends and supporters with government jobs.

CONCLUSION

This chapter viewed public goods and how preferences are reflected in public choices. After examining public goods, we discussed the problems arising from representative democracy and then looked at bureaus, the organizations that usually implement public choices. We also considered indirect income transfers, or rent seeking, which arise because of changes in the rules governing economic activity in the private sector.

Governments attempt to address market failures in the private economy. But simply turning problems of perceived market failure over to government may not always be the best solution, because government has failings of its own. Participation in markets is based on voluntary exchange. Governments, however, have the legal power to enforce public choices. We should employ at least as high a standard in judging the performance of government, where allocations have the force of law, as we do in judging the private market, where allocations are decided by voluntary exchange between consenting parties.

Take the Post-Test to assess your overall understanding of the key ideas in this chapter. The Post-Test provides a comprehensive selection of exam-style questions addressing the main topics and concepts of the chapter. At the completion of each Post-Test, you will receive a score and instructive feedback on how you answered each question, and a direct link to the part of the chapter addressed in the question. Take the Post-Test as often as you need to—a record of your progress for each attempt is kept for you to revisit and gauge your improvement. And each Post-Test is randomly generated, so every attempt is new.

Post-Test

endofchaptermaterial

- **Summary**
- **Questions for Review**
- **Problems and Exercises**

- **Experiential Exercises**
- **Wall Street Journal Exercise**

CHAPTER 17

Externalities and the Environment

What do the following have to do with economics? The rivers in Jakarta, Indonesia, are dead—killed by acid, alcohol, and oil. Coral reefs in the South Pacific have been ripped apart by dynamite fishing. Breathing the air in Bombay is reportedly equivalent to smoking 10 cigarettes a day. In Mexico City, some people buy oxygen tanks for home use. Five of the world's 10 most polluted cities are in China, where pollution levels are two to five times the guidelines for safe exposure. The air in some U.S. cities does not meet health standards, and some streams in Colorado are still considered toxic from gold mining that ended more than a century ago.

What does all this have to do with economics? Plenty! Market prices can allocate resources efficiently only as long as property rights are well defined and can be easily enforced. But property rights to clean water, air, and soil, to fish in the ocean, to peace and quiet, and to scenic vistas are hard to establish and enforce. This chapter examines the difficulty of assigning property rights to some key resources, and why the lack of property rights results in inefficient use.

As you learned in Chapter 4, externalities, which are unpriced by-products of production or consumption, may be either negative, such as air pollution, or positive, such as the general improvement in the civic climate that results from better education. This chapter concentrates mostly on negative externalities. The focus is on how externalities affect resource allocation and on how properly designed public policies can increase efficiency. Topics discussed in this chapter include:

- Exhaustible resources
- Renewable resources
- Common-pool problem
- Private property rights
- Optimal pollution

- Marginal social cost
- Marginal social benefit
- Coase theorem
- Markets for pollution rights
- Environmental protection

\<interactive\>exercise

ECONDEBATE ONLINE: ECONOMICS AND THE ENVIRONMENT

\<interactive\>update

- ECONDATA ONLINE: ECONOMICS AND THE ENVIRONMENT
- ECONLINKS ONLINE: ECONOMICS WEB LINKS
- ECONNEWS ONLINE: ECONOMICS AND THE ENVIRONMENT

EXTERNALITIES AND THE COMMON-POOL PROBLEM

Let's begin by distinguishing between *exhaustible* resources and *renewable* resources. An **exhaustible resource,** such as oil, coal, or copper ore, does not renew itself and so is available in a finite amount. Each gallon of oil burned is gone forever. Sooner or later, all oil wells will run dry. The world's oil reserves are exhaustible.

Renewable Resources

A resource is **renewable** if, when used conservatively, it can be drawn on indefinitely. Thus, timber is a renewable resource if felled trees are replaced to provide a steady supply. The atmosphere and rivers are renewable resources to the extent that they can absorb and neutralize a certain level of pollutants. More generally, biological resources like fish, game, forests, rivers, grasslands, and agricultural soil are renewable if managed appropriately.

Some renewable resources are also *open-access goods,* an idea introduced in the previous chapter. An open-access resource is rival in consumption, but preventing access to it is expensive. Fish caught in the ocean, for example, are not available for others to catch, so fish are rival in consumption. Yet it would be difficult for a person or firm to "own" fish still swimming in the ocean and prevent others from catching them, so exclusion is costly. An open-access good is often subject to the **common-pool problem,** which results because people consume such a good until the marginal value of additional use drops to zero. People will fish the ocean until fishing grounds become "fished out." Open-access goods are overfished, overhunted, overused, and overharvested.

Because the atmosphere is an open-access resource, the air gets used as a dump for unwanted gases. Air pollution is a negative externality imposed by polluters on society. As noted already, *negative externalities* are unpriced by-products of production or consumption that impose costs on other consumers or other firms. For example, some spray cans release fluorocarbons into the atmosphere; these gases are said to cause a thinning of the ozone layer that protects us from the sun's ultraviolet rays.

In a market system, specific individuals usually own the rights to resources and therefore have a strong interest in using those resources efficiently. **Private property rights** allow individuals to use resources or to charge others for their use. Private property rights are defined and enforced by government, by informal social actions, and by ethical norms. But because specifying and enforcing property rights to open-access resources, such as the air, are quite costly, these resources usually are not owned as private property.

Pollution and other negative externalities arise because there are no practical, enforceable, private property rights to open-access resources, such as the air. Market prices usually fail to include the costs that negative externalities impose on society. For example, the cost of a can of hair spray powered by fluorocarbons does not reflect the effect of gas emissions on the atmosphere's ozone layer. The price you pay for a gallon of gasoline does not reflect the costs imposed by the dirtier air and the greater traffic congestion your driving creates. And electric rates in the Midwest do not reflect the negative externalities, or *external* costs, that sulfur dioxide emissions impose on people living downwind from fossil-fueled power plants. Note that externalities are unintended side effects of actions that are themselves useful and purposeful. Electricity producers, for example, did not go into business to pollute.

ASK THE INSTRUCTOR: WHAT DOES BARBED WIRE HAVE TO DO WITH EXTERNALITIES?

ECONDEBATE ONLINE: SHOULD THE STRATEGIC PETROLEUM RESERVE BE USED TO REDUCE FLUCTUATIONS IN OIL PRICES?

Resolving the Common-Pool Problem

Users of the atmosphere, waterways, wildlife, or other open-access resources tend to ignore the impact of their use on the resource's renewal ability. As quality and quantity diminish from overuse, the resource grows more scarce and could disappear. For example, Georges Bank, located off the New England coast, long one of the world's most productive fishing grounds, became so depleted by overfishing that by the 1990s the catch was down 85 percent from peak years.[1] The United Nations reports that 11 of the world's 15 primary fishing grounds are seriously depleted.

By imposing restrictions on resource use, government regulations may be able to reduce the common-pool problem. Output restrictions or taxes could force firms to use the resource at a rate that is socially optimal. For example, in the face of the tendency to overfish and to catch fish before they are sufficiently mature, the government has imposed a variety of restrictions on the fishing industry. There are limits on the total catch, on the size of fish, on the length of the fishing season, on the equipment used, and on other aspects of the business.

More generally, *when imposing and enforcing private property rights would be too costly, government regulations may improve allocative efficiency.* For example, stop signs and traffic lights allocate the scarce road space at an intersection, minimum-size restrictions control lobster fishing, hunting seasons control the stock of game, and official study hours may calm the din in the dormitory.

But not all regulations are equally efficient. For example, fishing authorities sometimes limit the *total* industry catch and allow all firms to fish until that total is reached. Consequently, when the fishing season opens, there is a mad scramble to catch as much as possible before the industry limit is reached. Since time is of the essence, firms make no effort to fish selectively. And the catch reaches processors all at once, creating congestion throughout the supply chain. Also, each firm has an incentive to expand its fishing fleet to catch more in those precious few weeks. Thus, large fleets of technologically efficient fishing vessels sit in port for most of the year, except during the beginning of the fishing season. *Each firm is acting rationally, but the collective effect of the regulation is grossly inefficient in terms of social welfare.* Consider the complicated and sometimes confounding nature of fishing regulations in Iceland:

> *The Icelandic government realized that it would have to curb the capacity of its own fleet. But the fishermen compensated by buying more trawlers. Then the government restricted the size of the fleet and the number of days at sea; the fishermen responded by buying larger, more efficient gear. The cod stocks continued to decline. In 1984, the government introduced quotas on species per vessel per season. This was a controversial and often wasteful system. A groundfish hauled up from fifty fathoms [300 feet] is killed by the change in pressure. But if it is a cod and the cod quota has been used up, it is thrown overboard. Or if the price of cod is low that week and cod happens to come in the haddock net, the fishermen will throw them overboard because they do not want to use up their cod quota when they are not getting a good price.[2]*

[1]Deborah Cramer, "Troubled Waters," *Atlantic Monthly* (June 1995): 22–26.
[2]Mark Kurlansky, *Cod: A Biography of the Fish That Changed the World* (New York: Walker & Co., 1997), p. 172.

Chapter 17 Externalities and the Environment

Fish remain a common-pool resource because the technology has not yet been developed to establish and enforce rights to particular schools of fish. But advances in technology may some day allow the creation of private property rights to ocean fish, migrating birds, and even the air we breathe. At one time, establishing property rights to cattle on the Great Plains seemed impossible, but the invention of barbed wire allowed ranchers to fence the range. In a sense, barbed wire tamed the Wild West.

<interactive>example

NETBOOKMARK: U.S. ENVIRONMENTAL PROTECTION AGENCY (EPA) AND THE ACID RAIN PROGRAM

OPTIMAL LEVEL OF POLLUTION

Research suggests (though the issue is far from resolved) that the sulfur dioxide emitted by coal-fired power plants during electricity production mixes with moisture in the air to form sulfuric acid, which is carried by the prevailing winds and falls as acid rain. Many argue that acid rain has killed lakes and forests and has corroded buildings, bridges, and other structures. Electricity production, therefore, involves the external cost of using the atmosphere as a gas dump. For example, Ohio is the largest polluter in the United States based on coal-fired plants located there.[3] In this section, we examine how to analyze this externality problem.

External Costs with Fixed-Production Technology

Suppose *D* in Exhibit 1 depicts the demand for electricity in the Midwest. Recall that a demand curve reflects consumers' marginal benefit for each level of consumption. The lower horizontal line reflects the *marginal private cost* of electricity production. If producers base their pricing and output decisions on their private marginal costs, the equilibrium quantity of electricity used per month is 50 million kilowatt-hours and the equilibrium price is $0.10 per kilowatt-hour. At that price and output level, the marginal private cost of production just equals the marginal benefit enjoyed by consumers of electricity.

EXHIBIT 1

Negative Externalities: The Market for Electricity in the Midwest

If producers base their output on marginal private cost, 50 million kilowatt-hours of electricity are produced per month. The marginal external cost of electricity production reflects the cost of pollution imposed on society. The marginal social cost curve includes both the marginal private cost and the marginal external cost. If producers base their output decisions on marginal social cost, only 35 million kilowatt-hours are produced, which is the optimal level of output. The total social gain from basing production on marginal social cost is reflected by the blue-shaded triangle.

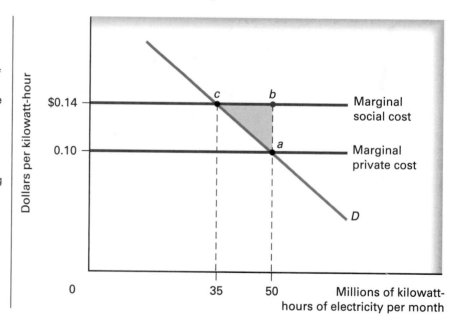

[3]Robert Melnbardis, "Report: Coal, Oil-Fired Power Plants Top Polluters," Reuters, 20 July 2001.

Electricity production involves not only the private cost of the resources employed but also the external cost of using the atmosphere as a gas dump. Suppose that the marginal external cost imposed on the environment by the generation of electricity is $0.04 per kilowatt-hour. When the only way of reducing emissions is by reducing the generation of electricity, then the relationship between the production of electricity and the production of pollution is fixed; the pollution in this case occurs with **fixed-production technology.**

The vertical distance between the marginal private cost curve and the marginal social cost curve in Exhibit 1 shows the marginal external cost of $0.04 per kilowatt-hour. The **marginal social cost** includes both the marginal private cost and the *marginal external cost* that production imposes on society. Because the marginal external cost is assumed to be constant, the two cost curves are parallel. Notice that at the private-sector equilibrium output level of 50 million kilowatt-hours, the marginal social cost, identified at point *b,* exceeds society's marginal benefit from that unit of electricity, identified at point *a* on the demand curve. The last kilowatt-hour of electricity produced costs society $0.14 but yields a marginal benefit of only $0.10. Because the marginal social cost exceeds the marginal benefit, the firm's choice of output results in a *market failure.* Too much pollution is produced because the price of electricity fails to reflect the social cost.

From society's point of view, the efficient output rate of 35 million kilowatts per month occurs where the demand, or marginal benefit, curve intersects the marginal social cost curve—a point identified as c in Exhibit 1. How could output be restricted to the socially efficient level? If government policy makers knew the demand and marginal cost curves, they could simply restrict electric utilities to produce that optimal level. Or they could impose a *pollution tax* on each unit of output equal to the marginal external cost. If correctly determined, such a tax would raise the marginal private cost curve up to the marginal social cost curve. Thus, the tax brings private costs in line with public costs.

With a tax of $0.04 per kilowatt-hour, the equilibrium combination of price and output moves from point *a* to point *c.* The price rises from $0.10 to $0.14 per kilowatt-hour, and output falls to 35 million kilowatt-hours. Setting the tax equal to the marginal external cost results in a level of output that is socially efficient; at point c, the marginal social cost of production equals the marginal benefit.

Notice that pollution is not eliminated at point *c,* but the utilities no longer generate electricity for which marginal social cost exceeds marginal benefit. The total social gain from reducing production to the socially optimal level is shown by the blue-shaded triangle in Exhibit 1. This triangle also measures the total social cost of ignoring the negative externalities in the production decision. Although Exhibit 1 offers a tidy solution, the external costs of pollution often cannot be easily calculated or taxed. At times, government intervention may result in more or less production than the optimal solution requires.

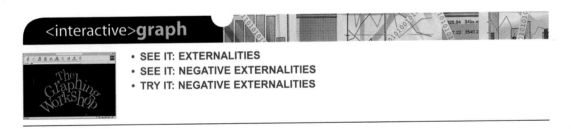

- **SEE IT: EXTERNALITIES**
- **SEE IT: NEGATIVE EXTERNALITIES**
- **TRY IT: NEGATIVE EXTERNALITIES**

External Costs with Variable Technology

The preceding example assumes that the only way to reduce the total amount of pollution is to reduce output. But power companies can usually change their resource mix to reduce emissions for a given level of output, particularly in the long run. Because pollution can be reduced by altering the production process rather than by simply adjusting the rate of output, these externalities are said to be produced under conditions of **variable technology.**

To examine the optimal amount of pollution for a given level of output under variable technology, let's look at Exhibit 2. The horizontal axis measures air quality. Air quality can be improved by adopting cleaner production technology. For example, coal-burning plants can be fitted with smoke "scrubbers" to reduce toxic emissions. Yet the production of cleaner air, like the production of other goods, is subject to diminishing returns. Cutting emissions of the largest particles may involve simply putting a screen over the smokestack, but eliminating successively finer particles requires more sophisticated and more expensive processes. Thus, the marginal social cost curve of cleaning the air slopes upward, as shown in Exhibit 2.

The **marginal social benefit** curve reflects the additional benefit society derives from improving air quality. When air quality is poor, an improvement can save lives and will be valued by society more than when air quality is excellent. Cleaner and cleaner air, like other goods, has a declining marginal benefit to society (though the total benefit still increases). The marginal social benefit curve from cleaner air therefore slopes downward, as shown in Exhibit 2.

The optimal level of air quality for a given level of production is found at point *a*, where the marginal social benefit of cleaner air equals the marginal social cost. In this example, the optimal level of air quality is *A*. Firms would not reach this optimal level voluntarily. If firms made their production decisions based simply on their private cost—that is, if the cost of pollution is external to the firm—then firms would have no incentive to search for production methods that reduce pollution, so too much pollution would occur.

What if the government decrees that the level of air quality should exceed *A*? For example, suppose a law sets *A'* as the minimum acceptable level. The marginal social cost, identified as *c*, of achieving that level of clean air exceeds the marginal social benefit, identified as *b*. The total social waste associated with imposing a greater-than-optimal level of air quality is shown by the pink- shaded triangle, *abc*. This is the total amount by which the additional social costs of cleaner air (associated with a move from *A* to *A'*) exceed the additional social benefits.

The idea that all pollution should be eliminated is a popular misconception. Usually, some pollution is consistent with efficiency. *Improving air quality benefits society as a whole as long as the marginal benefit of cleaner air exceeds its marginal cost.*

What would happen to the optimal level of air quality if either the marginal cost curve or the marginal benefit curve changed? Suppose, for example, that some technological breakthrough reduces the marginal cost of cleaning the air. As shown in panel (a) of Exhibit 3, the marginal social cost curve of reducing pollution would shift downward to *MSC'*, thereby increasing the optimal level of air quality from *A* to *A'*. The simple logic is that *the lower the marginal cost of reducing pollution, other things constant, the greater the optimal level of air quality.*

An increase in the marginal benefit of air quality would have a similar effect. For example, recent research finds that deaths from heart and lung disease would decrease 0.7% in large cities if suspended particulates decrease by just 1/100,000 gram per cubic meter of air.[4] This finding increases the perceived benefits of cleaner air. Thus, the marginal benefit of cleaner air would increase, as reflected in panel (b) of Exhibit 3 by a shift upward in the marginal social benefit curve to *MSB'*. As a result, the optimal level of air quality would increase. *The greater the marginal benefit of cleaner air, other things constant, the greater the optimal level of air quality.*

EXHIBIT 2

The Optimal Level of Air Quality

The optimal level of air quality is found at point *a*, where the marginal social cost of cleaner air equals its marginal social benefit. If some higher level of air quality were dictated by the government, the marginal social cost would exceed the marginal social benefit, and social waste would result. The total social waste resulting from a higher-than-optimal air quality is indicated by the pink-shaded triangle.

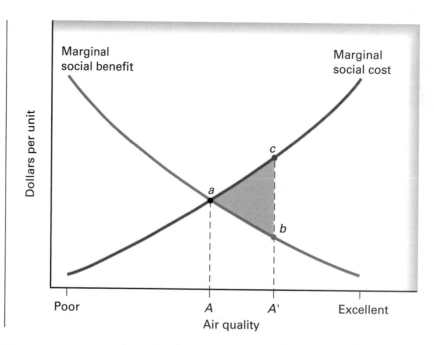

[4]Research published in the *New England Journal of Medicine* (December 2000), reported in Todd Zwillich, "Link Confirmed Between Air Pollution and Death Risk," *Reuters Health,* 13 December 2000.

EXHIBIT 3

Effect of Changes in Costs and Benefits on the Optimal Level of Air Quality

Either a reduction in the marginal social cost of cleaner air, as shown in panel (a), or an increase in the marginal social benefit of cleaner air, as shown in panel (b), will increase the optimal level of air quality.

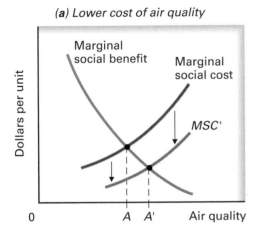

(a) Lower cost of air quality

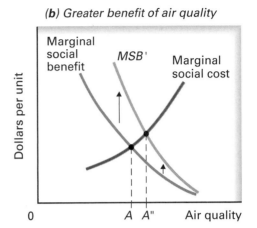

(b) Greater benefit of air quality

The atmosphere has the ability to cleanse itself of some emissions, but the destruction of the tropical rain forest has reduced this ability, as discussed in the following case study.

<interactive>video

ASK THE INSTRUCTOR: HOW DOES GOVERNMENT AFFECT THE ECONOMY?

CASESTUDY | Destruction of the Tropical Rain Forest

● *Public Policy*

The tropical rain forests have been called the lungs of the world because they naturally recycle carbon dioxide into oxygen and wood, thus absorbing heat-trapping gases and helping to maintain the world's atmospheric balance. These rain forests also contain over *half* of the world's species of plants and animals, representing an abundant source of fruits, crops, and medicines, including up to 70 percent of all new cancer drugs. The Amazon rain forest, for example, contains the largest collection of plant and animal life on Earth, along with 20 percent of the world's fresh water supply.

But the world's rain forests are located in countries that are relatively poor, such as Brazil, Indonesia, Bolivia, Colombia, Venezuela, Sudan, and the Philippines. Landless peasants and settlers burn down these forests to create farmland and pastures. Worse yet, the high world demand for timber has encouraged loggers to strip rain forests. Since claiming forestland for timber and agriculture is usually "first come, first served," poor settlers and timber companies often pursue a slash-and-burn approach with this open-access resource.

Burning the world's rain forests has a triple-barreled effect. The burning adds more harmful gases to the atmosphere, the loss of trees reduces the atmosphere's ability to cleanse itself, and the forest subsoil usually contains huge quantities of carbon subject to oxidization when the trees are removed. Since the world's atmosphere is a common pool, the costs of deforestation are imposed on people around the globe. Once the forests are cut down, the soil gets eroded by rains and baked by the sun and usually runs out of nutrients after just two seasons of crops. When the nutrients are lost, the system is not very resilient—it takes a century for a clear-cut forest to return to its original state.

The loss of the tropical forests involves other costs. As long as the tropical forest has its canopy of trees, it remains a rich, genetically diverse ecosystem. Tropical forests cover only 6 percent of the Earth's land surface (down from 12 percent 50 years ago), but, as previously noted, contain over half of the world's species of plants and animals. Of the tens of millions of species on the Earth, scientists have named only about 1.5 million and have studied even fewer in depth. The world loses an estimated 30 million acres—an area the size of Pennsylvania—of tropical forest each year in developing countries.

The tropical rain forests, by serving as the lungs of the world, confer benefits around the globe. But these benefits are usually ignored in the decision to clear the land. *It is not the greed of peasants and timber companies that leads to inefficient, or wasteful, uses of resource but the fact that the rain forests and the atmosphere are open-access resources that can be degraded with little immediate personal cost to those who clear the land.*

Poverty in the rainforest countries combined with the lack of legal title to the land encourages people to exploit that timber and soil rather than follow an approach that maximizes the long-term value of these resources. For example, a secure right to the land would reduce the need to clear a lot to claim it for agricultural purposes. A farmer with title to the land could also leave a forest bequest to children. Research on those people granted rights to land as part of a colonization effort in the Amazon forest indicates that having title encourages landowners to manage the land more conservatively. Property rights promote efficient harvesting of hardwoods and reforestation activities. For example, the frequency of reforestation among those with title was about 15 times greater than among those without title. Owners have a far greater incentive to conserve the value of the land than do those without title, who can claim the value only through a slash-and-burn approach.

Government programs that encourage selective cutting and replanting allow the forest to remain an air filter and a renewable source for forest products. There are efforts under way to protect the rain forests. With help from the World Bank and the World Wildlife Fund, Brazil plans to protect an area of rain forest the size of Colorado. And a timber company has given up harvesting rights to what is considered the most pristine rain forest in Africa. The United States now cancels some developing countries' government debts in return for efforts to preserve their rain forests. Other ideas are on the drawing board, but a systematic solution is still a long way off.

\<interactive\>exercise

eACTIVITY: DESTRUCTION OF THE TROPICAL RAIN FOREST

Sources: Gary Libecap et al., "Property Rights and the Preconditions for Markets: The Case of the Amazon Frontier," *Journal of International and Theoretical Economics,* 151 (March 1995): 89–107; Claudia Rosett, "Pity the Planet?" *Wall Street Journal,* 30 July 2001; Charles Wood and Robert Walker, "Saving the Trees by Helping the Poor," *Resources for the Future* (Summer 1999): 14–17; Jenny Lin, "Pristine Congo Rain Forest Spared from Logging," Reuters, 6 July 2001; "US House Votes to Protect Global Rain Forest," Dow Jones Newswire, 20 July 2001; and Gerald Urquhart et al., "Tropical Deforestation," *NASA Earth Observatory* at http://earthobservatory.nasa.gov/Library/Deforestation/.

The Coase Theorem

The traditional analysis of externalities assumes that market failures arise because people ignore the external effects of their actions. Suppose a research laboratory that tests delicate equipment locates next to a manufacturer of heavy machinery. The vibrations caused by the manufacturing process throw off the delicate machinery in the lab next door. Professor Ronald Coase, who won the Nobel Prize in 1991, would point out that the negative externality in this case is not necessarily imposed by the machinery producer on the testing lab—rather, *it arises from the incompatible activities of the two parties.* The externality is the result both of vibrations created by the factory and of the location of the testing lab next door. One efficient solution to this externality problem might be to modify the machines in the factory; another might be to make the equipment in the testing lab more shock resistant or to move the lab elsewhere.

According to Coase, *the efficient solution to an externality problem depends on which party can avoid the problem at the lower cost.* Suppose the factory determines that it would cost $2 million to reduce vibrations enough to allow the lab to function normally. For its part, the testing lab concludes that it cannot alter its equipment to reduce the effects of the vibrations, so its only recourse would be to move the lab elsewhere at a cost of $1 million. Based on these costs, the least-cost, or most efficient, resolution to the externality problem is for the testing lab to relocate.

Coase argues that *when property rights are assigned to one party or another, the two parties will agree on the efficient solution to an externality problem as long as transaction costs are low. This efficient solution will be achieved regardless of which party gets the property right.* Suppose the testing lab is granted the right to operate free of vibrations from next door, so the testing lab has the right to ask the factory to reduce its vibration. Rather than cut vibrations at a cost of $2 million, the factory can offer to pay the lab to relocate. Any payment by the factory owners that is greater than $1 million but less than $2 million will make both firms better off, since the lab will receive more than its moving cost and the factory will pay less than its cost of reducing vibrations. Thus, the lab will move, which is the efficient outcome.

Alternatively, suppose the factory is granted the right to generate vibrations in its production process, regardless of any effects on the testing lab. For the factory, this means business as usual. The lab may consider paying the factory to alter its production method, but since the minimum payment the factory would accept is $2 million, the lab would rather move itself at a cost of $1 million. Thus, whether property rights are granted to the lab or to the factory, the lab will move, which is the more efficient, or least-cost, solution. The **Coase theorem** says that as long as bargaining costs are small, the assignment of property rights will generate an efficient solution to an externality problem regardless of which party is assigned property rights. A particular assignment of property rights determines only who incurs the externality costs, not the efficient outcome.

Inefficient outcomes do occur, however, when the transaction costs of arriving at a solution are high. For example, an airport located in a populated area would have difficulty negotiating with all the surrounding residents about noise levels. Or a power plant emitting sulfur dioxide would have trouble negotiating with the millions of people scattered across the downwind states. Or a would-be farmer contemplating clearing a portion of the tropical rain forest cannot negotiate with the millions, and perhaps, billions, of people ultimately affected by that decision. When the number of parties involved in the transaction is large, the chance for a voluntary solution is small.

<interactive>**update**

- **ECONNEWS ONLINE: PAYING THE PRICE OF POLLUTION**
- **ECONNEWS ONLINE: AN INTERNATIONAL MARKET IN POLLUTION**

Markets for Pollution Rights

According to the Coase theorem, the assignment of property rights is often sufficient to resolve the market failure typically associated with externalities. Additional government intervention is not necessary. If pollution can be easily monitored and polluters easily identified, the government may be able to achieve an efficient solution to the problem of pollution simply by assigning the right to pollute. To see how this could work, let's look at an example. Firms that dump waste into a river evidently value the ability to discharge waste in this way. For them, the river provides an inexpensive outlet for pollutants that otherwise would have to be disposed of at greater cost. The river provides disposal services, and the demand curve for this pollutant transportation system slopes downward, like the demand for other resources.

The demand for the river as a discharge system is presented as *D* in Exhibit 4. The horizontal axis measures the tons of pollutants dumped into the river per day, and the vertical axis measures firms' marginal benefits of disposing of their waste in this way. The demand curve thus measures the marginal value to firms of using the river as a resource for discharging pollutants. With no restrictions on river pollution—that is, if all were free to dump waste into the river—dumping would continue as long as it yields some private marginal benefit. The discharge rate would occur where the private marginal benefit falls to zero, which is 250 tons per day in Exhibit 4.

The river, like the atmosphere and the soil, can absorb and neutralize a certain amount of pollution per day without deteriorating in quality. What if voters make the public choice that the river should be clean enough for swimming and fishing? Suppose engineers determine this level of water quality can be maintained as long as no more than 100 tons are discharged per day. Thus, if the river is to be preserved at the specified level of quality, the "supply" of the river

EXHIBIT 4

Optimal Allocation of Pollution Rights

Suppose the demand for a river as an outlet for pollution is *D*. In the absence of any environmental controls, pollution would be 250 tons per day, where the marginal benefit of further pollution equals zero. If regulatory authorities establish 100 tons as the maximum allowable level of pollution and then sell the rights to pollution, the market for these pollution rights will clear at $25 per ton. If the demand for pollution rights increases to *D'*, the market-clearing price will rise to $35 per ton.

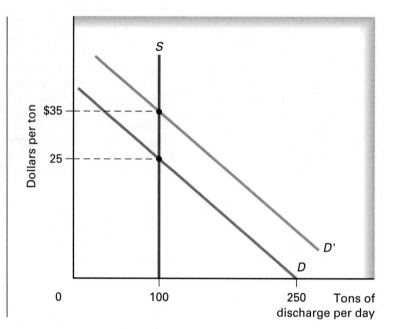

available as a discharge resource must be fixed at 100 tons per day, shown by the vertical supply curve, *S*, in Exhibit 4.

If government regulators can easily identify polluters and monitor their behavior, authorities can allocate permits to discharge 100 tons per day. If polluters are simply given these permits (that is, if the price of permits is zero), there will be an excess demand for them, since the quantity supplied is 100 tons but the quantity demanded at a price of *zero* would be 250 tons. An alternative is to *sell* permits for 100 tons of pollution at the market-clearing price. The intersection of supply curve *S* and demand curve *D* yields a permit price of $25 per ton, which is the marginal value of dumping the 100th ton into the river each day. To most purchasers, the marginal value of a permit will exceed $25 per ton.

The beauty of this system is that producers who value the discharge rights the most will ultimately end up with them. Producers who attach a lower marginal value obviously have cheaper ways of resolving their waste problems, including changing production techniques. And if conservation groups, such as the Sierra Club, want a higher river quality than the government's standard, such as water clean enough to drink, they can purchase pollution permits but not exercise them.

What if additional firms spring up along the river and want to discharge wastes? This added demand for discharge rights is reflected in Exhibit 4 by *D'*. This increase in demand would bid up the market price of pollution permits to $35 per ton. Some existing permit holders will sell their rights to those who value them more. Regardless of the comings and goings of would-be polluters, the total quantity of discharge rights is restricted to 100 tons per day, so the river's quality will be maintained. Thus, the value of pollution permits, but not the total amount of pollution, may fluctuate over time.

If the right to pollute could be granted, monitored, and enforced, then what had been a negative externality problem could be solved through market allocation. Historically, the U.S. government has relied on setting discharge standards and fining offenders. But in 1989, a pollution rights market for fluorocarbon emissions was established and was followed in 1990 by a market for sulfur dioxide. During the 1990s, sulfur dioxide emissions in the nation fell by more than half, exceeding the goals of the authorizing legislation. So the market for pollution rights is alive and growing.[5]

Unfortunately, legislation dealing with pollution is affected by the same problems of representative democracy that trouble other public policy questions. Polluters have a special inter-

[5]For a discussion of the market for sulfur dioxide emissions, see Paul Joskow, Richard Schmalensee, and Elizabeth Bailey, "The Market for Sulfur-Dioxide Emissions," *American Economic Review* 88 (September 1998): 669–685.

est in government proposals relating to pollution, and they fight measures to reduce pollution. But members of the public remain rationally ignorant about pollution legislation. So pollution regulations may be less in accord with the public interest than with the special interests of polluters. This is why a portion of pollution permits are often given free to existing firms. For example, under the sulfur dioxide program, the nation's 101 dirtiest power plants receive credits equal to between 30 and 50 percent of the pollution they emitted before the program began. Because they receive something of value, polluters were less inclined to fight the introduction of the program. Once the permits were granted, some recipients found it profitable to sell their permits to other firms that valued them more. Thus, a market emerged that led to an efficient allocation of pollution permits. According to some analysts, the sulfur dioxide program saves up to $3 billion annually compared with the old system. More generally, a system of marketable pollution rights can reduce the cost of pollution abatement by as much as 75 percent.

Before 1990, traditional **command-and-control environmental regulations** were the norm—an approach that required polluters, such as electric utilities, to introduce particular technologies to reduce emissions by specific amounts. These regulations were based on engineering standards and did not recognize unique circumstances across generating plants, such as plant design, ability to introduce scrubbers, and the ease of switching to low-sulfur fuels. But the market for pollution rights reflects an **economic efficiency approach** that offers each electrical utility the flexibility to reduce emissions in the most cost-effective manner, given its unique costs. Firms with the lowest emission-control costs have an incentive to implement the largest reduction in emissions and then sell unused allowances to those with greater control costs.

Now that you know something about the theory of externalities, let's turn to an important application of the theory—environmental protection.

ENVIRONMENTAL PROTECTION

Federal efforts to address the common-pool problems of air, water, and soil are coordinated by the *Environmental Protection Agency (EPA)*. Four federal laws and subsequent amendments underpin U.S. efforts to protect the environment: the Clean Air Act of 1970, the Clean Water Act of 1972, the Resource Conservation and Recovery Act of 1976 (which governs solid waste disposal), and the *Superfund* law of 1980 (legislation focusing on toxic waste dumps). In 1970, the EPA had about 4,000 employees and a budget of $200 million. By 2000, it had about 18,000 employees and a budget exceeding $5 billion.

According to EPA estimates, compliance with pollution control regulations costs U.S. producers and consumers an amount equivalent to 2 percent of gross domestic product, the market value of all final goods and services produced in the economy in a given year. We can divide pollution control spending into three categories: spending for air pollution abatement, spending for water pollution abatement, and spending for solid waste disposal. About 40 percent of the pollution control expenditures in the United States goes toward cleaner air, another 40 percent goes toward cleaner water, and 20 percent goes toward disposing of solid waste. In this section, we will consider, in turn, air pollution, water pollution, Superfund activities, and disposing of solid waste.

Air Pollution

In the Clean Air Act of 1970 and in subsequent amendments, Congress set national standards for the amount of pollution that could be emitted into the atmosphere. Congress thereby recognized the atmosphere as an economic resource, which, like other resources, has alternative uses. The air can be used as a source of life-giving oxygen, as a prism for viewing breathtaking vistas, or as a dump for carrying away unwanted soot and gases. The 1970 act gave Americans the right to breathe air of a certain quality and at the same time gave producers the right to emit particular amounts of specified pollutants.

Smog is the most visible form of air pollution. Automobile emissions account for 40 percent of smog. Another 40 percent comes from consumer products, such as paint thinner, fluorocarbon sprays, dry-cleaning solvents, and baker's yeast by-products. Surprisingly, only 15 percent of smog comes from manufacturing. The 1970 Clean Air Act mandated a reduction of 90 percent in auto emissions, leaving it to the auto industry to achieve this target. At the time, automakers said the target was impossible. Between 1970 and 1990, however, average emissions of lead fell 97 percent, carbon monoxide emissions fell 41 percent, and sulfur oxide emissions fell 25 percent. In fact, a recent EPA study concluded that because auto emissions and industrial smoke have been reduced, air pollution now is greater *indoors* than *outdoors*. For example, in the Los Angeles area, a smog alert, meaning the air reached dangerous levels, occurred on a weekly basis during the 1980s, but in 2000 there were no smog alerts. *U.S. air quality is now considered good compared to the air quality in much of the world.* Only one U.S. city, New York, ranks among the world's 20 worst when it comes to nitrogen oxide, and no U.S. city ranks among the world's 20 worst in sulfur dioxide.

Despite recent improvements in air quality, the United States is still a major source of carbon dioxide emissions. As you can see from Exhibit 5, which shows the world's 20 worst nations in carbon dioxide emissions per year, the United States ranks 4th worst with 20 tons per capita. Efforts are under way to improve air quality on a global scale. A tentative accord reached in Kyoto, Japan, in 1997, would require the 38 industrial countries to reduce emissions of carbon dioxide and other so-called greenhouse gases by one-third over 10 years. The measure would impose a carbon tax on coal, natural gas, and oil. The cost to the U.S. economy could reach $300 billion a year, according to one study. Only industrial countries would be required to reduce emissions; developing countries need not participate. Thus, even if industrial nations meet their Kyoto targets, carbon dioxide emissions would continue to rise since most of the projected global increase would come from exempted countries. The treaty requires approval by legislative bodies in the United States and in the other countries, which appears doubtful

EXHIBIT 5

Carbon Dioxide Emissions per Capita: The 20 Worst Nations

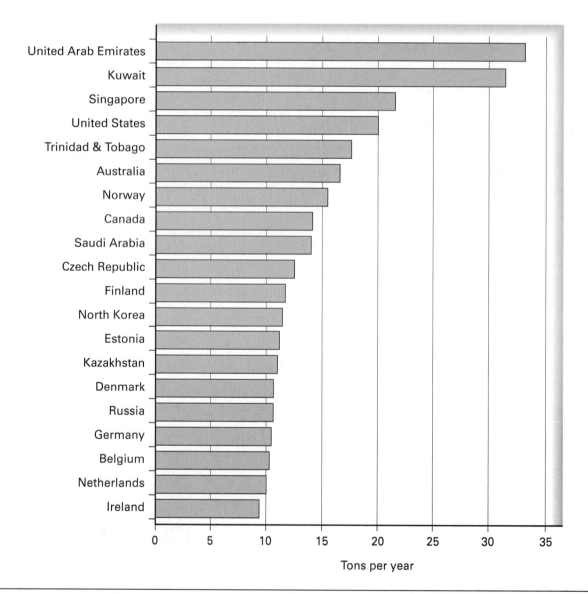

Source: Based on figures for 1996 as reported in *The Economist World in Figures: 2001 Edition* (London: Profile Books, 2001), 94.

at this point. Critics of the treaty argue that cleaner air should require a greater commitment from the developing world, such as China and India, which are major polluters. Argentina is the first developing nation offering to cut back greenhouse emissions.

The following case study examines the problem of cleaning up the polluted air in the capital city of one developing country.

<interactive>update

ECONNEWS ONLINE: DYING FOR FRESH AIR

CASESTUDY | City in the Clouds

● *Public Policy*

Prior to 1940, Mexico City was known for its spectacular views of snow-capped volcanoes. Now the distant hills seldom make an appearance. The problem? Population surged from 3 million in 1950 to 20 million today. More people mean more industry and more vehicles, which are increasing an average of 6 percent a year. More than half of Mexico's industrial output is produced in or near Mexico City. Millions of vehicles and tens of thousands of small, poorly regulated businesses spew a soup of pollution into the atmosphere. For example, brick makers fire their kilns with old rubber tires and sawdust soaked in kerosene—fuels that generate black, acrid smoke.

The city's geography and altitude compound pollution problems. Mountains surround Mexico City on three sides, so the wind that blows in from the north (the open side) traps pollution over the city. Worse yet, the city is 7,400 feet above sea level, reducing the oxygen content of the atmosphere by about one-quarter. The combination of high pollution, low oxygen, and a tropical sun makes for unhealthy air—which is why the place has been called "Makesicko City." In 1998, an estimated 7.2 million doctor visits were made to treat respiratory ailments, up 20 percent from the year before. In 1999, the World Resources Institute named the city's air as the most dangerous in the world for children. Foreign countries advise their diplomats not to have babies while stationed there.

City officials have taken steps to address the common-pool problem, but their efforts seem halfhearted. The price of gasoline in Mexico City is among the lowest in the world, so price is not much of a check on fuel consumption. Regulations prohibit half of the city's cars from traveling the streets during weekdays, yet fuel consumption has actually increased and, worse yet, subway and bus use has actually declined. And, although stricter regulations have been imposed on business activity, enforcement has been lax. Part of the problem is that low incomes in Mexico make environmental protection a costly luxury. To give you some idea, the minimum wage is the equivalent of less than $5 per day.

Despite all this, there are some hopeful signs. Catalytic converters on new vehicles and greater use of unleaded fuel are starting to brighten the picture. More importantly, NAFTA provides incentives for producers to locate closer to the U.S. border. As industry moves out of Mexico City, levels of lead, carbon dioxide, and sulfur dioxide are beginning to show some improvement. Make no mistake, the air in Mexico City is still filthy, but for the first time in a long while, a patch of blue sky is showing through.

<interactive>exercise

eACTIVITY: CITY IN THE CLOUDS

Sources: *World Development Report: Knowledge for Development 1999/2000, World Bank* (New York: Oxford University Press, 2000); Tim Weiner, "Terrific News in Mexico City: Air Is Sometimes Breathable," *New York Times*, 5 January 2001; Howard LaFranchi, "20,000 Lightpost Filters Scrub Mexico City's Dirty Air," *Christian Science Monitor*, 24 September 1999; "Mexico Volcano Spews Ash on Towns," Associated Press, 31 December 2000; and "Mexico City Chokes on Record Air Pollution," *Planet Ark*, 2 February 2000 at http://www.planetark.org.

Water Pollution

Two major sources of water pollution are sewage and chemicals. For decades, U.S. cities had an economic incentive to dump their sewage directly into waterways rather than incur the expense of cleaning it up first. Frequently, the current or tides would carry off the waste to become someone else's problem. Although each community found it rational, based on a narrow view of the situation, to dump into waterways, the combined effect of these individual choices was water pollution, a negative externality imposed by one community on other communities.

Federal money over the years has funded sewage treatment plants that have cut water pollution substantially. Hundreds of once-polluted waterways have been cleaned up enough to permit swimming and fishing. Nearly all U.S. cities now have modern sewage control systems. A notable exception is New York City, which teams up with New Jersey to dump raw sewage into the Atlantic Ocean, using a discharge point about 100 miles out to sea.

Chemicals are another source of water pollution. Chemical pollution may conjure up an image of a pipe spewing chemicals into a river, but only about 10 percent of chemical pollution in the water comes from *point* pollution—pollution from factories and other industrial sites. About two-thirds come from what is called *nonpoint* pollution—mostly runoff from agricultural pesticides and fertilizer. Congress has been reluctant to limit the use of pesticides, although they pollute water and contaminate food. Industrial America seems an easier target than Old MacDonald's farm.

In 1970, Congress shifted control of pesticides from the U.S. Department of Agriculture to the newly formed Environmental Protection Agency (EPA). But the EPA already had its hands full administering the Clean Water Act, so it turned pesticide regulation over to the states. Most states gave the job to their departments of agriculture. But these state agencies usually *promote* the interests of farmers, not *restrict* what farmers can do. The EPA now reports that in most states, pesticides have fouled some groundwater. *The EPA also argues that pesticide residues on food pose more health problems than do toxic waste dumps or air pollution.* The EPA's inspector general said that federal and state officials failed to enforce the nation's clean air and water laws. For example, most streams in Missouri are not clean enough for swimming. So that state failed to achieve the Clean Water Act's central goal.[6]

ECONNEWS ONLINE: SEWAGE IN PARADISE

Hazardous Waste and the Superfund

The U.S. synthetic chemical industry has flourished in the last 40 years, and about 55,000 chemicals are now in common use. Some have harmful effects on humans and other living creatures. These chemicals can pose risks at every stage of their production, use, and disposal. New Jersey manufactures more toxic chemicals than any other state and, not surprisingly, has the worst toxic waste burden. Prior to 1980, the disposal of toxic waste created get-rich-quick opportunities for anyone who could rent or buy a few acres of land to open a toxic waste dump. As an extreme example, one site in New Jersey took in 71 million gallons of hazardous chemicals during a three-year period.[7]

Before 1980, once a company paid someone to haul away its hazardous waste, the company was no longer responsible. The Comprehensive Environmental Response, Compensation, and Liability Act of 1980, known more popularly as the *Superfund* law, now requires any company that generates, stores, *or* transports hazardous wastes to pay to clean up any wastes that are improperly disposed of. A producer or hauler that is the source of even one barrel of pollution dumped at a site can be held liable for cleaning up the entire site.

The Superfund law gives the federal government authority over sites contaminated with toxins. But to get an offending company to comply, the EPA frequently must sue. The process is slow, and nearly half the budget goes to lawyers, consultants, and administrators rather than to site cleanups. The law did not require that benefits exceed costs or even that such comparisons be attempted. As of August 2001, there were 1,230 sites, with about 10 percent in New Jersey.

[6]John Cushman, "E.P.A. and States Found to Be Lax on Pollution Law," *New York Times,* 7 June 1998.
[7]Jason Zweig, "Real-Life Horror Story," *Forbes,* 12 December 1988.

Chapter 17 Externalities and the Environment

Construction work required for a cleanup has been completed at over half the sites, but the actual cleanup could take years.

Although billions have been spent so far, a recent EPA study concluded that the health hazards of Superfund sites have been vastly exaggerated. Chemicals in the ground often move slowly, sometimes taking years to travel a few feet, so any possible health threat may be confined to the site itself. In contrast, air pollution represents a more widespread danger because the air is so mobile and polluted air is drawn directly into the lungs. People know when they live near toxic waste sites, and they can exert political pressure to get something done. But people exposed to polluted air or water may develop some disease from the pollution, but they are not infected now. Thus, most people see no reason to press public officials for legislation that mandates cleaner air and water. *Because of their greater political urgency and media appeal, toxic waste dumps tend to receive more attention than air or water pollution.*

Solid Waste: "Paper or Plastic?"

Throughout most of history, households tossed their trash outside as fodder for pigs and goats. New York City, like other cities, had no trash collection, so domestic waste was thrown into the street, where it mixed with mud and horse manure. Decades of such behavior explains why the oldest Manhattan streets are anywhere from 3 to 15 feet above their original levels. About 200 years ago, people began to bury their trash near their homes or take it to the town dump. Now U.S. households generate about 4 pounds of garbage per resident per day—more than twice the amount in 1960 and the largest per capita in the world. Much of our solid waste consists of packaging material. The question is, how do we dispose of the more than 200 million tons of household garbage generated in this country each year?

Advanced economies produce and buy more than less developed economies, so there is more to throw away. And because of higher incomes in advanced economies, the opportunity cost of time is higher, so we tend to discard items rather than repair or recycle them. For example, it's cheaper to buy a new toaster for $25 than to pay someone $40 an hour to fix it, assuming you can even find a repair service. (Look up "Appliance Repair, Small" in the *Yellow Pages* of the Internet's Super Pages and see if you can find even one such shop in your area.)

About 70 percent of the nation's garbage is bulldozed and covered with soil in landfills. Although a well-managed landfill poses few environmental concerns, at one time, communities dumped all kinds of toxic materials in them—stuff that could leach into the soil, contaminating wells and aquifers. So landfills developed a bad reputation. The prevailing attitude with landfills is *Nimby* (Not in my back yard). We all want our garbage picked up but nobody wants it put down anywhere nearby.

As the cost of solid waste disposal increases, state and local governments are economizing, such as requiring households to sort their trash, charging households by the pound for trash pickups, and requiring returnable bottles. Nearly half of U.S. households participate in curbside recycling programs. **Recycling** is the process of converting waste products into reusable materials. Still, according to the EPA, only about 15 percent of U.S. garbage gets recycled; about 15 percent is incinerated and, as noted already, the remaining 70 percent goes into landfills. Of the recycled material, three-quarters consists of corrugated boxes, newspapers, and office paper. Some of the paper product is shipped to Korea and Taiwan, where it becomes packaging material for U.S. imports such as VCRs, DVD players, and computer components. Exhibit 6 ranks the top 20 paper recyclers. Germany heads the list, recycling 70 percent of its paper. The United States ranks 15th, recycling 41 percent.

Most of the 15 percent of garbage that is incinerated gets burned in trash-to-energy plants, which generate electricity using the heat from incineration. Until recently, such plants looked like the wave of the future, but less favorable tax treatment and environmental concerns over the siting of incinerators (Nimby strikes again) have taken the steam out of the trash-to-energy movement.

To repeat, about 70 percent of U.S. garbage goes to landfills, and only 30 percent is incinerated or recycled. In contrast, the Japanese recycle 40 percent of their waste and incinerate 33 percent, leaving only 27 percent to be deposited in landfills. Japanese households sort their trash into as many as 21 categories. Because land is scarcer in Japan—we know this because it costs relatively more—it is not surprising that the Japanese deposit a smaller share of their garbage in landfills.

Some recycling is clearly economical—such as aluminum cans, which are a cheap source of aluminum compared to producing raw aluminum. About two out of three aluminum cans now get recycled, though only 10 states require return deposits. Recycling paper and cardboard is also economical and occurred long before the environmental movement. Still, despite promotional efforts, curbside programs account for only one-sixth of U.S. recycling. Such old standbys as paper drives, drop-off bins, and redemption centers still collect more tonnage than

EXHIBIT 6 |

Paper Recycling: The 20 Best Nations

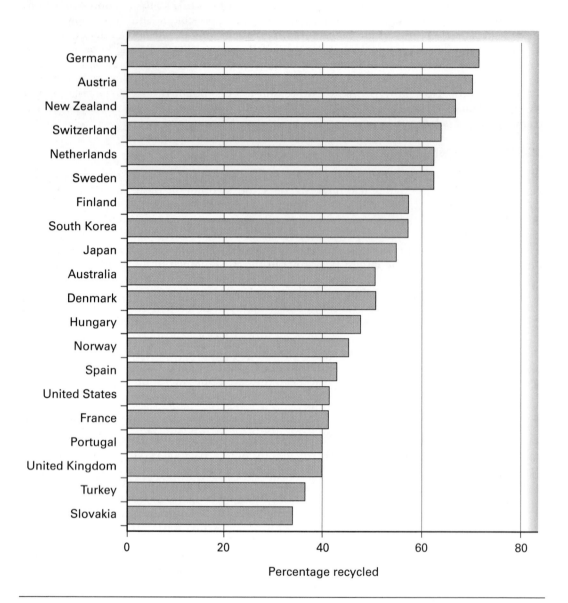

Percentage recycled

Source: Based on figures for 1997 as reported in *The Economist World in Figures: 2001 Edition* (London: Profile Books, 2001), 96.

curbside programs. Most recycling results from salvaging scrap material from business and industry, a practice that goes back decades.

Governments have tried to stimulate demand for recycled material—for example, by requiring newspapers to use a certain amount of recycled newsprint. Other recycled products are not in such demand. In fact, some recycled products have become worthless and must be hauled to land fills. Plastic containers, for example, have limited recycling potential.

Recycling imposes its own cost on the environment. Curbside recycling requires fleets of trucks that pollute the air. Newsprint must first be de-inked, creating a sludge that must be disposed of. But greater environmental awareness has made consumers more receptive to more efficient packaging material. For example, liquid laundry detergent is now available in a concentrated "ultra" form, which cuts volume in half. And labels for all kinds of products proudly identify the recycled content of the packaging.

POSITIVE EXTERNALITIES

To this point, we have considered only negative externalities. But externalities are sometimes positive, or beneficial. *Positive externalities* occur when the unpriced by-products of consumption or production benefit other consumers or other firms. For example, people who get inoculated against a disease reduce their own likelihood of contracting the disease, but in the process they also reduce the risk of transmitting the disease to others. Inoculations thus provide *external benefits* to others. Society as a whole receives external benefits from education because those who acquire more education become better citizens, can read road signs, are better able to support themselves and their families, and are less likely to require public assistance or to resort to crime for income. Thus, education provides private benefits but it also confers additional social benefits to others.

The effect of external benefits on the optimal level of consumption is illustrated in Exhibit 7, which presents the supply and demand for education. The demand curve, *D*, represents the private demand for education, which reflects the *marginal private benefit* for those who acquire the education. More education is demanded at a lower price than at a higher price.

The benefit of education, however, spills over to others in society. If we add this positive externality, or *marginal external benefit*, to the marginal private benefit of education, we get the marginal social benefit of education. The *marginal social benefit* includes all the benefit society derives from education, both private and public. The marginal social benefit curve is above the private demand curve in Exhibit 7. At each level of education, the marginal social benefit exceeds the marginal private benefit by the amount of marginal external benefit generated by that particular level of education.

If education were a strictly private decision, the amount purchased would be determined by the intersection of the private demand curve *D* with supply curve *S*. The supply curve reflects the marginal cost of producing each unit of the good. This intersection at point *e* yields education level *E*, where the marginal private benefit of education equals its marginal cost.

But at level *E*, the marginal social benefit of education exceeds its marginal cost. Net social welfare will increase if education expands beyond *E*. *As long as the marginal social benefit of education exceeds its marginal cost, social welfare increases if education expands.* Social welfare is maximized at point *e'* in Exhibit 7, where *E'* units of education are provided—that is, where the marginal social benefit equals the marginal cost, as reflected by the supply curve. The blue-shaded triangle identifies the net increase in social welfare that results from increasing the quantity of education to *E'*.

Thus, society is better off if the level of education exceeds the private equilibrium. *When positive externalities are present, decisions based on private marginal benefits result in less than the socially*

EXHIBIT 7

Education and Positive Externalities

In the absence of government intervention, the quantity of education demanded is *E*, at which the marginal cost equals the marginal private benefit of education. However, education also confers a positive externality on the rest of society, so the marginal social benefit exceeds the private benefit. At quantity *E*, the marginal social benefit exceeds the marginal cost, so more education is in society's best interest. In this situation, government will try to encourage an increase in the quantity of education to *E'*, where the marginal cost equals the marginal social benefit.

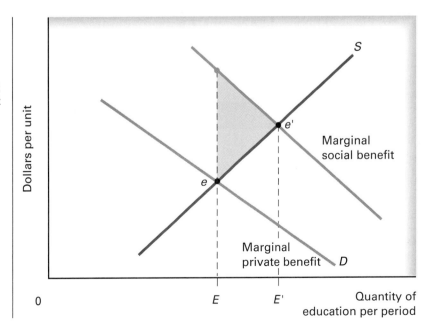

optimal quantity of the good. Thus, like negative externalities, positive externalities typically point to *market failure,* which is why government often gets into the act. When there are external benefits, public policy aims to increase the level of output beyond the private optimum. For example, governments try to increase education by providing free primary and secondary education, by requiring students to stay in school until they reach 16 years of age, by subsidizing public higher education, and by offering tax breaks for some education expenditures.

<interactive>exercise

ECONDEBATE ONLINE: DOES PUBLIC INVESTMENT IN MUNICIPAL SPORTS STADIUMS PAY OFF?

CONCLUSION

More than 6 billion people inhabit the globe, with about 90 million added each year. World population is projected to reach 9 billion by the middle of the 21st century, with most of this growth occurring in less developed countries, where most people barely eke out a living. Population pressure coupled with a lack of incentives to conserve open-access resources results in deforestation, dwindling fish stocks, and polluted air, land, and water. Market prices can direct the allocation of resources only as long as property rights are well defined and can be enforced at a reasonable cost. Pollution of air, land, and water arises not so much from the greed of producers and consumers as from the fact that these open-access resources are subject to the common-pool problem.

Ironically, because of tighter pollution controls, industrial countries tend to be less polluted than developing countries, where there is more pollution per capita from what little industry there is. Most developing countries have such profound economic problems that environmental quality is not a high priority. For example, when India's Supreme Court recently tried to close some dirty factories in New Delhi to cut air pollution, thousands of workers torched buses, threw stones, and blocked major roads, demanding the factories stay open.[8] Although New Delhi's air is so filthy that it often masks any trace of a blue sky, workers believe their jobs are more important. Here's an account of New Delhi's air quality:

> *In the heat of the afternoons, a yellow-white mixture hung above the city, raining acidic soot into the dust and exhaust fumes. At night the mixture condenses into a dry, choking fog that envelops the headlights of passing cars, and crept its stink into even the tightest houses. The residents could do little to keep the poison out of their lungs or the lungs of their children, and if they were poor, they could not even try.[9]*

<interactive>exercise

READING IT RIGHT: WALL STREET JOURNAL EXERCISE

endofchaptermaterial

- **Summary**
- **Questions for Review**
- **Problems and Exercises**

- **Experiential Exercises**
- **Wall Street Journal Exercise**

[8]Celia Duggar, "A Cruel Choice in New Delhi: Jobs vs. A Safer Environment," *New York Times,* 24 November 2000.
[9]William Langewiesche, "The Shipbreakers," *Atlantic Monthly* (August 2000): 42.

Take the Post-Test to assess your overall understanding of the key ideas in this chapter. The Post-Test provides a comprehensive selection of exam-style questions addressing the main topics and concepts of the chapter. At the completion of each Post-Test, you will receive a score and instructive feedback on how you answered each question, and a direct link to the part of the chapter addressed in the question. Take the Post-Test as often as you need to—a record of your progress for each attempt is kept for you to revisit and gauge your improvement. And each Post-Test is randomly generated, so every attempt is new.

CHAPTER 18

Income Distribution and Poverty

Why are some families poor even in the most productive economy on Earth? Who are the poor, and how did they get that way? What's been the trend in poverty over time? How has the changing family structure affected poverty? What public programs try to reduce poverty, and how well have they worked? Answers to these and related questions are addressed in this chapter, which discusses income distribution and poverty in America.

To establish a reference point, we first examine the distribution of income, paying special attention to trends in recent years. We then evaluate the "social safety net"—government programs aimed at helping poor people. We also consider the impact of the changing family structure on poverty, focusing in particular on the increase in households headed by women. We close by examining recent welfare reforms. Topics discussed in this chapter include:

- Distribution of income
- Official poverty level
- Public policy and poverty
- The feminization of poverty
- Poverty and discrimination
- Welfare reforms

Pre-Test

Take the Pre-Test to assess your initial knowledge of the key ideas in this chapter. The Pre-Test provides exam-style questions addressing the main topics and concepts of the chapter. At the completion of each Pre-Test, you will receive a score and instructive feedback on how you answered each question, and a direct link to the part of the chapter addressed in the question. Take the Pre-Test as often as you need to—a record of your progress for each attempt is kept for you to revisit and gauge your improvement.

<interactive>exercise

ECONDEBATE ONLINE: INCOME DISTRIBUTION AND POVERTY

<interactive>update

- ECONDATA ONLINE: INCOME DISTRIBUTION AND POVERTY
- ECONLINKS ONLINE: ECONOMICS WEB LINKS
- ECONNEWS ONLINE: INCOME DISTRIBUTION AND POVERTY

THE DISTRIBUTION OF HOUSEHOLD INCOME

In a market economy, income depends primarily on earnings, which depend on the productivity of one's resources. The problem with allocating income according to productivity is that some people have difficulty earning income. Individuals born with mental or physical disabilities tend to be less productive and may be unable to earn a living. Others may face limited job choices and reduced wages because of advanced age, poor education, discrimination, bad luck, or the demands of caring for small children.

Income Distribution by Quintiles

As a starting point, let's consider the distribution of income in the economy and see how it has changed over time, focusing on the household as the economic unit. After dividing the total number of U.S. households into five groups of equal size, or *quintiles,* ranked according to income, we can examine the percentage of income received by each group. Such a division is presented in Exhibit 1 since 1970. Take a moment to look over this exhibit. Notice that households in the lowest, or poorest, fifth of the population received only 4.1 percent of the income in 1970, whereas households in the highest, or richest, fifth received 43.3 percent of the income. The U.S. Census Bureau measures income after cash transfer payments are received but before taxes are paid.

EXHIBIT 1

Share of Aggregate Household Income by Quintile: 1970, 1980, 1990, and 2000

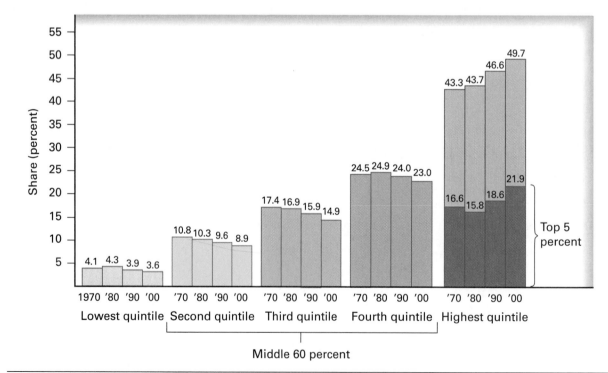

Source: U.S. Census Bureau, *Money Income in the United States: 2000,* Current Population Reports, September 2001, Table C, http://www.census.gov/hhes/www/income00.html.

In recent years, the share of income going to the top fifth has increased, and the share going to the bottom fifth has declined slightly. The richest group's share of income increased from 43.3 percent in 1970 to 49.7 percent in 2000. A primary contributor to the larger share of income going to the highest group has been the growth of two-earner households in the top group and the growth of single-parent households in the bottom group. Also shown in Exhibit 1 is the share of income going to the top 5 percent of households; that share has grown since 1980, accounting for all the growth of the top 20 percent of households. Because of substantial reductions in the top marginal tax rates in 1981 and 1986, high-income people had less incentive to engage in tax avoidance and tax evasion, so their reported income increased, boosting the share of reported income going to the richest 5 percent of households.

<interactive>exercise

ECONDEBATE ONLINE: WHAT ACCOUNTS FOR RECENT INCREASES IN INCOME INEQUALITY?

The Lorenz Curve

We have just examined the distribution of income using a bar chart. The Lorenz curve is another way to picture the distribution of income in an economy. The **Lorenz curve s**hows the percentage of total income received by any given percentage of households when incomes are arrayed from smallest to largest. As shown in Exhibit 2, the cumulative percentage of households is measured along the horizontal axis, and the cumulative percentage of income is measured along the vertical axis. Any given distribution of income can be compared to an equal distribution of income among households. If income were evenly distributed, each 20 percent of households would receive 20 percent of the total income, and the Lorenz curve would be a straight line with a slope equal to 1.0, as shown in Exhibit 2.

As the distribution becomes more uneven, the Lorenz curve is pulled down to the right, away from the line of equal distribution. The Lorenz curves in Exhibit 2 were calculated for 1970 and 2000, based on the data in Exhibit 1. As a reference, point *a* on the 1970 Lorenz curve indicates that in that year, the bottom 80 percent of families received 56.7 percent of the income, and the top 20 percent received 43.3 percent of the income. Point *b* on the 2000 curve shows that the bottom 80 percent received 50.3 percent of the income and the top 20 percent received 49.7 percent of the income. The Lorenz curve for 2000 is farther from the line of even distribution than is the Lorenz curve for 1970, showing that income among households has become more unevenly distributed.

EXHIBIT 2

Lorenz Curves Show That U.S. Income in 2000 Was Less Evenly Distributed Across Households Than in 1970

The Lorenz curve is a convenient way of showing the percentage of total income received by any given percentage of households when households are arrayed from smallest to largest based on income. For example, point *a* shows that in 1970, the bottom 80 percent of households received 56.7 percent of all income. Point *b* shows that in 2000, the share of all income going to the bottom 80 percent of households was lower than in 1970. If income were evenly distributed across households, the Lorenz curve would be a straight line.

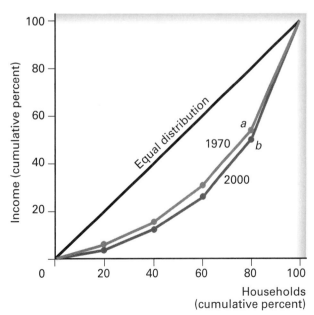

A College Education Pays More

Also contributing to the dominance of the top group is a growing premium paid those with a college education. In the last two decades, the median wage (adjusted for inflation) for people with only high school diplomas declined 6 percent, while the median wage for college graduates rose 12 percent. Why have more-educated workers done better? First, trends such as industry deregulation, declining unionization, and freer international trade have reduced the demand for workers with less education. Labor unions, for example, increase the wages of many workers who would otherwise end up in the bottom half of the income distribution. But the share of the labor force that is unionized declined from 26 percent in 1973 to only 14 percent in 2000.

Second, new computer-based information technologies have reduced the demand for low-skilled clerical workers, since their jobs became computerized. Computers also offered more timely and accurate information to management, allowing for organizational innovations that made managers and other professionals more productive.[1] So computers reduced the demand for workers with low skills, such as clerical staff and bank tellers, and increased the demand for those who use computers to boost labor productivity, such as managers and accountants.

Third, the supply of less-educated workers increased more than the supply of more-educated workers, thus increasing the rewards of education. For example, recent U.S. immigrants tend to be less educated than existing residents, including an estimated 6 million illegal aliens in the workforce. Thus, immigration has increased the supply of relatively poorly educated workers, which has depressed wages of the less educated generally. The Hispanic population more than doubled between 1980 and 2000, and the percentage of Hispanics in the United States who were foreign-born increased. Among males age 25 and older, only 57 percent of Hispanics had at least a high school education in 2000, compared with 85 percent of whites and 79 percent of blacks. More generally, the foreign-born share of the U.S. population doubled from 5 percent in 1970 to 11 percent in 2000, the largest share since the 1930s.

So economic trends in recent years have benefited the better educated, and this helps explain the growing disparity in household income. Income in the United States is less evenly distributed than in other developed countries throughout the world, such as Canada, France, Great Britain, Italy, and Australia, but is more evenly distributed than in most developing countries, such as Brazil, Chile, Mexico, Nigeria, and the Philippines. Some countries also have far more extensive redistribution programs than does the United States, basing a variety of public policies on income. For example, Finland bases traffic fines on the driver's income. One young tycoon clocked doing 43 miles per hour in a 25-mile-an-hour zone paid a fine of $71,000.[2]

NETBOOKMARK: INCOME—U.S. CENSUS BUREAU'S WEB SITE

Problems with Distribution Benchmarks

One problem with looking at income distributions is that there is no objective standard for evaluating them. The usual assumption is that a more equal distribution of income is more desirable, but is a perfectly even distribution most preferred? If not, then how uneven should the distribution be? For example, among major league baseball players, well over half the pay goes to 20 percent of the players. The 10-year contract of Alex Rodriguez for $252 million works out to be about $43,000 for each at bat, or about $173,000 per game. Professional basketball pay is even more skewed toward the top players. Does this mean the economy, as a whole, is in some sense "fairer" than these professional sports?

A second problem is that because Exhibits 1 and 2 measure money income after cash transfers but before taxes, it omits the effects of taxes and in-kind transfers, such as food stamps and free medical care for poor families. The tax system as a whole is progressive, meaning that families with higher incomes pay a larger fraction of their incomes in taxes. In-kind transfers benefit the lowest-income groups the most. Consequently, if Exhibit 1 incorporated the effects of taxes and in-kind transfers, the share of income going to the lower groups would increase, the share going to the higher groups would decrease, and income would be more evenly distributed.

---

[1]Timothy Bresnahan, "Computerization and Wage Dispersion: An Analytical Reinterpretation," *Economic Journal* (June 1999).
[2]Seven Stecklow, "Finnish Drivers Don't Mind Sliding Scale, But Instant Calculation Gets Low Marks," *Wall Street Journal,* 2 January 2001.

Third, focusing on the share of income going to each income quintile overlooks the fact that household size differs across quintiles. Most households in the bottom quintile consist of one person living alone. Only one in sixteen households in the top quintile consist of one person living alone. Households at the top average two-thirds larger than those at the bottom, which helps in part to explain the difference in income share going to each quintile.

Fourth, Exhibits 1 and 2 include only *reported* sources of income. If people receive payment "under the table" to evade taxes, or if they earn money through illegal activities, their actual income will exceed their reported income. The omission of unreported income will distort the data if unreported income as a percentage of total family income differs across income levels.

Finally, Exhibit 1 focuses on the distribution of income, but a better measure of household welfare would be the distribution of expenditures. Evidence on expenditures by households is not collected as systematically as income data are, but available evidence indicates that spending by quintiles is much more evenly distributed than income by quintiles.

<interactive>**video**

- **ASK THE INSTRUCTOR: WILL THERE ALWAYS BE POVERTY?**
- **ASK THE INSTRUCTOR: HOW DOES INCOME DISTRIBUTION IN THE U.S. COMPARE?**

Why Do Household Incomes Differ?

The **median income** of all households is the middle income when incomes are ranked from lowest to highest. In any given year, half the households are above the median income and half are below it. Income differences across households stem in part from differences in the *number* of workers in each household. Thus, *one reason household incomes differ is that the number of household members who are working differs.* For example, among households in the bottom 20 percent based on income, only one in five has a full-time, year-round worker.

The median income for households with two earners is 87 percent higher than for households with only one earner and about four times higher than for households with no earners. Incomes also differ for all the reasons labor incomes differ, such as differences in education, ability, job experience, and so on. At every age, people with more education earn more, on average. For example, according to the U.S. Census Bureau, men with a professional degree earn about four times more than men with only a high school education. Age itself also has an important effect on income. As workers mature, they acquire valuable job experience, get promoted, and earn more.

Differences in earnings based on age and education reflect a normal *life cycle* pattern of income. In fact, most income differences across households reflect the normal workings of resource markets, whereby workers are rewarded according to their productivity. Because of these lifetime patterns, it is not necessarily the same households that remain rich or poor over time. Indeed, one study of income mobility found that more than three-quarters of people in the bottom 20 percent in 1975 had moved into the top 40 percent for at least one year by 1991.[3] Despite this mobility over time, we can still characterize rich and poor households at a point in time. That is, a high-income household typically consists of a well-educated couple with both people employed. A low-income household is typically headed by a single parent who is young, female, poorly educated, and not employed. Low incomes are a matter of public concern, especially when children are involved, as we will see in the next section.

<interactive>**update**

ECONNEWS ONLINE: THE RICH GET RICHER, THE POOR GET SLIGHTLY RICHER

POVERTY AND THE POOR

Since poverty is such a relative concept, how do we measure it objectively, and how do we ensure that our measure can be applied with equal relevance over time? The federal government has developed a method for calculating an official poverty level, which has become the benchmark for poverty analysis in the United States.

[3]W. Michael Cox and Richard Arm, "By Our Own Bootstraps," *Federal Reserve Bank of Dallas: 1995 Annual Report.*

Official Poverty Level

To derive the **U.S. official poverty level,** the U.S. Department of Agriculture in 1959 first estimated the cost of a nutritionally adequate diet. Then, based on the assumption that the poor spend about one-third of their income on food, the official poverty level was calculated by multiplying this food cost by three. The U.S. Census Bureau tracks the official poverty level, making adjustments for family size and inflation. The official poverty level of money income for a family of four was $17,601 in 2000; a family of four at or below that income threshold was regarded as living in poverty. Poverty levels in 2000 ranged from $8,787 for a person living alone to $35,574 for a family of nine or more. The poverty definition is based on pretax money income, including cash transfers, but it excludes the value of noncash transfers such as food stamps, Medicaid, subsidized housing, or employer-provided health insurance.

Each year since 1959, the Census Bureau has conducted a survey comparing individual families' annual cash incomes to the annual poverty level applicable to that family. Results of this survey are presented in Exhibit 3, which indicates both the millions of people living below the official poverty level and the percentage of the U.S. population below that level. Periods of U.S. recession are also shown (a recession is defined as two or more successive quarters of declining gross domestic product). Note that poverty increased during recessions.

The biggest decline in poverty occurred before 1970; *the poverty rate dropped from 22.4 percent in 1959 to 12.1 percent in 1969.* During that period, the number of poor people decreased from about 40 million to 24 million. The poverty rate has not shown huge fluctuations since that initial drop. Most recently, the rate declined from 15.1 percent in 1993 to 11.3 percent in 2000, the lowest since 1973. The 31.1 million people in poverty in 2000 shows a drop of 8.2 million below the 1993 level.

Poverty is a relative term. If we examined the distribution of income across countries, we would find huge gaps between rich and poor nations. The U.S. official poverty level of income is many times greater than the average income for three-fourths of the world's population.[4] For example, the poverty level for a family of four in the United States works out to be about $12 per person per day, while China uses a poverty level of about $0.30 per person per day.

EXHIBIT 3

Number and Percentage of U.S. Population in Poverty: 1959–2000

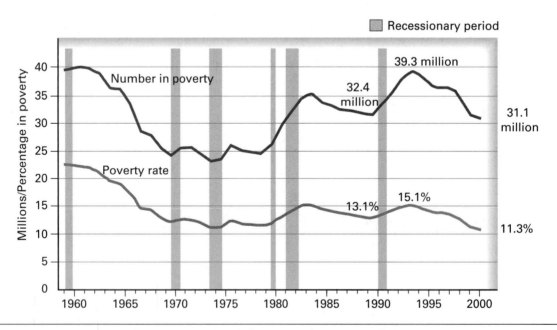

Source: U.S. Census Bureau, *Poverty in the United States: 2000,* Current Population Reports, September 2001, Figure 3, http://www.census.gov/hhes/poverty/poverty00/pov00.html.

[4]World Bank, *World Development Report 2000/2001* (New York: Oxford University Press, 2001), Table 1.

Programs to Help the Poor

What should society's response to poverty be? *Families with a full-time worker are nine times more likely to escape poverty than are families with no workers.* Thus, the government's first line of defense in fighting poverty is to promote a healthy economy. Yet even when the unemployment rate is low, some people remain poor. Although some government programs to help the poor involve direct market intervention, such as minimum-wage laws, the most visible programs redistribute income after the market has provided an initial distribution. Since the mid-1960s, social welfare expenditures at all levels of government have increased significantly. We can divide these programs into two broad categories: social insurance and income assistance.

Social Insurance. **Social insurance** programs are designed to help make up for the lost income of people who worked but are now retired, temporarily unemployed, or unable to work because of disability or work-related injury. The major social insurance program is **Social Security,** established during the Great Depression of the 1930s to supplement retirement income of those with a work history and a record of contributing to the program. **Medicare,** another social insurance program, provides health insurance for short-term medical care, mostly to those age 65 and older, regardless of income. There were about 40 million Social Security and Medicare beneficiaries in 2001. Other social insurance programs include *unemployment insurance* and *workers' compensation,* which supports workers injured on the job; both programs require that beneficiaries have a prior record of employment.

The social insurance system deducts "insurance premiums" from workers' pay to provide benefits to other retired, disabled, and unemployed individuals. These programs protect some families from poverty, particularly the elderly receiving Social Security, but they are aimed more at those with a work history. Still, the social insurance system tends to redistribute income from rich to poor and from young to old. Most current Social Security beneficiaries receive far more in benefits than they paid into the program, especially those with a brief work history or a record of low wages.

Income Assistance. **Income assistance programs**—what we usually call welfare programs—provide money and in-kind assistance to the poor. Unlike social insurance programs, income assistance programs do not require the recipient to have a history of work or to have contributed to the program. Income assistance programs are means tested. In a **means-tested program,** a household's income and assets must fall below a certain level to qualify for benefits. The federal government funds two-thirds of welfare spending, and state and local governments fund one-third.

The two primary *cash transfer* programs are **Temporary Assistance for Needy Families (TANF),** which provides cash to poor families with dependent children, and **Supplemental Security Income (SSI),** which provides cash to the elderly poor and the disabled. Cash transfers vary inversely with family income from other sources. In 1997, TANF replaced Aid for Families with Dependent Children (AFDC), which began during the Great Depression and was originally aimed at providing support for widows with young children. Whereas AFDC was a federal *entitlement* program, meaning that anyone who met the criteria was *entitled* to benefits, TANF is under the control of each state and carries no federal entitlement. The federal government gives each state a fixed grant to help fund TANF programs.

The SSI program provides support for the elderly and disabled poor. It is the fastest-growing cash transfer program, with outlays quadrupling from $8 billion in 1980 to nearly $32 billion in 2000. SSI coverage has been broadened to include people addicted to drugs and alcohol, children with learning disabilities, and, in some cases, the homeless. The federal portion of this program is uniform across states, but states can supplement federal aid. Benefit levels in California average twice those in Alabama. Most states also offer modest *General Assistance* aid to those who are poor but do not qualify for TANF or SSI.

The federal government also provides an **earned-income tax credit,** which supplements wages of the working poor. For example, a family with two children and earning $13,000 in 2000 would not only pay no federal income tax but would receive a cash transfer of $3,900. More than 12 million workers received such transfers in 2000, resulting in a federal outlay of $30 billion, nearly double federal spending on TANF.

In addition to cash transfer programs, a variety of *in-kind transfer* programs provide health care, food stamps, and housing assistance to the poor. **Medicaid** pays for medical care for those with incomes below a certain level who are aged, blind, disabled, or are living in families with dependent children. Medicaid is by far the largest welfare program, costing nearly twice as much as all cash transfer programs combined. It has grown more than any other poverty program, quadrupling in the last decade and accounting for nearly a quarter of the typical state's budget (though states receive federal grants covering half or more of their Medicaid budget).

The qualifying level of income is set by each state, and some states are quite strict. Therefore, the proportion of poor covered by Medicaid varies greatly across states. In 2000, about 36 million people received free medical care under Medicaid at a total cost of over $200 billion; outlays averaged about $5,600 per recipient. For many elderly, Medicaid pays for long-term nursing care (Medicaid pays half the nation's nursing home costs). Although half the nation's welfare budget goes for health care, nearly 43 million U.S. residents, or one in seven people, had no health insurance in 2000.

Food stamps are vouchers that can be redeemed for food. The program, funded by the federal government, is uniform across states and is aimed at reducing hunger and providing nutrition to poor families. In 2000, 17.2 million people received food stamps in the average month, down from an all-time high of 27.5 million recipients in 1994. Monthly benefits averaged $72 per recipient in 2000.

Housing assistance programs include direct assistance for rental payments and subsidized low-income housing. Spending for housing assistance has more than doubled since 1990. About 10 million people receive some form of housing assistance. Other in-kind transfer programs include the *school lunch program* for poor children; supplemental food vouchers for pregnant women, infants, and children; *energy assistance* to help pay the energy bills of poor families; and *education and training assistance* for poor families, such as Head Start. *In all, there are about 75 means-tested federal welfare programs.*

WHO ARE THE POOR?

Who are the poor, and how has the composition of this group changed over time? We will slice poverty statistics in several ways to examine the makeup of the group. Keep in mind that we are relying on official poverty estimates, which ignore the value of in-kind transfers and the earned-income tax credit, so, to that extent, official estimates overstate poverty.

<interactive>video

CNN VIDEO: "WELFARE REFORM: FROM GOVERNMENT HANDOUTS TO PRIVATE HANDOUTS"

<interactive>update

• ECONNEWS ONLINE: POVERTY PERSISTS
• ECONNEWS ONLINE: FOR RICHER OR POORER
• ECONNEWS ONLINE: DRAWING THE LINE—POVERTY REVISITED

Poverty and Age

Earlier we looked at the poverty rate for the entire population. Now we focus on poverty and age. Exhibit 4 presents the poverty rates for three age groups since 1959: people younger than 18 years old, those between 18 and 64, and those 65 and older. As you can see, poverty rates for each group declined between 1959 and 1968. Between the mid-1970s and the early 1980s, the rate among those under 18 trended upward, but has declined since 1993 to 16.2 percent in 2000.

In 1959, the elderly were the poorest group, with a poverty rate of 35 percent. Since then, poverty among the elderly has declined to 10.2 percent in 2000, slightly above the rate of 9.4 percent for people 18 to 64 years of age. The decline in poverty among the elderly stems from tremendous growth in spending for Social Security and Medicare. In real terms, those two programs grew tenfold from $62 billion in 1959 to over $620 billion in 2000 (measured in dollars of 2000 purchasing power). *Although not welfare programs in a strict sense, Social Security and Medicare have been extremely successful in reducing poverty among the elderly.*

Poverty and Public Choice

In a democratic country such as ours, public policies depend very much on the political power of the interest groups involved. In recent years, the elderly have become a powerful political force. The voter participation rate of those 65 and over is higher than that of any other age

EXHIBIT 4 |

Poverty Rates by Age: 1959–2000

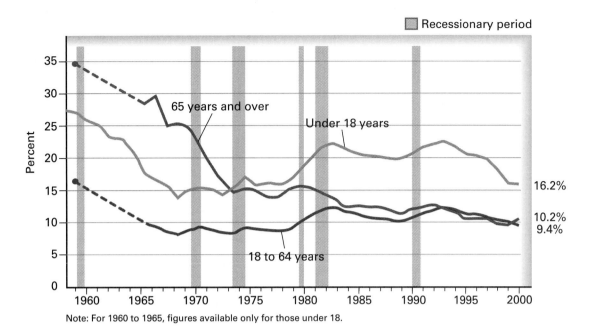

Note: For 1960 to 1965, figures available only for those under 18.

Source: U.S. Census Bureau, *Poverty in the United States: 2000,* Current Population Reports, September 2001, Figure 2, http://www.census.gov/hhes/poverty/poverty00/pov00.html.

group. For example, people 65 years of age and older show up at the polls at triple the rate of those between 18 and 24 and four times that of welfare recipients. The political muscle of the elderly has been flexed whenever a question of Social Security benefits has come up for a vote.

Unlike most interest groups, the elderly make up a group we all expect to join one day. The elderly are actually represented by five constituencies: (1) the elderly themselves; (2) people under 65 who are concerned about the current benefits to their parents or other elderly relatives; (3) people under 65 who are concerned about their own benefits in the future; (4) people who earn their living by caring for the elderly, such as doctors, nurses, and nursing-home operators; and (5) candidates for office who want to harvest the votes that seniors deliver. So the elderly have a broad constituency, and this pays off in terms of redistribution of wealth to the elderly.

The Feminization of Poverty

One way of classifying the incidence of poverty is by age. Another way is based on the marital status and race of the household head. Exhibit 5 compares, for black, non-Hispanic white, and Hispanic families, the poverty rates for married couples with the rates among families headed by women with no husbands present. Three trends are unmistakable. First, poverty rates among married couples average only one-third the rates among female householders. Second, Hispanic families have the highest poverty rates (individuals of Hispanic origin may be of any race) followed by black families and non-Hispanic white families. And third, since the middle of the 1990s, rates have trended down for all types of families. Not shown in the exhibit are poverty rates among male householders, which are higher than among married couples but still only about half the rates of female householders. Poverty rates among female householders remained high until recent declines.

The exhibit shows the poverty rate among female householders. What it doesn't show is the growth in the number of such households. The number of families headed by women has nearly tripled since 1960, while married-couple households grew just 40 percent. The percentage of births to unmarried mothers is five times greater today than in 1960. In 1960, only 1 in 200 children lived with a single parent who had never married. Today, 1 in 10 children lives with a single parent who has never married.

EXHIBIT 5

Poverty Rates Have Trended Down Recently for All Types of Families

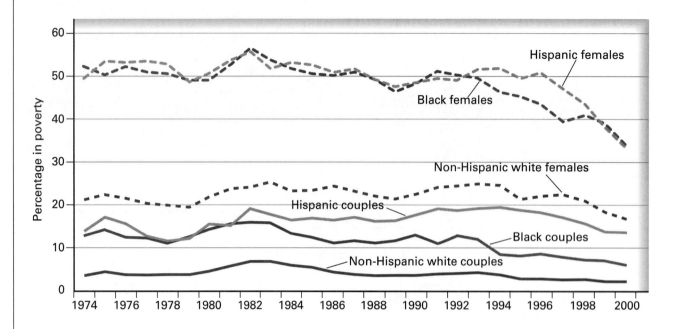

Source: Developed from data in U.S. Census Bureau, *Poverty in the United States: 2000,* Current Population Reports, September 2001, Table A-1, http://www.census.gov/hhes/poverty/poverty00/pov00.html.

The United States has the highest teenage pregnancy rate in the developed world—twice the rate of Great Britain and 15 times that of Japan. Since the father in such cases typically assumes little responsibility for child support, children born outside marriage are likely to be poorer than other children. The divorce rate has also increased since 1960. Because of the higher divorce rate, even children born to married couples now face a greater likelihood of living in a one-parent household before they grow up. Divorce usually reduces the resources available to the children.

The growth in the number of poor families since 1969 resulted overwhelmingly from a growth in the number of female householders. Since 1969, the U.S. economy has generated over 50 million new jobs. Families with a female householder were in the worst position to take advantage of this job growth. *Children of female householders are five times more likely to live in poverty than are other children.*

Young, single motherhood is a recipe for poverty. Often the young mother drops out of school, which reduces her future earning possibilities when and if she seeks work outside the home. Even a strong economy is little aid to households with nobody in the labor force. Worse yet, young, single mothers-to-be are less likely to seek adequate medical care; the result is a higher proportion of premature, underweight babies. This is one reason why the U.S. infant mortality rate exceeds that of many other industrialized countries. Compared to two-parent families, children in one-parent families are twice as likely to drop out of school, and girls from one-parent families are twice as likely to become single mothers themselves.

Because of a lack of education and limited job skills, most unwed mothers go on welfare. Before recently imposed lifetime limits on welfare, the average never-married mother had been on welfare for a decade, twice as long as divorced mothers on welfare. Of all teenagers who gave birth, the proportion unmarried was 13 percent in 1950, 30 percent in 1970, 67 percent in 1990, and 79 percent in 2000.[5]

Poverty has therefore become increasingly feminized, mostly because female householders have become more common. Children from mothers who finished high school, married before having a child, and gave birth after age twenty are 10 times less likely to be poor than children from mothers who fail to do these things.[6] Because the number of female householders has grown more rap-

[5]*National Vital Statistics Report,* Vol. 49, No.5 (24 July 2001), Table C.
[6]James Q. Wilson, "Human Remedies for Social Disorder," *Public Interest* (Spring 1998): 27.

idly among blacks, the feminization of poverty has been more dramatic in black households. Sixty-nine percent of all black births in 2000 were to unmarried women compared with 43 percent of all births among women of Hispanic origin and 22 percent of births among non-Hispanic whites.[7] But we should be careful in drawing conclusions about the role of race or ethnicity per se, since black and Hispanic households are poorer than white households and low income alone could account for much of the difference in birth rates. In other words, a better comparison would adjust for income differences across groups, but such data are not available.

Poverty and Discrimination

To what extent has racial discrimination limited job opportunities and increased poverty among minorities? Discrimination can occur in many ways: in school funding, in housing, in employment, in career advancement. Also, discrimination in one area can affect opportunities in another. For example, housing discrimination can reduce job opportunities if a black family cannot move within commuting distance of the best employers. Job-market discrimination can take many forms. An employer may fail to hire a black job applicant because the applicant lacks training. But this lack of training can arise from discrimination in the schools, in union apprenticeship programs, or in training programs run by other employers. For example, evidence suggests that black workers receive less on-the-job training than otherwise similar white workers.

Let's first consider the difference between the earnings of white and nonwhite workers. After adjusting for a variety of factors that could affect the wage, such as education and work experience, research shows that whites earn more than blacks. The gap between the two narrowed between 1940 and 1976 to the point where black workers earned only 7 percent less than white workers; then it widened a bit.[8] Since 1993, the gap has again narrowed.

Could explanations besides job discrimination account for the wage gap? Though the data adjust for *years* of schooling, some research suggests that black workers received a lower *quality* of schooling than white workers. For example, black students are less likely to use computers in school. Inner-city schools often have more problems with classroom discipline, which takes time and attention away from instruction. Such quality differences could account for at least a portion of the remaining gap in standardized wages.

Direct evidence of discrimination comes from audit studies, where otherwise similar white and minority candidates are sent to the same source to seek jobs, rent apartments, or apply for mortgage loans. For example, white and black job applicants with similar qualifications and résumés applied for the same job. These studies find that employers are less likely to interview or offer a job to minority applicants. Minority applicants also tend to be treated less favorably by real estate agents and lenders. The President's Council of Economic Advisers concluded that discrimination against members of racial and ethnic minorities, while "far less pervasive and overt" than it was, still persists.[9]

Affirmative Action

The Equal Employment Opportunity Commission, established by the Civil Rights Act of 1964, monitors cases involving unequal pay for equal work and unequal access to promotion. All companies doing business with the federal government had to set numerical hiring, promotion, and training goals to ensure that these firms did not discriminate in hiring on the basis of race, sex, religion, or national origin. Black employment increased in those firms required to file affirmative action plans.[10] The fraction of the black labor force employed in white-collar jobs increased from 16.5 percent in 1960 to 40.5 percent in 1981—an increase that greatly exceeded the growth of white-collar jobs in the labor force as a whole. Research also suggests that civil rights legislation played a role in narrowing the black-white earnings gap between 1960 and the mid-1970s.[11]

Attention focused on hiring practices and equality of opportunity at the state and local levels as well, as governments introduced so-called set-aside programs to guarantee minorities a share of contracts. But a 1995 U.S. Supreme Court decision challenged affirmative action programs, ruling that Congress must meet a rigorous legal standard to justify any contracting or

[7]*National Vital Statistics Report,* Vol. 49, No. 5 (24 July 2001), Table 5.

[8]M. Boozer, A. Krueger, and S. Wolken, "Race and School Quality Since Brown v. Board of Education," *Brookings Papers on Economic Activity: Microeconomics* (1992): 269–326.

[9]*Economic Report of the President,* February 1998, 152.

[10]James Smith and Finis Welch, "Black Economic Progress After Myrdal," *Journal of Economic Literature* 27 (June 1989): 519–563.

[11]David Card and Alan Krueger, "Trends in Relative Black-White Earnings Revisited," *American Economic Review* 83 (May 1993): 85–91.

hiring practice based on race, especially programs that reserve job slots for minorities and women. Programs must be shown to be in response to injustices created by past discrimination, said the Court.

In summary, evidence suggests that blacks earn less than whites after adjustment for other factors that could affect wages, such as education and job experience. Part of this wage gap may reflect differences in the quality of education, differences that could themselves be the result of discrimination. Keep in mind that unemployment rates are higher among blacks than among whites and are higher still among black teenagers, the group most in need of job skills and job experience. *But we should also note that black families are not a homogeneous group. In fact, the distribution of income is more uneven among black families than it is among the population as a whole.*

On the upside, according to the *Economic Report of the President:* Since 1993, the median income of black families has risen faster than that of white families. The proportion of black families living below the poverty line has fallen to a record low. And there is a growing middle class among black households. Since 1970, the number of black doctors, nurses, college professors, and newspaper reporters has more than doubled; the number of black engineers, computer programmers, accountants, managers, and administrators has more than tripled; the number of black elected officials has quadrupled; and the number of black lawyers has increased sixfold. Three of the most admired Americans are black—talk show host Oprah Winfrey, basketball legend Michael Jordan, and Secretary of State Colin Powell, who arguably could get elected president if he chose to run.

UNINTENDED CONSEQUENCES OF INCOME ASSISTANCE

On the plus side, antipoverty programs increase the consumption possibilities of poor families, and this is significant, especially since children are the largest poverty group. But programs to assist the poor may have secondary effects that limit their ability to reduce poverty. Here we consider some unintended consequences.

Disincentives

Society, through government, tries to provide families with an adequate standard of living, but society also wants to ensure that only those in need receive benefits. As we have seen, income assistance consists of a combination of cash and in-kind transfer programs. Because these programs are designed to help the poor and only the poor, the level of benefits varies inversely with income from other sources. This has resulted in a system where transfers decline sharply as earned income increases, in effect imposing a high marginal tax rate on that earned income. An increase in earnings may reduce benefits from TANF, Medicaid, food stamps, housing assistance, energy assistance, and other programs. With a bite taken from each program as earned income increases, working may lead to little or no increase in total income. Over certain income ranges, the welfare recipient may lose more than $1 in transfer benefits for each additional $1 in earnings. Thus, *the marginal tax rate* on earned income could exceed 100 percent.

Holding even a part-time job involves additional expenses—for transportation and child care, for instance—not to mention the loss of free time. Such a system of perverse incentives can frustrate people trying to work their way off welfare. *The high marginal tax rate discourages employment and self-sufficiency.* In many cases, the value of welfare benefits exceeds the disposable income resulting from full-time employment.

The longer people are out of the labor force, the more their job skills deteriorate, so when they do look for work, their productivity and their pay are lower than when they were last employed. This lowers their expected wage, making work less attractive. Some economists argue that in this way, welfare benefits can lead to long-term dependency. While welfare seems to be a rational choice in the short run, it has unfavorable long-term consequences for both the family and society.

Welfare programs can cause other disincentives. For example, children may be eligible for Supplemental Security Income if they have a learning disability. According to one firsthand account, some low-income parents encouraged poor behavior in school so their children would qualify for this program.[12]

Does Welfare Cause Dependency?

A relatively brief stay on welfare would be evidence of little dependency. But a same family staying on welfare year after year is a matter of concern. To explore the question of whether welfare causes dependency, a University of Michigan study tracked 5,000 families over a number

[12]Jacqueline Goldwyn Kingon, "Education Life: A View from the Trenches," *New York Times,* 8 April 2001.

of years, paying particular attention to economic mobility both from year to year and from one generation to the next.[13] The study first examined poverty from year to year, or dependency within a generation. It found that most recipients received welfare for less than a year, but about 30 percent remained on welfare for at least eight years. Thus there was a core of long-term recipients.

A second and more serious concern is whether the children of the poor end up in poverty as well. Is there a cycle of poverty? Why might we expect one? Children in welfare households may learn the ropes about the welfare system and may come to view welfare as a normal way of life rather than as a temporary bridge over a rough patch. Research indicates that daughters from welfare families are more likely than daughters in other families to participate in the welfare system themselves and are more likely to have premarital births.[14] It is difficult to say whether welfare "causes" the link between mother and daughter, because the same factors that contribute to a mother's welfare status can also contribute to her daughter's welfare status. The evidence of a link is weaker when it comes to sons from welfare families.

WELFARE REFORM

There has been much dissatisfaction with the welfare system, both among those who pay for the programs and among direct beneficiaries. Welfare reforms introduced in recent years have been aimed at reducing long-term dependency.

Recent Reforms

Some analysts believe that one way to reduce poverty is to provide welfare recipients with job skills and make them find jobs. Even before the 1996 federal reform of welfare, to be discussed shortly, some sort of "workfare" component for welfare recipients operated in most states. In these states, as a condition of receiving welfare, the head of the household had to participate in education and training programs, search for work, or take some paid or unpaid position. The idea was to acquaint people on welfare with the job market. Evidence from various states indicates that programs involving mandatory job searches, short-term unpaid work, and training could operate at low cost and increase employment. The government saved money because those in welfare-to-work programs left welfare rolls sooner.

Reforms at the state level set the stage for federal reforms. By far the biggest reform in the welfare system in the last 60 years came with the 1996 legislation that replaced Aid to Families with Dependent Children (AFDC) with Temporary Assistance for Needy Families (TANF). Whereas the AFDC program set eligibility rules and left federal costs open-ended through matching grants to the states, TANF offers a block grant to the states to run their welfare programs. States ended AFDC and began TANF by July 1, 1997. The total state grant was fixed at $16.4 billion per year from 1997 to 2002, though supplementary grants go to the states with higher population growth. Under the new system, states have wide latitude to run their own welfare programs. But concerns about welfare dependency fostered some special provisions. The act imposes a lifetime limit of five years that a recipient can be on welfare.

Aside from the time limits and work participation rates imposed by the federal government, states are free to set benefit levels and experiment however they choose. For example, about half the states impose time limits shorter than five years. Some observers fear that states now have an incentive to keep welfare costs down by cutting benefits. To avoid becoming destinations for poor people—that is, to avoid becoming "welfare magnets"—states may be tempted to offer relatively low levels of benefits. The fear is that states will undercut benefits in what has been called a "race to the bottom."

The following case study surveys some results of welfare reform so far.

CASE**STUDY**	Is Welfare-to-Work Working?
	● *Public Policy*

Here are some preliminary conclusions about the course of welfare reform. Work requirements do seem to yield substantial declines in caseloads. In January 1994, the number of welfare recipients in America peaked at 14.2 million, mostly single women with children. By 2000 the rolls had fallen to 5.8 million, or 60 percent below the peak. Exhibit 6 shows the percentage of the

[13]Greg J. Duncan et al., *Years of Poverty, Years of Plenty* (Ann Arbor: University of Michigan Press, 1984).
[14]Robert Moffit, "Incentive Effects of the U.S. Welfare System: A Review," *Journal of Economic Literature* 30 (March 1992): 37.

EXHIBIT 6

Welfare Recipients as a Percentage of the U.S. Population Declined Sharply After 1994

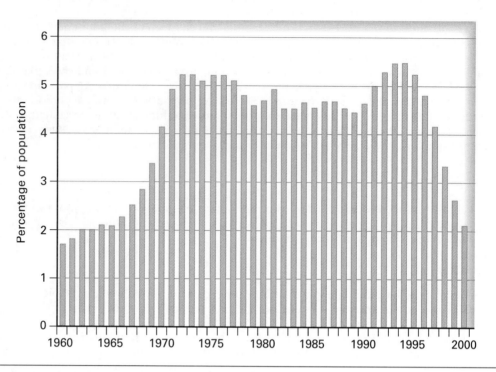

Source: Developed from data from the U.S. Department of Health and Human Services. Figures are for AFDC recipients before 1997 and TANF recipients after 1997.

U.S. population on welfare since 1960. Note the sharp decline in recent years. As a share of the population, welfare recipients fell from 5.5 percent in 1994 to 2.1 percent in 2000, the lowest rate since 1963. Fortunately, the reforms occurred during an expanding economy, with jobs plentiful, and the unemployment rate the lowest in three decades. But welfare rolls declined both in good economies, such as in Wisconsin, and in lagging economies, such as in New York City. In 2000 alone, 1.2 million parents on welfare went to work.

Many on welfare had other ways to support themselves. One expert who counted everything from food stamps to income from unreported jobs said cash transfers accounted for only about 34 percent of the average welfare recipient's income. Food stamps provided about 25 percent, and 36 percent came from unreported sources such as secret jobs, boyfriends, contributions from relatives, or private charities. (Medicaid was not counted as income, although it costs taxpayers more than other welfare programs put together.)

Since most people on welfare are poorly educated and have few job skills, wage levels for those who find jobs remain low. Part-time work is also common, as is job loss among those who initially found jobs. On the plus side, the earned-income tax credit in 2000 provided up to $3,900 a year in additional income to low-income workers. Most of those going to work can also receive food stamps, child care, and Medicaid.

Because the welfare rolls have declined but federal grants to states remain constant, welfare spending per recipient has increased significantly. Most states are combining tough new rules with an expanded menu of welfare services. States have made large investments in work-related services such as job placement, transportation, and especially child care.

Other positive developments include falling rates of crime and drug abuse; the greatest decline in child poverty, especially black child poverty, since the 1960s; and a substantial increase in employment among mothers who head families, especially those who have never been married. The proportion of black children living with married parents increased from 35 percent in 1995 to 39 percent in 2000. And a Michigan study found that former welfare mothers with jobs are significantly less likely than mothers still on welfare to report domestic violence or homelessness.

One effect of the work requirements of welfare reform has been to raise the "price" of welfare to recipients. Raising the price of going on welfare reduced the amount of welfare demanded. As one welfare director noted, a lot of people who are leaving welfare say, "It's not worth the hassle." We might say that the demand curve for welfare is downward sloping, with "hassle" measuring the price on the vertical axis. The greater the "hassle," the less welfare is demanded.

Welfare rolls declined more in states where efforts to get people to work are greater. For example, Wisconsin and Minnesota had similar economies, as reflected by identical unemployment rates, but Wisconsin's more aggressive work requirements cut welfare rolls there three times faster than in Minnesota. Wisconsin's success was no doubt behind President Bush's appointment of that state's governor, Tommy Thompson, to head the Department of Health and Human Services, the agency that runs federal welfare programs. During his 14 years as governor, Thompson reduced welfare payments to parents whose children skipped school and paid teenage parents more if they got married. During his tenure, the number of welfare families in the state dropped from about 100,000 in 1986 to only 16,000 in 2000. Reported cases of domestic violence have declined in Wisconsin since 1995.

Despite the good news on welfare, poor people are still having a hard time. The demand for emergency shelters increased 15 percent in 2000, the largest jump in a decade, according to the U.S. Conference of Mayors. Requests for emergency food climbed 17 percent. And, as mentioned earlier, although Medicaid is by far the most costly welfare program, an estimated 43 million Americans lacked health insurance in 2000.

The welfare reform law expires in 2002 and must be reauthorized or modified by Congress if it is to continue.

\<interactive\>exercise

- eACTIVITY: IS WELFARE-TO-WORK WORKING?
- READING IT RIGHT: WALL STREET JOURNAL EXERCISE
- ECONDEBATE ONLINE: IS WORKFARE WORKING?

Sources: June O'Neill and M. Anne Hill, "Gaining Ground? Measuring the Impact of Welfare Reform on Welfare and Work," Manhattan Institute, Civic Report 17, July 2001; Blaine Harden, "Two-Parent Families Rise After Changes in Welfare," *New York Times,* 12 August 2001; Mark Zawislak, "Use of Food Pantries, Shelters Rises Sharply," *Chicago Daily Herald,* 15 December 2000; William Julius Wilson and Andrew J. Cherlin, "The Real Test of Welfare Reform Still Lies Ahead," *New York Times,* 13 July 2001; and the federal site on welfare reform at http://www.acf.dhhs.gov/news/welfare/index.htm.

Along with Wisconsin, one of the most successful welfare reforms in the country is taking place in Oregon, as discussed in our final case study.

CASE**STUDY**	Oregon's Program of "Tough Love"
	● *Public Policy*

The number of Oregonians receiving welfare fell from 116,390 in January 1994 to 38,667 by September 2000, for a drop of 67 percent (the U.S. average was 60 percent). The decline came not as a result of strict time limits or tougher eligibility standards but by providing strong work incentives and working more closely with clients. TANF in Oregon offers a benefit level in the upper third for all states.

After leaving TANF for work, people in Oregon continue to qualify for health benefits for at least a year, child care until income reaches 200 percent of the federal poverty level, for food stamps for those who are income eligible, and the federal earned-income tax credit, which in effect can raise the wage more than $1 an hour. By working full time at the state's minimum wage of $6 an hour, a family's living standard increases to 130 percent of the poverty level. In comparison, the typical family on welfare and food stamps was living at only 75 percent of the poverty level. Thus, work is more attractive than welfare. The average starting wage in the first job after welfare exceeded $7 an hour.

One federal study tracked 5,500 welfare applicants and recipients in Oregon over a two-year period. Half the group participated in the welfare-to-work program and half did not. Taking part in the welfare-to-work program increased employment by 18 percent, raised average earnings over the two years by 35 percent, and boosted the proportion of individuals with employer-provided health insurance by 71 percent.

Oregon became the first state to require drug addicts to attend treatment as a condition of receiving welfare. An evaluation of that program found that clients who completed drug treatment earned 65 percent more than similar clients in a comparison group. Those completing treatment for addiction were 45 percent less likely to be arrested and only half as likely to be investigated for child abuse or neglect. The study also found that every dollar Oregon spent on drug treatment saved $5.60 on other social services. The approach in most other states is simply to ban recent drug felons from receiving aid.

The Oregon program offers abundant services, but welfare applicants must first spend a month looking for work before getting help. The federal government requires states to enroll 50 percent of their recipients in job-related activity by 2002. But as early as October 1997, Oregon had 89 percent of its recipients in job-related activity. Perhaps the most persuasive evidence that Oregon's approach of tough love is working is that after 18 months, only 8 percent of those who left welfare returned to the rolls.

Still, the road to welfare reform has not been smooth, even in Oregon. People coming off welfare often start near the poverty line. A University of Oregon study followed 1,000 Oregon families who left welfare during the first quarter of 1998. After two years, about 70 percent were employed and about 70 percent had health-care coverage, though wages for many still hovered around the federal poverty level.

\<interactive\>exercise

eACTIVITY: OREGON'S PROGRAM OF "TOUGH LOVE"

Sources: Kate Taylor, "Poverty Shadows Those Leaving Welfare," *The Oregonian,* 6 July 1999; *National Evaluation of Welfare Strategies,* Manpower Demonstration Research Corporation, June 2000; "Welfare and Food Stamp Caseloads in Oregon," December 2000, Oregon Department of Human Services; and Gary Weeks, "Oregon's Welfare Reform Produces Results," December 2000, Oregon Department of Human Services. An overview of Oregon's welfare-to-work program and current caseload information are available at http://www.afs.hr.state.or.us/services.html. State-by-state caseload information appears at http://www.acf.dhhs.gov/news/tables.htm.

CONCLUSION

Government redistribution programs have been most successful at reducing poverty among the elderly. But until quite recently, poverty rates among children increased because of the growth in the number of female householders. We might ask why transfer programs have reduced poverty rates more among the elderly than among female householders. Transfer programs do not encourage people to get old; that process occurs naturally and is independent of the level of transfers. But the level and availability of transfer programs at the margin influences some young unmarried women as they are deciding whether to have a child and may, at the margin, influence a married mother's decision to get divorced.

Most transfers in the economy are not from the government but rather are in-kind transfers within the family, from parents to children. Thus any change in a family's capacity to earn income has serious consequences for dependent children. Family structure is a primary determinant of family income. One in six children in the United States lives in poverty. Children are the innocent victims of the changing family structure. Recent welfare reforms are aimed at breaking the cycle of poverty.

endofchaptermaterial

- **Summary**
- **Questions for Review**

- **Experiential Exercises**
- **Wall Street Journal Exercise**

Take the Post-Test to assess your overall understanding of the key ideas in this chapter. The Post-Test provides a comprehensive selection of exam-style questions addressing the main topics and concepts of the chapter. At the completion of each Post-Test, you will receive a score and instructive feedback on how you answered each question, and a direct link to the part of the chapter addressed in the question. Take the Post-Test as often as you need to—a record of your progress for each attempt is kept for you to revisit and gauge your improvement. And each Post-Test is randomly generated, so every attempt is new.

International Trade

This morning you pulled up your Levi's jeans from Mexico, pulled over your Benetton sweater from Italy, and laced up your Timberland boots from Thailand. After a breakfast that included bananas from Honduras and coffee from Brazil, you climbed into your Volvo from Sweden fueled by Saudi Arabian oil and headed for a lecture by a visiting professor from Hungary. If the United States is such a rich and productive nation, why do we import so many goods and services? Why don't we produce everything ourselves? And why do some groups try to restrict foreign trade? Answers to these and other questions are addressed in this chapter.

The world is a giant shopping mall, and Americans are big spenders. Americans buy Japanese cars, French wine, Swiss watches, European vacations, and thousands of other goods and services from around the globe. But foreigners spend a lot on American products too—grain, personal computers, aircraft, movies, trips to Disney World, and thousands of other goods and services. In this chapter, we examine the gains from international trade and the effects of trade restrictions on the allocation of resources. The analysis is based on the familiar tools of supply and demand. Topics discussed in this chapter include:

- Gains from trade
- Absolute and comparative advantage revisited
- Tariffs
- Import quotas
- Welfare loss from trade restrictions
- Arguments for trade restrictions

<interactive>exercise

ECONDEBATE ONLINE: INTERNATIONAL TRADE

<interactive>update

- ECONDATA ONLINE: INTERNATIONAL TRADE
- ECONLINKS ONLINE: ECONOMICS WEB LINKS
- ECONNEWS ONLINE: INTERNATIONAL TRADE

THE GAINS FROM TRADE

A family from Virginia that sits down for a meal of Kansas prime rib, Idaho potatoes, and California string beans, with Georgia peach cobbler for dessert, is benefiting from interstate trade. You already understand why the residents of one state trade with those of another. Back in Chapter 2, you learned about the gains arising from specialization and exchange. You may recall the discussion of how you and your roommate could maximize output by each specializing. The law of comparative advantage says that the individual with the lowest opportunity cost of producing a particular good should specialize in producing that good. Just as individuals benefit from specialization and exchange, so do states and, indeed, nations. To reap the gains that arise from specialized production, countries engage in international trade. *With trade, each country specializes in the goods that it produces at the lowest opportunity cost.*

A Profile of Imports and Exports

Just as some states are more involved in interstate trade than others, some nations are more involved in international trade than others. For example, exports account for about one-quarter of the gross domestic product (GDP) in Canada and the United Kingdom; about one-third of GDP in Germany, Sweden, and Switzerland; and about half of GDP in the Netherlands. Despite the perception that Japan has a giant export sector, exports there make up only about one-seventh of GDP.

In the United States, exports of goods and services amounted to about 12 percent of GDP in 2000. Although small relative to GDP, exports play a growing role in the U.S. economy. The four main U.S. exports are (1) technology products, such as computer software and hardware, aircraft, telecommunication equipment, and military hardware; (2) industrial supplies and materials; (3) agricultural products, especially wheat, corn, and soybeans; and (4) entertainment products, such as movies and recorded music.

The United States depends on imports for some key raw materials, especially oil and metals. The four main U.S. imports are (1) manufactured consumer goods, such as automobiles from Japan and Germany and electronic equipment from Taiwan; (2) capital goods, such as high-tech printing presses from Germany; (3) oil; and (4) metals, such as lead, zinc, and copper. *U.S. imports of goods and services were 14 percent the size of GDP in 2000.*

The big change in U.S. exports over the last 25 years has been a growth in the dollar value of machinery exports; nearly half the capital goods produced in the United States are exported. The big change in U.S. imports over the last 25 years has been the increase in spending on foreign oil. Canada is our largest trading partner, followed by Japan and Mexico. Other key trading partners include Germany, Great Britain, South Korea, France, Hong Kong, Italy, and Brazil.

Let's focus just on raw materials. Exhibit 1 shows, for 12 key commodities, U.S. production as a percentage of U.S. consumption. If production exceeds consumption, the United States exports the difference. If production falls short of consumption, the United States imports the difference. For example, since the United States grows no coffee, U.S. production is 0 percent of U.S. consumption, so all coffee is imported. The exhibit also shows that U.S. production falls short of consumption for oil and metals such as lead, zinc, copper, and aluminum. At the other extreme, U.S. grown wheat amounts to 184 percent of U.S. wheat consumption, so nearly half of U.S. grown wheat is exported. U.S. production also exceeds consumption for other crops, including cotton, oil seeds (soybeans, sunflower seeds, cottonseeds), and coarse grains (corn, barley, oats). In short, when it comes to basic commodities, the United States is a net importer of oil and metals and a net exporter of crops.

<interactive>graph

TRY IT: FREE TRADE EQUILIBRIUM USING SUPPLY AND DEMAND ANALYSIS

Production Possibilities Without Trade

The rationale behind some international trade is obvious. The United States grows no coffee beans because our climate is not suited to coffee. More revealing, however, are the gains from trade where the comparative advantage is not so obvious. Suppose that just two goods—food and clothing—are produced and consumed and that there are only two countries in the world—the United States, with a labor force of 100 million workers, and the mythical country of Izodia, with 200 million workers. The conclusions derived from this simple model will have general relevance to the pattern of international trade.

Exhibit 2 presents production possibilities tables for each country, based on the size of the labor force and the productivity of workers in each country. The exhibit assumes that each country has a given technology and labor is fully and efficiently employed. If no trade occurs between countries, Exhibit 2 presents each country's *consumption possibilities* table as well, reflecting each country's consumption alternatives. The production numbers imply that each worker in the United States can produce either 6 units of food or 3 units of clothing per day. If all 100 million U.S. workers are employed in the food industry, they produce 600 million units per day, as shown in column U_1 in panel (a). If all U.S. workers make clothing, they turn out 300 million units per day, as shown in column U_6. The columns in between show some workers making food and some making clothing. Because a U.S. worker can produce either 6 units of food or 3 units of clothing, *the opportunity cost of 1 more unit of food is ½ unit of clothing.*

EXHIBIT 1

U.S. Production as a Percentage of U.S. Consumption for Various Commodities

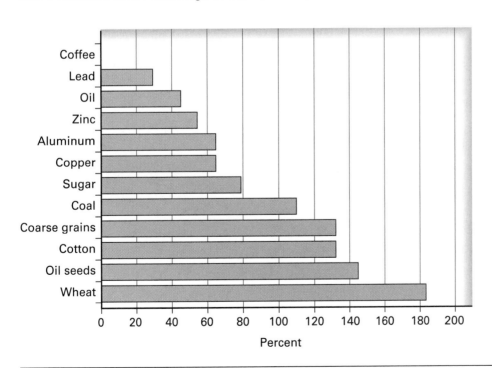

Source: Based on annual figures from *The Economist World in Figures: 2001 Edition* (London: Profile Books, 2001).

Chapter 19 International Trade

317

EXHIBIT 2

Production Possibilities Schedules for the United States and Izodia

(a) United States

	Production Possibilities with 100 Million Workers (millions of units per day)					
	U_1	U_2	U_3	U_4	U_5	U_6
Food	600	480	360	240	120	0
Clothing	0	60	120	180	240	300

(b) Izodia

	Production Possibilities with 200 Million Workers (millions of units per day)					
	I_1	I_2	I_3	I_4	I_5	I_6
Food	200	160	120	80	40	0
Clothing	0	80	160	240	320	400

Suppose Izodian workers are less educated, work with less capital, and farm less-fertile soil than U.S. workers, so each can produce only 1 unit of food or 2 units of clothing per day. If all 200 million Izodians specialize in food, they can produce 200 million units of food per day, as shown in column I_1 in panel (b) of Exhibit 2. If they all make clothing, total output is 400 million units of clothing per day, as shown in column I_6. Some intermediate production possibilities are also listed in the exhibit. Because an Izodian worker can produce either 1 unit of food or 2 units of clothing, *the opportunity cost of 1 more unit of food is 2 units of clothing.*

We can convert the data in Exhibit 2 to a production possibilities frontier for each country, as shown in Exhibit 3. In each diagram, the amount of food produced is measured on the vertical axis and the amount of clothing on the horizontal axis. U.S. combinations are shown in the left panel by U_1, U_2, and so on; Izodian combinations are shown in the right panel by I_1, I_2, and so on. Because we assume that resources are perfectly adaptable to the production of each commodity, each production possibilities curve is a straight line reflecting constant opportunity cost.

Exhibit 3 illustrates the possible combinations of food and clothing that residents of each country can produce and consume if all resources are fully and efficiently employed and there is no trade between the two countries. **Autarky** is the situation of national self-sufficiency, in

EXHIBIT 3

Production Possibilities Frontiers for the United States and Izodia Without Trade (millions of units per day)

Panel (a) shows the U.S. production possibilities curve; its slope indicates that the opportunity cost of an additional unit of food is ½ unit of clothing. Panel (b) shows production possibilities in Izodia; an additional unit of food costs 2 units of clothing. Food is relatively cheaper to produce in the United States.

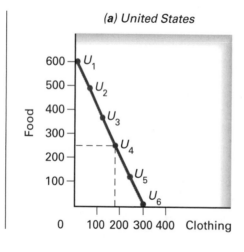

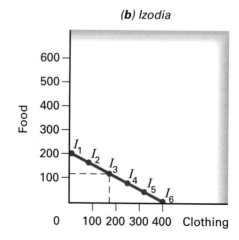

which there is no economic interaction with foreign producers or consumers. Suppose that U.S. producers maximize profit and U.S. consumers maximize utility with the combination of 240 million units of food and 180 million units of clothing—combination U_4. This combination will be called the *autarky equilibrium*. Suppose also that Izodians are in autarky equilibrium, identified as combination I_3, of 120 million units of food and 160 million units of clothing.

Consumption Possibilities Based on Comparative Advantage

In our example, each U.S. worker can produce both more clothing and more food per day than can each Izodian worker, so U.S. workers have an *absolute advantage* in the production of both goods. Recall from Chapter 2 that having an absolute advantage means being able to produce something using fewer resources than other producers require. Should the U.S. economy remain in autarky—that is, self-sufficient in both food and clothing productions—or could there be gains from trade?

As long as the opportunity cost of production differs between the two countries, there are gains from specialization and trade. The opportunity cost of producing 1 more unit of food is ½ unit of clothing in the United States compared with 2 units of clothing in Izodia. *According to the law of comparative advantage, each country should specialize in producing the good with the lower opportunity cost.* Since the opportunity cost of producing food is lower in the United States than in Izodia, both countries will gain if the United States specializes in food and exports some to Izodia, and Izodia specializes in clothing and exports some to the United States.

Before countries can trade, they must somehow agree on how much of one good exchanges for another—that is, they must establish the **terms of trade.** As long as Americans can get more than ½ unit of clothing for each unit of food, and as long as Izodians can get more than ½ unit of food for each unit of clothing, both countries will be better off by specialization and exchange rather than autarky. Suppose that market forces shape terms of trade so that 1 unit of clothing exchanges for 1 unit of food. Americans thus trade 1 unit of food to Izodians for 1 unit of clothing. To produce 1 unit of clothing themselves, Americans would have to sacrifice 2 units of food. Likewise, Izodians trade 1 unit of clothing to Americans for 1 unit of food, which is only half what Izodians would sacrifice to produce 1 unit of food themselves.

Exhibit 4 shows that with 1 unit of food trading for 1 unit of clothing, Americans and Izodians can consume anywhere along or below their blue consumption possibilities frontiers. *The consumption possibilities frontier* shows a nation's possible combinations of goods available as a result of production and foreign trade. (Note that the U.S. consumption possibilities curve does not extend to the right of 400 million units of clothing, since that is the most Izodians

EXHIBIT 4

Production (and Consumption) Possibilities Frontiers with Trade (millions of units per day)

If Izodia and the United States can trade at the rate of 1 unit of clothing for 1 unit of food, both can benefit. Consumption possibilities at those terms of trade are shown by the blue lines. The United States was previously producing and consuming combination U_4. By trading with Izodia, it can produce only food and still consume combination U—a combination that contains more food and more clothing than combination U_4 does. Likewise, Izodia can attain the preferred combination I by trading its clothing for U.S. food. Both countries are better off as a result of international trade.

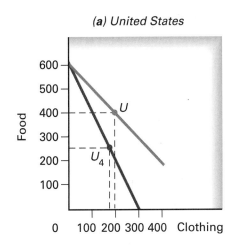

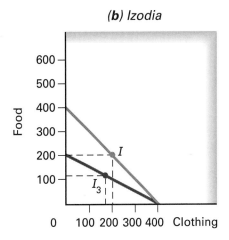

can produce.) The amount each country actually consumes will depend on the relative preferences for food and clothing. Suppose Americans select point *U* in panel (a) and Izodians select point *I* in panel (b).

Without trade, the United States produces and consumes 240 million units of food and 180 million units of clothing. With trade, the United States specializes in food by producing 600 million units; Americans eat 400 million units and exchange the rest for 200 million units of Izodian clothing. This consumption combination is reflected by point *U*. Through exchange, Americans increase their consumption of both food and clothing.

Without trade, Izodians produce and consume 120 million units of food and 160 million units of clothing. With trade, Izodians specialize to produce 400 million units of clothing, of which they wear 200 million units and exchange the rest for 200 million units of U.S. food. This consumption combination is shown by point *I*. Through trade, Izodians, like Americans, are able to increase their consumption of both food and clothing. How is this possible?

Since Americans are more efficient in the production of food and Izodians are more efficient in the production of clothing, total output increases when each specializes. Without specialization, total world production was 360 million units of food and 340 million units of clothing. With specialization, food increases to 600 million units and clothing to 400 million units. The only constraint on trade is that, for each good, *total world production must equal total world consumption*. In our two-country world, this means that the amount of food the United States exports must equal the amount of food Izodia imports. The same goes for Izodia's clothing exports.

Thus, both countries increase consumption with trade. *Although the United States has an absolute advantage in both goods, differences in the opportunity cost of production between the two nations ensure that specialization and exchange result in mutual gains.* Remember that comparative advantage, not absolute advantage, creates gains from specialization and trade.

We simplified trade relations in our example to highlight the gains from specialization and exchange. We assumed that each country would completely specialize in producing a particular good, that resources were equally adaptable to the production of either good, that the costs of transporting goods from one country to another were inconsequential, and that there were no problems in arriving at the terms of trade. The world is not that simple. For example, we don't expect a country to produce just one good. Regardless, the law of comparative advantage still leads to gains from trade.

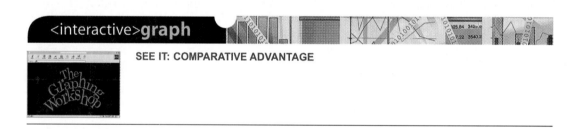

<interactive>graph

SEE IT: COMPARATIVE ADVANTAGE

Reasons for International Specialization

Countries trade with one another—or, more precisely, people and firms in one country trade with those in another—because each side expects to gain from exchange. How do we know what each country should produce and what each should trade?

Differences in Resource Endowments. Trade is often prompted by differences in resource endowments. Two key resources are labor and capital. Countries differ not only in their availability of labor and capital but also in the qualities of those resources. A well-educated and well-trained labor force is more productive than an uneducated and unskilled one. Similarly, capital that reflects the most recent technological developments is more productive than obsolete capital. Some countries, such as the United States and Japan, have an educated labor force and an abundant stock of modern capital. Both resources result in greater productivity per worker, making each nation quite competitive globally in producing goods that require skilled labor and sophisticated capital.

Some countries are blessed with an abundance of fertile land and favorable growing seasons. The United States, for example, has been called the "breadbasket of the world" because of its rich farmland. Honduras has the ideal climate for growing bananas. Coffee grows best in the climate and elevation of Colombia, Brazil, and Jamaica. Thus, the United States exports corn and imports coffee and bananas. Differences in the seasons across countries also serve as a basis for trade. For example, during the winter months, Americans import fruit from Chile, and Canadian tourists travel to Florida for sun and fun. During the summer months, Americans export fruit to Chile, and American tourists travel to Canada for fishing and camping.

Mineral resources are often concentrated in particular countries: oil in Saudi Arabia, bauxite in Jamaica, diamonds in South Africa. The United States has abundant coal supplies, but not enough oil to satisfy domestic demand. Thus, the United States exports coal and imports oil. More generally, *countries export products they can produce more cheaply in return for those that are unavailable domestically or are more costly to produce than to buy from other countries.*

Economies of Scale. If production is subject to *economies of scale*—that is, if long-run average cost falls as firms expand production—countries can gain from trade if each nation specializes. Such specialization allows firms in each nation to produce at a greater output rate, which reduces average production costs. The primary reason for establishing the single integrated market in Western Europe was to offer European producers a large, open market of over 320 million consumers so that producers can increase production, experience economies of scale, and in the process become more competitive in international markets.

Differences in Tastes. Even if all countries had identical resource endowments and combined those resources with equal efficiency, each country would still gain from trade as long as tastes and preferences differed among countries. Consumption patterns differ. For example, the Czechs and Irish drink three times as much beer per capita as do the Swiss and Swedes. The French drink three times as much wine as do Australians. The Danes eat twice as much pork as do Americans. Americans eat twice as much chicken as do Hungarians. Soft drinks are four times more popular in the United States than in Western Europe. The English like tea; Americans, coffee. Algeria has an ideal climate for growing grapes, but its large Muslim population abstains from alcohol; thus, Algeria exports wine.

NETBOOKMARK: U.S. CENSUS BUREAU'S TRADE DATA WEB SITE

ECONNEWS ONLINE: TRADE ORGANIZATION MORE WORLDLY

TRADE RESTRICTIONS AND WELFARE LOSS

Despite the benefits of international trade, nearly all countries at one time or another erect trade barriers across national borders. Trade restrictions usually benefit domestic producers but harm domestic consumers. In this section, we will consider the effects of restrictions and the reasons they are imposed.

<interactive>video

ASK THE INSTRUCTOR: WHAT ARE THE ARGUMENTS FOR TRADE RESTRICTIONS?

Tariffs

A *tariff*, a term first introduced in Chapter 4, is a tax on imports. (Tariffs can be applied to exports, too, but we will focus on import tariffs.) A tariff can be either *specific*, such as a tariff of $5 per barrel of oil, or *ad valorem*, such as 10 percent of the price of imported jeans. Consider the effects of a specific tariff on a particular good. In Exhibit 5, D is the U.S. demand for sugar and S is the supply of sugar from U.S. growers (there were about 10,000 U.S. sugar growers in 2001). Suppose that the world price of sugar is $0.10 per pound, as it was in 2001. The **world price** is determined by the world supply and demand for a product. It is the price at which any supplier can sell output on the world market and at which any demander can purchase output on the world market.

EXHIBIT 5

Effect of a Tariff

At a world price of $0.10 per pound, U.S. consumers demand 70 million pounds of sugar per month, and U.S. producers supply 20 million pounds per month; the difference is imported. With the imposition of a $0.05 per pound tariff, the U.S. price rises to $0.15 per pound, U.S. producers increase production to 30 million pounds, and U.S. consumers cut back to 60 million pounds. Imports fall to 30 million pounds. At the higher U.S. price, consumers are worse off; their loss of consumer surplus is the sum of areas *a, b, c,* and *d.* Area *a* represents an increase in producer surplus: a transfer from consumers to producers. Areas *b* and *f* reflect the portion of additional revenues to producers that is just offset by the higher production costs of expanding U.S. output by 10 million pounds. Area *c* shows government revenue from the tariff. The net welfare loss to society is the sum of area *d,* which reflects the loss of consumer surplus resulting from the drop in consumption, and area *b,* which reflects the higher marginal cost of domestically producing output that could have been produced more cheaply abroad.

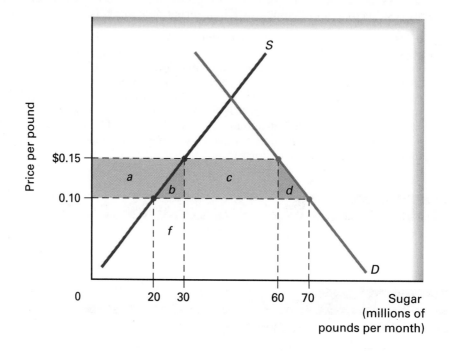

With free trade, U.S. consumers can buy any amount desired at the world price of $0.10 per pound, so the quantity demanded is 70 million pounds per month, of which U.S. producers supply 20 million pounds and 50 million pounds are imported. Since U.S. buyers can purchase sugar at the world price, U.S. producers can't charge more.

Now suppose that a specific tariff of $0.05 is imposed on each pound of imported sugar, raising the price of imported sugar from $0.10 to $0.15 per pound. U.S. producers can therefore raise their own price to $0.15 per pound as well without losing customers to imports. At the higher price, the quantity supplied by U.S. producers increases to 30 million pounds, but the quantity demanded by U.S. consumers declines to 60 million pounds. Because quantity demanded has declined and quantity supplied by U.S. producers has increased, U.S. imports fall from 50 million to 30 million pounds.

Since the price is higher after the tariff, consumers are worse off. Their loss in consumer surplus is identified in Exhibit 5 by the combination of the blue- and pink-shaded areas. Because both the U.S. price and the quantity supplied by U.S. producers have increased, U.S. producers' total revenue increases by the areas *a* plus *b* plus *f.* But only area *a* represents an increase in producer surplus. The increase in revenue represented by the areas *f* plus *b* merely offsets the higher marginal cost of expanding U.S. sugar production from 20 million to 30 million pounds. Area *b* represents part of the net welfare loss to the domestic economy because those 10 million pounds could have been imported for $0.10 per pound rather than produced domestically at a higher marginal cost.

Government revenue from the tariff is identified by area c, which equals the tariff of $0.05 per pound multiplied by the 30 million pounds that are imported, or $1.5 million per month. Tariff revenue represents a loss to consumers, but since the tariff goes to the government, it can be used to lower taxes or to increase public services. Area *d* shows a loss in consumer surplus because less sugar is consumed at the higher price. This loss is not redistributed to anyone else, so area *d* reflects part of the net welfare loss of the tariff. Therefore, areas *b* and *d* show the domestic economy's net welfare loss of the tariff; *the two triangles measure a loss in consumer surplus that is not offset by a gain to anyone in the domestic economy.*

In summary: Of the total loss in U.S. consumer surplus (areas *a, b, c,* and *d*) resulting from the tariff, area *a* is redistributed to U.S producers, area *c* becomes government revenue, and areas *b* and *d* reflect the net loss in domestic social welfare because of the tariff.

<interactive>**graph**

- **SEE IT: THE EFFECTS OF A TARIFF**
- **TRY IT: THE EFFECTS OF A TARIFF**

Import Quotas

An *import quota* is a legal limit on the amount of a particular commodity that can be imported. Quotas usually target imports from certain countries. For example, a quota may limit automobile imports from Japan or shoe imports from Brazil. To have an impact on the domestic market, or to be *effective,* a quota must limit imports to less than the amount imported under free trade.

Let's consider the impact of a quota on the U.S. market for sugar. In panel (a) of Exhibit 6, *D* is the U.S. demand curve and *S* is the supply curve of U.S. sugar producers. Suppose again that the world price of sugar is $0.10 per pound. With free trade, that price would prevail in

EXHIBIT 6

Effect of a Quota

In panel (a), *D* is the U.S. demand curve and *S* is the supply curve of U.S. producers. When the government establishes a sugar quota of 30 million pounds per year, the supply curve from both U.S. production and imports becomes horizontal at the world price of $0.10 per pound and remains horizontal until the supply reaches 50 million pounds. For higher prices, the supply curve equals the horizontal sum of the U.S. supply curve, *S,* and the quota. The new U.S. price, $0.15 per pound, is determined by the intersection of the new supply curve, *S'*, with the U.S. demand curve, *D*. Panel (b) shows the welfare effect of the quota. As a result of the higher U.S. price, consumer surplus is reduced by the amount of shaded area. Area *a* represents a transfer from U.S. consumers to U.S. producers. Rectangular area *c* shows the gain to those who can import sugar at the world price and sell it at the higher domestic price. Triangular area *b* reflects a net loss; it represents the amount by which the cost of producing an extra 10 million pounds of sugar in the United States exceeds the cost of buying it from abroad. Area *d* also reflects a net loss—a reduction in consumer surplus as consumption falls. Thus, the blue-shaded areas illustrate the loss in consumer surplus that is captured by domestic producers and those who are permitted to fulfill the quota, and the pink-shaded triangles illustrate the minimum net welfare cost.

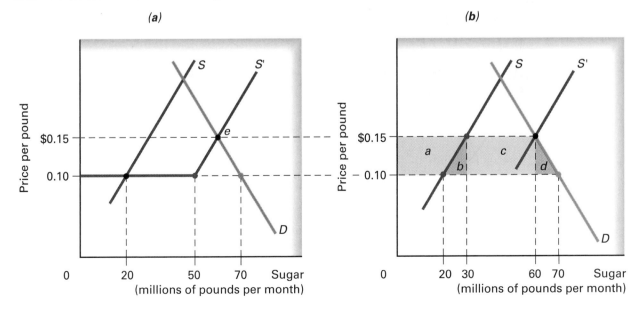

the U.S. market, and a total of 70 million pounds would be demanded. U.S. producers would supply 20 million pounds and importers, 50 million pounds. With a quota of 50 million pounds or more per month, the U.S. price would remain the same as the world price of $0.10 per pound, and quantity would be 70 million pounds per month. In short, a quota of at least 50 million pounds would not raise the U.S. price above the world price. A more stringent quota, however, would reduce imports, which, as we'll see, would raise the U.S. price.

Suppose U.S. trade officials impose a quota of 30 million pounds per month. As long as the U.S. price is at or above the world price of $0.10 per pound, foreign producers supply 30 million pounds. So at prices at or above $0.10 per pound, the total supply of sugar to the U.S. market is found by adding 30 million pounds of imported sugar to the amount supplied by U.S. producers. U.S. and foreign producers would never sell their output for less than $0.10 per pound in the U.S. market because they can always get that price on the world market. Thus, the supply curve that sums domestic production and imports is horizontal at the world price of $0.10 per pound and remains so until the quantity supplied reaches 50 million pounds.

Again, for prices above $0.10 per pound, the new supply curve, S', adds horizontally the 30-million-pound quota to S, the supply curve of U.S. producers. The U.S. price is found where this new supply curve, S', intersects the domestic demand curve, which in the left panel of Exhibit 6 occurs at point e. *An effective quota, by limiting imports, raises the domestic price of sugar above the world price and reduces quantity below the free-trade level.* (Note that to compare more easily the effects of tariffs and quotas, this quota was designed to yield the same equilibrium price and quantity as the tariff examined earlier.)

Panel (b) of Exhibit 6 shows the distribution and efficiency effects of the quota. As a result of the quota, U.S. consumer surplus declines by the combined blue and pink areas. Area a becomes producer surplus and thus involves no loss of U.S. welfare. Area c shows the increased profit to those permitted by the quota to sell Americans 30 million pounds at $0.15 per pound, or $0.05 above the world price. To the extent that foreign exporters rather than U.S. importers reap this profit, area c reflects a net loss in domestic welfare.

Area b shows by how much the marginal cost of producing another 10 million pounds in the United States exceeds the world price of the good. This is a welfare loss to the U.S. economy, because sugar could have been purchased abroad for $0.10 per pound, and the U.S. resources employed to increase sugar production could have been used more efficiently producing other goods. Area d is also a welfare loss because it reflects a reduction in consumer surplus with no offsetting gain to anyone. Thus, areas b and d in panel (b) of Exhibit 6 measure the minimum welfare cost imposed on the domestic economy by an effective quota. To the extent that the profit from quota rights (area c) accrues to foreign producers, this increases the U.S. welfare loss resulting from the quota.

SEE IT: EFFECTS OF A QUOTA

ECONNEWS ONLINE: CHIQUITA GOING BANANAS OVER QUOTAS

Quotas in Practice

The United States has granted quotas to specific countries. These countries, in turn, distribute these rights to their exporters through a variety of means. *By rewarding domestic producers with higher prices and foreign producers with the right to sell goods to the United States, the quota system creates two groups intent on securing and perpetuating these quotas.* Lobbyists for foreign producers work the halls of Congress, seeking the right to export to the United States. This strong support from producers, coupled with a lack of opposition from consumers (who remain rationally ignorant of all this), has resulted in quotas that have lasted for decades. Apparel quotas have been in effect for over 30 years, and sugar quotas for over 50 years.

Some economists have argued that if quotas are to be used, the United States should auction them off to foreign producers, thereby capturing the difference between the world price and the U.S. price. Auctioning off quotas would not only increase federal revenue but would reduce the profitability of quotas, which would reduce pressure on Washington to perpetuate quotas.

<interactive>update

ECONNEWS ONLINE: TO CONSUMERS, THE SUGAR PROGRAM IS ANYTHING BUT SWEET

Tariffs and Quotas Compared

Consider the similarities and differences between a tariff and a quota. Since the tariff and the quota in our example had identical effects on the price, they reflect the same change in quantity demanded. In both cases, U.S. consumers suffer the same loss of consumer surplus, and U.S. producers reap the same gain of producer surplus. The primary difference is that the revenue from the tariff goes to the domestic government, whereas the revenue from the quota goes to whoever secures the right to sell foreign goods in the U.S. market. *If quota rights accrue to foreigners, then the domestic economy is worse off with a quota than with a tariff.* But even if quota rights go to domestic importers, quotas, like tariffs, still increase the domestic price, restrict quantity, and thereby reduce consumer surplus. Quotas and tariffs also encourage foreign governments to retaliate with quotas and tariffs of their own, thus shrinking U.S. export markets, so the loss in welfare is greater than shown in Exhibits 5 and 6.

Other Trade Restrictions

Besides tariffs and quotas, a variety of other measures affect free trade. A country may provide *export subsidies* to encourage exports and *low-interest loans* to foreign buyers to promote exports of large capital goods. Some countries impose *domestic content requirements* specifying that a certain portion of a final good must be produced domestically. Other requirements concerning health, safety, or technical standards often discriminate against foreign goods. For example, European countries prohibit beef from hormone-fed cattle, a measure aimed at U.S. beef. Purity laws in Germany bar many non-German beers. Until the European Community adopted uniform standards, differing technical requirements forced manufacturers to offer as many as seven different models of the same TV for that market. Sometimes exporters will voluntarily limit exports, as when Japanese automakers agreed to cut exports to the United States. *The point is that tariffs and quotas are only two of many devices that restrict foreign trade.*

Recent research on the cost of protectionism indicates that international trade barriers slow the introduction of new goods and improved technologies. So, rather than simply raising domestic prices, trade restrictions slow economic progress.

Freer Trade by Multilateral Agreement

Mindful of the welfare loss from trade restrictions, the United States, after World War II, invited its trading partners to negotiate less stringent measures. The result was the **General Agreement on Tariffs and Trade (GATT),** an international trade treaty adopted in 1947 by 23 countries, including the United States. Each member of GATT agreed to (1) treat all member-nations equally with respect to trade, (2) reduce tariff rates through multinational negotiations, and (3) reduce import quotas. The agreement resulted in thousands of tariff reductions.

Major improvements in trade liberalization have come through trade negotiations among many countries, or "trade rounds," under the auspices of GATT. Trade rounds offer a package approach rather than an issue-by-issue approach to trade negotiations. Concessions that are necessary but otherwise difficult to defend in domestic political terms can be made more acceptable in the context of a package that also contains politically and economically attractive benefits. Most early GATT trade rounds were aimed at reducing tariffs. The Kennedy Round in the mid-1960s included new provisions against **dumping,** which is selling a commodity abroad for less than is charged in the home market. The Tokyo Round of the 1970s was a more sweeping attempt to extend and improve the system.

The most recent round of negotiations was launched in Uruguay in September 1986 and ratified by 123 participating countries in 1994 with 550 pages of details. The number of countries signing on to the agreement grew to 142 by 2001. This so-called **Uruguay Round,** the most comprehensive of the eight postwar multilateral trade negotiations, phased in tariff reductions on 85 percent of world trade and eventually will eliminate quotas. The Uruguay Round also created the World Trade Organization (WTO) to succeed GATT.

<interactive>update

- ECONDEBATE ONLINE: DOES THE U.S. ECONOMY BENEFIT FROM FOREIGN TRADE?
- ECONNEWS ONLINE: A SUPERSIZED NAFTA

The World Trade Organization

The **World Trade Organization (WTO)** now provides the legal and institutional foundation for the multilateral trading system. Whereas GATT was a multilateral agreement with no institutional foundation, the WTO is a permanent institution in Geneva, Switzerland, with a staff of 450 headed by a director general. Staff responsibilities include supporting delegate bodies, providing trade policy analyses, helping resolve trade disputes, and providing technical support to developing countries.

Whereas GATT involved only merchandise trade, the WTO includes services and trade-related aspects of intellectual property, such as books, movies, and computer programs. Quotas will eventually be outlawed by the WTO, but tariffs and customs duties remain legal. Average tariffs will fall from 6 percent to 4 percent (when GATT began in 1947, tariffs averaged 40 percent). In November 2001, members of the WTO agreed to launch a new round of multilateral trade talks to help boost economic growth around the world. The agreement, reached at a meeting in Qatar, outlined talks expected to last at least three years. These talks will focus on lowering tariffs on a wide range of industrial and agricultural products.

Whereas GATT relied on voluntary cooperation, the WTO has a dispute settlement body that should be faster, more automatic, and less susceptible to blockage than the GATT system. So far, the United States is the major user of the WTO's dispute settlement system. Charges brought by the United States include accusing Japan of unfair liquor taxes, Canada of discrimination against U.S. magazine publishers, Pakistan of violating pharmaceutical copyrights, and Turkey of excessively taxing U.S. movies. The WTO has also taken the U.S. side in disputes with the European Union over beef and bananas. In all, the United States filed about one-third of the cases filed with the WTO and has been successful in most of them.

The WTO has become a lightning rod for globalization issues, as discussed in the following case study.

<interactive>exercise

ECONDEBATE ONLINE: DOES THE U.S. ECONOMY BENEFIT FROM THE WORLD TRADE ORGANIZATION (WTO)?

CASE**STUDY**	The WTO and the "Battle in Seattle"
	● *Bringing Theory to Life*

When WTO members met in Seattle in November 1999 to set an agenda and timetable for the next round of trade talks, all hell broke loose, as 50,000 protesters disrupted the city. Most were peaceful, but police arrested more than 500 over three days, and property damage reached $3 million. T-shirts sold a week before the meeting dubbed the event the "Battle in Seattle," and so it was. The less-peaceful protestors targeted multinational companies, smashing windows at Starbucks, McDonald's, Nike Town, and Old Navy, and burning khakis in front of Gap. Across the Atlantic, about 2,000 sympathy demonstrators also protested in London, where 40 were arrested for overturning vehicles and starting fires.

The "Battle in Seattle" was by far the largest demonstration against free trade in the United States. Protest organizers used free trade as an organizing and fund-raising focus for a variety of groups, including labor unions and environmental groups. Protestors could pick their favorite cause—union members fear losing jobs overseas, environmentalists fear pollution anywhere, and other groups fear developments such as hormone-fed beef and genetically modified food.

Protestors would probably be surprised to learn that WTO members are not of one mind about trade issues. For example, the United States and Europe are pushing to protect workers around the world, but developing countries, including Mexico, Egypt, India, and Pakistan, object strenuously to discussing labor rights. These poorer nations are concerned that the clothing, shoes, and textiles they produce have not been allowed entry to the markets of rich nations quickly enough. Many developing countries view attempts to impose labor and environmental standards as just the latest effort to keep poor countries poor.

Without international groups such as the WTO to provide a forum for discussing labor and environmental issues around the world, conditions in poor countries would probably be worse. Working conditions, especially in poor countries, are improving, thanks to trade opportunities along with pressure for labor rights from WTO and other international groups. For example, Cambodia is one of the poorest countries in the world, but the highest wages in the country are earned by the 1 percent of the population working in the export sector. Protestors in Seattle should talk with Deth, who sews T-shirts and shorts, mostly for Nike and Gap, at the June Textile factory in Cambodia. She works from 6:15 a.m. to 2:15 p.m. with a half-hour for lunch. She gets time and a half for overtime and double for holidays. Though her pay is low by U.S. standards, it allows her to support her family and is more than twice what judges and doctors average in Cambodia. Her pay and working conditions are also far more attractive than in her previous line of work—prostitution.

Child labor still occurs in poor countries, but it's more likely to be on the family farm than in a factory. One in six 10-to-14-year-olds in Cambodia works, the highest rate in Southeast Asia. But the manufacturing and trade sectors account for only about 10 percent of Cambodia's estimated 600,000 child workers, according to the United Nations Development Program. The rest work on family farms or fisheries, with some hired out to neighboring families for work. Some children try to use fake IDs to get hired in factories, where the minimum age is 15.

The Seattle WTO meeting adjourned without a date or an agenda for the next round of trade talks, so demonstrators succeeded in disrupting deliberations. In part because of media pressure, Nike ended its contract with the June Textile factory in Cambodia at the end of 2000. Deth is worried. "I don't know what the fate of my children will be if I lose my job," she told *Asiaweek.*

The reduction in trade barriers resulting from the Uruguay Round is projected to boost world income by $510 billion in 2005 (the target date for full implementation), or about $100 per person on Earth. That payoff from freer trade may not impress those who smashed windows in Seattle, but in Cambodia and in other poor countries around the world it can be a lifesaver.

\<interactive\>exercise

- eACTIVITY: THE WTO AND THE "BATTLE IN SEATTLE"
- READING IT RIGHT: WALL STREET JOURNAL EXERCISE

Sources: Gina Chon, "Dropped Stitches," *Asiaweek,* 22 December 2000; Naomi Koppel, "Bush Policy May Break WTO Deadlock," Associated Press, 27 December 2000; David Postman and Linda Mapes, "Why WTO Unified So Many Foes," *Seattle Times,* 6 December 1999; Leslie Kaufman and David Gonzalez, "Labor Standards Clash with Global Reality," *New York Times,* 24 April 2001; and the Web site for the World Trade Organization at http://www.wto.org.

Common Markets

Some countries have looked to the success of the U.S. economy, which is essentially a free trade zone across 50 states, and have tried to develop free trade pacts of their own. The largest and best known is the European Union, which began in 1958 with a half-dozen countries and has expanded to more than a dozen. The idea was to create a barrier-free European market like the United States in which goods, services, people, and capital are free to flow to their highest-valued use. Twelve members of the European Union have adopted a common currency, the *euro,* which replaces national currencies in 2002.

The United States, Canada, and Mexico have developed a free trade pact called the North American Free Trade Agreement (NAFTA). Through NAFTA, Mexico hopes to attract increased U.S. investment by guaranteeing companies who build factories in Mexico duty-free access to U.S. markets, which is where over two-thirds of Mexico's exports go. The United States is interested in NAFTA because Mexico's 100 million people represent an attractive export market for U.S. producers, and because Mexico's huge oil reserves could ease U.S. energy problems. The United States would also like to bolster Mexico's move toward a more market-oriented economy, as is reflected, for example, by Mexico's privatization of its phone system and banks. But U.S. labor unions fear job losses to Mexico.

Free trade areas are proliferating. A half-dozen Latin American countries form Mercosur, the association of Southeast Asian nations make up ASEAN, and South Africa and its four neighboring countries make up the Southern African Customs Union. Regional trade agreements require an exception to WTO rules because bloc members can make special deals among themselves and thus discriminate against outsiders. Under WTO's requirements, any trade concession granted one country must be granted to *all other* WTO members.

ECONNEWS ONLINE: A TARIFF-IC PROPOSAL

ARGUMENTS FOR TRADE RESTRICTIONS

Trade restrictions often appear to be little more than handouts for the domestic industries they protect. Given the loss in social welfare that results from these restrictions, it would be more efficient simply to transfer money from domestic consumers to domestic producers. But such a bald transfer would be politically unpopular. Arguments for trade restrictions avoid mention of transfers to domestic producers and instead cite loftier goals. As we shall now see, some of these arguments are more valid than others.

ASK THE INSTRUCTOR: WHAT ARE THE ARGUMENTS FOR TRADE RESTRICTIONS?

National Defense Argument

Some industries claim they need protection from import competition because their output is vital to national defense. Products such as strategic metals and military hardware are often insulated from foreign competition by trade restrictions. Thus national defense considerations outweigh concerns about efficiency and equity. How valid is this argument? Trade restrictions may shelter the defense industry, but other means, such as government subsidies, might be more efficient. Or the government could stockpile basic military hardware so that maintaining an ongoing productive capacity would become less essential, though technological change soon makes certain weapons obsolete. Since most industries can play some role in national defense, instituting trade restrictions on this basis can get out of hand. For example, U.S. wool producers gained protection by successfully claiming that wool is critical for military uniforms.

CNN VIDEO: "THE ART OF THE TRADE WAR"

Infant Industry Argument

The infant industry argument was formulated as a rationale for protecting emerging domestic industries from foreign competition. According to this "Made in America" line of reasoning, in industries where a firm's average cost per unit falls as production expands, new domestic firms may need protection from imports until these firms grow big enough to be competitive.

Trade restrictions let new firms achieve the economies of scale needed to compete with mature foreign producers.

But how do we identify industries that merit protection, and when do they become old enough to look after themselves? The very existence of protection could foster inefficiencies that firms may not be able to outgrow. The immediate cost of such restrictions is the net welfare loss from higher domestic prices. These costs may become permanent if the industry never realizes the expected economies of scale and thus never becomes competitive. As with the national defense argument, policy makers should be careful in adopting trade restrictions based on the infant industry argument. Here again, temporary production subsidies may be more efficient than import restrictions.

Antidumping Argument

As we have noted already, *dumping* is selling a product abroad for less than the price in the home market. Exporters may be able to sell the good for less overseas because of export subsidies, or firms may simply find it profitable to sell for less in foreign markets where demand is more price elastic—that is, firms price discriminate. Critics of dumping call for a tariff to raise the price of dumped goods.

Why should U.S. consumers be prevented from buying products for as little as possible, even if these low prices are the result of a foreign subsidy or price discrimination? If dumping is persistent, the lower price may increase consumer surplus by an amount that more than offsets losses to domestic producers. *There is no good reason why consumers should not be allowed to buy imports for a persistently lower price.*

An alternative form of dumping, termed *predatory dumping*, is the *temporary* sale abroad at prices below the home market or even below cost to get rid of competing producers in that foreign market. Once the competition has been eliminated, so the story goes, the exporting firm can raise the price in the foreign market. The trouble with this argument is that if dumpers try to take advantage of their monopoly position by sharply increasing the price, then other firms, either domestic or foreign, could enter the market and sell for less. There are few documented cases of predatory dumping.

Sometimes dumping may be *sporadic*, as firms occasionally sell at a discount to unload excess inventories; retailers hold periodic "sales" for the same reason. Sporadic dumping can be unsettling for domestic producers, but the economic impact is not a matter of great public concern. Regardless, all dumping is prohibited in the United States by the Trade Agreements Act of 1979, which calls for the imposition of tariffs when a good is sold for less in the United States than in its home market. In addition, WTO rules allow for the imposition of offsetting tariffs when products are sold for "less than fair value" and when there is "material injury" to domestic producers. For example, U.S. producers of lumber and beer have accused their Canadian counterparts of dumping.

Jobs and Income Argument

One rationale for trade restrictions that is commonly heard in the United States, and was voiced by Seattle protestors, is that they protect U.S. jobs and wage levels. Using trade restrictions to protect domestic jobs is a strategy that dates back centuries. One problem with such a policy is that other countries will likely retaliate by restricting *their* imports to save *their* jobs, so international trade is reduced, jobs are lost in export industries, and potential gains from trade fail to materialize.

Wage rates in other countries, especially developing countries, are often a small fraction of wage rates in the United States. Looking simply at differences in wage rates, however, narrows the focus too much. Wages represent just one component of the total production cost and may not necessarily be the most important. Employers are interested in the labor cost per unit of output, which depends on both the wage rate and labor productivity.

Wage rates are high in the United States partly because U.S. labor productivity remains the highest in the world. This high productivity can be traced to education and training and to the abundant computers, machines, and other physical capital that make workers more productive. Workers in the United States also benefit from a business climate that is relatively stable and that offers appropriate incentives to produce.

But what about the lower wages in many developing countries? These low wages can often be linked to workers' lack of education and training, the meager physical capital available to each worker, and a business climate that is less stable and less attractive for producers. In U.S. industries with high wages supported by high output per worker, the labor cost per unit of output may be as low as or lower than labor costs in countries with low wages and low productivity.

For example, although total hourly compensation is more than twice as high at Birmingham Steel, a U.S. corporation, as at South Korean steel plants, Birmingham's labor productivity is four times greater, so the labor cost per ton is lower for Birmingham.

Once multinational firms build plants and provide technological know-how in developing countries, however, U.S. workers lose some of their competitive edge, and their relatively high wages could price some U.S. products out of the world market. This has already happened in the stereo and consumer electronics industries, and General Motors is planning to make more cars in Mexico. Most apparel and shoe production has also gone overseas.

Over time, as labor productivity in developing countries increases, wage differentials among countries will narrow, much as wage differentials between northern and southern U.S. states have narrowed. As technology and capital spread, U.S. workers, particularly unskilled workers, cannot expect to maintain wage levels that are far above those in other countries. The U.S. government may promote research and development to keep U.S. producers on the cutting edge of technological developments, but staying ahead in the technological race is a constant battle.

Domestic producers do not like to compete with foreign producers whose costs are lower, so they often push for trade restrictions. But if restrictions negate any cost advantage a foreign producer might have, the law of comparative advantage becomes inoperative and domestic consumers are denied access to the lower-priced goods.

Declining Industries Argument

Where an established domestic industry is in jeopardy of closing because of lower-priced imports, there could be a rationale for *temporary* import restrictions to allow the orderly adjustment of the domestic industry. After all, domestic producers employ many industry-specific resources—both specialized machines and specialized labor. This physical and human capital is worth less in its best alternative use. If the extinction of the domestic industry is forestalled through trade restrictions, specialized machines can be allowed to wear out naturally, and specialized workers can retire voluntarily or can gradually pursue more promising careers.

Thus, in the case of declining domestic industries, trade protection can help lessen shocks to the economy and can allow for an orderly transition to a new industrial mix. But the protection offered should not be so generous as to encourage continued investment in the industry. Protection should be of specific duration and should be phased out over that period.

The clothing industry is an example of a declining U.S. industry. The 22,000 U.S. jobs saved as a result of one recent trade restriction paid an average of about $23,000 per year. But a Congressional Budget Office study estimated that, because of higher domestic prices, U.S. consumers paid between $39,000 and $74,000 per year for each textile and apparel job saved. Trade restrictions in the U.S. clothing and textile industry are scheduled to be phased out under the Uruguay Round of trade agreements.

Free trade may displace some U.S. jobs through imports, but it also creates U.S. jobs through exports. When people celebrate a ribbon-cutting ceremony for a new software firm, nobody credits free trade for those jobs, but when a steel plant closes, everyone talks about how those jobs went overseas. What's more, many foreign companies have built plants in the United States and employ U.S. workers. For example, a dozen foreign television manufacturers and all major Japanese automobile manufacturers now have U.S. plants.

The number of jobs in the United States has more than doubled since 1960. To recognize this job growth is not to deny the problems facing workers who are displaced by imports. Some displaced workers, particularly those in blue-collar jobs in steel and other unionized industries, are not likely to find jobs that will pay as well as the ones they lost. As with infant industries, however, the problems posed by declining industries need not require trade restrictions. To support the affected industry, the government could offer wage subsidies or special tax breaks that decline over time. The government has also funded programs to retrain workers for jobs that are in greater demand.

Problems with Protection

Trade restrictions raise a number of problems in addition to the ones already mentioned. First, protecting one stage of production often requires protecting downstream stages of production. Protecting the U.S. textile industry from foreign competition, for example, may raise the cost of cloth to U.S. clothing manufacturers, reducing their competitiveness. Thus, if the government protects domestic textile manufacturers, it may also need to protect the domestic garment industry.

Second, the cost of protection includes not only the welfare loss arising from the higher domestic price but also the cost of the resources used by domestic producers and groups to secure the favored protection. The cost of *rent seeking*—lobbying fees, propaganda, and legal actions—can equal or exceed the direct welfare loss from restrictions. A third problem with imposing trade restrictions is that other countries usually retaliate, thus shrinking the gains from trade. Retaliation can set off still greater trade restrictions, leading to an outright trade war. A final problem with trade restrictions is the transaction costs of enforcing the myriad quotas, tariffs, and other restrictions. These policing and enforcement costs are discussed in the following case study.

CASE**STUDY**	Enforcing Trade Restrictions
	● *Public Policy*

The United States is the richest, most attractive market in the world. Trade restrictions often make U.S. markets even more appealing to foreign producers because U.S. prices exceed world prices. With thousands of different quota and tariff classifications and with tariffs ranging from zero to over 100 percent, the transaction costs of monitoring all this are huge and must be added to the welfare cost of trade restrictions. The U.S. Customs Service operates 24 hours a day, 365 days a year and must also inspect the luggage of nearly 500 million people who enter the country each year by air and sea as well as some 300 points of entry by land. For example, on highway I-35 in Laredo, Texas, just one of dozens of border crossings, some 6,000 18-wheelers roll in from Mexico every day.

We should not be surprised that some importers try to skirt trade restrictions, either evading them by redefining the product slightly or illegally importing goods that are restricted by quotas. For example, lumber from Canada is subject to quota restrictions. But take a 2-by-4, which is considered lumber, and drill a few small holes in it for electrical wiring, and that 2-by-4 becomes "carpentry," which is not subject to a quota. A diverse array of goods is imported in violation of quotas, including clothing, sugar, coffee, gems, and steel pipes. It has been estimated that more than 10 percent of all imports are illegal.

Restrictions affect not only the quantity of imports but also the quality. Nearly all schemes to import clothing illegally involve misrepresenting the clothing so that it fits into some quota or qualifies for a lower tariff. Sometimes the garments are altered to evade detection. For example, because men's running shorts are controlled by a quota, manufacturers often added a flimsy inner lining so the shorts could pass for swimming trunks, which faced no quotas.

Because the United States allows some countries more generous quotas than others, exporters in countries under tight control sometimes ship their goods through countries with a more generous ceiling. For example, Japan makes so little clothing for export that the United States imposes no quota for clothing imports from Japan. As a result, clothing made in Korea is often shipped through Japan to evade U.S. quotas on Korea. Similarly, because Nepal is not subject to a clothing quota but India is, India ships clothing to the United States through Nepal. To get around U.S. quotas on sugar imports, Brazil exports molasses to Canada that is then brought into the United States without a quota.

Some foreign producers and U.S. importers engage in "port shopping," or testing various ports to see where inspections are most lax. Documents are often forged. U.S. Customs inspectors are responsible for policing all this activity. These inspectors must remain alert because of the thousands of tariffs, quotas, and other trade restrictions in effect and the myriad ways to get around them. All this effort is aimed at protecting U.S. producers from foreign competition, but at what cost to U.S. consumers and taxpayers?

<interactive>**exercise**

eACTIVITY: ENFORCING TRADE RESTRICTIONS

Sources: Michael Fletcher, "Fewer People Searched by Customs in Past Year," *Washington Post,* 19 October 2000; Alex Keto, "White House Watch: Bush Put on Notice on Trade," Dow Jones Newswire, 2 August 2001; Daniel Machulaba, "U.S. Ports Are Losing the Battle to Keep Up with Overseas Trade," *Wall Street Journal,* 9 July 2001; Jim Yardley, "Truck-Choked Border City Fears Being Bypassed," *New York Times,* 15 March 2001; and the U.S. Customs Service home page at http://www.customs.treas.gov/.

Import Substitution Versus Export Promotion

A nation's economic progress frequently involves an evolution from the production of raw materials and agricultural products to manufacturing. If a country is fortunate, this transformation occurs gradually through natural market forces. Sometimes government pushes along the evolution. Many developing countries, including Argentina and India, pursued a development policy called **import substitution,** whereby the country manufactures products that until then had been imported. To insulate domestic producers from foreign competition, the government imposes tariffs and quotas. This development strategy became popular for several reasons. First, demand already existed for these products, so the "what to produce" question was readily answered. Second, import substitution provided infant industries a protected market. Finally, import substitution was popular with those who supplied capital, labor, and other resources to the favored domestic industries.

Like all protection measures, however, import substitution erased the gains from specialization and comparative advantage among countries. Often the developing country replaced low-cost foreign goods with high-cost domestic goods. And domestic producers, shielded from foreign competition, usually fail to become efficient. Worse still, other countries often retaliated with their own trade restrictions.

Critics of the import substitution approach claim that export promotion is a surer path to economic development. **Export promotion** is a development strategy that concentrates on producing for the export market. This approach begins with relatively simple products, such as textiles. As a developing country builds its technological and educational base—that is, as the developing economy learns by doing—producers can then export more complex products. Economists tend to favor export promotion over import substitution because the emphasis is on comparative advantage and trade expansion rather than on trade restriction. Export promotion also forces producers to grow more efficient in order to compete on world markets. Research shows that global competition has a profound effect on domestic efficiency.[1] What's more, export promotion requires less government intervention in the market than does import substitution.

Export promotion has been the more successful development strategy, as reflected, for example, by the newly industrialized countries of East Asia (Taiwan, South Korea, Hong Kong, and Singapore), which in recent decades have grown much more than import-substituting countries such as Argentina, India, and Peru. Since 1965, the four newly industrialized economies of East Asia raised their average real incomes from 20 percent to 70 percent of industrial economies. Most Latin American nations, which for decades had favored import substitution, are now pursuing free trade agreements with the United States. Even India is in the process of dismantling trade barriers, although the emphasis has been on importing high-technology capital goods. One slogan of Indian trade officials is "Microchips, yes! Potato chips, no!"

CONCLUSION

International trade arises from voluntary exchange among buyers and sellers pursuing their self-interest. Since 1950 world output has risen 7-fold, while world trade has increased 17-fold. World trade offers many advantages to the trading countries: access to markets around the world, lower costs through economies of scale, the opportunity to utilize abundant resources, better access to information about markets and technology, improved quality honed by competitive pressure, and lower prices for consumers. Comparative advantage, specialization, and trade allow people to use their scarce resources most efficiently to satisfy their unlimited wants.

Despite the clear gains from free trade, restrictions on international trade date back centuries, and pressure to impose trade restrictions continues today. Domestic producers (and their resource suppliers) benefit from trade restrictions because they are able to sell their output for a higher domestic price. Protection insulates domestic producers from the rigors of global competition, in the process stifling innovation and leaving the industry vulnerable to technological change elsewhere. Under a system of quotas, the winners also include those who have secured the right to import goods at the world prices and sell them at the domestic prices.

Consumers who must pay higher prices for protected goods suffer from trade restrictions, as do the domestic producers who use imported resources. Other losers are U.S. exporters,

[1]See Martin Baily and Hans Gersbach, "Efficiency in Manufacturing and the Need for Global Competition," in *Brookings Papers on Economic Activity: Microeconomics,* M. Baily, P. Reiss, and C. Winston, eds. (Washington D.C.: Brookings Institution, 1995), 307–347.

who face higher trade barriers as foreigners retaliate with their own trade restrictions. Even if other countries do not retaliate, U.S. trade restrictions reduce the gains from comparative advantage and thereby cut world income. With world income lower, U.S. exporters find that their foreign markets have shrunk. Some of these exporters may go out of business; other potential producers never even start.

Producer groups have a laser-like focus on trade legislation, but consumers remain largely oblivious. Consumers purchase thousands of different goods and thus have no special interest in the effects of trade policy on any particular good. Congress tends to support the group that makes the most noise, so trade restrictions persist, despite the clear gains from free trade.

endofchaptermaterial

- **Summary**
- **Questions for Review**
- **Problems and Exercises**

- **Experiential Exercises**
- **Wall Street Journal Exercise**

Take the Post-Test to assess your overall understanding of the key ideas in this chapter. The Post-Test provides a comprehensive selection of exam-style questions addressing the main topics and concepts of the chapter. At the completion of each Post-Test, you will receive a score and instructive feedback on how you answered each question, and a direct link to the part of the chapter addressed in the question. Take the Post-Test as often as you need to—a record of your progress for each attempt is kept for you to revisit and gauge your improvement. And each Post-Test is randomly generated, so every attempt is new.

Post-Test

Introduction to Macroeconomics

What's the big deal with macroeconomics? Why do macroeconomists typically focus on the national economy? How do we measure the performance of the economy over time? Which has more impact on your standard of living, the economy's ups and downs or its long-term growth? Answers to these and related questions are provided in this chapter, which introduces macroeconomics.

In macroeconomics we think big—not about the market for Dunkin' Donuts but about the market for everything produced in the economy; not about the price of gasoline but about the average price of all goods and services produced in the economy; not about consumption by the Ramoz household but about consumption by all households; not about investment by the Disney Corporation but about investment by all firms in the economy.

Macroeconomists develop and test theories about how the economy as a whole works—theories that can help predict the consequences of economic policies and events. Macroeconomists are concerned not only with what determines such big-picture measures as production, employment, and the economy's price level but also with understanding how and why these variables change over time. Macroeconomists are especially interested in what makes an economy grow over time, because a growing economy creates more job opportunities and more goods and services—in short, faster growth means a higher standard of living. What determines the economy's ability to use resources productively, to adapt, to grow? In this chapter, we begin to explore these questions. In the next chapter, we will hone in on the major macroeconomic focus—economic growth. Topics discussed in this chapter include:

- The national economy
- Economic fluctuations
- Aggregate demand
- Aggregate supply
- Equilibrium level of price and aggregate output
- Short history of the U.S. economy
- Demand-side economics
- Supply-side economics

<interactive>**exercise**

ECONDEBATE ONLINE

<interactive>**update**

- **ECONDATA ONLINE**
- **ECONLINKS ONLINE: ECONOMICS WEB LINKS**
- **ECONNEWS ONLINE**

<interactive>video

ASK THE INSTRUCTOR: WHAT IS MACROECONOMICS?

THE NATIONAL ECONOMY

Macroeconomics concerns the overall performance of the *economy*. The term **economy** describes the structure of economic life, or economic activity, in a community, a region, a country, a group of countries, or the world. We could talk about the Chicago economy, the Illinois economy, the Midwest economy, the U.S. economy, the North American economy, or the world economy. We measure an economy's size in different ways, such as the amount produced, the number of people employed, or their total income. The most commonly used measure of an economy's size is its *gross product,* which measures the market value of final goods and services produced in a particular geographical region during a given period, usually one year.

If the focus is the Illinois economy, we consider the *gross state product.* If the focus is the U.S. economy, we consider the **gross domestic product, or GDP,** which measures the market value of all final goods and services produced in the United States during a given period, usually a year. GDP helps us keep track of the economy's incredible variety of goods and services, from trail bikes to pedicures. We can use the gross domestic product to track the same economy over time or to compare different economies at the same time.

What's Special About the National Economy?

The national economy deserves special attention. Here's why. If you were to drive west on Interstate 10 in Texas, you would hardly notice crossing the state line into New Mexico. But if you took the Juarez exit south into Mexico, you would be stopped at the border, asked for identification, and possibly searched. You would be quite aware of crossing an international border. Like most countries, the United States and Mexico usually allow people and goods to move more freely *within* their borders than *across* their borders.

The differences between the United States and Mexico are far greater than the differences between Texas and New Mexico. For example, each country has its own standard of living and currency, its own culture and language, its own communication and transportation system, its own system of government, and its own "rules of the game"—that is, its own laws, regulations, customs, and conventions for conducting economic activity both within and across its borders.

Macroeconomics typically focuses on the performance of the national economy, including how the national economy interacts with other economies around the world. The U.S. economy is the largest and most complex in the world, with about 110 million households, 24 million businesses, and 87,400 separate government jurisdictions. The world economy includes more than 200 sovereign nations, ranging from tiny Liechtenstein, with a population of only 30,000, to China, with 1.3 billion people. These numbers offer snapshots of economic decision makers, but the economy is a moving picture, a work in progress—too complex to describe in snapshots. This is why we use theoretical models to simplify the key relationships. To help you get your mind around the economy, let's begin with a simple analogy.

The Human Body and the U.S. Economy

Consider the similarities and differences between the human body and the economy. The body consists of millions of cells, each performing particular functions yet each linked to the operation of the entire body. Similarly, the U.S. economy is composed of millions of economic decision makers, each acting with some independence yet each connected with the economy as a whole. The economy, like the body, is continually renewing itself, with new households, new businesses, a changing set of public officials, and new foreign competitors and customers. Blood circulates throughout the body, facilitating the exchange of oxygen and vital nutrients among cells. Similarly, *money* circulates throughout the economy, facilitating the exchange of resources and products among individual economic units. In fact, money is called a *medium of exchange*. Earlier we saw that the movement of money, products, and resources throughout the economy follows a *circular flow*, as does the movement of blood, oxygen, and nutrients, throughout the body.

Flow and Stock Variables. Just as the same blood recirculates as a medium of exchange in the body, the same dollars recirculate as a medium of exchange in the economy to finance transactions. The dollars you spend on croissants are spent by the baker on butter and then spent by the dairy farmer on work boots. Dollars *flow* through the economy. To measure a flow, we use a **flow variable,** which is an amount per period of time, such as your average spending per week or your heartbeats per minute. In contrast, a **stock variable** is an amount measured at a particular point in time, such as the amount of cash you have with you right now or your body weight this morning.

Testing New Theories. Physicians and other natural scientists can test theories using controlled experiments. Macroeconomists, however, have no laboratories and little ability to run experiments of any kind. Granted, they can study different economies throughout the world, but each economy is unique, so comparisons across countries are tricky. Controlled experiments also provide natural scientists with something seldom available to macroeconomists—the chance, or serendipitous, discovery (such as penicillin). But macroeconomists studying the U.S. economy have only one patient, so they can't introduce particular policies in a variety of ways. Cries of "Eureka!" are seldom heard from macroeconomists.

Knowledge and Performance

Throughout history, little was known about the human body, yet many enjoyed good health. For example, the fact that blood circulates in our bodies was not discovered until 1638; it took scientists another 150 years to figure out why. Similarly, over the millennia, various complex economies developed and flourished, although there was little understanding or even concern about how these economies worked.

The economy is much like the body: As long as it functions smoothly, policy makers need not understand how it works. But if a problem develops—severe unemployment, high inflation, or sluggish growth, for example—we must know how a healthy economy works before we can consider if and how the problem can be corrected. We need not know every detail of the economy, just as we need not know every detail of the body. But we must understand the essential relationships among key economic variables. For example, we would like to know the extent to which the economy is self-adjusting. Does the economy work well enough on its own, or does it often perform poorly? If the economy performs poorly, what policy options are available, and can we be sure that the proposed remedy won't do more harm than good?

When doctors did not understand how the human body works, their cures were often worse than the diseases. Much of the history of medicine describes misguided attempts to deal with maladies. Even today, medical care is based on less scientific evidence than you might think. According to one researcher, only one in seven medical interventions is supported by reliable scientific evidence.[1]

[1]Sherwin Nuland, "Medical Fads: Bran, Midwives and Leeches," *New York Times*, 25 January 1995.

Likewise, national policy makers have sometimes implemented the wrong economic prescription because of a flawed theory about how the economy works. At one time, for example, a nation's economic vitality was thought to spring from the stock of precious metals accumulated in the public treasury. This theory spawned a policy called **mercantilism,** which held that, as a way of accumulating gold and silver, a nation should sell more output to foreigners than it bought from them. To achieve this, nations restricted imports by such devices as tariffs and quotas. But these restrictions reduced international trade, thereby reducing the gains from specialization that arise from trade. Another flawed economic theory prompted President Herbert Hoover to introduce a major tax *increase* during the Great Depression. We have since learned that such a policy does more harm than good.

Let's turn now to the performance of the U.S. economy over time.

ECONOMIC FLUCTUATIONS AND GROWTH

The U.S. economy and other industrial market economies historically have experienced alternating periods of expansion and contraction in the level of economic activity. **Economic fluctuations** are the rise and fall of economic activity relative to the long-term growth trend of the economy. These fluctuations, or *business cycles,* vary in length and intensity, yet some features appear common to all. The ups and downs usually involve the entire nation and often the world, and they affect nearly all dimensions of economic activity, not simply employment and production.

NETBOOKMARK: JOSEPH HAIMOWITZ'S "THE LONGEVITY OF EXPANSIONS"

U.S. Economic Fluctuations

Perhaps the easiest way to understand economic fluctuations is to examine their components. During the 1920s and 1930s, Wesley C. Mitchell, director of the National Bureau of Economic Research (NBER), analyzed economic fluctuations, noting that the economy has two phases: periods of expansion and periods of contraction. Before World War II, a contraction might be so severe as to be called a **depression,** which is a sharp reduction in the nation's total production lasting more than a year and accompanied by high unemployment. A milder contraction is called a **recession,** which is a decline in total output lasting at least two consecutive quarters, or at least six months. The U.S. economy experienced both recessions and depressions before World War II. Since then, there have been recessions but no depressions, so things have gotten better.

Despite these ups and downs, the U.S. economy has grown dramatically over the long run. The economy in 2001 was more than 11 times larger than in 1929, as measured by *real gross domestic product,* or *real GDP.* With real GDP, the effects of changes in the economy's price level have been stripped away, so the remaining changes reflect real changes in the value of goods and services produced (more on this later). Production tends to increase over the long run because of (1) increases in the amount and quality of resources, especially labor and capital; (2) better technology; and (3) improvements in the *rules of the game* that facilitate production and exchange, such as property rights, patent laws, the legal system, and customs of the market.

Exhibit 1 shows such a long-term growth trend in real GDP as an upward-sloping straight line. Economic fluctuations reflect movements around this growth trend. A recession begins after the previous expansion has reached its *peak,* or high point, and continues until the economy reaches a *trough,* or low point. The period between a peak and trough is a *recession,* and the period between a trough and subsequent peak is an **expansion.** Note that expansions last longer than recessions, but the length of the full cycle varies.

Analysts at NBER have been able to track the U.S. economy back to 1854. Since then, the nation has experienced 31 full peak-to-trough fluctuations. No two have been exactly alike. The longest expansion began in the spring of 1991 and broke the record during the first quarter of 2001. The longest contraction lasted five and a half years from 1873 to 1879.

Output changes since 1929 appear in Exhibit 2, which shows the annual percentage change in real GDP, with declines in red and increases in blue. The big decline during the Great Depression of the early 1930s and the sharp jump during World War II stand in stark contrast. Growth has averaged 3.4 percent a year. Since 1948, the economy has completed nine full

EXHIBIT 1

Hypothetical Business Fluctuations

Business fluctuations reflect movements of economic activity around a trend line that shows long-term growth. A recession (shown in pink) begins after a previous expansion (shown in blue) has reached its peak and continues until the economy reaches a trough. An expansion begins when economic activity starts to increase and continues until the economy reaches a peak.

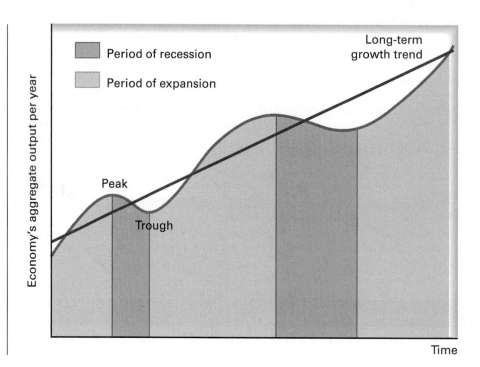

EXHIBIT 2

Annual Percentage Change in U.S. Real GDP from 1929 to 2001

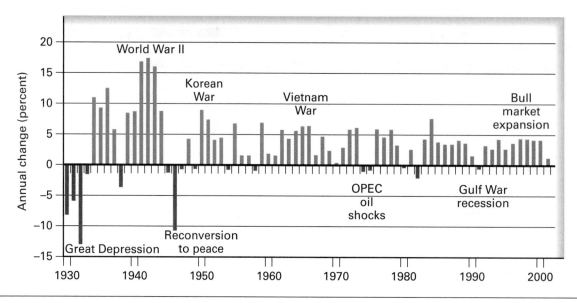

Source: "GDP and Other Major NIPA Series," *Survey of Current Business* 82 (August 2001). Figure for 2001 is projected as of September. For the latest data, go to http://www.bea.doc.gov/bea/pubs.htm.

cycles, with expansions averaging just under five years and recessions just under one year. Notice that recessions have been shorter and milder since 1948.

The intensity of the economic fluctuations varies from region to region across the United States. A recession hits hardest regions that produce durable goods, such as appliances, furniture, and automobiles, since the demand for these goods falls more during hard times than does the demand for other goods and services. Because of seasonal fluctuations and random disturbances, the economy does not move smoothly through phases of economic fluctuations. We cannot always distinguish at the time between temporary setbacks in economic activity and the beginning of a downturn. The drop in production in a particular quarter may result from a snowstorm or a poor harvest rather than mark the onset of a recession. Turning points—peaks and troughs—are thus identified by the NBER only after the fact. Since a recession means that output declines for at least two consecutive quarters, a recession is not so designated until at least six months after it begins.

As noted, fluctuations usually involve the entire nation. Indeed, economies around the world often move together. The following case study compares the year-to-year output change in the United States with another leading economy, the United Kingdom.

CASE**STUDY**	The Global Economy
	● *The World of Business*

Though economic fluctuations are not perfectly synchronized across countries, a link is often apparent. Consider the recent experience of two leading economies—the United States and the United Kingdom, economies separated by the Atlantic Ocean. Exhibit 3 shows for both economies the year-to-year percentage change since 1985 in total output—their real GDP. Again *real* means that the effects of inflation have been erased, so remaining changes reflect *real* changes in the total amount of goods and services produced.

If you spend a little time following the annual changes in each economy, you will see the similarities. For example, in 1991, U.S. real GDP declined, or had a negative growth rate, reflecting a recession. The United Kingdom also experienced a recession that year. Likewise, in both economies, growth in 1994 jumped to at least 4 percent and then slowed the following year.

One problem with the linkage across economies is that a slump in other major economies could worsen a recession in the United States, and vice versa. For example, there were fears in 2001 that difficulties in the top two economies in the world, the United States and Japan, would feed into each other, dragging other economies down with them. The terrorist attacks

EXHIBIT 3

U.S. and U.K. Growth Rates in Output Are Similar

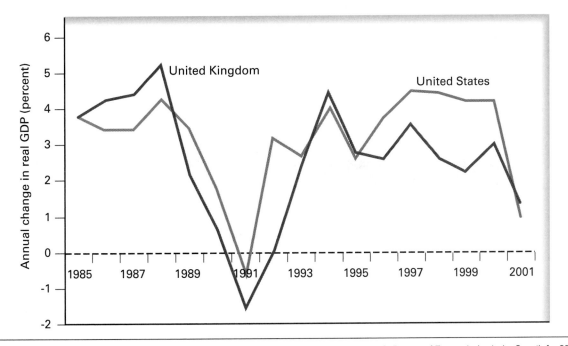

Source: Growth estimates from *OECD Economic Outlook* 69 (June 2001), Annex Table 1, and U.S. Bureau of Economic Analysis. Growth for 2001 estimated as of September. For the latest U.S. data, go to http://www.bea.doc.gov/bea/dn1.htm.

on the United States in September 2001 affected economies around the world, reducing airline travel and lowering stock prices.

Although year-to-year fluctuations in output are of interest, even more important to an economy's standard of living is its long-term growth trend. U.S. real GDP growth averaged 3.2 percent per year between 1985 and 2001 compared with 2.6 percent in the United Kingdom. This seemingly small difference compounded over the years to raise the level of real GDP much more in the United States. For example, if U.S. GDP had averaged only 2.6 percent growth since 1985, output by 2001 would have been $900 billion below that achieved with its 3.2 percent growth. This lower growth rate would have reduced U.S. production and income in 2001 by about $3,200 per capita, or $12,800 for a family of four. That would represent a significant cut in the U.S. standard of living.

Thus, even though the ups and downs of changing real GDP seemed similar across the two countries, Americans did relatively better because of the higher average growth rate here.

<interactive>exercise

eACTIVITY: THE GLOBAL ECONOMY

Sources: Edmund Andrews, "America's Economic Cloud Extends to Europe," *New York Times,* 28 September 2001; Michael Williams et al., "Japan Must Finish Its Stalled Reform," *Wall Street Journal,* 16 March 2001; "America's Economy: What a Peculiar Cycle," *Economist,* 8 March 2001; *Economic Report of the President,* January 2001; *OECD Economic Outlook* 69 (June 2001), Annex Table 1; and the Bureau of Economic Analysis Web site at http://www.bea.doc.gov/.

Leading Economic Indicators

Certain events foreshadow a turning point in economic activity. Months before a recession is fully under way, changes in these leading economic indicators point to the coming storm. In the early stages of a recession, business slows down, firms reduce overtime and new hiring, orders for machinery and computers slip, and the stock market, anticipating lower profits, turns down. Consumer confidence in the economy also begins to sag, so households spend less, especially on big-ticket items like automobiles and new homes, and unsold goods pile up. For example, the September 2001 terrorist attacks led to the biggest drop in consumer confidence in a decade.[2] All these activities are called **leading economic indicators** because they usually predict, or *lead to,* a downturn. Upturns in leading indicators point to an economic recovery. But leading indicators cannot predict precisely *when* a turning point will occur, or even whether one will occur. Sometimes the leading indicators sound a false alarm, and sometime output growth slows but does not actually decline.

Our introduction to economic fluctuations has been largely mechanical, focusing on the history and measurement of these fluctuations. We have not discussed why economies fluctuate, in part because such a discussion requires a firmer footing in macroeconomic theory and in part because the causes remain in dispute. In the next section, we begin to build a macroeconomic framework by introducing a key model of analysis.

<interactive>exercise

READING IT RIGHT: WALL STREET JOURNAL EXERCISE

<interactive>video

CNN VIDEO: "FOOD FOR FORECASTERS"

[2]Gregg Ip and Patrick Barta, "Consumer Confidence Index Takes Biggest Drop Since the Gulf War," *Wall Street Journal,* 26 September 2001.

AGGREGATE DEMAND AND AGGREGATE SUPPLY

The economy is so complex that we need to simplify, or to abstract from the millions of relationships, to isolate the important ones. We must step back from all the individual economic transactions to survey the resulting mosaic.

Aggregate Output and the Price Level

Let's begin our discussion with something you know. Picture a pizza. Got that? Now picture food more generally. Food, of course, includes not just pizza but thousands of other edibles. Although food is more general than pizza, you probably have no difficulty picturing food. Now make the leap from food to all goods and services produced in the economy—food, housing, clothing, entertainment, transportation, medical care, and so on. Economists call this **aggregate output.** Since *aggregate* means total, aggregate output is the total amount of goods and services produced in the economy during a given period. A unit of aggregate output is a composite measure of all output in the same sense that a unit of food is a composite measure of all food. The best measure of aggregate output is *real GDP.*

Just as we can talk about the demand for pizza, or the demand for food, we can talk about the demand for aggregate output. **Aggregate demand** is the relationship between the average price of aggregate output and the quantity of aggregate output demanded. The average price of aggregate output is called the **price level.** You are more familiar than you may think with these aggregate measures. Headlines refer to changes in the growth of aggregate output—as in "Growth Slows in Second Quarter." News accounts also report on changes in the "cost of living," reflecting movements in the economy's price level—as in "Prices Up Slightly in June."

In a later chapter, you will learn how the economy's price level is computed. All you need to know now is that the price level in any year is an *index number,* or reference number, comparing average prices that year to average prices in some base, or reference, year. If we say that the price level is higher, we mean compared with where it was. In Chapter 3, we talked about the price of a particular product, such as pizza, *relative to the prices of other products.* Now we talk about the *average price* of all goods and services produced in the economy *relative to the price level in some base year.*

The price level in the *base year* has a benchmark value of 100, and price levels in other years are expressed relative to the base-year price level. For example, in 2001, the U.S. price level, or price index, was 109, indicating that the price level that year was 9 percent higher than its value of 100 in the base year of 1996. The price level, or price index, is used not only to make comparisons in prices across time but also to make accurate comparisons of real aggregate output over time. Economists use a GDP *price index* to eliminate any year-to-year changes in GDP due solely to changes in the average price level. After this adjustment is made, remaining changes are simply changes in real output—the amount of goods and services produced. After adjusting GDP for price changes, we end up with what is called the **real gross domestic product, or real GDP.** So the price index (1) shows how the economy's general price level changes over time and (2) can be used to convert production in different years into dollars of constant purchasing power, so we can focus on real GDP. You will get a better idea of these two roles as we discuss the U.S. economy.

The Aggregate Demand Curve

In Chapter 3, you learned about the demand for a particular product. Now let's talk about the demand for our composite measure of output—aggregate output, or real GDP. The **aggregate demand curve** shows the relationship between the price level in the economy and the real GDP demanded, other things constant. Exhibit 4 shows a hypothetical aggregate demand curve, *AD.* The vertical axis measures an index of the economy's price level relative to a 1996 base-year price level of 100. The horizontal axis shows real GDP, which measures output in dollars of constant purchasing power (here we use 1996 prices).

The aggregate demand curve in Exhibit 4 reflects an inverse relationship between the price level in the economy and real GDP demanded. Aggregate demand sums demands of the four economic decision makers: households, firms, governments, and the rest of the world. As the price level increases, other things constant, households demand less housing and furniture, firms demand fewer trucks and tools, governments demand less computer software and military hardware, and the rest of the world demands less U.S. grain and U.S. aircraft.

The reasons behind this inverse relationship will be examined more closely in later chapters, but here's a quick summary. Real GDP demanded depends in part on household *wealth.* Some wealth is typically held in bank accounts and currency. An increase in the price level, other things constant, decreases the purchasing power of bank accounts and currency. Households

EXHIBIT 4

Aggregate Demand Curve

The quantity of output demanded is inversely related to the price level, other things constant. This inverse relationship is reflected by the aggregate demand curve *AD*.

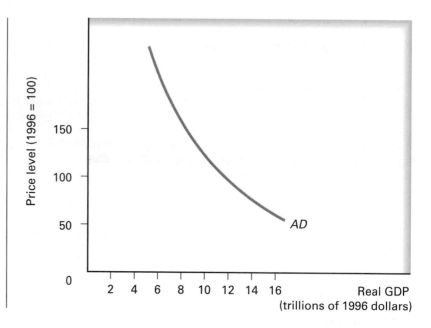

are therefore poorer when the price level increases, so the quantity of real GDP demanded decreases. Conversely, a reduction in the price level increases the purchasing power of bank accounts and currency. Because households are richer as the price level decreases, the quantity of real GDP demanded increases.

Among the factors held constant along a given aggregate demand curve are the price levels in other countries as well as the exchange rates between the U.S. dollar and foreign currencies. When the U.S. price level increases, U.S. products become more expensive relative to foreign products. Consequently, households, firms, and governments both here and abroad decrease the quantity of U.S. real GDP demanded. On the other hand, a lower U.S. price level makes U.S. goods relatively cheap compared with foreign goods, so the quantity of U.S. real GDP demanded increases.

<interactive>video

CNN VIDEO: "CONSUMER TALES"

The Aggregate Supply Curve

The **aggregate supply curve** shows how much output U.S. producers are willing and able to supply at each price level, other things constant. How does the quantity supplied respond to changes in the price level? The upward-sloping aggregate supply curve *AS* in Exhibit 5 shows a positive relationship between the price level and the quantity of aggregate output that producers supply, other factors remaining constant. Assumed constant along an aggregate supply curve are (1) resource prices, (2) the state of technology, and (3) the rules of the game that provide production incentives, such as patent and copyright laws. Wage rates are typically assumed to be constant along the aggregate supply curve. With wages constant, firms find a higher price level more profitable, so they increase real GDP supplied. *Whenever the prices firms receive rise faster than the cost of production, firms find it profitable to expand output, so real GDP supplied varies directly with the economy's price level.*

Equilibrium

The intersection of the aggregate demand curve and aggregate supply curve determines the equilibrium levels of price and real GDP in the economy. Exhibit 5 is a rough depiction of aggregate demand and supply in 2001. Equilibrium real GDP in 2001 was about $9.3 trillion

EXHIBIT 5

Aggregate Demand and Supply

The total output of the economy and its price level are determined at the intersection of the aggregate demand and aggregate supply curves. The equilibrium reflects real GDP and the price level for 2001, using 1996 as the base year.

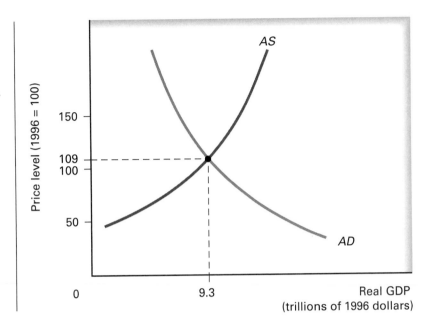

(measured in dollars of 1996 purchasing power). The equilibrium price level in 2001 was 109 (compared with a price level of 100 in the base year of 1996). At any other price level, quantity demanded would not match quantity supplied.

Incidentally, although employment is not measured directly along the horizontal axis, firms usually must hire more workers to produce more output. So higher levels of real GDP can be beneficial because (1) more goods and services are available in the economy, and (2) more people are employed.

Perhaps the best way to understand aggregate demand and aggregate supply is to apply these tools to the U.S. economy. In the following section we simplify U.S. economic history to review changes in the price and output levels over time.

A SHORT HISTORY OF THE U.S. ECONOMY

The history of the U.S. economy can be crudely divided into four economic eras: (1) before and during the Great Depression, (2) after the Great Depression to the early 1970s, (3) from the early 1970s to the early 1980s, and (4) since the early 1980s. The first era was marked by recessions and depressions, culminating in the Great Depression of the 1930s. These depressions were often accompanied by a falling price level. The second era was one of generally strong economic growth, with only moderate increases in the price level. The third era saw episodes of both high unemployment and high inflation. And the fourth era was more like the second, with good economic growth on average and only moderate increases in the price level.

The Great Depression and Before

Before World War II, the U.S. economy alternated between periods of prosperity and periods of sharp economic decline. As noted earlier, the longest contraction on record occurred between 1873 and 1879, when 80 railroads went bankrupt and most of the steel industry was shut down. During the depression of the 1890s, the unemployment rate topped 18 percent. In October 1929, the stock market crashed, beginning what was to become the deepest, though not the longest, economic contraction in our nation's history, the Great Depression of the 1930s.

In terms of aggregate demand and aggregate supply, the Great Depression can be viewed as a shift to the left of the aggregate demand curve, as shown in Exhibit 6. AD_{1929} is the aggregate demand curve in 1929, before the onset of the depression. Real GDP in 1929 was $822 billion (measured in dollars of 1996 purchasing power), and the price level was 12.6 (relative

EXHIBIT 6

The Decrease in Aggregate Demand Between 1929 and 1933

The Great Depression of the 1930s can be represented by a shift to the left of the aggregate demand curve, from AD_{1929} to AD_{1933}. In the resulting depression, real GDP fell from $822 billion to $603 billion, and the price level dropped from 12.6 to 9.3.

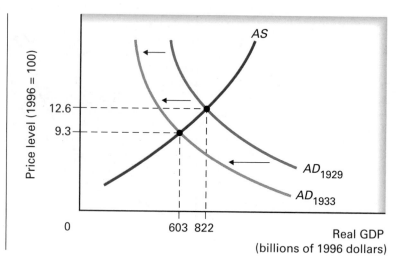

to a 1996 base-year price level of 100). By 1933, aggregate demand had shifted leftward, decreasing to AD_{1933}.[3] Why did aggregate demand decline so much? Though the causes are still debated, the stock market crash of 1929, grim business expectations, a drop in consumer spending, widespread bank failures, a sharp decline in the nation's money supply, and severe restrictions on world trade all contributed to the drop in aggregate demand.

Because of the decline in aggregate demand, both the price level and real GDP dropped. Real GDP fell 27 percent, from $822 billion in 1929 to $603 billion in 1933, and the price level fell 26 percent, from 12.6 to 9.3. As real GDP declined, the unemployment rate soared, climbing from about only 3 percent in 1929 to 25 percent in 1933, the highest U.S. rate ever recorded.

Before the Great Depression, macroeconomic policy was based primarily on the *laissez-faire* philosophy of Adam Smith. Smith, you may recall, argued in his book *The Wealth of Nations* that if people were allowed to pursue their self-interest in free markets, resources would be guided as if by an "invisible hand" to produce the greatest, most efficient level of aggregate output. Although the U.S. economy had suffered several sharp contractions since the beginning of the 19th century, most economists of the day viewed these as a natural phase of the economy—unfortunate but ultimately therapeutic and essentially *self-correcting*.

The Age of Keynes: After the Great Depression to the Early 1970s

The Great Depression was so severe that it stimulated new thinking about how the economy worked (or didn't work). In 1936, John Maynard Keynes (1883–1946) published *The General Theory of Employment, Interest, and Money*, the most famous economics book of the 20th century. In it, Keynes argued that aggregate demand was inherently unstable, in part because investment decisions were often guided by the unpredictable "animal spirits" of business expectations. If businesses grew pessimistic about the economy, they would cut investment spending, which would reduce aggregate demand, output, and employment. For example, investment dropped more than 80 percent between 1929 and 1933. Keynes saw no natural market forces operating to ensure that the economy, even if allowed a reasonable time to adjust, would return to a higher level of output and employment.

Keynes proposed that the government jolt the economy out of its depression by increasing aggregate demand. He recommended an *expansionary fiscal policy* to deal with contractions. The government could achieve this stimulus directly by increasing its own spending, or indirectly by cutting taxes to stimulate the primary components of private-sector demand, consumption and investment. But either action could create a federal budget deficit. A **federal budget deficit** is a flow variable that measures, for a particular period, the amount by which total federal outlays exceed total federal revenues.

---

[3]The aggregate supply curve probably also shifted somewhat during this period, but for simplicity, we assume it was unchanged. Most economists agree that the shift in the aggregate demand curve was the dominant factor.

To understand what Keynes had in mind, imagine federal budget policies that would increase aggregate demand in Exhibit 6, shifting the aggregate demand curve to the right, back to its original position. Such a shift would raise equilibrium real GDP, which would increase employment. According to the Keynesian prescription, the miracle drug of government fiscal policy—changes in government spending and taxes—was needed to compensate for what he viewed as the inherent instability of private spending, especially investment. If demand in the private sector declined, Keynes said the government should pick up the slack. We can think of the Keynesian approach as **demand-side economics** because it focused on how changes in aggregate demand could promote full employment. Keynes argued that government stimulus could shock the economy out of its depression and back to health. Once investment returned to normal levels, the government stimulus would no longer be necessary.

The U.S. economy bounced back some during the second half of the 1930s (see Exhibit 2); then World War II broke out, boosting war-related demand for tanks, ships, aircraft, and the like. This increased output and employment, seeming to confirm the powerful impact that government spending could have on the economy. The increase in government spending, with no increase in tax rates, created federal deficits during the war. Immediately after the war, memories of the Great Depression were still vivid. Trying to avoid another depression, Congress approved the *Employment Act of 1946,* which imposed a clear responsibility on the federal government to foster, in the language of the act, "maximum employment, production, and purchasing power." The act also required the president to report annually on the state of the economy and to appoint a *Council of Economic Advisers,* a three-member group of economists, with a professional staff, to provide the president with economic advice.

The economy seemed to prosper during the 1950s largely without the added stimulus of fiscal policy. The 1960s, however, proved to be the *golden age of Keynesian economics,* a period when fiscal policy makers thought they could "fine-tune" the economy to avoid recessions—just as a mechanic fine-tunes a racecar to achieve top performance. During the early 1960s, nearly all advanced economies around the world enjoyed low unemployment and healthy growth in output with only modest **inflation,** which is a sustained increase in the price level. In short, the world economy was booming, and the U.S. economy was on top of the world.

The economy was on such a roll that toward the end of the 1960s some economists began to think the business cycle was history. As a sign of the times, the federal government changed the name of its publication *Business Cycle Developments* to *Business Conditions Digest.* In the early 1970s, however, fluctuations returned with a fury. Worse yet, the problem of recession was compounded by inflation, which increased during the recessions of 1974–1975 and 1979–1980. Until then, inflation was limited primarily to periods of expansion. Confidence in demand-side policies was shaken, and the expression "fine-tuning" disappeared from economists' vocabularies. What ended the golden age of Keynesian economics?

<interactive>video

ASK THE INSTRUCTOR: IS ONE TYPE OF INFLATION WORSE THAN ANOTHER?

The Great Stagflation: 1973 to 1980

During the late 1960s, federal spending increased on both the war in Vietnam and social programs at home. This combined stimulus increased aggregate demand enough that in 1968 the *inflation rate,* the annual percentage increase in the price level, jumped to 4.4 percent, after averaging only 2.0 percent during the previous decade. Inflation climbed to 4.7 percent in 1969 and to 5.3 percent in 1970. These rates were so alarming that in 1971, President Richard Nixon introduced measures aimed at putting a ceiling on prices and wages.

The ceiling was eliminated in 1973, about the time that crop failures around the world caused grain prices to climb. To compound these problems, the Organization of Petroleum Exporting Countries (OPEC) cut its supply of oil, thus increasing the world price of oil. Decreases in the supplies of grain and oil reduced aggregate supply in the economy. This reduction in aggregate supply, shown in Exhibit 7 by the leftward shift of the aggregate supply curve from AS_{1973} to AS_{1975}, created the **stagflation** of the 1970s, meaning a *stag*nation, or a contraction, in the economy's aggregate output combined with in*flation,* or a rise, in the economy's price level. Real GDP declined by about $40 billion a year between 1973 and 1975, while the price level jumped nearly 20 percent. The unemployment rate climbed from 4.9 percent in 1973 to 8.5 percent in 1975. You could think of stagflation as higher unemployment and higher inflation.

EXHIBIT 7

Stagflation Between 1973 and 1975

The stagflation of the mid-1970s can be represented as a reduction in aggregate supply from AS_{1973} to AS_{1975}. Aggregate output fell from $4.12 trillion to $4.08 trillion (stagnation), and the price level rose from 33.6 to 40.0 (inflation).

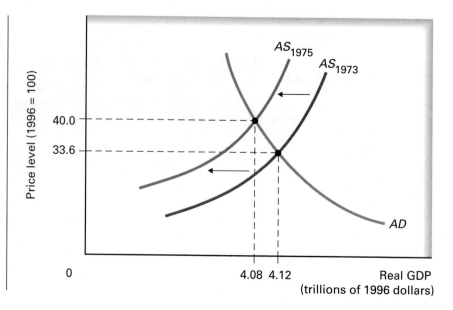

Stagflation occurred again at the end of 1980, fueled partly by another OPEC boost in oil prices. Between 1979 and 1980, real GDP declined and the price level increased by 9.2 percent. Macroeconomics has not been the same since. Because the problem of stagflation was primarily on the supply side, not on the demand side, the demand-management prescriptions of Keynes seemed ineffective. Government increasing aggregate demand might reduce unemployment but would worsen inflation.

Experience Since 1980

Increasing aggregate supply seemed an appropriate way to combat stagflation, for such a move would both lower the price level and increase output and employment. Attention therefore turned from aggregate demand to aggregate supply. A key idea behind **supply-side economics** was that the federal government, by lowering tax rates, would increase after-tax earnings, which would provide incentives to increase the supply of labor and other resources. According to advocates of the supply-side approach, the resulting increase in aggregate supply would achieve the happy result of expanding real GDP and reducing the price level. But this was easier said than done.

In 1981, to provide economic incentives and thereby increase aggregate supply, President Ronald Reagan and Congress cut personal income tax rates by an average of 23 percent to be phased in over three years. Their hope was that aggregate output would increase enough so that the lower tax rate would actually result in more tax revenue. Put another way, they believed the tax cuts would stimulate economic growth enough that the government's smaller share of a bigger pie would exceed what had been its larger share of a smaller pie.

But before the tax cut was fully implemented, recession hit in 1982, and the unemployment rate shot up to 10 percent. After the recession, the economy began what at the time was the longest peacetime expansion on record. During the rest of the 1980s, output grew, unemployment declined, and inflation remained relatively low. But the growth in federal spending exceeded the growth in federal tax revenues during this period, so federal budget deficits swelled.

Deficits worsened with the onset of a recession in 1990. Even though that recession officially ended in March 1991, the deficit continued to grow, topping $290 billion in 1992. Annual deficits accumulated as a huge federal debt. **Government debt** is a stock variable that measures the net accumulation of prior deficits. Measured relative to GDP, the federal debt nearly doubled from 33 percent in 1980 to 64 percent in 1992.

During the 1990s, policy makers began to worry more about huge federal deficits. To reduce them, President George H. W. Bush increased taxes in 1990, President William Clinton increased taxes on the rich in 1993, and a newly elected Republican Congress reduced federal spending growth beginning in 1995. Higher tax rates and a slower growth in federal spending combined with an improving economy to reduce federal deficits. By 1998, the federal budget yielded a surplus. By early 2001, the U.S. economic expansion became the longest on record, a stretch during which 22 million jobs were added, the unemployment rate dropped from 7.5 percent to 4.2 percent, and inflation remained low. But after achieving this record, the economy softened in 2001. Job losses accelerated after the terrorist attacks of September 2001, adding to a recession, which began in March of 2001.

We close this chapter with a case study that summarizes price and output movements for the period covered during our brief history of the U.S. economy.

CASE**STUDY**	Seven Decades of Real GDP and Price Levels
	● *Public Policy*

Exhibit 8 traces the U.S. real GDP and price level since 1929. Aggregate demand and aggregate supply curves are shown as an example for 2001, but all points in the series reflect such intersections. Years of growing GDP are indicated as blue points and years of declining GDP as red ones. Despite the Great Depression of the 1930s and eight recessions after World War II, the long-term trend of economic growth is unmistakable. Real GDP, measured along the horizontal axis in 1996 constant dollars, grew from $0.8 trillion in 1929 to $9.3 trillion in 2001—more than an 11-fold increase and an average annual growth rate of 3.4 percent. The price level also rose, but not as much, rising from only 12.6 in 1929 to 109.2 in 2001—more than an 8-fold increase and an average inflation rate of 3.0 percent per year.

Because the U.S. population is growing all the time, the economy must create new jobs just to employ the additional people looking for work. For example, the U.S. population grew from 122 million in 1929 to 284 million in 2001, a rise of 133 percent. Fortunately, employment grew even faster, from 47 million in 1929 to 135 million in 2001, for a growth of 187 percent. So during the last seven decades, employment grew more than enough to keep up with a growing population. The United States has been an impressive job machine, creating more jobs than any other economy in the world.

EXHIBIT 8

Tracking U.S. Real GDP and Price Level Since 1929

As you can see, both real GDP and the price level increased since 1929. Blue points indicate years of growing real GDP, and red points are years of declining real GDP. Real GDP in 2001 was more than 11 times greater than it was in 1929, and the price level was more than 8 times greater.

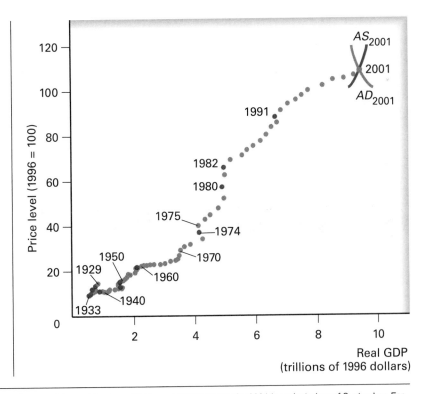

Source: Developed from data in *Survey of Current Business* 82 (August 2001). Figure for 2001 is projected as of September. For the latest data, go to http://www.bea.doc.gov/bea/pubs.htm.

Chapter 20 Introduction to Macroeconomics

Not only did the number of workers more than double, but workers' average level of education increased as well. Employment of other resources, especially capital, also rose sharply. What's more, the level of technology improved steadily, thanks to breakthroughs like the computer chip. The availability of more and higher-quality human capital and physical capital increased the productivity of each worker, contributing to the 11-fold jump in real GDP since 1929.

Real GDP is important, but the best measure of the average standard of living in an economy is **real GDP per capita,** which tells us how much an economy produces on average per resident. Because real GDP grew much faster than the population since 1929, real GDP *per capita* jumped fivefold from $6,740 in 1929 to about $34,000 in 2001. The United States is the largest economy in the world and has been the leader in real GDP per capita. We will examine U.S. productivity and growth more closely in the next chapter.

\<interactive\>exercise

eACTIVITY: SEVEN DECADES OF REAL GDP AND PRICE LEVELS

Source: "National Income and Product Account Tables," *Survey of Current Business* 81 (August 2001); *Economic Report of the President,* January 2001; *Economic Report of the President,* January 1980; and *OECD Economic Outlook* 69 (June 2001). For the latest real GDP and price level data, go to http://www.bea.doc.gov/bea/pubs.htm.

CONCLUSION

Because macroeconomists have no test subjects and cannot rely on serendipitous discoveries, they hone their craft by developing models of the economy and then observing the economy's performance for evidence to support or reject these models. In this sense, macroeconomics is largely retrospective, always looking at recent history for hints about which model works best. The macroeconomist is like a traveler who can only view the road behind and must find the way using a collection of poorly drawn maps. The traveler must continually check each map (or model) against the landmarks passed to see whether one map appears more consistent with the terrain than the others. Each new batch of information about the economy causes macroeconomists to shuffle through their "maps" to reevaluate their models.

Different economists may have different interpretations of the events discussed in this chapter. At this point, there is no dominant macroeconomic theory about how the economy works. Some books lay out the competing theories, leaving it to the reader to choose sides. Rather than describe each theory of the economy in detail, this book will attempt to integrate theories whenever possible to find common ground.

Macroeconomics often emphasizes what can go wrong with the economy. Problems associated with faltering economic growth, high unemployment, and rising inflation capture much of the attention. In the next chapter, we consider in greater detail the record of economic growth in the United States. In a subsequent chapter, we discuss two potential problems confronting the economy: unemployment and inflation. Our approach to growth, unemployment, and inflation at this stage will be more descriptive than prescriptive. We must understand how a healthy economy operates before we can consider remedial policies when the economy stalls.

Take the Post-Test to assess your overall understanding of the key ideas in this chapter. The Post-Test provides a comprehensive selection of exam-style questions addressing the main topics and concepts of the chapter. At the completion of each Post-Test, you will receive a score and instructive feedback on how you answered each question, and a direct link to the part of the chapter addressed in the question. Take the Post-Test as often as you need to—a record of your progress for each attempt is kept for you to revisit and gauge your improvement. And each Post-Test is randomly generated, so every attempt is new.

Post-Test

endofchaptermaterial

- **Summary**
- **Questions for Review**
- **Problems and Exercises**

- **Experiential Exercises**
- **Wall Street Journal Exercise**

21

Productivity and Growth

Why is the average standard of living so much higher in some countries than in others? What's needed to raise the standard of living? Why is the economy's long-term growth rate more important than short-term fluctuations in economic activity? What's labor productivity and why has it grown faster in recent years? What's the impact of that surge on your standard of living? Answers to these and other questions are addressed in this chapter, which focuses on arguably the most important criteria for judging an economy's performance—productivity and growth.

The single most important determinant of a nation's standard of living over the long run is the productivity of its resources. A nation prospers by getting more from its resources. Even a relatively small growth in productivity can, if sustained for years, have a profound effect on the average living standard—that is, on the average availability of goods and services per capita. Growing productivity is therefore critical to a rising standard of living and has kept the U.S. ahead of every other nation on Earth.

Economic growth is a complicated process, one that economists do not yet fully understand. Since before Adam Smith inquired into the *Wealth of Nations*, economists have puzzled over what makes some economies prosper while others founder. Because a market economy is not the product of conscious design, it does not reveal its secrets readily, nor can it be easily manipulated in pursuit of growth. We can't simply push here and pull there to achieve the desired result. Changing the economy is not like remodeling a home by knocking out a wall and adding on to the kitchen. Because we have no clear blueprint of the economy, we cannot make changes to specifications.

Still, there is much that is known. In this chapter, we first develop a few simple models to examine productivity and growth. Then we use these models to help explain why some nations are rich and some poor. U.S. performance gets special attention, particularly compared with other major economies around the world. We close with some current issues of technology and growth. Topics discussed in this chapter include:

- Labor productivity
- Worlds apart
- U.S. productivity and growth

- Technological change and unemployment
- Research and development
- Convergence

\<interactive\>exercise

ECONDEBATE ONLINE: PRODUCTIVITY AND GROWTH

\<interactive\>update

- ECONDATA ONLINE: PRODUCTIVITY AND GROWTH
- ECONLINKS ONLINE: ECONOMICS WEB LINKS
- ECONNEWS ONLINE: PRODUCTIVITY AND GROWTH

THEORY OF PRODUCTIVITY AND GROWTH

Two centuries ago, most Americans worked in agriculture, where the hours were long and rewards unpredictable. Others had it no better, toiling from sunrise to sunset for a wage that bought just the bare necessities. People had little intellectual stimulation and little contact with the outside world. A typical worker's home in 1800 was described as follows: "Sand sprinkled on the floor did duty as a carpet. . . . What a stove was he did not know. Coal he had never seen. Matches he had never heard of. . . . He rarely tasted fresh meat. . . . If the food of an artisan would now be thought coarse, his clothes would be thought abominable."[1]

Over the last two centuries, there has been an incredible increase in the U.S. *standard of living* as measured by the amount of goods and services available on average per person. An economy's standard of living grows over the long run because of (1) increases in the amount and quality of resources, especially labor and capital, (2) better technology, and (3) improvements in the *rules of the game* that facilitate production and exchange, such as tax laws, property rights, patent laws, the legal system, and customs of the market. Perhaps the easiest way to introduce the idea of economic growth is by beginning with something you have already read about, the production possibilities frontier.

Growth and the Production Possibilities Frontier

The *production possibilities frontier,* or *PPF,* first introduced in Chapter 2, shows alternative combinations of goods that the economy can produce if available resources are used efficiently. Let's briefly review the assumptions made in developing the frontier shown in Exhibit 1. During the period under consideration, usually a year, the quantity of resources in the economy and the level of technology are assumed to be fixed. Although not mentioned in Chapter 2, also assumed fixed during the period are the rules of the game that facilitate production and exchange. We classify all production into two broad categories—in this case, consumer goods

[1]E. L. Bogart, *The Economic History of the United States* (New York: Longmans, Green, and Co., 1912), pp. 157–158.

and capital goods. Capital goods are used to produce other goods. For example, the economy can make pizzas and pizza ovens. Pizzas are consumer goods and ovens are capital goods.

When resources are employed efficiently, the production possibilities frontier *CI* in each panel of Exhibit 1 shows the possible combinations of consumer goods and capital goods that can be produced in a given year. Point *C* depicts the quantity of consumer goods produced if all the economy's resources are employed efficiently to produce them. Point *I* depicts the same for capital goods. Points inside the frontier show inefficient combinations, and points outside the frontier are unattainable, given the resources, technology, and rules of the game. The production possibilities frontier is bowed out because resources are not perfectly adaptable to the production of both goods; some resources are specialized.

Economic growth is an outward shift of the production possibilities frontier, as shown in each panel of Exhibit 1. What can cause this growth? Any increase in the availability of resources, such as a growth in the labor supply or the capital stock, shifts the frontier outward. Labor can increase either because the population increases or because the existing population supplies more labor. The capital stock expands if the economy produces more capital goods this year. The more capital goods produced this year, the more the economy grows, as reflected by an outward shift in the production frontier.

Any improvement in technology also expands the frontier by making more efficient use of existing resources. Technological change often improves the quality of capital, but it can enhance the productivity of any resource. Finally, any improvement in the rules of the game that nurtures production and exchange promotes growth and expands the frontier. For example, the economy can grow as a result of a patent law revision that encourages more inventions or legal reforms that reduce transaction costs. Thus, *the economy grows because of a greater availability of resources, an improvement in the quality of resources, technological change that makes better use of resources, or improvements in the rules of the game that enhance production.*

The amount of capital produced this year will affect the location of the PPF next year. For example, in panel (a) of Exhibit 1, the economy has chosen point *A* from possible points along *CI.* The capital produced this year shifts the PPF from *CI* this year out to *C'I'* next year. But if more capital goods are produced this year, as reflected by point *B* in panel (b), the PPF will shift outward farther next year, to *C"I"* .

An economy that produces more capital this year is said to *invest* more in capital. As you can see, to invest more, people must give up some consumer goods. Thus, the opportunity cost of more capital is having fewer consumer goods available. More generally, we can say that people in the economy must *save* more now—that is, forgo some current consumption—to invest in capital. Investment cannot occur without saving, which is forgoing some current consumption. Economies that save more can invest more, as we'll see later. First, let's get back to production.

EXHIBIT 1

Economic Growth Shown by Shifts Outward in the Production Possibilities Frontier

An economy that produces more capital goods will grow more, as reflected by a shifting outward of the production possibilities frontier. More capital goods and fewer consumer goods are produced in panel (b) than in panel (a), so the PPF shifts outward more in panel (b).

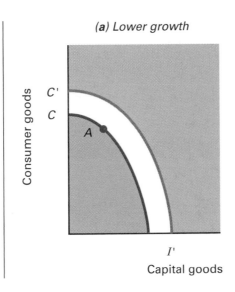

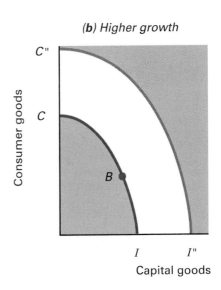

What Is Productivity?

Production is a process that transforms resources into products. Resources coupled with technology produce output. Productivity measures how efficiently resources are employed. In simplest terms, the greater the productivity, the more goods and services can be produced from a given amount of resources, and the farther out will be the production possibilities frontier. Economies that use resources more efficiently create a higher standard of living, meaning that more goods and services are produced per capita.

Productivity is defined as the ratio of total output to a specific measure of input. It usually reflects an average, expressing total output divided by the amount of a particular kind of resource employed. For example, **labor productivity** is the output per unit of labor and measures total output divided by the hours of labor employed to produce that output.

We can talk about the productivity of any resource, such as labor, capital, or land. When agriculture produced made up the bulk of output in the economy, land productivity, or bushels of grain per acre, was a key measure of economic welfare. Where soil was rocky and barren, people were less prosperous than where soil was fertile and fruitful. Even today, in many countries around the world, soil productivity determines the standard of living.

Industrialization and trade, however, have liberated many economies from dependence on soil fertility. Today some of the world's most productive economies have relatively little land or have land of poor fertility. For example, Japan has a relatively high living standard even though its population, which is nearly half that of the United States, lives on a land area that is only 4 percent of the U.S. land area.

<interactive>**update**

ECONNEWS ONLINE: INFLATIONARY PRODUCTIVITY SLOWDOWN?

Labor Productivity

Labor is the resource most commonly used to measure productivity. Why labor? First, it accounts for a relatively large share of the cost of production—about 70 percent on average. Second, labor is more easily measured than other inputs, whether we speak of hours per week or full-time workers per year. Statistics about employment and hours worked are more readily available and more reliable than those about other resources used.

But the resource most responsible for increasing labor productivity is capital. As introduced in Chapter 1, the two broad categories of capital are human capital and physical capital. *Human capital* is the accumulated knowledge, skill, and experience of the labor force. As individual workers acquire more human capital, their productivity and their incomes grow. That's why surgeons earn more than butchers and accountants earn more than file clerks. You are reading this book right now to enhance your human capital. *Physical capital* includes the machines, buildings, roads, airports, communication networks, and other manufactured creations used to produce goods and services. Think about the difference between digging a ditch with your bare hands and digging it with a shovel. Now compare that shovel to a backhoe. More physical capital obviously makes a digger more productive.

As an economy accumulates more capital per worker, labor productivity increases and the standard of living grows. The most productive combination of all is human capital combined with physical capital. For example, one certified public accountant with a computer and specialized software can sort out a company's finances more quickly and more accurately than can a thousand high-school-educated file clerks with pencils and paper.

<interactive>**update**

- **ECONDATA ONLINE: LABOR PRODUCTIVITY**
- **ECONNEWS ONLINE: PRODUCTIVITY GAINS**

The Per-Worker Production Function

We can express the relationship between the amount of capital per worker and the output per worker as an economy's **per-worker production function.** Exhibit 2 shows the relationship between the amount of capital per worker, measured along the horizontal axis, and average

EXHIBIT 2

Per-Worker Production Function

The per-worker production function, *PF,* shows a direct relationship between the amount of capital per worker, *k,* and the output per worker, *y.* The bowed shape of *PF* reflects the law of diminishing marginal returns.

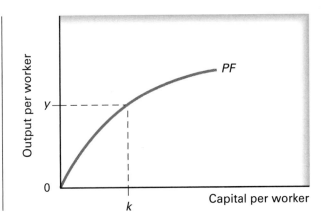

output per worker, or labor productivity, measured along the vertical axis, other things constant—including the level of technology and rules of the game. Any point on the production function, *PF,* shows how much output per worker can be produced for a given amount of capital per worker. For example, when there are *k* units of capital per worker, average output per worker in the economy is *y.* The curve slopes upward from left to right because an increase in capital per worker helps each worker produce more output. For example, a bigger truck makes the driver more productive.

As the quantity of capital per worker increases, output per worker increases as well but at a diminishing rate, as reflected by the shape of the per-worker production function. The diminishing slope of this curve reflects the *law of diminishing marginal returns,* which when applied to capital says that the more capital per worker there is already, the less additional output can be gained by increasing capital stock per worker still more. For example, adding to the size and number of trucks at a shipping company initially increases the productivity of drivers. Once all drivers have big trucks, however, additional trucks add little to total output. Thus, given the supply of other resources, the level of technology, and the rules of the game, additional gains from more capital eventually diminish. An increase in the amount of capital per worker is called **capital deepening** and is one source of rising productivity. *Capital deepening contributes to labor productivity and economic growth.*

Held constant along a per-worker production function is the level of technology in the economy. Technological change usually improves the *quality* of capital and represents another source of increased productivity. For example, a tractor is more efficient than a horse-drawn plow, a word processor more efficient than a typewriter, and an Excel spreadsheet more efficient than a pencil and paper. Better technology is reflected in Exhibit 3 by an upward rotation in the per-worker production function from *PF* to *PF'.* As a result of a technological breakthrough, more output is produced at each level of capital per worker. For example, if there are *k* units of capital per worker, the improvement in technology increases the output per worker in the economy from *y* to *y'.*

Simon Kuznets, who won a Nobel Prize in part for his analysis of economic growth, claimed that technological change and the ability to apply such breakthroughs to all aspects of production were the driving forces behind modern economic growth in industrial market economies. Kuznets argued that changes in the *quantities* of labor and capital account for only one-tenth of the increase in economic growth. Nine-tenths results from improvements in the *quality* of inputs. As technological breakthroughs become *embodied* in new capital, resources are combined in more efficient ways, so total output increases. *From the wheel to the assembly-line robot, capital embodies the fruits of scientific inquiry and serves as the primary engine for economic growth.*

Thus, two kinds of changes in capital improve worker productivity: (1) an increase in the *quantity* of capital per worker, as reflected by a movement along the per-worker production function, and (2) an improvement in the *quality* of capital per worker, as reflected by technological change that rotates the curve upward. More capital per worker and better capital per worker result in more output per worker, which, over time, usually translates into more output per capita, meaning a higher standard of living.

EXHIBIT 3

Impact of a Technological Breakthrough on the Per-Worker Production Function

A technological break-through increases output per worker at each level of capital per worker. Better technology makes workers more productive.

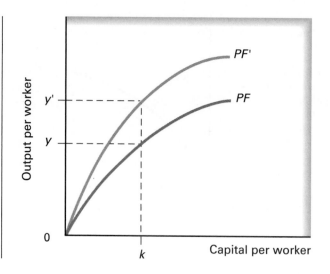

<interactive>update

ECONNEWS ONLINE: PLEASING PRODUCTIVITY PATH

Rules of the Game

Perhaps the most elusive ingredients for productivity and growth are the **rules of the game,** the formal and informal institutions that promote economic activity: the laws, customs, conventions, and other institutional elements that encourage people to undertake productive activity. A stable political environment and system of well-defined property rights are important. Little investment will occur if potential investors believe their capital might be appropriated by government, stolen by thieves, destroyed by civil unrest, or blown up by terrorists. Improvements in the rules of the game could result in more output for each level of capital per worker, thus reflected in a rotation up in the per-worker production function. Simply put, a more stable political climate could have a similar beneficial effect on productivity as a technological improvement. Conversely, events that foster instability can harm an economy's productivity and rotate the per-worker production function downward. The terrorist attack of the World Trade Center was such a destabilizing event. According to Albert Abadie, a Harvard economist, the attack affected "the spinal cord of any favorable business environment"—the ability of business and workers "to meet and communicate effectively without incurring risks."[2]

Now that you have some idea about the theory of productivity and growth, let's look at them in practice, beginning with the vast difference in performance among economies around the world and then focusing on the United States.

<interactive>exercise

READING IT RIGHT: WALL STREET JOURNAL EXERCISE

PRODUCTIVITY AND GROWTH IN PRACTICE

Differences in the standard of living among countries are profound. To give you some idea, per capita output in the United States, the world leader, is more than 50 times that of the world's poorest countries. With only 5 percent of the world's population, the United States

---

[2]As quoted in Greg Ip and John McKinnon, "Economy Likely Won't See Gain from War Against Terrorism," *Wall Street Journal,* 25 September 2001.

produces more than all the nations comprising the bottom 50 percent of the world's population put together. At the risk of appearing simplistic, we might say that poor countries are poor because they experience low labor productivity. We can sort the world's economies into two broad groups. **Industrial market countries,** or *developed countries,* make up about 20 percent of the world's population. They consist of the economically advanced capitalist countries of Western Europe, North America, Australia, New Zealand, and Japan. Industrial market countries were the first to experience long-term economic growth during the 19th century, and today they have the world's highest standard of living based on abundant human and physical capital. The rest of the world, the remaining 80 percent of the population, consists of **developing countries,** which have a lower standard of living because of relatively less human and physical capital. Developing countries are also known as *third-world countries.* On average, more than half the workers in developing countries are in agriculture. Because farming methods there are relatively primitive, labor productivity is low and most people barely subsist, much like Americans in the early 19th century.

<interactive>update

ECONNEWS ONLINE: PRODUCTIVITY SLACKENS

Education and Economic Development

Another important source of productivity is the quality of labor—the skill, experience, and education of workers. If knowledge is lacking, other resources may not be used efficiently. For example, a country may be endowed with fertile land, but farmers may lack knowledge of irrigation and fertilization techniques. Or farmers may not know how to rotate crops and avoid soil depletion. What exactly is the contribution of education to the process of economic development? Education makes workers aware of the latest production techniques and more receptive to new ideas and methods. Countries with the most advanced educational systems were also the first to develop. The importance of education in Japan during the 19th century contributed to a ready acceptance of technology and thus to Japan's remarkable economic growth in the 20th century. America led the world in education during the last century and is today the world's premier economy.

Exhibit 4 shows the average years of schooling of the working-age population in the United States and six other leading industrial market economies (together called the Group of Seven, or G-7). In 1970, the average education of the U.S. working population was 11.6 years, which was higher than any other nation in the world. Among other advanced economies, average education ranged from a low of 6.6 years in Italy to 11.3 years in Canada. By 1998, the U.S. education average had grown to 12.7 years, but other countries became even more educated, so Americans ranked third behind Germany, at 13.6 years, and Canada, at 12.9 years.

Developing economies, not shown in Exhibit 4, have far lower levels of education. Among countries that comprise the poorest third of the world's population, most adults are illiterate, while the illiteracy rate is less than 5 percent among industrial market economies.

U.S. Labor Productivity

What has been the growth of labor productivity in the United States? Exhibit 5 offers a long-run perspective, showing productivity growth stretching back more than a century as measured by growth in real output per work hour. Annual productivity growth is averaged by decade. The huge dip during the 1930s because of the Great Depression and the rebound during the 1940s because of World War II are unmistakable. Productivity growth slowed during the 1970s and 1980s but recovered somewhat during the 1990s.

For the entire period since 1870, productivity grew an average of 2.1 percent per year. This may not seem like much, but because of the power of compounding, output per work hour has grown about 1,500 percent since 1870. To put this growth in perspective, if a roofer in 1870 could shingle a single roof in a day, today's roofer could shingle 16 roofs in a day.

Over long periods, small differences in productivity growth can make huge differences in the economy's ability to produce and therefore in the standard of living. For example, if productivity growth had averaged only 1.1 percent instead of 2.1 percent, output per work hour since 1870 would have increased by only 325 percent, not 1,500 percent. On the other hand, if productivity growth averaged 3.1 percent per year, output per work hour since 1870 would have jumped 5,700 percent! The wheels of progress seem to grind slowly but they grind very fine, and the cumulative effect is powerful.

EXHIBIT 4

Average Years of Education of Working-Age Populations in 1970 and 1998

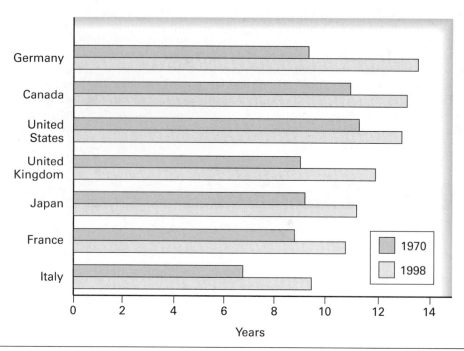

Source: Based on estimates developed in *OECD Economic Outlook* 68 (December 2000). Figure IV.1. The 1998 figure for Japan is based on 1990 data.

So far, we have been discussing the average growth in productivity for all workers. Productivity has grown more in some industries than in others. In ocean shipping, for example, cargo carried per worker is now 65 times greater than it was in 1900, for an average annual productivity growth of 4.3 percent. On the other hand, labor productivity in making wooden office furniture is only about three times greater today than in 1900, for an average growth of 1.1 percent.

Slowdown and Rebound in Productivity Growth

You can see in Exhibit 5 that productivity growth declined during the 1970s and 1980s and recovered a bit during the 1990s. By breaking the data down into intervals other than decades, we can better examine productivity trends since World War II. Exhibit 6 offers average annual growth for four periods. The growth in labor productivity declined from an average of 2.9 percent per year between 1948 and 1973 to 0.8 percent between 1974 and 1982. So the rate of growth in labor productivity from 1974 to 1982 was less than a third the rate during the quarter century following World War II, and, except for the Great Depression, less than the average for any decade during the previous century.

Why the slowdown? First, as noted in the previous chapter, the price of oil quadrupled from 1973 to 1974 as a result of OPEC actions. Spikes in energy prices boosted inflation during the period and contributed to three recessions, which slowed productivity growth. Second, in the early 1970s, several laws were passed to protect the environment and improve the quality and safety of the workplace. These measures ultimately led to cleaner air and water and safer factories, but they also required more costly production methods, and productivity growth slowed as these costlier methods were introduced.

Fortunately, productivity rebounded off the lows that occurred from 1974 to 1982, growing 1.7 percent from 1983 to 1995 and 2.3 percent from 1996 to 2001. Why the rebound? The most dramatic technological development in recent years has been the information revolution powered by the computer chip. The following case study looks at the impact of computers on productivity.

EXHIBIT 5

Long-Term Trend in U.S. Labor Productivity Growth: Annual Average by Decade

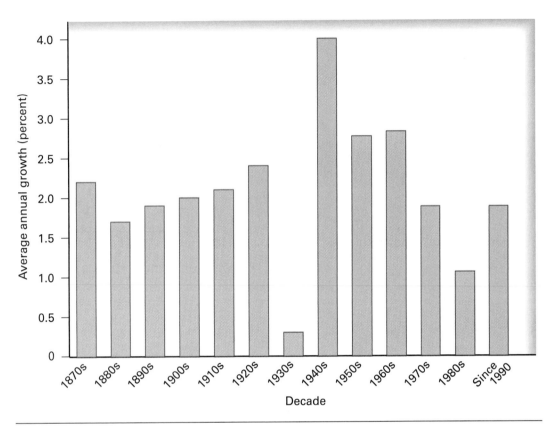

Sources: Angus Maddison, *Phases of Capitalist Development* (New York: Oxford University Press, 1982) and U.S. Bureau of Labor Statistics. "Since 1990" includes 2000 and 2001. For the latest data, go to http://www.bls.gov/lprhome.htm.

EXHIBIT 6

U.S. Labor Productivity Growth Slowed During 1974 to 1982 and Then Rebounded

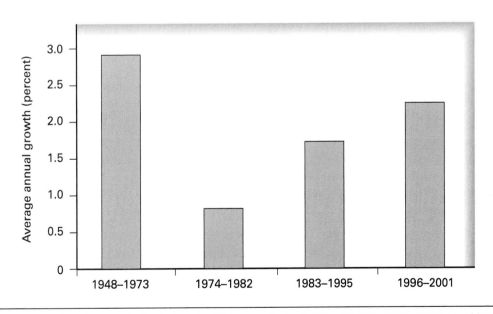

Source: Averages based on annual estimates from the U.S. Bureau of Labor Statistics. Figure for 2001 is projected as of September. For the latest data go to: http://www.bls.gov/lprhome.htm.

Chapter 21 Productivity and Growth

357

● *The Information Economy*

The first microprocessor, the Intel 4004, could execute about 400 computations per second when it hit the market in 1971. IBM's first personal computer, introduced a decade later, could execute 330,000 computations per second. Today a $650 PC can handle at least 1 billion computations per second, and upscale desktops can crunch 2 billion computations per second, *or 5 million* times what the 1971 Intel 4004 could handle.

Such advances in computing power have fueled a boom in computer use. In 2000, there were about 57 PCs per 100 persons in the United States, the world leader. There are now more computers in the United States than there are automobiles. Since 1982, growth of the computer sector has averaged 26 percent annually. U.S. companies and universities are well ahead of those in other countries in high-technology applications, ranging from software to biotechnology.

PCs are moving beyond word processing and spreadsheet analysis to help people work together. For example, design engineers in California can use the Internet to test new ideas with marketers in New York, cutting development time in half. Sales representatives on the road can use laptops or wireless devices to log orders and provide customer service. U.S. insurance companies can coordinate data entry done as far away as India to handle claims more efficiently. An owner of many restaurants can use the Internet to track sales up to the minute, check the temperatures of freezers, refrigerators, and fryers, and observe each restaurant through a live video feed. A new generation of machines monitor themselves and send messages to a service center, detailing problems when they arise. For example, General Electric uses the Internet to keep tabs on factory equipment thousands of miles away. Many home appliances have also become Internet compatible. Computers not only improve the quality and safety in the automobile and airline industries but increase the versatility of machines, which can be reprogrammed for different tasks.

A study by Stephen Oliner and Daniel Sichel, economists with the Federal Reserve System in Washington, D.C., concludes that information technology (IT) has been a leading force behind the improved productivity growth during the second half of the 1990s, and they expect this growth to persist. Labor productivity growth increased from 1.5 percent per year between 1990 and 1995 to 2.3 percent between 1996 and 2001. Computers affect productivity through two channels: (1) efficiency gains in the production of computers and semiconductors and (2) greater computer use by industry. According to Oliner and Sichel, these two channels accounted for most of the increase in productivity growth during the second half of the decade.

Although computer hardware manufacturers make up only a small fraction of the U.S. economy, their pace of innovation quickened enough since 1995 to boost overall U.S. productivity growth. For example, in 2001, Intel sold its new 1.7-gigahertz Pentium 4 processor for $342, versus $990 for the 1.1-gigahertz Pentium 3. What's more, the efficiency in semiconductor production and the price declines since 1995 advanced IT use by business more generally, which also enhanced labor productivity. Granted, IT investment in late 2000 and 2001 slowed to a crawl as the Internet stock bubble burst and firms pulled back on investment, but all investment is swayed by the vagaries of the business cycle. More important is the long-term trend. America invested more and earlier in IT than did other big economies, so economic benefits should show up here first. If America's average rate of labor productivity growth since 1995 continues in the long run, GDP per capita, a good measure of living standards, will grow about 2.7 percent a year, which is much faster than its growth during the first Industrial Revolution.

<interactive>exercise

- eACTIVITY: COMPUTERS AND PRODUCTIVITY GROWTH
- ECONDEBATE ONLINE: IS THERE A NEW ECONOMY?

<interactive>video

ASK THE INSTRUCTOR: HAVE COMPUTERS AFFECTED WORKER PRODUCTIVITY?

Sources: "Solving the Paradox," *Economist*, 23 September 2000; David Morgan, "Dot-Coms May Play Sleeper Role in U.S. Slowdown," Reuters, 17 January 2001; Leila Jason, "Software Lets Managers Watch Their Business from a Distance," *Wall Street Journal*, 30 August 2001; and Stephen Oliner and Daniel Sichel, "The Resurgence of Growth in the Late 1990s: Is Information Technology the Story?" Working Paper (May 2000), Federal Reserve Board, at http://www.federalreserve.gov/Pubs/FEDS/2000/200020/200020pap.pdf.

Higher labor productivity growth can easily make up for output lost during recessions. For example, if over the next 10 years the U.S. labor productivity grew an average of 2.3 percent per year (the average from 1996 to 2001) instead of 1.5 percent (the average from 1990 to 1995), that higher growth would add nearly $1 trillion to GDP in the 10th year—more than enough to make up for the output lost during two typical recessions. *This cumulative power of productivity growth is why economists now pay less attention to short-term fluctuations in output and more to long-term growth.*

Output per Capita

So far, we have focused on rising labor productivity as an engine of economic growth—that is, growth achieved by getting more output from each hour worked. But even if labor productivity did not increase, total output would grow if the quantity of labor increased. After all, since labor productivity equals real GDP divided by the quantity of labor, then real GDP equals labor productivity times the quantity of labor. Therefore, total output can grow as a result of greater labor productivity, more labor, or both.

As noted earlier, the best measure of an economy's standard of living is output per capita. *Output per capita,* or real GDP divided by the population, indicates how much an economy produces on average per resident. Let's relate output per capita to labor productivity by using an example. Suppose labor productivity in the economy is $60,000 per worker per year. If there is one worker for every two people in the economy, then *output per capita* equals output per worker divided by two, which is $60,000/2, or $30,000.

Even if labor productivity does not change over time, output per capita would grow if the number of workers grows faster than the population—that is, if the worker-population ratio increases. More generally, output per capita increases if (1) labor productivity increases for a given worker-population ratio, (2) the worker-population ratio increases for given labor productivity, or (3) labor productivity and the worker-population ratio both increase. In fact, output per capita would increase as long an increase in one of the variables more than offsets any decrease in the other one. For example, if labor productivity increases 2.3 percent but the worker-population ratio declines 2.0 percent, output per capita would increase. Before you go on, take a minute now to reread this paragraph and give it some thought.

Exhibit 7 presents real GDP per capita since 1959 for the United States. Notice the general upward trend, interrupted by seven recessions, indicated by the pink shading. Real GDP per capita nearly tripled (in 1996 dollars) from about $13,100 in 1959 to about $34,000 in 2001 for an average annual growth rate of 2.3 percent. Incidentally, since 1959, labor productivity grew an average of 2.1 percent. Output per capita grew faster than did labor productivity because the number of workers grew faster than did the population, so the worker-population ratio increased.

ECONNEWS ONLINE: REAL PER-CAPITA DISPOSABLE PERSONAL INCOME

International Comparisons

How does U.S. output per capita compare with that of other industrial countries? Exhibit 8 compares GDP per capita in 1999 for the United States and the six other leading industrial nations. The United States stands alone, with a per capita income 28 percent above that of second-ranked Canada and 52 percent above that of France, ranked last. Thus, the United States produced more output per capita in 1999 than any other major economy.

Exhibit 8 looks at the *level* of output per capita. What about the *growth* in output per capita? Exhibit 9 shows growth in real GDP per capita since 1983. With an average growth of 2.5 percent per year, the United States again ranked first among major industrial nations. Growth in the six other nations averaged 2.0 percent. Incidentally, America's growth advantage resulted from both higher labor productivity growth than the other major economies and a faster increase in the worker-population ratio.

To review, over the last 130 years, U.S. labor productivity has grown an average of 2.1 percent per year. Output per hour of work is now about 16 times its 1870 level. Labor productivity growth slowed between 1974 and 1982, because of spikes in energy prices and costly new environmental and workplace regulations. Since 1983 labor productivity growth has picked up, especially since 1996, due primarily to information technology. Among the seven major industrial economies, the United States experienced the fastest growth in living standards since 1983 and most recently had the highest standard of living, as measured by per capita output.

EXHIBIT 7

U.S. Real GDP per Capita Has Nearly Tripled Since 1959

Despite the recessions since 1959, real GDP per capita nearly tripled. Periods of recession are indicated by the pink-shaded bars.

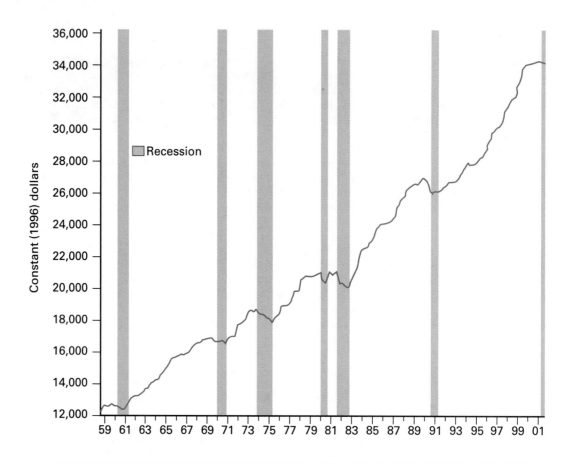

Source: *Survey of Current Business* 81 (July 2001). For the latest data, go to http://www.bea.doc.gov/bea/pubs.htm. Select the most recent month, go to the "National Data" section toward the end of the page, and then select "Charts."

OTHER ISSUES OF TECHNOLOGY AND GROWTH

In this section we consider some other issues of technology and growth, beginning with the question of whether technological change creates unemployment.

Does Technological Change Lead to Unemployment?

Technological change can sometimes free resources for new uses. For example, AT&T controls most of the world's known stock of copper in the form of existing wires and cables that are gradually being replaced by fiber-optic cables and cellular technology.

Technological change usually reduces the number of workers needed to produce a given amount of output. Consequently, some observers fear that new technology will throw people out of work and lead to higher unemployment. True, technological change can lead to unemployment in some industries and so create dislocations as workers must find new jobs. But technological change can also increase production and employment by making products more affordable. For example, the introduction of the assembly line cut the cost of automobiles, making them more affordable to the average household. This stimulated production and employment in the auto industry. The same happened with personal computers. Even in industries where some workers are displaced by machines, those who keep their jobs are more productive, so they earn more. And as long as human wants are unlimited, displaced workers will usually find jobs producing other goods and services demanded in a growing economy.

EXHIBIT 8

U.S. GDP per Capita Is Highest Among Major Economies

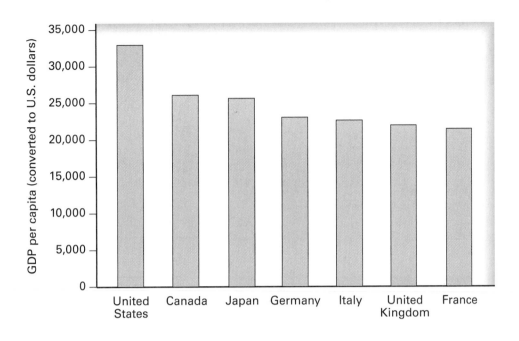

Source: Based on OECD figures, which are adjusted across countries using the purchasing power of the local currency as of 1999. For the latest data, go to the Organization for Economic Cooperation and Development Web page at http://www1.oecd.org/std/gdpperca.htm.

EXHIBIT 9

U.S. Real GDP per Capita Outgrew Other Major Economies Since 1983

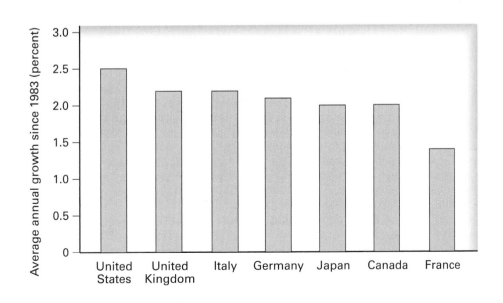

Source: Based on annual figures from 1983 through 1998 from the U.S. Bureau of Labor Statistics. Figures were converted into U.S. dollars based on the purchasing power of local currency. For the latest data, go to http://stats.bls.gov/flsdata.htm.

Chapter 21 *Productivity and Growth*

Although data from the 19th century are sketchy, there is no evidence that the unemployment rate is any higher today than it was in 1870. Since then, worker productivity has increased about 1,500 percent, and the length of the average workweek has been cut nearly in half. Although technological change may displace some workers in the short run, long-run benefits include higher real incomes on average and more leisure—in short, a higher standard of living.

If technological change caused unemployment, then the slowdown in productivity growth that occurred from 1974 to 1982 should have resulted in lower unemployment than during the period of higher productivity growth from 1996 to 2001. But the unemployment rate, the percentage of the workforce looking for jobs, averaged 7.2 percent during 1974 to 1982, compared to only 4.6 percent since 1996. And if technological change causes unemployment, then unemployment rates should be lower where the latest technology has not yet been introduced, such as in developing countries. But unemployment rates are usually much higher in such countries, and workers there earn relatively little because they are not very productive.

Again, there is no question that technological change sometimes creates job dislocations and hardships in the short run, as workers scramble to adjust to a changing world. Some workers with specialized skills made obsolete by technology may be unable to find jobs that pay as well as the ones they lost. These temporary dislocations are one price of progress. Over time, however, most displaced workers find other jobs, often in new industries created by technological change. In a typical year, the U.S. economy eliminates about 10 million jobs but creates nearly 12 million new ones. Out with the old, in with the new.

<interactive>video

ASK THE INSTRUCTOR: DOES NEW TECHNOLOGY DESTROY JOBS?

<interactive>exercise

ECONDEBATE ONLINE: DO TECHNOLOGICAL ADVANCES RESULT IN HIGHER UNEMPLOYMENT?

Research and Development

As noted several times already, a major contributor to productivity growth has been an improvement in the quality of human and physical capital. In terms of human capital, this improvement results from more education and more job training. In terms of physical capital, this improvement springs from better technology embodied in this capital. For example, because of extensive investments in cellular transmission, new satellites, and fiber-optic technology, labor productivity in the telecommunications industry increased by an average of 5.5 percent per year during the past three decades.

Improvements in technology arise from scientific discovery, which is the fruit of research. We can distinguish between basic research and applied research. **Basic research,** the search for knowledge without regard to how that knowledge will be used, is a first step toward technological advancement. In terms of economic growth, however, scientific discoveries are meaningless until they are implemented, which requires applied research. **Applied research** seeks to answer particular questions or to apply scientific discoveries to the development of specific products. Since technological breakthroughs may or may not have commercial possibilities, the payoff is less immediate with basic research than with applied research. Yet basic research seems to yield a higher rate of return to society as a whole than does applied research.

Because technological change is the fruit of research and development (R&D), investment in R&D reflects the economy's efforts to improve productivity through technological discovery. One way to track R&D spending is to measure it relative to gross domestic product, or GDP. Exhibit 10 shows R&D spending as a share of GDP for the United States and the six other major economies for the 1980s and 1990s. Overall R&D spending in the United States averaged 2.7 percent of GDP in both the 1980s and the 1990s. During the 1990s, R&D as a share of GDP ranked the United States second among the major economies, slightly behind Japan, at 2.9 percent, but well ahead of last placed Italy, at only 1.1 percent.

Bar segments in the chart distinguish between R&D by businesses and R&D by governments and nonprofit institutions. Business R&D is more likely to be targeted toward applied research and innovations. R&D spending by governments and nonprofits, such as universities, may gen-

EXHIBIT 10

R&D Spending as a Percentage of GDP for Major Economies During the 1980s and 1990s

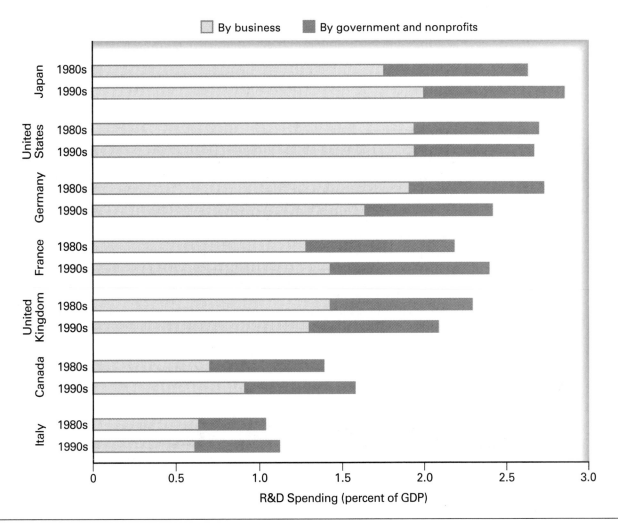

Source: Based on figures published in *OECD Economic Outlook* 68 (December 20001). Figure IV.2.

erate basic knowledge that has specific applications in the long run (for example, the Internet sprang from R&D spending on national defense). R&D by U.S. businesses averaged 1.9 percent of GDP in the 1990s, the same as in the 1980s. Three of the six other major countries experienced an increase in business R&D between the 1980s and 1990s, and three saw a decrease. Again, only Japan had higher business R&D than the United States had in the 1990s, at 2.0 percent of GDP. Italy had the lowest at 0.6 percent.

In short, the United States devotes relatively more resources to R&D than most other advanced economies, and this should help America maintain a higher standard of living.

Do Economies Converge?

If given enough time, will poor countries eventually catch up with rich ones? The **convergence** theory argues that developing countries can grow faster than advanced ones and should eventually close the gap. Here's why: It is easier to copy new technology once it is developed than to develop that technology in the first place. Countries that start out far behind can grow faster by copying existing technology. But economies that are already using the latest technology can boost productivity only with a steady stream of new breakthroughs.

Advanced countries, such as the United States, will find their growth limited by the rate of creation of new knowledge and improved technology. But follower countries can grow more quickly by, for example, adding computers where they previously had none. Until 1995, the

United States, which makes up just 5 percent of the world's population, accounted for the majority of home purchases of personal computers. By 2000, most PC purchases were made outside the United States.

What's the evidence on convergence? Some poor countries have begun to catch up with richer ones. For example, the newly industrialized Asian economies of Hong Kong, Singapore, South Korea, and Taiwan have invested heavily in technology acquisition and human resources and are closing the gap with the world leaders, moving them from the ranks of developing nations to the ranks of industrial market economies. But these so-called Asian Tigers are more the exception than the rule. Among the nations that comprise the poorest third of the world's population, consumption per capita has grown only about 1.0 percent per year over the last two decades compared with a 2.5 percent growth in the rest of the world,[3] so the standard of living in the poorest third of the world has grown somewhat in absolute terms but has fallen further behind in relative terms.

One reason per-capita consumption has grown so slowly in the poorest economies is that birth rates there are double those in richer countires, so poor economies must produce still more just to keep up with a growing population. Another reason why convergence has not begun, particularly for the poorest third of the world, is the vast difference in the quality of human capital across countries. Whereas technology is indeed portable, the knowledge, skill, and training usually required to take advantage of that technology are not. Countries with a high level of human capital can make up for other shortcomings. For example, much of the capital stock in Japan and Germany was destroyed during World War II. But the two countries retained enough of their well-educated and highly skilled labor force to join elite industrial market economies again in little more than a generation. But some countries, such as those in Africa, simply do not have the human capital needed to identify and absorb new technology. As noted already, such poor economies tend to have low education levels and low literacy rates. What's more, some countries lack the stable macroeconomic environment and the established institutions needed to nurture economic growth. Many developing countries have serious deficiencies in their infrastructures, lacking, for example, the reliable source of electricity needed to power new technologies. And some of the poorest nations have been ravaged by civil war for years.

NETBOOKMARK: MARY C. DALY'S "ASSESSING THE BENEFITS OF ECONOMIC GROWTH"

Industrial Policy

Policy makers have debated whether government should become more involved in shaping an economy's technological future. One concern is that technologies of the future will require huge sums to develop and implement, sums that an individual firm cannot easily raise and put at risk. Another concern is that some technological breakthroughs spill over to other firms and other industries, but the firm that develops the breakthrough may not be in a position to reap benefits from these spillover effects, so individual firms may underinvest in such research. One possible solution is more government involvement.

Industrial policy is the idea that government, using taxes, subsidies, regulations, and coordination in the private sector, could help nurture the industries and technologies of the future to give domestic industries an advantage over foreign competition. The objective is to secure a leading global role for domestic industry. One example of European industrial policy is Airbus Industrie, a four-nation aircraft consortium. With an estimated $20 billion in government aid, the aircraft producer has become Boeing's main rival. When Airbus seeks aircraft orders around the world, it can draw on government backing to promise special terms, such as landing rights at key European airports and an easing of regulatory constraints. U.S. producers do not get such government support. Industrial policy is discussed in the following case study.

CNN VIDEO: "VARIATIONS ON AN ENIGMA"

[3]Based on figures developed by the World Bank in *World Development Report 2001/2002* (New York: Oxford University Press, 2001), Tables 1 and 2.

<interactive>exercise

ECONDEBATE ONLINE: IS MORE SPENDING ON INFRASTRUCTURE THE KEY TO ECONOMIC GROWTH?

CASE**STUDY**	Picking Technological Winners
	● *Public Policy*

U.S. industrial policy over the years was aimed at creating the world's most advanced military production capacity. With the demise of the Soviet Union, however, defense technologies became less important. Some argue that U.S. industrial policy should shift from a military to a civilian focus. Former President Clinton once talked about establishing a powerful agency to help finance and coordinate R&D for what he called "cutting-edge products and technologies." He also proposed bringing together businesses, universities, and laboratories to carry out R&D in civilian technologies.

Many state governments are also trying to identify the industries that should be promoted in their states. Economists have long recognized that firms in some industries gain a performance advantage by *clustering*—that is, by locating in a region already thick with firms in the same industry or in related industries. Clusters such as Hollywood's show business, Madison Avenue's advertising business, Wall Street's financial business, and Silicon Valley's computer business facilitate communication and promote healthy competition among cluster members. The flow of information and cooperation between firms, as well as the competition among firms in close proximity, stimulates regional innovation and propels growth. By locating in a region where there are similar firms, a firm can tap into established local markets for specialized labor and for other inputs.

But skeptics wonder whether the government should be trusted to identify emerging technologies and to pick the industry clusters that will lead the way. Critics of industrial policy believe that markets allocate scarce resources better than governments do. For example, the costly attempt of European governments to develop the supersonic transport Concorde has not worked. As another example, in the early 1980s, the U.S. government spent $1 billion to help military contractors develop a high-speed computer circuit. But Intel, a company getting no federal support, was the first to develop the circuit. Japan has had the most aggressive policy for regulating and supporting favored industries, an approach that includes discouraging competition in the industry and encouraging joint research. But those Japanese industries subject to the most regulation and support, like chemicals and aircraft manufacturing, simply became uncompetitive in the world market. Meanwhile, the Japanese industries that had received little government backing, like automobiles, cameras, and video games, turned out to be dynamic, innovative world competitors.

There is also concern that an industrial policy would evolve into another government giveaway program. Rather than going to the most promising technologies, the money and the competitive advantages would be awarded based on political connections. Critics also wonder how wise it is to sponsor corporate research when beneficiaries may share their expertise with foreign companies and may even build factories abroad. Most economists would prefer to let Microsoft, General Electric, or some start-up bet on the important technologies of the future.

Sources: "The Complications of Clustering," *Economist,* 2 January 1999; "The President Bets on Technology," *New York Times,* 23 October 1997; Michael Porter, "Japan: What Went Wrong," *Wall Street Journal,* 21 March 2001; Ron Martin, "The New 'Geographical' Turn in Economics," *Cambridge Journal of Economics,* January 1999; and Minnesota's home page for its clustering efforts at http://www.hhh.umn.edu/centers/slp/edweb/home.htm.

CONCLUSION

Productivity and growth depends on the supply and quality of resources, the level of technology, and the rules of the game that nurture production and exchange. These elements tend to be correlated with one another. An economy with an unskilled and poorly educated workforce will usually be deficient in physical capital, in technology, and in the institutional tissue that promotes production and exchange. Similarly, an economy with a high-quality workforce will likely excel in the other sources of productivity and growth.

We should distinguish between an economy's standard of living, as measured by output per capita, and improvements in that standard of living, as measured by the growth in output per capita. Growth in output per capita can occur when labor productivity increases or when the number of workers in the economy grows faster than the population. *In the long run, productivity growth and the growth in workers relative to the growth in population will determine whether or not the United States continues to enjoy the world's highest standard of living.*

In the next chapter, you will learn how to measure economic activity and how to adjust data for inflation. In later chapters, you will develop aggregate demand and aggregate supply curves to build a model of the economy. Once you have an idea how a healthy economy works, you can consider the policy options in the face of high unemployment, high inflation, or both.

endofchaptermaterial

- **Summary**
- **Questions for Review**
- **Problems and Exercises**

- **Experiential Exercises**
- **Wall Street Journal Exercise**

Take the Post-Test to assess your overall understanding of the key ideas in this chapter. The Post-Test provides a comprehensive selection of exam-style questions addressing the main topics and concepts of the chapter. At the completion of each Post-Test, you will receive a score and instructive feedback on how you answered each question, and a direct link to the part of the chapter addressed in the question. Take the Post-Test as often as you need to—a record of your progress for each attempt is kept for you to revisit and gauge your improvement. And each Post-Test is randomly generated, so every attempt is new.

Post-Test

CHAPTER *22*

Measuring Economic Aggregates and the Circular Flow of Income

How do we keep track of the most complex economy in world history? What's gross about the gross domestic product? What's domestic about it? If you make yourself a tuna sandwich, how much does your effort add to the gross domestic product? Since prices change over time, how can we compare the economy's production in one year with that in other years? Answers to these and other questions are addressed in this chapter, which introduces an economic scorecard for a $10 trillion economy.

As mentioned earlier, although Americans account for only 5 percent of the world's population, they produce 20 percent of the world's output. In this chapter, you will learn how economists keep track of the billions of economic transactions that make up the U.S. economy. The scorecard is the national income accounting system, which reflects the performance of the economy as a whole by reducing a huge network of economic activity to a few aggregate measures.

As you will see, aggregate output can be measured by either the total spending on that output or the total income derived from producing it. We examine both approaches, see why they are equivalent, and learn how to adjust for the effects of inflation over time. The major components and important equalities built into the national income accounts are offered here as another way of understanding how the economy works—not as a foreign language to be mastered before the next exam. The emphasis is more on economic intuition than on accounting precision. The main part of this chapter provides the background sufficient for later chapters. More details about the national income accounts are offered in the appendix to this chapter. Topics discussed in this chapter include:

- National income accounts
- Expenditure approach to GDP
- Income approach to GDP
- Circular flow of income and expenditure
- Leakages and injections
- Limitations of national income accounting
- The consumer price index
- The GDP price index

<interactive>exercise

ECONDEBATE ONLINE: PRODUCTIVITY AND GROWTH

<interactive>update

- ECONDATA ONLINE: PRODUCTIVITY AND GROWTH
- ECONLINKS ONLINE: ECONOMICS WEB LINKS
- ECONNEWS ONLINE: PRODUCTIVITY AND GROWTH

THE PRODUCT OF A NATION

How do we measure the economy's performance? During much of the 17th and 18th centuries, when the dominant economic policy was mercantilism, many thought that economic prosperity was best measured by the *stock* of precious metals a nation accumulated. Mercantilism led to tariffs and quotas aimed at restricting imports, which had the unintended consequence of limiting the gains from comparative advantage and trade.

In the latter half of the 18th century, François Quesnay became the first to measure economic activity as a *flow*. In 1758, he published his *Tableau Économique,* which described the *circular flow* of output and income through different sectors of the economy. His insight was probably inspired by his knowledge of the circular flow of blood in the body—Quesnay was court physician to King Louis XV of France.

Rough measures of national income were developed in England some two centuries ago, but detailed calculations built up from microeconomic data were refined in the United States during the Great Depression. The resulting *national income accounting system* organizes huge quantities of data collected from a variety of sources across America. These data are summarized, assembled into a coherent framework, and reported periodically by the federal government. The conception and implementation of these accounts has been hailed as one of the greatest achievements of the 20th century. The U.S. national income accounts are the most widely reported and among the most highly regarded in the world and earned their developer, Simon Kuznets, the Nobel Prize.

<interactive>video

ASK THE INSTRUCTOR: WHAT IS INCLUDED IN THE CALCULATION OF GDP?

National Income Accounts

How do the national income accounts keep track of the economy's incredible variety of goods and services, from hiking boots to guitar lessons? Again, the *gross domestic product,* or GDP, measures the market value of all final goods and services produced during a year by resources located in the United States, regardless of who owns those resources. For example, GDP includes production in the United States by foreign firms, such as a Japanese auto plant in Kentucky, but excludes foreign production by U.S. firms, such as a General Motors plant in Mexico.[1]

The national income accounts are based on the idea that *one person's spending is another person's income.* The idea that spending equals income is expressed in a double-entry bookkeeping system, in which spending on aggregate output is recorded on one side of the ledger and income created by that spending is recorded on the other side. GDP can be measured either by total spending on U.S. production or by total income received from that production. The **expenditure approach** adds up the aggregate expenditure on all final goods and services produced during the year. The **income approach** adds up the aggregate income earned during the year by those who produce that output.

Gross domestic product includes only **final goods and services,** which are goods and services sold to the final, or ultimate, user. A toothbrush, a pair of contact lenses, and a bus ride are examples of final goods and services. Whether a sale is to the final user depends on who buys the product. Your purchase of chicken from a grocer is reflected in GDP. When Kentucky Fried Chicken purchases chicken, however, this transaction is not directly recorded in GDP because KFC is not the final consumer. Only after the chicken purchased by KFC is prepared, fried, and sold to consumers is a sale recorded as part of GDP.

Intermediate goods and services are those purchased for additional processing and resale, like the chicken purchased by KFC. This additional processing may be imperceptible, as when a grocer buys canned goods to stock the shelves. Or the intermediate goods can be dramatically altered, as when paint and canvas are transformed into a work of art.

Sales of intermediate goods and services are excluded from GDP to avoid the problem of **double counting,** which is counting an item's value more than once. For example, suppose the grocer buys a can of tuna for $0.60 and sells it for $1.00. If GDP counted both the intermediate transaction of $0.60 and the final transaction of $1.00, that can of tuna would be counted twice in GDP, and its recorded value of $1.60 would exceed its final value of $1.00 by $0.60. Hence, GDP counts only the final value of the product. GDP also ignores most of the second-hand value of used goods, such as existing homes, used cars, and used textbooks. These goods were counted in GDP the year they were produced. But just as the value of services provided by the grocer is included in GDP, so is the value of services provided by realtors, used-car dealers, and used-book sellers.

ECONNEWS ONLINE: THE TIMES MAY BE CHANGING

GDP Based on the Expenditure Approach

As noted already, one way to measure the value of GDP is to add up all spending on final goods and services produced in the economy during the year. The easiest way to understand the spending approach is to divide aggregate expenditure into its four components: consumption, investment, government purchases, and net exports. Let's discuss each in turn.

Consumption, or more specifically, *personal consumption expenditures,* consists of purchases of final goods and services by households during the year. Consumption is the easiest to understand and the largest spending category, accounting on average for about two-thirds of U.S. GDP during the last decade. Along with *services* like dry cleaning, haircuts, and air travel, consumption includes purchases of *nondurable goods,* like soap and soup, and *durable goods,* like televisions and furniture. Durable goods are those expected to last at least three years.

Investment, or more specifically, *gross private domestic investment,* consists of spending on new capital goods and additions to inventories. More generally, investment consists of spending on current production that is not used for current consumption. The most important category of investment is new **physical capital,** such as new buildings and new machinery purchased by firms and used to produce goods and services. Investment also includes purchases of new **residential construction.** Although investment fluctuates from year to year, on average it accounted for about one-sixth of U.S. GDP during the last decade.

---

[1]Before 1992, the federal government's measure of output was gross national product, or GNP, which measures the market value of all goods and services produced by resources supplied by U.S. residents and firms, regardless of the location of the resources.

Changes in firms' inventories are another category of investment. **Inventories** are stocks of goods in process, such as computer parts, and stocks of finished goods, such as new computers awaiting sale. Inventories help manufacturers deal with unexpected changes in the supply of their resources or in the demand for their products. A *net* increase in inventories during the year counts as investment because a net increase in inventories represents current production not used for current consumption. Conversely, a net decrease in inventories during the year counts as negative investment, or *disinvestment*, because net inventory reductions represent the sale of output already credited to a prior year's GDP.

Although investment includes purchasing a new residence, it excludes household purchases of durable goods, such as furniture and major appliances, which are counted as consumption. Investment also excludes purchases of *existing* buildings and machines and purchases of financial assets, such as stocks and bonds. Existing buildings and machines were counted in GDP when they were produced. Although purchases of stocks and bonds sometimes provide firms the funds to invest, stocks and bonds are not investments but simply indications of ownership.

Government purchases, or more specifically, *government consumption and gross investment,* include spending by all levels of government for goods and services—from clearing snowy roads to clearing court dockets, from library books to the librarian's pay. Government purchases at all levels averaged a little less than one-fifth of U.S. GDP during the last decade. Government purchases, and therefore GDP, exclude transfer payments, such as Social Security, welfare benefits, and unemployment insurance. Such payments are outright grants from the government to the recipients and are not true purchases by the government or true earnings by the recipients.

The final component of aggregate expenditure results from the interaction between the U.S. economy and the rest of the world. **Net exports** equal the value of U.S. exports of goods and services minus the value of U.S. imports of goods and services. Net exports include the value of not only *merchandise* trade—that is, goods, or stuff you can drop on your feet—but also services, or so-called *invisibles,* such as tourism, insurance, accounting, and consulting. Spending on consumption, investment, and government purchases includes purchases of foreign goods and services, yet this spending on foreign products does not count as part of U.S. GDP. So in computing GDP, we must subtract imports from exports to get the net effect of the rest of the world on GDP. The value of U.S. imports has exceeded the value of our exports nearly every year since the 1960s, meaning U.S. net exports have been negative. During the last decade, net exports averaged −1 percent of GDP.

With the expenditure approach, the nation's **aggregate expenditure** equals the sum of consumption, *C,* investment, *I,* government purchases, *G,* and net exports, which is the value of exports, *X,* minus the value of imports, *M,* or $(X - M)$. Summing these spending components yields aggregate expenditure, or GDP:

$$C + I + G = (X - M) = \text{Aggregate expenditure} = \text{GDP}$$

ECONNEWS ONLINE: A SHRINKING PRODUCT

GDP Based on the Income Approach

The expenditure approach sums, or aggregates, spending on production. The income approach sums, or aggregates, income arising from that production. Again, double-entry bookkeeping ensures that the value of aggregate output equals the aggregate income paid for resources used to produce that output: the wages, interest, rent, and profit arising from production. The price of a Hershey Bar reflects income earned by all resource suppliers who bring the candy bar to the grocer's shelf. **Aggregate income** equals the sum of all the income earned by resource suppliers in the economy. Thus, we can say that

$$\text{Aggregate expenditure} = \text{GDP} = \text{Aggregate income}$$

A finished product is usually processed by several firms on its way to the consumer. A wooden desk, for example, starts as raw timber, which is usually cut by one firm, milled by another, made into a desk by a third, and retailed by a fourth. We avoid double counting either by including only the market value of the desk when it is sold to the final user or by *calculating the value added at each stage of production.* The **value added** by each firm equals that firm's selling price minus the amount paid for inputs from other firms. The value added at each stage represents income to individual resource suppliers at that stage. *The sum of the value added at all stages equals the market value of the final good, and the sum of the value added for all final goods and services equals GDP based on the income approach.* For example, suppose you buy a wooden desk for $200, which is the final market value added directly into GDP. Consider the history of that desk. Suppose the tree that gave its life for your studies was cut into a log that was sold to a miller for $20. That log was milled into lumber and sold for $50 to a manufacturer, who built your desk and sold it for $120 to a retailer, who sold it to you for $200.

Column (1) of Exhibit 1 lists the selling price at each stage of production. If all these transactions were added together, the total of $390 would exceed the $200 market value of the desk. To avoid double counting, we include only the value added at each stage of production, listed in column (3) as the difference between the purchase price and the selling price. Again, *the value added at each stage equals the income to all who supplied their resources at that stage.* For example, the $80 in value added by the retailer consists of income to resource suppliers at that final stage, from the salesperson to the janitor who cleans the showroom to the trucker who provides "free delivery" of your desk. The value added at all stages totals $200, which is both the final market value of the desk and the total income earned by all resource suppliers along the way.

To reinforce your understanding of the equality of income and spending, let's return to familiar ground, the circular-flow model.

THE CIRCULAR FLOW OF INCOME AND EXPENDITURE

Chapter 1 introduced a simple circular flow with just households and firms. The circular-flow model shown in Exhibit 2 outlines the flow of income and spending in the economy. The main stream flows clockwise around the circle, first as income from firms to households (in the lower half of the circle), and then as spending from households back to firms (in the upper half of the circle). For each flow of money, there is an equal and opposite flow of goods or resources. Here we focus on the spending and income flows, not the real flows of resources and products.

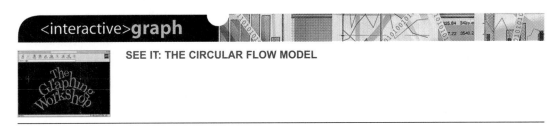

<interactive>graph

SEE IT: THE CIRCULAR FLOW MODEL

EXHIBIT 1

Computation of Value Added for a New Desk

The value added at each stage of production is the sale value minus the cost of intermediate goods, or column (1) minus column (2). The sum of the values added at all stages equals the market value of the final good, shown at the bottom of column (3).

Stage of Production	(1) Sale Value	(2) Cost of Intermediate Goods	(3) Value Added
Logger	$ 20	——	$ 20
Miller	50	$ 20	30
Manufacturer	120	50	70
Retailer	200	120	80
		Market value of final good	**$200**

The Income Half of the Circular Flow

In the process of developing a circular-flow model of income and expenditure, we must make some simplifying assumptions that allow us to depict the flows without complicating the model so much that we lose sight of the big picture. Specifically, by assuming that capital does not wear out (no depreciation) and that firms pay out all profits to firm owners (firms retain no earnings), we can say that *GDP equals aggregate income.*

The circular flow is a continuous process, but the logic of the model is clearest if we begin at juncture (1) in Exhibit 2, where firms in the United States make production decisions. After all, production must occur before output is sold and income is earned. As Henry Ford said, "It is not the employer who pays the wages—the employer only handles the money. It is the product that pays wages." Production of aggregate output, or GDP, gives rise to an equal amount of aggregate income. Households supply their labor, capital, land, and entrepreneurial ability to firms and are paid wages, interest, rent, and profit.

Thus, at juncture (1), aggregate output equals aggregate income. But not all that income is available for household spending. At juncture (2), governments collect taxes. Some of these tax dollars are returned to the income stream as transfer payments at juncture (3). By subtracting taxes and adding transfers, we transform aggregate income into **disposable income, DI,** which flows to households at juncture (4). Disposable income is take-home pay, which households can spend or save.

The bottom half of this circular flow is the *income half* because it focuses on what happens to the income arising from production. Aggregate income is the total income from producing GDP, and disposable income is the income remaining after taxes are subtracted and transfers added. To simplify the discussion, we define **net taxes, NT,** as taxes minus transfer payments. So *disposable income equals GDP minus net taxes.* Put another way, we can say that aggregate income equals disposable income plus net taxes:

$$GDP = \text{Aggregate income} = DI + NT$$

At juncture (4), firms have produced output and have paid resource suppliers; governments have collected taxes and made transfer payments. Households, with disposable income in hand, must now decide how much to spend and how much to save. Since firms have already produced the output and have paid resource suppliers, firms wait to see how much consumers want to spend. Suppliers will be stuck with any unsold output, which will become unplanned additions to firm inventories.

The Expenditure Half of the Circular Flow

Disposable income splits at juncture (5). Part is spent on consumption, *C,* and the remainder is saving, *S.* Thus,

$$DI = C + S$$

Spending on consumption remains in the circular flow and is the major aggregate expenditure, about two-thirds of the total. Household saving flows to **financial markets,** which consist of banks and other financial institutions that link savers and borrowers. For simplicity, Exhibit 2 shows households as the only savers, though governments, firms, and the rest of the world could save too. The primary borrowers are firms and governments, but households borrow as well, particularly for new homes, and the rest of the world also borrows. In reality, financial markets should be connected to all four economic decision makers, but we have simplified the flows to keep the model from looking like a plate of spaghetti.

In our simplified model firms pay resource suppliers an amount equal to the entire value of output. With nothing left for investment, firms must borrow in financial markets to finance purchases of physical capital plus any increases in their inventories. Households also borrow from financial markets to purchase new homes. Therefore, investment, *I,* consists of spending on new capital by firms, including inventory changes, plus spending on residential construction. Investment spending enters the circular flow at juncture (6), so aggregate spending at that point totals $C + I$.

Governments must also borrow whenever they incur deficits, that is, whenever their total outlays—transfer payments plus purchases of goods and services—exceed government revenues. Government purchases of goods and services, represented by *G,* enter the spending stream in the upper half of the circular flow at juncture (7). Remember that *G excludes* transfer payments, which already entered the stream as income at juncture (3).

Some spending by households, firms, and governments goes for imports. Since spending on imports, *M,* flows to foreign producers, not U.S. producers, import spending leaks from the circular flow at juncture (8). But the rest of the world buys U.S. products, so foreign spending

EXHIBIT 2

Circular Flow of Income and Expenditure

The circular-flow diagram captures important relationships in the economy. The bottom half of the diagram depicts the income flow arising from production. At juncture (1), GDP equals aggregate income. Taxes leak out of the flow at (2), but transfer payments augment the flow at (3). Taxes minus transfer payments equals net taxes, *NT*. Aggregate income minus taxes plus transfer payments equals disposable income, *DI,* which flows to households at juncture (4).

The top half of the diagram shows the flow of expenditures on GDP. At (5), households split their disposable income between consumption and saving. The saving stream flows into financial markets, where it is channeled to government borrowing and to business investment. At (6), the injection of investment augments the spending stream. At (7), government purchases represent another injection into the circular flow. At (8), imports are a leakage of spending, and at (9) exports are an injection of spending into the circular flow. Consumption plus investment plus government purchases plus exports minus imports, or net exports, equals the aggregate expenditure of GDP received by firms at (10).

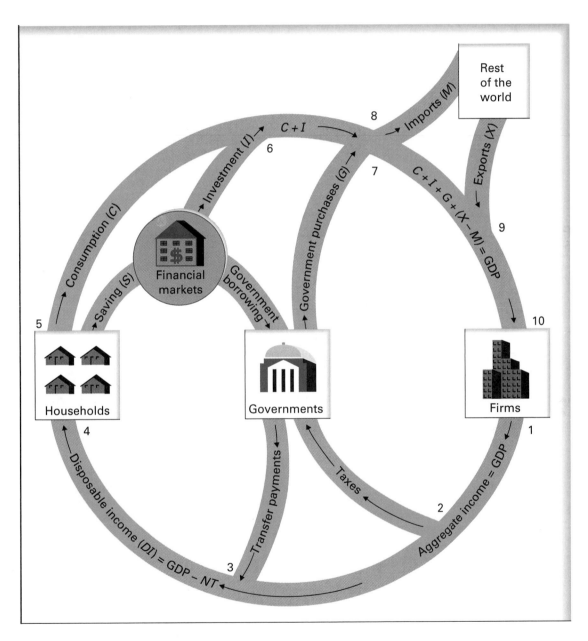

on U.S. exports, *X,* enters the circular flow at juncture (9). The net impact of the *rest of the world* on aggregate expenditure, or net exports, equals exports minus imports, *X − M,* which can be positive, negative, or zero.

The upper half of the circular flow is the *expenditure half* because it focuses on the components that make up aggregate expenditure: consumption, *C,* investment, *I,* government purchases, *G,* and net exports, *X − M.* Aggregate spending flows into firms at juncture (10).

Aggregate spending on U.S. output equals the market value of aggregate output in the economy, or GDP. In other words,

$$C + I + G + (X - M) = \text{Aggregate expenditure} = GDP$$

Leakages Equal Injections

Let's step back now to view the big picture. In the lower half of the circular flow, aggregate income equals disposable income plus net taxes. In the upper half, aggregate expenditure equals the total spending on U.S. output. *The aggregate income arising from production equals the aggregate expenditure on that production.* This is the first accounting identity. Thus, aggregate income (disposable income plus net taxes) equals aggregate expenditure (spending by each sector), or

$$DI + NT = C + I + G + (X - M)$$

Aggregate income = Aggregate expenditure

Since disposable income equals consumption plus saving, we can substitute $C + S$ for DI in the above equation to yield

$$C + S + NT = C + I + G + (X - M)$$

After subtracting C from both sides and adding M to both sides, the equation reduces to

$$S + NT + M = I + G + X$$

Note that at various points around the circular flow, some of the flow leaks from the main stream. Saving, S, net taxes, NT, and imports, M, are **leakages** from the circular flow. **Injections** into the main stream also occur at various points around the circular flow. Investment, I, government purchases, G, and exports, X, are *injections* of spending into the circular flow. As you can see from the preceding equation, *leakages from the circular flow equal injections into that flow.* This leakages-injections equation demonstrates a second accounting identity based on the principles of double-entry bookkeeping.

Planned Investment Versus Actual Investment

As you have learned already, at juncture (1) in the circular flow, firms produce the aggregate output expected to meet demand. But aggregate expenditure may not match production. Suppose, for example, that firms produce $10.0 trillion in output, but the spending components add up to only $9.8 trillion. Firms will end up with $0.2 trillion in unsold products, which they must add to their inventories. Since increases in inventories are counted as investment, *actual* investment turns out to be $0.2 trillion greater than firms had *planned.*

Note the distinction here between **planned investment,** the amount firms plan to invest before they know how much output they sell, and **actual investment,** which includes both planned investment and any unplanned changes in inventories. Unplanned increases in inventories cause firms to smarten up and decrease their production next time around so as not to get stuck with more unsold goods. Only when there are no unplanned changes in inventories will GDP be at an *equilibrium level*—that is, *a level that can be sustained period after period. Only in equilibrium will planned investment equal actual investment.*

The relationship between actual and planned investment will be examined more closely later. For now, you need only understand that the national income accounting system reflects *actual* investment, not necessarily *planned* investment. *The national income accounts always look at things after the dust has settled.* Although planned leakages may differ from planned injections, actual leakages always equal actual injections.

LIMITATIONS OF NATIONAL INCOME ACCOUNTING

Imagine the difficulty of developing an accounting system that must capture the subtleties of a such a complex and dynamic economy. In the interest of clarity and simplicity, certain features get neglected. In this section, we examine some limitations of the national income accounting system, beginning with productive activity that is not captured by GDP.

ECONNEWS ONLINE: HOW DOMESTIC IS GDP?

Some Production Is Not Included in GDP

With some minor exceptions, GDP includes only those products that are sold in markets, thereby neglecting all do-it-yourself household production—child care, meal preparation, house cleaning, and home repair. Thus an economy in which householders are largely self-sufficient will have a lower GDP than will an otherwise similar economy in which households specialize and sell products to one another.

During the 1950s, more than 80 percent of American mothers with small children stayed at home caring for the family, but all this care added not one cent to GDP. Today more than half of mothers with small children are in the workforce, where their market labor gets counted in U.S. GDP. What's more, GDP has increased because meals, child care, and the like are now more apt to be purchased in markets rather than provided in the home. In less developed economies, more economic activity is do-it-yourself or provided by the extended family. *Because official GDP figures ignore most home production, these figures understate the value of household production.*

GDP also ignores production for which no official records are kept. The term **underground economy** describes all market activity that goes unreported either because it's illegal or those involved want to evade taxes on otherwise legal activity. Although there are no official estimates on the extent of the underground economy, most economists agree that it is substantial. A federal study suggests the equivalent of 7.5 percent of GDP is underground production; this would amount to about $750 billion in 2001.

For some economic activity, income must be *imputed,* or estimated, because market exchange does not occur. For example, included in GDP is an *imputed rental income* that homeowners receive from home ownership, even though no rent is actually paid or received. Also included in GDP is an imputed dollar amount for (1) wages paid in *kind,* such as employers' payments for employees' medical insurance, and (2) food produced by farm families for their own consumption. GDP therefore includes some economic production that does not involve market exchange.

<interactive>exercise

READING IT RIGHT: WALL STREET JOURNAL EXERCISE

Leisure, Quality, and Variety

The average U.S. workweek is much shorter now than it was a century ago, so people work less to produce today's output. People also retire now at a much earlier age and they live longer after retirement. Over the years, there has been an increase in the amount of leisure available. But leisure time is not reflected in GDP because leisure is not explicitly bought and sold in a market. The quality and variety of products available have on average also improved over the years because of technological advances and competition, yet most of these improvements are not reflected in GDP. For example, improvements have occurred in recording systems, computers, tires, running shoes, and hundreds of other products. Also, new products are introduced all the time, such as high-definition television. *The gross domestic product fails to capture changes in the availability of leisure time and often fails to reflect changes in the quality of existing products and the availability of new products.* The special problem of measuring production in an economy shaped by changing technology is discussed in the following case study.

CASE**STUDY**	Tracking a $10 Trillion Economy
	● *The Information Economy*

How does the government keep track of the most sophisticated economy in history? Ever since Article I of the U.S. Constitution required a decennial population census, the federal government has been gathering data. The three main data-gathering agencies are the Census Bureau, the Bureau of Economic Analysis, and the Bureau of Labor Statistics. Since 1980, real GDP has doubled, employment has increased nearly 40 million, and real foreign trade has tripled. Yet the federal budget for these agencies has declined in real terms. Only 0.2 percent of the federal budget goes toward keeping track of the economy.

Federal budget cuts have eliminated some data-collection efforts and have slowed down others. For example, computations of monthly international trade statistics have become so overwhelming that as many as half the imports counted for a particular month reflect a "carryover" from previous months. And, in a cost saving move, the monthly household sample that tracks unemployment was cut from 60,000 to 50,000. Some agencies must do more with the same staff. For example, in 1980, the Bureau of Labor Statistics had 18 analysts to monitor productivity in 95 different industries. The number of industries they now track has quadrupled, but the number of analysts has changed little. The Census Bureau proposed collecting new data on the digital economy, but Congress said no.

The traditional ways of monitoring economic activity were originally developed in the 1930s and 1940s, when manufacturing dominated. Manufacturing output is relatively easy to measure because it is tangible, such as automobiles, toasters, or in-line skates. But service output, such as medical care, yoga lessons, or online services, is intangible and more difficult to measure, though services now account for 80 percent of GDP. It has proven difficult and costly to develop new measures for the service economy.

Because services are intangible, measures for the service sector tend to be less reliable than those for the manufacturing sector. Measures of service output often fail to reflect improvements in the speed or quality of services. For example, a Wisconsin trucking firm uses onboard computers in its vehicles to map the most efficient route and remap the route should priorities change. The firm has become so efficient that the number of ton-miles (tonnage times miles) carried per month has declined. Yet, according to federal statisticians, these truck drivers are less productive because ton-miles measures output in this industry.

Official productivity data indicate that industries that rely more on computers such as banking, education, and health care have the lowest measured growth in productivity. Does this mean that information technology is a waste of money in these industries? No. More likely the measure of output is flawed. For example, according to official figures, productivity in health care declined 20 percent in the last decade. But because of technological advances, diagnosis is now more accurate, treatments are less invasive and less painful, and people recover more quickly, so hospital stays are shorter. These improvements suggest big cost savings and greater convenience for patients. But since output in health care is usually measured by inputs, such as the doctor's time and hospital-bed days, these measures miss improved quality.

Federal statisticians are working on improvements, but they have difficulty measuring output in a wide range of industries, including medicine, banking, education, software, legal services, wholesale trade, and communications. There are indications that output and productivity in the service sector may be rising faster than official estimates show. For example, capital investment in the service sector has grown more in recent years than has investment in the manufacturing sector. And the United States has experienced a growing trade surplus in services, suggesting that the U.S. service sector is competitive and relatively productive, at least when compared with services produced abroad. In contrast, the trade balance on goods has been in deficit for decades, and this deficit has been growing.

One final problem is the decentralized structure of the U.S. statistical system. In contrast to those of most other industrialized countries, U.S. statistical agencies do not share data collected in closely related programs. For example, both the Census Bureau and the Bureau of Labor Statistics collect industry employment data, mostly from the same firms. This is wasteful both for the agencies themselves and for the reporting firms. A centralized statistical agency would free up resources to attack problems already discussed. Most other countries have a central data-collection system.

<interactive>exercise

eACTIVITY: TRACKING A $10 TRILLION ECONOMY

Sources: "The U.S. Statistical System and a Rapidly Changing Economy," *Brookings Policy Brief*, no. 63 (July 2000): 2–8; Leonard Nakamura, "Is the U.S. Economy Really Growing Too Slowly? Maybe We're Measuring Growth Wrong," *Federal Reserve Bank of Philadelphia Business Review* (March–April 1997): 1–12; and *Economic Report of the President*, January 2001. For the latest labor productivity data, go to http://www.bls.gov/lprhome.htm.

GDP Ignores Depreciation

In the course of producing GDP, some capital wears out, such as the delivery truck that finally dies, and some capital becomes obsolete, such as an aging computer that can't run the latest software. A new truck that logs 100,000 miles its first year has been subject to wear and tear, and therefore has a diminished value as a resource. A truer picture of the *net* production that actually occurs during a year is found by subtracting this *depreciation* from GDP. **Depreciation** measures the value of the capital stock that is used up or becomes obsolete in the production process. Gross domestic product is called "gross" because it fails to take into account this depreciation. **Net domestic product** equals gross domestic product minus depreciation, the value of the capital stock used up in the production process.

We can now distinguish between two definitions of investment. *Gross investment* measures the value of all investment during a year. Gross investment is used in computing GDP. *Net investment* equals gross investment less depreciation. The economy's production possibilities depend on what happens to net investment. If net investment is negative—that is, if depreciation exceeds gross investment—the capital stock declines, so its contribution to output will decline as well. If net investment is zero, the capital stock remains constant, as does its contribution to output. And if net investment is positive, the capital stock grows, as does its contribution to output.

As the names imply, *gross* domestic product reflects gross investment and *net* domestic product reflects net investment. But developing a figure for depreciation involves much guesswork. For example, what is the appropriate measure of depreciation for the roller coasters at Busch Gardens, the metal display shelves at Wal-Mart, the parking lots at Disney World, or the Library of Congress building in Washington, D.C.?

GDP Does Not Reflect All Costs

Some production and consumption degrades the quality of our environment. Trucks and automobiles pump carbon monoxide into the atmosphere. Housing developments displace forests. Paper mills foul the lungs and burn the eyes. These negative externalities—costs that fall on those not directly involved in the transactions—are largely ignored in GDP accounting, even though they diminish the quality of life and may limit future production. To the extent that growth in GDP also involves growth in such negative externalities, a rising GDP may not be as attractive as it would first appear.

Although the national income accounts reflect the depreciation of buildings, machinery, vehicles, and other manufactured capital, this accounting ignores the depletion of natural resources, such as standing timber, fish stocks, and soil fertility. So national income accounts reflect depreciation of the manufactured capital stock but not the natural capital stock. For example, intensive farming may raise productivity temporarily and boost GDP, but this depletes soil fertility. Worse still, some economic development may cause the extinction of certain plants and animals. The U.S. Commerce Department is now in the process of developing so-called green accounting, or green GDP, to reflect the impact of production on air pollution, water pollution, lost trees, soil depletion, and the loss of other natural resources.

GDP and Economic Welfare

In computing GDP, the market price of output is the measure of its value. Therefore, each dollar spent on handguns or cigarettes is counted in GDP the same as each dollar spent on baby formula or bibles. Positive economic analysis tries to avoid making value judgments about how people choose to spend their money. Because the level of GDP provides no information about its composition, some economists question whether GDP is a good measure of the nation's economic welfare. For example, at a time when some people in the nation are hungry and homeless, Americans spend billions on tobacco products, even though these products are linked to illness and death.

Despite the limitations and potential distortions associated with official GDP estimates, the trend of GDP over time provides a fairly accurate picture of the overall movement of the U.S. economy. Inflation, however, distorts the direct comparability of dollar amounts from one year to the next. In the next section, we discuss how to adjust GDP for changes in the economy's price level.

ACCOUNTING FOR PRICE CHANGES

As noted earlier, the national income accounts are based on the market values of final goods and services produced in a particular year. Gross domestic product measures the value of output in *current dollars*—that is, in the dollar values at the time the output is produced. When GDP is based on current dollars, the national income accounts measure the *nominal value* of national output. Thus, the current-dollar GDP, or **nominal GDP,** is based on the prices prevailing when the output is produced.

The system of national income accounting based on current, or nominal, dollars allows for comparisons among income or expenditure components in a particular year. Since the economy's average price level changes over time, however, current-dollar comparisons across years can be misleading. For example, between 1979 and 1980, nominal GDP increased by about 9 percent. That sounds impressive, but the economy's average price level rose more than 9 percent. So the growth in nominal GDP resulted entirely from inflation. Real GDP, or GDP measured in terms of the goods and services produced, in fact declined.

If nominal GDP increases in a given year, part of this increase may simply result from inflation—pure hot air. To make meaningful comparisons of GDP across years, we must take out the hot air, or *deflate* nominal GDP. We focus on *real* changes in production by eliminating changes due solely to inflation.

<interactive>video

ASK THE INSTRUCTOR: WAS THERE A RECESSION IN 1974?

<interactive>update

ECONDATA ONLINE: REAL GDP

Price Indexes

To compare the price level over time, let's first establish a point of reference, a base year to which prices in other years can be compared. An *index number* compares the value of some variable in a particular year to its value in a base year, or reference year. Think about the simplest index number imaginable. Suppose bread is the only good produced in an economy. As a reference point, let's look at the price in some specific year. The year selected is called the **base year;** prices in other years are expressed relative to the base-year price.

Suppose the base year is 2000, when a loaf of bread in our simple economy sold for $1.25. Let's say the price of bread increased to $1.30 in 2001 and to $1.40 in 2002. We construct a **price index** by dividing each year's price by the price in the base year and then multiplying by 100, as shown in Exhibit 3. For 2000, the base year, we divide the base price of bread by itself, $1.25/$1.25, which equals 1, so the price index in 2000 equals $1 \times 100 = 100$. *The price index in the base year is always 100.* The price index in 2001 is $1.30/$1.25, which equals 1.04, which when multiplied by 100 equals 104. In 2002, the index is $1.40/$1.25, or 1.12, which when multiplied by 100 equals 112. Thus, the index is 4 percent higher in 2001 than in the base year and 12 percent higher in 2002.

The price index permits comparisons between any two years. For example, what if you were presented with the indexes for 2001 and 2002 and asked what happened to the price level between the two years? By dividing the 2002 price index by the 2001 price index, 112/104, you find that the price level rose by 7.7 percent.

EXHIBIT 3

Hypothetical Example of a Price Index (base year = 2000)

The price index equals the price in the current year divided by the price in the base year, all multiplied by 100.

Year	(1) Price of Bread in Current Year	(2) Price of Bread in Base Year	(3) Price Index (3) = (1)/(2) × 100
2000	$1.25	$1.25	100
2001	1.30	1.25	104
2002	1.40	1.25	112

This section has shown how to develop a price index assuming we already know the price level each year. Determining the price level is a bit more involved, as we'll now see.

Consumer Price Index

The price index most familiar to you is the **consumer price index,** or **CPI,** which measures changes over time in the cost of buying a "market basket" of goods and services purchased by a typical family. For simplicity, suppose a typical family's market basket for the year includes 365 packages of Twinkies, 500 gallons of fuel oil, and 12 months of cable TV. Prices in the base year are listed in column (2) of Exhibit 4. The total cost of each product in the base year is found by multiplying price by quantity, as shown in column (3). The cost of the market basket in the base year is shown at the bottom of column (3) to be $1,184.85.

Prices in the current year are listed in column (4). Notice that not all prices changed by the same percentage since the base year. The price of fuel oil increased by 50 percent, but the price of Twinkies declined. The cost of purchasing that same basket in the current year is $1,398.35, shown as the total of column (5). To compute the consumer price index for the current year, we simply divide the total cost in the current year by the total cost of that same basket in the base year, $1,398.35/$1,184.85, and then multiply by 100. This yields a price index of 118. We could say that between the base period and the current year, the "cost of living" increased by 18 percent, although not all prices increased by the same percentage.

The federal government uses the years 1982 to 1984 as the base period for calculating the CPI for a market basket of 400 goods and services in eight major categories. The CPI is reported monthly based on prices collected from about 23,000 sellers across the country. In reality, each household consumes a unique market basket, so we could theoretically develop about 110 million CPIs—one for each U.S. household.

<interactive>update

ECONDATA ONLINE: CONSUMER PRICE INDEX (CPI)

Problems with the CPI

There is no perfect way to measure changes in the price level. As we have already seen, the quality and variety of some products are improving all the time, so some price increases may be as much a reflection of improved quality as of inflation. Thus, there is a *quality bias* in the CPI, since it assumes that the quality of the market basket remains relatively constant over time. *As a result of ignoring quality improvements, the CPI overstates the true extent of inflation.*

The CPI tends to overstate inflation for another reason. Recall that the CPI holds constant over time the kind and amount of goods and services in the typical market basket. Since not all items in the market basket experience the same rates of price change, relative prices change

EXHIBIT 4

Hypothetical Market Basket Used to Develop the Consumer Price Index

The cost of a market basket in the current year, shown at the bottom of column (5), sums the quantities of each item in the basket, shown in column (1), times the price of each item in the current year, shown in column (4).

Good or Service	(1) Quantity in Market Basket	(2) Prices in Base Year	(3) Cost of Basket in Base Year (3) = (1) × (2)	(4) Prices in Current Year	(5) Cost of Basket in Current Year (5) = (1) × (4)
Twinkies	365 packages	$ 0.84/package	$ 324.85	$ 0.79	$ 288.35
Fuel Oil	500 gallons	1.00/gallon	500.00	1.50	750.00
Cable TV	12 months	30.00/month	360.00	30.00	360.00
			$1,184.85		$1,398.35

over time. A household would respond to changes in relative prices by purchasing less of the relatively more expensive products and more of the relatively cheaper products. But, because the CPI holds the composition of the market basket constant for long periods, the CPI is slow to incorporate consumer responses to changes in relative prices. *The CPI calculations, by not allowing households to shift away from goods that have become relatively more costly, overestimates the true extent of inflation experienced by the typical household.*

The CPI has also failed to keep up with the consumer shift toward discount stores such as Wal-Mart, Target, and Home Depot. Government statisticians consider goods sold at discount retailers as distinct from similar or identical goods sold by traditional retailers. The discounter is assumed to be offering a different good, one with lower services and fewer consumer amenities. Hence the discounter's lower price does not translate into a reduction in the cost of living.

Researchers conclude the CPI has overestimated inflation by about 1 percent per year. This problem is of more than academic concern because the index determines changes in tax brackets and in an array of payments, including wage agreements that include a cost-of-living allowance, Social Security benefits, and welfare payments. In fact, about 30 percent of federal outlays are tied to changes in the CPI. A 1 percent correction in the upward bias of the CPI would save the federal budget $180 billion annually by the year 2008.

Overstating the CPI also distorts other measures of the economy that use the CPI to adjust for inflation, such as the real wage. For example, based on the official CPI, the average real wage fell by a total of about 2 percent between 1980 and 2000. But if the CPI overstates inflation by 1 percent per year, as researchers conclude, then the real wage, instead of dropping by 2 percent during the period, actually increased by about 20 percent.

The Bureau of Labor Statistics, the group that estimates the CPI, is now working on these problems and has introduced an experimental version of the CPI that would reduce measured inflation. One experiment uses scanner data at supermarkets to find out how consumers respond, for example, to a rise in the price of romaine lettuce relative to iceberg lettuce, two products assumed to be reasonable substitutes.

<interactive>example

NETBOOKMARK: BRIAN MOTLEY'S "BIAS IN THE CPI: ROUGHLY RIGHT OR PRECISELY WRONG?"

<interactive>update

- **ECONNEWS ONLINE: WILL THE NEW CPI MEASURE UP?**
- **ECONNEWS ONLINE: MEASURE TO MEASURE**

The GDP Price Index

Price indexes are weighted sums of various prices. Whereas the CPI focuses on just a sample of consumer purchases, a more complex and more comprehensive price index, the **GDP price index,** measures the average level of prices of all goods and services included in GDP. To calculate the GDP price index, we use the formula

$$\text{GDP price index} = (\text{Nominal GDP}/\text{Real GDP}) \times 100$$

where nominal GDP is the dollar value of this year's GDP measured in current-year prices, and real GDP is the dollar value of this year's GDP measured in base-year prices. If we know both nominal GDP and real GDP, then finding the GDP price index is easy. Nominal GDP is simply current-dollar GDP. The challenge is finding real GDP. Any measure of real GDP is constructed as the weighted sum of thousands of different goods and services produced in the economy. The question is what weights, or prices, to use. Between World War II and 1995, the Bureau of Economic Analysis (BEA) used prices of a particular base year (most recently, 1987) to estimate real GDP. In this case, the quantity of each output in a particular year was valued by using the 1987 price of each output. So real GDP in, say, 1994 was the sum of 1994 outputs valued at 1987 prices.

Moving from Fixed Weights to Chain Weights

Estimating real GDP by using prices from a base year yields an accurate measure of real GDP as long as the year in question is close to the base year. But BEA used prices that prevailed in 1987 to value production in years from 1929 to 1995. In early 1996, BEA switched from a fixed-

EXHIBIT 5

U.S. Gross Domestic Product in Current Dollars and Chained (1996) Dollars

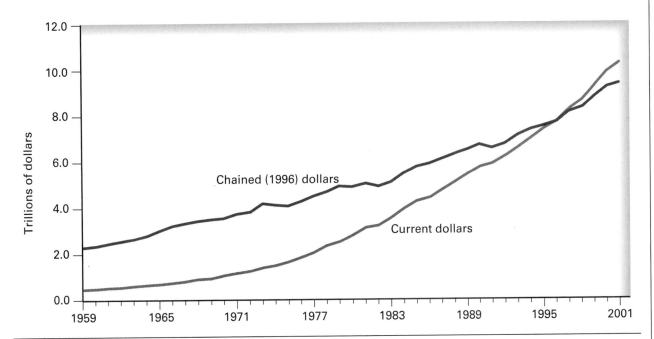

Source: Based on annual estimates from the Bureau of Economic Analysis, U.S. Dept. of Commerce. Figures for 2001 are projected as of September. For the latest data, go to http://www.bea.doc.gov/bea/dn1.htm.

price weighting system to a **chain-weighted system,** using a complicated process that changes price weights from year to year. All you need to know is that the chain-weighted real GDP adjusts the weights in calculating a price index more or less continuously from year to year, getting rid of much of the bias caused by a fixed-price weighting system.

Even though the chain-type index adjusts the weights from year to year, any index, by definition, must still use some year as an anchor, or reference point—that is, any index must answer the question, Compared to what? To provide such a reference point, BEA measures U.S. real GDP and its components in *chained (1996) dollars.* Exhibit 5 presents current-dollar estimates of GDP as well as chained (1996) dollar estimates of real GDP. The blue line indicates current-dollar GDP, or nominal GDP, since 1959. The red line indicates real GDP since 1959, or GDP measured in chained (1996) dollars. The two lines intersect at 1996, when real GDP equaled nominal GDP. Nominal, or current-dollar, GDP is below real GDP in years prior to 1996 because real GDP is based on chained (1996) prices, which on average are higher than prices prior to 1996. Current-dollar GDP growth reflects growth in real GDP and in the price level. Chained-dollar GDP growth reflects only growth in real GDP. So current-dollar GDP grows more than chained-dollar GDP.

An example of the bias resulting from a fixed-price weighting system involves computers, as discussed in this closing case study.

CASE**STUDY**	Computer Prices and GDP Estimation
	● *Public Policy*

As noted already, until 1996, federal statisticians based their real GDP estimates on 1987 prices. Relying on such estimates, most observers believed that the economic recovery that began in the spring of 1991 was spurred primarily by investment spending, especially spending on new computers. In this case study, we reconsider the role of computer production as an economic stimulus to that recovery.

Computer prices have fallen by an average of about 13 percent per year since 1982. Based on this rate of decline, a computer that cost, say, $10,000 in 1982 cost about $5,000 in 1987 but only about $650 in 2001. According to these prices, that computer cost about the same in 1982 as a Chrysler minivan; in 2001, you could buy about 35 computers for the cost of a minivan. So computers became much less expensive between 1982 and 2001.

The sharp decline in computer prices spurred purchases for offices and homes. Suppose the number of computers purchased jumped from 1 million in 1982 to 5 million in 2001. If computers are valued at their 1987 price of $5,000, computer spending would have increased fivefold, from $5 billion in 1982 to $25 billion in 2001. But if priced in current, or nominal, dollars, of $10,000 in 1982 and $650 in 2001, computer spending would have declined two-thirds from $10 billion in 1982 to only $3.3 billion in 2001. Using the 1987 price understates the value of computer production in 1982, overstates it in 2001, and thus exaggerates the growth between 1982 and 2001. It was this exaggeration in the value of computer production in 1991 that led to the incorrect belief that the recovery resulted primarily from a jump in investment spending.

The chain-weighted measure adjusts for some of the distortion that comes from using 1987 fixed prices. Under the chain-weighted measure, investment grew less rapidly during the recovery that began in 1991 than during the four previous recoveries, so investment turned out to be less of a factor in stimulating economic expansion than it had been in the previous two decades. The chain-weighted system, although it is more complicated than the fixed-price weighting system, provides a more reliable picture of year-to-year changes in real output.

\<interactive\>exercise

eACTIVITY: COMPUTER PRICES AND GDP ESTIMATION

Sources: Gary McWilliams, "Dell Fine-Tunes Its PC Pricing to Gain an Edge in Slow Market," *Wall Street Journal,* 8 June 2001; "Improved Estimates of the National Income and Product Accounts for 1959–95: Results of the Comprehensive Revision," *Survey of Current Business* 76 (January/February 1996); *Survey of Current Business* 81 (August 2001); and "From Investment Boom to Bust," *Economist,* 1 March 2001. The home page for the Bureau of Economic Analysis is at http://www.bea.doc.gov/.

CONCLUSION

This chapter examined how GDP is measured and how it is adjusted for changes in the economy's price level over time. Subsequent chapters will refer to the distinction between real and nominal values. Although no price index is perfect, the price indexes now in use provide reasonably good measures of the trend in price levels over time. The national income accounts have limitations, but they do offer a reasonably accurate measure of year-to-year movements in the economy. The national income accounts are published in much greater detail than the preceding discussion suggests. The appendix to this chapter provides some flavor of the detail available.

endofchaptermaterial

- **Summary**
- **Questions for Review**
- **Problems and Exercises**

- **Experiential Exercises**
- **Wall Street Journal Exercises**
- **Appendix Questions**

NATIONAL INCOME ACCOUNTS

This chapter has focused on the gross domestic product, or GDP, the measure of output that will be of most interest in subsequent chapters. Other economic aggregates also convey useful information and receive media attention. One of these, *net domestic product,* has already been introduced. Exhibit 6 shows that net domestic product equals gross domestic product minus depreciation. In this appendix we examine other aggregate measures.

NATIONAL INCOME

So far, we have been talking about the value of production from resources located in the United States, regardless of who owns them. Sometimes we want to know how much American resource suppliers earn for their labor, capital, land, and entrepreneurial ability. **National income** captures all income earned by American-owned resources, whether located in the United States or abroad. National income results from several adjustments to net domestic product. First, to get the net value of production from American-owned resources, we add income earned by American resources abroad and subtract income earned by foreign-owned resources in the United States.

Second, the value of final goods and services is computed at market prices, but because of **government subsidies,** such as payments to suppliers of low-income housing, some products sell for less than resource suppliers receive. Because subsidies are received as income, they should be included in national income, even though they are not part of the selling price.

Third, because of **indirect business taxes,** such as sales, excise, and property taxes, some products sell for more than resource suppliers receive. For example, a gallon of gasoline may sell for $1.50, but about $0.40 in taxes must be paid to the government before any resource supplier earns a penny. Because indirect business taxes are not received as income by any individual, they should not be included in national income, even though they are part of the selling price. Indirect business taxes are about 20 times greater than government subsidies, so we simplify the reporting by computing *indirect business taxes net of subsidies.*

National income therefore equals net domestic product plus net earnings from American resources abroad minus indirect business taxes (net of subsidies). Exhibit 6 shows how to go from net domestic product to national income. We have now moved from gross domestic product to net domestic product to national income. Next we peel back another layer of the onion to arrive at personal income, the income people actually receive.

EXHIBIT 6

Deriving Net Domestic Product and National Income Using 2001 Data (in trillions of dollars)

Gross domestic product (GDP)	$10.20
Minus depreciation	−1.34
Net domestic product	8.86
Plus net earnings of American resources abroad minus indirect business taxes (net of subsidies)	−0.65
National income	$8.21

Source: Figures are current, or nominal, projections as of September 2001. For the latest figures, go to http://www.bea.doc.gov/bea/dn/nipaweb/populartables.asp.

Chapter 22 Measuring Economic Aggregates and the Circular Flow of Income

383

PERSONAL INCOME

Some of the income received this year was not earned this year, and some of the income earned this year was not received this year by those who earned it. By adding to national income the income received but not earned and subtracting the income earned but not received, we move from national income to the total income *received* by individuals, which is called **personal income,** a widely reported measure of economic welfare. The federal government computes and reports personal income monthly.

The adjustment from national income to personal income is shown in Exhibit 7. Income *earned but not received* in the current period includes the employer's share of Social Security taxes, corporate income taxes, and undistributed corporate profits, which are profits the firm retains rather than pays as dividends. Income *received but not earned* in the current period includes government transfer payments, receipts from private pension plans, and interest paid by government and by consumers.

DISPOSABLE INCOME

Although several taxes have been considered so far, we have not yet discussed personal taxes, which consist mainly of federal, state, and local personal income taxes and the employee's share of the Social Security tax. Subtracting personal taxes and other government charges from personal income yields *disposable income,* which is the amount available for spending or saving—the amount that can be "disposed of" by the household. Think of disposable income as take-home pay. Exhibit 7 shows that personal income minus personal taxes and other government charges yields disposable income.

SUMMARY OF NATIONAL INCOME ACCOUNTS

Let's summarize the income side of national income accounts. We begin with *gross domestic product,* or *GDP,* the market value of all final goods and services produced during the year by resources located in the United States. We subtract depreciation from GDP to yield the *net domestic product.* To net domestic product we add net earnings from American resources abroad and subtract indirect business taxes (net of subsidies) to yield *national income.* We obtain *personal income* by subtracting from national income all income earned but not received this year (for example, undistributed corporate profits) and by adding all income received but not earned this year (for example, transfer payments). By subtracting personal taxes and other government charges from personal income, we arrive at the bottom line: *disposable income,* the amount people are actually free either to spend or to save.

EXHIBIT 7

Deriving Personal Income and Disposable Income Using 2001 Data (in trillions of dollars)

National income	$8.21
Minus income earned but not received (Social Security taxes, corporate income taxes, undistributed corporate profits)	−2.05
Plus income received but not earned (government and business transfers, net personal interest income)	2.56
Personal income	8.72
Minus personal tax and nontax charges	−1.35
Disposable income	$7.37

Source: Figures are current, or nominal, projections as of September 2001. For the latest figures, go to http://www.bea.doc.gov/bea/dn/nipaweb/populartables.asp.

SUMMARY INCOME STATEMENT OF THE ECONOMY

Exhibit 8 presents an annual income statement for the entire economy. The upper portion lists aggregate expenditure, which consists of consumption, gross investment, government purchases, and net exports. Because imports exceeded exports, net exports are negative. The income from this expenditure is allocated as shown in the lower portion of Exhibit 8. After subtracting both depreciation and net indirect business taxes, and adding net earnings from American resources abroad to the remaining forms of income, we get national income. National income is the sum of all earnings from resources supplied by U.S. residents and firms; it can be divided into its five income sources: employee compensation, proprietors' income, corporate profits, net interest, and rental income of persons. **Employee compensation,** by far the largest income source, includes both money wages and employer contributions to cover Social Security taxes, medical insurance, and other fringe benefits. **Proprietors' income** includes the earnings of unincorporated businesses. **Corporate profits** are the net revenues received by incorporated businesses before subtracting corporate income taxes. **Net interest** is the interest received by individuals, excluding interest paid by consumers to businesses and interest paid by government.

Each family that owns its own home is viewed as a tiny firm that rents that home to itself. Since homeowners do not, in fact, rent homes to themselves, an imputed rental value is estimated based on what the market rent would be. **Rental income of persons** consists primarily of the imputed rental value of owner-occupied housing minus the cost of owning that property (such as property taxes, insurance, depreciation, and interest paid on the mortgage). From the totals in Exhibit 8, you can see that *aggregate spending in the economy equals the income generated by that spending.*

EXHIBIT 8

Expenditure and Income Statement for the U.S. Economy Using 2001 Data (in trillions of dollars)

Aggregate Expenditure	
Consumption (C)	$7.05
Gross investment (I)	1.67
Government purchases (G)	1.84
Net exports ($X - M$)	−0.36
GDP	$10.20
Allocation of Income	
Depreciation	$1.34
Net earnings of American resources abroad	−0.02
Net indirect business taxes	0.63
Compensation of employees	6.01
Proprietors' income	0.75
Corporate profits	0.76
Net interest	0.55
Rental income of persons	0.18
GDP	$10.20

Source: Figures are current, or nominal, projections as of September 2001. For the latest figures, go to http://www.bea.doc.gov/bea/dn/nipaweb/populartables.asp.

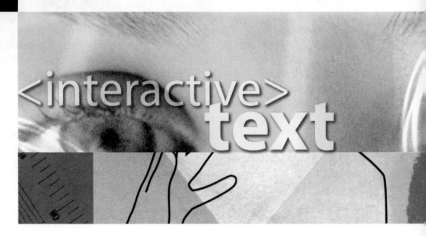

Unemployment and Inflation

Who among the following would be counted as unemployed: a college student who is not working, a bank teller displaced by an automatic teller machine, Julia Roberts between movies, or baseball slugger Barry Bonds in the off-season? What type of unemployment might be healthy for the economy? What's so bad about inflation? Why is anticipated inflation better than unanticipated inflation? These and other questions are answered in this chapter, where we explore two macroeconomic problems: unemployment and inflation.

To be sure, unemployment and inflation are not the only problems an economy could face. Sluggish growth and widespread poverty are some others. But low unemployment and low inflation go a long way toward helping diminish the effects of other economic problems. Although unemployment and inflation are often related, we initially describe each separately. We focus more on the extent and consequences of these problems than on their causes. The causes of each and the relationship between the two will become clearer in later chapters, as you learn more about how the economy works.

This chapter shows that not all unemployment or all inflation harms the economy. Even in a healthy economy, a certain amount of unemployment reflects the voluntary choices of workers and employers seeking their best opportunities. And inflation that is fully anticipated creates fewer distortions than does unanticipated inflation. Topics discussed in this chapter include:

- Measuring unemployment
- Frictional, structural, seasonal, and cyclical unemployment
- Full employment
- Sources and consequences of inflation

- Relative price changes
- Nominal and real interest rates

<interactive>exercise

ECONDEBATE ONLINE: EMPLOYMENT, UNEMPLOYMENT, AND INFLATION

<interactive>update

- ECONDATA ONLINE: EMPLOYMENT, UNEMPLOYMENT, AND INFLATION
- ECONLINKS ONLINE: ECONOMICS WEB LINKS
- ECONNEWS ONLINE: EMPLOYMENT, UNEMPLOYMENT, AND INFLATION

UNEMPLOYMENT

"They scampered about looking for work. . . . They swarmed on the highways. The movement changed them; the highways, the camps along the road, the fear of hunger and the hunger itself, changed them. The children without dinner changed them, the endless moving changed them."[1] There is no question, as John Steinbeck wrote in *The Grapes of Wrath,* that a long stretch of unemployment profoundly affects the individual and the family. The most obvious loss is a steady paycheck, but those who are unemployed often suffer a loss of self-esteem as well. According to psychologists, in terms of stressful events, the loss of a job ranks only slightly below the death of a loved one or a divorce. Moreover, unemployment appears to be linked to a greater incidence of crime and to a variety of afflictions, including heart disease, suicide, and mental illness.[2] No matter how much people complain about their jobs, they rely on those same jobs not only for income but also for part of their personal identity. When strangers meet, the "what do you do" question is usually one of the first to come up. The loss of a long-held job usually involves some loss of one's personal identity.

In addition to these personal costs, unemployment imposes a cost on the economy as a whole because fewer goods and services are produced. When the economy does not generate enough jobs to employ all who are willing and able to work, that unemployed labor service is lost forever. *This lost output coupled with the economic and psychological damage to unemployed workers and their families represents the true cost of unemployment.* As we begin our analysis, keep in mind that unemployment statistics reflect millions of individuals with their own stories. As President Harry Truman remarked, "It's a recession when your neighbor loses his job; it's a depression when you lose your own." For some lucky people, unemployment is a brief vacation between jobs. For others, a long stretch of unemployment can have a lasting effect on self-esteem, family stability, and economic welfare.

Measuring Unemployment

The unemployment rate is perhaps the most widely reported measure of the nation's economic health. What does the unemployment rate measure? What are the sources of unemployment? How has unemployment changed over time? These are some of the questions explored in this section. Let's start by considering how to measure unemployment.

We begin with the U.S. *civilian noninstitutional adult population,* which consists of all civilians 16 years of age and older, except those institutionalized in prisons or mental hospitals. The adjective *civilian* means that the definition excludes those in the military. In this chapter, when we refer to the *adult population,* we mean the civilian noninstitutional adult population. The **labor force** consists of members of the adult population who are either working or looking for work. *Those with no job who are looking for work are counted as unemployed.* The Bureau of Labor Statistics surveys 50,000 households monthly and counts people as unemployed if they have no job but want one and have looked for work at least once during the preceding four weeks. Thus, the college student, the displaced bank teller, Julia Roberts, and Barry Bonds would all

---

[1]John Steinbeck, *The Grapes of Wrath* (New York: Viking Press, 1939), p. 392.
[2]For a study linking a higher incidence of suicides to recessions, see Christopher Ruhm, "Are Recessions Good for Your Health," *Quarterly Journal of Economics* 115 (May 2000): 617–650.

be counted as unemployed if they want a job and looked for work in the previous month. The unemployment rate measures the percentage of those in the labor force who are unemployed. Hence, the **unemployment rate,** which is reported monthly, equals the number unemployed—that is, people without jobs who are looking for work—divided by the number in the labor force.

Only a fraction of adults who are not working are considered unemployed. The others may have retired, are students, are caring for children at home, or simply don't want to work. Others may be unable to work because of long-term illness or disability. Some may have become so discouraged by a long, unfruitful job search that they have given up in frustration. These **discouraged workers** have, in effect, dropped out of the labor force, so they are not counted as unemployed. Finally, about one-third of those working part time would prefer to work full time, yet all part-time workers are counted as employed. Because the official unemployment rate does not include discouraged workers and counts all part-time workers as employed, it may underestimate the true extent of unemployment in the economy. Later we will consider some factors that work in the opposite direction.

These definitions are illustrated in Exhibit 1, where circles represent the various groups, and the number (in millions) of individuals in each category and subcategory is shown in parentheses. The circle on the left depicts the entire U.S. labor force, including both employed and unemployed people. The circle on the right represents members of the adult population who, for whatever reason, are not working. Together, these two circles include the entire adult population. The overlapping area identifies the number of *unemployed* workers—that is, people in the labor force who are not working. The unemployment rate is found by dividing the number of unemployed by the number in the labor force; in August 2001, 7.0 million people were unemployed in a labor force of 141.5 million, yielding an unemployment rate of 4.9 percent.

The productive capability of any economy depends in part on the proportion of adults in the labor force, measured as the *labor force participation rate.* Let's step back from the unemployment rate to bring into the picture this more fundamental measure. In Exhibit 1, the U.S. adult population equals those in the labor force (141.5 million) plus those not in the labor force (70.7 million)—a total of 212.2 million. The **labor force participation rate** therefore equals the number in the labor force divided by the adult population, or 66.7 percent (141.5/212.2). So, on average, two out of three adults are in the labor force. The labor force participation rate increased from about 60 percent in 1970 to about 67 percent in 1990 and has remained relatively constant since.

EXHIBIT 1

Composition of Adult Population, August 2001 (in millions)

The labor force consists of employed and unemployed people. Those not working consist of individuals not in the labor force and those unemployed. The adult population sums the employed, the unemployed, and people not in the labor force.

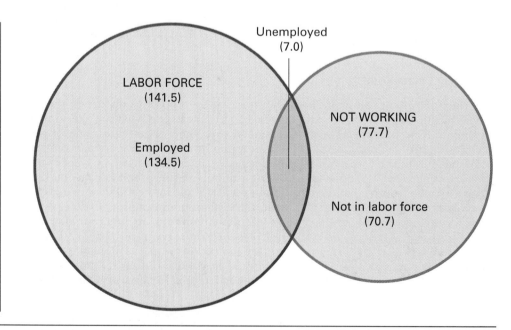

Source: U.S. Bureau of Labor Statistics. For the latest data, go to http://www.bls.gov/news.release/empsit.toc.htm.

Changes over Time in Unemployment Statistics

The noninstitutional adult population changes slowly over time. The only way to join that group is to become 16 years of age, get released from prison or a mental hospital, or immigrate to the United States. The only way to leave the adult population is to die, become institutionalized, or emigrate from the United States to another country. Over the last half century, the adult population in the United States has grown by an average of 1.4 percent per year.

The labor force participation rate can change more quickly than the adult population because moving in and out of the labor force is easier than moving in and out of the adult population. One striking development since World War II has been the convergence in the labor force participation rates of men and women. In 1950, only 34 percent of adult women were in the labor force; today 60 percent are, with the greatest increase among younger women. The labor force participation rate among men has declined from 86 percent in 1950 to about 75 percent today, primarily because of earlier retirement. The participation rate is slightly higher among white males than black males but higher among black females than white females.

Over time, what changes even more quickly than the labor force participation rate or the adult population is the unemployment rate. Exhibit 2 shows the U.S. unemployment rate since 1900, with shading to indicate periods of recession and depression. As you can see, the rate rises during recessions and falls during expansions. Perhaps the most striking feature of the graph is the dramatic jump that occurred during the Great Depression of the 1930s, when the unemployment rate reached 25 percent. Note that the rate trended upward from the end of World War II in the mid-1940s until the early 1980s; then it came back down, from a high of 9.7 percent in 1982 to 4.0 percent in early 2000, before edging up in 2001.

Why did the unemployment rate trend down from the early 1980s to 2000? First, the overall economy was on a roll during that period, interrupted by only a brief recession in

EXHIBIT 2

The U.S. Unemployment Rate Since 1900

Since 1900, the unemployment rate has fluctuated widely, rising during recessions and falling during expansions. During the Great Depression of the 1930s, the rate rose as high as 25.2 percent.

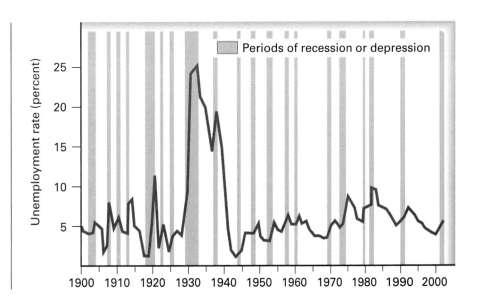

Sources: U.S. Census Bureau, *Historical Statistics of the United States: Colonial Times to 1970* (Washington, D.C.: U.S. Government Printing Office, 1975); *Economic Report of the President*, January 2001; and U.S. Bureau of Labor Statistics. For the latest data, go to http://www.bls.gov/news.release/empsit.toc.htm.

Chapter 23 Unemployment and Inflation

389

1990–1991 triggered by the Gulf War. The economy has added 35 million jobs since 1982 and has been called an incredible job machine, the envy of the world. Unemployment also trended down because there are now relatively fewer teenagers in the workforce. Teenagers have an unemployment rate about four times that of adult workers, so the declining share of teenage workers helped cut the overall unemployment rate.

NETBOOKMARK: BUREAU OF LABOR STATISTICS—U.S. ECONOMY AT A GLANCE

ASK THE INSTRUCTOR: WHY WAS UNEMPLOYMENT HIGHER IN THE 1970s THAN IN THE 1990s?

Unemployment in Various Groups

The unemployment rate says nothing about who is unemployed or for how long. Even a low overall rate often hides wide differences in unemployment rates across age, race, gender, and geographic area. For example, when the unemployment rate in 2001 was 4.9 percent, the rate was 16.1 percent among teenagers, 9.1 percent among blacks, and 6.3 percent among Hispanics. Why are unemployment rates among teenagers so much higher than among older workers? Since young workers enter the job market with little training, they take unskilled jobs from which they are the first to be fired if demand stalls. Young workers also move in and out of the job market more frequently during the year as they juggle school demands. Even those who have left school often shop around more than older workers, quitting one job and searching for another that suits them better.

Unemployment rates for different groups appear in Exhibit 3. Each panel shows the rate by race and by gender since 1972 (historical data are not available for Hispanics). Panel (a) shows the rates for people 20 years of age and older, and panel (b) the rates for those 16 to 19 years old. Years of recession are shaded. As you can see, rates are higher among blacks than among whites, and rates are higher among teenagers than among those aged 20 and older. During recessions, the rates climbed for all groups. Rates peaked during the recession of 1982 and then trended down. After the recession of the early 1990s, unemployment rates continued downward, with the rate among blacks falling in 2000 to the lowest on record.

Unemployment also varies by occupational group. Professional and technical workers experience lower unemployment rates than blue-collar workers. Construction workers have the highest average unemployment rate because that business is seasonal and is subject to wide swings over the business cycle.

Unemployment Differences Across the Country

The national unemployment rate masks much variation in rates across the country. For example, in 2001, unemployment rates in Alaska, New Mexico, and West Virginia were more than double those in Nebraska, North Dakota, and South Dakota. To look behind the numbers, read the following case study about one troubled county in West Virginia.

CASE**STUDY**	Poor King Coal
	● *The World of Business*

For decades McDowell County, West Virginia, prospered by supplying the coal that fired the nation's steel mills. Mining jobs were abundant, accounting for half of all jobs in the county. And mining wages were attractive, paying in 1980 an average of $80,000 in today's dollars. Most young people, rather than finishing high school, became miners (more than half of those over age 25 in 1980 were high school dropouts). Mining companies dominated the county, owning most of the property.

But two developments in the early 1980s hurt West Virginia's coal industry. First, the value of the dollar rose relative to foreign currencies, so American steel became more expensive overseas and foreign steel became cheaper here. Consequently, steel imports rose substantially, reducing the demand for U.S. steel and the coal used to make it. Second, more stringent pollution controls reduced the demand for the kind of coal mined in McDowell County. As a result, many coal mines there shut down, putting most miners out of work. By 1983, the county's unemployment rate topped 40 percent.

The county tried to attract new industry—even a nuclear waste dump—but met with little success. The poor roads and bridges and a labor force trained only for mining scared off potential employers. Between 1980 and 2000, mining jobs in the county fell from 7,200 to only 700 while all private-sector jobs dropped by more than half. As jobs disappeared, people left. County population dropped from about 50,000 in 1980 to 29,000 in 2000. The unemployment rate in 2001 was still nearly triple the national average and double the state average. In short,

EXHIBIT 3

Unemployment Rates Among Various Groups Since 1972

Unemployment affects different groups in different ways. The unemployment rate is higher for blacks than for whites and higher for teenagers than for older persons.

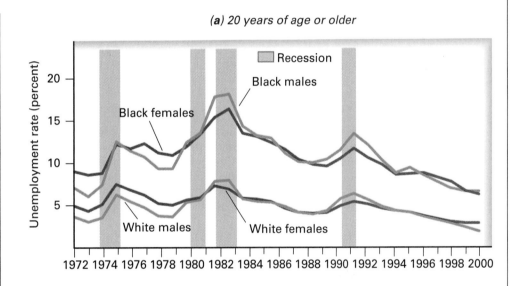

(a) 20 years of age or older

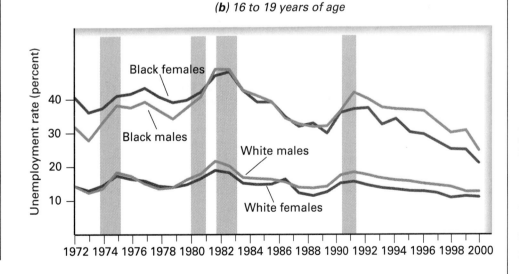

(b) 16 to 19 years of age

Source: *Economic Report of the President,* January 2001; U.S. Bureau of Labor Statistics. For the latest data, go to http://www.bls.gov/news.release/empsit.toc.htm.

the county had all its eggs in one basket—mining—but that basket fell, and the county has not recovered.

<interactive>exercise

eACTIVITY: POOR KING COAL

Sources: Walter Adams, "Steel," in *The Structure of American Industry,* edited by Walter Adams and James Brock (Englewood Cliffs, N.J.: Prentice-Hall, 1995), pp. 93–118. General information about McDowell County can be found at http://www. capitolimpact.com/cgi-local/cio_county_detail.pl?GetFile=wv~54047. For recent employment and income figures for McDowell County go to http://www.state.wv.us/bep/lmi/cntyprof/CP99mcdo.htm.

Types of Unemployment

Pick up any metropolitan newspaper and thumb through the classifieds. The Help Wanted section may include thousands of jobs, from accountants to X-ray technicians. Why, when millions are unemployed, are so many jobs open? To understand this paradox, we must take a closer look at the reasons behind unemployment.

Think about all the ways people can become unemployed. They may quit or be fired from their last job. They may be looking for a first job, or they may be reentering the labor force after an absence. An examination of the reasons behind unemployment in 2000 indicates that 42 percent of the unemployed lost their previous jobs, 13 percent quit their previous jobs, 9 percent were entering the labor market for the first time, and 36 percent were reentering the market. *Thus, 58 percent were unemployed either because they quit jobs or because they were just joining or rejoining the labor force.*

There are four sources of unemployment: frictional, structural, seasonal, and cyclical.

Frictional Unemployment. Just as employers do not always hire the first applicant who comes through the door, job seekers do not always accept their first offer. Both employers and job seekers need time to explore the job market. Employers need time to learn about the talent available, and job seekers need time to learn about employment opportunities. The time required to bring together labor suppliers and labor demanders causes **frictional unemployment.** Although unemployment often creates economic and psychological hardships, not all unemployment is necessarily bad. Frictional unemployment does not usually last long and results in a better match-up between workers and jobs, so the entire economy becomes more efficient.

Structural Unemployment. A second reason why job vacancies and unemployment coexist is that unemployed workers often do not have the skills demanded by employers or do not live where their skills are in demand. For example, the Lincoln Electric Company in Euclid, Ohio, could not fill 200 job openings because few of the thousands who applied could operate computer-controlled machines. Unemployment arising from a mismatch of skills or geographic location is called **structural unemployment.** *Structural unemployment occurs because changes in tastes, technology, taxes, or competition reduce the demand for certain skills and increase the demand for other skills.* In our dynamic economy, some workers, such as coal miners in West Virginia, are stuck with skills that are no longer in demand. Likewise, golf carts replaced caddies, ATMs put many bank tellers out of work, and better office technology is replacing clerical staff. For example, because of e-mail, voice mail, PCs, and Palm handhelds, the number of secretaries, typists, and administrative assistants in the United States fell from 5.2 million in 1987 to 3.4 million in 2001.

Whereas most frictional unemployment is short-term and voluntary, structural unemployment poses more of a problem because workers must seek jobs elsewhere or develop the skills that are in demand. For example, unemployed coal miners and bank tellers must seek work in other industries or in other regions. But moving to where the jobs are is easier said than done. Most people prefer to remain near friends and relatives. Those laid off from good jobs may be reluctant to leave the area because they hope to get rehired. Families in which one spouse is still employed may not want to give up one job to seek two elsewhere. Finally, available jobs may be in regions where the cost of living is much higher. So those unemployed often stay put, remaining structurally unemployed.

Seasonal Unemployment. Unemployment caused by seasonal changes in labor demand during the year is called **seasonal unemployment.** During cold winter months, demand for farm hands, lifeguards, landscapers, and construction workers shrinks, as it does for dozens of other seasonal occupations. Likewise, tourism in places such as Miami and Phoenix melts in the summer heat. The Christmas season increases the demand for sales clerks, postal workers, and Santa Clauses. Those with seasonal jobs know they will probably be unemployed in the off-season. Some may have even chosen a seasonal occupation to complement their lifestyles or academic schedules. To eliminate seasonal unemployment, we would have to outlaw winter and abolish Christmas. Monthly employment statistics are "seasonally adjusted" to smooth out the bulges that result from seasonal factors.

Cyclical Unemployment. As output declines during recessions, firms reduce their demand for inputs, including labor. **Cyclical unemployment** is the fluctuation in unemployment caused by the business cycle. Cyclical unemployment increases during recessions and decreases during expansions. Between 1932 and 1934, when unemployment averaged about 24 percent, there was clearly much cyclical unemployment. Between 1942 and 1945, when the rate averaged less than 2 percent, there was no cyclical unemployment. Government policies to stimulate aggregate demand during recessions are aimed at reducing cyclical unemployment.

‹interactive›video

ASK THE INSTRUCTOR: WHAT ARE THE FOUR TYPES OF UNEMPLOYMENT?

‹interactive›update

- **ECONDATA ONLINE: CIVILIAN UNEMPLOYMENT RATE**
- **ECONNEWS ONLINE: ENERGIZED CEOs—THEY KEEP GOING AND GOING**

The Meaning of Full Employment

In a dynamic economy such as ours, changes in product demand and changes in technology continually alter the supply and demand for particular types of labor. Thus, even in a healthy economy, there will be some frictional, structural, and seasonal unemployment. The economy is viewed as operating at *full employment* if there is no cyclical unemployment. When economists talk about "full employment," they do not mean zero unemployment but relatively low unemployment, with estimates ranging from 4 to 6 percent. Even when the economy is at **full employment,** there will be some frictional, structural, and seasonal unemployment. After all, more than half of those unemployed have quit their last job or are new entrants or reentrants into the labor force. We can't expect them to find jobs overnight. Most of this group would be considered frictionally unemployed.

‹interactive›exercise

READING IT RIGHT: WALL STREET JOURNAL EXERCISE

‹interactive›update

ECONNEWS ONLINE: RETIREES MODEL THE ENERGIZER BUNNY—THEY KEEP GOING AND GOING AND GOING

Unemployment Compensation

As noted at the outset, unemployment often imposes an economic and psychological hardship. For a variety of reasons, however, the burden of unemployment on the individual and the family may not be as severe today as it was during the Great Depression. Today, a large proportion of households have two workers in the labor force, so if one becomes unemployed, another is likely to have a job—a job that may provide health insurance and other benefits. Having more than one family member in the labor force cushions the economic shock of unemployment.

Moreover, unlike the experience during the Great Depression, workers who lose their jobs now often receive unemployment benefits. In response to the massive unemployment of the Great Depression, Congress passed the Social Security Act of 1935, which provided unemployment insurance financed by a tax on employers. Unemployed workers who meet certain qualifications can receive **unemployment benefits** for up to six months, provided they actively seek work. During recessions, benefits often extend beyond six months in states with especially high unemployment rates. Insurance benefits go mainly to people who have lost jobs. Individuals just entering or reentering the labor force are not covered, nor are those who quit their last job or those fired for just cause, such as excessive absenteeism or theft. Because of these restrictions, fewer than half of all unemployed workers receive unemployment benefits.

Unemployment insurance replaces on average about 40 percent of a person's take-home pay, with a higher share for those whose jobs paid less. Benefits averaged $220 per week in 2000. Because unemployment benefits reduce the opportunity cost of remaining unemployed, they may reduce incentives to find work. For example, if you faced the choice of taking a job washing dishes that pays $200 per week or collecting $150 per week in unemployment benefits, which would you choose? Evidence suggests that unemployed workers who receive benefits tend to search less actively than those who don't. So although unemployment insurance provides a safety net for the unemployed, it may also reduce the urgency of finding work, thereby increasing the average duration of unemployment and the unemployment rate. On the plus side, unemployment insurance allows for a higher-quality search, since the insured job seeker has walking-around money and need not take the first job that comes along. As a result of a better search, there is a better match between job skills and job requirements, and this promotes economic efficiency.

International Comparisons of Unemployment

How do U.S. unemployment rates compare with those around the world? Exhibit 4 shows rates since 1982 for the United States, Japan, and the average of four major European economies—France, Germany, Italy, and the United Kingdom. During the past two decades, the unemployment rate trended down in the United States, trended up in Japan, and remained relatively high in Europe. At the beginning of the period, the United States had the highest unemployment rate among the three economies; most recently, the U.S. rate was lowest, just below Japan's.

EXHIBIT 4

In the Last Two Decades, Unemployment Rates Fell in the United States, Rose in Japan, and Remained High in Europe

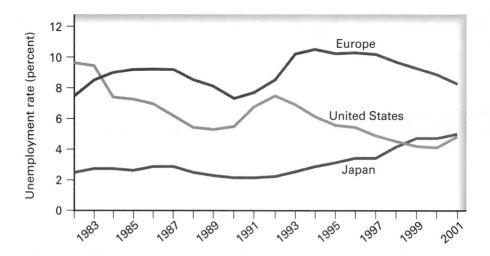

Source: Based on standardized rates on *OECD Economic Outlook* 69 (June 2001), Annex 22. Figures for Europe are the averages of those for France, Germany, Italy, and the United Kingdom. For the latest data, go to http://stats.bls.gov/flsdata.htm.

Why are rates so high in Europe? The ratio of unemployment benefits to average pay is higher in Europe than in the United States, and unemployment benefits last longer there, sometimes years. So unemployed workers have less incentive to find new jobs. What's more, government regulations make employers in Europe reluctant to hire new workers because firing them is quite difficult. For example, Germany imposes penalties on firms for "socially unjustified" layoffs.

Historically, unemployment has been low in Japan because many firms have offered job security for life. Thus, some employees there who do little or no work are still carried on company payrolls. Both labor laws and social norms limit layoffs in Japan. Unemployment has increased there lately only because many firms have gone bankrupt and had no alternative but to lay off workers.

Problems with Official Unemployment Figures

Official unemployment statistics are not without their problems. As we saw earlier, not counting discouraged workers in the official labor force understates unemployment. Official employment data also ignore the problem of **underemployment,** which arises because people are counted as employed even if they can find only part-time jobs or are vastly overqualified for their job, as when someone with a Ph.D. in English can find work only as a bookstore clerk. Counting overqualified and part-time workers as employed tends to understate the actual amount of unemployment.

On the other hand, because unemployment insurance and most welfare programs require recipients to seek employment, some people may act as if they are looking for work just to qualify. If these people do not in fact want to work, their inclusion among the unemployed tends to overstate the official unemployment figures. Likewise, some people who would prefer to work part time can find only full-time positions, and some forced to work overtime and weekends would prefer to work fewer hours. To the extent that people must work more than they would like to, the official unemployment rate overstates the amount of unemployment in the economy. Finally, people working in the underground economy may not readily acknowledge their jobs on a government survey because their intent is to evade taxes or skirt the law. *On net, however, most experts believe that official U.S. unemployment figures tend to underestimate unemployment because of the exclusion of discouraged workers and because underemployed workers are counted as employed.* Still, the size of this underestimation may not be large. For example, counting discouraged workers as unemployed would have raised the unemployment rate in August 2001 from 4.9 percent to 5.1 percent.

Despite several qualifications and limitations, the unemployment rate is a useful measure of unemployment trends over time. We turn next to another major concern: inflation.

<interactive>update

ECONDATA ONLINE: CIVILIAN UNEMPLOYMENT RATE

INFLATION

Let's begin our discussion of inflation with a case study that underscores the cost of high inflation.

CASE**STUDY**	Hyperinflation in Brazil
	● *Bringing Theory to Life*

Between 1988 and 1994, annual inflation rates in Brazil were 1,300 percent, 2,900 percent, 440 percent, 1,000 percent, 1,260 percent, and 1,740 percent, respectively. Six years of such inflation meant that prices on average were about *3.6 million* times higher in 1994 than in 1988! To put this in perspective, with such inflation in the United States, the price of gasoline would have climbed from $1.25 a gallon in 1988 to $4.5 million a gallon in 1994. A pair of jeans that sold for $25 in 1988 would cost $90 million in 1994!

Those were crazy times in Brazil. With the value of the Brazilian currency, the cruzeiro, cheapening by the hour, people understandably did not want to hold any. Workers insisted on getting paid at least once a day. They immediately tried to either spend the day's pay before prices increased or exchange cruzeiros for a more stable currency, such as the U.S. dollar. With such wild inflation, everyone, including merchants, had difficulty keeping track of prices. Different price increases among sellers of the same product encouraged shoppers to incur the "shoe-leather cost" of looking around for the lowest price.

The huge increase in the average price level meant carrying out even the simplest transactions required piles of cash. Think again in terms of dollars. As a consequence of such inflation, dinner for two would cost more than $120 million. Even in $100 bills, that pile of cash would weigh more than a ton, literally. Because carrying even modest purchasing power became physically impossible, Brazilian officials issued currencies in larger and larger denominations. Between the mid-1980s and 1994, new currency denominations were issued five separate times, with each issue a huge multiple of the previous one. For example, the 1994 issue of the new *cruzeiro real* (now called simply the *real*) exchanged for 2,750 of the cruzeiro it replaced. New currency issues made transactions easier.

Lugging money around, shopping for the lowest price, and a constant preoccupation with money all sucked up time and energy and so reduced actual production. High and unpredictable inflation led to activity that was rational for each individual but wasteful for the economy as a whole. Inflation in Brazil dropped from the runaway levels of the early 1990s to single digits since then. For example, the rate in 2001 was about 8 percent. Fernando Henrique Cordoso, the finance minister credited with taming inflation, became such a hero that he was elected Brazil's president in 1994 and reelected in 1998.

Although Brazil ended its inflation nightmare, hyperinflation is usually a problem somewhere in the world. Congo, the most recent victim, averaged 1,700 percent inflation a year during the 1990s.

<interactive>exercise

eACTIVITY: HYPERINFLATION IN BRAZIL

Sources: "Battle Begins for Cordoso's Successor," *Economist,* 6 January 2001; "Brazil," *Britannica Book of the Year* (Chicago: Encyclopaedia Britannica, 1995); and Andriana Brasileiro, "Brazil Inflation to Cool Off in 2001 as Fuel Prices Ease," Dow Jones Newswire, 12 January 2001. For a focus on the Brazilian economy, go to http://www. latin-focus.com/countries/brazil/brazil.htm.

We have already discussed inflation in different contexts. *Inflation* is a sustained increase in the average price level. If the price level bounces around—moving up one month, falling back another—any particular increase in the price level would not necessarily be called inflation in a meaningful sense. Extremely high inflation, as in Brazil, is called **hyperinflation.** A sustained *decrease* in the average price level is called **deflation,** as occurred in the United States during the Great Depression and most recently in Japan, Hong Kong, and Argentina. And a reduction in the rate of inflation is called **disinflation.**

We typically measure inflation on an annual basis. The annual *inflation rate* is the percentage increase in the average price level from one year to the next. For example, between August 2000 and August 2001, the U.S. *consumer price index* increased 2.7 percent. In this section, we first consider two sources of inflation. We then examine the extent and consequences of inflation in the United States and around the world.

<interactive>update

- **ECONNEWS ONLINE: AND NOW DEFLATION?**
- **ECONNEWS ONLINE: NOT MUCH "IN" IN INFLATION**

Two Sources of Inflation

Inflation is a sustained increase in the economy's price level resulting from an increase in aggregate demand or a decrease in aggregate supply. Panel (a) of Exhibit 5 shows an increase in aggregate demand that raises the price level from P to P'. Inflation resulting from increases in aggregate demand is often called **demand-pull inflation.** In such cases, a shift to the right of the aggregate demand curve *pulls up* the price level. To generate continuous demand-pull inflation, the aggregate demand curve would have to keep shifting out along a given aggregate supply curve. Rising U.S. inflation rates during the late 1960s resulted from demand-pull inflation, when federal spending for the Vietnam War and for expanded social programs boosted aggregate demand.

Alternatively, inflation can arise from reductions in aggregate supply, as shown in panel (b) of Exhibit 5, where a leftward shift of the aggregate supply curve raises the price level. For example, crop failures and cuts in oil supplies reduced aggregate supply during 1974 and 1975, thereby raising the price level. Inflation stemming from decreases in aggregate supply is called **cost-push inflation,** suggesting that increases in the cost of production *push up* the price level. Prices increase and real GDP decreases, a combination identified earlier as *stagflation.* Again, to generate sustained and continuous cost-push inflation, the aggregate supply curve would have to keep shifting to the left along a given aggregate demand curve.

ECONNEWS ONLINE: WITHERING WAGES

A Historical Look at Inflation and the Price Level

The consumer price index is the price measure you most often encounter, so we give it more attention here. As you learned in the previous chapter, the *consumer price index,* or *CPI,* measures the cost of a "market basket" of consumer goods and services over time. Exhibit 6 shows prices in the United States since 1913, using the consumer price index. Panel (a) shows the price *level,* measured by an index relative to the base period of 1982 to 1984. As you can see, the price level was lower in 1940 than in 1920. Since 1940, however, it has risen steadily, especially during the 1970s.

People are concerned less about the price level and more about year-to-year changes in that level. The lower panel shows the annual *rate of change* in the CPI, or the annual rate of *inflation* or *deflation.* The decade of the 1970s was not the only period of high inflation. Inflation climbed above 10 percent from 1916 to 1919 and in 1947—periods associated with world wars. Prior to the 1950s, inflation was war related and was usually followed by deflation. Such an inflation-deflation cycle stretches back during the last two centuries. In fact, between the Revolutionary War and World War II, the price level fell in about as many years as it rose. At the end of World War II, the price level was about where it had been at the end of the Civil War.

EXHIBIT 5

Inflation Caused by Shifts in the Aggregate Demand and Aggregate Supply Curves

Panel (a) illustrates demand-pull inflation. An outward shift of the aggregate demand to *AD'* "pulls" the price level up from *P* to *P'*.
Panel (b) shows cost-push inflation, in which a decrease in aggregate supply to *AS'* "pushes" the price level up from *P* to *P'*.

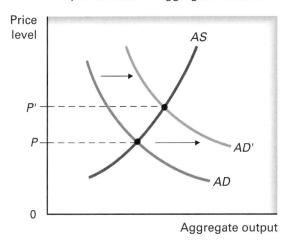

(a) *Demand-pull inflation: inflation induced by an increase in aggregate demand*

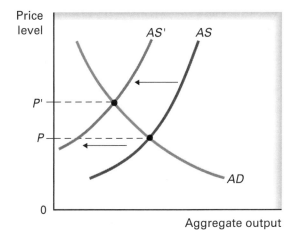

(b) *Cost-push inflation: inflation induced by a decrease in aggregate supply*

EXHIBIT 6

Consumer Price Index Since 1913

Panel (a) shows that, despite fluctuations, the price level, as measured by the consumer price index, was lower in 1940 than in 1920. Since 1940, the price level has risen almost every year. Panel (b) shows the annual rate of change in the price level. Since 1947, the inflation rate has averaged 3.9 percent annually.

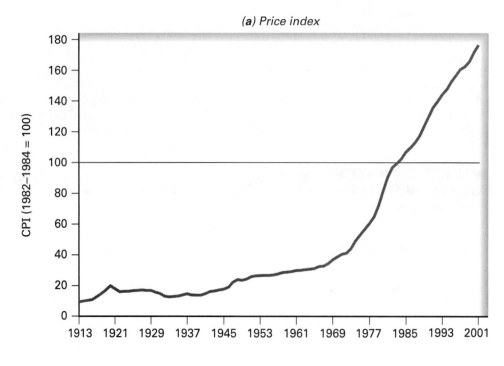

(a) Price index

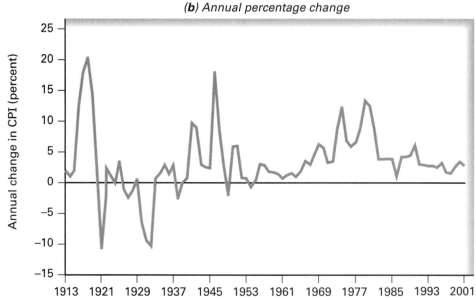

(b) Annual percentage change

Source: The CPI home page of the U.S. Bureau of Labor Statistics at http://www.bls.gov/cpihome.htm.

So changes in the price level are nothing new. But prior to World War II, periods of inflation and deflation balanced out over the long run. Therefore, people had good reason to believe the dollar would retain its purchasing power when averaged over the long term. Since the end of World War II, however, the CPI has increased by an average of 3.9 percent per year. That may not sound like much, but it translates into an *eightfold* increase in the consumer price index since 1947. *Inflation erodes confidence in the value of the dollar over the long term.*

Anticipated Versus Unanticipated Inflation

What is the effect of inflation on the economy's performance? *Unanticipated inflation* creates more problems for the economy than does *anticipated inflation*. To the extent that inflation is higher or lower than anticipated, it arbitrarily creates economic winners and losers. If inflation is higher than expected, the winners are the people who had contracted to pay a price that anticipates lower inflation. The losers are those who agreed to sell at that price. If inflation is lower than expected, the situation is reversed: The winners are the people who contracted to sell at a price that anticipates higher inflation, and the losers are all those who contracted to buy at that price.

Suppose inflation next year is expected to be 3 percent, and you agree to work for a *nominal*, or money, wage that is 4 percent higher than this year. In this case, you expect your *real* wage—that is, your wage measured in dollars of constant purchasing power—to increase by 1 percent. If inflation turns out to be 3 percent, you and your employer will both be satisfied with your nominal wage increase of 4 percent. If inflation turns out to be 5 percent, your real wage will fall, so you will be a loser and your employer will be a winner. If inflation turns out to be only 1 percent, your real wage will increase by 3 percent, so you will be a winner and your employer, a loser. *The arbitrary gains and losses arising from unanticipated inflation are one reason that inflation is so unpopular.*

The Transaction Costs of Variable Inflation

During long periods of price stability, people correctly believe that they can predict future prices and can therefore plan accordingly. But if inflation changes unexpectedly, the future is cloudier, so planning gets harder. Uncertainty about inflation undermines the ability of money to serve as a link between the present and the future.

Firms that deal with the rest of the world face added complications, for they must not only plan for U.S. inflation, they must also anticipate how the value of the dollar might change relative to foreign currencies. Inflation uncertainty and the resulting exchange-rate uncertainty increase the difficulty of making international business decisions. In this more uncertain environment, managers must shift their attention from production to anticipating the effects of inflation and exchange-rate variations on the firm's finances. The *transaction costs* of contracts, particularly long-term contracts, increase as inflation becomes more unpredictable. Some economists suspect that the high and variable inflation rates in the United States during the 1970s and early 1980s contributed to the slower growth of the economy during that period.

Inflation Obscures Relative Price Changes

Even with no inflation, some prices would go up and some would go down, reflecting the healthy workings of supply and demand for different products. For example, during the last two decades, the U.S. price level nearly doubled, yet the prices of color televisions, DVD players, pocket calculators, computers, and many other items declined sharply. Because the prices of various goods change by different amounts, *relative prices* change. Whereas the economy's price level describes the terms at which some representative bundle of goods exchanges for *money*, relative prices describe the terms at which individual goods exchange for *one another*.

Inflation does not necessarily cause the change in relative prices, but it can obscure the change. During periods of volatile inflation, there is greater uncertainty about the price of one good relative to another—that is, about relative prices. In his Nobel Prize address, Milton Friedman noted, "The more volatile the rate of general inflation, the harder it becomes to extract the signal about relative prices from the absolute prices; the broadcast about relative prices is, as it were, being jammed by the noise coming from the inflation broadcast."[3] But relative price changes are important for allocating the economy's resources efficiently.

If all prices moved together, producers could simply link the selling prices of their goods to the overall inflation rate. Since prices usually do not move in unison, however, tying a particular product's price to the overall inflation rate may result in a price that is too high or too low based on market conditions. The same is true of agreements by employers to raise wages in accord with inflation. If the price of an employer's product grows more slowly than the rate of inflation in the economy, the employer may be hard-pressed to increase wages by the rate of inflation. Consider the problem confronting oil refiners who signed labor contracts agreeing to pay their workers cost-of-living wage increases. In some years, those employers had to provide pay increases at a time when the price of oil was falling like a rock.

<interactive>update

ECONNEWS ONLINE: A BITTER PILL

International Comparisons of Inflation

Exhibit 7 shows the annual rates of inflation based on the CPI for the past two decades in the United States, Japan, and Europe, where Europe is the average of France, Germany, Italy, and the United Kingdom. All three economies show a similar trend, with falling inflation rates, or disinflation, during the 1980s, a rise during the middle that peaked in the early 1990s, and then another trend lower. So the overall trend during the two decades was toward lower inflation. Inflation rates in Europe were similar to those in the United States; rates in Japan were consistently lower, even dipping into deflation in recent years. Inflation for the past 20 years averaged 4.5 percent in Europe, 3.8 percent in the United States, and 1.5 percent in Japan.

So in major industrial economies, inflation is not as high as it once was. Still, inflation has averaged more than 10 percent a year since 1996 in some other economies, including Greece,

EXHIBIT 7

Inflation Rates in Major Economies Have Trended Lower During the Past Two Decades

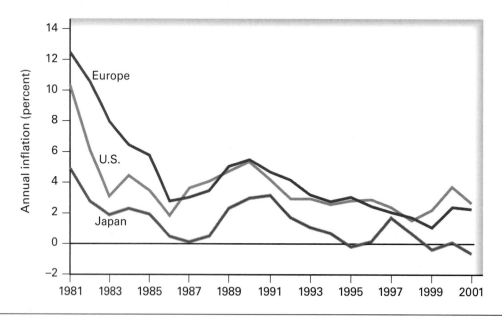

Source: Developed from annual CPI inflation reported in *OECD Economic Outlook* 69 (June 2001), Annex Table 16. Figures for Europe are the averages of those for France, Germany, Italy, and the United Kingdom. For the latest data, go to the Web site for the *Economist* at http://economist.com and search for "prices and wages."

---

[3]Milton Friedman, "Nobel Lecture: Inflation and Unemployment," *Journal of Political Economy* 85 (June 1977): 467.

Hungary, Mexico, and Poland. Inflation averaged more than 100 percent a year during the 1990s in most countries that once belonged to the former Soviet Union.

The quantity and quality of data collected to compute the price level vary across countries. Governments in less-developed countries sample fewer products and measure prices only in the capital city. Whereas prices for some 400 items are sampled to determine the U.S. consumer price index, as few as 30 might be sampled in some less-developed countries.

Inflation and Interest Rates

No discussion of inflation would be complete without some mention of the interest rate. **Interest** is the dollar amount paid by borrowers to lenders; lenders must be rewarded for forgoing present consumption. The **interest rate** is the interest per year as a percentage of the amount loaned. For example, an interest rate of 5 percent means $5 per year on a $100 loan. The greater the interest rate, other things constant, the greater the reward for lending money. Thus, the amount of money people are willing to lend, called *loanable funds*, increases as the interest rate rises, other things constant. The supply curve for loanable funds therefore slopes upward, as indicated by line *S* in Exhibit 8.

These funds are demanded by households, firms, and governments to finance purchases, such as homes, buildings, machinery, and a college education. The higher the interest rate, other things constant, the higher the cost of borrowing. So the quantity of loanable funds demanded decreases as the interest rate increases, other things constant. That is, the interest rate and the quantity of loanable funds demanded are inversely related. The demand curve therefore slopes downward, as indicated by curve *D* in Exhibit 8. The downward-sloping demand curve for loanable funds and the upward-sloping supply curve intersect at the equilibrium point to yield the equilibrium nominal rate of interest, *i*.

The **nominal interest rate** measures interest in terms of the current dollars paid. The nominal rate is the one that appears on the borrowing agreement; it is the rate discussed in the news media and is often of political significance. The **real interest rate** equals the nominal rate of interest minus the inflation rate:

$$\text{Real interest rate} = \text{Nominal interest rate} - \text{Inflation rate}$$

The real interest rate is expressed in dollars of constant purchasing power as a percentage of the amount loaned. For example, if the nominal interest rate is 5 percent and the inflation rate is 3 percent, the real interest rate is 2 percent. With no inflation, the nominal interest rate and the real interest rate would be identical. But with inflation, the nominal interest rate exceeds the real interest rate. If inflation were unexpectedly high enough—higher, for example, than the nominal interest rate—then the real interest rate would turn out to be negative. In this case, nominal interest would not even offset the loss in spending power because of inflation. Lenders would lose purchasing power. This is why lenders and borrowers are concerned more about the real rate than the nominal rate. The real rate of interest, however, is known only after the fact—that is, only after inflation actually occurs.

EXHIBIT 8

The Market for Loanable Funds

The upward-sloping supply curve, S, shows that more funds are supplied to financial markets at higher interest rates. The downward-sloping demand curve, D, shows that the quantity of loanable funds demanded is greater at lower interest rates. The two curves intersect to determine the equilibrium interest rate, i.

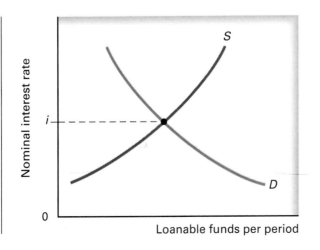

Because the future is uncertain, lenders and borrowers must form expectations about inflation, and they base their willingness to lend and to borrow on these expectations. Other things constant, the higher the *expected* rate of inflation, the higher the nominal rate of interest that lenders require and that borrowers are willing to pay. Lenders and borrowers base their decisions on the *expected* real interest rate, which equals the nominal rate of interest minus the expected inflation rate.[4]

Why Is Inflation Unpopular?

Whenever the price level increases, more money must be spent to buy the same goods and services. If you think of inflation only in terms of spending, you consider only the problem of paying those higher prices. But if you think of inflation in terms of the higher money incomes that result, you see that higher prices mean higher receipts for resource suppliers, usually including higher wages for workers. When viewed from the income side, inflation is not such a bad thing.

If every higher price is received by some resource supplier, why are people so troubled by inflation? People view their higher incomes as well-deserved rewards for their labor, but they see inflation as a penalty that unjustly robs them of purchasing power. Most people do not stop to realize that, unless their labor productivity increases, higher wages *must* result in higher prices. Prices and wages are simply two sides of the same coin. To the extent that nominal wages on average keep up with inflation, workers on average do not suffer a loss of real income as a result of inflation. But in a survey of 1,000 adults, more than two-thirds believed that price increases are due to companies trying to manipulate prices to increase profits.[5] Less than one-third attributed price increases to the workings of supply and demand.

Presidents Ford and Carter could not control inflation and were turned out of office. Inflation slowed significantly during President Reagan's first term, and he won reelection easily, even though the unemployment rate was higher during his first term than during President Carter's tenure. During the 1988 election, George H. W. Bush won in part by reminding voters what inflation was in 1980, the last time a Democrat had been president. But he lost his bid at reelection in part because inflation spiked to 6.0 percent in 1990, the highest in a decade. Inflation remained under 3.0 percent during President Clinton's first term, and he was reelected. In the 2000 election, inflation was so low that it was not a factor.

Although inflation affects everyone, it hits hardest individuals whose incomes are fixed in nominal terms. For example, pensions are often fixed amounts and are eroded by inflation. But the benefits paid by the largest pension program, Social Security, are adjusted annually for changes in the CPI. Retirees who rely on fixed nominal interest income also see their incomes eroded by inflation.

In summary, to the extent that inflation is fully anticipated by market participants, it is of less concern than unanticipated inflation. *Unanticipated inflation arbitrarily redistributes income and wealth from one group to another, reduces the ability to make long-term plans, and forces buyers and sellers to pay more attention to prices.* The more variable and unpredictable inflation is, the greater the difficulty of negotiating long-term contracts. The overall productivity of the economy falls because people must spend more time coping with the uncertainty created by inflation, leaving less time for production.

<interactive>**exercise**

ECONDEBATE ONLINE: SHOULD THE FEDERAL RESERVE AIM AT A ZERO INFLATION POLICY?

CONCLUSION

This chapter has focused on two macroeconomic problems: unemployment and inflation. Although we have discussed them separately, they are related in a variety of ways, as we will see in later chapters. Politicians sometimes add the unemployment rate to the rate of inflation to come up with what they refer to as the "misery index." In 1980, for example, an unemployment

---

[4]Although the discussion has implied that there is only one rate of interest, there are actually many rates. Rates differ depending on such factors as the risk, the maturity of different loans, and tax treatment of the interest.
[5]As reported in Robert J. Blendon et al., "Bridging the Gap Between the Public's and Economists' Views of the Economy," *Journal of Economic Perspectives* 11 (Summer 1997): 116.

rate of 7.1 percent combined with a CPI increase of 13.6 percent to yield a misery index of 20.7—a number that explains why President Carter was not reelected that year. By 1984 the misery index had dropped to 11.8, and by 1988 to 9.6; Republicans retained the White House in both elections. In 1992, the index climbed slightly to 10.4 percent, an increase that spelled trouble for President Bush. And in 1996, the index fell back to 8.4 percent, assuring President Clinton's reelection. During the election of 2000, the misery index was down to 7.7, which should have helped Al Gore, the candidate of the incumbent party. But during the campaign, Gore distanced himself from President Clinton and thus was not able to capitalize on the strong economy.

endofchaptermaterial

- Summary
- Questions for Review
- Problems and Exercises
- Experiential Exercises
- Wall Street Journal Exercise

Take the Post-Test to assess your overall understanding of the key ideas in this chapter. The Post-Test provides a comprehensive selection of exam-style questions addressing the main topics and concepts of the chapter. At the completion of each Post-Test, you will receive a score and instructive feedback on how you answered each question, and a direct link to the part of the chapter addressed in the question. Take the Post-Test as often as you need to—a record of your progress for each attempt is kept for you to revisit and gauge your improvement. And each Post-Test is randomly generated, so every attempt is new.

Post-Test

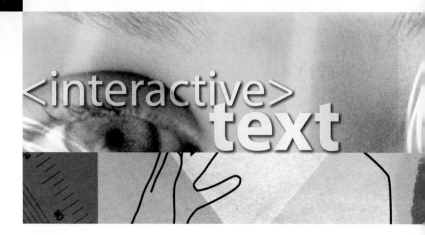

CHAPTER 24

Aggregate Expenditure Components

When driving through a neighborhood new to you, how can you figure out the income level of the residents? What's the most predictable and useful relationship in macroeconomics? How would your spending change if you won the lottery? Why is so much attention paid to consumer and business confidence? Answers to these and other questions are addressed in this chapter, which focuses on the components of aggregate expenditure. Consumption is the most important spending component, accounting for about two-thirds of all spending, but in this relatively short chapter, we also discuss investment, government purchases, and net exports. We will discuss how each relates to the level of income in the economy.

Let's preview where this leads. In the next chapter, we will combine these spending components and show the link between income and spending to derive the aggregate demand curve. Next we will develop the aggregate supply curve and see how it interacts with the aggregate demand curve to determine the economy's equilibrium levels of price and output. Topics discussed in this chapter include:

- Consumption and income
- Marginal propensities to consume and to save
- Changes in consumption and in saving
- Investment
- Government purchases
- Net exports
- Composition of spending

`<interactive>exercise`

- ECONDEBATE ONLINE: PRODUCTIVITY AND GROWTH
- ECONDEBATE ONLINE: EMPLOYMENT, UNEMPLOYMENT, AND INFLATION

`<interactive>update`

- ECONDATA ONLINE: PRODUCTIVITY AND GROWTH
- ECONDATA ONLINE: EMPLOYMENT, UNEMPLOYMENT, AND INFLATION
- ECONDATA ONLINE: AGGREGATE DEMAND/AGGREGATE SUPPLY
- ECONLINKS ONLINE: ECONOMICS WEB LINKS
- ECONNEWS ONLINE: PRODUCTIVITY AND GROWTH
- ECONNEWS ONLINE: EMPLOYMENT, UNEMPLOYMENT, AND INFLATION
- ECONNEWS ONLINE: AGGREGATE DEMAND/AGGREGATE SUPPLY

CONSUMPTION

Suppose a new college friend invites you home for the weekend. On your visit, you would get some impression of the family's standard of living. Is their house a mansion, a dump, or in between? Do they drive a new BMW or take the bus? The simple fact is that consumption tends to reflect income. Although some people can temporarily live well beyond their means and others still have the first nickel they ever earned, by and large consumption depends on income. *The positive and stable relationship between consumption and income, both for the household and for the economy as a whole, is the main point of this chapter.* Got it?

A key decision in the circular-flow model developed two chapters back is how much households spend on consumption. Consumption depends primarily on income, and income depends on production. Although this seems obvious, the link between income and consumption is fundamental to an understanding of how the economy works. Let's look at this income-consumption link in the U.S. economy over time.

An Initial Look at Income and Consumption

The blue line in Exhibit 1 shows *disposable income* in the United States for the last four decades, and the red line shows consumer spending, or consumption. Data have been adjusted for inflation so that dollars are of constant purchasing power—in this case, 1996 dollars. Disposable

EXHIBIT 1

Disposable Income, Consumption, and Saving in the United States: 1960–2001

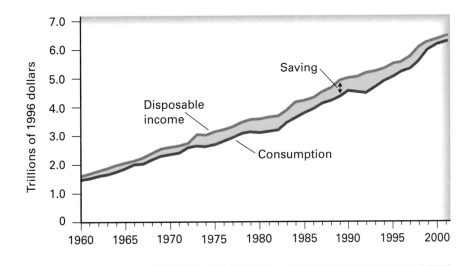

income, remember, is the income actually available for spending and saving. Notice that consumer spending and disposable income move together over time. Both increased nearly every year, and the relationship between the two has been relatively stable. Specifically, consumer spending averaged 90 percent of disposable income during the 1960s, 89 percent during the 1970s, 90 percent during the 1980s, and 92 percent from 1990 through 2001.

Saving is the difference between disposable income and consumption. In Exhibit 1, the vertical distance between the two lines measures saving. Saving averaged 10 percent of disposable income during the 1960s, 11 percent during the 1970s, 10 percent during the 1980s, and 8 percent since 1990.

Another way to graph the relationship between U.S. income and consumption over time is shown in Exhibit 2, where disposable income is measured along the horizontal axis and consumption along the vertical axis. Notice that each axis measures the same units: trillions of 1996 dollars. Each year is depicted by a point that reflects two values: disposable income and consumption. In 1986, for example, disposable income (measured along the horizontal axis) was $4.5 trillion and consumption (measured along the vertical axis) was $4.0 trillion.

As you can see, there is a clear and direct relationship between consumption and disposable income, a relationship that should come as no surprise after examining Exhibit 1. You need little imagination to see that by connecting the points on the graph in Exhibit 2, you could trace a line relating consumption to income. That relationship has special significance in macroeconomics.

The Consumption Function

After examining the link between consumption and income, we found it to be quite stable. Given their level of disposable income, households decide how much to consume and how much to save. So consumption depends on disposable income. *Consumption is the dependent variable and disposable income, the independent variable.* Because consumption depends on income, we say that consumption is a *function* of income. Exhibit 3 presents a hypothetical **consumption function,** which shows a positive relationship between the level of disposable income

EXHIBIT 2

U.S. Consumption Depends on Disposable Income

Notice that each axis measures trillions of 1996 dollars. Consumption is on the vertical axis and disposable income on the horizontal axis. For example, in 1986, consumption was $4.0 trillion and disposable income was $4.5 trillion. There is a clear and direct relationship over time between consumption and disposable income. As disposable income increases, so does consumption.

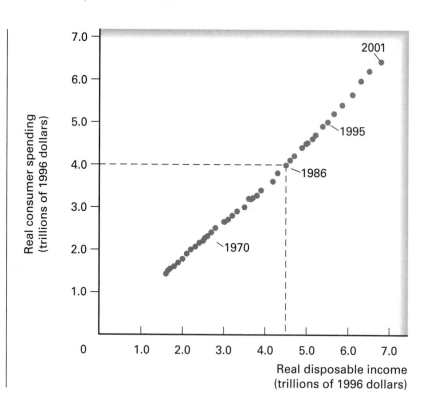

Source: Based on estimates from the Bureau of Economic Analysis, U.S. Department of Commerce. The point for 2001 was projected as of September. For the latest data, go to http://www.bea.doc.gov/bea/dn1.htm.

EXHIBIT 3

The Consumption Function

The consumption function, *C*, shows the relationship between consumption expenditure and disposable income, other things constant.

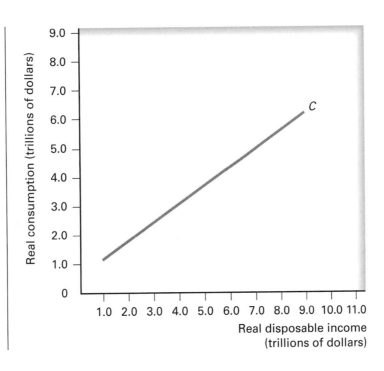

in the economy and the amount spent on consumption, with other determinants of consumption assumed to be constant. Again, both disposable income and consumption are measured in real terms, or in inflation-adjusted dollars. Notice that our hypothetical consumption function in Exhibit 3 looks like the historical relationship between consumption and income shown in Exhibit 2.

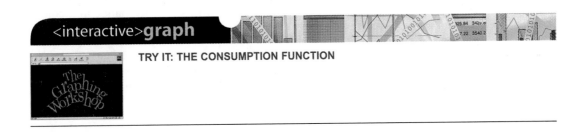

TRY IT: THE CONSUMPTION FUNCTION

ASK THE INSTRUCTOR: CAN WE MAKE SENSE OUT OF THE CONSUMPTION FUNCTION?

Marginal Propensities to Consume and to Save

In Chapter 1, you learned that economic analysis focuses on activity at the margin. For example, what happens to consumption if income changes by a certain amount? To study such changes, we must apply marginal analysis to the relationship between changes in disposable income and changes in consumption. Suppose U.S. households receive another billion dollars in disposable income. Some of this additional income will be spent on consumption and the rest will be saved. The fraction of the additional income that is spent on consumption is called the marginal propensity to consume. More precisely, the **marginal propensity to consume,** or **MPC,** equals the change in consumption divided by the change in income. Likewise, the fraction of that additional income that is saved is called the marginal propensity to save. More precisely,

the **marginal propensity to save,** or **MPS,** equals the change in saving divided by the change in income.

These propensities can be best understood by looking at Exhibit 4, which presents hypothetical data underlying a consumption function. The table shows, for a range of possible incomes, how much consumers would like to spend and how much they would like to save. Column (1) presents alternative levels of disposable income, *DI,* beginning with $8.0 trillion and ranging up to $10.0 trillion in increments of $0.5 trillion.

As you can see from the table, if income increases from $8.0 trillion to $8.5 trillion, consumption increases by $0.4 trillion and saving by $0.1 trillion. The marginal propensity to consume equals the change in consumption divided by the change in income. In this case, the change in consumption is $0.4 trillion and the change in income is $0.5 trillion, so the marginal propensity to consume is 0.4/0.5, or 4/5. Notice that each time income increases by $0.5 trillion, as indicated in column (2), consumption increases by $0.4 trillion, as indicated in column (4). Therefore, the MPC, listed in column (7), is 4/5 at all levels of income shown.

Income not spent on consumption is saved. Saving increases by $0.1 trillion with each $0.5 trillion increase in income, so the marginal propensity to save equals 0.1/0.5, or 1/5, at all levels of income shown. The MPS is listed in column (8). Since disposable income is either spent or saved, the marginal propensity to consume plus the marginal propensity to save must sum to 1. In our example, 4/5 + 1/5 = 1. We can say more generally that MPC + MPS = 1.

MPC, MPS, and the Slope of the Consumption and Saving Functions

You may recall from the appendix to Chapter 1 that the slope of a straight line is the vertical distance between any two points divided by the horizontal distance between those same two points. Consider, for example, the slope between points *a* and *b* on the consumption function in panel (a) of Exhibit 5, where Δ means "change in." The horizontal distance between these points shows the change in disposable income, denoted as ΔDI—in this case, $0.5 trillion. The vertical distance shows the change in consumption, denoted as ΔC—in this case, $0.4 trillion. The slope equals the vertical distance divided by the horizontal distance, or 0.4/0.5, which equals the marginal propensity to consume of 4/5.

Thus, *the marginal propensity to consume is measured graphically by the slope of the consumption function.* After all, the slope is nothing more than the increase in consumption divided by the increase in income. *Because the slope of any straight line is constant everywhere along the line, the MPC for any linear, or straight-line, consumption function is constant at all levels of income.* We are assuming for convenience that the consumption function is a straight line, though it need not be.

Panel (b) of Exhibit 5 presents the **saving function,** *S,* which relates saving to the level of income, reflecting the hypothetical data presented in Exhibit 4. The slope between any two points on the saving function measures the change in saving divided by the change in income. For example, between points *c* and *d* in panel (b) of Exhibit 5, the change in income is $0.5 trillion and the resulting change in saving is $0.1 trillion. The slope between these two points therefore equals 0.1/0.5, or 1/5, which by definition equals the marginal propensity to save. Since the marginal propensity to consume and the marginal propensity to save are simply different sides of the same coin, from here on we focus mostly on the marginal propensity to consume.

$$MPC + MPS = 1$$

EXHIBIT 4

Marginal Propensity to Consume and Marginal Propensity to Save (trillions of dollars)

(1) Income (Real *DI*)	(2) Change in Income (ΔDI)	(3) Consumption (*C*)	(4) Change in *C* (ΔC)	(5) Saving (*S*)	(6) Change in Saving (ΔS)	(7) MPC ($\Delta C/\Delta DI$) = (4) ÷ (2)	(8) MPS ($\Delta S/\Delta DI$) = (6) ÷ (2)
8.0		7.5		0.5		0.4/0.5 = 4/5	0.1/0.5 = 1/5
8.5	0.5	7.9	0.4	0.6	0.1	4/5	1/5
9.0	0.5	8.3	0.4	0.7	0.1	4/5	1/5
9.5	0.5	8.7	0.4	0.8	0.1	4/5	1/5
10.0	0.5	9.1	0.4	0.9	0.1		

EXHIBIT 5

Marginal Propensities to Consume and to Save

The slope of the consumption function equals the marginal propensity to consume. For the straight-line consumption function in panel (a), the slope is the same at all levels of income and is given by the change in consumption divided by the change in disposable income that causes it. Thus, the marginal propensity to consume equals $\Delta C/\Delta DI$, or $0.4/0.5 = 4/5$. The slope of the saving function in panel (b) equals the marginal propensity to save, $\Delta S/\Delta DI$, or $0.1/0.5 = 1/5$.

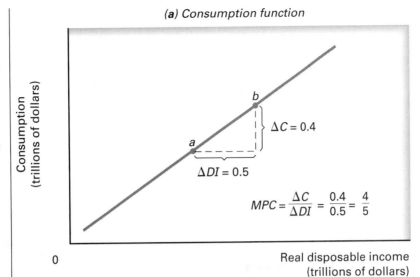

(a) Consumption function

$$MPC = \frac{\Delta C}{\Delta DI} = \frac{0.4}{0.5} = \frac{4}{5}$$

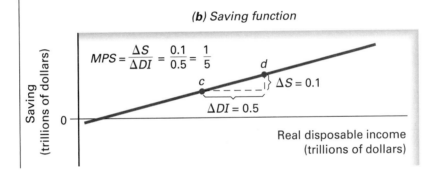

(b) Saving function

$$MPS = \frac{\Delta S}{\Delta DI} = \frac{0.1}{0.5} = \frac{1}{5}$$

Nonincome Determinants of Consumption

Along a given consumption function, consumer spending depends on the level of disposable income in the economy, other things constant. Now let's see what's held constant and how changes in these factors could cause the entire consumption function to shift.

Net Wealth and Consumption Given the level of income in the economy, an important influence on consumption is each household's **net wealth**—that is, the value of all assets that each household owns minus any liabilities, or debts owed. Consider your own family. Your family's assets may include a home, cars, furniture, bank accounts, cash, and the value of stocks, bonds, and pension funds. Your family's liabilities, or debts, may include a mortgage, car loans, student loans, credit card balances, and the like. To increase net wealth, your family can either save or pay off debts.

Net wealth is assumed to be constant along a given consumption function. A decrease in net wealth would make consumers less inclined to spend and more inclined to save at each level of income. To see why, suppose prices fall sharply on the stock market. Because of the decrease in wealth, households that own corporate stock are poorer than they were, so they spend less. For example, when stock market prices fell sharply in October 1987, the decrease in stockholders' net wealth prompted them to reduce consumption and increase saving at each level of income. Household saving as a percentage of disposable income increased from 3.9 percent in the quarter before the crash to 5.7 percent in the quarter following the crash. Spending on new homes and cars declined. As another example, a decline in the stock market in 2000 and 2001 cut the value of U.S. stock holdings by more than $5 trillion, which contributed to a decline in retail sales. Research by the Federal Reserve indicates that consumer spending eventually rises, or falls, between three to five cents for every $1 change in stock market wealth. Our original consumption function is depicted as line C in Exhibit 6. If net wealth declines, the consumption function shifts from C down to C', because households now want to spend less and save more at every level of income.

Conversely, suppose stock prices increase sharply. This increase in net wealth increases the desire to spend. For example, stock prices surged in 1999, increasing stockholders' net wealth. Consumers spent 94 percent of disposable income that year compared with an average of about 90 percent during the first half of the decade. Purchases of homes and cars soared. Because of an increase in net wealth, the consumption function shifts from C up to C'', reflecting households' desire to spend more at every level of income. Again, *it is a change in net wealth not a change in disposable income that shifts the consumption function. A change in disposable income, other things remaining constant, means a movement along a given consumption function, not a shift of that function.* Be mindful of the difference between a *movement along* the consumption function, which results from a change in income, and a *shift of* the consumption function, which results from a change in one of the nonincome determinants of consumption, such as net wealth.

<interactive>video

ASK THE INSTRUCTOR: HOW WOULD A STOCK MARKET CRASH AFFECT THE ECONOMY?

<interactive>update

ECONNEWS ONLINE: THE BULLS AND THEIR BOUNTY

EXHIBIT 6

Shifts of the Consumption Function

A downward shift of the consumption function, such as from C to C', can be caused by a decrease in wealth, an increase in the price level, an unfavorable change in consumer expectations, or an increase in the interest rate. An upward shift, such as that from C to C'', can be caused by an increase in wealth, a decrease in the price level, a favorable change in expectations, or a decrease in the interest rate.

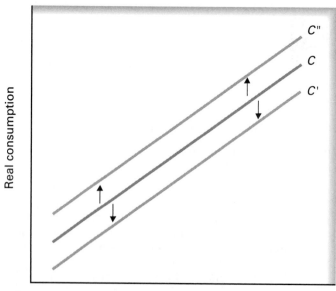

The Price Level Another variable that can affect the consumption function is the price level prevailing in the economy. As we have seen, households' net wealth is an important determinant of consumption. The greater the net wealth, other things constant, the greater consumption will be at each income level. Some household wealth is held in dollar-denominated assets, such as bank accounts and cash. When the price level changes, so does the real value of bank accounts, cash, and other dollar-denominated financial assets.

For example, suppose your wealth consists of $20,000 in a bank account. If the price level increases by 5 percent, your bank account will purchase about 5 percent fewer real goods and services. You feel poorer because you are poorer. The real value of your wealth has declined. To rebuild your wealth to some desired level, you decide to spend less and save more. An increase in the price level reduces the purchasing power of wealth held in fixed-dollar assets and, as a consequence, causes households to consume less and save more at each income level. So the consumption function shifts downward from C to C', as shown in Exhibit 6.

Conversely, should the price level ever fall, as it did frequently before World War II and just recently in Japan, the real value of dollar-denominated assets would increase. Households would be wealthier, so they would be willing and able to consume more at each level of income. For example, if the price level declined by 5 percent, your $20,000 bank account would then buy about 5 percent more real goods and services. A drop in the price level shifts the consumption function from C up to C''. *At each level of income, a change in the price level influences consumption by affecting the real value of net wealth.*

The Interest Rate Interest is the reward savers earn for deferring consumption and the cost paid by borrowers for current spending power. When graphing the consumption function, we assume a given interest rate. If the interest rate increases, other things constant, savers or lenders are rewarded more, and borrowers are charged more. The higher the interest rate, the less is spent on those items typically purchased on credit, such as cars. Thus, at a higher rate of interest, households save more, borrow less, and spend less. Greater saving at each level of income means less consumption. Simply put, *a higher interest rate, other things constant, shifts the consumption function downward.* Conversely, *a lower interest rate, other things constant, shifts the consumption function upward.*

Expectations Expectations influence economic behavior in a variety of ways. For example, suppose as a college senior, you land a high-paying job that starts when you graduate. Your consumption will probably jump long before the job actually begins because you expect an increase in your income. Conversely, a worker who gets a layoff notice to take effect at the end of the year will likely reduce consumption immediately, well before the actual date of the layoff. More generally, if people grow concerned about their job security, they will reduce the amount they consume at each level of income.

Changing expectations about price levels and interest rates also affect consumption. For example, a change that leads householders to expect higher car prices or higher interest rates in the future will prompt some to purchase new cars now. On the other hand, a change leading householders to expect lower prices or lower interest rates in the future will cause some to defer car purchases. Thus, expectations affect spending at each level of income, and a change in expectations can shift the consumption function. This is why economic forecasters monitor consumer confidence so closely.

Keep in mind the distinction between *movements along a given consumption function* as a result of a change in income and *shifts in the consumption function* as a result of a change in one of the factors assumed to remain constant along a given consumption function. We conclude our introduction to consumption with the following case study, which discusses consumption and saving patterns over a lifetime.

CNN VIDEO: "CONSUMER TALES"

CASE**STUDY**	The Life-Cycle Hypothesis
	● *Bringing Theory to Life*

Do people with high incomes save a larger fraction of their incomes than do those with low income? Both theory and evidence suggest that they do. The easier it is to make ends meet, the more income left over for saving. Does it follow from this that richer economies save more than poorer ones—that economies save a larger fraction of total disposable income as they grow? In his famous book, *The General Theory of Employment, Interest, and Money,* published in 1936, John Maynard Keynes drew that conclusion. But as later economists studied the data—such as that presented in Exhibit 2—it became clear that Keynes was wrong. *The fraction of total disposable income saved in an economy seems to stay constant as the economy grows.*

So how can it be that richer people save more than poorer people, yet richer countries do not necessarily save more than poorer countries? Several answers have been proposed. One of the most important is the *life-cycle model of consumption.* According to this model, people tend to borrow when they are young to finance education and home purchases. In middle age, people pay off debts and save more; in old age, they draw down their savings, or dissave. Some still have substantial wealth at death, because they are not sure when death will occur and because some parents want to pass wealth to their children. But net savings over a person's entire lifetime tend to be relatively small.

The life-cycle hypothesis suggests that the saving rate for an economy as a whole depends on, among other things, the relative number of savers and dissavers in the population. Other factors that influence the saving rate across countries include the way saving is taxed, the convenience and reliability of saving institutions, national customs, and the relative cost of each household's major purchase—housing. In Japan, for example, about 24,000 post offices nationwide offer convenient savings accounts, and more than half the population have such accounts. In fact, Japan's postal savings system holds about $2.4 trillion in savings deposits, more than all Japanese banks combined. Also, a homebuyer in Japan must come up with a substantial down payment, one that represents a relatively large fraction of the home's purchase price, and housing there is more expensive than in the United States. Finally, borrowing in Japan is considered by many to be shameful, so consumers save to avoid having to borrow. Since saving in Japan is necessary, convenient, and consistent with the aversion to borrowing, the country has one of the highest saving rates in the world. In 2000, for example, the Japanese saved 13 percent of their disposable income compared with a saving rate of only about 4 percent in the United States.

<interactive>exercise

eACTIVITY: THE LIFE-CYCLE HYPOTHESIS

Sources: Martin Browning and Thomas Crossley, "The Life-Cycle Model of Consumption and Saving," *Journal of Economic Perspective* 15 (Summer 2001): 3-22; Stephanie Strom, "In Japan, Golden Years Have Lost Their Glow," *New York Times,* 16 February 2000; "Credit Cards in Japan: A Borrower Be," *The Economist,* 21 April 2001; *OECD Economic Outlook* 69 (June 2001), Annex Table 26; and Brian Bremner, "Will They Liberate the Postal Office Loot?," *BusinessWeek Online,* 30 January 2001, at http://www.businessweek.com/bwdaily/dnflash/jan2001/nf20010130_100.htm.

We now turn to the second component of aggregate expenditure—investment. Keep in mind that our ultimate objective is to understand the relationship between total spending in the economy and the level of income.

INVESTMENT

The second component of aggregate expenditure is investment, or, more precisely, *gross private domestic investment.* Again, by *investment* we do not mean buying stocks, bonds, or other financial assets. Investment consists of spending on (1) new factories and new equipment, such as computers; (2) new housing; and (3) net increases in inventories.

Firms invest in capital goods now in the expectation of a future return. Since the return is in the future, a would-be investor must estimate how much a particular investment will yield this year, next year, the year after, and in all years during the productive life of the investment. *Firms buy new capital goods only if they expect this investment to yield a greater return than other possible uses of their funds.*

<interactive>update

ECONDATA ONLINE: HOUSING STARTS

The Demand for Investment

To understand the investment decision, let's study a simple example. The operators of the Hacker Haven Golf Club are contemplating buying solar-powered golf carts to rent to golfers. The model under consideration, called the Weekend Warrior, sells for $2,000, requires no maintenance or operating expenses, and is expected to last indefinitely. *The expected rate of return equals the annual dollar earnings expected from the investment divided by the purchase price.* The first cart purchased is expected to generate rental income of $400 per year. This income, divided by the cost of the cart, yields an expected rate of return on the investment of $400/$2,000, or 20 percent per year. Additional carts will be used less. A second is expected to generate $300 per year in rental income, yielding a rate of return of $300/$2,000, or 15 percent; a third cart, $200 per year, or 10 percent; and a fourth cart, $100 per year, or 5 percent. A fifth cart would not get rented at all, so it has a zero expected rate of return.

Should the operators of Hacker Haven invest in golf carts, and if so, how many? Suppose they plan to borrow the money to buy the carts. The number of carts they purchase will depend on the interest rate they must pay to borrow money. If the market interest rate were more than 20 percent, the cost of borrowing would exceed the expected rate of return for even the first cart, so the club would not buy any carts. What if the operators have enough money on hand to buy the carts? The market interest rate also reflects what the club owners could earn on savings. If the interest rate paid on savings were more than 20 percent, they would earn a higher rate of return by saving any funds on hand than by investing these funds in golf carts, so the club would not buy any carts. *The market interest rate is the opportunity cost of investing in capital.*

Suppose the market interest rate is 8 percent per year. At that rate, the first three carts, all with expected rates of return exceeding 8 percent, would more than pay for themselves. A fourth cart would lose money, since its expected rate of return is only 5 percent. Exhibit 7 measures the nominal interest rate along the vertical axis and the amount invested in golf carts along the horizontal axis. The steplike relationship shows the expected rate of return earned on additional dollars invested in golf carts. This relationship also indicates the amount invested in golf carts at each interest rate, so you can view this steplike relationship as Hacker Haven's demand curve for this type of investment. For example, the first cart costs $2,000 and earns a rate of return of 20 percent. A firm should reject any investment with an expected rate of return that falls below the market rate of interest.

The horizontal line at 8 percent indicates the market interest rate, which is Hacker Haven's opportunity cost of investing. Recall that the course operators' objective is to choose an investment strategy that maximizes profit. Profit is maximized when $6,000 is invested in the carts—that is, when three carts are purchased. The expected return from a fourth cart is 5 percent, which is below the opportunity cost of funds. Therefore, investing in four or more carts would lower total profit.

EXHIBIT 7

Rate of Return on Golf Carts and the Opportunity Cost of Funds

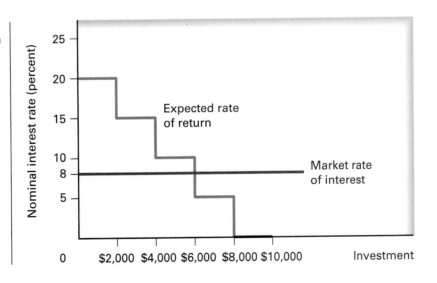

An individual firm will invest in any project with a rate of return that exceeds the market interest rate. At an interest rate of 8 percent, Hacker Haven would purchase three golf carts, investing $6,000.

 SEE IT: DEMAND FOR INVESTMENT

From Micro to Macro

So far, we have examined the investment decision for a single golf course, but there are about 13,000 golf courses in the United States. The industry demand for golf carts shows the relationship between the amount all course operators invest and the expected rate of return. Like the steplike relationship in Exhibit 7, the investment demand curve for the golf industry slopes downward.

Let's move beyond golf carts and consider the investment decisions of all industries: publishing, hog farming, fast foods, trail bikes, and hundreds more. Individual industries generally have downward-sloping demand curves for investment. More is invested when the opportunity cost of borrowing is lower, other things constant. A downward-sloping investment demand curve for the entire economy can be derived, with some qualifications, from a horizontal summation of all industries' downward-sloping investment demand curves. The economy's *investment demand curve* is represented as *D* in Exhibit 8, which shows the inverse relationship between the quantity of investment demanded and the market interest rate, other things—including business expectations—held constant. For example, in Exhibit 8, when the market interest rate is 8 percent, the quantity of investment demanded is $0.8 trillion. If the interest rate rises to 10 percent, investment spending declines to $0.7 trillion, and if the interest rate falls to 6 percent, investment increases to $0.9 trillion. Assumed constant along the investment demand curve are business expectations about the economy. If firms grow more optimistic about profit prospects, the demand for investment increases, so the investment curve shifts to the right.

<interactive>example

NETBOOKMARK: "CAIRNCROSS ON KEYNES"

EXHIBIT 8

Investment Demand Curve for the Economy

The investment demand curve for the economy is obtained by summing the amount of investment undertaken by each firm at each interest rate. At lower interest rates, more investment projects become profitable for individual firms, so total investment in the economy increases.

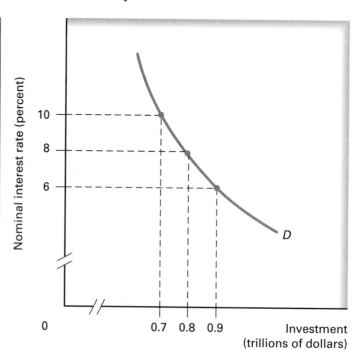

Planned Investment and the Economy's Level of Income

To integrate the discussion of investment with our earlier analysis of consumption, we need to know if and how investment varies with the level of income in the economy. Whereas we were able to present empirical evidence relating consumption to disposable income over time, the link between investment and disposable income is weaker. Over the last dozen years, for example, investment in a particular year has shown little relation to the level of income that year. *Investment depends more on interest rates and on business expectations than on the prevailing level of income.* One reason investment is less related to the level of income is that some investments, such as a new power plant, take years to complete. And investment, once in place, is expected to last for years, sometimes decades. The investment decision is thus said to be "forward looking," based more on expected profit than on current levels of income and output.

So how does planned investment relate to disposable income? The simplest **investment function** assumes that planned investment is unrelated to the current level of disposable income. Investment is assumed to be **autonomous** with respect to income. For example, suppose that, given current business expectations and an interest rate of 8 percent, firms plan to invest $0.8 trillion, regardless of the economy's income level. Exhibit 9 measures disposable income on the horizontal axis and planned investment on the vertical axis. Investment of $0.8 trillion is shown by the flat investment function, *I*. As you can see, along *I*, planned investment does not vary even though real disposable income does.

Nonincome Determinants of Investment

The investment function isolates the relationship between the level of income in the economy and *planned investment*—the amount firms would like to invest, other things constant. We have already mentioned two determinants that are assumed to remain constant: the interest rate and business expectations. Now let's look at the effect of changes in these factors on investment.

Market Interest Rate Exhibit 8 showed that if the interest rate is 8 percent, planned investment is $0.8 trillion. This level of investment is also shown as *I* in Exhibit 9. If the interest rate increases because of, say, a change in the nation's monetary policy (as happened in 1999), the cost of borrowing increases, which increases the opportunity cost of investment. For example, if the interest rate increases from 8 percent to 10 percent, planned investment drops from $0.8 trillion to $0.7 trillion; this decrease is reflected in Exhibit 9 by a downward shift of the investment function from *I* to *I* '. Conversely, if the interest rate decreases because of, say, a change in the nation's monetary policy (as happened in 2001), the cost of borrowing decreases, which reduces the opportunity cost of investment. For example, a drop in the rate of interest from 8 percent to 6 percent, other things remaining constant, will reduce the cost of borrowing and increase planned investment from $0.8 trillion to $0.9 trillion, as reflected by the upward shift

---

EXHIBIT 9

Autonomous Investment Function

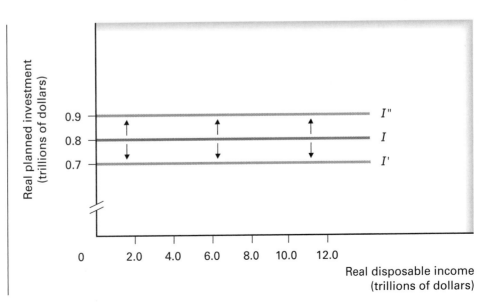

Autonomous investment spending is assumed to be independent of income, as shown by the horizontal lines. An increase in the interest rate or declining business expectations can decrease autonomous investment, as shown by the downward shift from *I* to *I*'. A decrease in the interest rate or upbeat business expectations can shift the investment function up to *I*".

of the investment function from *I* to *I* ". Notice that the shifts in Exhibit 9 mirror interest rate movements along the investment demand curve in Exhibit 8.

Business Expectations Investment depends primarily on business expectations, or on what Keynes called the "animal spirits" of business. Suppose planned investment initially is $0.8 trillion, as depicted by *I* in Exhibit 9. If firms now become more pessimistic about profit prospects, perhaps expecting the worst, as in 2001 when terrorists leveled the World Trade Center, planned investment will decrease at every level of income, as reflected in Exhibit 9 by a shift of the investment function from *I* down to *I* '. On the other hand, if profit expectations become rosier, as they did in 1999, firms will be more willing to invest, thereby increasing the investment function from *I* up to *I* ". *Examples of factors that could affect business expectations, and thus investment plans, include wars, technological change, changes in the tax structure, and destabilizing events such as terrorist attacks.* Changes in business expectations also shift the investment demand curve in Exhibit 8.

Now that we have examined consumption and investment individually, let's take a look at their year-to-year variability in the following case study.

<interactive>exercise

READING IT RIGHT: WALL STREET JOURNAL EXERCISE

CASE**STUDY**	Investment Varies Much More than Consumption
	● *Public Policy*

We already know that consumption makes up about two-thirds of GDP and that investment varies from year to year, averaging about one-sixth of GDP over the last decade. Now let's compare their year-to-year variability. Exhibit 10 shows the annual percentage changes since 1960 in GDP, consumption, and investment, all measured in real terms.

EXHIBIT 10|

Annual Percentage Change in U.S. Real GDP, Consumption, and Investment

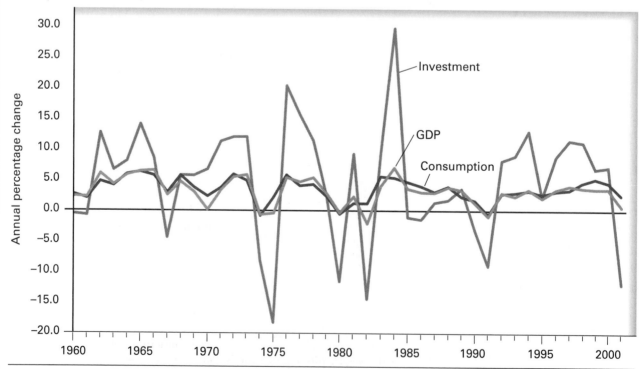

Source: Bureau of Economic Analysis, U.S. Department of Commerce. Figures for 2001 are based on the first two quarters. For the latest data, go to http://www.bea.doc.gov/bea/rels.htm.

Two points are obvious. First, fluctuations in consumption and in GDP appear to be entwined, although consumption varies a bit less than GDP. Consumption varies less that GDP because consumption depends on disposable income, which varies less than GDP. Second, investment fluctuates much more than either consumption or GDP. For example, in the recession year of 1982, GDP declined 2.0 percent but investment crashed 14.1 percent; consumption actually increased 1.2 percent. In 1984, GDP increased 7.3 percent, consumption rose 5.4 percent, but investment soared 29.2 percent.

GDP fell during recession years since 1960, with an average decline of 0.9 percent. During those recession years, investment dropped an average of 11.7 percent, but consumption increased 0.4 percent. So *while consumption is the largest spending component, investment varies much more than consumption and accounts for nearly all the variability in real GDP.* And a big drop in investment in 2001 dragged down the growth in real GDP. This is why economic forecasters pay special attention to business expectations and investment plans.

\<interactive\>exercise

eACTIVITY: INVESTMENT VARIES MUCH MORE THAN CONSUMPTION

Sources: *Economic Report of the President,* January 2001; U.S. Department of Commerce, *Survey of Current Business* 81 (November 2001); and *OECD Economic Outlook* 69 (June 2001). For data and articles about economic aggregates, go to the Bureau of Economic Analysis site at http://www.bea.doc.gov/.

GOVERNMENT

The third component of aggregate expenditure is government purchases of goods and services. Federal, state, and local governments purchase thousands of goods and services, ranging from weapon systems to road signs. In the United States, government purchases in 2001 accounted for about 18 percent of GDP—about one-third was spending by the federal government and about two-thirds by state and local governments.

Government Purchase Function

The **government purchase function** relates government purchases to the level of income in the economy, other things constant. Decisions about government purchases are largely under the control of public officials, such as the decision to build an interstate highway system or to reduce military spending. These purchases do not depend directly on the level of income in the economy. We therefore assume that *government purchases* are autonomous, or independent of the level of income. Such a function would relate to income as a flat line similar to the investment function shown in Exhibit 9. An increase in government purchases would result in an upward shift of the government purchase function. And a decrease in government purchases would result in a downward shift of the government purchase function.

Net Taxes

As noted earlier, government purchases represent only one of the two components of government outlays; the other is *transfer payments,* such as Social Security, welfare benefits, and unemployment benefits. Transfer payments, which make up about a third of government outlays, are outright grants from governments to households and are thus not considered part of aggregate expenditure. Transfer payments vary inversely with income—as income increases, transfer payments decline.

To fund government outlays, governments impose taxes. Taxes vary directly with income; as income increases, so do taxes. *Net taxes* equal taxes minus transfers. Since taxes tend to increase with income but transfers tend to decrease with income, for simplicity, let's assume that net taxes do not vary with income. Thus, we assume that *net taxes* are *autonomous,* or independent of the level of income.

Net taxes affect aggregate spending indirectly by changing disposable income, which in turn changes consumption. We saw from the discussion of circular flow that by subtracting net taxes, we transform real GDP into *disposable income.* Disposable income is take-home pay—the income households can spend or save. We will examine the impact of net taxes in the next few chapters.

NET EXPORTS

The rest of the world affects aggregate expenditure through imports and exports and has a growing influence on the U.S. economy. The United States, with only one-twentieth of the world's population, accounts for about one-sixth of the world's imports and one-eighth of the world's exports.

ECONDATA ONLINE: CURRENT ACCOUNT BALANCE

Net Exports and Income

How do imports and exports relate to the level of income in the economy? When their incomes rise, Americans spend more on all normal goods, including imports. Higher incomes lead to more spending on Persian rugs, French wine, Korean VCRs, trips to Europe, and thousands of other foreign goods and services.

How does the value of U.S. exports relate to the economy's level of income? The amount of U.S. exports purchased by the rest of the world depends on the income of foreigners, not on the U.S. level of income. The level of disposable income in the United States does not influence the desire of the French to purchase U.S. computers or the desire of Saudi Arabians to purchase U.S. military hardware.

The **net export function** shows the relationship between net exports and the level of income in the economy, other things constant. Since our exports are relatively insensitive to the level of U.S. income but our imports tend to increase with income, *net exports,* which equal the value of exports minus the value of imports, tend to decline as U.S. incomes increase. Such an inverse relationship is developed graphically in the appendix to this chapter. For now, we simplify the analysis by assuming that net exports are *autonomous,* or independent of the level of disposable income.

If exports exceed imports, net exports are positive; if imports exceed exports, net exports are negative; and if exports equal imports, net exports equal zero. U.S. net exports have been negative in nearly every year during the past three decades, so let's suppose net exports are autonomous and equal to −$0.1 trillion, or −$100 billion, as shown by the net export function $X - M$ in Exhibit 11.

Nonincome Determinants of Net Exports

Factors assumed constant along the net export function include the U.S. price level, price levels in other countries, interest rates here and abroad, foreign income levels, and the exchange rate between the dollar and foreign currencies. Consider the effects of a change in one of these factors. Suppose the value of the dollar increases relative to foreign currencies such as those of Asia, as happened in 1998. With the dollar worth more on world markets, foreign products become cheaper for Americans, and U.S. products become more costly for foreigners. A rise in the dollar's exchange value will increase imports and decrease exports, resulting in a decrease in net exports, shown in Exhibit 11 by a parallel drop in the net export line from $X - M$ down to $X' - M'$, a decline from −$100 billion to −$120 billion.

A decline in the value of the dollar, as occurred in 1994, will have the opposite effect, increasing exports and decreasing imports. An increase in autonomous net exports is shown in our example by a parallel increase in the net export function, from $X - M$ up to $X'' - M''$, reflecting an increase in autonomous net exports from −$100 billion to −$80 billion. Countries sometimes try to devalue their currency in an attempt to increase their net exports and increase employment. The effect of changes in net exports on aggregate spending will be taken up in the next chapter.

- **ECONNEWS ONLINE: WORLDLY QUESTIONS**
- **ECONNEWS ONLINE: TRADE TROUBLES**

EXHIBIT 11

Autonomous Net Export Function

Autonomous net exports are assumed to be independent of disposable income, as shown by the horizontal lines. $X - M$ is the net export function if net exports equal $-\$100$ billion. An increase in the value of the dollar relative to other currencies would cause net exports to decrease, as shown by the shift down to $X' - M'$. A decrease in the value of the dollar would cause net exports to increase, as shown by the shift up to $X'' - M''$.

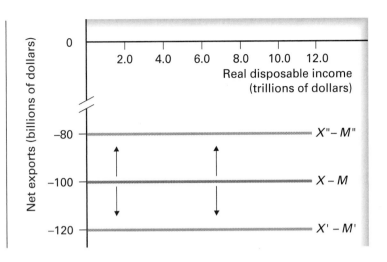

COMPOSITION OF AGGREGATE EXPENDITURE

Now that we have examined each component of aggregate spending, let's get some idea of the breakdown of GDP among the spending components over time. Exhibit 12 shows the composition of spending in the United States for the last four decades. As you can see, consumption's share of GDP seemed relatively stable from year to year, but the long-term trend shows an increase from an average of 62 percent during the 1960s to 67 percent during the last decade. Investment bounced around the most from year to year, with a slight trend upward over the four decades, from an average of 15 percent of GDP during the 1960s to 16 percent during the last decade.

Government purchases declined from an average of 22 percent of GDP during the 1960s to an average of 19 percent since 1990, the smallest share since before World War II. Net exports averaged 0.3 percent of GDP in the 1960s but have been negative nearly every year since then, averaging -1 percent of GDP since 1990. Negative net exports mean that the sum of spending on consumption, investment, and government purchases exceeds GDP, the amount produced in the U.S. economy. Americans are spending more than they make, and they are covering the difference by borrowing from abroad. So U.S. spending exceeds U.S. GDP by the amount shown as negative net exports. Since the spending components must sum to GDP, *negative* net exports are expressed in Exhibit 12 by that portion of spending that exceeds 100 percent of GDP.

In summary: During the last four decades, consumption's share of total spending increased and government purchases decreased, primarily because of declines in defense spending. Investment spending bounced around and net exports turned negative, meaning that imports exceeded exports.

CONCLUSION

This chapter has focused on the relationship between spending and income. We studied the four components of aggregate expenditure: consumption, investment, government purchases, and net exports. Consumption relates positively to the level of income in the economy. Investment relates more to factors like interest rates and business expectations than it does to income. Government purchases are also assumed to be autonomous, or independent of income. And net exports are assumed, for now, to be affected more by such factors as the exchange rate than by the level of U.S. income. The appendix to this chapter develops a more realistic but also more complicated picture by showing how net exports decline as income increases. In the next chapter, we will see how aggregate spending depends on income and how this relationship helps determine the amount demanded.

EXHIBIT 12

U.S. Spending Components as Percentages of GDP Since 1960

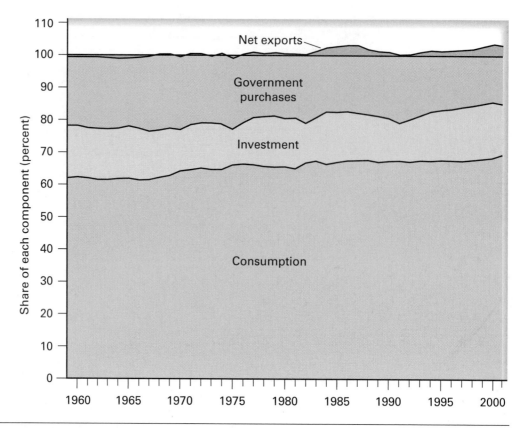

Source: Computed from annual estimates in *Survey of Current Business* 81 (August 2001). Figures for 2001 are projected based on the first two quarters. For the latest data, go to http://www.bea.doc.gov/bea/dn1.htm.

endofchaptermaterial

- **Summary**
- **Questions for Review**
- **Problems and Exercises**

- **Experiential Exercises**
- **Wall Street Journal Exercise**
- **Appendix Questions**

Take the Post-Test to assess your overall understanding of the key ideas in this chapter. The Post-Test provides a comprehensive selection of exam-style questions addressing the main topics and concepts of the chapter. At the completion of each Post-Test, you will receive a score and instructive feedback on how you answered each question, and a direct link to the part of the chapter addressed in the question. Take the Post-Test as often as you need to—a record of your progress for each attempt is kept for you to revisit and gauge your improvement. And each Post-Test is randomly generated, so every attempt is new.

VARIABLE NET EXPORTS

In this appendix, we examine more closely the relationship between net exports and the U.S. level of income. We first look at exports and imports separately and then consider exports minus imports, or net exports.

NET EXPORTS AND INCOME

As noted in the chapter, the amount of U.S. output purchased by foreigners depends not on the U.S. level of income but on income levels in their own countries. We therefore assume that U.S. exports do not vary with U.S. income. Specifically, suppose the rest of the world spends $0.8 trillion per year on U.S. exports of goods and services. The export function, X, is as shown in panel (a) of Exhibit 13. On the other hand, when disposable income increases, U.S. consumers spend more on all goods and services, including imported goods and services. Thus, the relationship between imports and income is positive, as expressed by the upward-sloping import function, M, in panel (b) of Exhibit 13. If Americans spend 10 percent of their disposable income on imports, when disposable income is $8.0 trillion, imports are $0.8 trillion.

So far, we have considered imports and exports as separate functions of income. What matters in terms of total spending on U.S. products are exports, X, minus imports, M, or net exports, $X - M$. Since money spent on imports goes to foreign producers, not U.S. producers, imports are subtracted from the circular flow of spending. By subtracting the import function depicted in panel (b) from the export function in panel (a), we derive the *net export function*, depicted as $X - M$ in panel (c) of Exhibit 13.

Since exports in panel (a) equal $0.8 trillion at all levels of income, net exports equal zero when U.S. disposable income equals $8.0 trillion. At income levels less that $8.0 trillion, net exports are positive because exports exceed imports. At income levels greater than $8.0 trillion, net exports are negative because imports exceed exports. The United States has experienced

EXHIBIT 13

Imports, Exports, and Net Exports (in trillions of dollars)

Exports are independent of the level of income, as shown in panel (a). Imports are positively related to income, as shown in panel (b). Net exports equal exports minus imports; net exports are negatively related to income, as shown in panel (c).

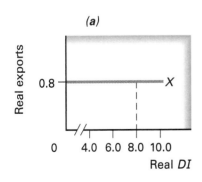
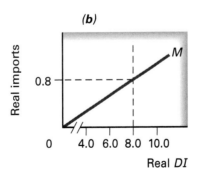
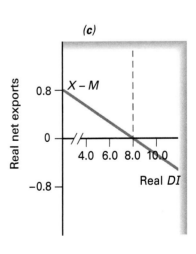

negative net exports during most of the last four decades. The trade deficit shrank during the recession of the early 1990s, but then increased again as the U.S. economy recovered during the rest of the decade. The trade deficit also declined in late 2001 as the economy slowed down.

SHIFTS IN NET EXPORTS

The net export function, $X - M$, shows the relationship between net exports and disposable income, other things constant. Suppose the value of the dollar increases relative to foreign currencies, as it did in 2000. With the dollar worth more on world markets, foreign products become cheaper for Americans, and U.S. products become more expensive for foreigners. The impact of a rising dollar is to decrease exports but increase imports at each level of income. This decreases net exports, as shown in Exhibit 14 by the shift from $X - M$ down to $X' - M'$. A decline in the dollar's value will have the opposite effect, increasing exports and decreasing imports, as reflected in Exhibit 14 by an upward shift of the net export function from $X - M$ to $X'' - M''$.

In summary, in this appendix we assumed that *imports relate positively to the level of income, whereas exports are independent of the domestic level of income. Thus, net exports, which equal exports minus imports, vary inversely with the level of income.* The net export function shifts upward if the value of the dollar falls and shifts downward if the value of the dollar rises.

EXHIBIT 14

Shifts in Net Exports (in trillions of dollars)

A rise in the value of the dollar, other things held constant, will decrease exports and increase imports, thereby contributing to a decrease in net exports, as shown by the shift from $X - M$ down to $X' - M'$. A decrease in the value of the dollar will increase exports and decrease imports, causing net exports to rise, as shown by the shift from $X - M$ up to $X'' - M''$.

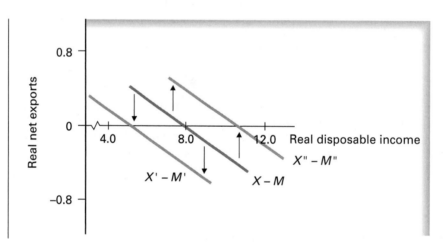

CHAPTER 25

Aggregate Expenditure and Aggregate Demand

How does spending in the economy relate to income? What is the effect of a change in the price level on spending? What does all this have to do with aggregate demand? And why might a change in the amount people plan to spend ripple through the economy, causing an impact greater than that made by the initial change in spending? For instance, how did the drop in air travel following the terrorist attacks of September 11 affect the economy as a whole? Answers to these and other questions are covered in this chapter, which develops the aggregate demand curve.

Your economic success depends to a large extent on the overall performance of the economy. When the economy expands, job opportunities grow, so your chances of finding a good one increase. When the economy contracts, job opportunities shrink, as do your job prospects. Thus, you should have a personal interest in the economy's success. In this chapter, we continue to build a model that will help us determine the economy's equilibrium level of output, or real GDP.

The previous chapter discussed the components of aggregate spending—consumption, investment, government purchases, and net exports—showing how each relates to the level of income in the economy. In this chapter, these components get added up to explain how total spending, or aggregate expenditure, relates to the level of income. We then use this information to derive the aggregate demand curve. Aggregate supply will be developed in the next chapter; then, a fuller treatment of the effects of government spending and taxing will be examined in the chapter after that.

In Appendix A, you can see what happens when imports increase with income. An algebraic approach to the aggregate expenditure framework is developed in Appendix B. Topics discussed in this chapter include:

- Aggregate expenditure line
- Real GDP demanded
- Effect of changes in aggregate expenditure
- Simple spending multiplier
- Effect of changes in the price level
- Aggregate demand curve

<interactive>exercise

- ECONDEBATE ONLINE: PRODUCTIVITY AND GROWTH
- ECONDEBATE ONLINE: EMPLOYMENT, UNEMPLOYMENT, AND INFLATION

<interactive>update

- ECONDATA ONLINE: PRODUCTIVITY AND GROWTH
- ECONDATA ONLINE: EMPLOYMENT, UNEMPLOYMENT, AND INFLATION
- ECONDATA ONLINE: AGGREGATE DEMAND/AGGREGATE SUPPLY
- ECONLINKS ONLINE: ECONOMICS WEB LINKS
- ECONNEWS ONLINE: PRODUCTIVITY AND GROWTH
- ECONNEWS ONLINE: EMPLOYMENT, UNEMPLOYMENT, AND INFLATION
- ECONNEWS ONLINE: AGGREGATE DEMAND/AGGREGATE SUPPLY

AGGREGATE EXPENDITURE AND INCOME

In the previous chapter, the big idea was the link between income and consumption, a link that is the most stable in all of macroeconomics. In this section, we build on the income-consumption connection to uncover the tie between income and total spending. If we try to confront the economy head-on, it soon becomes a bewildering maze, which is why we often make progress only by beginning with a simple model. In this chapter, we continue to assume, as we did in developing the circular-flow model, that there is no capital depreciation and no business saving. Thus, we can say that *each dollar spent on production translates directly into a dollar of aggregate income.* Therefore, gross domestic product, or GDP, equals aggregate income. We also continue to assume that investment, government purchases, and net exports are *autonomous,* or independent of the level of income.

The Components of Aggregate Expenditure

Let's begin developing the aggregate demand curve by asking how much aggregate output would be demanded at a given price level. By finding the quantity demanded at a given price level, we'll identify a single point on the aggregate demand curve. We want to consider the relationship between aggregate spending in the economy and aggregate income, or real GDP. By *real* GDP, we mean GDP measured in terms of real goods and services produced.

To get us started, let's suppose the price level in the economy is 130, meaning that it is 30 percent higher than in the base year. We want to find out how much will be spent at various levels of real income, or real GDP. Exhibit 1 presents the hypothetical data that will serve as building blocks for constructing the relation between aggregate spending and income. Don't panic. This exhibit simply puts into tabular form relationships that were introduced in the previous chapter—consumption, saving, planned investment, government purchases, net taxes, and net exports. Although the entries are hypothetical, they bear some relation to levels observed in the U.S. economy. For example, real GDP in the U.S. economy is now about $10 trillion a year.

EXHIBIT 1

Real GDP with Net Taxes and Government Purchases (trillions of dollars)

(1) Real GDP (Y)	(2) Net Taxes (NT)	(3) Disposable Income (Y − NT) (3) = (1) − (2)	(4) Consumption (C)	(5) Saving (S)	(6) Planned Investment (I)	(7) Government Purchases (G)	(8) Net Exports (X − M)	(9) Planned Aggregate Expenditure (AE)	(10) Unintended Inventory Adjustment (Y − AE) (10) = (1) − (9)
9.0	1.0	8.0	7.5	0.5	0.8	1.0	−0.1	9.2	−0.2
9.5	1.0	8.5	7.9	0.6	0.8	1.0	−0.1	9.6	−0.1
10.0	**1.0**	**9.0**	**8.3**	0.7	**0.8**	**1.0**	**−0.1**	**10.0**	**0.0**
10.5	1.0	9.5	8.7	0.8	0.8	1.0	−0.1	10.4	+0.1
11.0	1.0	10.0	9.1	0.9	0.8	1.0	−0.1	10.8	+0.2

Column (1) in Exhibit 1 lists a range of possible levels of real GDP in the economy, symbolized by Y. Column (2) shows *net taxes,* or *NT,* which are assumed to be $1.0 trillion at each level of real GDP. Subtracting net taxes from real GDP yields *disposable income,* listed in column (3) as Y − NT. Note that at all levels of real GDP, disposable income equals real GDP minus net taxes of $1.0 trillion. Since net taxes do not vary with income, each time real GDP increases by $0.5 trillion, disposable income also increases by $0.5 trillion.

Households have only two possible uses for disposable income: consumption and saving. Columns (4) and (5) show that the levels of *consumption, C,* and *saving, S,* increase with disposable income. Each time real GDP and disposable income increase by $0.5 trillion, consumption increases by $0.4 trillion and saving increases by $0.1 trillion. Thus, as in the previous chapter, the marginal propensity to consume is 4/5, or 0.8, and the marginal propensity to save is 1/5, or 0.2.

Columns (6), (7), and (8) list three now-familiar injections of spending into the circular flow: *planned investment* of $0.8 trillion, *government purchases* of $1.0 trillion, and *net exports* of −$0.1 trillion. In the table, government purchases equal net taxes, so the government budget is balanced. We first want to see how a balanced budget works before we look at the effects of budget deficits or surpluses, which are discussed the chapter after next. *The sum of consumption, C, planned investment, I, government purchases, G, and net exports, X − M, is listed in column (9) as planned aggregate expenditure, AE, which indicates the amount that households, firms, governments, and the rest of the world plan to spend on U.S. output at each level of real GDP.* Note that the only spending component that varies with the level of real GDP is consumption. As real GDP increases, so does disposable income, which increases the amount households spend on consumption.

The final column in Exhibit 1 lists any unplanned inventory adjustment, which equals real GDP minus planned aggregate expenditure, or Y − AE. For example, when real GDP is $9.0 trillion, planned aggregate expenditure is $9.2 trillion. Since planned spending exceeds the amount produced by $0.2 trillion, firms must reduce inventories by $0.2 trillion to make up the shortfall in output. So when real GDP is $9.0 trillion, the unplanned inventory adjustment in the final column is −$0.2 trillion. Because firms cannot reduce inventories indefinitely, they respond to such reductions by increasing production, and they continue to do so until they produce the amount people want to buy—that is, until real GDP equals planned aggregate expenditure.

If the amount produced exceeds planned spending, firms get stuck with unsold goods, which become unplanned increases in inventories. For example, if real GDP is $11.0 trillion, planned aggregate expenditure is only $10.8 trillion, so $0.2 trillion in output remains unsold. Thus, inventories increase by $0.2 trillion. Firms respond by reducing output and do so until they produce the amount people want to buy—planned spending.

When the amount people plan to spend equals the amount produced, there are no unplanned inventory adjustments. More precisely, *for a given price level, the quantity of real GDP demanded occurs when real GDP equals planned aggregate expenditure.* In Exhibit 1, this occurs where planned aggregate expenditure and real GDP equal $10.0 trillion.

Real GDP Demanded

Using a table, we have seen how firms adjust output until production just equals desired spending. You may find graphs easier to understand. Graphs are also more general than tables and can show relationships between variables without focusing on specific numbers. The tabular relationship between real GDP and planned aggregate expenditure in Exhibit 1 can be expressed as an **aggregate expenditure line** in Exhibit 2. Like the aggregate expenditure amounts shown in column (9) of Exhibit 1, the aggregate expenditure line in Exhibit 2 reflects the sum of consumption, investment, government purchases, and net exports, or $C + I + G + (X - M)$. Planned aggregate expenditure is measured on the vertical axis.

Real GDP, measured along the horizontal axis in Exhibit 2, can be viewed in two ways—as the value of *aggregate output* and as the *aggregate income* generated by that level of output. Because real GDP, or income, is measured on the horizontal axis and aggregate expenditure is measured on the vertical axis, this graph is often called the **income-expenditure model.**[1]

To gain perspective on the relationship between income and expenditure, we use a handy analytical device: the 45-degree ray from the origin. The special feature of this line is that any point along it is the same distance from both axes. Thus, the 45-degree line identifies all points where planned expenditure equals real GDP. *Aggregate output demanded at a given price level occurs where real GDP, measured along the horizontal axis, equals planned aggregate expenditure, measured along the vertical axis.* In Exhibit 2, this occurs at point *e*, where the aggregate expenditure line intersects the 45-degree line. At point *e*, the amount people plan to spend equals the amount produced. Keep in mind that this approach was based on a given price level. We conclude that, at the given price level of 130, the quantity of real GDP demanded equals $10.0 trillion.

- SEE IT: DETERMINING AGGREGATE OUTPUT DEMANDED
- TRY IT: THE AGGREGATE EXPENDITURE MODEL

EXHIBIT 2 |

Deriving the Aggregate Output Demanded for a Given Price Level

The aggregate output demanded, given the price level, is found where aggregate expenditure equals real GDP—that is, where desired spending equals the amount produced.

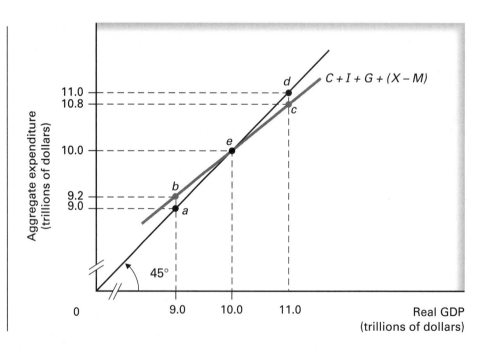

[1]Notice in Exhibit 2 that the horizontal axis measures real GDP. In exhibits in the previous chapter, the horizontal axis measured disposable income. There is not much of a difference because real GDP minus net taxes equals disposable income. Since net taxes in our example are $1.0 trillion, every level of real GDP implies a level of disposable income that is $1.0 trillion lower. The link between real GDP and each spending component was spelled out in Exhibit 1.

When Output and Planned Spending Differ

To find the real GDP demanded at the given price level, consider what happens when real GDP is initially less than $10.0 trillion. As you can see from Exhibit 2, when real GDP is less than $10.0 trillion, the planned aggregate expenditure line is above the 45-degree line, indicating that planned spending exceeds the amount produced. For example, if real GDP is $9.0 trillion, planned spending is $9.2 trillion, as indicated by point *b* on the aggregate expenditure line, so planned spending exceeds output by $0.2 trillion. When the amount people plan to spend exceeds the amount firms produce, something has to give. Ordinarily what gives is the price, but remember that we are seeking the real GDP demanded for a given price level, so the price level is assumed to be constant, at least for now. What gives in this model are firms' *inventories.* Firms are forced to sell from inventories to make up the $0.2 trillion by which spending exceeds real GDP. Since firms cannot draw down inventories indefinitely, *unplanned inventory reductions* prompt firms to produce more. That increases employment and consumer income, leading to more spending. As long as planned spending exceeds output, firms increase production to make up the difference. This process of more output, more income, and more spending will continue until planned spending equals real GDP, an equality achieved at point *e.*

When output reaches $10.0 trillion, planned spending exactly matches output, so no unintended inventory adjustments occur. More importantly, when output reaches $10.0 trillion, planned spending equals the amount produced and equals the total income generated by that production. Earlier we assumed a price level of 130. Therefore, $10.0 trillion is the real GDP demanded at that given price level.

To reinforce the logic of the model, consider what happens when real GDP initially exceeds $10.0 trillion—that is, when the aggregate expenditure line is below the 45-degree line. Notice in Exhibit 2 that, to the right of point *e,* planned spending falls short of production. For example, if the amount produced in the economy is $11.0 trillion, planned spending, as indicated by point *c* on the aggregate expenditure line, is $0.2 trillion less than real GDP, indicated by point *d* on the 45-degree line. Because real GDP exceeds the amount people want to spend, unsold goods accumulate. This swells inventories by $0.2 trillion more than firms want. Rather than allow inventories to pile up indefinitely, firms reduce production, which reduces employment and income. As an example of such behavior, a recent news account read, "General Motors will idle two assembly plants in a move to trim inventories in the wake of slowing sales."[2] *Unplanned inventory buildups* cause firms to cut production until the amount they produce equals aggregate spending, which occurs, again, where real GDP is $10.0 trillion. Given the price level, real GDP demanded is found where the amount people plan to spend equals the amount produced. Hence, *for a given price level, there is only one point along the aggregate expenditure line at which planned spending equals real GDP.*

We have now discussed the forces that determine real GDP demanded for a given price level. In the next section, we examine changes that can shift planned spending.

THE SIMPLE SPENDING MULTIPLIER

In the previous section, we employed the aggregate expenditure line to determine real GDP demanded for a particular price level. In this section, we continue to assume that the price level remains unchanged as we trace the effects of changes in planned spending on aggregate output demanded. Like a stone thrown into a still pond, the effect of any shift in planned spending ripples through the economy, generating changes in aggregate output that may far exceed the initial shift in planned spending.

NETBOOKMARK: ALAN GREENSPAN DISCUSSES A LOOMING ECONOMIC SLOWDOWN AND FED BOARD MEMBER'S VIEWS ON THE FORCES AFFECTING AGGREGATE DEMAND

An Upward Shift of the Aggregate Expenditure Line

We begin at point *e* in Exhibit 3, where planned spending equals real GDP at $10.0 trillion. Now let's consider the effect of an increase in one of the components of spending. Suppose that firms become more optimistic about future profit prospects and increase their planned investment.

[2]"GM Plans to Idle Two Factories in an Effort to Deplete Inventories," *Wall Street Journal,* 9 March 2001.

Specifically, suppose planned investment increases from $0.8 trillion to $0.9 trillion per year, as reflected in Exhibit 3 by a change in the aggregate expenditure line, which shifts upward by $0.1 trillion, from $C + I + G + (X - M)$ to $C + I' + G + (X - M)$.

What happens to real GDP demanded? An instinctive response is to say that real GDP demanded increases by $0.1 trillion. In this case, however, instinct is a poor guide. As you can see, the new spending line intersects the 45-degree line at point e', where real GDP demanded is $10.5 trillion. How can a $0.1 trillion increase in planned spending increase real GDP demanded by $0.5 trillion? What's going on?

The idea of the circular flow is central to an understanding of the adjustment process. As noted earlier, real GDP can be thought of as both the value of production and the income arising from that production. Recall that production yields income, which generates spending. We can think of each trip around the circular flow as a "round" of income and spending.

Round One. An upward shift of the aggregate expenditure line means that, at the initial real GDP level of $10.0 trillion, planned spending now exceeds output by $0.1 trillion, or $100 billion. This is shown in Exhibit 3 by the distance between point e and point f. Initially, this increased spending is satisfied by reducing inventories, but shrinking inventories prompt firms to expand production by $100 billion, as shown by the movement from point f to point g. This increased production generates $100 billion in increased income.

Thus, output and income increase by $100 billion in the first round of new spending arising from the increase in planned investment of $100 billion. The movement from e to g shows the first round in the multiplier process. The income-generating process does not stop there, however, because those who receive this additional income spend some of it and save the rest, laying the basis for round two of spending and income.

Round Two. Given a marginal propensity to consume, or MPC, of 0.8, those who receive the additional $100 billion as income will spend a total of $80 billion on toasters, movies, backpacks, and thousands of other goods and services. The other $20 billion will be saved. This $80 billion spending increase is shown by the move from point g to point h in Exhibit 3. Firms respond by increasing their output by $80 billion, shown by the movement from point h to point i. Thus, the initial $100 billion in new income increases real GDP by $80 billion in round two.

Round Three and Beyond. Focus now on the $80 billion that went toward consumption in round two. Production increases of $80 billion in the second round generated an equal amount of income for resource suppliers. Again, based on the MPC, we know that four-fifths of the additional income will be spent and one-fifth will be saved. Thus, $64 billion will be spent on still

EXHIBIT 3

Effect of an Increase in Autonomous Investment on Real GDP Demanded

The economy is initially at point e, where spending and real GDP both equal $10.0 trillion. A $0.1 trillion increase in autonomous investment shifts the aggregate expenditure line up vertically by $0.1 trillion from $C + I + G + (X - M)$ to $C + I' + G + (X - M)$. Real GDP rises until it equals spending at point e'. As a result of the $0.1 trillion increase in autonomous investment, real GDP demanded increases by $0.5 trillion, to $10.5 trillion.

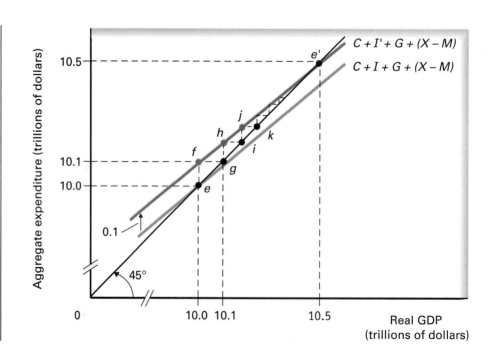

more goods and services, as reflected by the movement from point *i* to point *j*. The remaining $16 billion gets saved. The additional spending causes firms to increase output by $64 billion, as shown by the movement from point *j* to point *k*. This increase in real GDP means that income also increases by $64 billion, laying the basis for subsequent rounds of spending, output, and income. *As long as planned spending exceeds output, production will increase, thereby creating more income, which will generate still more spending.*

Exhibit 4 summarizes the multiplier process, showing the first three rounds, round 10, and the cumulative effect of all rounds. The new spending generated in each round is shown in the second column, and the accumulation of new spending appears in the third column. For example, the new spending accumulated as of the third round is $244 billion—the sum of the first three rounds of spending ($100 billion + $80 billion + $64 billion). The new saving from each round appears in the fourth column, and the accumulation of new saving appears in the final column.

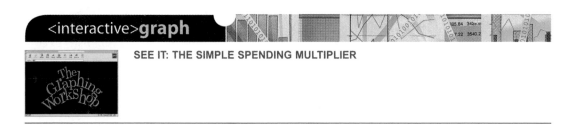

<interactive>graph

SEE IT: THE SIMPLE SPENDING MULTIPLIER

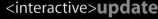

<interactive>update

- **ECONNEWS ONLINE: WITH A LITTLE BIT OF LUCK**
- **ECONDATA ONLINE: STOCK PRICES—S&P 500**

Using the Simple Spending Multiplier

Consumers spend four-fifths of their income each round, with each new round equal to spending from the previous round times the MPC. This goes on round after round, leaving less and less spending to fuel more spending and income. At some point, the new rounds of income and spending become so small that they disappear and the process stops. The question is, by how much does total spending increase in the process? We can get some idea of the total by

EXHIBIT 4 |

Tracking the Rounds of Spending Following a $100 Billion Increase in Planned Investment (billions of dollars)

Round	New Spending This Round	Cumulative New Spending	New Saving This Round	Cumulative New Saving
1	100	100	—	—
2	80	180	20	20
3	64	244	16	36
⋮	⋮	⋮	⋮	⋮
10	13.4	446.3	3.35	86.6
⋮	⋮	⋮	⋮	⋮
∞	0	500	0	100

working through a limited number of rounds. For example, as shown in Exhibit 4, total new spending after 10 rounds sums to $446.3 billion. But calculating the exact total would require us to work through an infinite series of rounds—an impossible task.

Fortunately, we can borrow a shortcut from mathematicians, who have found that the sum of an infinite series of rounds, each of which is MPC times the previous round, equals $1/(1 - MPC)$ times the initial change. Translated, this means that the cumulative spending resulting from an infinite series of rounds equals $1/(1 - MPC)$, or $1/0.2$ in our example, which is 5, times the initial increase in spending, which is $100 billion. In short, the increase in planned investment eventually boosts real GDP demanded by 5 times $100 billion, or $500 billion.

The **simple spending multiplier** is the factor by which real GDP demanded changes for a given initial change in spending.

$$\text{Simple spending multiplier} = \frac{1}{1 - MPC}$$

The simple spending multiplier provides a shortcut to the total change in real GDP demanded. This multiplier depends on the value of the MPC. *The larger the fraction of an increase in income that is spent each round, the larger the spending multiplier.* The marginal propensity to consume and the multiplier are therefore directly related; the larger the MPC, the larger the simple spending multiplier. If the MPC was 0.9 instead of 0.8, the denominator would equal $1 - 0.9$, or 0.1, so the simple spending multiplier would be $1/0.1$, which is 10. So with an MPC of 0.9, a $0.1 trillion investment increase would generate a $1.0 trillion increase in real GDP demanded. On the other hand, an MPC of 0.75 would yield a denominator of 0.25 and a simple spending multiplier of 4. So a $0.1 trillion investment increase would raise real GDP demanded by $0.4 trillion.

Let's return to Exhibit 3. The $0.1 trillion rise in autonomous investment has boosted real GDP demanded from $10.0 trillion to $10.5 trillion. Note that real GDP demanded would have increased by the same amount if consumers had decided to spend $0.1 trillion more at each level of income—that is, if the consumption function, rather than the investment function, had shifted up by $0.1 trillion. Real GDP demanded would likewise have increased if government purchases or net exports increased $0.1 trillion. *The change in aggregate output demanded depends on how much the aggregate expenditure line shifts, not on which spending component causes the shift.*

In our example, planned investment increased by $0.1 trillion in the year in question. *If this higher level of planned investment is not sustained the following year, real GDP demanded will fall back.* For example, if planned investment returns to its initial level, other things constant, real GDP demanded would return to $10.0 trillion.

Finally, recall from the previous chapter that the MPC and the MPS add up to 1, so 1 minus the MPC equals the MPS. With this information, we can define the simple spending multiplier in terms of the MPS as follows:

$$\text{Simple spending multiplier} = \frac{1}{1 - MPC} = \frac{1}{MPS}$$

When we express it this way, we can see that the smaller the MPS, the larger the fraction of each fresh round of income that is spent and the less that leaks out as saving, so the larger the spending multiplier. Incidentally, this spending multiplier is called "simple" because consumption is the only spending component that varies with income.

As an example of how a decline in aggregate expenditure can ripple through the economy, let's look what happened to air travel in the wake of the recent terrorist attacks.

<interactive>video

- ASK THE INSTRUCTOR: WHAT DO ECONOMISTS MEAN BY THE TERM "MULTIPLIER"?
- ASK THE INSTRUCTOR: DOES THE MULTIPLIER WORK IN BOTH DIRECTIONS?

<interactive>update

ECONNEWS ONLINE: JOBS DOWN, CONFIDENCE UP

When hijacked planes slammed into the World Trade Center and the Pentagon, America's sense of domestic security changed. The thousands of lives lost and the billions of dollars of property destroyed have been chronicled at length in the media. Let's look at the impact of the tragedy on just one industry—air travel—to see how slumping demand there had a multiplier effect on aggregate expenditure.

Once aviation regulators became aware of the hijackings, they grounded all nonmilitary aircraft immediately. This cost the airlines hundreds of millions of dollars a day during the week of the shutdown. Television footage of the second plane crashing into the twin towers was shown again and again during the days following the attack, freezing this image in people's minds and heightening concerns about airline safety. These worries, coupled with the added time required (passengers were told to arrive up to three hours before flights), reduced the demand for air travel. Two weeks after the attack, airlines were operating only 75 percent of their flights, and these flights were only 30 percent full instead of the usual 75 percent. Reservations dropped 40 percent, and airline revenue declined 45 percent in September. Airlines requested federal assistance, saying they would go bankrupt without it. Congress quickly approved a $15 billion package of loans and grants.

Despite the promise of federal aid, all the major airlines, reeling from losses, announced flight cuts and layoffs totaling over 85,000 jobs, or about 20 percent of their workforce. Flight reductions meant that as many as 900 aircraft would be parked indefinitely, so investment in new planes collapsed. Boeing, the major producer of new planes, said 30,000 workers would get laid off. This touched off a cascade of other layoffs among suppliers of airline parts, ranging from jet engines to electronic components. For example, Rockwell Collins, an electronics supplier, said it would lay off 15 percent of its workforce. Other suppliers in airline food chain also cut jobs. Sky Chef, a major airline caterer, announced it would lay off 4,800 of its 16,000 employees.

Airports began rethinking their investment plans. Half the major U.S. airports said they were reevaluating their capital improvement plans to see if these investments made sense in this new environment. Honolulu airport, for example, suspended plans to add extra gates and renovate its overseas terminals.

Just within the first three weeks after the attacks, announced job cuts in the industry exceeded 150,000. These were part of only the first round of reduced consumption and investment. In an expanding economy, job losses in one sector can be made up by job expansions in other sectors. But the U.S. economy had already been softening at the time of the attack. People who lost jobs and faced a job market that was growing grimmer would be forced to reduce their demand for housing, clothing, entertainment, restaurant meals, and other goods and services. For example, unemployed flight attendants would be less likely to buy a new car, reducing the income of autoworkers and suppliers. People who lost jobs in this declining auto industry would reduce *their* demand for goods and services. So the reductions in airline jobs had a multiplier effect.

Airlines are only one part of the travel industry. With fewer people traveling, fewer people needed hotels, rental cars, taxi rides, restaurant meals, and tickets to tourist attractions. Each of those sectors generated a cascade of job losses. The terrorist attacks also shook consumer confidence, which in September 2001 suffered its largest monthly drop since October 1990, when the nation readied for the Persian Gulf War.

Within 10 days after the attacks, the number of people filing for unemployment benefits jumped to a nine-year high. Again, these early job losses could be viewed as just part of the first round of reduced aggregate expenditure. The second round would occur when people who lost jobs or who feared they would lose their jobs started reducing their consumption.

Offsetting to some extent job losses within the airline industry were job gains from federal spending to beef up airline security, increase the number of armed marshals aboard domestic flights, fortify cockpit doors against hijackers, and improve the air traffic control system. More generally, rebuilding New York City and repairing the Pentagon would boost investment spending and jobs, but perhaps not enough to offset jobs lost from the attacks.

<interactive>exercise

• eACTIVITY: FEAR OF FLYING
• READING IT RIGHT: WALL STREET JOURNAL EXERCISE

Sources: Will Pinkston, "Airports Reconsider Expansion Plans as Future of Air Travel Gets Murkier," *Wall Street Journal,* 27 September 2001; Luke Timmerman, "Boeing Warns Bad May Get Worse," *Seattle Times,* 21 September 2001; Sherri Day, "Delta and Sky Chefs Announce Cuts," *Wall Street Journal,* 27 September 2001; "Consumer Confidence Plunges Even More Than Expected," *Wall Street Journal,* 25 September 2001; Scott McCarthy, "Airline Revenue Drop as Fares, Traffic Slide Following Attacks," *Wall Street Journal,* 24 October 2001; and the Federal Aviation Administration at http://www.faa.gov/.

DERIVING THE AGGREGATE DEMAND CURVE

In this chapter, we have used the aggregate expenditure line to find real GDP demanded *for a given price level.* But what happens to the aggregate expenditure line if the price level changes? As you will see, for each price level, there is a specific aggregate expenditure line, which yields a unique real GDP demanded. By altering the price level, we can derive the aggregate demand curve.

A Higher Price Level

What is the effect of a higher price level on the economy's aggregate expenditure line and, in turn, on real GDP demanded? Recall that consumers hold many assets that are fixed in dollar terms, such as currency and bank accounts. A higher price level decreases the real value of these dollar-denominated assets. Consumers are poorer, so they are less willing to spend at each level of income. For reasons that will be more fully explained in a later chapter, a higher price level also tends to increase the market interest rate, and a higher interest rate reduces investment. Finally, a higher U.S. price level means that foreign goods become relatively cheaper for U.S. consumers, and U.S. goods become relatively more expensive abroad. So imports rise and exports fall, decreasing net exports. Therefore, *a higher price level reduces consumption, planned investment, and net exports, which all reduce aggregate spending.* This decrease in the aggregate expenditure line reduces real GDP demanded.

Exhibit 5 represents different ways of expressing the effects of a change in the price level on real GDP demanded. Panel (a) offers the income-expenditure model, and panel (b) offers the aggregate demand curve, showing the inverse relationship between the price level and real GDP demanded. The idea is to find, for a given price level, the real GDP demanded in panel (a) and show that price-quantity combination as a point on the aggregate demand curve in panel (b).

The two panels align so that levels of real GDP on the horizontal axes correspond. At the initial price level of 130 in panel (a), the aggregate expenditure line, now denoted by *AE,* intersects the 45-degree line at point *e* to yield $10.0 trillion in real GDP demanded. Panel (b) shows more directly the link between real GDP demanded and the price level. As you can see, when the price level is 130, real GDP demanded is $10.0 trillion. This combination of price level and real GDP is identified by point *e* on the aggregate demand curve.

What if the price level increases from 130 to, say, 140? As you've just learned, an increase in the price level reduces consumption, investment, and net exports. This reduction in planned spending is reflected in panel (a) by a downward shift of the aggregate expenditure line from *AE* to *AE'*. As a result of this decrease in planned spending, real GDP demanded declines from $10.0 trillion to, say, $9.5 trillion. Panel (b) shows that an increase in the price level from 130 to 140 decreases real GDP demanded from $10.0 trillion to $9.5 trillion, as reflected by point *e'*.

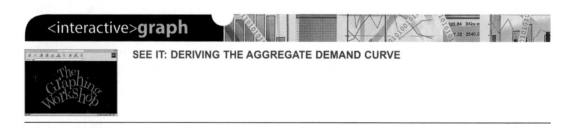

SEE IT: DERIVING THE AGGREGATE DEMAND CURVE

A Lower Price Level

The opposite holds if the price level falls. At a lower price level, the value of bank accounts, currency, and other dollar-denominated assets increases. Consumers on average are richer and thus more inclined to consume more at each level of real GDP. A lower price level also tends to decrease the market interest rate, which increases investment. Finally, a lower U.S. price level, other things constant, makes U.S. products relatively cheaper abroad and foreign prod-

EXHIBIT 5

The Income-Expenditure Approach and the Aggregate Demand Curve

At the initial price level of 130, the aggregate expenditure line is *AE*, which identifies real GDP demanded of $10.0 trillion. This combination of a price level of 130 and a real GDP demanded of $10.0 trillion determine one point (point *e*) on the aggregate demand curve in panel (b).

At the higher price level of 140, the aggregate expenditure line is lower at *AE'*, and real GDP demanded is less at $9.5 trillion. This price-output combination is plotted as point *e'* in panel (b).

At the lower price level of 120, the aggregate expenditure line is higher at *AE"* and so is real GDP demanded. That price-output combination is plotted as point *e"* in panel (b).

Connecting points *e*, *e'*, and *e"* gives us the downward-sloping aggregate demand curve, which shows how much real GDP is demanded at each price level.

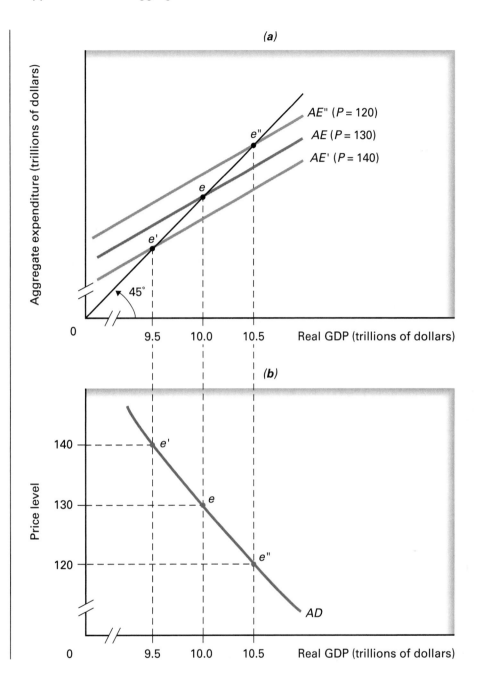

ucts relatively more expensive here, so exports increase and imports decrease. *Because of a decline in the price level, consumption, investment, and net exports increase at each level of real GDP. A higher aggregate expenditure line leads to a higher real GDP demanded.*

Refer again to Exhibit 5 and consider the effect of a decrease in the price level. Suppose the price level declines from 130 to, say, 120. As explained already, a decline in the price level causes consumption, planned investment, and net exports to increase, as reflected in panel (a) by an upward shift in the spending line from *AE* to *AE"*. An increase in planned spending at each level of income increases real GDP demanded from $10.0 trillion to, say, $10.5 trillion, as indicated by the intersection of the top aggregate expenditure line with the 45-degree line at point *e"*. This same price decrease can be viewed more directly in panel (b). As you can see, when the price level decreases to 120, real GDP demanded increases to $10.5 trillion.

The aggregate expenditure line and the aggregate demand curve portray real output from different perspectives. The aggregate expenditure line shows, for a given price level, how planned spending relates to the level of real GDP in the economy. Real GDP demanded is found where planned spending equals real GDP. The aggregate demand curve shows, for various price levels, the quantities of real GDP demanded.

The Multiplier and Shifts in Aggregate Demand

Now that you have some idea how changes in the price level shift the aggregate expenditure line to generate the aggregate demand curve, lets reverse course and return to the situation where the price level is assumed to be constant. What we want to do now is trace through the effects of a shift in a component of spending, such as consumption or investment, on aggregate demand, while assuming the price level does not change. For example, suppose that a bounce in business confidence spurs a $0.1 trillion increase in planned investment at each level of real GDP. Each panel of Exhibit 6 represents a different way of expressing the effects

EXHIBIT 6

A Shift of the Aggregate Expenditure Line That Shifts the Aggregate Demand Curve

A shift of the aggregate expenditure line that is not the result of a change in the price level will shift the aggregate demand curve. In panel (a), an increase in investment of $0.1 trillion, with the price level constant at 130, causes the aggregate expenditure line to increase from $C + I + G + (X - M)$ to $C + I' + G + (X - M)$. As a result, real GDP demanded increases from $10.0 trillion to $10.5 trillion. In panel (b), the aggregate demand curve has shifted from AD to AD'. At the prevailing price level of 130, the amount of output demanded has increased by $0.5 trillion.

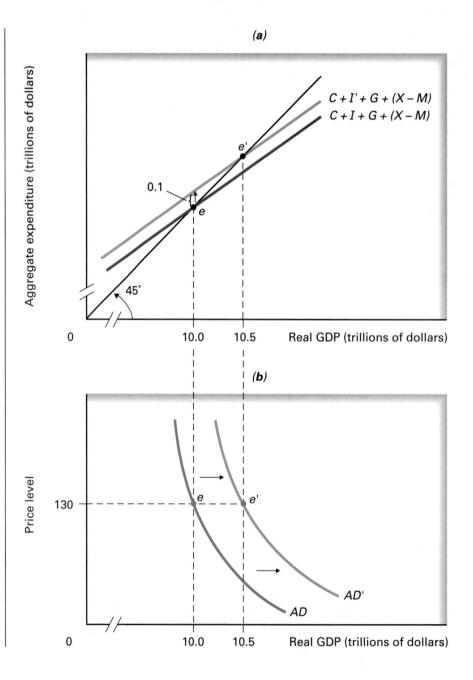

of an increase in planned spending on real GDP demanded, assuming the price level remains unchanged. Panel (a) presents the income-expenditure model and panel (b) the aggregate demand model. Again, the two panels align so that levels of real GDP on the horizontal axes correspond. At a price level of 130 in panel (a), the aggregate expenditure line, $C + I + G + (X - M)$, intersects the 45-degree line at point e to yield \$10.0 trillion in real GDP demanded. Panel (b) shows more directly the link between real GDP demanded and the price level. As you can see, when the price level is 130, real GDP demanded is \$10.0 trillion. This combination of price level and real GDP is identified by point e on the aggregate demand curve AD.

Exhibit 6 shows how shifts of the aggregate expenditure line relate to shifts of the aggregate demand curve, given a constant price level. In panel (a), a \$0.1 trillion increase in investment shifts the aggregate expenditure line up by \$0.1 trillion, from $C + I + G + (X - M)$ to $C + I' + G + (X - M)$. As we have seen, because of the multiplier effect, such an increase in spending raises real GDP demanded from \$10.0 trillion to \$10.5 trillion. Panel (b) shows the effect of the increase in spending on the aggregate demand curve, which shifts to the right, from AD to AD'. At the prevailing price level of 130, real GDP demanded increases from \$10.0 trillion to \$10.5 trillion as a result of the \$0.1 trillion increase in investment.

Our discussion of the simple spending multiplier exaggerates the actual effect we might expect from a given shift of the aggregate expenditure line. For one thing, we have assumed that the price level remains constant. As we shall see in the next chapter, incorporating aggregate supply into the analysis reduces the impact of a given shift in aggregate expenditure because of the resulting price change. Moreover, as income increases there are leakages from the circular flow in addition to saving, such as higher income taxes and increased spending on imports, and these leakages cut the size of the multiplier. Finally, although we have presented the process in a timeless framework, the spending multiplier takes time to work itself out—perhaps a year or more.

In summary: For a given price level, the aggregate expenditure line relates planned spending to the level of income in the economy, or to real GDP. A change in the price level will shift the aggregate expenditure line, changing real GDP demanded. Changes in the price level and consequent changes in real GDP demanded generate points along an aggregate demand curve. But at a given price level, a shift in a spending component, such as planned investment, consumer spending, or government purchases, will shift the aggregate demand curve.

We close with a case study that considers the problem created when Japanese consumers decided to spend less and save more at each level of income.

SEE IT: SHIFTING THE AGGREGATE DEMAND CURVE

- ECONNEWS ONLINE: HARD LANDING AHEAD
- ECONNEWS ONLINE: THE PAUPER EFFECT

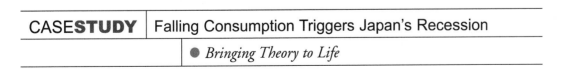

CASE**STUDY** | Falling Consumption Triggers Japan's Recession

● *Bringing Theory to Life*

As noted already, consumer spending is the largest component of aggregate expenditure, accounting for about two-thirds of the total. Consumption depends primarily on household income. But at any given income level, consumption depends on several other factors, including household wealth, the interest rate, and consumer expectations. Look at what's been happening in Japan, where by 2001 the stock market stood two-thirds below its 1990 level, taking a big bite from the wealth of Japanese households. A collapse in the once-booming real estate market cut household wealth even more.

This sharp reduction in household wealth, combined with an erosion of consumer confidence in the economy, prompted Japanese households to save more and consume less. Japan's consumption function shifted downward, and their saving function shifted upward. The drop in consumption reduced aggregate expenditure and shifted the aggregate demand curve to the left. The decline in aggregate demand resulted in Japan's longest economic downturn in 50 years, with the unemployment rate doubling between 1990 and 2001. Japan, the second largest economy in the world (after the United States), is by far the largest economy in Asia. A weak economy in Japan hurts the already troubled economies across Asia because Japan is a customer for their exports. Thus, the decline in consumption in Japan has global implications.

<interactive>exercise

eACTIVITY: FALLING CONSUMPTION TRIGGERS JAPAN'S RECESSION

<interactive>video

CNN VIDEO: "WILL THE SUN RISE AGAIN?"

Sources: *OECD Economic Outlook* 69 (December 2001); "Japan Stock Market: Support Systems," *Economist,* 8 February 2001; "Report Underlines Risk of Japan Recession," Reuters, 28 February 2001; Phred Dvorak, "Japan Begins to Discuss Bolder Revamping Plans." *Wall Street Journal,* 19 September 2001; and Howard French, "In Stagnant Japan, Economic and Social Ills Match," *New York Times,* 6 February 2001. For a survey of the 2000 Japanese economy, go to http://www.oecd.org/eco/surv/esu-jap.htm.

CONCLUSION

Three ideas central to this chapter are (1) certain forces determine the real GDP demanded at a given price level, (2) changes in the price level generate the aggregate demand curve, and (3) at a given price level, changes in planned spending shift the aggregate demand curve. The simple multiplier provides a crude idea how a change in planned spending affects real GDP demanded, but, as we'll see, this effect is exaggerated.

This chapter focused on aggregate spending. A simplifying assumption used throughout was that net exports did not vary with income. Appendix A adds realism by considering what happens when imports increase with income. Because imports leak from the circular flow, this more realistic approach reduces the spending multiplier.

So far, we have determined real GDP demanded using several approaches, including intuition, tables, and graphs. With the various approaches, we find that for each price level there is a specific real GDP demanded, other things constant. Appendix B uses algebra to derive real GDP and the spending multiplier.

Take the Post-Test to assess your overall understanding of the key ideas in this chapter. The Post-Test provides a comprehensive selection of exam-style questions addressing the main topics and concepts of the chapter. At the completion of each Post-Test, you will receive a score and instructive feedback on how you answered each question, and a direct link to the part of the chapter addressed in the question. Take the Post-Test as often as you need to—a record of your progress for each attempt is kept for you to revisit and gauge your improvement. And each Post-Test is randomly generated, so every attempt is new.

endofchaptermaterial

- **Summary**
- **Questions for Review**
- **Problems and Exercises**
- **Experiential Exercises**
- **Wall Street Journal Exercise**

- **Appendix A Questions**
- **Appendix B Questions**
- **Graphing Workshop: Apply It Exercises**

Post-Test

VARIABLE NET EXPORTS REVISITED

This chapter has assumed that net exports do not vary with income. A more realistic approach has net exports varying inversely with income. Such a model was developed in the appendix to the last chapter. The resulting net export function, $X - M$, is presented in panel (a) of Exhibit 7. Recall that the higher the income level in the economy, the more spent on imports, so the lower the net exports. (If this is not clear, review the appendix to the previous chapter.) Panel (b) of Exhibit 7 shows what happens when variable net exports are added to consumption, government purchases, and investment. We add the variable net export function to $C + I + G$ to get $C + I + G + (X - M)$. Perhaps the easiest way to see how introducing net exports affects planned spending is to begin where real GDP equals $9.0 trillion. Since net exports equal zero when real GDP equals $9.0 trillion, the addition of net exports has no effect on planned spending when real GDP is $9.0 trillion. So the $C + I + G$ and $C + I + G + (X - M)$ lines intersect where real GDP equals $9.0 trillion. At real GDP levels less than $9.0 trillion, net exports are positive, so the $C + I + G + (X - M)$ line is above the $C + I + G$ line. At real GDP levels greater than $9.0 trillion, net exports are negative, so the $C + I + G + (X - M)$ line is below

---

EXHIBIT 7

Net Exports and the Aggregate Expenditure Line

In panel (a), net exports, $X - M$, equal exports minus imports. Net exports are added to consumption, investment, and government purchases in panel (b) to yield $C + I + G + (X - M)$. The addition of net exports has the effect of rotating the spending line about the point where net exports are zero, which occurs where real GDP is $9.0 trillion.

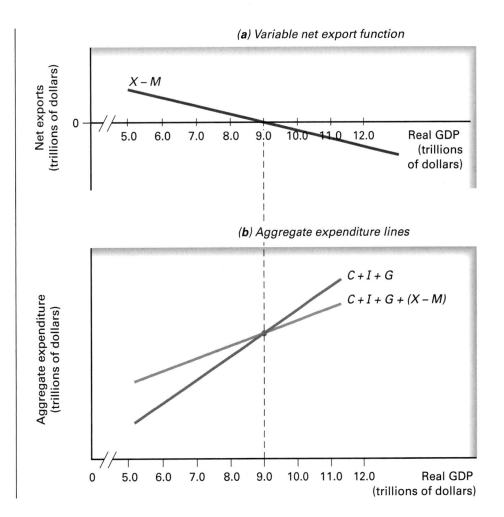

(a) Variable net export function

(b) Aggregate expenditure lines

the $C + I + G$ line. *Because variable net exports and real GDP are inversely related, the addition of variable net exports has the effect of flattening out, or reducing the slope of, the aggregate expenditure line.*

NET EXPORTS AND THE SPENDING MULTIPLIER

The inclusion of variable net exports makes the model more realistic but more complicated, and it requires a reformulation of the spending multiplier. If net exports are autonomous, or independent of income, only the marginal propensity to consume determines how much gets spent and how much gets saved as income increases. The inclusion of variable net exports means that, as income increases, U.S. residents spend more on imports. The **marginal propensity to import,** or **MPM,** is the fraction of each additional dollar of disposable income spent on imported products. Imports leak from the circular flow. Thus, there are now two leakages that grow with income: saving and imports. This additional leakage changes the value of the multiplier from 1/MPS to the following:

$$\text{Spending multiplier with variable net exports} = \frac{1}{MPS + MPM}$$

The larger the marginal propensity to import, the greater the leakage during each round of spending and the smaller the resulting spending multiplier. Suppose the MPM equals 1/10, or 0.1. If the marginal propensity to save is 0.2 and the marginal propensity to import is 0.1, then only $0.70 of each additional dollar of disposable income gets spent on output produced in the United States. We can compute the new multiplier as follows:

$$\text{Spending multiplier with variable net exports} =$$

$$\frac{1}{MPS + MPM} = \frac{1}{0.2 + 0.1} = \frac{1}{0.3} = 3.33$$

Thus, the inclusion of net exports reduces the spending multiplier in our hypothetical example from 5 to 3.33. *Because some of each additional dollar of income is spent on imports, less is spent on U.S. products, so any given shift of the aggregate expenditure line has less of an impact on the quantity of output demanded.*

A CHANGE IN AUTONOMOUS SPENDING

Given the net export function described in the previous section, what is the level of real GDP demanded, and how does income change when there is a change in autonomous spending? To answer these quesitons, let's begin in Exhibit 8 with an aggregate expenditure line of $C +$

EXHIBIT 8

Effect of a Shift in Autonomous Spending on Real GDP Demanded

An increase in planned investment, other things constant, shifts the spending line up from $C + I + G + (X - M)$ to $C + I' + G + (X - M)$, increasing the quantity of real GDP demanded.

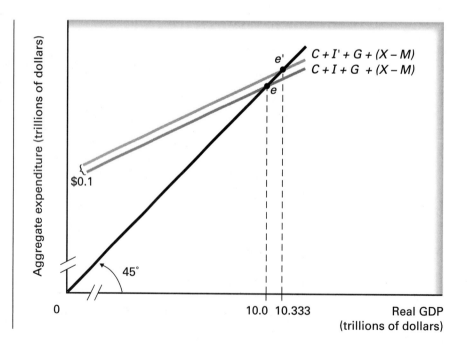

$I + G + (X - M)$, where net exports vary with income. This aggregate expenditure line intersects the 45-degree line at point e, determining real GDP demanded of $10.0 trillion. Suppose now that investment increases by $0.1 trillion at every level of income, with the price level unchanged. This increase in investment will shift the entire aggregate expenditure line up by $0.1 trillion, from $C + I + G + (X - M)$ to $C' + I' + G + (X - M)$, as shown in Exhibit 8. As you can see, output demanded increases from $10.0 trillion to $10.333 trillion, representing an increase of $0.333 trillion, or $333 billion, which is $0.1 trillion times the spending multiplier with variable exports of 3.33. We explain the derivation of the output level and the size of the multiplier in Appendix B.

APPENDIX B

THE ALGEBRA OF INCOME AND EXPENDITURE

This appendix explains the algebra behind real GDP demanded. You should see some similarity between this and the circular-flow explanation of national income accounts.

THE AGGREGATE EXPENDITURE LINE

We first determine where planned spending equals output and then derive the relevant spending multipliers, assuming a given price level. Initially, let's assume net exports are autonomous. Then we'll incorporate variable net exports into the framework.

Real GDP demanded for a given price level occurs where planned spending equals income, or real GDP. Planned spending is equal to the sum of consumption, C, investment, I, government purchases, G, and net exports, $X - M$. Algebraically, we can write the equality as

$$Y = C + I + G + (X - M)$$

where Y equals income, or real GDP. To find where real GDP equals planned spending, we begin with the heart of the income-expenditure model: the consumption function. The consumption function used throughout this chapter is a straight line; the equation for this line can be written as

$$C = 1.1 + 0.8\,(Y - 1.0)$$

The marginal propensity to consume is 0.8, Y is income, or real GDP, and 1.0 is autonomous net taxes in trillions of dollars. Thus $(Y - 1.0)$ is real GDP minus net taxes, which equals disposable income. The consumption function can be simplified to

$$C = 0.3 + 0.8Y$$

Consumption at each level of real GDP, therefore, equals \$0.3 trillion (which could be called autonomous consumption—that is, consumption that does not vary with income), plus 0.8 times the level of income, which is the marginal propensity to consume times income.

The second component of spending is investment, I, which we have assumed is autonomous and equal to \$0.8 trillion. The third component of spending is autonomous government purchases, G, which we assumed to be \$1.0 trillion. Net exports, $X - M$ the final spending component, we assumed to be −\$0.1 trillion at all levels of income. Substituting the numerical values for each spending component in planned spending, we get

$$Y = 0.3 + 0.8Y + 0.8 + 1.0 - 0.1$$

Notice there is only one variable in this expression: Y. If we rewrite the expression as

$$Y - 0.8Y = 0.3 + 0.8 + 1.0 - 0.1$$
$$0.2Y = 2.0$$

we can solve for real GDP demanded:

$$Y = \frac{2.0}{0.2}$$

$$Y = \$10.0 \text{ trillion}$$

A MORE GENERAL FORM OF INCOME AND EXPENDITURE

The advantage of algebra is that it allows us to derive the equilibrium quantity of real GDP demanded in a more general way. Let's begin with a consumption function of the general form

$$C = a + b(Y - NT)$$

where b is the marginal propensity to consume and NT is net taxes. Consumption can be rearranged as

$$C = a + bNT + bY$$

where $a - bNT$ is *autonomous* consumption (the portion of consumption that is independent of the level of income) and bY is *induced* consumption (the portion of consumption generated by the level of income in the economy). Real GDP demanded equals the sum of consumption, C, autonomous investment, I, autonomous government purchases, G, and autonomous net exports, $X - M$, or

$$\text{Income} = \text{Expenditure}$$

$$Y = a - bNT + bY + I + G + (X - M)$$

Again, by rearranging terms and isolating Y on the left side of the equation, we get

$$Y = \frac{1}{1 - b}(a - bNT + I + G + X - M)$$

The $(a - bNT + I + G + X - M)$ term represents autonomous spending—that is, the amount of spending that is independent of income. And $(1 - b)$ equals 1 minus the MPC. In the chapter, we showed that $1/(1 - \text{MPC})$ equals the simple spending multiplier. One way of viewing what's going on is to keep in mind that autonomous spending is *multiplied* through the economy to arrive at real GDP demanded.

The formula that yields real GDP demanded can be used to derive the spending multiplier. We can increase autonomous spending by, say, \$1, to see what happens to real GDP demanded.

$$Y' = \frac{1}{1 - b}(a - bNT + I + G + X - M + \$1)$$

The difference between this expression and the initial one (that is, between Y' and Y) is $\$1/(1 - b)$. Since b equals the MPC, the simple multiplier equals $1/(1 - b)$. Thus, the change in equilibrium income equals the change in autonomous spending times the multiplier.

VARYING NET EXPORTS

Here we explore the algebra behind variable net exports, first introduced in the appendix to the last chapter. We begin with the equality

$$Y = C + I + G + (X - M)$$

Exports are assumed to equal \$0.8 trillion at each level of income. Imports increase as disposable income increases, with a marginal propensity to import of 0.1. Therefore, net exports equal

$$(X - M) = 0.8 - 0.1\,(Y - 1.0)$$

After incorporating the values for C, I, and G presented earlier, we can express the equality as

$$Y = 0.3 + 0.8Y + 0.8 + 1.0 + 0.8 - 0.1(Y - 1.0)$$

which reduces to $0.3Y = \$3.0$ trillion, or $Y = \$10.0$ trillion. Algebra can be used to generalize these results. If m represents the marginal propensity to import, net exports become $X - m(Y - NT)$. Real GDP demanded can be found by solving for Y in the expression

$$Y = a + b(Y - NT) + I + G + X - m(Y - NT)$$

which yields

$$Y = \frac{1}{1 - b + m}(a - bNT + I + G + X - mNT)$$

The expression in parentheses represents autonomous spending. In the denominator, $1 - b$ is the marginal propensity to save and m is the marginal propensity to import. Appendix A demonstrated that $1/(\text{MPS} + \text{MPM})$ equals the spending multiplier when variable net exports are included. Thus, real GDP demanded equals the spending multiplier times autonomous spending. And an increase in autonomous spending times the multiplier gives us the resulting increase in real GDP demanded.

Aggregate Supply

What is your normal capacity for academic work, and when do you usually exceed that effort? If the economy is already operating at full employment, how can it produce more? What valuable piece of information do employers and workers lack when they negotiate wage agreements? Why do employers and workers fail to agree on pay cuts that might save jobs? How might a long stretch of high unemployment reduce the economy's ability to produce in the future? These and other questions are answered in this chapter, which develops the aggregate supply curve in the short run and the long run.

Up to this point, we have focused on real GDP demanded at a given price level. We have not yet introduced a theory of aggregate supply. Perhaps no other macroeconomic theory is more debated. The debate involves the shape of the aggregate supply curve and the reasons for that shape. In this chapter, we attempt to develop a single, coherent framework for aggregate supply.

Although our focus continues to be on economic aggregates, you should keep in mind that aggregate supply reflects billions of individual production decisions made by millions of individual resource suppliers and firms in the economy. Each firm operates in its own little world, dealing with its own suppliers and customers, and keeping a watchful eye on existing and potential competitors. Yet each firm also recognizes that success depends in part on the performance of the economy as a whole. The theory of aggregate supply we describe here must be consistent with both the microeconomic behavior of individual suppliers and the macroeconomic behavior of the economy. Topics discussed in this chapter include:

- Expected price level and long-term contracts
- Potential output
- Short-run aggregate supply
- Long-run aggregate supply
- Expansionary gaps and contractionary gaps
- Changes in aggregate supply

Pre-Test

<interactive>**exercise**

ECONDEBATE ONLINE: PRODUCTIVITY AND GROWTH

<interactive>**update**

- ECONDATA ONLINE: PRODUCTIVITY AND GROWTH
- ECONDATA ONLINE: AGGREGATE DEMAND/AGGREGATE SUPPLY
- ECONLINKS ONLINE: ECONOMICS WEB LINKS
- ECONNEWS ONLINE: PRODUCTIVITY AND GROWTH
- ECONNEWS ONLINE: AGGREGATE DEMAND/AGGREGATE SUPPLY

AGGREGATE SUPPLY IN THE SHORT RUN

As you know, *aggregate supply* is the relationship between the price level in the economy and the aggregate output firms are willing and able to supply, with other things constant. Assumed constant along a given aggregate supply curve are resource prices, the state of technology, and the set of formal and informal institutions that structure production incentives, such as the system of property rights, patent laws, tax systems, respect for the laws, and the customs and conventions of the market. The greater the supply of resources, the better the technology, and the more effective the production incentives provided by the economic institutions, the greater the aggregate supply. Let's begin by looking at the key resource—labor.

Labor and Aggregate Supply

Labor is the most important resource, accounting for about 70 percent of production cost. The supply of labor in an economy depends on the size and abilities of the adult population and household preferences for work versus leisure. Along a given labor supply curve—that is, for a given adult population with given preferences for work versus leisure—the quantity of labor supplied depends on the wage rate. The higher the wage, other things constant, the more people are willing and able to work.

So far, so good. But things start getting complicated once we recognize that the purchasing power of any given nominal wage depends on the economy's price level. *The higher the price level, the less any given money wage will purchase, so the less attractive that wage is to workers.* Consider wages and the price level over time. Suppose a worker in 1970 was offered a job paying $20,000 per year. That salary may not impress you today, but its real purchasing power would exceed $75,000 in today's dollars.

Because the price level matters, we must distinguish between the **nominal wage,** which measures the wage in current dollars (the number of dollars in your pay), and the **real wage,** which measures the wage in constant dollars—that is, dollars measured by the goods and services they will buy. A higher real wage means workers can buy more goods and services.

Both workers and employers care more about the real wage than about the nominal wage. The problem is that nobody knows for sure what price level will prevail during the life of the wage agreement, so labor contracts must be negotiated in terms of nominal wages. Some resource prices, such as wages set by long-term contracts, remain in force for extended periods, often for two or three years. Workers as well as other resource suppliers must therefore reach agreements based on the *expected* price level.

Even where there are no explicit labor contracts, there is often an implicit agreement that the wage, once negotiated, will not change for a while. For example, in many firms, the standard practice is to revise wages annually. So wage agreements may be either *explicit* (based on a labor contract) or *implicit* (based on labor market practices). These explicit and implicit agreements make it difficult to change contract terms during the life of the agreement, even if the price level in the economy turns out to be higher or lower than expected.

ECONNEWS ONLINE: STEADY AS SHE GOES

Potential Output and the Natural Rate of Unemployment

Here's how resource owners and firms negotiate resource price agreements for a particular period, say, a year. Firms and resource suppliers expect a certain price level to prevail in the economy during the year. You could think of this as the price level resulting from the *consensus* view of inflation for the upcoming year. Based on consensus expectations, firms and resource suppliers reach agreements on resource prices, such as wages. For example, firms and workers may expect the price level to increase 3 percent next year, so they agree on a nominal wage increase of 4 percent, which will increase the real wage by 1 percent. If these price-level expectations are realized, the agreed-on nominal wage translates into the expected real wage, so everyone is satisfied with the way things work out—after all, that's what they willingly negotiated. When the actual price level turns out as expected, we call the resulting level of output the economy's potential output. *The potential output is the amount produced when there are no surprises associated with the price level.* So, at the agreed-on real wage, workers are supplying the quantity of labor they want to and firms are hiring the quantity of labor they want to. Both sides are content with the arrangement.

We can think of the **potential output** level as the economy's maximum sustainable output level, given the supply of resources, the state of technology, and the formal and informal production incentives. Potential output is also referred to by other terms, including the *natural rate of output* and the *full-employment rate of output.*

The unemployment rate that occurs when the economy is producing its potential GDP is called the **natural rate of unemployment.** The natural rate of unemployment is the rate that prevails when cyclical unemployment is zero. When the economy is producing its potential output, the number of job openings equals the number of people unemployed for frictional, structural, and seasonal reasons. Widely accepted estimates of the natural rate of unemployment range from about 4 percent to about 6 percent of the labor force.

In summary, potential output provides a reference point, an anchor, for the analysis in this chapter. *When the actual price level turns out as anticipated, the expectations of both workers and firms are fulfilled, and the economy produces its potential level of output.* Complications arise, however, when the actual price level that occurs in the economy differs from expectations, as we'll see next.

CNN VIDEO: "VARIATIONS ON AN ENIGMA"

An Actual Price Level Higher than Expected

As you already know, each firm's objective is to maximize profit. Profit equals total revenue minus total cost. Suppose workers and firms, based on their expectations about the price level, have reached a wage agreement. What if the economy's price level then turns out to be higher than expected? What happens *in the short run* to aggregate output supplied? The **short run** is a period during which many resource prices remain fixed by contract. Does output in the short run exceed the economy's potential, fall short of that potential, or equal that potential?

The prices of many resources have been fixed for the duration of contracts, so firms welcome a price level that is higher than expected. After all, the selling prices of their products, on average, are higher than expected, while the costs of at least some of the resources they employ remain constant. *Because a price level that is higher than expected results in higher profits, firms have an incentive in the short run to expand production beyond the economy's potential level.*

At first it might appear contradictory to talk about producing beyond the economy's potential, but remember that potential output means the natural rate of unemployment, not zero unemployment. Even in an economy producing its potential output, there is some unemployed labor and some unused production capacity. If you think of potential GDP as the economy's *normal capacity,* you get a better idea of how the economy can temporarily exceed that capacity. For example, during World War II, the United States pulled out all the stops to win the war. Factories operated around the clock. The unemployment rate fell under 2 percent—well below the natural rate. Overtime was common. People worked longer and harder for the war effort than they normally would have.

Think about your own study habits. During most of the term, you display your normal capacity for academic work. As the end of the term draws near, however, you may shift into high gear, finishing term papers, studying late into the night for final exams, and generally running yourself ragged trying to pull things together. During those final frenzied days of the term, you study beyond your normal capacity, beyond the schedule you would follow on a regular or sustained basis. We often observe workers exceeding their normal capacity for short bursts: fireworks displayers around the Fourth of July, accountants during tax time, farmers during harvest time, and elected officials during the closing days of a campaign or a legislative session. Similarly, firms and their workers are able, *in the short run,* to push output beyond the economy's potential.

ECONDATA ONLINE: CONSUMER PRICE INDEX

Why Costs Rise When Output Exceeds Potential

The economy is flexible enough to expand output above potential GDP, but as output expands, the cost of additional output increases. Although many workers are bound by contracts, wage agreements may require overtime pay for extra hours or weekend work. As the economy expands and the unemployment rate declines, additional workers are harder to find. Retirees, homemakers, and students may want extra pay to draw them into the labor force. Some firms may resort to hiring workers who are not properly prepared for the available jobs—those who had been structurally unemployed. If few additional workers are available, if available workers are less qualified, or if workers require additional pay for overtime, the nominal cost of labor will increase as output expands in the short run, even though most workers' nominal wages are fixed by long-term agreements.

As production increases, the demand for nonlabor resources increases as well, so the prices of those resources purchased in markets where prices are flexible—such as the market for oil—will increase, reflecting their greater scarcity. Also, as production increases, firms use their machines and trucks more intensively, so this equipment wears out faster and is more subject to breakdown. Thus, the nominal cost per unit of output rises when production is pushed beyond the economy's potential output. But *because the prices of some resources are fixed by contracts, the price level rises faster than the per-unit production cost, so firms find it profitable to increase the quantity supplied.*

When the actual price level exceeds the expected price level, the real value of an agreed-on nominal wage declines. We might ask why workers would be willing to increase the quantity of labor they supply when the price level is higher than expected. One answer is that since labor agreements require workers to offer their labor at the agreed-on nominal wage, workers are simply complying with their contracts, at least until they have a chance to renegotiate.

In summary: If the price level is higher than expected, firms have a profit incentive to increase the quantity of goods and services supplied. At higher rates of output, however, the per-unit cost of additional output increases. Firms will expand output as long as the revenue from additional production exceeds the cost of that production.

NETBOOKMARK: CNN AND MONEY MAGAZINE, MARKETPLACE, AND THE ECONOMIST

An Actual Price Level Lower than Expected

We have discovered that if the price level is greater than expected, firms expand output in the short run, but as they do, the per-unit cost of additional production increases. Now let's look at the effects of a price level that turns out to be lower than expected. Again, suppose that resource suppliers and firms expect a certain price level. If the price level turns out to be lower than expected, production is less attractive to firms. The prices they receive for their output are on average lower than they expected, yet many of their production costs, such as the nominal wage, do not fall.

Because production is less profitable when the price level is lower than expected, firms reduce their quantity supplied, so the economy's output is below its potential. As a result, some workers are laid off, those who keep their jobs may work fewer hours, and unemployment exceeds the natural rate. Not only is less labor employed, but machines go unused, delivery trucks sit idle, and entire plants may shut down—for example, automakers sometimes halt production for weeks.

Just as some costs increase in the short run when output is pushed beyond the economy's potential, some costs decline when output falls below the economy's potential. As output falls below potential, some resources become unemployed, so the prices of resources decline in markets where the price is flexible. Moreover, with an abundance of unemployed resources, firms can become more selective about which resources to retain, laying off the least productive first (recent hires, who typically are least experienced, are usually the first to go).

To review: If the price level turns out to be higher than expected, firms maximize profit by increasing the quantity supplied beyond the economy's potential output. As output expands, the per-unit cost of additional production increases, but firms expand production as long as prices rise more than costs. If the price level turns out to be lower than expected, firms reduce output below the economy's potential output because prices fall more than costs. All of this is a long way of saying that *there is a direct relationship in the short run between the actual price level and real GDP supplied.*

The Short-Run Aggregate Supply Curve

What we have been describing so far can be used to trace out the **short-run aggregate supply (SRAS) curve,** which shows the relationship between the actual price level and real GDP supplied, other things remaining constant. Again, the *short run* in this context is the period during which some resource prices, especially those for labor, are fixed by implicit or explicit agreement. For simplicity, we can think of the short run as the duration of labor contracts, which are based on the expected price level.

Suppose the expected price level is 130. The short-run aggregate supply curve in Exhibit 1, $SRAS_{130}$, is based on that expected price level (hence the subscript 130). If the price level turns out to be 130, as expected, producers supply the economy's *potential level of output*, which in Exhibit 1 is $10.0 trillion. Although not shown in the exhibit, for the price level to turn out as expected, the aggregate demand curve would have to intersect the aggregate supply curve at point a. So, given the economy's potential output, the short-run aggregate supply curve depends on the expected price level, which depends on expectations about aggregate demand.

If the economy produces its potential output level, unemployment is at the *natural rate.* Nobody is surprised, and all are content with the outcome. There is no tendency to move away from point *a* even if workers and firms have a chance to renegotiate their contracts.

In Exhibit 1, levels of output that fall short of the economy's potential are shaded red, and levels of output that exceed the economy's potential are shaded blue. The slope of the short-run aggregate supply curve depends on how sharply the cost of additional production rises as aggregate output expands. If, in the short run, increases in per unit costs are modest as output expands, the supply curve will be relatively flat. If these costs increase sharply as output expands, the supply curve will be relatively steep. Much of the controversy about the short-run aggregate supply curve involves its shape. Shapes range from relatively flat to relatively steep. Notice that the short-run aggregate supply curve becomes steeper as output increases, because resources become scarcer and thus more costly as output increases.

<interactive>graph

- SEE IT: AGGREGATE SUPPLY
- TRY IT: TEMPORARY SUPPLY SHOCKS IN THE AGGREGATE SUPPLY AND DEMAND MODEL

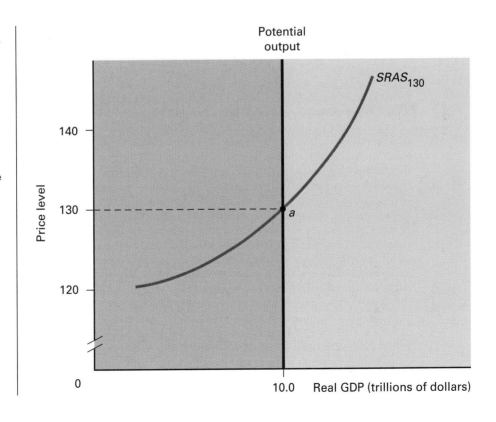

<interactive>video

ASK THE INSTRUCTOR: CAN THE AGGREGATE SUPPLY CURVE TAKE ON DIFFERENT SHAPES?

FROM THE SHORT RUN TO THE LONG RUN

In this section, we begin with a short-run equilibrium price level that is higher than expected to see what happens in the long run. The long run is long enough that firms and resource suppliers can renegotiate all agreements based on knowledge of the actual price level. *So in the long run, there are no surprises about the price level.*

Closing an Expansionary Gap

Let's begin our look at the long-run adjustment in Exhibit 2 with an expected price level of 130. The short-run aggregate supply curve for that expected price level is *SRAS*$_{130}$. Given this short-run aggregate supply curve, the equilibrium price level and real GDP depend on the aggregate demand curve. The actual price level will equal the expected price level only if the aggregate demand curve intersects the aggregate supply curve at point *a*—that is, where the short-run quantity equals potential output. Point *a* reflects a potential output level of $10.0 trillion and a price level of 130, which is the expected price level.

But what if aggregate demand turns out to be greater than expected, as shown by curve *AD*, which intersects the short-run aggregate supply curve *SRAS*$_{130}$ at point *b*. Point *b* is the **short-run equilibrium,** reflecting a price level of 135 and a real GDP of $10.2 trillion. The actual price level in the short run is higher than expected, and the level of output exceeds the economy's potential of $10.0 trillion.

The amount by which short-run equilibrium output exceeds the economy's potential is often referred to as the **expansionary gap.** In Exhibit 2, that gap is the short-run output of

EXHIBIT 1

Short-Run Aggregate Supply Curve When the Expected Price Level Is 130

The short-run aggregate supply curve is drawn for a given expected price level of 130. Point *a* shows that if the actual price level equals the expected level, producers supply the potential level of output. If the price level exceeds 130, firms increase the quantity supplied. With a price level below 130, firms decrease the quantity supplied. Levels of output that fall short of the economy's potential are shaded red; levels of output that exceed the economy's potential are shaded blue.

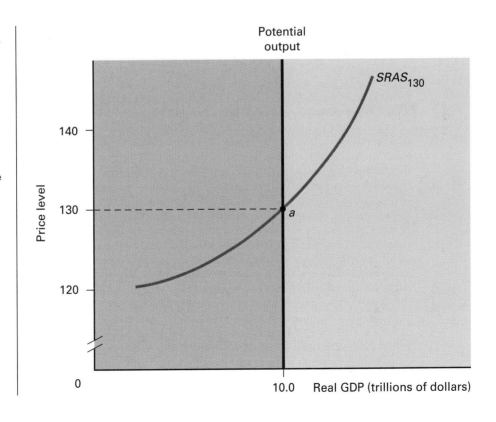

EXHIBIT 2

Short-Run Equilibrium When the Price Level Exceeds Expectations

If the expected price level is 130, the short-run aggregate supply curve is $SRAS_{130}$. If the actual price level turns out as expected, the quantity supplied is the potential output, $10.0 trillion. However, given the aggregate demand curve shown here, the price level ends up being higher than expected, and output exceeds potential, as shown by the short-run equilibrium at point *b*. The amount by which output of $10.2 trillion exceeds the economy's potential output is referred to as the expansionary gap. In the long run, price expectations will be revised upward. Costs will rise and the short-run aggregate supply curve will shift leftward to $SRAS_{140}$. Eventually, the economy will move to long-run equilibrium at point *c*.

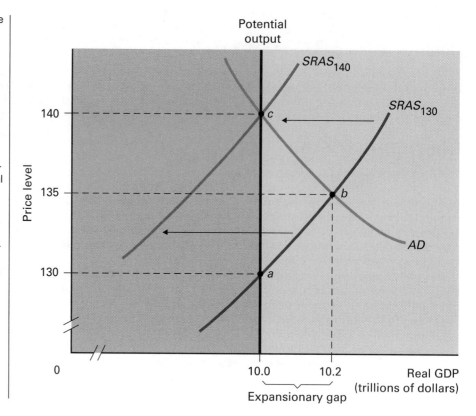

$10.2 trillion minus potential output of $10.0 trillion, or $0.2 trillion. When real GDP exceeds potential output, the actual unemployment rate is below its natural rate. Employees are working overtime, machines are being pushed to the limit, and farmers are sandwiching extra crops between usual plantings. Because the price level prevailing in the short run exceeds the expected price level, the nominal wage based on an expected price level of 130 translates into a real wage lower than expected. As we will see, output exceeding potential GDP creates inflationary pressure in the economy. *The more that short-run output exceeds the economy's potential, the larger the expansionary gap and the greater the upward pressure on the price level.*

What happens in the long run? The **long run** is a period during which firms and resource suppliers know about market conditions, particularly aggregate demand and the actual price level, and have the time to renegotiate resource payments based on that knowledge. Because the higher-than-expected price level erodes the real value of the nominal wage originally agreed to, workers will try to negotiate a higher nominal wage at their earliest opportunity. Workers and other resource suppliers negotiate higher nominal payments, raising production costs for firms, so the short-run aggregate supply curve shifts leftward. In Exhibit 2, the expansionary gap causes the short-run aggregate supply curve to shift leftward to $SRAS_{140}$, which results in an expected price level of 140. Notice that the short-run aggregate supply curve shifts until the equilibrium quantity equals the economy's potential output. *Actual output can exceed the economy's potential in the short run but not in the long run.*

As shown in Exhibit 2, the expansionary gap is closed by long-run market forces that shift the short-run aggregate supply curve from $SRAS_{130}$ left to $SRAS_{140}$. Whereas $SRAS_{130}$ was based on resource contracts reflecting an expected price level of 130, $SRAS_{140}$ is based on resource contracts reflecting an expected price level of 140. Because the expected price level and the actual price level are identical at point *c*, the economy at that point is not only in short-run equilibrium but also in **long-run equilibrium.** Consider all the equalities that hold at point *c*: (1) the actual price level equals the expected price level; (2) the quantity supplied in the short run equals potential output, which also equals the quantity supplied in the long run; and (3) the quantity supplied equals the quantity demanded. Put another way, *long-run equilibrium occurs where the aggregate demand curve intersects the vertical line drawn at potential output.* Point *c* will continue to be the equilibrium point unless there is some change in aggregate demand or in aggregate supply.

Note that the situation at point *c* is no different *in real terms* from what had been expected at point *a*. At both points, firms are willing and able to supply the economy's potential level of output of $10.0 trillion. The same amounts of labor and other resources are employed, and although the price level, the nominal wage rate, and other nominal resource payments are higher at point *c*, the real wage and the real return to other resources are the same as they would have been at point *a*. For example, suppose the nominal wage rate was $13 per hour when the expected price was 130. If the expected price level increased from 130 to 140, an increase of 7.7 percent, the nominal wage rate would also increase by that same percentage to $14 per hour, leaving the real wage unchanged. With no change in the real wage between points *a* and *c*, firms demand enough labor and workers supply enough labor to produce $10.0 trillion in aggregate output.

Thus, if the price level turns out to be higher than expected, the short-run response is to increase quantity supplied. But production exceeding the economy's potential creates inflationary pressure in the economy that in the long run causes the short-run aggregate supply curve to shift to the left, reducing output, increasing the price level, and closing the expansionary gap.

If an increase in the price level were predicted accurately year after year, firms and resource suppliers would build these expected price levels into their long-term agreements. The price level would move up each year by the expected amount, but the economy's output would remain at potential GDP, thereby skipping the round-trip beyond the economy's potential and back.

Closing a Contractionary Gap

Let's begin again with an expected price level of 130 as presented in Exhibit 3, where blue shading indicates output levels above potential and red shading indicates output levels below potential. Again, if the price level turned out as expected, the resulting equilibrium combination would occur at *a*, which would be both a short-run and a long-run equilibrium. Suppose this time that the aggregate demand curve intersects the short-run aggregate supply curve to the left of potential output, yielding a price level below that expected. The intersection of the

EXHIBIT 3

Short-Run Equilibrium When the Price Level Is Below Expectations

When the price level is below expectations, as indicated by the intersection of the aggregate demand curve *AD* with the short-run aggregate supply curve $SRAS_{130}$, short-run equilibrium occurs at point *d*. Production of $9.8 trillion is below the economy's potential by the amount of the contractionary gap, $0.2 trillion. In the long run, resource suppliers and firms will lower their price expectations. As nominal resource costs fall, the short-run aggregate supply curve eventually shifts rightward to $SRAS_{120}$ and the economy moves to long-run equilibrium at point *e*, with output at the potential level, $10.0 trillion.

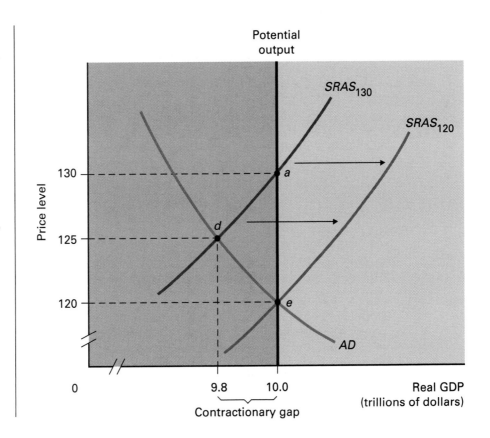

aggregate demand curve, *AD*, with $SRAS_{130}$ establishes the short-run equilibrium point, *d*, where the price level is below expectations and production is less than the economy's potential. The amount by which actual output falls short of potential GDP is called the **contractionary gap.** In this case, the contractionary gap is $0.2 trillion, and unemployment exceeds its natural rate.

Because the prevailing price level of 125 is below the expected level of 130, the nominal wage, which is based on the expected price level, translates into a higher real wage in the short run. What happens in the long run? With the price level lower than expected, employers are no longer willing to pay as high a nominal wage. And with the unemployment rate higher than the natural rate, more workers are competing for jobs, putting downward pressure on the nominal wage. If the price level and the nominal wage are flexible enough, the combination of a lower price level and a pool of unemployed workers competing for jobs should make workers more willing to accept a lower nominal wage when wage agreements are negotiated.

If firms and workers negotiate a lower nominal wage, the cost of production decreases, shifting the short-run aggregate supply curve rightward. The short-run supply curve will continue to shift rightward until it intersects the aggregate demand curve where the economy produces its potential output. This increase in supply is reflected in Exhibit 3 by a rightward shift of the short-run aggregate supply curve from $SRAS_{130}$ to $SRAS_{120}$. *If the price level and nominal wage are flexible enough, the short-run aggregate supply curve will move rightward until the economy produces its potential output.* The new short-run aggregate supply curve is based on an expected price level of 120. Because the expected price level and the actual price level are now identical, the economy is in long-run equilibrium at point *e*.

Although the nominal wage is lower at point *e* than that originally agreed to when the expected price level was 130, the real wage is the same at point *e* as it was at point *a*. Since the real wage is the same, the amount of labor that workers supply is the same and real output is the same. All that has changed between points *a* and *e* are nominal measures—the price level, the nominal wage, and other nominal resource prices.

We conclude that when incorrect expectations cause firms and resource suppliers to overestimate the actual price level, output in the short run falls short of the economy's potential. As long as wages and prices are flexible, however, firms and workers should be able to renegotiate wage agreements based on a lower expected price level. The negotiated drop in the nominal wage will shift the short-run aggregate supply curve to the right until the economy once again produces its potential level of output. If wages and prices are not flexible, they will not adjust quickly to a contractionary gap, so shifts in the short-run aggregate supply curve may be slow to move the economy to its potential output. The economy can therefore be stuck at an output and employment level below its potential.

We are now in a position to provide an additional interpretation of the red- and blue-shaded areas of our exhibits. *If a short-run equilibrium occurs in the blue-shaded area, that is, to the right of potential output, then market forces in the long run will increase nominal resource costs, shifting the short-run aggregate supply to the left. If a short-run equilibrium occurs in the red-shaded area, then market forces in the long run will reduce nominal resource costs, shifting the short-run aggregate supply curve to the right.*

Tracing Potential Output

If wages and prices are flexible enough, the economy will produce its potential output in the long run, as indicated in Exhibit 4 by the vertical line drawn at the economy's potential GDP of $10.0 trillion, called the economy's **long-run aggregate supply (LRAS) curve.** *The long-run aggregate supply curve depends on the supply of resources in the economy, the level of technology, and the production incentives provided by the formal and informal institutions of the economic system.*

Note that as long as wages and prices are flexible, the economy's potential GDP is consistent with any price level. *In the long run, equilibrium output equals long-run aggregate supply, which is also potential output. The equilibrium price level depends on the aggregate demand curve.* In Exhibit 4, the initial price level of 130 is determined by the intersection of *AD* with the long-run aggregate supply curve. If the aggregate demand curve shifts out to *AD'*, then in the long run, the equilibrium price level will increase to 140 and equilibrium output will remain at $10.0 trillion, the economy's potential GDP. Conversely, a decline in aggregate demand from *AD* to *AD"* will, in the long run, lead only to a fall in the price level from 130 to 120, with no change in output. Note that these long-run movements are more like tendencies than smooth and timely adjustments. It may take a long time for resource prices to adjust, particularly when the economy in the short run faces a contractionary gap.

EXHIBIT 4

Long-Run Aggregate Supply Curve

In the long run, when the expected price level equals the actual price level, output will be at the potential level. In the long run, $10.0 trillion will be supplied regardless of the actual price level. As long as wages and prices are flexible, the economy's potential GDP is consistent with any price level. Thus, shifts of the aggregate demand curve will in the long run not affect potential output. The long-run aggregate supply curve, *LRAS*, is a vertical line at potential GDP.

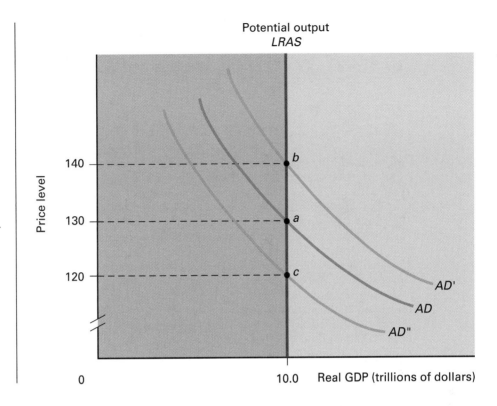

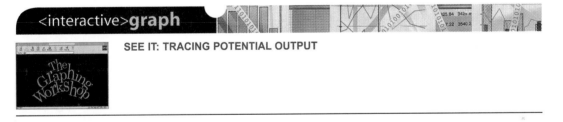

SEE IT: TRACING POTENTIAL OUTPUT

Wage Flexibility and Employment

What evidence is there that a vertical line drawn at the economy's potential GDP can depict the long-run aggregate supply curve? Except during the Great Depression, unemployment over the last century has varied from year to year but typically has returned to what would be viewed as a natural rate of unemployment— estimates range from 4 percent to 6 percent.

An *expansionary* gap creates a labor shortage that eventually results in a higher nominal wage and a higher price level. But a *contractionary* gap does not necessarily generate enough downward pressure to lower the nominal wage. Studies indicate that nominal wages are slow to adjust to high unemployment. Nominal wages have declined in particular industries; during the 1980s, for example, nominal wages fell in airlines, steel, and trucking. But seldom have we observed actual declines in nominal wages across the economy, especially since World War II.

Nominal wages do not adjust downward as quickly or as substantially as they adjust upward, and the downward response that does occur tends to be slow and relatively modest. Consequently, we say that nominal wages tend to be "sticky" in the downward direction. *Since nominal wages fall slowly, if at all, the natural supply-side adjustments needed to close a contractionary gap may take so long as to seem ineffective.* What, in fact, often closes a contractionary gap is an increase in aggregate demand.

Although the nominal wage seldom falls, an actual decline in the nominal wage is not necessary to close a contractionary gap. All that is needed is a fall in the real wage. And *the real wage will fall as long as the price level increases more than the nominal wage.* For example, if the price level increases by 4 percent and the nominal wage increases by 2 percent, the real wage falls by 2 percent. If the real wage falls enough, firms will be willing to demand enough additional labor to produce the economy's potential output.

In the following case study, we look more at output gaps and discuss why wages are not more flexible.

CASE**STUDY**	U.S. Output Gaps and Wage Flexibility
	● *Public Policy*

Let's look at estimates of actual and potential GDP since 1983. Exhibit 5 measures actual GDP minus potential GDP as a percentage of potential GDP. When actual output exceeds potential output, the output gap is positive and the economy has an expansionary gap. For example, actual output in 2000 was 1.8 percent above potential output, amounting to an expansionary gap of about $165 billion (in 1996 dollars). When actual output falls short of potential output, the output gap is negative and the economy suffers a contractionary gap. For example, actual output in 1993 was 1.6 percent below potential output, amounting to a contractionary gap of $110 billion (in 1996 dollars). Note that the economy need not be in recession for actual output to fall below potential output. For example, from 1992 to 1995, real GDP increased, yet actual output remained below potential output. In fact, actual output was below its potential in more than half the years since 1983, but only in the recession year of 1991 did output actually decline.

Employers and employees clearly would have been better off if these contractionary gaps had been reduced or eliminated. After all, more workers would have been employed, and more goods and services would have been produced and available. If workers and employers fail to reach an outcome that seems possible and that all would prefer, then they have failed to coordinate in some way. Contractionary gaps can thus be viewed as resulting from a **coordination failure.**

If employers and workers can increase output and employment by agreeing to lower nominal wages, why doesn't such an agreement occur quickly? As we have already seen, some workers are operating under long-term contracts, and wages established by such contracts are not very flexible, particularly in the downward direction. But if long-term contracts reduce the ability to achieve potential output, why not negotiate shorter-term contracts? First, contract

EXHIBIT 5 |

U.S. Output Gap Measures Actual GDP Minus Potential GDP as a Percentage of Potential GDP

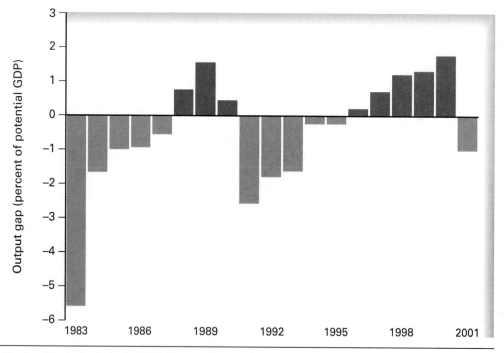

Source: Developed from estimates by the *OECD Economic Outlook* 69 (June 2001), Annex Table 11. The figure for 2001 is a projection by the author as of October.

negotiations are costly, so longer contracts reduce the frequency, and consequently the average annual cost, of negotiations. Second, long-term contracts reduce the frequency of strikes, lockouts, and other settlement disputes that can arise in the course of contract negotiations. Thus, both workers and employers gain from longer contracts, even though such contracts make wages more sticky and contractionary gaps more likely to linger.

When unemployment is high, why do employers appear reluctant to cut nominal wages or to replace existing employees with lower-paid workers from the pool of the unemployed? Yale economist Truman Bewley talked to over 300 managers, union officials, and employment recruiters and concluded that resistance to pay cuts comes, not from workers or unions, but from employers. Employers think pay cuts damage worker morale more than layoffs. By lowering morale, pay cuts increase labor turnover and reduce productivity. In contrast, the damage from layoffs is brief and limited because laid off workers are soon gone and cannot disrupt the workplace. What's more, even during the sharpest of recessions, more than nine in ten workers still keep their jobs, so most workers have little incentive to support a wage cut to increase employment.

Another reason workers may be reluctant to accept lower nominal wages is unemployment benefits. When a worker is laid off, the incentive to accept a lower wage is reduced by the prospect of unemployment benefits. The greater these benefits and the longer their duration, the less the pressure to accept a lower wage. For example, in the latter part of the 1920s, unemployment benefits nearly tripled in Great Britain and eligibility requirements were relaxed. Despite record high unemployment, money wages remained unchanged during the period. For some people, unemployment benefits had become a viable alternative to employment.

\<interactive\>exercise

eACTIVITY: U.S. OUTPUT GAPS AND WAGE FLEXIBILITY

Sources: Truman Bewley, *Why Wages Don't Fall During a Recession* (Cambridge, MA: Harvard University Press, 2000); Laurence Ball and David Romer, "Sticky Prices and Coordination Failures," *American Economic Review* 81 (June 1991): 539–552; Daniel Benjamin and Levis Kochin, "Searching for an Explanation of Unemployment in Interwar Britain," *Journal of Political Economy* 87 (June 1979): 441–470; and *Survey of Current Business* 81 (November 2001).

To review: Given potential output, or the long-run aggregate supply curve, the location of the short-run aggregate supply curve depends on the expected price level. An increase in the expected price level would shift the short-run aggregate supply curve leftward, and a decrease in the expected price level would shift the curve rightward. When the actual price level differs from the expected price level, output in the short run will depart from the economy's potential. In the long run, however, market forces will shift the short-run aggregate supply curve until the economy once again produces its potential level of output. Thus, surprises about the price level will change real GDP in the short run but not in the long run. Shifts in the aggregate demand curve change the price level but do not affect potential output, or long-run aggregate supply.

CHANGES IN AGGREGATE SUPPLY

So far, our focus has been on how changes in the expected price level shift the short-run aggregate supply curve. In this section, we consider factors other than changes in the expected price level that may affect aggregate supply. We begin by distinguishing between long-term trends in aggregate supply and **supply shocks,** which are unexpected events that affect aggregate supply, sometimes only temporarily.

\<interactive\>video

ASK THE INSTRUCTOR: WHAT CIRCUMSTANCES CAN SHIFT THE AGGREGATE SUPPLY CURVE?

\<interactive\>update

ECONNEWS ONLINE: HOT GAS PRICES MAY COOL THE ECONOMY

Increases in Aggregate Supply

The economy's potential output is based on the willingness and ability of households to supply resources to firms, the level of technology, and the institutional underpinnings of the economic system. Any change in these could affect the economy's potential output.[1] The supply of labor may change over time because of a change in the size, composition, or quality of the labor force or a change in household preferences for labor versus leisure. For example, the U.S. labor force has doubled since 1948 as a result of population growth and a growing labor force participation rate, especially among women with children. At the same time, job training, education, and on-the-job experience increased the quality of labor. Increases in both the quantity and the quality of the labor force have increased the economy's potential GDP, or long-run aggregate supply.

The quantity and quality of other resources also change over time. The capital stock—the amount of machines, buildings, and trucks—increases whenever the economy's gross investment exceeds the depreciation of capital. Even the quantity and quality of land can be increased—for example, by claiming land from the sea, as is done in the Netherlands and Hong Kong, or by revitalizing soil that has lost its fertility. These increases in the quantity and quality of resources increase the economy's potential output.

Finally, institutional changes that define property rights more clearly or make contracts more enforceable, such as the introduction of clearer patent and copyright laws, will increase the incentives to undertake productive activity, thereby increasing potential output. *Changes in the labor force, in the supply of other key resources, and in the institutional arrangements of the economic system tend to occur gradually.* Exhibit 6 depicts a gradual shift of the economy's potential output from $10.0 trillion to $10.5 trillion. The long-run aggregate supply curve shifts from *LRAS* out to *LRAS'*.

In contrast to the gradual, or long-term, changes that often occur in the supply of resources, *supply shocks* are unexpected events that change aggregate supply, sometimes only temporarily. **Beneficial supply shocks** increase aggregate supply; examples include (1) abundant harvests that increase the supply of food, (2) discoveries of natural resources, such as oil in Alaska and the North Sea, (3) technological breakthroughs that allow firms to combine resources more efficiently, such as new generations of computer chips, and (4) sudden changes in the economic system that promote more production, such as legislation that reduces the number of frivolous product liability suits or major tax cuts that stimulate production incentives.

Exhibit 7 shows the effect of a beneficial supply shock from a technological breakthrough. The beneficial supply shock shown here shifts the short-run and long-run aggregate supply curves. Along the aggregate demand curve, *AD*, the equilibrium combination of price and out-

EXHIBIT 6

Effect of a Gradual Increase in the Supply of Resources

A gradual increase in the supply of resources increases the potential level of real GDP—in this case, from $10.0 trillion to $10.5 trillion. The long-run aggregate supply curve shifts to the right.

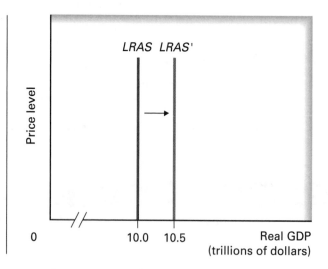

---

[1]Changes in the economy's potential GDP over time were discussed in greater detail in the earlier chapter that focused on U.S. productivity and growth.

EXHIBIT 7

Effects of a Beneficial Supply Shock on Aggregate Supply

Given the aggregate demand curve, a beneficial supply shock expected to have a lasting effect, such as a break-through in technology, will permanently shift both the short-run aggregate sup-ply curve and the long-run aggregate supply curve, or potential output. A ben-eficial supply shock lowers the price level and increases output, as reflected by the change in equilibrium from point *a* to point *b*. A temporary beneficial sup-ply shock, such as would result from an unusually favorable growing season, will shift the aggregate supply curves only temporarily. If the next growing season returns to normal, the aggregate supply curves will return to their original equi-librium position at point *a*.

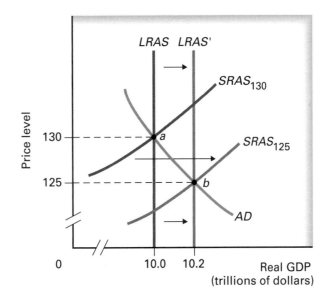

put moves from point *a* to point *b*. *For a given aggregate demand curve, the happy outcome of a ben-eficial supply shock is an increase in output and a decrease in the price level.* The new equilibrium at point *b* is a short-run and a long-run equilibrium in the sense that there is no tendency to move from that point as long as whatever caused the beneficial effect continues. Substantial new oil discoveries would also have a permanent beneficial effect on the economy. On the other hand, the beneficial supply shock resulting from an unusually favorable growing season is likely to be only temporary. If the next growing season returns to normal, the aggregate supply curves will return to their original equilibrium position—point *a* in Exhibit 7.

READING IT RIGHT: WALL STREET JOURNAL EXERCISE

Decreases in Aggregate Supply

Adverse supply shocks are sudden, unexpected events that reduce aggregate supply, some-times only temporarily. For example, a drought could reduce the supply of a variety of resources, such as food, building materials, and water- powered electricity. A government that had been stable could be toppled, destabilizing the economy in the process, as has occurred in Russia and Indonesia. Or terrorist attacks could shake the institutional underpinnings of the economy, such as the September 2001 plane hijackings and crashes, which killed thou-sands, destroyed capital worth billions, and eroded the civil liberties of a free nation. The attacks increased the cost of doing business in the United States—everything from airline travel to building security.

An adverse supply shock is depicted as a leftward shift of both the short-run and long-run aggregate supply curves, as shown in Exhibit 8, moving the equilibrium combination from point *a* to point *c* and reducing potential output from $10.0 trillion to $9.8 trillion.

As mentioned earlier, the combination of reduced output and a higher price level is often referred to as stagflation. The United States encountered stagflation during the 1970s, when the economy was rocked by a series of adverse supply shocks, such as crop failures around the globe and the hikes in oil prices achieved by OPEC in 1974 and 1979. If the effect of the adverse supply shock is temporary, such as a bad growing season, the aggregate supply curve returns to its original position once things return to normal.

EXHIBIT 8

Effects of an Adverse Supply Shock on Aggregate Supply

Given the aggregate demand curve, an adverse supply shock shifts aggregate supply curves to the left, increasing the price level and reducing aggregate output. This change is shown by the move in equilibrium from point *a* to point *c*.

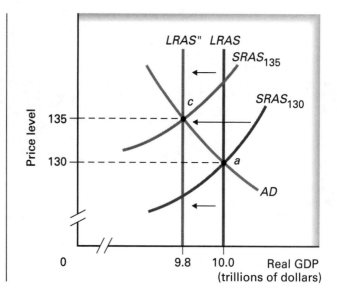

Some economists question an economy's ability to bounce back from recessions, as discussed in the following case study.

CASE**STUDY** | Why Is Unemployment So High in Europe?

● *Public Policy*

Between World War II and the mid-1970s, unemployment in Western Europe was relatively low. From 1960 to 1974, for example, the unemployment rate in France and the United Kingdom never even reached 4 percent. The worldwide recession of the mid-1970s, however, jacked up unemployment rates. But unemployment continued to climb in Europe long after the recession was over. Unemployment in France and Italy remained above 10 percent for most of the 1980s. After a modest decline in the late 1980s, rates again topped 10 percent in the 1990s. In 2001, the rate was 9 percent in Germany, France, and Italy and 13 percent in Spain.

Some observers argue that the rise in unemployment in Europe reflects an increase in the underlying natural rate of unemployment there. Some economists who have studied the issue have borrowed a term from physics, **hysteresis** (pronounced *his-ter-eé-sis*), to explain that the natural rate of unemployment depends in part on the recent history of unemployment. *The longer the actual unemployment rate remains above what had been considered the natural rate, the more the natural rate itself will increase.*

Here are some possible explanations for hysteresis: First, people out of work can lose valuable job skills, thereby reducing their ability to find a job even after the economy recovers. Second, as weeks of unemployment turn into months and years, the shock and stigma may diminish, so the work ethic weakens. Reinforcing this second point is that some European countries offer generous unemployment benefits indefinitely, reducing the hardship of unemployment. Some Europeans have collected unemployment benefits *for more than a decade.*

No consensus exists among economists regarding the validity of hysteresis. The theory seems to be less relevant in the United States, where unemployment rates dropped throughout most of the 1980s and declined again after the 1990–1991 recession from 7.5 percent in 1992 to 4.0 percent in 2000 (though rates since 2000 have begun to increase).

An alternative explanation for high unemployment rates in Europe is that legislation introduced in the 1970s made it more difficult to lay off workers. In most European countries, job dismissals must be approved by work councils, which consider such factors as the worker's health, marital status, and number of dependents. Severance pay has also become mandatory.

With such tight restrictions on the ability to dismiss workers, hiring became almost an irreversible decision for the employer, so firms have grown reluctant to add workers, particularly untested workers with little job experience. Also, relatively high minimum wages throughout Europe, high payroll taxes, and an expanded list of worker rights have increased the cost of hiring labor.

Regardless of the explanation, the result is that the quantity of labor demanded in Europe decreased and unemployment increased, particularly among young workers. Compared to the United States, relatively few private sector jobs have been created in Europe during the last two decades. If Western Europe had the same unemployment rate and the same labor participation rate as the United States, about 30 million more people would now be working there.

<interactive>exercise

eACTIVITY: WHY IS UNEMPLOYMENT SO HIGH IN EUROPE?

Sources: Horst Siebert, "Labor Market Rigidities: At the Root of Unemployment in Europe," *Journal of Economic Perspectives* 11 (Summer 1997): 37–54; Daniel McGinn and Keith Naughton, "How Safe Is Your Job?" *Newsweek,* 5 February 2001; "Economic and Financial Indicators," *The Economist,* 8 September 2001, p. 112; *OECD Economic Outlook* 69 (June 2001); and "Should Europe Be More Like America?" *BusinessWeek Online,* 29 January 2001, at http://www.businessweek.com/bwdaily/dnflash/jan2001/nf20010129_163.htm.

CONCLUSION

This chapter calls attention to the expected price level as a key determinant of the nominal resource prices that shape aggregate supply in the short run. Unexpected changes in the price level can move output in the short run from its potential level. But as firms and resource suppliers fully adjust to price surprises, the economy will return in the long run to its potential output.

<interactive>update

ECONNEWS ONLINE: BUSH'S ENERGY PLAN—MORE POWER? OR HOT AIR?

endofchaptermaterial

- **Summary**
- **Questions for Review**
- **Problems and Exercises**

- **Experiential Exercises**
- **Wall Street Journal Exercise**

Take the Post-Test to assess your overall understanding of the key ideas in this chapter. The Post-Test provides a comprehensive selection of exam-style questions addressing the main topics and concepts of the chapter. At the completion of each Post-Test, you will receive a score and instructive feedback on how you answered each question, and a direct link to the part of the chapter addressed in the question. Take the Post-Test as often as you need to—a record of your progress for each attempt is kept for you to revisit and gauge your improvement. And each Post-Test is randomly generated, so every attempt is new.

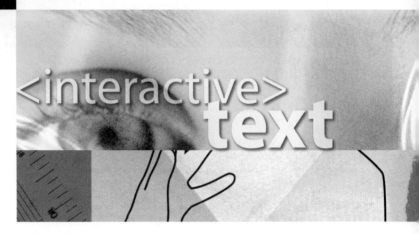

Fiscal Policy

What is the proper government role of taxing and spending in macroeconomic policy? Can fiscal policy reduce swings in the business cycle? Why did fiscal policy fall on hard times in recent decades? How might fiscal policy affect aggregate supply? When might the spending multiplier be zero? Answers to these and other questions are addressed in this chapter, which examines the theory and practice of fiscal policy.

The Japanese government cut taxes and increased spending to stimulate its troubled economy. In his first state-of-the-union message, President George W. Bush proposed a tax cut to "get the country moving again." These are examples of *fiscal policy*, which focuses on the effect of government purchases, transfer payments, taxes, and borrowing on aggregate economic activity.

In this chapter, we first explore the effects of fiscal policy on aggregate demand. Next, we bring aggregate supply into the picture to consider the impact of taxes and government purchases on the level of income and employment in the economy. Then we examine the role of fiscal policy in moving the economy to its potential level of output. Finally, we review fiscal policy as it has been practiced since World War II.

Throughout the chapter, we use relatively simple tax and spending programs to explain fiscal policy. A more complex treatment, along with the algebra behind the numbers, appears in the appendix to this chapter. Topics discussed in this chapter include:

- Fiscal policy theory
- Discretionary fiscal policy
- Automatic stabilizers
- Lags in fiscal policy
- Limits of fiscal policy
- The supply-side experiment

Take the Pre-Test to assess your initial knowledge of the key ideas in this chapter. The Pre-Test provides exam-style questions addressing the main topics and concepts of the chapter. At the completion of each Pre-Test, you will receive a score and instructive feedback on how you answered each question, and a direct link to the part of the chapter addressed in the question. Take the Pre-Test as often as you need to—a record of your progress for each attempt is kept for you to revisit and gauge your improvement.

\<interactive\>exercise

- ECONDEBATE ONLINE: FISCAL POLICY
- ECONDEBATE ONLINE: EMPLOYMENT, UNEMPLOYMENT, AND INFLATION
- ECONDEBATE ONLINE: TAXES, SPENDING, AND DEFICITS

\<interactive\>update

- ECONDATA ONLINE: FISCAL POLICY
- ECONDATA ONLINE: EMPLOYMENT, UNEMPLOYMENT, AND INFLATION
- ECONDATA ONLINE: TAXES, SPENDING, AND DEFICITS
- ECONLINKS ONLINE: ECONOMICS WEB LINKS
- ECONNEWS ONLINE: FISCAL POLICY
- ECONNEWS ONLINE: EMPLOYMENT, UNEMPLOYMENT, AND INFLATION
- ECONNEWS ONLINE: TAXES, SPENDING, AND DEFICITS

THEORY OF FISCAL POLICY

Our macroeconomic model so far has viewed government as relatively passive. But government purchases and transfer payments at all levels today in the United States total $3 trillion per year, making government an important player in a $10 trillion economy. From welfare reform to balancing the budget, fiscal policy affects the economy in myriad ways. We now move fiscal policy to center stage.

As introduced in Chapter 4, *fiscal policy* refers to government purchases, transfer payments, taxes, and borrowing as they affect macroeconomic variables such as real GDP, employment, the price level, and economic growth. When economists study fiscal policy, they usually focus on the federal government, although governments at all levels affect the economy.

The tools of fiscal policy sort into two categories: automatic stabilizers and discretionary fiscal policy. **Automatic stabilizers** are revenue and spending items in the federal budget that automatically change with the ups and downs of the economy to stabilize disposable income and, consequently, consumption and real GDP. For example, the federal income tax is an automatic stabilizer because (1) it reduces the drop in disposable income during recessions and reduces the jump in disposable income during expansions and (2) once adopted, it requires no congressional action to operate year after year, so it's "automatic." **Discretionary fiscal policy,** on the other hand, requires ongoing congressional decisions involving the deliberate manipulation of government purchases, taxation, and transfers to promote macroeconomic goals like full employment, price stability, and economic growth. President Bush's 2001 tax cut was an example of discretionary fiscal policy.

Using the income-expenditure framework developed earlier, we will initially focus on the demand side to consider the effect of changes in government purchases, transfer payments, and taxes on real GDP demanded. The short story is that *at any given price level, an increase in government purchases or in transfer payments increases real GDP demanded, and an increase in net taxes decreases real GDP demanded, other things constant.* In this section, we see how and why.

\<interactive\>video

ASK THE INSTRUCTOR: WHAT IS FISCAL POLICY ALL ABOUT?

EXHIBIT 1

Effect of a $0.1 Trillion Increase in Government Purchases on Aggregate Expenditure and Real GDP Demanded

As a result of a $0.1 trillion increase in government purchases, the aggregate expenditure shifts up by $0.1 trillion, increasing the level of real GDP demanded by $0.5 trillion. This model assumes the price level remains unchanged.

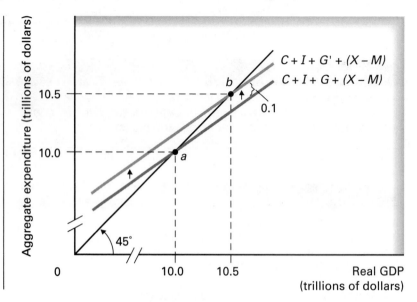

Changes in Government Purchases

Let's begin by looking at Exhibit 1, with real GDP demanded of $10.0 trillion, as reflected at point *a*, where the aggregate expenditure line crosses the 45-degree line. This equilibrium was determined two chapters back, where government purchases and net taxes each equaled $1.0 trillion and did not vary with income. Since government purchases equal net taxes, the government budget is balanced.

Now suppose the federal government, to stimulate aggregate demand, increased purchases by $0.1 trillion, or by $100 billion, assuming other things, including net taxes and the price level, remain constant. This additional spending shifts the aggregate expenditure line up by $0.1 trillion, to $C + I + G' + (X - M)$. At real GDP of $10.0 trillion, planned spending now exceeds output, so production will increase. This increase in production increases income, which in turn increases planned spending, and so it goes through the series of spending rounds.

The initial increase of $0.1 trillion in government purchases eventually increases real GDP demanded at the given price level from $10.0 trillion to $10.5 trillion, shown as point *b* in Exhibit 1. Because output demanded increases by $0.5 trillion as a result of an increase of $0.1 trillion in government purchases, the government purchases multiplier in our example is equal to 5. *As long as consumption is the only spending component that varies with income, the multiplier for a change in government purchases, other things constant, equals* $1/(1 - \text{MPC})$, or $1/(1 - 0.8)$ in our example. Thus, we can say that for a given price level, and assuming that only consumption varies with income,

$$\Delta \text{ Real GDP} = \Delta G \times \frac{1}{1 - MPC}$$

where, again, Δ means "change in." This same multiplier appeared two chapters back, when we discussed shifts in consumption, investment, and net exports.

<interactive>**example**

NETBOOKMARK: A CITIZEN'S GUIDE TO THE FEDERAL BUDGET

Changes in Net Taxes

A change in net taxes also affects real GDP demanded, but the effect is less direct. A *decrease* in net taxes, other things constant, *increases* disposable income at each level of real GDP, so consumption increases. In Exhibit 2, we begin again at equilibrium point *a*, with real GDP demanded equal to $10.0 trillion. To stimulate aggregate demand, suppose government cuts net taxes by $0.1 trillion, or by $100 billion, other things constant. We continue to assume that net taxes are autonomous—that is, that they do not vary with income. A $100 billion reduction in net taxes could result from a tax cut, an increase in transfer payments, or some combination of the two. The $100 billion decrease in net taxes increases disposable income by $100 billion at each level of real GDP. Because households now have more disposable income, they spend more and save more at each level of real GDP.

But because households save some of the tax cut, consumption increases in the first round of spending by less than the full tax cut. Specifically, *consumption spending at each level of real GDP rises by the decrease in net taxes multiplied by the marginal propensity to consume.* In our example, desired consumption at each level of real GDP increases by $100 billion times 0.8, or $80 billion. Decreasing net taxes by $100 billion causes the aggregate expenditure line to shift up by $80 billion, or $0.08 trillion, at all levels of income, as shown in Exhibit 2. This initial increase in spending triggers subsequent rounds of spending, following a now-familiar pattern in the income-consumption cycle based on the marginal propensities to consume and to save. For example, the $80 billion increase in consumption increases output and income by $80 billion, which in the second round leads to $64 billion in consumption and $16 billion in saving, and so on through successive rounds. As a result, real GDP demanded eventually increases from $10.0 trillion to $10.4 trillion per year, or by $400 billion.

The effect of a change in net taxes on real GDP demanded equals the resulting shift in the consumption function times the simple spending multiplier. Thus we can say that the effect of a change in net taxes is

$$\Delta \text{ Real GDP} = (-MPC \times \Delta NT) \times \frac{1}{1 - MPC}$$

The simple spending multiplier is applied to the shift in consumption that results from the change in net taxes. This equation can be rearranged as

$$\Delta \text{ Real GDP} = \Delta NT \times \frac{-MPC}{1 - MPC}$$

EXHIBIT 2

Effect of a $0.1 Trillion Decrease in Autonomous Net Taxes on
Aggregate Expenditure and Real GDP Demanded

As a result of a decrease in autonomous net taxes of $0.1 trillion, or $100 billion, consumers, who are assumed to have a marginal propensity to consume of 0.8, spend $80 billion and save $20 billion. The consumption function shifts up by $80 billion, or $0.08 trillion, as does the aggregate expenditure line. An $80 billion increase in the aggregate expenditure line eventually increases the level of real GDP demanded by $0.4 trillion. Keep in mind that the price level is assumed to remain constant.

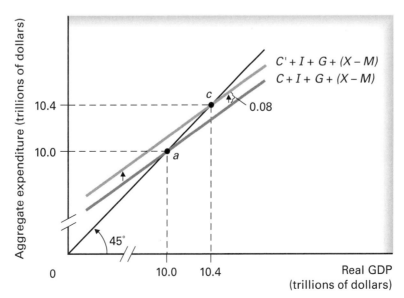

where $-MPC/(1 - MPC)$ is the **simple tax multiplier**, which can be applied directly to the change in net taxes to yield the change in the quantity of real GDP demanded at a given price level. This tax multiplier is called *simple* because, by assumption, only consumption varies with income. For example, with an MPC of 0.8, the simple tax multiplier equals -4. In our example, a *decrease* of $0.1 trillion in net taxes results in an *increase* in real GDP demanded of $0.4 trillion, assuming a given price level. As another example, an *increase* in net taxes of $0.2 trillion would, other things constant, *decrease* real GDP demanded by $0.8 trillion.

Note two differences between the government purchase multiplier and the simple tax multiplier. First, the government purchase multiplier is positive, so an increase in government purchases leads to an increase in real GDP demanded. The tax multiplier is negative, so an increase in net taxes leads to a decrease in real GDP demanded. Second, the multiplier for a given change in government purchases is larger by 1 than the absolute value of the multiplier for an identical change in net taxes. In our example, the government purchase multiplier is 5, while the absolute value of the tax multiplier is 4. This holds because changes in government purchases affect aggregate spending directly—a $100 billion increase in government purchases increases spending in the first round by $100 billion. In contrast, a $100 billion decrease in net taxes increases consumption indirectly by way of a change in disposable income. Thus, each $100 decrease in net taxes increases disposable income by $100, which, given an MPC of 0.8, increases consumption in the first round by $80; people save the other $20. In short, an increase in government purchases has a greater impact than does an identical tax cut because some of the tax cut is saved.

To summarize: An increase in government purchases or a decrease in net taxes, other things constant, increases real GDP demanded. Although not shown, the combined effect of changes in government purchases and in net taxes is found by adding their individual effects.

To this point, in the chapter, we have focused on the amount of real GDP demanded at a given price level. We are now in a position to bring aggregate supply into the picture.

ASK THE INSTRUCTOR: IN THEORY HOW DOES A TAX CUT WORK TO STIMULATE THE ECONOMY?

ECONNEWS ONLINE: ARE MORE TAX CUTS NEEDED? NOT EXACTLY

ECONDEBATE ONLINE: HOW SHOULD WE REFORM THE CURRENT TAX SYSTEM?

INCLUDING AGGREGATE SUPPLY

The previous chapter introduced the idea that natural market forces may take a long time to close a contractionary gap. Let's consider the possible remedial effect of discretionary fiscal policy in such a situation.

Discretionary Fiscal Policy for a Contractionary Gap

Let's begin with a short-run aggregate supply curve, $SRAS_{130}$ in Exhibit 3. This curve implies that if the price level turns out to be 130, the economy will produce its potential output of $10.0 trillion. Suppose instead that the aggregate demand curve, *AD*, intersects aggregate supply at point *e*, yielding the short-run output of $9.5 trillion and price level of 125. Because output falls short of its potential, this opens a contractionary gap of $0.5 trillion, as Exhibit 3 shows, which means unemployment exceeds the natural rate.

If markets adjusted naturally to high unemployment, nominal resource prices would drop enough in the long run that the short-run aggregate supply curve would shift rightward to

EXHIBIT 3 |

Discretionary Fiscal Policy to Close a Contractionary Gap

The aggregate demand curve *AD* and the short-run aggregate supply curve, *SRAS*₁₃₀, intersect at point *e*. Because the price level of 125 is below the expected price level of 130, output falls short of the economy's potential. The resulting contractionary gap is $0.5 trillion. This gap could be closed by discretionary fiscal policy that increases aggregate demand by just the right amount. An increase in government purchases, a decrease in net taxes, or some combination of the two could shift aggregate demand to *AD**, moving the economy to its potential level of output at *e**.

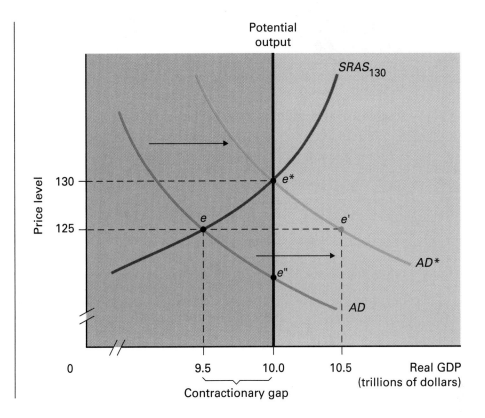

achieve an equilibrium at the economy's potential output, point *e"* in Exhibit 3. History suggests, however, that wages and other resource prices could be slow to respond to a contractionary gap.

Suppose policy makers believe that natural market forces will take too long to return the economy to potential output. They also believe that the appropriate increase in government purchases, decrease in net taxes, or some combination of the two could increase aggregate demand enough to return the economy to its potential output. A $0.2 trillion increase in government purchases reflects an **expansionary fiscal policy** that increases aggregate demand, as shown in Exhibit 3 by the rightward shift from *AD* to *AD**. If the price level remains at 125, the additional spending would increase the quantity demanded from $9.5 to $10.5 trillion. This increase of $1.0 trillion reflects the simple multiplier effect, given a constant price level.

At the original price level of 125, however, excess quantity demanded causes the price level to rise. As the price level rises, real GDP supplied increases, but real GDP demanded decreases. The price level will rise until quantity demanded equals quantity supplied. In Exhibit 3, the new aggregate demand curve intersects the aggregate supply curve at *e**, where the price level is 130, the one originally expected, and output equals potential GDP of $10.0 trillion.

Since 130 was the price level on which producers originally based their production plans, the intersection at point *e** is not only a short-run equilibrium but a long-run equilibrium. If fiscal policy makers are accurate enough (or lucky enough), the appropriate fiscal stimulus can close the contractionary gap and foster a long-run equilibrium at potential GDP. However, the increase in output results in a higher price level. What's more, if the federal budget was in balance before the fiscal stimulus, the increase in government spending creates a budget deficit. In fact, the federal government ran substantial deficits from the early 1970s to the mid-1990s.

What if policy makers overshoot the mark and stimulate aggregate demand more than needed to achieve potential GDP? In the short run, real GDP will exceed potential output. In the long run, firms and resource owners will adjust to the unexpectedly high price level. The short-run supply curve will shift back until it intersects the aggregate demand curve at potential output, increasing the price level further but reducing real GDP to $10.0 trillion, the potential output. Note that an expansionary fiscal policy is employed to close a contractionary gap.

Chapter 27 Fiscal Policy

463

Discretionary Fiscal Policy for an Expansionary Gap

Suppose the short-run equilibrium price level exceeds the level on which long-term contracts are based, so output exceeds potential GDP. In Exhibit 4, the short-run aggregate supply curve is again based on an expected price level of 130, but its intersection with the aggregate demand curve, *AD'*, yields the higher actual price level of 135. So short-run output is $10.5 trillion, an amount exceeding potential output of $10.0 trillion, and the economy faces an expansionary gap of $0.5 trillion. Ordinarily, this gap would be closed by a leftward shift of the short-run aggregate supply curve, which would return the economy to the potential level of output but at a higher price level, as shown by point *e''*.

But the use of discretionary fiscal policy introduces another possibility. By reducing government purchases, increasing net taxes, or employing some combination of the two, the government can implement a **contractionary fiscal policy** to reduce aggregate demand, moving the economy to potential output without increasing prices. If the policy succeeds, aggregate demand in Exhibit 4 will shift leftward from *AD'* to *AD**, establishing a new equilibrium at point *e**. Again, with just the right reduction in aggregate demand, output will fall to $10.0 trillion, the potential GDP. Closing an expansionary gap through fiscal policy rather than through natural market forces results in a lower price level, not a higher one. Increasing net taxes or reducing government purchases also reduces a government deficit or increases a surplus. Note that a contractionary fiscal policy is used to close an expansionary gap.

Such precisely calculated expansionary and contractionary fiscal policies are difficult to achieve, for their proper execution assumes that (1) the relevant spending multiplier can be predicted accurately, (2) aggregate demand can be shifted by just the right amount, (3) the potential level of output is accurately gauged, (4) various government entities can somehow

EXHIBIT 4

Discretionary Fiscal Policy to Close an Expansionary Gap

With the price level above the expected level of 130, there is an expansionary gap of $0.5 trillion. The gap could be eliminated by discretionary fiscal policy aimed at reducing aggregate demand by just the right amount. An increase in net taxes, a decrease in government purchases, or some combination of the two could shift the aggregate demand curve back to *AD** and move the economy to potential output at point *e**.

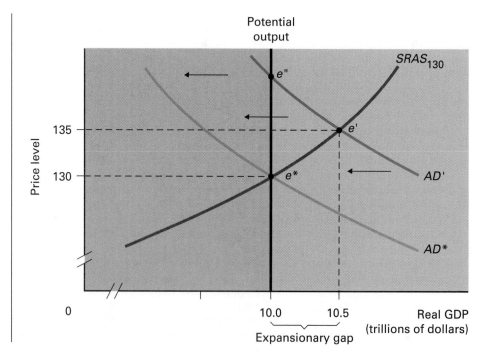

coordinate their fiscal efforts, and (5) the shape of the short-run aggregate supply curve is known and will remain unaffected by the fiscal policy.

The Multiplier and the Time Horizon

In the short run, the aggregate supply curve slopes upward, so a shift in aggregate demand changes both the price level and the level of output. When aggregate supply gets in the act, we find that the simple multiplier overstates the amount by which output changes. The exact change in equilibrium output in the short run depends on the steepness of the aggregate supply curve, which in turn depends on how sharply production costs increase as output expands. *The steeper the short-run aggregate supply curve, the less impact a given shift in the aggregate demand curve has on output and the more impact it has on the price level, so the smaller the spending multiplier.*

If the economy is already producing its potential, then in the long run, any change in fiscal policy aimed at stimulating demand will increase the price level but will not affect output. Thus, *if the economy is already at potential output, the spending multiplier in the long run is zero.*

You now have some idea of how fiscal policy can work in theory. Let's take a look at fiscal policy in practice.

THE EVOLUTION OF FISCAL POLICY

Before the 1930s, discretionary fiscal policy was seldom used to influence the performance of the macroeconomy. Prior to the Great Depression, public policy was shaped by the views of **classical economists,** who advocated *laissez-faire,* the belief that free markets were the best way to achieve national economic prosperity. Classical economists did not deny the existence of depressions and high unemployment, but they argued that the sources of such crises lay outside the market system, in the effects of wars, tax increases, poor growing seasons, and changing tastes. Such external shocks could reduce output and employment, but classical economists believed that natural market forces, such as changes in prices, wages, and interest rates, would correct these problems.

Simply put, classical economists argued that if the economy's price level was too high to sell all that was produced, prices would fall until the quantity supplied equaled the quantity demanded; if wages were too high to employ all who wanted to work, wages would fall until the quantity of labor supplied equaled the quantity demanded; and if the interest rate was too high to invest all that had been saved, interest rates would fall until the amount invested equaled the amount saved.

So the classical approach implied that natural market forces, through flexible prices, wages, and interest rates, would move the economy toward its potential GDP. There appeared to be no need for government intervention in the economy. What's more, the idea of government running a deficit was considered immoral; the government, like households, was expected to live within its means. Thus, before the onset of the Great Depression, most economists believed that an active fiscal policy would do more harm than good. Besides, the federal government itself was a bit player in the economy. At the onset of the Great Depression, for example, federal outlays were less than 3 percent of GDP (versus about 20 percent today).

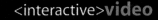

<interactive>video

CNN VIDEO: "A MATTER OF PRIORITIES"

The Great Depression and World War II

Although classical economists acknowledged that capitalistic, market-oriented economies could experience temporary unemployment, the prolonged depression of the 1930s strained belief in the economy's ability to correct itself. The Great Depression was marked by unemployment reaching 25 percent and much unused plant capacity. With vast unemployed resources, output and income fell far short of the economy's potential.

The stark contrast between the natural market adjustments predicted by classical theory and the years of high unemployment during the Great Depression represented a collision of theory and fact. In 1936, John Maynard Keynes of Cambridge University, England, published *The General Theory of Employment, Interest, and Money,* a book that challenged the classical view and touched off what would later be called the Keynesian revolution. *Keynesian theory and policy were developed to address the problem of unemployment arising from the Great Depression.* Keynes's main quarrel with the classical economists was that prices and wages did not appear flexible enough to ensure the full employment of resources. According to Keynes, prices and wages were relatively inflexible—they were "sticky"—so natural market forces would not return the economy to full employment in a timely fashion. Keynes also believed business expectations might at times become so bleak that even very low interest rates would not spur firms to invest all that consumers might save.

It is said that geologists learn more about the nature of the Earth's crust from one major upheaval, such as a huge earthquake or major volcanic eruption, than from a dozen more-common events. Likewise, economists learned more about the economy from the Great Depression than from many more-modest economic fluctuations. Even though this depression began more than seven decades ago, economists continue to sift through the rubble, looking for hints about how the economy really works.

Three developments in the years following the Great Depression bolstered the use of discretionary fiscal policy in the United States. The first was the influence of Keynes's *General Theory,* in which he argued that natural forces would not necessarily close a contractionary gap. Keynes thought the economy could get stuck at a level of output that was well below its potential, requiring the government to increase aggregate demand so as to boost output and employment. The second development was the impact of World War II on output and employment. The demands of war greatly increased production and in the process eliminated cyclical unemployment during the war years, pulling the U.S. economy out of its depression. The third development, largely a consequence of the first two, was the passage of the Employment Act of 1946, which gave the federal government responsibility for promoting full employment and price stability.

Prior to the Great Depression, the dominant fiscal policy was a balanced budget. Indeed, to head off a modest deficit in 1932, federal taxes were increased, which deepened the depression. In the wake of Keynes's *General Theory* and World War II, however, policy makers grew more receptive to the idea that fiscal policy could improve economic stability. The objective of fiscal policy was no longer to balance the budget but to promote full employment with price stability even if deficits occurred in the process.

Automatic Stabilizers

This chapter has focused mostly on discretionary fiscal policy—conscious decisions to change taxes and government spending. Now let's get a clearer picture of automatic stabilizers. *Automatic stabilizers smooth fluctuations in disposable income over the business cycle, thereby boosting aggregate demand during periods of recession and dampening aggregate demand during periods of expansion.*

Look at the federal income tax. For simplicity, we assumed net taxes to be independent of income. In reality, the federal income tax system is progressive, meaning that the fraction of income paid in taxes increases as income increases. During an economic expansion, taxes claim a growing fraction of income, slowing the growth in disposable income and, hence, the growth in consumption. Therefore, the progressive income tax relieves some of the inflationary pressure that might otherwise arise when output increases above its potential during an economic expansion. Conversely, when the economy is in recession, real GDP declines, but taxes decline faster, so disposable income does not fall as much as real GDP. Thus, the progressive income tax cushions declines in disposable income, in consumption, and in aggregate demand.

Another automatic stabilizer is unemployment insurance. During an economic expansion, the unemployment insurance system automatically increases the flow of unemployment insurance taxes from the income stream into the unemployment insurance fund, thereby moderating aggregate demand. During a recession, unemployment increases and the system reverses itself. Unemployment payments automatically flow from the insurance fund to people who become unemployed, increasing disposable income and propping up consumption and aggregate demand. Likewise, welfare spending automatically increases as more people become eligible during hard times. *Because of these automatic stabilizers, real GDP fluctuates less than it otherwise would, and disposable income varies proportionately less than does real GDP.* And because disposable income varies less than does real GDP, consumption also fluctuates less than does real GDP (as we saw in an earlier case study).

Unemployment insurance, welfare benefits, and the progressive income tax were initially designed not so much as automatic stabilizers but as income redistribution programs. Their beneficial roles as automatic stabilizers are secondary effects of the legislation. Automatic stabilizers do not eliminate economic fluctuations, but they do reduce their magnitude. The stronger and more effective the automatic stabilizers are, the less need there is for discretionary fiscal policy. Because of the greater influence of automatic stabilizers, *the economy is more stable today than it was during the Great Depression and before.* As a measure of just how successful these automatic stabilizers have been in cushioning the impact of recessions, real consumption increased on average during the last four recession years. Without much fanfare, automatic stabilizers have been quietly doing their work, keeping the economy on a more even keel.

From the Golden Age to Stagflation

The 1960s were the Golden Age of fiscal policy. John F. Kennedy was the first president to propose a federal budget deficit to stimulate an economy experiencing a contractionary gap. Fiscal policy was also used on occasion to provide an extra kick to an expansion already under way, as in 1964, when Kennedy's successor, Lyndon Johnson, cut income tax rates to keep an expansion alive. *This tax cut, introduced to stimulate business investment, consumption, and employment, was perhaps the shining example of the successful use of fiscal policy during the 1960s.* The tax cut seemed to work wonders, increasing disposable income and consumption. The unemployment rate dropped below 5 percent for the first time in seven years, the inflation rate dipped under 2 percent, and the federal budget deficit in 1964 equaled only about 1 percent of GDP (compared with an average of 4 percent between 1982 and 1996).

Discretionary fiscal policy is a type of demand-management policy because the objective is to increase or decrease aggregate demand to smooth economic fluctuations. Demand-management policies were applied during much of the 1960s. But the 1970s were different. During the 1970s, the problem was stagflation—the double trouble of higher inflation and higher unemployment resulting from a decrease in aggregate supply. The aggregate supply curve shifted left because of crop failures around the world, sharply higher oil prices, and other adverse supply shocks. Demand-management policies were ill suited to solving the problem of stagflation because an increase in aggregate demand would worsen inflation, whereas a decrease in aggregate demand would worsen unemployment.

Other concerns also caused economists and policy makers to question the effectiveness of discretionary fiscal policy: the difficulty of estimating the natural rate of unemployment, the time lags involved in implementing fiscal policy, the distinction between current and permanent income, and the possible feedback effects of fiscal policy on aggregate supply. We will consider each of these concerns in turn.

Fiscal Policy and the Natural Rate of Unemployment

As we have seen, the unemployment rate that occurs when the economy is producing its potential GDP is called the *natural rate of unemployment.* Before adopting discretionary policies, public officials must correctly estimate this natural rate. Suppose the economy is producing its potential output of $10.0 trillion, as in Exhibit 5, where the natural rate of unemployment is 5.0 percent. Also suppose that public officials mistakenly believe the natural rate is 4.0 percent, and they attempt to increase output and reduce unemployment through discretionary fiscal

EXHIBIT 5

When Discretionary Fiscal Policy Overshoots

If public officials underestimate the natural rate of unemployment, they may attempt to stimulate aggregate demand even if the economy is producing its potential output, as at point a. In the short run, this expansionary policy yields a short-run equilibrium at point b, where the price level and output are higher and unemployment is lower, so the policy appears to succeed. But the resulting expansionary gap will, in the long run, reduce the short-run aggregate supply curve from SRAS₁₃₀ to SRAS₁₄₀, eventually reducing output to its potential level of $10.0 trillion while increasing the price level to 140. Thus, attempts to increase production beyond potential GDP lead only to inflation in the long run.

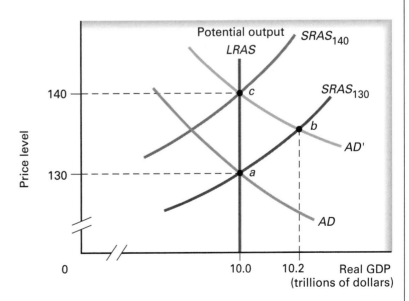

policy. As a result of their policy, the aggregate demand curve shifts to the right, from AD to AD'. In the short run, this stimulation of aggregate demand expands output to $10.2 trillion and reduces unemployment to 4.0 percent, so the policy appears successful. But stimulating aggregate demand opens up an expansionary gap, which pushes up nominal resource prices in the long run, resulting in a leftward shift in short-run aggregate supply from $SRAS_{130}$ to $SRAS_{140}$. This reduction in aggregate supply pushes up prices and reduces real GDP to $10.0 trillion, the economy's potential. Thus, increases in output may temporarily persuade policy makers that their plan was a good one, but attempts to increase production beyond potential GDP in the long run lead only to inflation.

Lags in Fiscal Policy

The time required to approve and implement fiscal legislation may hamper its effectiveness and weaken discretionary fiscal policy as a tool of macroeconomic stabilization. Even if a fiscal prescription is appropriate for the economy at the time it is proposed, the months and some-times years required to approve and implement legislation means the medicine could do more harm than good. The policy might kick in only after the economy has already turned itself around. Because a recession is not usually identified as such until at least six months after it begins, and because the nine recessions since 1949 lasted an average of only 11 months, a nar-row window remains open in which to execute discretionary fiscal policy. (More will be said about timing problems in a later chapter.)

READING IT RIGHT: WALL STREET JOURNAL EXERCISE

Discretionary Fiscal Policy and Permanent Income

It was once believed that discretionary fiscal policy could be turned on and off like a faucet, stimulating the economy at the right time by just the right amount. Given the marginal propensity to consume—a relationship that is among the most stable in macroeconomics—tax changes could increase or decrease disposable income to bring about desired change in con-sumption. A more recent view is that people base their consumption decisions not merely on changes in their current income but on changes in their permanent income.

Permanent income is the income a person expects to receive on average over the long term. Changing tax rates for a year or two will not have the desired effects on consumption as long as people view the changes as only temporary. In 1967, for example, the escalating war in Viet-nam increased military spending, pushing real GDP beyond its potential. The combination of a booming domestic economy and higher war-related spending opened up an expansionary gap by 1968. That year, Congress approved a *temporary* tax increase, which raised income tax rates for 18 months. The idea was that higher tax rates would soak up some disposable income, thereby reducing consumption to relieve inflationary pressure in the economy. But the reduc-tion in aggregate demand turned out to be disappointingly small, and inflation was hardly affected. Although several factors help explain why higher taxes failed to reduce consumption, most economists agree that the *temporary* nature of the tax increase meant that consumers faced only a small cut in their permanent income. Because permanent income changed little, consumption spending changed little. Consumers simply saved less. In late 1997, Japanese offi-cials announced an income tax cut intended to stimulate Japan's flat economy. People expected the cut to be repealed after a year, so economists were skeptical that the plan would work, and it didn't.[1] In short, *to the extent that consumers base spending decisions on their permanent income, attempts to fine-tune the economy with tax changes believed to be temporary will be less effective.*

The Feedback Effects of Fiscal Policy on Aggregate Supply

So far we have limited our discussion of fiscal policy to its effect on aggregate demand. Fiscal policy may also affect aggregate supply, although often the effect is unintentional. For exam-ple, suppose the government increases unemployment benefits and finances these transfer payments with higher taxes on current workers. If the marginal propensity to consume is the

[1]See David Hamilton, "Japan's Prime Minister Slashes Taxes in Surprise Move to Boost Nikkei," *Wall Street Journal,* 17 December 1997.

same for both groups, the reduction in spending by people whose taxes increase should just offset the increase in spending by transfer recipients. According to a theory of fiscal policy focusing on aggregate demand, there should be no change in aggregate demand and thus no change in equilibrium real GDP, simply a redistribution of disposable income from the employed to the unemployed.

But what about the possible effects of these changes on the labor supply? The unemployed, who benefit from increased transfers, now have less incentive to find work, so they may search at a more leisurely pace. Conversely, workers who find their after-tax wage reduced by the higher tax rates may be less willing to work extra hours or to work a second job because the higher marginal tax rates they face cut their opportunity cost of leisure. In short, the supply of labor could decrease as a result of offsetting changes in taxes and transfers. A decrease in the supply of labor would decrease aggregate supply, reducing the economy's potential GDP.

Both automatic stabilizers, such as unemployment insurance and the progressive income tax, and discretionary fiscal policies, such as changes in tax rates, may affect individual incentives to work, spend, save, and invest, although these effects are usually unintended. We should keep these secondary effects in mind when we evaluate fiscal policies. It was concern about the effects of taxes on the supply of labor that motivated the tax cuts approved in 1981, as we will see next.

U.S. Budget Deficits of the 1980s and 1990s

In 1981, President Reagan and Congress agreed on a 23 percent reduction in average income tax rates and a major buildup in defense programs, with no substantial offsetting reductions in domestic programs. This tax cut reflected a philosophy that reductions in tax rates would make people more willing to work and to invest because they could keep more of what they earned. Lower taxes would increase the supply of labor and the supply of other resources in the economy, thereby increasing aggregate supply and the economy's potential GDP. In its strongest form, this supply-side theory held that enough additional real GDP would be generated by the tax cuts that total tax revenue would actually increase—that is, a smaller tax share of a bigger pie would exceed a larger tax share of a smaller pie. What happened as a result of the tax cut? Let's review events during the 1980s in the following case study.

CASE**STUDY**	The Supply-Side Experiment
	● *Public Policy*

Taking 1981 to 1988 as the time frame for examining the supply-side experiment, we can make some tentative observations about the effects of the 1981 federal income tax cut, which was phased in over three years. After the tax cut was approved but before it took effect, a recession hit the economy and the unemployment rate climbed to nearly 10 percent in 1982.

Although it is difficult to untangle the growth generated by the tax cuts from the cyclical upswing following the recession of 1981–1982, we can say that between 1981 and 1988, employment climbed by 15 million and unemployment fell by 2 million. Real GDP per capita, a good measure of the standard of living, increased by about 2.5 percent per year between 1981 and 1988. This rate was higher than the 1.4 percent average annual increase between 1973 and 1981 but lower than the 3.1 percent annual growth rate between 1960 and 1973.

Does the growth in employment and in real GDP mean the supply-side experiment was a success? Part of the growth in employment and output could be explained by the economic boost provided by the huge federal stimulus resulting from deficits during the period. Although policy makers did not make a conscious decision to do so, their tax cuts, in effect, resulted in an expansionary fiscal policy. *The stimulus from the tax cut helped sustain a continued expansion during the 1980s—the longest peacetime expansion to that point in the nation's history.*

Despite the growth in employment, government revenues did not expand enough to offset the combination of tax cuts and increased government spending. Between 1981 and 1988, federal outlays grew an average of 7.1 percent per year, and federal revenues averaged 6.3 percent. So the tax cut failed to generate the revenue required to fund growing government spending. Before 1981, deficits had been relatively small—typically less than 1 percent compared with GDP. But deficits grew to about $175 billion a year by the middle of the 1980s, averaging about 4 percent compared with GDP. These deficits were the largest the nation had ever experienced during peacetime. The recession of the early 1990s pushed the federal deficit up to 5 percent of GDP by 1992. Because government spending grew faster than revenue, the resulting deficits accumulated into a huge national debt. *The national debt, which is the accumulation of annual deficits, nearly doubled relative to GDP from 33 percent in 1981 to 64 percent in 1992.*

<interactive>**exercise**

eACTIVITY: THE SUPPLY-SIDE EXPERIMENT

<interactive>**update**

ECONNEWS ONLINE: TO SPEND OR TO SAVE? THAT IS THE QUESTION

Sources: *Economic Report of the President*, January 2001; Herbert Stein, *The Fiscal Revolution in America*, 2nd ed. (Washington, D.C.: The AIE Press, 1996).

Given the effects of fiscal policy, particularly in the short run, we should not be surprised that elected officials might use it to enhance their reelection prospects. Let's look at how political considerations may shape fiscal policies.

CASE**STUDY**	Discretionary Fiscal Policy and Presidential Elections
	● *Public Policy*

After the recession of 1990–1991, the economy was slow to recover. At the time of the 1992 presidential election, the unemployment rate still languished at 7.5 percent, up two percentage points from where it stood in 1988 when President George H. W. Bush was elected. The higher unemployment rate was too much of a hurdle to overcome, and President Bush lost his reelection bid to Bill Clinton.

The link between economic performance and reelection success goes back a long way. Ray Fair of Yale University examined presidential elections dating back to 1916 and found, not surprisingly, that the state of the economy had a clear impact on the election outcomes. Specifically, he found that a declining unemployment rate and strong growth of real GDP per capita during an election year increased the chances of election for the candidate of the incumbent party.

Another Yale economist, William Nordhaus, developed a theory of **political business cycles,** arguing that incumbent presidents use expansionary policies to stimulate the economy, often only temporarily, during an election year. They try to increase their chances of reelection by pursuing policies that stimulate real GDP and reduce unemployment. For example, observers claim that President Nixon used expansionary policies to increase his chances for reelection in 1972.

The evidence to support the theory of political business cycles is not entirely convincing. One problem is that the theory limits presidential motives to reelection, when in fact presidents may have other objectives. For example, President Bush passed up an opportunity in 1992 to sign a tax cut for the middle class because that measure would also have increased taxes on a much smaller group—upper-income taxpayers.

An alternative to the theory of political business cycles is that Democrats care relatively more about unemployment and relatively less about inflation than do Republicans. This view is supported by evidence indicating that during Democratic administrations, unemployment is more likely to fall and inflation is more likely to rise than during Republican administrations. Republican presidents tend to pursue contractionary policies soon after taking office and are more willing to endure a recession to reduce inflation. The country suffered a recession in the first term of the last six Republican administrations, including one during President George W. Bush's first term. Democratic presidents tend to pursue expansionary policies to reduce unemployment and are willing to put up with higher inflation to do so.

<interactive>**exercise**

eACTIVITY: DISCRETIONARY FISCAL POLICY AND PRESIDENTIAL ELECTIONS

Sources: *Economic Report of the President,* January 2001; Ray Fair, "The Effects of Economic Events on Votes for President," *Review of Economics and Statistics* (May 1978): 159–172; and William Nordhaus, "Alternative Approaches to the Political Business Cycle," *Brookings Papers on Economic Activity,* no. 2 (1989): 1–49.

The large federal budget deficits of the 1980s and first half of the 1990s reduced the use of discretionary fiscal policy as a tool for economic stabilization. Because deficits were already large during economic expansions, it was hard to justify increasing deficits still more during a recession. For example, President Clinton proposed a modest stimulus package in early 1993 to boost the recovery that was under way. His opponents blocked the measure, arguing that it would increase the deficit.

Balancing the Federal Budget

Clinton did not get his way with the stimulus package, but in 1993, he did manage to substantially increase taxes on high-income households, a group that now pays the lion's share of federal income taxes. The Republican Congress elected in 1994 imposed more fiscal discipline on federal spending as part of a plan to balance the budget. Meanwhile, the economy experienced a vigorous recovery fueled by growing consumer spending and rising business optimism based on technological innovation, market globalization, and the strongest stock market in history. The confluence of these events—tax increases on the rich, restraints on federal spending, and a strengthening economy—changed the dynamic of the federal budget. Revenues gushed into Washington, growing an average of 8.3 percent per year between 1993 and 1998; meanwhile, federal outlays remained in check, growing only 3.2 percent per year. By 1998, that one-two punch knocked out the federal deficit, a deficit that only six years earlier reached a record $290 billion. The federal surplus grew from $70 billion in 1998 to more than $200 billion in 2000. Federal debt relative to GDP fell from 67 percent in 1996 to 57 percent in 2000.

But by early 2001, U.S. economic growth was slowing, so newly elected President George W. Bush pushed through an across-the-board $1.35 trillion, 10-year cut in income tax rates to "get the economy moving again." To stimulate consumer spending, policy makers provided tax rebates of up to $600 per tax filer, though the bulk of the tax cuts were not scheduled to take effect for several years.

On September 11, 2001, 19 men in four hijacked airplanes ended thousands of lives and squelched chances of a quick rebound in economic growth. The terrorist attacks worsened a recession that began in March 2001. The unemployment rate jumped from 4.5 percent in July 2001 to 5.7 percent in November 2001. Treasury Secretary Paul O'Neill said the attack hit the economy in a "resounding way." Consumers became more cautious. Federal Reserve Chairman Alan Greenspan said taxpayers were spending only about one-fifth of the tax rebate checks on new goods and services—an amount far below the levels policy makers had hoped for. Given the softening economy and uncertainty created by the terrorist attacks, consumers were taking a wait-and-see approach.

The attack prompted the president and Congress to enact swiftly a $40 billion spending package to help rebuild New York City and beef up domestic security. Congress also passed a $15 billion package aimed at keeping U.S. airlines flying. Both measures were also viewed as a short-run economic stimulus. Other stimulative measures were also being considered. Discretionary fiscal policy was in play again because the huge budget deficits of the previous two decades had been erased. But the recession was cutting into the federal surplus for 2001. In April 2001, the White House projected a surplus of $281 billion. In August, the projection was $158 billion, and after the terrorist attack it slipped to $120 billion. By 2002, federal deficits were back in the picture. Despite the short-term problems, most economists agreed that the long-term outlook for the economy remained bright.

<interactive>**update**

ECONNEWS ONLINE: A DISAPPEARING ACT

CONCLUSION

This chapter reviewed several factors that reduce the size of the spending multiplier. In the short run, the aggregate supply curve slopes upward, so the impact on equilibrium output of any change in aggregate demand is blunted by a change in the price level. In the long run, the aggregate supply curve is vertical, so if the economy is already producing at its potential, the spending multiplier is zero. To the extent that consumers respond primarily to changes in their permanent incomes, temporary changes in net taxes affect consumption less, so the net-tax multiplier will be smaller.

Throughout this chapter, we assumed constant net taxes and constant net exports. In the real world, income taxes increase with income and net exports decrease with income. The appendix develops the spending multiplier that introduces these more realistic assumptions. The resulting spending multipliers and tax multipliers are smaller than those developed to this point.

Because of huge federal deficits between 1982 and 1996, discretionary fiscal policy fell out of favor in the 1980s and most of the 1990s. During the time when discretionary fiscal policy was dormant, discretionary monetary policy took center stage as a tool of economic stabilization. Monetary policy is the regulation of the money supply by the Federal Reserve. In the next three chapters, we will introduce money and financial institutions, review monetary policy, and discuss the impact of monetary and fiscal policy on economic stability and growth. After we introduce money, we will consider yet another reason why the simple spending multiplier is overstated.

endofchaptermaterial

- Summary
- Questions for Review
- Problems and Exercises

- Experiential Exercises
- Wall Street Journal Exercise
- Appendix Questions

Take the Post-Test to assess your overall understanding of the key ideas in this chapter. The Post-Test provides a comprehensive selection of exam-style questions addressing the main topics and concepts of the chapter. At the completion of each Post-Test, you will receive a score and instructive feedback on how you answered each question, and a direct link to the part of the chapter addressed in the question. Take the Post-Test as often as you need to—a record of your progress for each attempt is kept for you to revisit and gauge your improvement. And each Post-Test is randomly generated, so every attempt is new.

THE ALGEBRA OF DEMAND-SIDE EQUILIBRIUM

In this appendix, we continue to focus on aggregate demand, using algebra. In Appendix B two chapters back, we solved for real GDP demanded at a particular price level and then derived the simple spending multiplier for changes in spending, including government purchases. As derived in that appendix, the change in real GDP demanded, here denoted as ΔY, resulting from a change in government purchases, ΔG, is

$$\Delta Y = \Delta G \times \frac{1}{1 - MPC}$$

The government spending multiplier is $1/(1 - MPC)$. In this appendix, we first derive the multiplier for net taxes that do not vary with income. Then we incorporate proportional income taxes and variable net exports into the framework. *Note that multiplier effects assume a given price level, so we limit the analysis to shifts in the aggregate demand curve, thereby exaggerating the size of the multiplier.*

NET TAX MULTIPLIER

How does a $1 increase in net taxes that do not vary with income affect the quantity of GDP demanded? We begin with Y, the real GDP demanded, which was derived in Appendix B two chapters back:

$$Y = \frac{1}{1 - b}(a - bNT + I + G + X - M)$$

where b is the marginal propensity to consume and $a - bNT$ is that portion of consumption that is independent of the level of income (review Appendix B two chapters back if you need a refresher).

Now let's increase net taxes by $1 to see what happens to the level of real GDP demanded. Increasing net taxes by $1 yields

$$Y' = \frac{a - b(NT + \$1) + I + G + X - M}{1 - b}$$

The difference between Y' and Y is

$$Y' - Y = \frac{\$1(-b)}{1 - b}$$

Since b is the marginal propensity to consume, this difference can be expressed as $1 \times -MPC/(1 - MPC)$, which is the net tax multiplier discussed in this chapter. With the MPC equal to 0.8, the net tax multiplier equals $-0.8/0.2$, or -4, so the effect of increasing net taxes by $1 is to reduce GDP demanded by $4, with the price level assumed constant. For any change larger than $1, we simply scale up the results. For example, the effect of increasing net taxes by $10 billion is to reduce GDP demanded by $40 billion. A different marginal propensity to consume will yield a different multiplier. For example, if the MPC equals 0.75, the net tax multiplier equals $-0.75/0.25$, or -3.

THE MULTIPLIER WHEN BOTH G AND NT CHANGE

Although we did not discuss in the chapter the combined effects of changes in both government purchases and net taxes, we can easily summarize these effects. Suppose both increase by $1. We can bring together the two changes in the following equation:

$$Y^* = \frac{a - b(NT + \$1) + I + G + \$1 + X - M}{1 - b}$$

The difference between this equilibrium and Y (the income level before introducing any changes in G or NT) is

$$Y^* - Y = \frac{\$1(-b) + \$1}{1 - b}$$

which we can simplify to

$$Y^* - Y = \frac{\$1(-b)}{1 - b} = \$1$$

Equilibrium aggregate output demanded increases by $1 as a result of $1 increases in both government purchases and net taxes. This result is referred to as the *balanced budget multiplier*, which is equal to 1.

More generally, we can say that if ΔG represents the change in government purchases and ΔNT represents the change in net taxes, the resulting change in aggregate output demanded, ΔY, can be expressed as

$$\Delta Y = \frac{\Delta G - b\Delta NT}{1 - b}$$

THE MULTIPLIER WITH A PROPORTIONAL INCOME TAX

A net tax of a fixed amount is relatively easy to manipulate, but it is not very realistic. Instead, suppose we introduce a **proportional income tax** rate equal to t, where t lies between zero and 1. Incidentally, the proportional income tax is also the so-called *flat tax* discussed as an alternative to the existing progressive income tax. Tax collections under a proportional income tax equal real GDP, Y, times the tax rate, t. With tax collections of tY, disposable income equals

$$Y - tY = (1 - t)Y$$

We plug this value for disposable income into the equation for the consumption function to yield

$$C = a + b(1 - t)Y$$

To consumption, we add the other components of aggregate expenditure, I, G, and $X - M$, to get

$$Y = a + b(1 - t)Y + I + G + (X - M)$$

Moving the Y terms to the left side of the equation yields

$$Y - b(1 - t)Y = a + I + G + (X - M)$$

or

$$Y[1 - b(1 - t)] = a + I + G + (X - M)$$

By isolating Y on the left side of the equation, we get

$$Y = \frac{a + I + G + (X - M)}{1 - b(1 - t)}$$

The numerator on the right side consists of the autonomous spending components. A $1 change in any of these components would change income by

$$\Delta Y = \frac{\$1}{1 - b(1 - t)}$$

Thus, the spending multiplier with a proportional income tax equals

$$\frac{1}{1 - b(1 - t)}$$

As the tax rate increases, the denominator increases, so the multiplier gets smaller. *The higher the proportional tax rate, other things constant, the smaller the multiplier.* A higher tax rate reduces consumption during each round of spending.

INCLUDING VARIABLE NET EXPORTS

The previous section assumed that net exports remained independent of the level of disposable income. If you have been reading the appendixes along with the chapters, you already know how variable net exports fit into the picture. *The addition of variable net exports causes the aggregate expenditure line to flatten out because net exports decrease as real income increases.* Real GDP demanded with a proportional income tax and variable net exports is

$$Y = a + b(1 - t)Y + I + G + X - m(1 - t)Y$$

where $m(1 - t)Y$ shows that imports are an increasing function of disposable income. The above equation reduces to

$$Y = \frac{a + I + G + X}{1 - b + m + t(b - m)}$$

The higher the proportional tax rate, t, or the higher the marginal propensity to import, m, the larger the denominator, so the smaller the spending multiplier. If the marginal propensity to consume is 0.8, the marginal propensity to import is 0.1, and the proportional income tax rate is 0.2, the spending multiplier would be about 2.3, or less than half the simple spending multiplier of 5. And this still assumes the price level remains unchanged.

Since we first introduced the simple spending multiplier, we have examined several factors that reduce that multiplier: (1) a marginal propensity to consume that responds primarily to permanent changes in income, not transitory changes; (2) a marginal propensity to import; (3) a proportional income tax; and (4) the upward-sloping aggregate supply curve in the short run and a vertical aggregate supply curve in the long run. After we introduce money in the next two chapters, we will consider still other factors that reduce the size of the spending multiplier.

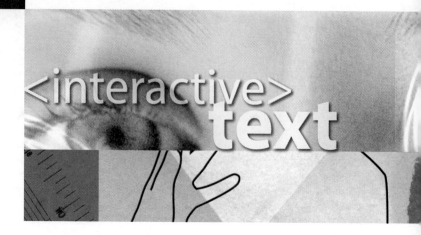

CHAPTER 28

Money and the Financial System

Why are you willing to exchange a piece of paper bearing Alexander Hamilton's portrait and the number 10 in each corner for a pepperoni pizza with extra cheese? If Russia can't pay its bills, why not simply print more rubles? Why are so few of the largest banks in the world American? Why was someone able to cash a check written on a pair of underpants? And why is there so much fascination with money? These and other questions are answered in this chapter, which introduces money and banking.

The word *money* comes from the name of the goddess in whose temple Rome's money was coined. Money has come to symbolize all personal and business finance. You can read *Money* magazine and the "Money" section of *USA Today*, watch TV shows such as *Moneyline*, *Moneyweek*, and *Your Money*, and go to Web sites such as http://money.cnn.com, http://moneycentral.msn.com/home.asp, and http://smartmoney.com. With money, you can articulate your preferences—after all, money talks. And when it talks, it says a lot, as in, "Put your money where your mouth is" and "Show me the money." Money is the oil that lubricates the wheels of commerce. Just as oil makes for an easier fit among gears, money reduces the friction—the transaction costs—of market exchange. Too little can leave some parts creaking; too much can gum up the works.

This chapter is obviously about money. We begin with the evolution of money, tracing its use from the most primitive economies to our own. Then we turn to monetary developments in the United States.

Topics discussed in this chapter include:

- Barter
- Functions of money
- Commodity and fiat money

- The Federal Reserve System
- Depository institutions
- Banking developments

<interactive>exercise

ECONDEBATE ONLINE: MONEY AND THE FINANCIAL SYSTEM

<interactive>update

- ECONDATA ONLINE: MONEY AND THE FINANCIAL SYSTEM
- ECONLINKS ONLINE: ECONOMICS WEB LINKS
- ECONNEWS ONLINE: MONEY AND THE FINANCIAL SYSTEM

THE EVOLUTION OF MONEY

In the beginning, there was no money. The earliest families were largely self–sufficient. Each produced all it consumed and consumed all it produced, so there was little need for exchange. Without exchange, there was no need for money. When specialization first emerged, as some people went hunting and others took up farming, hunters and farmers had to trade. Thus, the specialization of labor resulted in exchange, but the kinds of goods traded were limited enough that people could easily exchange their products directly for other products—a system called *barter.*

<interactive>video

ASK THE INSTRUCTOR: WHAT HAS BEEN MONEY IN THE PAST AND WHAT IS MONEY TODAY?

Barter and the Double Coincidence of Wants

Barter depends on a **double coincidence of wants,** which occurs when one trader is willing to exchange his or her product for something another trader offers. If a hunter was willing to exchange hides for a farmer's corn, that was a coincidence. But if the farmer was also willing to exchange corn for the hunter's hides, that was a double coincidence—a *double coincidence of wants.* As long as specialization was limited, say to two or three goods, mutually beneficial trades were relatively easy to discover—that is, trade wasn't much of a coincidence. As the economy developed, however, greater specialization increased the difficulty of finding the particular goods that each trader wanted to exchange.

In a barter system, traders must not only discover a double coincidence of wants, they must also agree on an exchange rate. How many hides should the farmer get for a bushel of corn? If only two goods are produced, only one exchange rate need be determined. As the number of goods produced in the economy increases, however, the number of possible exchange rates grows. Increased specialization raises the transaction costs of the barter system of exchange. A huge difference in the values of the units to be exchanged can make barter difficult. For example, suppose the hunter wanted to buy a home that exchanged for 2,000 hides. A hunter would be hard-pressed to find a home seller in need of so many hides. High transaction costs of barter gave birth to money.

The Earliest Money and Its Functions

Nobody actually recorded the emergence of money. We can only speculate about how it first came into use. Through experience accumulated from barter, traders may have found they could always find ready buyers for certain goods. If a trader could not find a good that he or she desired personally, some good with a ready market could be accepted instead. So traders began to accept certain goods not for immediate consumption but because the goods were readily accepted by others and therefore could be retraded later. For example, corn might become accepted because traders knew that it was always in demand. As one good became generally accepted in return for all other goods, that good began to function as **money.** *Any commodity that acquires a high degree of acceptability throughout an economy becomes money.*

Money fulfills three important functions: a *medium of exchange,* a *unit of account,* and a *store of value.* Let's consider each function.

Medium of Exchange.
Separating the sale of one good from the purchase of another requires an item acceptable to each party involved in the transactions. If a society, by luck or by design, can find one commodity that everyone will accept in exchange for whatever is sold, traders can save time, disappointment, and sheer aggravation. Suppose corn plays this role, a role that clearly goes beyond its role as food. We then call corn a medium of exchange because it is accepted in exchange by all buyers and sellers, whether or not they want corn for food. A **medium of exchange** is anything that is generally accepted in payment for goods and services sold. The person who accepts corn in exchange for some product believes the corn can be used later to purchase whatever is desired.

In this example, corn is both a *commodity* and *money,* so we call it a **commodity money.** The earliest money was commodity money. Cattle served as money, first for the Greeks, then for the Romans. In fact, the word *pecuniary* (meaning "of or relating to money") comes from the Latin word for cattle, *pecus.* Salt also served as money. Roman soldiers received part of their pay in salt; the salt portion was called the *salarium,* the origin of the word *salary.* The precious metals gold and silver have been used as money for at least 4,000 years. Other commodity moneys used at various times include wampum (polished strings of shells) and tobacco in colonial America, tea pressed into small cakes in Russia, and palm dates in North Africa.

Unit of Account.
As one commodity, such as corn, becomes widely accepted, it becomes a **unit of account,** a standard on which prices are based. The price of shoes or pots or hides is measured in bushels of corn. Thus, corn serves not only as a medium of exchange, it also becomes a common denominator, a yardstick, for *measuring the value* of all goods and services. Rather than having to determine how much of each good can be exchanged for every other good, as is the case in a barter economy, people can price everything using a common denominator, such as corn. For example, if a pair of shoes sells for 2 bushels of corn and a 5-gallon pot sells for 1 bushel of corn, then a pair of shoes has the same value in exchange as two 5-gallon pots.

Store of Value.
Because people do not want to make purchases every time they sell something, the purchasing power acquired through a sale must somehow be preserved. Money serves as a **store of value** when it retains purchasing power over time. The better it preserves purchasing power, the better money serves as a store of value. Consider again the distinction between a stock and a flow. Recall that a *stock* is an amount measured at a particular point in time, such as the amount of food in your refrigerator, or the amount of money you have with you right now. In contrast, a *flow* is an amount per unit of time, such as the calories you consume per day, or the income you earn per week. *Money* is a stock and *income* is a flow. Don't confuse money with income. The role of money as a stock is best reflected by money's role as a store of value.

<interactive>**video**

ASK THE INSTRUCTOR: WHAT ARE THE PRINCIPAL FUNCTIONS OF MONEY?

Problems with Commodity Money

The introduction of commodity money reduced the transaction costs of exchange compared with barter, but commodity money also involves some transaction costs. First, if the commodity money is perishable, as is corn, it must be properly stored or its quality deteriorates; even then, it won't maintain its quality for long. So money should be *durable.* Second, if the commodity money is bulky, exchanges for major purchases can become unwieldy. For example, if a new home cost 5,000 bushels of corn, many cartloads of corn would be needed to purchase that home. So money should be *portable.* Third, some commodity money is not easily divisible into smaller units. For example, when cattle served as money, any price involving a fraction of a cow posed an exchange problem. So money should be *divisible.*

Fourth, if commodity money like corn is valued equally in exchange, regardless of its quality, people will tend to keep the best corn and trade away the rest. As a result, the quality remaining in circulation will decline, reducing its acceptability. Sir Thomas Gresham wrote back in the 16th century that "bad money drives out good money"; this has come to be known as **Gresham's law.** People tend to trade away inferior money and hoard the best. Over time, the supply of money shrinks and the quality remaining in circulation becomes less acceptable. So money should be of *uniform quality.*

Fifth, commodity money usually ties up otherwise valuable resources, so it has a relatively high opportunity cost compared with, say, paper money. For example, corn that is used for money cannot at the same time be used for corn on the cob, corn flour, or other food. So the creation of money should have a *low opportunity cost.*

A final problem of commodity money is that its supply and demand determine the prices of all other goods; if the supply or demand for money fluctuates unpredictably so will the economy's price level. For example, if a bumper crop increases the supply of corn, more corn is required to purchase other goods. This is what we call *inflation.* Likewise, any change in the demand for corn *as food,* such as occurred with the development of corn chips, would alter the amount available as a medium of exchange, and this, too, would affect the exchange value of corn. Erratic fluctuations in the market for corn limit its usefulness as money, particularly as a unit of account and a store of value. So the value of money *should not fluctuate erratically.*

If people cannot rely on the value of corn over time, they will be reluctant to hold it or to agree on future contracts quoted in terms of corn. More generally, *since the value of money depends on its limited supply, anything that can be easily gathered or produced does not serve well as commodity money.* For example, tree leaves or common rocks would not serve well as commodity monies. What all this boils down to is that *the best money is durable, portable, divisible, and of uniform quality; has a low opportunity cost; and does not fluctuate erratically in value.*

<interactive>update

ECONNEWS ONLINE: WILL CASH BECOME SCARCE?

Coins

The division of commodity money into units was often quite natural, as in bushels of corn or heads of cattle. When rock salt was used as money, it was cut into uniform bricks. Since salt was usually of consistent quality, a trader had only to count the bricks to determine the amount of money. When silver and gold were used as commodity money, both their quantity and quality were open to question. Because precious metals could be *debased* with cheaper metals, the quantity and the quality of the metal had to be determined with each exchange.

This quality control problem was addressed by coining the metal, a practice more than 2,000 years old. *Coinage determined both the amount and quality of the metal.* The use of coins allowed payment by count rather than by weight. A table on which this money was counted came to be called the *counter,* a term still used today. Initially, coins were stamped on one side only, but undetectable amounts of the metal could be shaved from the smooth side of the coin. To prevent such shaving, coins were stamped on both sides. But another problem arose because small amounts of the metal could be clipped from the edge. To prevent clipping, coins were bordered with a well-defined rim and were milled around the edges. If you have a dime or a quarter, notice the tiny serrations on the edge and the wording along the border. These features, throwbacks from the time when coins were silver or gold rather than cheaper metals, reduce your chances of "getting clipped."

The power to coin, which was vested in the *seignior,* or feudal lord, was considered an act of sovereignty. Counterfeiting was considered an act of treason. If the face value of the coin exceeded the cost of coinage, the minting of coins became a source of revenue to the seignior. **Seigniorage** (pronounced "seen´-your-edge") refers to the revenue earned from coinage by the seignior. **Token money** is money whose face value exceeds its cost of production. Coins and paper money now in circulation in the United States are token money. For example, the 25-cent coin costs the U.S. Mint only about 3 cents to make. Coin production nets the federal government about $500 million per year in seigniorage. Paper money is a far greater source of seigniorage, as we'll see later.

Money and Banking

The word *bank* comes from the Italian word *banca,* meaning "bench," because Italian money changers originally conducted their business on benches. Banking spread from Italy to England, where London goldsmiths offered the community "safekeeping" for money and other valuables. The goldsmith gave depositors their money back on request, but since deposits by some people tended to offset withdrawals by others, the amount of idle cash, or gold, in the vault remained relatively constant over time. Goldsmiths found that they could earn interest by making loans from this pool of idle cash.

Keeping money on deposit with a goldsmith was safer than leaving it where it could be easily stolen, but visiting the goldsmith every time money was needed was a pain. For example, a farmer might visit the goldsmith to withdraw enough money to buy a horse. The farmer would then pay the horse trader, who would promptly deposit the receipts with the goldsmith. Thus, money took a round trip from goldsmith to farmer to horse trader and back to goldsmith. Depositors grew tired of visiting the goldsmith every time they needed to make a purchase, so goldsmiths instituted a practice whereby a purchaser, such as the farmer, could write the goldsmith instructions to pay someone else, such as the horse trader, a given amount from the purchaser's account. The payment amounted to moving gold from one stack (the farmer's) to another (the horse trader's). *These written instructions to the goldsmith were the first checks.* Checks have since become official-looking instruction forms, but they need not be, as evidenced by the actions of a Montana man who paid a speeding fine with a check written on a clean but frayed pair of underpants. The Western Federal Savings and Loan of Missoula honored the check.

By combining the ideas of cash loans and checks, the goldsmith soon discovered how to make loans by check. Rather than lend idle cash, the goldsmith could create a checking account for the borrower. *The goldsmith could extend a loan by creating an account against which the borrower could write checks. In this way goldsmiths, or banks, were able to create a medium of exchange, or to "create money."* This money, based only on an entry in the goldsmith's ledger, was accepted because of the public's confidence that these claims would be honored.

The total claims against the goldsmith consisted of claims by people who had deposited their money plus claims by people to whom the goldsmith extended loans. Because these claims exceeded the value of gold on reserve, this was the beginning of a **fractional reserve banking system,** a system in which the goldsmith's reserves amounted to just a fraction of total deposits. The *reserve ratio* measured reserves as a share of total claims against the goldsmith, or total deposits. For example, if the goldsmith had gold reserves valued at $5,000 but deposits totaling $10,000, the reserve ratio was 50 percent.

NETBOOKMARK: AMERICAN CURRENCY EXHIBIT

Paper Money

Another way a bank could create money was by issuing bank notes. **Bank notes** were pieces of paper promising the bearer specific amounts of gold or silver when the notes were presented to the issuing bank for redemption. In London, goldsmith bankers introduced bank notes about the same time they introduced checks. *Whereas checks could be redeemed only if endorsed by the payee, notes could be redeemed by anyone who presented them.* Paper money was often "as good as gold," since the bearer could redeem it for gold. In fact, paper money was more convenient than gold because it was less bulky and more portable.

The amount of paper money issued by a bank depended on that bank's estimate of the proportion of notes that would be redeemed. The greater the redemption rate, the fewer notes could be issued based on a given amount of reserves. Initially, these promises to pay were issued by private individuals or banks, but over time, governments took a larger role in printing and circulating notes. Once paper money became widely accepted, it was perhaps inevitable that governments would begin issuing **fiat money,** which derives its status as money from the power of the state, or by *fiat.* Fiat (pronounced "fee´at") money is money because the government says so. The word is from the Latin and means, "let it be done." Fiat money is not redeemable for anything other than more fiat money; it is not backed by something of intrinsic value. You can think of fiat money as mere paper money. It is acceptable not because it is intrinsically useful or valuable—as is corn or gold—but because the government says it's money. Fiat money is declared **legal tender** by the government, meaning that you have made a valid and legal offer of payment of your debt when you pay with this money. *Gradually, people came to accept fiat money because they believed that others would accept it as well.* The currency issued in the United States today, and indeed paper money throughout most of the world, is fiat money.

In a way, a well-regulated system of fiat money is more efficient for an economy than commodity money. Fiat money uses only paper (a dollar bill costs about 5 cents to print), but commodity money ties up something intrinsically valuable. Paper money makes up only part of the money supply. Modern money also includes checking accounts, which are electronic entries in bank computers.

The Value of Money

Money has grown increasingly more abstract—from a physical commodity, to a piece of paper representing a claim on a physical commodity, to a piece of paper of no intrinsic value, to an electronic entry representing a claim on a piece of paper of no intrinsic value. So why does money have value? The commodity feature of early money bolstered confidence in its acceptability. Commodities such as corn, tobacco, and gold had value in use even if for some reason they became less acceptable in exchange. When paper money came into use, its acceptability was initially fostered by the promise to redeem it for gold, silver, or other items of value. But since most paper money throughout the world is now fiat money, there is no promise of redemption. So why can a piece of paper bearing the portrait of Alexander Hamilton and the number 10 in each corner be exchanged for a large pepperoni pizza or anything else selling for $10? *People accept these pieces of paper because, through experience, they have reason to believe that others will do so as well.* The acceptability of money, which we now take for granted, is based on our years of experience with the stability of its value and with the willingness of others to accept it as payment. As we will soon see, when money's value becomes questionable, so does its acceptability.

The *purchasing power* of money is the rate at which it exchanges for goods and services. The higher the price level, the less can be purchased with each dollar, so the less each dollar is worth. The purchasing power of each dollar over time varies inversely with the price level. As the price level increases, the purchasing power of money falls. To measure the purchasing power of the dollar in a particular year, you first compute the price index for that year and then divide 100 by that price index. For example, relative to the base period of 1982 through 1984, the consumer price index for September 2001 was 178.3. The purchasing power of a dollar was therefore 100/178.3, or about $0.56, measured in 1982–1984 dollars. Exhibit 1 chronicles the steady decline in the value of the dollar since 1960.

When Money Performs Poorly

One way to understand the functions of money is to look at situations in which money did not perform well. In an earlier chapter, we examined hyperinflation in Brazil. With prices growing by the hour, money no longer represented a stable store of value, so people couldn't wait to

EXHIBIT 1

Purchasing Power of a Dollar Measured in 1982–1984 Constant Dollars

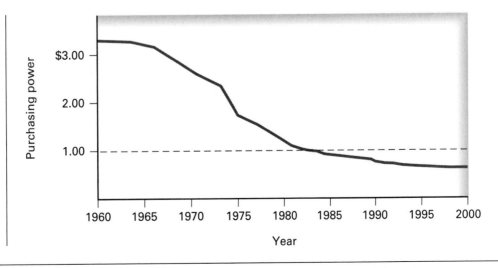

An increase in the price level reduces the amount of goods and services that can be purchased with a dollar. Since 1960, the price level has risen every year, so the purchasing power of the dollar has fallen continually.

Source: Developed from estimates by the U.S. Bureau of Labor Statistics. For the latest information on the consumer price index, go to http://www.bls.gov/news.release/cpi.toc.htm.

exchange rapidly inflating money for goods or for a "hard" currency—that is, one whose value was more stable. And with the price level rising rapidly, some merchants were quicker to raise their prices than others, so relative prices became distorted. Thus, money became less useful as a store of value and as a unit of account—that is, as a way of comparing the price of one good with the price of another.

At some point, the inflation rate may become so high that people no longer accept the nation's money and instead resort to some other medium of exchange or to barter. Likewise, if the supply of money dries up or if the price system is not allowed to function properly, barter may be the only alternative. The following case study discusses instances when money performed poorly because of too much money, too little money, or a hobbled price system.

CASE**STUDY**	When Monetary Systems Break Down
	● *Public Policy*

What happens when there is too much money in circulation? We already discussed the transaction costs and distortions of hyperinflation in Brazil. As a different example, hyperinflation of the ruble in Russia following the breakup of the Soviet Union increased Russian demand for so-called hard currencies, especially the dollar. In keeping with Gresham's law, Russians traded their rubles and hoarded their dollars. A Russian central banker claimed that the value of Russians' dollar holdings in 1995 exceeded the value of their ruble holdings. Advertisers even quoted prices in "bucks."

Let's consider the opposite problems: What if there isn't enough money to go around? Money became extremely scarce during the 19th century in Brazil because a copper shortage halted minting of copper coins. Money-financed transactions were difficult as people hoarded rather than traded the limited supply of coins available. In response, some merchants and tavern keepers printed vouchers redeemable for goods and services. These vouchers circulated as money until enough copper coins reappeared. Similarly, people coped with the shortage of money in the early American colonies by maintaining careful records, showing who owed what to whom.

For a more recent example of a money shortage, consider Panama, a Central American country that relies on the U.S. dollar as its currency. In 1988, the United States, in response to charges that the leader of Panama was involved in drug dealing, froze Panamanian assets in the United States. This touched off a panic in Panama as bank customers tried to withdraw their deposits. Banks were forced to close for nine weeks. Dollars were hoarded, so people resorted to barter. Because barter is less efficient than a smoothly functioning monetary system, Panama's GDP fell by 30 percent in 1988.

Finally, what happens when the price system is not allowed to operate? After Germany lost World War II, money in that country became almost useless because, despite tremendous inflationary pressure in the economy, those who won the war imposed strict price controls on Germany. Because most prices were set well below what people thought they should be, sellers stopped accepting money, and this forced people to barter. Experts estimate that because of the lack of a viable medium of exchange, the German economy produced only half the output that it would have with a smoothly functioning monetary system. The "economic miracle" in Germany immediately after 1948 can be credited in large part to that country's adoption of a reliable monetary system.

Thus, when the supply of money shrinks as a result of hoarding or when the official money fails to serve as a medium of exchange because of price controls or hyperinflation, some other mechanism often emerges to facilitate exchange. But this second-best alternative is seldom as efficient as a smoothly functioning monetary system, because more resources must be diverted from production to exchange. A poorly functioning monetary system results in higher transaction costs. *It has been said that no machine increases the economy's productivity as much as properly functioning money.* Indeed, it seems hard to overstate the value of a reliable monetary system. This is why we pay so much attention to money and banking.

<interactive>exercise

- eACTIVITY: WHEN MONETARY SYSTEMS BREAK DOWN
- READING IT RIGHT: WALL STREET JOURNAL EXERCISE

Sources: Peter White, "The Power of Money," *National Geographic*, January 1993; Frederic Dannen and Ira Silverman, "The Supernote," *New Yorker*, 23 October 1995; "Russia Official Nods to Money Boost," *New York Times*, 30 September 1998; and Michael Bryan et al. "Who Is That Guy on the $10 Bill?" *Economic Commentary: Federal Reserve Bank of Cleveland*, July 2000.

Let's turn now to the development of money and banking in the United States.

FINANCIAL INSTITUTIONS IN THE UNITED STATES

You have already learned about the origin of modern banks: Goldsmiths lent money from deposits they held for safekeeping. So you already have some idea of how banks work. Recall from the circular-flow model discussed earlier that household saving flows into financial markets, including banks, where it is lent to investors. Financial institutions accumulate funds from savers and lend these funds to borrowers, thereby serving as intermediaries between savers and borrowers. Financial institutions, or **financial intermediaries,** earn a profit by "buying low and selling high"—that is, by paying a lower interest rate to savers than they charge borrowers.

<interactive>update

- ECONDATA ONLINE: MONEY SUPPLY (M2)
- ECONNEWS ONLINE: BANKS BEHAVING BADLY?

Commercial Banks and Thrifts

A wide variety of financial intermediaries respond to the economy's demand for financial services. **Depository institutions**—such as commercial banks, savings and loan associations, mutual savings banks, and credit unions—obtain funds primarily by accepting customer *deposits*. We focus on depository institutions in this section because they play a key role in providing the nation's money supply. Depository institutions can be classified broadly into two types: commercial banks and thrift institutions.

Commercial banks are the oldest, largest, and most diversified of depository institutions. They are called **commercial banks** because historically they made loans primarily to *commercial* ventures, or businesses, rather than to households. Commercial banks hold two-thirds of all deposits held by depository institutions. Until 1980, commercial banks were the only depository institutions that offered demand deposits, or checking accounts. **Demand deposits** are so named because a depositor with such an account can write a check *demanding* those deposits.

Thrift institutions, or **thrifts,** include savings and loan associations, mutual savings banks, and credit unions. Historically, savings and loan associations and mutual savings banks specialized in making home mortgage loans. Credit unions, which account for four of five thrifts, extend loans only to their "members" to finance homes or other major consumer purchases, such as new cars.

Development of the Dual Banking System

Before 1863, commercial banks in the United States were chartered by the states in which they operated, so they were called *state banks*. These banks, like the English goldsmiths, issued bank notes. Thousands of different notes circulated and nearly all were redeemable for gold. The National Banking Act of 1863 and its later amendments created a new system of federally chartered banks called *national banks*. National banks were authorized to issue notes and were regulated by the Office of the Comptroller of the Currency, part of the U.S. Treasury. At the time, a tax was introduced on the notes issued by state-chartered banks, the idea being to tax state bank notes out of existence. But state banks survived by substituting checks for notes. Borrowers were issued checking accounts rather than bank notes. State banks held on, and to this day, the United States has a *dual banking system* consisting of both state banks and national banks.

Birth of the Federal Reserve System

During the 19th century, the economy experienced a number of panic "runs" on banks by depositors seeking to withdraw their funds. A panic was usually set off by the failure of some prominent financial institution. *As people became frightened and tried to withdraw their money, they couldn't because each bank held only a fraction of its deposits as reserves.* Following such a failure, fearful customers besieged other banks. Borrowers wanted additional loans and extensions of credit, and depositors wanted their money back. Similar bank panics have occurred recently in Russia and in parts of Asia. The failure of the Knickerbocker Trust Company in New York triggered the Panic of 1907. This banking calamity so aroused the public that Congress authorized a study that led to the creation of the **Federal Reserve System** in 1913 as the central bank and monetary authority of the United States.

Nearly all industrialized countries had formed central banks by 1900—the Bundesbank in Germany, the Bank of Japan, the Bank of England. The American public's suspicion of such monopoly power led to the establishment of not one central bank but 12 separate banks in 12 Federal Reserve districts around the country. The new banks were named after the cities in which they were located—the Federal Reserve Banks of Boston, New York, Chicago, San Francisco, and so on, as shown in Exhibit 2. (Which district are you in?) *Throughout most of its history, the United States had what is called a decentralized banking system. The Federal Reserve Act moved the country toward a system that was partly centralized and partly decentralized.* All national banks became members of the Federal Reserve System and were thus subject to new regulations issued by the *Fed,* as it came to be called. For state banks, membership was voluntary; most state banks did not join because their owners did not want to comply with the new regulations.

Powers of the Federal Reserve System

The founding legislation established the Federal Reserve Board "to exercise general supervision" over the Federal Reserve System and to ensure sufficient money and credit in the banking system needed to support a growing economy. The power to issue bank notes was taken away from national banks and turned over to the Federal Reserve Banks. (Take out a $1 bill and notice what it says across the top: "Federal Reserve Note." On the $1 bill only, the seal to the left of George Washington's portrait identifies which Federal Reserve Bank issued the note.) The Federal Reserve was also given other powers: *to buy and sell government securities, to extend loans to member banks, to clear checks, and to require that member banks hold reserves equal to at least a specified fraction of their deposits.*

Federal Reserve Banks do not deal with the public directly. Each may be thought of as a bankers' bank. Reserve Banks hold deposits of member banks, just as depository institutions hold deposits of the public, and they extend loans to member banks, just as depository institutions extend loans to the public. The name Reserve Bank comes from the responsibility to hold member bank *reserves* on deposit. **Reserves** are cash that banks have on hand or on deposit with the Fed to promote banking safety, to facilitate interbank transfers of funds, to satisfy the cash demands of their customers, and to comply with Federal Reserve regulations. By holding bank reserves, a Reserve Bank can clear a check written by a depositor at one bank and deposited in another bank. This check clearance process is, on a larger scale, much like the goldsmith's moving of gold reserves from the farmer's account to the horse trader's account. Reserve Banks also lend to banks. The interest rate charged to banks for these *dis-*

EXHIBIT 2

The Twelve Federal Reserve Districts

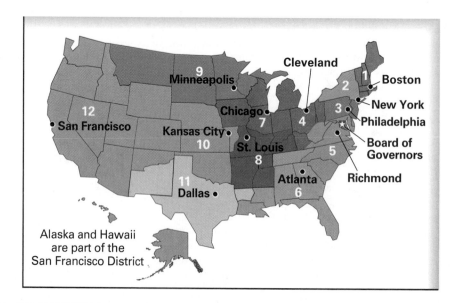

Source: Federal Reserve Board Web page at http://www.federalreserve.gov/otherfrb.htm.

count loans is called the *discount rate.* By making discount loans to banks, the Fed can increase reserves in the banking system.

A member bank is required to own stock in its district Federal Reserve Bank, and this entitles the bank to a specified dividend. Any additional profit earned by the Reserve Banks is turned over to the U.S. Treasury.

Banking During the Great Depression

From 1913 to 1929, both the Federal Reserve System and the national economy performed relatively well. But the stock market crash of 1929 was followed by the Great Depression, creating a new set of problems for the Fed, such as bank runs caused by panicked depositors. The Fed, however, dropped the ball by failing to act as a lender of last resort—that is, the Fed did not lend banks the money they needed to satisfy deposit withdrawals in cases of runs on otherwise sound banks.

The Federal Reserve System was established precisely to prevent such panics and to add stability to the banking system. What went wrong? In a word, everything. Between 1930 and 1933, the support offered by the Federal Reserve System seemed to crumble in stages. As businesses failed, they were unable to repay their loans. These loan defaults led to the initial bank failures. As the crisis deepened, the public worried about the safety of bank deposits, so cash withdrawals increased. To satisfy the greater demand for currency, banks were forced to sell their holdings of stocks and bonds. But with many banks trying to sell and with few buyers, securities prices collapsed, sharply reducing the market value of bank assets. Many banks did not have the resources to survive. Between 1930 and 1933, about one-third of all U.S. banks failed.

Because the Fed failed to understand its role as the lender of last resort, it failed to extend loans on a large scale to banks experiencing short-run shortages of cash (in contrast, the Fed was a ready source of loans a half century later during the stock market crash of 1987). The Fed viewed bank failure as a regrettable but inevitable consequence of poor management, prior speculative excesses, or simply as the effect of a collapsing economy. The Fed did not seem to understand that the banking system's instability was contributing to the deterioration of the economy. For example, the stock market collapsed between 1929 and 1933 in part because many banks were trying to sell their securities at the same time. And the collapse came just when banks were badly in need of cash. Fed officials appeared concerned primarily with the solvency of the Federal Reserve Banks. They did not realize they had unlimited money-creating power, so they could not fail.

Roosevelt's Reforms

In his first inaugural address in 1933, President Franklin D. Roosevelt said, "The only thing we have to fear is fear itself," a statement especially apt for a fractional reserve banking system. Most banks were sound as long as people had confidence in the safety of their deposits. But if many depositors tried to withdraw their money, they could not do so because each bank held only a fraction of deposits as reserves. When he took office, Roosevelt declared a "banking holiday," closing all banks for a week. Such a drastic measure was considered a welcome sign that something would be done. The Banking Acts of 1933 and 1935 shored up the banking system and centralized the power of the Federal Reserve System. Let's consider the most important features of these acts.

Board of Governors. The Federal Reserve Board was renamed the Board of Governors and became responsible for setting and implementing the nation's monetary policy. *Monetary policy,* a term introduced in Chapter 4, is the regulation of the economy's money supply and interest rates to promote macroeconomic objectives. All 12 Reserve Banks are under the authority of the Board of Governors, which consists of seven members appointed by the president and confirmed by the Senate. Each member serves one 14-year nonrenewable term, with one member appointed every two years; one governor is also appointed to chair the Board of Governors for a four-year renewable term. Board membership is relatively stable because a new president can be sure of appointing or reappointing only two members in a presidential term. *The Board structure was designed to insulate monetary authorities from short-term political pressure by elected officials.*

Federal Open Market Committee. Originally, the power of the Federal Reserve System was vested in each of the 12 Reserve Banks. The Banking Acts established the **Federal Open Market Committee (FOMC)** to consolidate decisions about an important tool of monetary policy—**open-market operations,** which are purchases and sales of U.S. government securities by the Fed (open-market operations and other tools of monetary policy will be examined in the next chapter). The FOMC consists of the seven board governors plus 5 of the 12 presidents of the Reserve Banks; the chair of the Board of Governors heads the group. The New York Federal Reserve Bank carries out open-market operations, and the president of the New York Fed is always an FOMC member. The organizational structure of the Federal Reserve System as it now stands is presented in Exhibit 3. The presidential appointment of Board members is subject to Senate confirmation. The FOMC and, less significantly, the Federal Advisory Committee (which consists of a commercial banker from each of the 12 Reserve Bank districts) advise the Board.

Regulating the Money Supply. As we saw earlier, because reserves amount to just a fraction of deposits, we have a *fractional reserve* banking system. The Banking Acts gave the Board of Governors more discretion in setting reserve requirements, thereby giving the Fed an additional tool of monetary policy. Thus, as of 1935, the Federal Reserve System has a variety of tools to regulate the money supply, including *(1) conducting open-market operations—buying and selling U.S. government securities; (2) setting the discount rate—the interest rate charged by Reserve Banks for loans to member banks; and (3) setting legal reserve requirements for member banks.* We will explore these tools in greater detail in the next chapter.

Deposit Insurance. Panic runs on banks stemmed from fears about the safety of bank deposits. The *Federal Deposit Insurance Corporation (FDIC)* was established in 1933 to insure the first $2,500 of each deposit account. Today the insurance ceiling is $100,000 per account. Members of the Federal Reserve System must purchase FDIC insurance; the program is voluntary for other banks. About 97 percent of commercial banks and about 90 percent of savings and loan associations are FDIC insured. Private companies or state reserve funds insure the rest. *Deposit insurance, by calming fears about the safety of deposits, worked wonders to reduce bank runs.*

Restricting Bank Investment Practices. As part of the Banking Act of 1933, commercial banks could no longer own corporate stocks and bonds, financial assets that could fluctuate widely in value and contribute to instability of the banking system. The act limited bank assets primarily to loans and government securities—bonds issued by federal, state, and local governments. A *bond* is an IOU, so a government bond is an IOU from the government. Also, bank failures were thought to have resulted in part from fierce interest-rate competition among banks for customer deposits. To curb such competition, the Fed was empowered to set a ceiling on the interest that banks could pay depositors.

EXHIBIT 3

Organization Chart for the Federal Reserve System

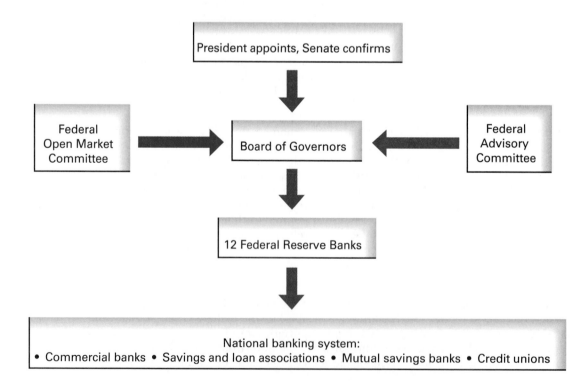

Objectives of the Fed. Over the years, the Fed has accumulated additional responsibilities. Six goals are frequently mentioned as objectives of the Fed's policies: (1) a high level of employment in the economy, (2) economic growth, (3) price stability, (4) stability in interest rates, (5) stability in financial markets, such as the stock market, and (6) stability in foreign exchange markets. *We can boil these goals down to high employment; economic growth; and stability in prices, interest rates, financial markets, and exchange rates.* As we will see, not all of these objectives can be achieved simultaneously.

Banks Lost Deposits When Inflation Increased

Restrictions imposed on depository institutions during the 1930s made banking a heavily regulated industry. Depository institutions lost much of their freedom to wheel and deal, and the federal government insured most deposits. The assets banks could acquire were carefully limited, as were the interest rates they could offer depositors (checking deposits earned no interest). Banking thus became a highly regulated, even stuffy, industry. Bankers operated on what was facetiously called the "3-6-3 rule"—borrow at 3 percent, lend at 6 percent, and get on the golf course by 3 p.m.

Ceilings on interest rates reduced interest-rate competition for deposits *among* banks. But a surge of inflation during the 1970s increased interest rates in the economy. Banking has not been the same since. When market interest rates rose above what banks could legally offer, many customers withdrew their deposits and put them into higher-yielding alternatives. In 1972, Merrill Lynch, a major brokerage house, introduced an account combining a **money market mutual fund** with limited check-writing privileges. Money market mutual fund shares are claims on a portfolio, or collection, of short-term interest-earning assets. These mutual funds proved to be stiff competition for bank deposits, especially demand deposits, which paid no interest.

Depository institutions used savers' deposits to make loans. When savers withdrew their deposits, banks and thrifts had to support their loans by borrowing at prevailing interest rates, which were typically higher than the rates they earned on their existing loans. Commercial banks, because their loans were usually for short periods, got in less trouble than thrifts did when interest rates rose. Thrifts had made loans for long-term mortgages, loans that would not be fully repaid for 30 years. Because thrifts had to pay more interest to borrow funds than they were earning on these mortgages, they were in big trouble, and many failed.

Bank Deregulation

In response to the loss of deposits and other problems of depository institutions, Congress tried to ease regulations, giving banks and thrifts greater discretion in their operations. For example, interest-rate ceilings for deposits were eliminated, and all depository institutions were allowed to offer money market deposit accounts. Such accounts jumped from only $8 billion in 1978 to $200 billion in 1982. Some states, like California and Texas, deregulated state-chartered savings and loan associations. The combination of deposit insurance, unregulated interest rates, and wider latitude in the kinds of assets that thrifts could purchase gave them a green light to compete for large deposits in national markets and to acquire assets as they pleased. Once-staid financial institutions moved into the fast lane.

Thrifts could wheel and deal but with the benefit of deposit insurance. The combination of deregulation and deposit insurance encouraged some thrifts on the verge of failing to take bigger risks—to "bet the bank"—since their depositors would be protected by deposit insurance. This created a *moral hazard,* which in this case is the tendency of bankers to take unwarranted risks because depositors were insured. Banks that were already virtually bankrupt—so-called "zombie" banks—were able to attract additional deposits because of deposit insurance. Zombie banks, by offering higher interest rates, also drew deposits away from healthy banks.

Meanwhile, since depositors were insured, most paid little attention to their banks' health. Thus, *deposit insurance, originally introduced during the Great Depression to prevent bank panics, caused depositors to become complacent about the safety of their deposits. Worse still, it caused those who ran the banks and thrifts to take wild gambles to survive.*

<interactive>**exercise**

ECONDEBATE ONLINE: SHOULD U.S. FINANCIAL MARKETS BE DEREGULATED?

Bailing Out the Thrifts

Many of these gambles, particularly loans to real estate developers, failed, and thrifts lost a ton. The result was a disaster, and depository institutions, particularly thrifts, failed at record rates. Thrift failures grew in the mid-1980s. The insolvency and collapse of a growing number of thrifts prompted Congress in 1989 to approve the largest financial bailout of any U.S. industry in history—a measure that would eventually cost about $250 billion. Taxpayers paid nearly two-thirds of the total, and the thrift industry paid the remaining third through higher deposit insurance premiums. The money was spent to shut down failing thrifts and to pay off insured depositors. Exhibit 4 shows thrift failures in the United States by year since 1980. From their 1989 peak of 328, annual failures dropped to 2 or fewer since 1995. Because of failures, mergers, and acquisitions, the number of thrifts dropped 53 percent, from 3,400 in 1984 to 1,590 in 2000.

Commercial Banks Were Also Failing

The U.S. banking system experienced more change and upheaval during the 1980s and early 1990s than at any other time since the Great Depression. As was the case of thrifts, risky decisions based on deposit insurance coupled with a slump in real estate values hastened the demise of many commercial banks. Banks in Texas and Oklahoma failed when loans to oil drillers and farmers proved unsound. Banks in the Northeast failed because of falling real estate values, which caused borrowers to default. Hundreds of troubled banks, like Continental Illinois Bank, First Republic Bank of Dallas, and the Bank of New England, were taken over by the FDIC or forced to merge with healthier competitors. Exhibit 5 shows the number of commercial bank failures per year since 1980. The rising tide during the 1980s is clear, with failures peaking in 1988. But by the mid-1990s, failures settled down. Because of failures, mergers, and acquisitions, the number of commercial banks fell 43 percent, from 14,400 in 1985 to 8,300 in 2000.

EXHIBIT 4

Annual Failures of U.S. Thrift Institutions Peaked in 1989

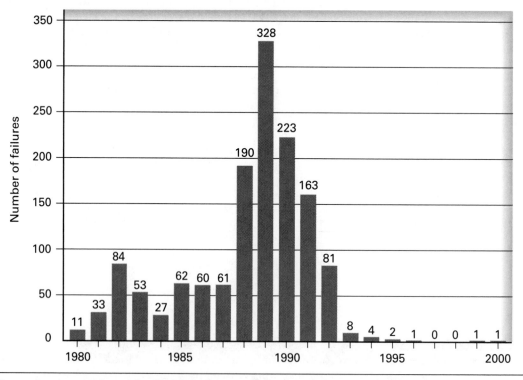

Source: Based on annual reports from the Federal Deposit Insurance Corporation. For the latest figures, go to http://www2.fdic.gov/hsob/SelectRpt.asp?EntryTyp=30.

EXHIBIT 5 |

Annual Failures of U.S. Commercial Banks Peaked in 1988

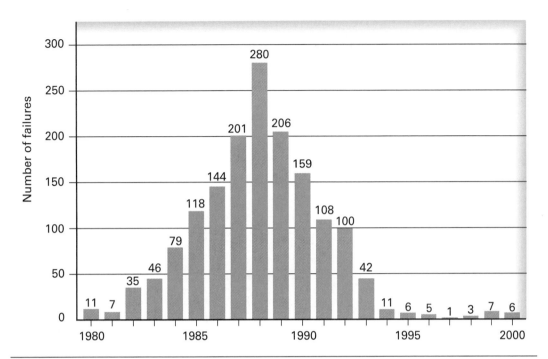

Source: Based on annual reports from the Federal Deposit Insurance Corporation. For the latest figures, go to http://www2.fdic.gov/hsob/SelectRpt.asp?EntryTyp=30.

The Structure of U.S. Banking

Despite the drop in the number of commercial banks, the United States still has more banks than any other country in the world. Other industrial countries have fewer than 1,000 commercial banks, and Japan has fewer than 100. The 10 largest U.S. commercial banks hold less than half the U.S. banking industry assets. In contrast, as few as a half dozen banks hold over half the assets in other advanced industrial countries such as Australia, Canada, Japan, and the United Kingdom. *So the United States has more banks than other countries, and U.S. bank assets are distributed more evenly across banks.*

The large number of banks in this country reflects past restrictions on branches, which are additional offices that carry out banking operations. Again, Americans feared monopoly power and did not want any one bank to become too powerful. The combination of intrastate and interstate restrictions on branching spawned the many commercial banks that exist today, most of which are relatively small. Branching restrictions create inefficiencies, since banks cannot achieve optimal size and cannot as easily diversify their portfolios of loans across different regions.

In recent years, two developments have allowed banks to get around branching restrictions: bank holding companies and mergers. A **bank holding company** is a corporation that may own several different banks. Many states now let holding companies cross state lines, thereby skirting federal prohibitions against interstate banking. Moreover, a holding company can provide other services that banks are not authorized to offer, such as financial advising, leasing, insurance, credit cards, and securities trading. The *Graham-Leach-Bliley Act of 1999* gave holding companies additional leeway in owning other types of businesses, repealing some Depression-era restrictions on the kinds of assets a bank could own. Thus, holding companies have blossomed in recent years; more than three-quarters of the nation's checking deposits are in banks owned by holding companies.

Another important development that allowed banks to expand their geographical reach is *bank mergers,* which have spread the presence of some banks across the country. Banks are merging because they want more customers and expect the higher volume of transactions to reduce operating costs per customer. Nationwide banking is also seen as a way of avoiding the concentration of bad loans that sometimes occur in one geographical area. The merger movement was fueled by a rising stock market during the 1990s and by federal legislation that

EXHIBIT 6

The Number of Commercial Banks Declined Recently, But Branches
Have Multiplied Since 1934

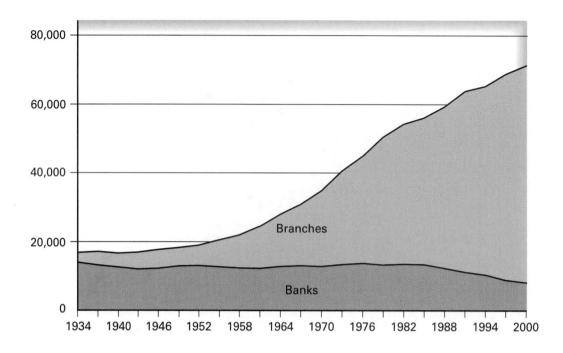

Source: FDIC-insured commercial banks in the United States based on FDIC data. For the latest figures, go to
http://www.fdic.gov/bank/statistical/statistics/0012/nmbank.html.

facilitates consolidation of merged banks. For example, NationsBank and BankAmerica
merged to create Bank of America, one of the nation's largest banks and the first to stretch
coast to coast. The new bank holds nearly $1 of every $12 Americans put in banks; its 4,300
branch offices and 13,000 ATMs span 21 states and 38 countries.

Bank holding companies and bank mergers have reduced the number of banks but have
increased the number of branches. Exhibit 6 shows the number of commercial banks and bank
branches in the United States since 1934. The number of banks remained relatively constant
between 1934 and the mid-1980s but then declined, falling from 14,400 in 1985 to 8,300 in
2000 as a result of failures, mergers, and holding companies. The number of bank branches
increased steadily, multiplying from 3,000 in 1934 to 63,300 in 2000. So the number of
branches per bank increased. In 1985, the average bank had about three branches; by 2000,
the average bank had eight branches.

As failed banks disappeared or merged with stronger banks, the industry got healthier. Bank
profits grew fourfold during the 1990s. As shown earlier in Exhibit 5, the number of bank failures dropped to only 6 in 2000, down from a high of 280 in 1988. Still, bank mergers and the
resulting national banking system is no guarantee against bank failure. The following case study
discusses recent banking problems in Japan, a country with fewer than 100 commercial banks.

CASE**STUDY**	Banking Troubles in Japan
	● *Public Policy*

Prior to the 1980s, financial markets in Japan were heavily regulated, with restrictions on the
interest rates that banks could offer. After deregulation, banks became more aggressive in attracting deposits and more willing to make riskier loans, particularly in real estate. For example, the
Kizu Credit Cooperative, by paying high interest rates, increased deposits from $2 billion in
1988 to $12 billion by 1995. Kizu lent these deposits to finance risky real estate purchases.

When Japanese property values collapsed in the 1990s, banks were in trouble. As the bad
loans piled up, Japan experienced its first bank failures since World War II. Banks that grew

the fastest during the go-go era, such as Kizu, were among the first casualties. According to the Japanese finance minister, bank losses in the country totaled $350 billion by 1997.

Although many Japanese banks failed, regulatory officials appear reluctant to close down banks that are financially insolvent. Much of the Japanese banking system still consists of zombies, living-dead banks kept alive by transfusions from the central bank. One problem with the banking crisis in Japan is that nobody knows how bad off banks really are because reporting requirements there are much looser than in the United States. For example, on a per-capita basis, there are 12 times more auditors in the United States than in Japan. The so-called *lack of transparency* in Japanese accounting magnifies the impact of whatever information does become public. For example, when Fuji Bank reported that its problem loans were 50 percent larger than it had previously disclosed, Fuji's share price plunged, along with shares of other banks.

To resolve its banking crisis, the Japanese government in 1998 began using public funds to bail out troubled banks. By early 1999, about $75 billion had been earmarked to shore up 15 major banks. In April 2001, new data showed Japanese banks and credit unions had as much as $1.2 trillion in problem loans, equivalent to about 30 percent of Japan's GDP. This makes Japan's banking problem about five times bigger, in relative terms, than the U.S. savings-and-loan problem. On a positive note, Japan's new Prime Minister Junichiro Koizumo asked banks to speed up plans to write off bad loans. Still, with Japan stuck in its worst economy in decades, the bank sector will likely get worse before it gets better. Bank regulators warned that because of corporate bankruptcies, loans will continue to turn bad at about the same rate that banks write off existing bad loans, so the country's banks will make little progress at reducing bad loan totals until 2004.

\<interactive\>exercise

eACTIVITY: BANKING TROUBLES IN JAPAN

Sources: "Duffer," *Economist,* 21 April 2001; David Ibison, "Japan Investment Banking," *Financial Times,* 12 April 2001; Jason Singer, "Regulators Admit That Japanese Banks Will Be Slow to Relieve Bad-Loan Burden," *Wall Street Journal,* 30 August 2001; and Stephanie Strom, "Japan's New Prime Minister Challenges Nation to Change," *New York Times,* 30 April 2001. An English-language Web site for Japan's central bank, the Bank of Japan, can be found at http://www.boj.or.jp/en/index.htm.

CONCLUSION

Money has grown increasingly more abstract over time, moving from commodity money to paper money that represented a claim on some commodity such as gold, to paper money with no intrinsic value. As you will see, paper money constitutes only a fraction of the money supply. Modern money also consists of electronic entries in the banking system's computers. So money has changed from a physical commodity to an electronic entry. Money today does not so much change hands as change computer accounts.

Money and banking have been intertwined ever since the early goldsmiths offered to hold customers' valuables for safekeeping. Banking has evolved from one of the most staid industries to one of the most competitive. Deregulation and branching innovations have increased competition and have expanded the types of bank deposits. Reforms have given the Federal Reserve System more uniform control over all depository institutions and have given the institutions greater access to the services provided by the Fed. Thus, all depository institutions can compete on more equal footing.

Deregulation provides greater freedom not only to prosper but also to fail. Failures of depository institutions create a special problem, however, because these institutions provide the financial underpinning of the nation's money supply, as you will see in the next chapter. There we will examine more closely how banks operate and supply the nation's money.

endofchaptermaterial

- **Summary**
- **Questions for Review**
- **Problems and Exercises**
- **Experiential Exercises**
- **Wall Street Journal Exercise**

Take the Post-Test to assess your overall understanding of the key ideas in this chapter. The Post-Test provides a comprehensive selection of exam-style questions addressing the main topics and concepts of the chapter. At the completion of each Post-Test, you will receive a score and instructive feedback on how you answered each question, and a direct link to the part of the chapter addressed in the question. Take the Post-Test as often as you need to—a record of your progress for each attempt is kept for you to revisit and gauge your improvement. And each Post-Test is randomly generated, so every attempt is new.

29

Banking and the Money Supply

How do banks create money? Why are banks called First Trust or Security National rather than Benny's Bank or Easy Money Bank and Trust? Why are we so interested in banks, anyway? After all, isn't banking a business like any other, such as dry cleaning, auto manufacturing, or home remodeling? Why not devote a chapter to the home-remodeling business? Answers to these and related questions are provided in this chapter, which examines banking and the money supply.

In this chapter, we take a closer look at the unique role banks play in the economy. Banks are special in macro-economics because, like the London goldsmith, they can convert a borrower's IOU into money, and an adequate supply of money is a key ingredient to a healthy economy. Because regulatory reforms have eliminated many of the distinctions between commercial banks and thrift institutions, and because thrifts represent a dwindling share of depository institutions, from here on, all depository institutions will usually be referred to more simply as *banks*.

We begin by going over definitions of money, from the narrowest to the broadest. Then we look at how banks work and how they create money. We also consider the operation of the Federal Reserve System in more detail. As we will see, the Federal Reserve, or the Fed, attempts to control the money supply directly by issuing currency and indirectly by controlling bank reserves. Topics discussed in this chapter include:

PHOTO: © IMAGE 100

- Money aggregates
- Checkable deposits
- Balance sheets
- Money creation
- Money multiplier
- Tools of the Fed

Pre-Test

Take the Pre-Test to assess your initial knowledge of the key ideas in this chapter. The Pre-Test provides exam-style questions addressing the main topics and concepts of the chapter. At the completion of each Pre-Test, you will receive a score and instructive feed-back on how you answered each question, and a direct link to the part of the chapter addressed in the question. Take the Pre-Test as often as you need to—a record of your progress for each attempt is kept for you to revisit and gauge your improvement.

\<interactive\>exercise

ECONDEBATE ONLINE: MONEY AND THE FINANCIAL SYSTEM

\<interactive\>update

- **ECONDATA ONLINE: MONEY AND THE FINANCIAL SYSTEM**
- **ECONLINKS ONLINE: ECONOMICS WEB LINKS**
- **ECONNEWS ONLINE: MONEY AND THE FINANCIAL SYSTEM**

MONEY AGGREGATES

When you think of money, what comes to mind is probably currency—dollar bills and coins. But as you learned in the last chapter, dollar bills and coins account for only a portion of the money supply. In this section, we consider three definitions of money.

The Narrow Definition of Money: M1

Suppose you have some cash with you right now—dollar bills and coins. Dollar bills and coins are part of the money supply as it is narrowly defined. If you were to deposit this cash in a checking account, you could then write checks directing your bank to pay someone from your account. **Checkable deposits,** or deposits against which checks can be written, are also part of the narrow definition of money. Checkable deposits can also be tapped with an ATM card, or debit card, which can be used at a growing number of retailers.

Banks hold a variety of checkable deposits. The most important over the years have been *demand deposits,* which are held mostly by commercial banks and do not earn interest. In recent years, financial institutions have developed other kinds of accounts that carry check-writing privileges but also earn interest, such as negotiable order of withdrawal (NOW) accounts.

Money aggregates are various measures of the money supply defined by the Federal Reserve. The narrowest definition, called **M1,** consists of currency (including coins) held by the nonbanking public, checkable deposits, and traveler's checks. Note that currency sitting in bank vaults is not counted as part of the money supply because it is not being used as a medium of exchange. But checkable deposits are money because their owners can write checks and use debit cards to tap them. Checkable deposits are the liabilities of the issuing banks, which stand ready to convert them into currency. But unlike cash, checks are not legal tender, as signs that say "No Checks!" attest.

The primary currency circulating in the United States consists of Federal Reserve notes, which are printed by the U.S. Bureau of Engraving and Printing and are issued by, and are liabilities of, the Federal Reserve Banks. Over three-fourths of the Fed's liabilities consist of Federal Reserve notes. The Fed spends about $700 million a year printing, storing, and distributing notes—the Fed's largest single expense. Because Federal Reserve notes are redeemable for nothing other than more Federal Reserve notes, U.S. currency is *fiat money,* as already mentioned. The other component of currency is coins, manufactured and distributed by the U.S. Mint. Like paper money, U.S. coins are token money because their metal values are less—usually much less—than their face values (as noted in the last chapter, a quarter costs about 3 cents to make).

More than half the Federal Reserve notes now in circulation are in foreign hands. Some countries, such as Panama, Ecuador, and El Salvador, use U.S. currency as their money. This is actually a good deal for Americans because a $100 bill that costs only about 5 cents to produce can be "sold" to foreigners for $100 worth of goods and services. It's as if these countries were granting us an interest-free loan during the period the dollar remains in circulation abroad, usually several years. But having our currency used around the world poses a special problem when it comes to counterfeiting, as discussed in the following case study.

CASE**STUDY**	Faking It
	● *Public Policy*

Until recently U.S. currency had changed little—so little, in fact, that on the back of a $10 bill the car driving by the U.S. Treasury building dated back to the 1920s. Since 1879, Crane & Company has been the exclusive supplier of U.S. currency paper. That paper is 75 percent cotton and 25 percent linen, with embedded red and blue fibers.

One threat to the integrity of U.S. currency is the so-called supernote—a counterfeit $100 bill of extremely high quality that began showing up around 1990. The supernote is a remarkable forgery, including sequential serial numbers and a polymer security thread that had taken Crane years to develop. By perfectly emulating the magnetic field generated by ferrous oxide inked into Benjamin Franklin's portrait, the supernote can fool currency-scanning machines at the nation's 12 Federal Reserve banks. Supernotes are ubiquitous abroad, especially in Europe. Up to one-fifth of the $100 bills circulating in Russia in a recent year were believed to be fake. Because of the supernote, merchants and bank tellers in Europe and the Far East grew reluctant to accept $100 bills.

Expert engravers produce the supernote, but technological improvements in copy machines, computers, and printers now allow even amateurs to make passable counterfeits. Of the fake bills found in the United States in 2000, half were produced with computers, copiers, and printers, up from just 1 percent five years earlier. On U.S. soil, the Secret Service has been able to seize most counterfeit money before it gets into circulation. But foreign counterfeiting poses a problem for the Secret Service, which is primarily a domestic police force (few of the 2,000 agents work abroad). Most counterfeit money seized in the United States is printed abroad, and the volume of seizures outside the United States has been growing.

To combat the supernote and other improvements in counterfeiting technology, U.S. currency was recently redesigned for the first time since 1929. But the new design is not a radical departure. The new bills are the same size as the old ones and printed on the same Crane paper in the same green and black ink. Changes to the $100 bill include a new off-center portrait of Franklin, microprinting around the portrait that repeats the phrase "The United States of America," a watermark image of Franklin, and a "100" that shifts from green to black when viewed from different angles. A new security thread buried in the paper repeats "USA 100" in print 42-thousandths of an inch tall. This lettering is visible when held up to light but is not reproducible in a photocopier, and the thread glows red under ultraviolet light.

New $50, $20, $10, and $5 bills have also been issued, each with its own security features, such as a security strip with a distinct color under ultraviolet light. The $1 bill is not scheduled for a makeover because it is not yet popular with counterfeiters. Apparently, the cost of counterfeiting a $1 bill and the risk of trying to pass it exceed the benefits.

Counterfeiters are fighting back. The watermark is faked by light printing. The security strip is faked by laboriously threading material between the two thin sheets that make up the bill. The hardest features to fake are microprinting, fine-line printing patterns, and details in the U.S. Treasury seal. The $20 bill is most popular among domestic counterfeiters, and the $100 bill most popular among foreign counterfeiters. Colombia is now the world's largest source of bogus American currency, accounting for 40 percent of the world total. Colombia borders on Ecuador, which converted to the U.S. dollar in 2000 and thus offers a ready outlet for counterfeits.

The United States has a policy of never recalling existing currency for fear that the world's hoarders of dollars might switch to other currencies, like euros or yen (remember, we want foreigners to hold onto U.S. dollars). Over time, preference for the new currency and the replacement of old bills as they pass through the Fed will eventually eliminate old bills. But the two types of currency will circulate for some time, especially $100 bills. To give you some idea how long this could take, U.S. bills of $500 and up were last printed in 1946, and the Fed began taking them out of circulation in 1969. Yet hundreds of thousands of these big bills are still hoarded by the public, more than a half century after they were last printed. Some still show up at Federal Reserve Banks, where they are destroyed.

<interactive>**exercise**

- eACTIVITY: FAKING IT
- READING IT RIGHT: WALL STREET JOURNAL EXERCISE

Sources: Frederic Dannen and Ira Silverman, "The Supernote," *New Yorker,* 23 October 1995, pp. 50–55; Dan Molinski, "Colombia Officials Raid Bogus Cash Ring in Medellin," Dow Jones Newswire, 29 March 2001; and Kirk Semple, "How They Make a Fake," *New York Times,* 15 October 2000. The U.S. Treasury has a Web site providing information about the new bills at http://www.moneyfactory.com/section.cfm/4 .

Broader Money Aggregates

We regard currency and checkable deposits as money because each serves as a medium of exchange, a unit of account, and a store of value. Some other financial assets perform the store-of-value function and sometimes can be readily converted into currency or to checkable deposits. Because these are so close to money, we call them money under a broader definition.

Savings deposits earn interest but have no specific maturity date. Banks often allow depositors to shift funds from savings accounts to checking accounts by using a phone, an ATM, or an online account, so distinctions between narrow and broad definitions of money have become blurred. **Time deposits** (also called *certificates of deposit,* or *CDs*) earn a fixed rate of interest if held for a specified period, ranging from several months to several years. Premature withdrawals are penalized by forfeiture of several months' interest. Neither savings deposits nor time deposits serve directly as media of exchange, so they are not included in M1, the narrowest definition of money.

Money market mutual fund accounts, mentioned in the previous chapter, represent another component of money when defined more broadly. But, because of restrictions on the minimum balance, on the number of checks that can be written per month, and on the minimum amount of each check, these popular accounts are not viewed as money when narrowly defined.

Recall that M1 consists of currency (including coins) held by the nonbanking public, checkable deposits, and traveler's checks. **M2** is a money aggregate that includes M1 as well as savings deposits, small-denomination time deposits, and money market mutual fund accounts. **M3** includes M2 plus large-denomination time deposits ($100,000 or more). M3 is less liquid than M2, which is less liquid than M1. The size and relative importance of each money aggregate are presented in Exhibit 1. As you can see, compared to M1, M2 is nearly five times larger and M3 is nearly seven times larger. Thus, the narrowest definition of money describes only a fraction of broader aggregates. And distinctions between M1 and M2 become less meaningful as banks allow depositors to transfer funds from one account to another.

You may be curious why the definitions of money include debit cards but not credit cards, such as VISA and MasterCard. After all, most sellers accept credit cards as readily as they accept cash or checks (some even prefer credit cards to checks), and credit cards account for 20 percent of all consumer spending. Credit cards themselves are not money but a convenient way of obtaining a short-term loan from the card issuer. If you buy an airline ticket with a credit card, the card issuer lends you the money to pay for the ticket. You don't use money until you repay the credit card issuer. The credit card has not eliminated your use of money; it has merely delayed it. On the other hand, when you use your debit card at a grocery store or drugstore, you tap directly into your checking account, paying with electronic money—part of M1.

HOW BANKS WORK

Banks are profit-making institutions in the business of taking people's money on deposit, lending out a large portion, and earning a profit on the difference between the interest paid on deposits and the interest received from loans. Banks attract funds from savers to lend to borrowers. Savers need a safe place for their money, and borrowers need credit; banks try to earn a profit by serving both groups. To inspire depositor confidence, banks usually present an image of sober dignity—an image meant to foster trust and assurance. For example, they are more apt to be called First Trust, Security National, or Federal Savings than Benny's Bank, Easy Money Bank and Trust, or Loans 'R' Us. In contrast, *finance companies* are financial intermediaries that do not get their funds from depositors, so they can choose names aimed at borrowers—names such as Household Finance, The Money Store, and Home Improvement Loan Online.

<interactive>video

ASK THE INSTRUCTOR: HOW ARE BANKS DIFFERENT FROM OTHER BUSINESSES?

EXHIBIT 1

Alternative Measures of the Money Supply (September 2001)

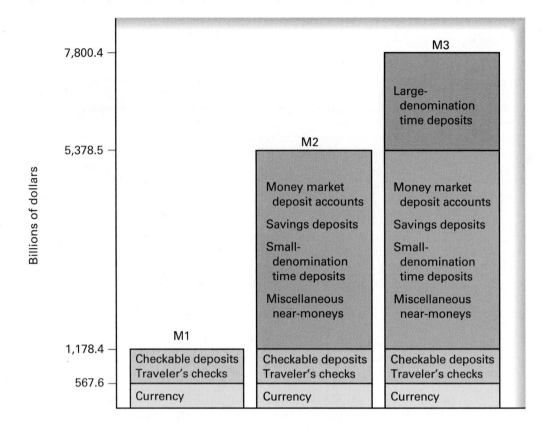

Source: Based on monthly estimates from the Federal Reserve Board. For the latest data, go to http://www. federalreserve.gov/releases/H6/current/.

Banks Are Financial Intermediaries

By bringing together the two sides of the money market, banks serve as financial intermediaries, or as go-betweens. They gather various amounts from savers and repackage these funds into the amounts demanded by borrowers. Some savers need their money next week, some next year, some only after retirement. Likewise, different borrowers want to borrow for different lengths of time. Banks, as intermediaries, offer desirable durations to both savers and borrowers. In short, *banks reduce the transaction costs of channeling savings to creditworthy borrowers.* Here's how.

Coping with Asymmetric Information. Banks, as lenders, try to identify borrowers who are willing to pay interest and are able to repay the loans. But borrowers have more reliable information about their own credit history and financial plans than do lenders. Thus, in the market for loans, there is **asymmetric information**—an inequality in what's known by each party to the transaction. Asymmetric information is unequal information. This asymmetry would not create a problem if borrowers could be trusted to report relevant details to lenders. Some borrowers, however, have an incentive to suppress important information, such as other debts, a troubled financial history, or plans to put the borrowed funds into a risky venture. Because they have experience and expertise in evaluating the creditworthiness of loan applicants, banks have a greater ability to cope with asymmetric information than an individual saver would. Moreover, because banks have experience in drawing up and enforcing contracts with borrowers, they can do so more cheaply than an individual saver could. Thus, savers are better off dealing with banks than making loans directly to the ultimate borrower. *The economy is more efficient because banks develop expertise in evaluating borrowers, structuring loans, and enforcing loan contracts.*

Reducing Risk Through Diversification. By developing a diversified portfolio of assets rather than lending funds to a single borrower, banks reduce the risk to each individual saver. A bank, in effect, lends a tiny fraction of each saver's deposits to each of its many borrowers. If one borrower fails to repay a loan, this failure will hardly affect a large, diversified bank. Certainly such a default does not represent the personal disaster it would if one saver's entire nest egg was loaned directly to that defaulting borrower.

<interactive>update

ECONNEWS ONLINE: BANKS BEHAVING BADLY?

Starting a Bank

Let's begin with the formation of a bank. We could consider the operation of any type of depository institution (commercial bank, savings and loan, mutual savings bank, or credit union), but we will focus on commercial banks because they are the most important in terms of total assets. Moreover, the operating principles apply to other depository institutions as well.

Suppose some business leaders in your hometown want to establish a commercial bank called Home Bank. To obtain a *charter,* or the right to operate, they must apply to the state banking authority in the case of a state bank or to the U.S. Comptroller of the Currency in the case of a national bank. The chartering agency reviewing the application considers the quality of management, the need for an additional bank in the region, and the likely success of the bank.

Suppose the founders plan to invest $500,000 in the bank, and they so indicate on their application for a national charter. If their application is approved, they incorporate, issuing themselves shares of stock—certificates of ownership. Thus, they exchange $500,000 for shares of stock in the bank. These shares are called the *owners' equity,* or the **net worth,** of the bank. Part of the $500,000, say $50,000, is used to buy shares in their district Federal Reserve Bank. So Home Bank is now a member of the Federal Reserve System. With the remaining $450,000, the owners acquire and furnish the bank building.

To focus our discussion, we will examine the bank's **balance sheet,** presented in Exhibit 2. As the name implies, a balance sheet shows a balance between the two sides of the bank's accounts. The left side lists the bank's assets. An **asset** is any physical property or financial claim owned by the bank. At this early stage, assets include the building and equipment owned by Home Bank plus its stock in the district Federal Reserve Bank. The right side lists the bank's liabilities and net worth. A **liability** is an amount the bank owes. So far the bank owes nothing, so the right side includes only the net worth of $500,000. The two sides of the ledger must always be equal, or in *balance,* which is why we call it a *balance sheet.* So assets must equal liabilities plus net worth:

$$\text{Assets} = \text{Liabilities} + \text{Net worth}$$

The bank is now ready for business. Opening day is the bank's lucky day, because the first customer carries in a briefcase full of $100 bills and deposits $1,000,000 into a new checking account. In accepting this, the bank promises to repay the depositor that amount. The deposit

EXHIBIT 2

Home Bank's Balance Sheet

Assets		Liabilities and Net Worth	
Building and furniture	$450,000	Net worth	$500,000
Stock in district Fed	50,000		
Total	$500,000	Total	$500,000

EXHIBIT 3

Home Bank's Balance Sheet After $1,000,000 Deposit

Assets		Liabilities and Net Worth	
Cash	$1,000,000	Checkable deposits	$1,000,000
Building and furniture	450,000	Net worth	500,000
Stock in district Fed	50,000		
Total	$1,500,000	Total	$1,500,000

therefore is an amount the bank owes—it's a liability of the bank. As a result of this deposit, the bank's assets increase by $1,000,000 in cash and its liabilities increase by $1,000,000 in checkable deposits. Exhibit 3 shows the effects of this transaction on Home Bank's balance sheet. The right side now shows two claims on the bank's assets: claims by the owners, called net worth, and claims by nonowners, called liabilities, which at this point consist of checkable deposits.

Reserve Accounts

Where do we go from here? As mentioned in the previous chapter, banks are required by the Fed to set aside, or to hold in reserve, a percentage of their checkable deposits. The dollar amount that must be held in reserve is called **required reserves**—checkable deposits multiplied by the required reserve ratio. The **required reserve ratio** dictates the minimum proportion of deposits the bank must hold in reserve. The current reserve requirement is 10 percent on checkable deposits (other types of deposits have no reserve requirement). All depository institutions are subject to the reserve requirements established by the Fed. Reserves are held either as cash in the bank's vault or as deposits at the Fed, but neither earns the bank any interest. Home Bank must therefore hold $100,000 as reserves, which equals 10 percent times $1,000,000.

Suppose Home Bank deposits $100,000 in a reserve account with its district Federal Reserve Bank. Home Bank's reserves now consist of $100,000 in required reserves on deposit with the Fed and $900,000 in **excess reserves** held as cash in the vault. So far Home Bank has not earned a penny. Excess reserves, however, can be used to make loans or to purchase interest-bearing assets, such as government bonds. By law, the bank's interest-bearing assets are limited primarily to loans and to government securities (if a bank is owned by a holding company, the holding company has broader latitude in the kinds of assets it can hold).

Liquidity Versus Profitability

Like the early goldsmiths, modern banks must be prepared to satisfy depositors' requests for funds. A bank loses reserves whenever a depositor withdraws cash or writes a check that is deposited in another bank. The bank must be in a position to satisfy all depositor demands, even if many depositors ask for their money at the same time. Required reserves are not meant to be used to meet depositor requests for funds; therefore, banks often hold some excess reserves or other assets, such as government bonds, that can be easily converted to cash to satisfy any unexpected demand for funds. Banks may also want to hold excess reserves in case a valued customer needs an immediate loan.

The bank manager must therefore structure the portfolio of assets with an eye toward liquidity but must not forget that the bank's survival also depends on profitability. **Liquidity** is the ease with which an asset can be converted into cash without a significant loss of value. *The objectives of liquidity and profitability are at odds.* For example, the bank will generally find that the assets offering a higher interest rate are less liquid than other assets offering a lower interest rate. The most liquid asset is bank reserves, either in the bank's vault as cash or on account with the Fed, but reserves earn no interest.

At one extreme, suppose a bank is completely liquid, holding all its assets as cash reserves. Such a bank would clearly have no difficulty meeting depositors' demands for funds. The bank is playing it safe—too safe. With no interest-earning assets, the bank earns no income and will fail. At the other extreme, suppose a bank uses all its excess reserves to acquire high-yielding but illiquid assets, such as long-term loans. Such a bank will run into problems whenever withdrawals exceed new deposits. There is a trade-off between liquidity and profitability. The portfolio manager's task is to strike just the right balance between liquidity, or safety, and profitability.

Because reserves earn no interest, banks usually try to keep excess reserves to a minimum. Banks continuously "sweep" their accounts to find excess reserves that can be put to some interest-bearing use. They do not let excess reserves remain idle even overnight. The **federal funds market** provides for day-to-day lending and borrowing among banks of excess reserves on account at the Fed. These funds usually do not leave the Fed—instead, they shift among accounts. For example, suppose that at the end of the business day, Home Bank has excess reserves of $100,000 on account with the Fed and wants to lend that amount to another bank that finished the day with a deficiency in required reserves of $100,000. These two banks are brought together by a broker who specializes in the market for federal funds—that is, the market for reserves at the Fed. The interest rate paid on this loan is called the **federal funds rate;** this is the rate the Fed targets as a tool of monetary policy, but more on that later.

Let's now discuss how the Fed, Home Bank, and the banking system as a whole can create money.

HOW BANKS CREATE MONEY

This section is about how the Fed and the banking system create fiat money. Our discussion focuses on the behavior of commercial banks because these are the largest and most important depository institutions, although thrifts can carry out similar functions. Excess reserves are the raw material the banking system employs to support the creation of money.

Creating Money Through Excess Reserves

Suppose Home Bank has already used its $900,000 in excess reserves to make loans and buy government bonds and has no excess reserves left. In fact, let's assume there are no excess reserves in the banking system. With that as a point of departure, let's walk through the money creation process.

Round One. To start, suppose the Fed buys a $1,000 U.S. government bond from a securities dealer, with the transaction handled by the dealer's bank—Home Bank. The Fed pays the dealer by crediting Home Bank's reserve account with $1,000, so Home Bank can increase the dealer's checking account by $1,000. Where does the Fed get these reserves? It makes them up—creates them out of thin air, out of electronic ether! The securities dealer has exchanged one asset, a U.S. bond, for another asset, checkable deposits. A U.S. bond is not money, but checkable deposits are, so the money supply increases by $1,000 in this first round. Exhibit 4 shows changes in Home Bank's balance sheet as a result of the Fed's bond purchase. On the assets side, Home Bank's reserves at the Fed increase by $1,000. On the liabilities side, checkable deposits increase by $1,000. Of the dealer's $1,000 checkable deposit, Home Bank must set aside $100 in required reserves (based on a 10 percent required reserve ratio). The remaining $900 is excess reserves, which can fuel a further increase in the money supply.

Round Two. Suppose Home Bank is your regular bank, and you apply for a $900 student loan to help pay student fees. Home Bank approves your loan and increases your checking account by $900. *Home Bank has converted your promise to repay, your IOU, into a $900 checkable deposit. Because checkable deposits are money, this action increases the money supply by $900.* The money supply has increased by a total of $1,900 to this point—the $1,000 increase in the securities dealer's checkable deposits and now the $900 increase in your checkable deposits. In the process, what had been $900 in Home Bank's excess reserves now back up its loan to you (remember, a bank can lend no more than its excess reserves). As shown in Exhibit 5, Home

EXHIBIT 4

Changes in Home Bank's Balance Sheet After the Fed Buys a
$1,000 Bond from a Securities Dealer

Assets		Liabilities and Net Worth	
Reserves at Fed	+ $1,000	Checkable deposits	+ $1,000

EXHIBIT 5

Changes in Home Bank's Balance Sheet After Lending $900 to You

Assets		Liabilities and Net Worth	
Loans	+$900	Checkable deposits	+$900

Bank's loans increase by $900 on the assets side because your IOU becomes the bank's asset. On the bank's liabilities side, checkable deposits increase by $900 because the bank has increased your account by that amount. In short, Home Bank has created $900 in checkable deposits based on your promise to repay the loan.

When you write a $900 check for college fees, your college promptly deposits the check into its checking account at Merchants Trust, which increases the college's account by $900, and sends your check to the Fed. The Fed transfers $900 in reserves from Home Bank's account to Merchants Trust's account. The Fed then sends the check to Home Bank, which reduces your checkable deposits by $900. The Fed has thereby "cleared" your check by settling the claim that Merchants Trust had on Home Bank. The $900 in checkable deposits has simply shifted banks, so the total increase in the money supply to this point is still $1,900.

Round Three. Merchants Trust now has $900 more in reserves on deposit with the Fed. After setting aside $90 as required reserves, or 10 percent of your college's checkable deposit increase, the bank has $810 in excess reserves. Suppose Merchants Trust loans this $810 to an English major who is starting a new business called "Note This," a note-taking service for students in large classes. Exhibit 6 shows assets at Merchants Trust are up by $810 in loans, and liabilities are up by $810 in checkable deposits. At this point, checkable deposits in the banking system, and the money supply in the economy, are up by a total of $2,710 (= $1,000 + $900 + $810), all engendered by the Fed's original $1,000 bond purchase.

The $810 loan is spent at the college bookstore, which deposits the check in its account at Fidelity Bank. Fidelity credits the bookstore's checkable deposits with $810 and sends the check to the Fed for clearance. The Fed reduces Merchants Bank's reserves by $810 and increases Fidelity's by the same amount. The Fed then sends the check to Merchants, which reduces the English major's checkable deposits by $810. So checkable deposits are down by $810 at Merchants and up by the same amount at Fidelity. Checkable deposits are still up by $2,710, as the $810 in checkable deposits has simply shifted from Merchants Trust to Fidelity Bank.

Round Four and Beyond. We could continue the process with Fidelity Bank setting aside $81 in required reserves and lending $729 in excess reserves, but you get the idea of money creation by now. Notice the pattern of deposits and loans emerging from the analysis. Each time a bank gets a fresh deposit, 10 percent goes to required reserves. The rest becomes excess reserves, which fuel new loans or other asset acquisitions. In our example, excess reserves are a prerequisite to support a loan that increases the borrower's checkable deposits. The borrower writes a check, which the recipient deposits in a checking account, thereby generating excess reserves to support still more loans. Because this example began with the Fed, the Fed can rightfully claim, "The buck starts here"—a slogan that appears on a large plaque in the Federal Reserve chairman's office.

EXHIBIT 6

Changes in Merchants Trust's Balance Sheet After Lending $810 to an English Major

Assets		Liabilities and Net Worth	
Loans	+ $810	Checkable deposits	+ $810

An individual bank can lend no more than its excess reserves. When the borrower spends the amount loaned, reserves at one bank usually fall, but total reserves in the banking system do not. The recipient bank uses most of the new deposit to extend more loans, creating more checkable deposits. The potential expansion of checkable deposits in the banking system therefore equals some multiple of the initial increase in reserves. Note that our example assumes that banks do not allow excess reserves to sit idle, that borrowed funds do not idle in checking accounts, and that the public does not choose to hold some of the newly created money as cash. If excess reserves remained just that or if borrowed funds idled in checking accounts, they obviously could not fuel an expansion of the money supply. And if people chose to hold some of the newly created money as cash rather than in checking accounts, then that portion of borrowed funds could not provide additional reserves in the banking system.

A Summary of the Rounds

Let's review the money creation process: *The initial and most important step is the Fed's injection of $1,000 in fresh reserves into the banking system.* By paying the securities dealer for the bond, the Fed instantly increased the money supply by $1,000. Home Bank set aside $100 as required reserves and lent you its $900 in excess reserves. You paid your college fees, and the $900 ended up in your college's checkable account. This fueled more money creation, as shown in a series of rounds of Exhibit 7. As you can see, during each round, the increase in checkable deposits (column 1) minus the increase in required reserves (column 2) equals the potential increase in loans (column 3). Checkable deposits in this example can potentially increase by as much as $10,000.

In our example, money creation results from the Fed's $1,000 bond purchase from the securities dealer, but excess reserves would also have increased if the Fed purchased a $1,000 bond from Home Bank, lent Home Bank $1,000 in the form of a discount loan, or freed up $1,000 in excess reserves by lowering the reserve requirement.

What if the Fed paid the securities dealer in cash? By exchanging Federal Reserve notes, which become part of the money supply in the hands of the public, for a U.S. bond, which is not part of the money supply, the Fed would have increased the money supply by $1,000. Once the securities dealer put this cash into a checking account—or spent the cash, so the money ended up in someone else's checking account—the banking system's money creation process would have been off and running.

Reserve Requirements and Money Expansion

The banking system as a whole eliminates excess reserves by expanding the money supply. With a 10 percent reserve requirement, the Fed's initial injection of $1,000 in fresh reserves could support up to $10,000 in new checkable deposits in the banking system as a whole, *assuming no bank holds excess reserves, borrowers do not let their funds sit idle, and borrowers do not want to hold cash.*

EXHIBIT 7

Summary of the Money Creation Process Resulting from the Fed's
Purchase of a $1,000 U.S. Government Bond

Bank	(1) Increase in Checkable Deposits	(2) Increase in Required Reserves	(3) Increase in Loans (3) = (1) − (2)
1. Home Bank	$ 1,000	$ 100	$ 900
2. Merchants Trust	900	90	810
3. Fidelity Bank	810	81	729
All remaining rounds	7,290	729	6,561
Totals	$10,000	$1,000	$9,000

The multiple by which the money supply increases as a result of an increase in the banking system's reserves is called the **money multiplier.** The **simple money multiplier** equals the reciprocal of the required reserve ratio, or $1/r$, where r is the reserve ratio. In our example, the reserve ratio was 10 percent, or 0.1, so the reciprocal is $1/0.1$, which equals 10. The formula for the multiple expansion of checkable deposits can be written as:

Change in checkable deposits (or the money supply) = Change in fresh reserves $\times 1/r$

Again, the simple money multiplier assumes that banks hold no excess reserves, that borrowers do not let the funds sit idle, and that people do not want to hold cash. The higher the reserve requirement, the greater the fraction of deposits that must be held as reserves, so the smaller the money multiplier. A reserve requirement of 20 percent instead of 10 percent would require each bank to set aside twice as much in required reserves. The simple money multiplier in this case would be $1/0.2$, which equals 5, and the maximum possible increase in checkable deposits resulting from an initial $1,000 increase in fresh reserves would therefore be $1,000 \times$ 5, or $5,000. *Excess reserves fuel the deposit expansion process, and a higher reserve requirement drains this fuel from the banking system, thereby reducing the amount of new money that can be created.*

On the other hand, with a reserve requirement of only 5 percent, banks would set aside less for required reserves, leaving more excess reserves available for loans. The simple money multiplier in that case would be $1/0.05$, or 20. With $1,000 in fresh reserves and a 5 percent reserve requirement, the banking system could increase the money supply by a maximum of $1,000 \times 20$, which equals $20,000. Thus, the change in the required reserve ratio affects the banking system's ability to create money.

In summary, money creation usually begins with the Fed injecting new reserves into the banking system. An individual bank lends an amount no greater than its excess reserves. The borrower's spending ends up in someone else's checking account, fueling additional loans. *The fractional reserve requirement is the key to the multiple expansion of checkable deposits.* If each $1 deposit had to be backed by $1 in required reserves, the money multiplier would be reduced to 1.

Limitations on Money Expansion

Various leakages from the multiple expansion process reduce the size of the money multiplier, which is why $1/r$ is called the *simple* money multiplier. To repeat, our example assumed (1) that banks do not let excess reserves sit idle, (2) that borrowers do something with the money, and (3) that people do not choose to increase their cash holdings. With regard to the first assumption, idle excess reserves represent an opportunity cost for banks, so banks have a profit incentive to make a loan or buy some other interest-bearing asset with excess reserves. The second assumption is also easy to defend. Why would people borrow money if they didn't plan to spend it? The third assumption is trickier. Cash may sometimes be preferable to checking accounts because cash is more versatile, so people may choose to hold some of the newly created money as cash. To the extent that people prefer to hold cash, this drains reserves from the banking system. With reduced reserves, banks are less able to make loans, reducing the money multiplier. Incidentally, for the money multiplier to operate, a particular bank need not use excess reserves in a specific way; it could use them to pay all its employees a Christmas bonus, for that matter. As long as that spending ends up as checkable deposits in the banking system, away we go with the money expansion process.

Multiple Contraction of the Money Supply

We have already outlined the money creation process, so the story of how the Federal Reserve System can reduce bank reserves, thereby reducing the money supply, can be a brief one. Again, we begin by assuming there are no excess reserves in the system and the reserve requirement is 10 percent. Suppose the Fed *sells* a $1,000 U.S. bond to a securities dealer and gets paid with a check drawn on the security dealer's account with Home Bank. So the Fed gets its money by drawing down Home Bank's reserves at the Fed by $1,000. The Fed has thereby reduced the money supply by $1,000 in this first round.

Home Bank's reserves at the Fed are down by $1,000. Because the dealer's checking account was reduced by $1,000, Home Bank no longer needs to hold $100 in required reserves. But Home Bank is still short $900 in required reserves (remember, when we started, there were no excess reserves in the banking system). To replenish reserves, Home Bank must recall loans (ask for repayment before the due date), sell some other asset, or borrow additional reserves. Suppose the bank calls in a $900 loan to a local business, and the loan is repaid with a check written against Merchants Bank. When the check clears, Home Bank's reserves are up by $900, just enough to satisfy its reserve requirement, but Merchants Bank's reserves are down by $900. Because there were no excess reserves at the outset, the loss of $900 in reserves leaves Merchants $810 short of its required level of reserves, forcing that bank to get more reserves.

And so it goes down the line. The Fed's sale of government bonds reduces bank reserves, forcing banks to recall loans or to somehow replenish reserves. *The maximum possible effect is to reduce the money supply by the original reduction in bank reserves times the simple money multiplier, which again equals 1 divided by the reserve requirement, or 1/r.* In our example, the Fed's sale of $1,000 in U.S. bonds could reduce the money supply by as much as $10,000.

For a change of pace, let's end this section with a case study that looks at new developments in banking sparked by the revolution in personal computers and the Internet.

CASE**STUDY** | Banking on the Net

● *The Information Economy*

Juniper Bank never closes. It's open 24 hours a day, 365 days a year. From anywhere in the world with Internet access, bank customers can pay bills, check account balances, and borrow money. Juniper was one of the nation's first virtual banks—one of the first authorized to offer banking services on the Internet. The bank can accept deposits from customers in all 50 states, and all accounts are FDIC insured. With the money saved on buildings and bank tellers, Internet banks can offer higher interest rates.

But even customers at a virtual bank need a physical connection when it comes to getting cash and making deposits. Juniper Bank customers can get cash at thousands of ATM locations. Deposits are accepted at ATMs, through the mail, direct deposit, electronic transfers, and at any of the 4,200 Mail Boxes Etc. locations.

Juniper Bank and the few other mostly virtual banks are exceptions in that they have little physical presence beyond ATMs. The overwhelming share of banks now accessible via the Internet consists of physical banks that offer Internet banking for added convenience. For example, Wells Fargo, a bank with 4,300 branches in 22 states, has invested $1 billion in online banking and claims to be the market leader. Like some other banks, Wells Fargo also offers customers the ability to verify online all account balances, *including accounts at other banks.* Some banks even offer wireless banking for customers with Web-enabled cell phones or personal digital assistants.

With such easy access, customers are increasingly shopping nationwide for the best rates for deposits, credit cards, and loans. So a customer in St. Louis can get a mortgage in Atlanta, a car loan in Phoenix, a credit card in Boston, a checking account in New York, and a savings account in Los Angeles. For example, ING Direct offers 4 percent interest on FDIC-insured savings accounts with no minimum balance and no fees. Customers can transfer funds online between this account and online checking accounts at other banks.

The Internet could become the biggest market in history, and banks want to be part of it. Over the long run, the Internet offers convenience for customers and potential cost savings for banks. Like telephone banking, which now accounts for one-fourth of all bank transactions, the Internet reduces the need for branches and branch personnel. Citibank, for example, encourages online use by eliminating fees for those who bank online. Since online banking reduces the search costs of shopping around for the best deal, banking will become more competitive, squeezing down interest rate differences across banks for similar products.

<interactive>**exercise**

eACTIVITY: BANKING ON THE NET

Sources: Stacy Forster, "Web Banks Seek Better Way to Take Customer Deposits," *Wall Street Journal,* 20 November 2000; and Pat Maio, "Wells Fargo CEO Sees Online Unit Profitable by April '02," Dow Jones Newswire, 19 April 2001. Juniper Bank's Web address is http://www.juniper.com/, Wells Fargo's is http://www.wellsfargo.com/, and ING Direct's is http://home.ingdirect.com/.

Now that we have some idea how fractional reserve banking works, we are in a position to summarize the Federal Reserve's role in the economy.

THE FED'S TOOLS OF MONETARY CONTROL

As mentioned in the previous chapter, in its capacity as a bankers' bank, the Fed clears checks for, extends loans to, and holds deposits of banks. The Fed, through its regulation of financial markets, also tries to prevent major disruptions and financial panics. For example, during the dark days following the terrorist attacks on America of September 11, 2001, people used their ATM cards to load up on cash. Some were hoarding cash. To provide the banking system with sufficient liquidity, the Fed bought all the government securities offered for sale, purchasing a record $150 billion worth in two days.[1] The Fed also eased some regulations to facilitate bank clearances, especially for banks hit by the attacks. Fed Chairman Alan Greenspan also worked behind the scenes to ensure that banks had sufficient liquidity to calm panics in 1987, 1989, and 1998, when financial crises threatened.

As noted already, about half of the money supply as narrowly defined (M1) consists of checkable deposits. The Fed's control over checkable deposits works indirectly through its control over reserves in the banking system. You are already familiar with the Fed's three tools for controlling reserves: (1) conducting open-market operations, or the buying and selling of U.S. government bonds; (2) setting the **discount rate,** which is the interest rate the Fed charges for loans it makes to banks; and (3) setting the required reserve ratio, which is the minimum fraction of reserves that banks must hold against deposits. Let's examine each of these in more detail.

<interactive>**example**

NETBOOKMARK: THE FED'S INFRASTRUCTURE AND OPERATIONS

<interactive>video

CNN VIDEO: "BRAKING NEWS"

Open-Market Operations and the Federal Funds Rate

The Fed carries out open-market operations whenever it buys or sells U.S. government bonds in the open market. To increase the money supply, the Fed directs the New York Fed to buy U.S. bonds. The purchase of a bond by the Fed is called an **open-market purchase.** To reduce the money supply, the Fed can carry out an **open-market sale.** Policy decisions about open-market operations are made by the Federal Open Market Committee, or FOMC, which meets every six weeks. Open-market operations are relatively easy to carry out. They require no change in laws or regulations and can be executed in any amount—large or small—chosen by the Fed. Their simplicity and ease of use make them the tool of choice for the Fed.

Through open-market operations, the Fed influences bank reserves and the *federal funds rate,* which is the interest rate banks charge one another for borrowing excess reserves at the Fed, typically overnight. Banks that are unable to meet their legal reserve requirements can borrow excess reserves from other banks, paying the federal funds rate. The federal funds rate serves as a good indicator of the "tightness" of monetary policy. For example, suppose the Fed buys bonds in the open market and thereby increases reserves in the banking system. As a result, more banks have excess reserves. Demand for excess reserves in the federal funds market will fall and supply will increase, so the federal funds rate—the interest rate for reserves in this market—will decline. We can expect that this lower federal funds rate will spread quickly to the economy at large: The excess reserves that have created the lower federal funds rate will prompt banks to lower short-term interest rates in general to increase the quantity of loans demanded.

[1]Anita Rachavan, Susan Pulliam, and Jeff Opdyke, "Banks and Regulators Drew Together to Calm Rattled Markets After Attack," *Wall Street Journal,* 18 October 2001.

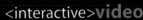 
- ECONNEWS ONLINE: THE ECONOMY RATES A 10
- ECONNEWS ONLINE: A DELICATE BALANCE

The Discount Rate

The second monetary policy tool available to the Fed is changes in the discount rate, which is the interest rate the Fed charges on loans it makes to banks. Banks can borrow from the Fed when they need reserves to satisfy their reserve requirements. If the Fed extends loans to banks, reserves increase, allowing the banking system to increase lending and thereby increasing the money supply. By lowering or raising the discount rate, the Fed encourages or discourages banks from borrowing, which alters reserves and affects the money supply. A lower discount rate reduces the cost of borrowing, encouraging banks to borrow reserves from the Fed. More bank reserves usually result in more bank lending and an increased money supply. On the other hand, a higher discount rate increases the cost of borrowing reserves from the Fed, resulting in less bank lending and a reduced money supply. The Fed's Board of Governors (not the FOMC) sets the discount rate by majority vote.

The discount rate is an imperfect tool for monetary policy because there is no guarantee that banks will necessarily borrow more even if the discount rate is reduced. If business prospects look poor and banks view lending as risky, then even a lower discount rate may not entice banks to borrow from the Fed. *The Fed uses the discount rate more as a signal to financial markets about its monetary policy than as a tool for increasing or decreasing the money supply.* The discount rate might also be thought of as an emergency tool for injecting liquidity into the banking system in the event of some financial crisis, such as a stock market crash. Banks would prefer to borrow reserves from other banks in the federal funds market rather than borrow reserves from the Fed. The Fed changes the discount rate from time to time, usually when announcing changes in the federal funds rate target, primarily to signal its intentions about interest rates. So the discount rate has become largely symbolic.

<interactive>video

ASK THE INSTRUCTOR: HOW DOES THE FED INFLUENCE INTEREST RATES?

Reserve Requirements

The Fed also influences the money supply through reserve requirements, which are regulations regarding the minimum amount of reserves that banks must hold to back up deposits. Reserve requirements influence how much money the banking system can create with each dollar of fresh reserves. If the Fed increases the reserve requirement, then banks must hold more reserves, reducing the fraction of each dollar on deposit that can be lent out. This reduces the banking system's ability to create money. On the other hand, a decrease in the reserve requirement increases the fraction of each dollar on deposit that can be lent out, which increases the banking system's ability to create money. Reserve requirements can be changed by a simple majority vote by the Board of Governors. But changes in the reserve requirement disrupt the banking system, so the Fed seldom employs this tool. As noted already, the current reserve requirement is 10 percent on checkable deposits and zero on other deposits. Some countries such as Canada, Switzerland, New Zealand, and Australia have no reserve requirement. Banks there still hold reserves to deal with everyday cash requirements and can borrow from their central banks (at high rates) if necessary.

The Fed Is a Money Machine

Over three-fourths of the Federal Reserve's assets are U.S. government bonds. These bonds, which are U.S. Treasury securities, are the result of open-market operations and are IOUs from the federal government and assets of the Fed. *Over three-fourths of the Fed's liabilities are Federal Reserve notes in circulation.* These notes—U.S. currency—are IOUs from the Fed and are therefore liabilities of the Fed. The Fed's primary asset—U.S. government bonds—earns interest, whereas the Fed's primary liability—Federal Reserve notes—requires no interest payments by the Fed.

The Fed is therefore both literally and figuratively a money machine. It is literally a money machine because it supplies the economy with Federal Reserve notes; it is figuratively a money machine because its main asset earns interest, but its main liability requires no interest payments. The Fed also earns revenue from various services it provides. After covering its operating costs, the Fed turns over any remaining income, in excess of $20 billion some years, to the U.S. Treasury.

We will learn more about how the Fed uses these tools during a discussion of monetary policy in the next chapter.

CONCLUSION

Banks play a unique role in the economy because they can transform someone's IOU into a checkable deposit, and a checkable deposit is money. The banking system's ability to expand the money supply depends on the amount of excess reserves in that system. In our example, it was the purchase of a $1,000 U.S. bond that started the ball rolling. The Fed can also increase reserves by lowering the discount rate enough to stimulate bank borrowing from the Fed (although the Fed uses changes in the discount rate more to signal its policy goals than to alter the money supply). And, by reducing the required reserve ratio, the Fed not only instantly creates excess reserves in the banking system but also increases the money multiplier. In practice, the Fed rarely changes the reserve requirement because of the disruptive effect of such a change on the banking system. *To control the money supply, the Fed relies primarily on open-market operations.*

Open-market operations can have a direct effect on the money supply, as when the Fed buys bonds from the public. But the Fed also affects the money supply indirectly, as when the Fed's bond purchase increases bank reserves, which then serve as fuel for the money multiplier. In the next chapter, we will consider the effects of changes in the money supply on the economy.

endofchaptermaterial

- **Summary**
- **Questions for Review**
- **Problems and Exercises**

- **Experiential Exercises**
- **Wall Street Journal Exercises**

CHAPTER 30

Monetary Theory and Policy

Why do people maintain checking accounts and have cash in their pockets, purses, wallets, desk drawers, coffee cans—wherever? In other words, why do people hold money? How does the stock of money in the economy affect your chances of finding a job, your ability to finance a new car, the interest rate you pay on credit cards, the ease of securing a student loan, and the interest rate on that loan? What have economic theory and the historical record taught us about the relationship between the quantity of money in the economy and other macroeconomic variables? Answers to these and related questions are addressed in this chapter, which examines monetary theory and policy.

The amount of money in the economy affects you in a variety of ways, but to understand those effects, we must dig a little deeper. So far, we have focused on how the banking system creates money. But a more fundamental question is how the quantity of money affects the economy. The study of the effect of money on the economy is called *monetary theory*. A central concern of monetary theory is the effect of the money supply on the economy's price level, employment, and real GDP. The Fed's role in supplying money to the economy is called *monetary policy*.

In the short run, changes in the money supply affect the economy by working through changes in the interest rate. In the long run, changes in the money supply affect the price level. In this chapter, we consider the theory behind each time frame. Topics discussed in this chapter include:

Take the Pre-Test to assess
your initial knowledge of the
key ideas in this chapter.
The Pre-Test provides
exam-style questions
addressing the main topics
and concepts of the chapter.
At the completion of each
Pre-Test, you will receive a
score and instructive feedback on how you answered
each question, and a direct
link to the part of the chapter addressed in the question. Take the Pre-Test as
often as you need to—a
record of your progress for
each attempt is kept for you
to revisit and gauge your
improvement.

- Demand and supply of money
- Money in the short run
- Federal funds rate
- Money in the long run
- Velocity of money
- Monetary policy targets

<interactive>exercise

- ECONDEBATE ONLINE: EMPLOYMENT, UNEMPLOYMENT, AND INFLATION
- ECONDEBATE ONLINE: MONETARY POLICY

<interactive>update

- ECONDATA ONLINE: EMPLOYMENT, UNEMPLOYMENT, AND INFLATION
- ECONDATA ONLINE: MONETARY POLICY
- ECONLINKS ONLINE: ECONOMICS WEB LINKS
- ECONNEWS ONLINE: EMPLOYMENT, UNEMPLOYMENT, AND INFLATION
- ECONNEWS ONLINE: MONETARY POLICY

THE DEMAND AND SUPPLY OF MONEY

Let's begin by reviewing the important distinction between the *stock of money* and the *flow of income*. How much money do you have with you right now? That amount is a *stock*. Income, in contrast, is a *flow*, indicating how much money you earn per period. Income has no meaning unless the period is specified. You would not know whether to be impressed that a friend earned $300 unless you knew whether this was earnings per week, per day, or per hour.

The **demand for money** is a relationship between how much money people want to hold and the interest rate. Keep in mind that the quantity of money held is a stock measure. It may seem odd at first to be talking about the demand for money. You might think people would demand all the money they could get their hands on. But remember that money, the stock, is not the same as income, the flow. People express their demand for income by selling their labor and other resources. People express their demand for money by holding some of their wealth as money rather than holding other assets that earn more interest.

But we are getting ahead of ourselves. The question is, why do people demand money? Why do people maintain checking accounts and have cash in their pockets, purses, wallets, desk drawers, coffee cans—wherever? The most obvious reason people demand money is that it is a convenient medium of exchange. *People demand money to carry out market transactions.*

<interactive>video

ASK THE INSTRUCTOR: WHY DO PEOPLE LISTEN TO ALAN GREENSPAN?

The Demand for Money

Because barter represents an insignificant portion of exchange in the modern industrialized economy, households, firms, governments, and foreigners need money to conduct their daily transactions. Consumers need money to buy products, and firms need money to buy resources. *Money allows people to carry out economic transactions more easily and more efficiently.* When credit cards are involved, the short-term loan delays the payment of money, but all accounts must eventually be settled with money.

The greater the value of transactions to be financed in a given period, the greater the demand for money. *So the more active the economy is—that is, the more goods and services exchanged, reflected by real output—the more money demanded.* Obviously an economy with a real GDP of $10 trillion will require more money than an economy half that size. *Also, the higher the price level, the greater the demand for money.* The more things cost on average, the more money is required to buy them.

Your demand for money supports expenditures you expect in the course of your normal economic affairs plus various unexpected expenditures. If you plan to buy lunch tomorrow, you will carry enough money to pay for it. But you may also want to be able to pay for other possible contingencies. For example, you could have car trouble or you could come across an unexpected sale on a favorite item. You can use credit cards for some of these unexpected purchases, but you still like to carry some cash. You may have a little extra money with you right now for who knows what. Even *you* don't know.

The demand for money is rooted in money's role as a medium of exchange. But as we have seen, money is more than a medium of exchange; it is also a store of value. People save for a new home, for college, for retirement. People can store their purchasing power as money or as other financial assets, such as corporate and government bonds. When people purchase bonds and other financial assets, they are lending their money and are paid interest for doing so.

The demand for any asset is based on the flow of services it provides. The big advantage of money as a store of value is its liquidity: Money can be immediately exchanged for whatever is for sale. In contrast, other financial assets, such as corporate or government bonds, must first be *liquidated,* or exchanged for money, which can then be used to buy goods and services. Money, however, has one major disadvantage when compared to other financial assets. Money in the form of currency and traveler's checks earns no interest, and the interest rate earned on checkable deposits is typically below that earned on other financial assets. So holding wealth in the form of money means forgoing some interest that could be earned by holding some other financial asset. For example, suppose a corporation could earn 3 percent more interest by holding financial assets other than money. The opportunity cost of holding $10 million as money rather than as some other financial asset would amount to $300,000 per year. *The interest forgone is the opportunity cost of holding money.*

<interactive>**video**

ASK THE INSTRUCTOR: WHY SHOULD WE CARE HOW FAST THE MONEY SUPPLY GROWS?

Money Demand and Interest Rates

When the market interest rate is low, other things constant, the cost of holding money—the cost of maintaining liquidity—is low, so people hold a larger fraction of their wealth in the form of money. When the market interest rate is high, the cost of holding money is high, so people hold less of their wealth in money and more in other financial assets that pay higher interest. Thus, *other things constant, the quantity of money demanded varies inversely with the market interest rate.*

The money demand curve, D_m, in Exhibit 1 shows the quantity of money people in the economy demand at alternative interest rates, other things constant. Both the quantity of

EXHIBIT 1

Demand for Money

The money demand curve, D_m, slopes downward. As the interest rate falls, so does the opportunity cost of holding money; the quantity of money demanded increases.

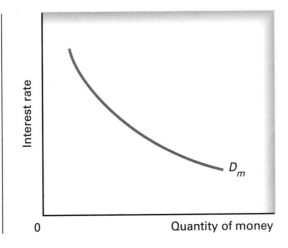

money and the interest rate are in nominal terms. *The money demand curve slopes downward because the lower the interest rate, the lower the opportunity cost of holding money.* Movements along the curve reflect the effects of changes in the interest rate on the quantity of money demanded, other things assumed constant. The quantity of money demanded is inversely related to the price of holding money, which is the interest rate. *Assumed constant along the curve are the price level and real GDP. If either increases, the demand for money increases, as reflected by a rightward shift of the money demand curve.*

The Supply of Money and the Equilibrium Interest Rate

The supply of money—the stock of money available in the economy at a particular time—is determined primarily by the Fed through its control over currency and over excess reserves in the banking system. The supply of money, S_m, is depicted as a vertical line in Exhibit 2. *A vertical supply curve implies that the quantity of money supplied is independent of the interest rate.*

The intersection of the demand for money, D_m, with the supply of money, S_m, determines the equilibrium interest rate, i—the interest rate that equates the quantity of money demanded in the economy with the quantity of money supplied. At interest rates above the equilibrium level, the opportunity cost of holding money is higher, so the quantity of money people want to hold is less than the quantity supplied. At interest rates below the equilibrium level, the opportunity cost of holding money is lower, so the quantity of money people want to hold exceeds the quantity supplied.

If the Fed increases the money supply, the money supply curve shifts to the right, as shown by the movement from S_m to S'_m in Exhibit 2. The quantity supplied now exceeds the quantity demanded at interest rate i. Because of the increased supply of money, people are *able* to hold a greater quantity of money. But at interest rate i they are *unwilling* to hold that much. Since people are now holding more of their wealth as money than they would like, they exchange some money for other financial assets, such as bonds.

As the demand for bonds increases, bond sellers can pay less interest yet still attract enough buyers. The interest rate falls until the quantity of money demanded just equals the quantity supplied. With the decline in the interest rate to i' in Exhibit 2, the opportunity cost of holding money falls enough that the public is willing to hold the now-larger stock of money. *For a given money demand curve, an increase in the supply of money drives down the market interest rate, and a decrease in the supply of money drives up the market interest rate.*

Now that you have some idea how money demand and supply determine the market interest rate, you are ready to see how money fits into the model of the macroeconomy we've developed so far. Specifically, let's see how changes in the supply of money affect aggregate demand and equilibrium output.

EXHIBIT 2

Effect of an Increase in the Money Supply

Because the supply of money is determined by the Federal Reserve, money supply can be represented by a vertical line. The intersection of the supply of money, S_m, and the demand for money, D_m, determines the equilibrium interest rate, i. Following an increase in the money supply to S'_m, the quantity of money supplied exceeds the quantity demanded at the original interest rate, i. People who are holding more money than they would like attempt to exchange money for bonds or other financial assets. In doing so, they drive the interest rate down to i', where quantity demanded equals the new quantity supplied.

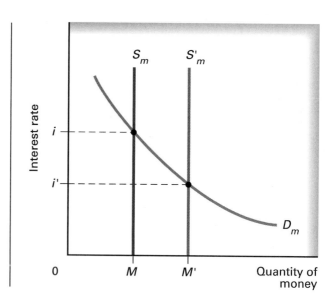

MONEY AND AGGREGATE DEMAND IN THE SHORT RUN

Monetary policy influences the market interest rate, which in turn affects the level of planned investment, a component of aggregate demand. *In the short run, money affects the economy through changes in the interest rate.* Let's work through the chain of causation for a specific economic setting.

Interest Rates and Planned Investment

Suppose the Federal Reserve believes that the economy is operating below its potential output and decides to stimulate output and employment by increasing the money supply. Recall from the previous chapter that the Fed can expand the money supply by (1) purchasing U.S. government securities, (2) lowering the discount rate—the rate at which banks can borrow from the Fed, or (3) lowering the reserve requirement.

The three panels of Exhibit 3 trace the links between changes in the money supply and changes in aggregate demand. We begin with equilibrium interest rate i, which is determined in panel (a) by the intersection of the money demand curve D_m with the money supply curve S_m. Suppose the Fed purchases U.S. government bonds and thereby increases the money supply, as shown by a rightward shift in the money supply curve from S_m to S'_m. After the increase in the supply of money, people are holding more of their wealth in money than they would prefer at interest rate i, so they try to exchange one form of wealth, money, for other financial assets. This greater willingness to exchange dollars for financial assets has no direct effect on aggregate demand, but it does reduce the market interest rate.

A decline in the interest rate to i', other things constant, reduces the opportunity cost of financing new plants and equipment, thereby making new business investment more profitable. Likewise, a lower interest rate reduces the cost of mortgages on new housing. So the decline in the interest rate increases the quantity of investment demanded. Panel (b) shows the demand for investment, D_I, first introduced several chapters back. When the interest rate falls from i to i', planned investment increases from I to I''.

EXHIBIT 3

Effects of an Increase in the Money Supply on Interest Rates, Investment, Aggregate Expenditure, and Aggregate Demand

In panel (a), an increase in the money supply drives the interest rate down to i'. With the cost of borrowing now lower, the level of investment spending increases from I to I', as shown in panel (b). The increased expenditure sets off the multiplier process, so the quantity of aggregate output demanded increases from Y to Y'. The increase is shown by the shift to the right in the aggregate demand curve in panel (c).

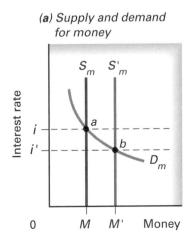

(a) Supply and demand for money

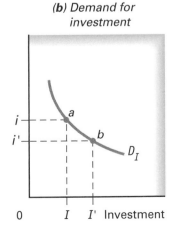

(b) Demand for investment

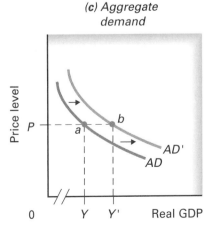

(c) Aggregate demand

The spending multiplier magnifies this increase in investment, leading to a greater increase in aggregate demand, reflected in panel (c) by a rightward shift of the aggregate demand curve from AD to AD'. At the given price level P, real GDP increases from Y to Y'. The sequence of events can be summarized as follows:

$$M\uparrow \rightarrow i\downarrow \rightarrow I\uparrow \rightarrow AD\uparrow \rightarrow Y\uparrow$$

An increase in the money supply, M, reduces the interest rate, i. The lower interest rate stimulates investment spending, I, which leads to an increase in aggregate demand from AD to AD'.[1] At a given price level, real GDP demanded increased from Y to Y'. The entire sequence is also traced out in each panel by the movement from point a to point b.

Let's now consider the effect of a Fed-orchestrated increase in interest rates. In Exhibit 3 such a policy can be traced by moving from point b to point a in each panel, but we will dispense with a blow-by-blow discussion of the graphs. Suppose the Federal Reserve decides to reduce the money supply to cool down an overheated economy. A decrease in the money supply would create an excess demand for money at the initial interest rate, so people will attempt to exchange other financial assets for money. These efforts to get more money result in an increase in the market interest rate—the opportunity cost of holding money. The interest rate increases until the quantity of money demanded declines just enough to equal the now-lower quantity of money supplied. At the higher interest rate, businesses find it more costly to finance plants and equipment, and households find it more costly to finance new homes. Hence a higher interest rate reduces investment. The resulting decline in investment is magnified by the spending multiplier, leading to a greater decline in aggregate demand.

As long as the interest rate is sensitive to changes in the money supply, and as long as investment is sensitive to changes in the interest rate, changes in the supply of money affect planned investment. The extent to which a given change in planned investment affects aggregate demand depends on the size of the spending multiplier.

<interactive>graph

- SEE IT: MONEY MARKET EQUILIBRIUM
- TRY IT: THE MONEY MARKET AND THE INTEREST RATE
- SEE IT: MONEY AND AGGREGATE DEMAND
- TRY IT: IMPACT OF AN INCREASE IN THE MONEY SUPPLY

<interactive>video

CNN VIDEO: "BRAKING NEWS"

Adding Short-Run Aggregate Supply

Even after tracing the effect of a change in the money supply on aggregate demand, we still have only half the story. To determine the effects of monetary policy on the equilibrium level of real GDP in the economy, we need the supply side. An aggregate supply curve can help show how a given shift in the aggregate demand curve affects real GDP and the price level. In the short run, the aggregate supply curve slopes upward, so the quantity supplied will expand only if the price level increases. *For a given shift of the aggregate demand curve, the steeper the short-run aggregate supply curve, the smaller the increase in real GDP and the larger the increase in the price level.*

Suppose the economy is producing at point a in Exhibit 4, where the aggregate demand curve AD intersects the short-run aggregate supply curve $SRAS_{130}$, yielding a short-run equilibrium output of \$9.8 trillion and a price level of 125. As you can see, the actual price level of 125 is below the expected price level of 130, and the short-run equilibrium output of \$9.8 trillion is below the economy's potential of \$10.0 trillion, yielding a contractionary gap of \$0.2 trillion.

[1]The graphs presented in Exhibit 3 are simplified versions. Since the demand for money depends on the level of real GDP, an increase in real GDP would shift the money demand curve to the right in panel (a). For simplicity, we have not shown a shift in the money demand curve. If we had shifted the money demand curve, the equilibrium interest rate would still have fallen, but not by as much, so investment and aggregate demand would not have increased by as much.

EXHIBIT 4

Expansionary Monetary Policy to Correct a Contractionary Gap

At point *a*, the economy is producing below potential. There is a contractionary gap equal to $0.2 trillion. If the Federal Reserve increases the money supply, the aggregate demand curve shifts to *AD'*. Equilibrium is reestablished at point *b*, with the price level at 130 and output at the potential level of $10.0 trillion.

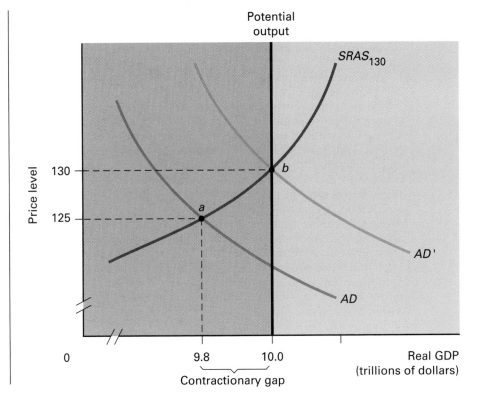

At point *a*, real wages are higher than had been negotiated and many people are looking for jobs. The Fed can wait to see whether natural market forces close the contractionary gap. Market forces could cause employers and workers to renegotiate lower nominal wages. This would lower production costs, pushing the short-run aggregate supply curve rightward, thus closing the contractionary gap. But if the Fed has little confidence in natural market forces or thinks it would take too long, the Fed could intervene and attempt to close the gap using an expansionary monetary policy. For example, during 2001, the Fed aggressively lowered the federal funds rate to stimulate aggregate demand. If the Fed lowers the rate by just the right amount, this stimulates investment, thus increasing the aggregate demand curve enough to achieve a new equilibrium at point *b*, where the economy produces its potential output. Given all the connections in the chain of causality between changes in the money supply and changes in equilibrium output, however, it would actually be quite remarkable for the Fed to execute monetary policy so precisely. If the Fed overshoots the mark and stimulates aggregate demand too much, this would create an expansionary gap, thus creating inflationary pressure in the economy.

To review: As long as the demand for money slopes downward and the amount invested is sensitive to changes in the interest rate, an increase in the money supply will reduce the market interest rate, increasing planned investment and consequently increasing aggregate demand. And as long as the short-run aggregate supply curve slopes upward, the short-run effect of an increase in the money supply is an increase in both real output and the price level. But one final caution: Lowering the interest rate may not always stimulate investment. The economic outlook may grow so grim that lower interest rates may fail to achieve the desired increase in aggregate demand. In Japan, for example, the central bank has lowered the interest rate to below 1 percent, yet that economy has been stagnant for a decade.

SEE IT: MONETARY POLICY WITH AGGREGATE SUPPLY

Fiscal Policy with Money

Now that we have considered the short-run effect that money has on aggregate demand and on equilibrium output, we can take another look at fiscal policy. Suppose there is an increase in government purchases, other things constant. Three chapters back, we found that an increase in government purchases increases aggregate demand, leading in the short run to both a greater output and a higher price level. Once money enters the picture, we must recognize that an increase in either real output or the price level increases the demand for money.

Thus, an increase in government purchases increases aggregate demand, which in the short run increases aggregate output and the price level. Increases in aggregate output and the price level increase money demand because more money is needed for the additional spending. For a given supply of money, an increase in money demand leads to a higher interest rate. And a higher interest rate *reduces* investment spending. We therefore say that the fiscal stimulus of government purchases *crowds out* some investment. This reduction in investment, to some extent, dampens the expansionary effects of fiscal policy on real output. *So the inclusion of money in the fiscal framework introduces yet another reason why the simple spending multiplier overstates the increase in real output arising from any given fiscal stimulus.*

Likewise, monetary effects will temper any fiscal policy designed to reduce aggregate demand. Suppose that the government, in an attempt to cool inflation, increases income taxes, which reduces consumption. As aggregate demand declines, equilibrium output and the price level fall in the short run. With a lower level of output and a lower price level, less money is needed to carry out transactions, so the demand for money falls. Again, with the supply of money unchanged, a drop in the demand for money leads to a lower interest rate. This drop in the interest rate stimulates investment spending, to some extent offsetting the effects of higher taxes. Thus, *given the supply of money, the impact of changes in the demand for money on interest rates reduces the effectiveness of fiscal policy.*

That's the theory of monetary policy in the short run. The following case study looks at how the Fed executes that policy.

CASE**STUDY**	Targeting the Federal Funds Rate
	● *Public Policy*

At 2:15 P.M. on November 6, 2001, immediately following a regular meeting, the Federal Open Market Committee (FOMC) announced that it would lower its target for the federal funds rate by half a percentage point to 2 percent. The last time the rate got that low was in 1961. As you know by now, the federal funds rate is the one that banks charge one another for overnight loans. Since lowering the rate reduces the cost of covering any reserve shortfall, banks are more willing to lend. In cutting the target rate, the FOMC said, "Heightened uncertainty and concerns about a deterioration in business conditions both here and abroad are damping economic activity." Since the beginning of 2001, the Fed cut the rate 4.5 percentage points in 10 steps, its most concentrated effort to stimulate the economy ever. To lower the federal funds rate, the FOMC authorized the New York Fed to make open-market purchases to increase bank reserves until the rate fell to the target level.

For nearly four decades, the Fed has reflected its monetary policy in this interest rate. (For a short time, the Fed targeted money aggregates, but more on that later.) There are many interest rates in the economy—for credit cards, new car sales, mortgages, home equity loans, and more. Why focus on such an obscure rate? First, by changing bank reserves through open-market operations, the Fed has a direct lever on the federal funds rate, so the Fed's grip on this rate is tighter than on any other market rate. Second, the federal funds rate also serves as a benchmark in the economy for determining other short-term interest rates. For example, after the Fed announced the November 6th rate cut of half a percent, major banks around the country lowered by the same amount their prime interest rate—the interest rate they charge their best corporate customers.

Exhibit 5 shows the federal funds rate since early 1996. Let's walk through developments during the period. Between early 1996 and late 1998, the economy grew nicely with low inflation, so the FOMC kept the rate relatively stable in a range of 5.25 percent to 5.5 percent. But in late 1998, fears of a global financial crisis caused by a default on Russian bonds and the near collapse of a U.S. financial institution prompted the FOMC to drop its target rate to 4.75 percent. By the summer of 1999, those fears abated, and instead the FOMC became concerned

EXHIBIT 5

Recent Ups and Downs in the Federal Funds Rate

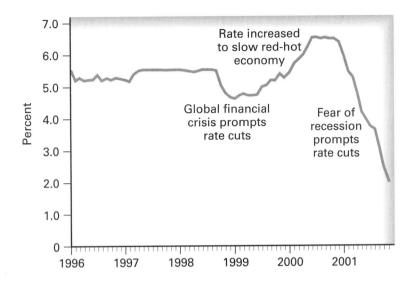

Source: Based on monthly averages from the St. Louis Federal Reserve Bank. For the latest rates, go to http://www.stls.frb.org/fred/index.html.

that robust economic growth would trigger inflation. In a series of six steps, the federal funds target rate was raised from 4.75 percent to 6.5 percent. The FOMC announced at the time that the moves "should markedly diminish the risk of rising inflation going forward." In early 2001, concerns about waning consumer confidence, weaker capital spending, falling manufacturing output, and a sinking stock market prompted the FOMC to reverse course, with the series of rate cuts discussed already.

In 1994, the Fed began announcing after each FOMC meeting whether the target interest rate would increase, decrease, or remain unchanged. Later it began indicating the probable "bias" in the near term—that is, whether or not its current direction of interest rate changes would continue. For example, with its November 2001 announcement, the FOMC said it would continue to cut the target rate if necessary (and, in fact, it cut the rate one-quarter point in December 2001). With such concrete news coming after each meeting, these FOMC meetings became media events. Some of the cuts during 2001 came between regular meetings. Such intermeeting actions have a more dramatic impact on markets, particularly the stock market, because of the surprise element. Still, in announcing target rate cuts, the FOMC has to be careful not to sound too concerned about the economy, because its doubts could harm business and consumer confidence further. Also, the Fed has to avoid overdoing rate cuts. As one member of the Board of Governors warned, the Fed must not cut the rate so much that it "ends up adding to price pressure as the growth strengthens."

Before making a decision about changes in the target interest rate, the Fed tracks a variety of indicators, including real GDP and the unemployment rate. One of Chairman Greenspan's favorites is the employment cost index, which measures changes in the cost of labor. If labor costs increase more than labor productivity, this signals to Greenspan that inflationary pressure is building in the economy, suggesting that an interest rate hike might be the appropriate policy.

<interactive>exercise

- **eACTIVITY: TARGETING THE FEDERAL FUNDS RATE**
- **READING IT RIGHT: WALL STREET JOURNAL EXERCISE**

Sources: Greg Ip, "U.S. Federal Reserve Cuts Funds Rate by Half a Point to 40-Year Low Level," *Wall Street Journal,* 7 November 2001; "How Low Can They Go?," *Economist,* 6 October 2001; "Minutes of the Federal Open Market Committee" and "FOMC Statement on Interest Rates," 3 January 2001, 30–31 January 2001, 20 March 2001, 18 April 2001, 15 May 2001, 2 October 2001, and 6 November 2001. Find the latest FOMC minutes and statements at http://www.federalreserve.gov/fomc/#calendars.

MONEY AND AGGREGATE DEMAND IN THE LONG RUN

When we looked at the impact of money on the economy in the short run, we found that money influences aggregate demand and equilibrium output through its effect on the interest rate. Here we look at the long-run effects of changes in the money supply on the economy. The long-run view of money is more direct in that if the central bank supplies more money to the economy, people eventually spend more. But since long-run aggregate supply is fixed at the economy's potential output, this greater spending simply increases the price level. Here are the details.

The Equation of Exchange

Every transaction in the economy involves a two-way swap: The seller surrenders goods for money, and the buyer surrenders money for goods. One way of expressing this relationship among key variables in the economy is the **equation of exchange,** first developed by classical economists. Although this equation can be arranged in different ways, depending on the variables to be emphasized, the basic version is

$$M \times V = P \times Y$$

where M is the quantity of money in the economy; V is the **velocity of money,** or the average number of times per year each dollar is used to purchase final goods and services; P is the price level; and Y is real national output, or real GDP. The equation of exchange says that the quantity of money in circulation, M, multiplied by V, the number of times that money turns over (changes hands), equals the average price level, P, times real output, Y. The price level, P, times real output, Y, equals the economy's nominal income and output, or nominal GDP.

By rearranging the equation of exchange, we find that velocity equals nominal GDP divided by the money stock. For example, U.S. nominal GDP in 2001 was about $10.2 trillion, and the money stock as measured by M1 averaged $1.15 trillion. The velocity of money indicates how often each dollar is used on average to pay for final goods and services during the year. So in 2001, velocity was nominal GDP of $10.2 trillion divided by $1.15 trillion, or 8.9. Given the value of total output and the money supply in that year, each dollar must have been spent about nine times on average to pay for final goods and services. There is no other way these market transactions could have occurred. The specific value of velocity is implied by the values of the other variables. Incidentally, velocity measures spending only on final goods and services—not on intermediate products, secondhand goods, or financial assets, even though such spending also takes place. So velocity is really a low estimate of how hard money works during the year.

Classical economists developed the equation of exchange as a way of explaining the economy's price level. The equation says that total spending ($M \times V$) is always equal to total receipts ($P \times Y$), as was the case in our circular-flow analysis. As described so far, however, the equation of exchange is simply an *identity*—a relationship expressed in such a way that it is true by definition. Another example of an identity would be a relationship equating miles per gallon to the distance driven divided by the gasoline required.

The Quantity Theory of Money

If velocity is relatively stable over time, or at least predictable, the equation of exchange turns from an identity into a theory—the quantity theory of money. The **quantity theory of money** states that if the velocity of money is stable, or at least predictable, then the equation of exchange can be used to predict the effects of changes in the money supply on *nominal* GDP, $P \times Y$. For example, if M is increased by 5 percent and V remains constant, then $P \times Y$, or nominal GDP, must also increase by 5 percent. For a while, some economists believed they could use the equation of exchange to predict nominal output in the short run. Now it's used primarily as a guide in the long run.

So an increase in the money supply results in more spending in the long run, which leads to a higher nominal GDP. How is this increase in $P \times Y$ divided between changes in the price level and changes in real GDP? The answer does not lie in the quantity theory, for that theory is stated only in terms of nominal GDP. The answer lies in the shape of the aggregate supply curve.

The long-run aggregate supply curve is vertical at the economy's potential level of output. With output, Y, fixed and the velocity of money, V, relatively stable or at least predictable, an increase in the stock of money translates directly into a higher price level, or inflation. Exhibit 6 shows the effect of an increase in the supply of money in the long run. An increase in the money supply causes a rightward shift of the aggregate demand curve, which increases the

EXHIBIT 6

In the Long Run, an Increase in the Money Supply Results in a
Higher Price Level, or Inflation

The quantity theory of money predicts that if velocity is stable, or at least predictable, then an increase in the supply of money in the long run results in a higher price level, or inflation. Because the long-run aggregate supply curve is fixed, increases in the money supply affect only the price level, not real output.

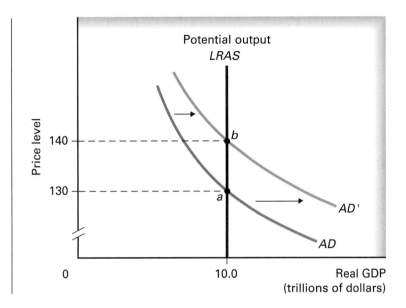

price level but leaves output unchanged at potential GDP. So the economy's potential output level is not affected by changes in the money supply. *In the long run, increases in the money supply result only in higher prices.*

To review: *If velocity is stable, or at least predictable, the quantity theory of money says that increases in the money supply will, in the long run, result in a higher price level, or inflation.* Velocity's stability and predictability are key to the quantity theory of money. Let's consider some factors that might influence velocity.

What Determines the Velocity of Money?

Velocity depends on the customs and conventions of commerce. In colonial times, money might be tied up in transit for days as a courier on horseback carried a payment from a merchant in Boston to one in Baltimore. Today the electronic transmission of funds takes only seconds, so the same stock of money can move around much more quickly to finance many more transactions. *The velocity of money has also been increased by a variety of commercial innovations that have facilitated exchange.* For example, a wider use of charge accounts and credit cards has reduced the need for shoppers to carry cash. Likewise, automatic teller machines have made cash more accessible any time. What's more, ATM cards can be used as debit cards at a growing number of retail outlets, such as grocery stores and drug stores, so people have reduced their "walking around" money.

Another institutional factor that determines velocity is the frequency with which workers get paid. Suppose a worker earns $26,000 per year and is paid $1,000 every two weeks. Earnings are spent evenly during the two-week period and are gone by the end of the period. In that case, a worker's average money balance during the pay period is $500. If a worker earns the same $26,000 per year but, instead, gets paid $500 weekly, the average money balance during the week falls to $250. *Thus, the more often workers get paid, other things constant, the lower their average money balances, so the more active the money supply and the greater its velocity.* Payment practices change slowly over time, and the effects of these changes on velocity are predictable.

The better money serves as a store of value, the more money people want to hold, so the lower its velocity. For example, the introduction of interest-bearing checking accounts made money a better store of value, so people were more willing to hold money in checking accounts and this financial innovation reduced velocity. When inflation increases unexpectedly, money turns out to be a poor store of value. People grow more reluctant to hold money and try to exchange it for some asset that retains its value better during inflation. This reduction in people's willingness to hold money during periods of high inflation increases the velocity of money. During hyperinflation, workers usually get paid daily, boosting velocity. Thus, *velocity increases with a rise in the inflation rate, other things constant.* Money becomes a hot potato.

The usefulness of the quantity theory in predicting changes in the price level in the long run hinges on how stable and predictable the velocity of money is over time.

How Stable Is Velocity?

Exhibit 7 graphs velocity since 1960, measured both as nominal GDP divided by M1 in panel (a) and as nominal GDP divided by M2 in panel (b). Between 1960 and 1980, M1 velocity increased steadily and in that sense could be considered at least predictable. M1 velocity

EXHIBIT 7

The Velocity of Money from 1960 to 2000

M1 velocity fluctuated so much during the 1980s that M1 growth was abandoned as a short-run policy target. M2 velocity appears more stable than M1 velocity, but both are considered by the Fed as too unpredictable for short-run policy use.

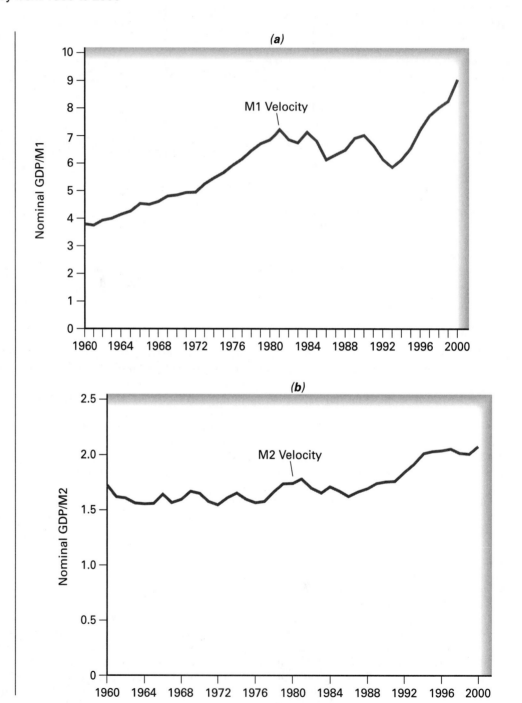

Source: *Economic Report of the President,* January 2001. To compute the latest velocity, go to http://w3.access.gpo.gov/eop/.

bounced around during the 1980s. But during the last decade, more and more banks began offering money market funds that included check-writing privileges, or what is considered M2. Deposits shifted from M1 to M2, which increased the velocity of M1. Also in recent years, more people began using their ATM, or debit, cards to pay directly at grocery stores, drug stores, and a growing number of outlets, and this too increased the velocity of M1 because people had less need for cash.

The velocity of M2 has been more stable than the velocity of M1, as you can see by comparing the two panels in Exhibit 7. For a few years, the Fed focused on changes in the money supply as a target for monetary policy in the short run. Because M1 velocity became so unstable during the 1980s, the Fed in 1987 switched from targeting M1 to targeting M2. But when M2 velocity became volatile in the early 1990s, the Fed announced in 1993 that money aggregates, including M2, would no longer be considered reliable guides for monetary policy in the short run. *Since 1993, the equation of exchange has been considered more of a rough guide linking changes in the money supply to inflation in the long run.*

What is the long-run relationship between increases in the money supply and inflation? Since the Federal Reserve System was established in 1913, the United States has suffered three major episodes of high inflation, and each was preceded and accompanied by a corresponding increase in the rate of growth in the money supply. These inflation episodes occurred from 1913 to 1920, 1939 to 1948, and 1967 to 1980. The following case study examines other evidence linking growth in the money supply with inflation in the long run worldwide.

CASESTUDY	The Money Supply and Inflation Around the World
	● *Public Policy*

If we think globally, what's the link between inflation and changes in the money supply in the long run? According to the quantity theory, as long as the velocity of money does not go through wild swings, there should be a positive relation in the long run between the percentage change in the money supply and the percentage change in the price level. Panel (a) of Exhibit 8 illustrates the relationship between the average annual growth rate in M2 from 1980 to 1990 and the average annual inflation rate from 1980 to 1990 for the 85 countries for which complete data are available. As you can see, the points fall rather neatly along the trend line,

EXHIBIT 8

Annual Inflation and Money Growth in 85 Countries: 1980–1990 (average annual percent)

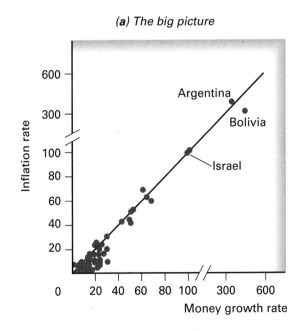
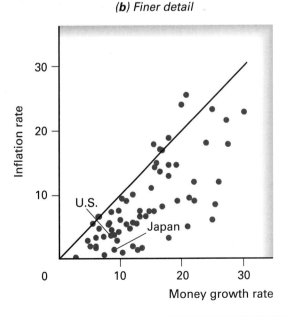

(a) The big picture   *(b) Finer detail*

Source: The World Bank, *World Development Report 1992* (New York: Oxford University Press, 1992), Table 13.

showing a positive relation between money growth and inflation. Because most countries are bunched below an inflation rate of 20 percent, let's break these points out in finer detail in panel (b). Although panel (a) shows a sharper link between money growth and inflation than does panel (b), in both panels, countries with higher rates of money growth tend to experience higher rates of inflation.

In panel (a), Argentina, Bolivia, and Israel—three countries with annual inflation averaging more than 100 percent—also had an annual growth in the money supply exceeding 100 percent. Hyperinflation is largely a 20th-century phenomenon, and in every case, it is accompanied by extremely rapid growth in the supply of paper money. For example, Argentina, which had the highest average annual inflation rate over the 10-year period in the sample, at 395 percent, also had the highest average annual rate of growth in the money supply, at 369 percent.

How does hyperinflation end? The monetary authority must somehow convince the public it is committed to halting the rapid growth in the money supply. The most famous hyperinflation was in Germany between August 1922 and November 1923, when inflation averaged 322 percent *per month.* Inflation was halted when the German government created an independent central bank that issued a new currency convertible on demand into gold. Argentina, Bolivia, and Israel all managed to tame inflation, with inflation under 3 percent by 2000. Incidentally, households in all three countries, perhaps mindful of their experience with hyperinflation, still hold a lot of U.S. currency. In fact, the currency of Argentina, the peso, exchanges 1 for 1 with the dollar.

eACTIVITY: THE MONEY SUPPLY AND INFLATION AROUND THE WORLD

Sources: Michael Salemi, "Hyperinflation," *The Fortune Encyclopedia of Economics,* edited by D. R. Henderson (New York: Warner Books, 1993), pp. 208–211; Central Intelligence Agency, *World Factbook: 2000,* at http://www.odci.gov/cia/publications/factbook; World Bank, *World Development Report 1997* (Oxford: Oxford University Press, 1997); and "Emerging Market Indicators," *Economist,* 13 October 2001.

TARGETS FOR MONETARY POLICY

In the short run, monetary policy affects the economy largely by influencing the interest rate. In the long run, changes in the money supply affect the price level, though with an uncertain lag. Should monetary authorities focus on the interest rates in the short run or the supply of money in the long run? As we will see, the Fed lacks the tools to focus on both at the same time.

Contrasting Policies

To demonstrate the effects of different policies, we begin with the money market in equilibrium at point e in Exhibit 9. The interest rate is i and the money stock is M, values the monetary authorities find appropriate. Suppose there is an increase in the demand for money in the economy, perhaps because of an increase in nominal GDP. The money demand curve shifts to the right, from D_m to D'_m.

When confronted with an increase in the demand for money, monetary authorities can choose to do nothing, thereby allowing the interest rate to rise, or they can increase the supply of money in an attempt to keep the interest rate constant. If monetary authorities do nothing, the quantity of money in the economy remains at M, but the interest rate rises because the greater demand for money will increase the equilibrium from point e up to point e'. Alternatively, monetary authorities can try to keep the interest rate at its initial level by increasing the supply of money from S_m to S'_m. In terms of possible combinations of the money stock and the interest rate, monetary authorities must choose from points lying along the new money demand curve, D'_m.

A growing economy usually needs a growing money supply to pay for the increase in aggregate output. If monetary authorities maintain a constant growth in the money supply, and if velocity remains stable, the interest rate will fluctuate unless the growth in the supply of money each period just happens to match the growth in the demand for money (as in the movement from e to e'' in Exhibit 9). Alternatively, monetary authorities could try to adjust the money supply each period by the amount needed to keep the interest rate stable. In this approach, changes in the money supply would have to offset any changes in the demand for money. This essentially is what the Fed does when it holds the federal funds target constant.

EXHIBIT 9

Targeting Interest Rates Versus the Supply of Money

An increase in the price level or in real GDP increases the demand for money from D_m to D'_m. If the Federal Reserve holds the money supply at S_m, the interest rate will rise from i (at point e) to i' (at point e'). Alternatively, the Fed could hold the interest rate constant by increasing the supply of money to S'_m. The Fed may choose any point along the money demand curve D'_m.

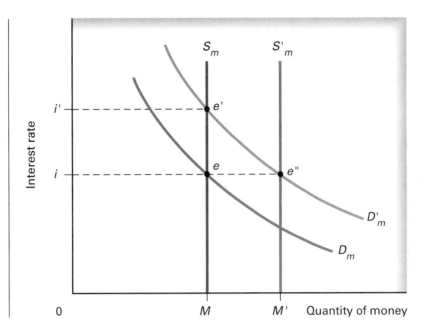

Interest rate fluctuations could be harmful if they created undesirable fluctuations in investment. For interest rates to remain stable during economic expansions, the money supply would have to grow at the same rate as the demand for money. Likewise, for interest rates to remain stable during economic contractions, the money supply would have to shrink at the same rate as the demand for money. Hence, for monetary authorities to maintain the interest rate at some specified level, the money supply must increase during economic expansions and decrease during contractions. But an increase in the money supply during an expansion would increase aggregate demand even more, and a decrease in the money supply during a contraction would reduce aggregate demand even more. *Such changes in the money supply would thus tend to worsen fluctuations in economic activity, thereby adding more instability to the economy.* With this in mind, let's examine monetary policy over the years.

Targets Before 1982

Between World War II and October 1979, the Fed attempted to stabilize interest rates. Stable interest rates were viewed as a prerequisite for an attractive investment environment and, thus, for a stable economy. Milton Friedman, the Nobel Prize winner, argued that this exclusive attention to interest rates made monetary policy a source of instability in the economy because changes in the money supply reinforced fluctuations in the economy. He said that the Fed should pay less attention to interest rates and instead should focus on a steady and predictable growth in the money supply. The debate raged during the 1970s, and Friedman won some important converts. Amid growing concern about the rising inflation rate, the Fed, under its new chairman, Paul Volcker, announced in October 1979 that it would deemphasize interest rates and would instead target the growth in specific money aggregates. Not surprisingly, the interest rate became much more volatile.

But many observers believe that a sharp reduction in money growth in the latter half of 1981 caused the recession of 1982. Inflation declined rapidly, but the unemployment rate jumped to more than 10 percent. People were worried. As you might expect, the Fed was widely criticized for its monetary policy. Farmers, politicians, and businesspeople denounced Volcker. Emotions ran high. Volcker was reportedly even given Secret Service protection. In October 1982, three years after the focus on interest rates was dropped, Volcker announced that the Fed would again pay more attention to interest rates.

Targets After 1982

The Fed is always feeling its way, looking for signs about the direction of the economy. The rapid pace of financial innovations and deregulation during the 1980s made the definition and measurement of the money supply more difficult. What's more, as we have seen, the relationship between M1 and nominal GDP began to break down. In 1987, the Fed announced it would no longer target M1 growth. The Fed switched to M2, which appeared to have a more stable link to economic activity. But by the early 1990s, the link between M2 and nominal GDP had also deteriorated.

Alan Greenspan, who became the Fed chairman in 1987, said that, in the short run, changes in the money supply "are not linked closely enough with those of nominal income to justify a single-minded focus on the money supply."[2] In 1993, he testified in Congress that the Fed would no longer target money aggregates, such as M1 and M2, as a guide to monetary policy. As we've seen, the Fed in recent years has targeted the federal funds rate. No central bank in a major economy now makes significant use of money aggregates to guide policy in the short run. Still, most policy makers also agree that in the long run, the money supply influenced the price level and inflation.

One final point: The Fed targets the federal funds rate, which is a short-term interest rate. The Fed has less control over *long-term interest rates*—rates of more than several years. Long-term rates depend more on inflationary expectations in the economy for the long term. Thus, the Fed could push down short-term rates without causing long-term rates to follow, as occurred in 2001. At the time, long-term lenders were concerned about the inflationary effects of an expansive monetary policy combined with an expansive fiscal policy aimed at warding off recession and giving the economy a boost in the wake of the terrorist attacks. So the Fed's control over the economy is limited.

CONCLUSION

This chapter has described two ways of viewing the effects of money on the economy's performance, but we should not overstate the differences. In the model that focuses on the short run, an increase in the money supply means that people are holding more money than they would like at the prevailing interest rate, so they exchange one form of wealth, money, for other financial assets, such as corporate or government securities. This increased demand for other financial assets has no direct effect on aggregate demand, but it does reduce the interest rate, and this lower interest rate stimulates investment. The increase in planned investment gets magnified by the spending multiplier, increasing aggregate demand. The effect of this increase in demand on real output and the price level depends on the shape of the short-run aggregate supply curve.

In the model that focuses on the long run, changes in the money supply act more directly on the price level. If velocity is relatively stable or at least fairly predictable, then changes in the money supply will have a predictable effect on the price level in the long run. Increase the supply of money in the economy, and people eventually spend more, increasing aggregate demand. But since long-run aggregate supply is fixed at the economy's potential output, increased aggregate demand leads simply to a higher price level, or to inflation.

endofchaptermaterial

- **Summary**
- **Questions for Review**
- **Problems and Exercises**
- **Experiential Exercises**

- **Wall Street Journal Exercise**
- **Graphing Workshop: Apply It Exercises**

[2]Quoted in "Greenspan Asks That Fed Be Allowed to Pay Interest," *Wall Street Journal,* 11 March 1992.

Take the Post-Test to assess your overall understanding of the key ideas in this chapter. The Post-Test provides a comprehensive selection of exam-style questions addressing the main topics and concepts of the chapter. At the completion of each Post-Test, you will receive a score and instructive feedback on how you answered each question, and a direct link to the part of the chapter addressed in the question. Take the Post-Test as often as you need to—a record of your progress for each attempt is kept for you to revisit and gauge your improvement. And each Post-Test is randomly generated, so every attempt is new.

CHAPTER 31

The Policy Debate: Active or Passive?

Does the private sector work fairly well on its own, or does it require active government intervention? If people expect intervention to prod the economy along, does this expectation affect their behavior? Does government intervention do more harm than good? What is the relationship between unemployment and inflation in the short run and in the long run? Answers to these and other questions are provided in this chapter, which examines the policy debate regarding the appropriate role for government in economic stabilization.

You have now studied both fiscal and monetary policy and are in a position to take a broader view of the impact of public policy on the U.S. economy. This chapter distinguishes between two general approaches: the *active approach* and the *passive approach*. The active approach views the private sector as relatively unstable and unable to recover from shocks when they occur. According to the active approach, economic fluctuations arise primarily from the private sector, particularly investment, and natural market forces may not help much when the economy gets off track. To move the economy to its potential output, the active approach calls for government intervention and discretionary policy. The passive approach, on the other hand, considers the private sector to be relatively stable and able to recover from shocks when they occur. When the economy derails, natural market forces nudge it back on track. Not only is government intervention unnecessary, but according to the passive approach, such activism may do more harm than good.

Pre-Test

Take the Pre-Test to assess your initial knowledge of the key ideas in this chapter. The Pre-Test provides exam-style questions addressing the main topics and concepts of the chapter. At the completion of each Pre-Test, you will receive a score and instructive feedback on how you answered each question, and a direct link to the part of the chapter addressed in the question. Take the Pre-Test as often as you need to—a record of your progress for each attempt is kept for you to revisit and gauge your improvement.

In this chapter, we consider the pros and cons of *active* intervention in the economy versus *passive* reliance on natural market forces. We also examine the role that expectations play in determining the effectiveness of stabilization policy. You will learn why unanticipated stabilization policies have more impact on employment and output than do anticipated ones. Finally, the chapter explores the trade-off between unemployment and inflation. Topics discussed in this chapter include:

- Active versus passive approaches
- Self-correcting mechanisms
- Rational expectations
- Policy rules and policy credibility

- The time-inconsistency problem
- Short-run and long-run Phillips curves
- Natural rate hypothesis

\<interactive\>exercise

- ECONDEBATE ONLINE: EMPLOYMENT, UNEMPLOYMENT, AND INFLATION
- ECONDEBATE ONLINE: MONETARY POLICY
- ECONDEBATE ONLINE: FISCAL POLICY

\<interactive\>update

- ECONDATA ONLINE: EMPLOYMENT, UNEMPLOYMENT, AND INFLATION
- ECONDATA ONLINE: MONETARY POLICY
- ECONDATA ONLINE: FISCAL POLICY
- ECONLINKS ONLINE: ECONOMICS WEB LINKS
- ECONNEWS ONLINE: EMPLOYMENT, UNEMPLOYMENT, AND INFLATON
- ECONNEWS ONLINE: MONETARY POLICY
- ECONNEWS ONLINE: FISCAL POLICY

ACTIVE POLICY VERSUS PASSIVE POLICY

According to the *active approach,* discretionary fiscal or monetary policy can reduce the costs of an unstable private sector, such as higher unemployment. According to the *passive approach,* discretionary policy may contribute to the instability of the economy and is therefore part of the problem, not part of the solution. The two approaches differ in their assumptions about how well natural market forces operate and the effectiveness of government intervention.

\<interactive\>exercise

ECONDEBATE ONLINE: SHOULD THE FED PURSUE A FIXED POLICY RULE?

Closing a Contractionary Gap

Perhaps the best way to describe each approach is by examining a particular macroeconomic problem. Suppose the economy is in short-run equilibrium at point a in panel (a) of Exhibit 1, with real GDP at $9.8 trillion, which is below the economy's potential output of $10.0 trillion. The contractionary gap of $0.2 trillion drives unemployment above the natural rate (the rate of unemployment when the economy is producing its potential output). This gap could have resulted from lower-than-expected aggregate demand. What should public officials do when confronted with this gap?

EXHIBIT 1

Closing a Contractionary Gap

At point *a* in both panels, the economy is in short-run equilibrium, with unemployment above the natural rate. According to the passive approach, shown in panel (a), that high unemployment eventually causes wages to fall, reducing firms' cost of doing business. The decline in costs causes the short-run aggregate supply curve to shift rightward to $SRAS_{120}$, moving the economy to its potential level of output at point *b*. In panel (b), the government employs an active approach to shift the aggregate demand curve from *AD* to *AD'*. If the policy works, the economy moves to its potential level of output at point *c*.

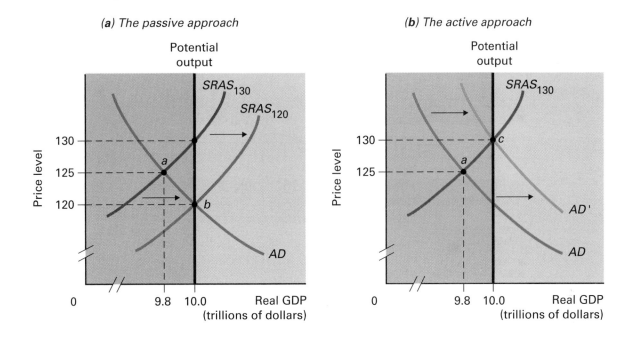

(a) *The passive approach*   **(b)** *The active approach*

Those who follow the passive approach, as did their classical predecessors, have more faith in the *self-correcting mechanisms* of the economy than do those who favor the active approach. In what sense is the economy self-correcting? According to the passive approach, wages and prices are flexible enough to adjust within a reasonable period to labor shortages or surpluses. High unemployment will cause wages to fall, which will reduce production costs, which will shift the short-run aggregate supply curve rightward in panel (a) of Exhibit 1. (Money wages need not actually fall; money wage increases may simply lag behind increases in the price level, so that real wages fall.) The short-run aggregate supply curve will, within a reasonable period, shift from $SRAS_{130}$ to $SRAS_{120}$, moving the economy to its potential level of output at point *b*. *According to the passive approach, the economy is inherently stable, gravitating in a reasonable amount of time toward potential GDP. Consequently, advocates of passive policy see little reason for active government intervention.* The passive approach is to let natural market forces close the contractionary gap. So the prescription of passive policy is to do nothing beyond the automatic stabilizers built into government policy.

Advocates of an active approach, on the other hand, believe that prices and wages are not very flexible, particularly in the downward direction. They think that when adverse supply shocks or sagging demand result in unemployment that exceeds the natural rate, the economy will not quickly adjust to eliminate this unemployment. Advocates of the active approach argue that even when there is much unemployment in the economy, the renegotiation of long-term wage contracts in line with a lower expected price level may take a long time. If so, the wage reductions required to shift the short-run aggregate supply curve rightward may also take a long time, even years. The longer it takes natural market forces to lower unemployment to the natural rate, the greater the output forgone during the adjustment period and the greater the economic and psychological costs to those unemployed during that period. *Because advocates of an active policy associate a high cost with the passive approach, they believe that the economy needs an active stabilization policy to alter aggregate demand and achieve the natural rate of output and price stability.*

A decision by public officials to intervene in the economy to speed the return to potential output—that is, a decision to use discretionary policy—reflects an active approach. In panel (b) of Exhibit 1, we begin at the same point *a* as in panel (a). At point *a*, short-run equilibrium output is below potential output, so the economy is experiencing a contractionary gap. Through discretionary monetary policy, discretionary fiscal policy, or some mix of the two, as occurred in 2001, active policy attempts to increase aggregate demand from *AD* to *AD'*, moving equilibrium from point *a* to point *c* and closing the contractionary gap.

In 2001, policy makers tried to revive a slowing economy using both fiscal and monetary policy. George W. Bush's tax cut, the largest in a decade, was approved by Congress in May and was aimed, in his words, at "getting the country moving again." Later in the year, Congress and the president also approved a multi-billion dollar package of federal outlays to support greater national security in the wake of the terrorist and anthrax attacks. Meanwhile, throughout 2001, the Fed cut its target interest rate a record amount. This combination of fiscal and monetary policy was the most concentrated attempt to boost aggregate demand since World War II. One possible cost of using discretionary policy to stimulate aggregate demand is an increase in the price level, or inflation. To the extent that the fiscal stimulus also reduces a federal budget surplus or increases a federal deficit, another cost of active fiscal policy is to delay efforts to pay off the national debt, a cost that we address in the next chapter.

READING IT RIGHT: WALL STREET JOURNAL EXERCISE

SEE IT: CLOSING A CONTRACTIONARY GAP

Closing an Expansionary Gap

Let's consider the situation in which the short-run equilibrium output exceeds the economy's potential. Suppose that the actual price level of 135 exceeds the expected price level of 130, causing an expansionary gap of $0.2 trillion, as shown in Exhibit 2. The passive approach argues that natural market forces will prompt firms and workers to negotiate higher wages. These higher nominal wages will increase production costs, shifting the short-run supply curve leftward, from $SRAS_{130}$ to $SRAS_{140}$, as shown in panel (a). Consequently, the price level will increase and output will decrease to the economy's potential. So the natural adjustment process will result in a higher price level, or inflation.

An active approach sees discretionary policy as a way of returning the economy to its potential output without increasing the price level. Advocates of active policy believe that if aggregate demand can be reduced from AD'' to AD', as shown in panel (b) of Exhibit 2, then the equilibrium point will move down along the initial aggregate supply curve from *d* to *c*. *Whereas the passive approach relies on natural market forces to close an expansionary gap through a decrease in short-run aggregate supply, the active approach relies on just the right discretionary policy to close the gap through a decrease in aggregate demand.* In the long run, the passive approach results in a higher price level and the active approach results in a lower price level. Thus, the correct discretionary policy can relieve the inflationary pressure associated with an expansionary gap. Whenever the Fed attempts to cool down an overheated economy by increasing its target interest rate, as it did in 2000, it employs an active monetary policy to close an expansionary gap. In 2000, when the economy was flying high, with output exceeding potential, the Fed tried to orchestrate a so-called soft landing to gently slow the rate of growth before that growth triggered inflation.

• SEE IT: RESPONSES TO AN EXPANSIONARY GAP
• TRY IT: THE SELF-CORRECTION PROCESS

EXHIBIT 2 |

Policy Responses to an Expansionary Gap

At point *d* in both panels, the economy is in short-run equilibrium, producing $10.2 trillion. Unemployment is below the natural rate. In the passive approach reflected in panel (a), the government makes no change in policy, so natural market forces eventually bring about a higher negotiated wage, shifting the short-run supply curve leftward to $SRAS_{140}$. The new equilibrium at point *e* results in a higher price level and a lower level of output and employment. An active policy reduces aggregate demand, shifting the equilibrium from point *d* to point *c* in panel (b), thus closing the expansionary gap without increasing the price level.

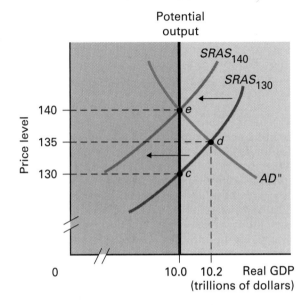

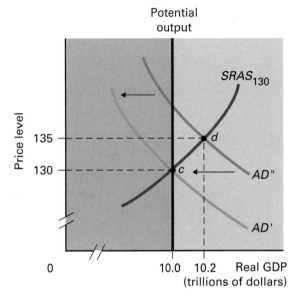

Problems with Active Policy

The timely adoption and implementation of an appropriate active policy is not easy. One problem is identifying the economy's potential output level and the unemployment rate at that level. Suppose the natural rate of unemployment is 5 percent, but policy makers believe it to be 4 percent. As they pursue their elusive goal of 4 percent unemployment, they find that output is constantly pushed beyond its potential, creating higher prices in the long run but no permanent reduction in unemployment. Recall that when output exceeds the economy's potential, this opens up an expansionary gap, causing a leftward shift of the short-run aggregate supply curve until the economy returns to its potential level of output at a higher price level.

Even if policy makers can accurately estimate the economy's potential level of output, formulating an effective policy requires detailed knowledge of current and future economic conditions. To pursue an effective active policy, policy makers must first be able to forecast what aggregate demand and aggregate supply would be without government intervention. Simply put, they must be able to predict what would happen with a passive approach. Second, they must have the tools necessary to achieve the desired result relatively quickly. Third, they must be able to forecast the effects of an active policy on the economy's key performance measures. Fourth, policy makers must work together, or at least not work at cross-purposes. Congress and the president pursue fiscal policy while the Fed directs monetary policy; these groups often fail to coordinate their efforts. To the extent that an active policy requires coordination, the policy may not work as desired. In early 1995, for example, Congress was considering an expansionary tax cut at the same time the Fed was pursuing a contractionary monetary policy. Fifth, policy makers must be able to implement the appropriate policy, even if this involves short-term political costs. For example, during inflationary times, the optimal policy may call for a tax increase or a tighter monetary policy—policies that may be unpopular because they increase unemployment. Finally, policy makers must be able to deal with a variety of timing lags. As we will see next, these lags compound the problems of pursuing an active policy.

The Problem of Lags

So far, we have ignored the time required to implement policy. That is, we have assumed that the desired policy is selected and implemented instantaneously. We have also assumed that, once implemented, the policy works as advertised—again, in no time. Actually, there may be

long, sometimes unpredictable lags at several stages in the process. These lags reduce the effectiveness and increase the uncertainty of active policies.

First, there is a **recognition lag,** which is the time it takes to identify a problem and determine how serious it is. For example, time is required to accumulate evidence that the economy is indeed performing below its potential. Even if initial data look troubling, these data are usually revised later. Therefore, policy makers must await additional evidence of trouble rather than risk responding to what may turn out to be a false alarm. Since a recession is not identified until more than 6 months after it begins and since the average recession lasts only about 11 months, a typical recession will be more than half over before it is officially recognized as such.

Even after enough evidence has accumulated, policy makers usually take additional time deciding what to do, so there is a **decision-making lag.** In the case of discretionary fiscal policy, Congress and the president must develop and agree on an appropriate course of action. Fiscal legislation usually takes months to approve; it could take more than a year. On the other hand, the Fed can decide on the appropriate monetary policy more quickly and does not even have to wait for regular meetings of the FOMC. For example, as the economy weakened in 2001, the Fed announced interest rate cuts three times between meetings. So the decision-making lag is shorter for monetary policy than for fiscal policy.

Once a decision has been made, the new policy must be introduced, which often involves an **implementation lag.** Again, monetary policy has the advantage: After a policy has been adopted, the Fed can immediately buy or sell bonds to influence bank reserves and thereby change the federal funds rate. The implementation lag is longer for fiscal policy. For example, if tax rates change, new tax forms must be printed and distributed advising employers of changes in tax withholding. If government spending changes, the appropriate government agencies must get involved. The implementation of fiscal policy can take more than a year. For example, in February 1983, the nation's unemployment rate reached 10.3 percent, with 11.5 million people unemployed. The following month, Congress passed the Emergency Jobs Appropriation Act, providing $9 billion to create what supporters claimed would be hundreds of thousands of new jobs. Fifteen months later, only $3.1 billion had been spent and only 35,000 new jobs had been created, according to a U.S. General Accounting Office study. By that time, the economy was already recovering on its own, lowering the unemployment rate to 7.1 percent and adding 6.2 million jobs. So this public spending program was implemented only after the recession had bottomed out and recovered. Likewise, in the spring of 1993, President Clinton proposed a $16 billion stimulus package to boost what appeared to be a sluggish recovery. The measure was defeated because it would have increased what already was a large federal deficit, yet the economy still added 5.6 million jobs over the next two years. As a final example, in early 2001, President Bush proposed a tax cut to stimulate the economy. Although Congress passed the measure relatively quickly, tax rebate checks were not mailed until six months after Bush introduced the legislation.

Once a policy has been implemented, there is an **effectiveness lag** before the full impact of the policy registers on the economy. One problem with monetary policy is that the lag between a change in the federal funds rate and the change in aggregate demand and output can take from months to a year or more. Fiscal policy, once enacted, usually requires 3 to 6 months to take effect and between 9 and 18 months to register its full effect.

These various lags make active policy difficult to execute. The more variable the lags, the harder it is to predict when a particular policy will take hold and what the state of the economy will be at that time. To advocates of passive policy, these lags are reason enough to avoid active discretionary policy. *Advocates of a passive approach argue that an active stabilization policy imposes troubling fluctuations in the price level and real GDP because it often takes hold only after self-correcting market forces have already returned the economy to its potential output level.*

Talk in the media about "jump-starting" the economy reflects the active approach, which views the economy as a sputtering machine that can be fixed by an expert mechanic. The passive approach views the economy as more like a supertanker on automatic pilot. The policy question then becomes whether to trust that automatic pilot (the self-correcting tendencies of the economy) or to try to override the mechanism with active discretionary policies.

A Review of Policy Perspectives

The active and passive approaches embody different views about the natural resiliency of the economy and the ability of Congress or the Fed to implement appropriate discretionary policies. So they disagree about the inherent stability of the private sector and the role of public policy in the economy. As we have seen, advocates of an active approach think that the natural adjustments of wages and prices can be excruciatingly slow, particularly when unemployment is high, as it was during the Great Depression. Prolonged high unemployment means that much output must be sacrificed, and the unemployed must suffer personal hardship during the slow adjustment period. If high unemployment lasts a long time, labor skills may grow rusty, and some long-term unemployed workers may drop out of the labor force. Therefore, prolonged unemployment may cause the economy's potential GDP to fall, as suggested in the case study of hysteresis several chapters back.

Thus, active policy associates a high cost with the failure to pursue a discretionary policy. And, despite the lags involved, advocates of the active approach prefer action—through discretionary fiscal policy, discretionary monetary policy, or some combination of the two—to inaction. Passive policy advocates, on the other hand, believe that uncertain lags and ignorance about how the economy works prevent policy makers from accurately determining and effectively implementing the appropriate active policy. Therefore, the passive approach, rather than pursuing a misguided activist policy, relies more on the economy's natural ability to correct itself just relying on government's automatic stabilizers.

Differences between active and passive approaches emerged during the presidential campaign of 1992, when the economy was slow to recover from a recession, as discussed in the following case study.

CASESTUDY | Active Versus Passive Presidential Candidates

● *Public Policy*

During the third quarter of 1990, after what at the time had become the longest peacetime economic expansion of the century, the U.S. economy slipped into a recession, triggered by Iraq's invasion of oil-rich Kuwait. Because of large federal deficits prevailing at the time, policy makers were reluctant to employ discretionary fiscal policy to stimulate the economy. That task was left to monetary policy. The recession lasted only nine months, but the recovery was sluggish—so sluggish that unemployment continued to edge up in what was derisively called a "jobless recovery."

That sluggish recovery was the economic backdrop for the presidential election of 1992 between Republican President George H. W. Bush and Democratic challenger Bill Clinton. Since monetary policy did not seem to be providing enough kick, was additional fiscal stimulus needed? With the federal budget deficit in 1992 already approaching $300 billion, a record level, would a higher deficit do more harm than good?

Bush's biggest economic liabilities during the campaign were the sluggish recovery and ballooning federal deficits; these were Clinton's biggest economic assets. Clinton argued that (1) Bush had not done enough to revive the economy; (2) Bush and his predecessor, Ronald Reagan, were responsible for the huge federal deficits; and (3) Bush could not be trusted because he broke his 1988 campaign pledge of "no new taxes" by signing a tax increase in 1990 to cut federal deficits. Clinton promised to raise tax rates on high-income taxpayers and cut them for the middle class. He also promised to create jobs through government spending that would "invest in America."

Bush tried to point out that, technically, the recession was over and the economy was on the right track. But that was a hard sell with unemployment averaging 7.6 percent during the six months leading up to the election. He blamed a Democratic Congress for blocking his recovery proposals, and he renewed his pledge of no new taxes (saying he really meant it this time). In fact, he promised to cut taxes by 1 percent, arguing that this would reallocate spending from government back to households.

Clinton saw a stronger role for government, and Bush saw a stronger role for the private sector. Clinton's approach was more *active* and Bush's more *passive*. In the end, the high unemployment rates during the campaign made people willing to gamble on Clinton. Evidently, during uncertain times, an active policy has more voter appeal than a passive one. Ironically, the economy at the time was stronger than conveyed by the media and by challenger Clinton. Real GDP in 1992 grew 3.0 percent, which was more than the 2.7 percent real GDP growth experienced during Clinton's first year in office. The unemployment rate began falling in October 1992, the month before the election (though too late to help Bush) and it continued to fall *for the next eight years.* Bush's timing was awful; Clinton's, incredible.

eACTIVITY: ACTIVE VERSUS PASSIVE PRESIDENTIAL CANDIDATES

Sources: David Wessel, "Wanted: Fiscal Stimulus Without Higher Taxes," *Wall Street Journal,* 5 October 1992; Herbert Stein, "The Inane Campaign Gives Me a Pain," *Wall Street Journal,* 7 October 1992; *Economic Report of the President,* January 2001; Bob Woodward, *The Agenda* (New York: Simon & Schuster, 1994); and the St. Louis Federal Reserve Bank's database at http://www.stls.frb.org/fred/index.html.

THE ROLE OF EXPECTATIONS

The effectiveness of a particular government policy depends in part on what people expect. As we saw in an earlier chapter, the short-run aggregate supply curve is drawn for a given expected price level reflected in long-term wage contracts. If workers and firms expect continuing inflation, their wage agreements will reflect these inflationary expectations. One approach in macroeconomics, called **rational expectations,** argues that people form expectations on the basis of all available information, including information about the probable future actions of policy makers. Thus, aggregate supply depends on what sort of macroeconomic course policy makers are expected to pursue. For example, if people were to observe policy makers using discretionary policy to stimulate aggregate demand every time output falls below potential, people would come to anticipate the effects of this policy on the price level and output. Robert Lucas, of the University of Chicago, won the 1995 Nobel Prize for his studies of rational expectations.

Monetary authorities are required to testify before Congress regularly, indicating the policy they plan to pursue. The Fed also announces, after each meeting of the FOMC, any changes in its interest rate targets and the likely direction of future changes. We will consider the role of expectations in the context of monetary policy by examining the relationship between policy pronouncements and equilibrium output. We could employ a similar approach with fiscal policy, but active discretionary fiscal policy for years was hobbled by high federal deficits and various lags. Monetary policy has been at center stage for the last two decades, and only in 2001 did it begin sharing the stage with fiscal policy.

<interactive>video

ASK THE INSTRUCTOR: CAN WE COUNT ON MONETARY AND FISCAL POLICY?

Monetary Policy and Expectations

Suppose the economy is producing potential output. At the beginning of the year, firms and employees must negotiate wage agreements. While negotiations are under way, the Fed announces that throughout the year, its monetary policy will aim at maintaining the potential level of output while keeping the price level stable. This seems the appropriate policy because unemployment is already at the natural rate. Firms and workers understand that the Fed's stable price policy appears optimal under the circumstances because an expansionary monetary policy would result simply in higher inflation in the long run. Until the year is under way and monetary policy is actually implemented, however, the public cannot be sure what the Fed will do.

As long as wage increases do not exceed the growth in labor productivity, the Fed's plan of a stable price level should work. Alternatively, workers could try for higher wage growth, but that option would ultimately lead to higher inflation. Suppose workers and firms believe the Fed's pronouncements and agree on wage settlements based on a constant price level. If the Fed follows through as promised, the price level should turn out as expected. Output will remain at the economy's potential, and unemployment will remain at the natural rate. The situation is depicted in Exhibit 3, in which the short-run aggregate supply curve, $SRAS_{130}$, is based on wage contracts reflecting an expected price level of 130. If the Fed follows the announced course, aggregate demand will be AD and equilibrium will be at point a, where the price level is as expected and the economy is producing $10.0 trillion, the potential level of output.

Suppose, however, that after workers and firms have agreed on nominal wages—that is, after the short-run aggregate supply curve has been determined—public officials become dissatisfied with the prevailing level of unemployment. Perhaps election-year concerns about unemployment, a false alarm about the onset of a recession, or an overestimate of potential output persuade the Fed to stimulate aggregate demand.

An expansionary monetary policy increases aggregate demand from AD, the level anticipated by firms and employees, to AD'. This unexpected policy stimulates output and employment in the short run to equilibrium point b. Output increases to $10.2 trillion, and the price level increases to 135. This temporary boost in output and reduction in unemployment may last long enough to help public officials get reelected.

So the price level is now higher than workers expected, and their agreed-on wage buys less in real terms than they bargained for. At their next opportunity, workers will negotiate higher wages. These higher wage agreements will eventually cause the short-run aggregate supply curve in Exhibit 3 to shift leftward, intersecting AD' at point c, the economy's potential output

EXHIBIT 3

Short-Run Effects of an Unexpected Expansionary Monetary Policy

At point *a*, firms and workers expect the price level to be 130; supply curve $SRAS_{130}$ reflects those expectations. If the Federal Reserve unexpectedly pursues an expansionary monetary policy, the aggregate demand curve will be *AD'* rather than *AD*. Output will temporarily rise above the potential rate (at point *b*), but in the long run, it will fall back to the potential rate at point *c*. The short-run effect of monetary policy is a higher level of output, but the long-run effect is just an increase in the price level.

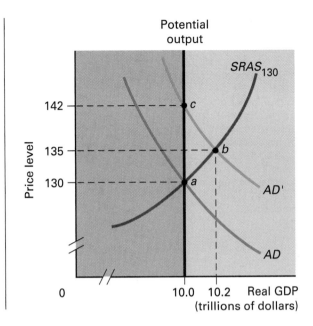

(to keep the diagram less cluttered, the shifted short-run aggregate supply curve is not shown). So output once again returns to the economy's potential GDP, but in the process the price level rises to 142.

Thus, the unexpected expansionary policy causes a short-run pop in output and employment. But in the long run, the increase in the aggregate demand results only in a higher price level, and a higher inflation rate, than had been expected. The **time-inconsistency problem** arises when policy makers have an incentive to announce one policy to influence expectations but then to pursue a different policy once those expectations have been formed and acted on.

Anticipating Monetary Policy

Workers may be fooled once by the Fed's actions, but they won't be fooled again. Suppose Fed policy makers become alarmed by the high inflation. The next time around, the Fed once again announces that it plans a monetary policy that will hold the price level constant at 142, a policy aimed at keeping real GDP at its potential. Based on their previous experience, however, workers and firms have learned that the Fed is willing to accept higher inflation in exchange for a temporary reduction in unemployment. Consequently, they take the Fed's announcement with a grain of salt. Workers, in particular, do not want to get caught again with their real wages down should the Fed implement a stimulative monetary policy, so a high wage-increase settlement is reached.

In effect, workers and firms are betting that monetary authorities will pursue an expansionary monetary policy regardless of their pronouncement to the contrary. The short-run aggregate supply curve reflecting these higher wage agreements is depicted by $SRAS_{152}$ in Exhibit 4, where 152 is the expected price level. Note that *AD'* is the aggregate demand that would result if the Fed's announced constant-price-level policy were pursued; that demand curve intersects the potential output line at point *c*, where the price level is 142. But *AD"* is the aggregate demand that firms and workers expect based on an expansionary monetary policy. They have agreed to wage settlements that will produce the economy's potential level of output if the Fed behaves as *expected,* not as *announced.* Thus, a price level of 152 is based on rational expectations. In effect, workers and firms expect the expansionary policy to shift aggregate demand from *AD'* to *AD".*

Monetary authorities must now decide whether to stick with their announced plan of holding the price level constant or follow a more expansionary monetary policy. If they pursue the constant-price-level policy, aggregate demand will turn out to be *AD'* and short-run equilibrium will occur at point *d.* Short-run output will fall below the economy's potential, resulting

EXHIBIT 4

Short-Run Effects of the Fed Pursuing a More Expansionary Policy Than Announced

The Fed announces a monetary policy that will keep the price level at 142. Firms and workers, however, do not believe the announcement; they think the monetary policy will be expansionary. The short-run aggregate supply curve, $SRAS_{152}$, reflects their forecasts of the price level. The Fed must then decide what to do. If it follows the noninflationary policy, aggregate demand will be AD', and output will fall below potential to point d. To keep the economy performing at its potential, the Fed must increase the money supply by as much as workers and firms expect.

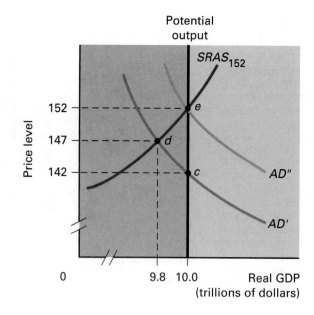

in unemployment exceeding the natural rate. If monetary authorities want to keep the economy performing at its potential, they have only one alternative—to match public expectations. Monetary authorities must pursue an expansionary monetary policy, a course of action that reinforces public skepticism of policy announcements. This expansionary policy will result in an aggregate demand of AD'', leading to equilibrium at point e, where the price level is 152 and output equals the economy's potential.

Thus, firms and workers enter their negotiations with the realization that the Fed has an incentive to pursue an expansionary monetary policy. So workers and firms agree to higher wage increases, and the Fed follows with an expansionary policy, one that results in more inflation. Once workers and firms come to expect an expansionary monetary policy and the resulting inflation, such a policy does not spur even a temporary boost in output beyond the economy's potential. *Economists of the rational expectations school believe that if the economy is already producing its potential, an expansionary monetary policy, if fully and correctly anticipated, will have no effect on output or employment. Only unanticipated or incorrectly anticipated changes in policy can temporarily influence output and employment.*

Policy Credibility

If the economy were already producing its potential, an unexpected expansionary monetary policy would increase output and employment temporarily. The costs, however, include not only inflation in the long term but also a loss of credibility the next time around. Is there any way out of this? For the Fed to pursue a policy consistent with a constant price level, its announcements must somehow be *credible*, or believable. Firms and workers must believe that when the time comes to make a hard decision, the Fed will follow through as promised. Perhaps the Fed could offer some sort of insurance policy to make everyone believe any deviation from the announced course will cost policy makers dearly—for example, the chairman of the Fed could promise to resign if the Fed does not pursue the announced course. Ironically, policy makers are often more credible and therefore more effective if they have their discretion taken away. In this case, a hard-and-fast rule could be substituted for a policy maker's discretion. We will examine policy rules in the next section.

Consider the problems facing central banks in countries that have experienced hyperinflation. For an anti-inflation policy to succeed at the least possible cost in forgone output, the public must believe the announcements of central bankers. How can central bankers in an economy ripped by hyperinflation establish credibility? Some economists believe that the most efficient anti-inflation policy is **cold turkey,** which is to announce and execute tough measures to stop inflation, such as halting the growth in the money supply. For example, in 1985, the annual rate of inflation in Bolivia was running at 20,000 percent when the new government announced a stern policy. The restrictive measures worked, and inflation was stopped within a month, with only a 5 percent loss in output. Around the world, credible anti-inflation policies have been successful.[1] Drastic measures may involve costs. For example, some economists argue that the Fed's dramatic efforts to curb high U.S. inflation during the early 1980s precipitated the worst recession since the Great Depression. Some say that the Fed's pronouncements were not credible and therefore resulted in a recession.

Much depends on the Fed's time horizon. If policy makers take the long view of their duties, they will be reluctant to risk their long-run policy effectiveness for a temporary reduction in unemployment. If Fed officials realize that their credibility is hard to develop but easy to undermine, they will be reluctant to pursue policies that will ultimately just increase inflation.

Often Congress tries to pressure the Fed to stimulate the economy. By law, the Fed must "promote effectively the goals of maximum employment, stable prices, and moderate long-term interest rates." The law leaves it up to the Fed how best to do this. The Fed does not rely on congressional appropriations, so Congress cannot attempt to influence the Fed by withholding funds. Thus, although the U.S. president appoints members of the Board of Governors, and the Senate must approve these appointments, the Fed operates somewhat independently of the president and Congress. Consider the link between central bank independence and inflation around the world in the following case study.

<interactive>exercise

ECONDEBATE ONLINE: SHOULD THE FEDERAL RESERVE AIM AT A ZERO INFLATION POLICY?

CASE**STUDY**	Central Bank Independence and Price Stability
	● *Public Policy*

Some economists argue that the Fed would do better in the long run if it were committed to the single goal of price stability. But to focus on price stability, a central bank should be insulated from political influence. When the Fed was established, several features insulated it from politics, such as the 14-year terms with staggered appointments for members of its Board of Governors. Also, since the Fed has its own source of income (interest on government securities and fees from bank services), it does not rely on Congress for a budget.

Does this independence affect performance? When central banks for 17 advanced industrial countries were ranked from least independent to most independent, inflation between 1973 and 1988 turned out to be the lowest in countries with the most independent central banks and highest in countries with the least independent central banks. For example, the most independent central banks were in Germany and Switzerland, and their inflation rates averaged about 3 percent per year during the 15-year span. The least independent banks were in Spain, New Zealand, Australia, and Italy, where inflation averaged 11.5 percent per year. The U.S. central bank is considered relatively independent; our inflation rate, which averaged 6.5 percent per year, fell between the most independent and least independent groups.

The trend around the world is toward greater central bank independence. Since 1988, for example, Australia and New Zealand have amended laws governing their central banks to make price stability the primary goal. Chile, Colombia, and Argentina—developing countries that experienced hyperinflation—have legislated more central bank independence. And the Maastricht agreement, which defined the framework for establishing a single European currency, the euro, identified price stability as the main objective of the new European Central Bank. That bank announced a policy rule that it would not lower its interest rate target as long as inflation exceeded 2.0 percent. In fact, the European Central Bank came under criticism recently for appearing reluctant to cut its interest rates target even though a recession loomed and the unemployment rate exceeded 8 percent.

<interactive>exercise

eACTIVITY: CENTRAL BANK INDEPENDENCE AND PRICE STABILITY

[1]For a discussion about how four hyperinflations in the 1920s ended, see Thomas Sargent, "The Ends of Four Big Inflations," in *Inflation: Causes and Consequences,* edited by Robert Hall (Chicago: University of Chicago Press, 1982), pp. 41–98.

Chapter 31 The Policy Debate: Active or Passive?

533

Sources: Alberto Alesina and Lawrence Summers, "Central Bank Independence and Macroeconomic Performance: Some Comparative Evidence," *Journal of Money, Credit and Banking* 25 (May 1993): 151–162; Patricia Pollard, "Central Bank Independence and Economic Performance," *Federal Reserve Bank of St. Louis* (July/August 1993): 21–36; and Neil Lipschutz, "Central Banks Can't Be Tied to Rules," Dow Jones Newswire, 4 May 2001. For links to more than 80 central bank Web sites, including all those discussed in this case study, go to http://www.bis.org/cbanks.htm.

POLICY RULES VERSUS DISCRETION

Again, the active approach views the economy as inherently unstable and in need of discretionary policy to eliminate excessive unemployment when it arises. The passive approach views the economy as so stable that discretionary policy is not only unnecessary but may actually worsen economic fluctuations. In place of discretionary policy, the passive approach often calls for predetermined rules to guide the actions of policy makers. In the context of fiscal policy, these rules take the form of automatic stabilizers, such as unemployment insurance, a progressive income tax, and transfer payments, all of which are aimed at reducing economic fluctuations. In the case of monetary policy, passive rules might be the decisions to allow the money supply to grow at a predetermined rate, to maintain interest rates at some predetermined level, and to keep inflation below a certain rate. For example, as noted in the previous case study, the European Central Bank announced a rule that it would not lower its target interest rate as long as inflation exceeded 2.0 percent a year. In the last decade a number of central banks have announced goals of achieving explicit inflation targets. In this section, we examine the arguments for policy rules versus discretion mostly in the context of monetary policy, since that's where the action has been in recent decades.

Limitations on Discretion

The rationale for the passive approach rather than the use of active discretion arises from different views of how the economy works. One view holds that *the economy is so complex and economic aggregates interact in such obscure ways and with such varied lags that policy makers cannot comprehend what is going on well enough to pursue an active monetary or fiscal policy.* For example, if the Fed adopts a discretionary policy that is based on a misreading of the current economy or a poor understanding of the lag structure, the Fed may be lowering interest rates when a more appropriate course is to leave rates unchanged or even raise them. As a case in point, during a meeting of the FOMC, one member lamented the group's difficulty in figuring out what was going on with the economy at the time, noting, "As a lesson for the future, I'd like to remind us all that as recently as two meetings ago [in September] we couldn't see the strength that was unfolding in the second half [of the year]. . . . It wasn't in our forecast; it wasn't in the other forecasts; and it wasn't in the anecdotal reports. We were standing right on top of it and we couldn't see it. That's just an important lesson to remember going forward."[2]

A comparison of economic forecasters and weather forecasters may help shed light on the position of those who advocate the passive approach. Suppose you are in charge of the heating and cooling system at a big shopping mall. You realize that weather forecasts are unreliable, particularly in the early spring, when days can be either warm or cold. Each day you must guess what the temperature will be and, based on that guess, decide whether to fire up the heater, turn on the air conditioner, or leave them both off. Because the mall is so large, you must start the system long before you know for sure what the weather will be. Once it's turned on, it can't be turned off until much later in the day.

Suppose you guess the day will be cold, so you turn on the heat. If the day turns out to be cold, your policy is correct and the mall temperature will be just right. But if the day turns out to be warm, the heater will make the mall unbearable. You would have been better off with nothing. In contrast, if you turn on the air conditioner expecting a warm day but the day turns out to be cold, the mall will be freezing. The lesson is that if you are unable to predict the weather, you should use neither heat nor air conditioning. Similarly, if policy makers cannot predict accurately the course of the economy, they should not try to fine-tune monetary or fiscal policy. Complicating the prediction problem is the fact that policy officials are not sure about the lags involved with discretionary policy. The situation is comparable to your not knowing how long the system actually takes to come on once you have flipped the switch.

This analogy applies only if the cost of doing nothing—using neither heat nor air conditioning—is relatively low. In the early spring, you can assume that there is little risk of the weather being so cold that water pipes will freeze or so hot that the walls will sweat. A similar assumption in the passive view is that the economy is inherently stable and periods of pro-

[2]FOMC board member Thomas Melzer, in a transcript of the December 22, 1992, meeting of the Federal Open Market Committee, p. 14. Meeting transcripts are published after a five-year lag and are available at http://www.federalreserve.gov/fomc/transcripts/.

longed unemployment are unlikely. In such an economy, the costs of *not* intervening are relatively low. In contrast, advocates of active policy believe that there can be wide and prolonged swings in the economy (analogous to wide and prolonged swings in temperature), so doing nothing involves significant risks.

NETBOOKMARK: *THE REGION*—INTERVIEWS WITH NOBEL PRIZE WINNERS

Rules and Rational Expectations

Another group of economists also advocates the passive approach, but not because they believe we know too little about how the economy works. Proponents of the rational expectations approach discussed earlier claim that people on average have a pretty good idea about how the economy works and what to expect from government policy makers. For example, individuals and firms know enough about the monetary policy pursued in the past to forecast, with reasonable accuracy, future policies and their effects on the economy. Some individuals will forecast too high and some too low, but on average, forecasts will turn out to be about right. *To the extent that monetary policy is fully anticipated by workers and firms, it has no effect on the level of output; it affects only the price level.* Thus only unexpected changes in policy can bring about short-run changes in output.

In the long run, changes in the money supply affect only the rate of inflation, not real output, so followers of the rational expectations theory believe that the Fed should not try to pursue a discretionary monetary policy. Instead, the Fed should follow a predictable monetary rule. A monetary rule would reduce monetary surprises and keep output near the natural rate. *Whereas some economists have favored rules over discretion because of ignorance about the lag structure of the economy, rational expectations theorists advocate a predictable rule to avoid surprises, which result in unnecessary departures from the natural rate of output.*

Despite support by some economists for explicit rules rather than discretion, central bankers appear reluctant to follow hard-and-fast rules about the course of future policy. Discretion has been used more than explicit rules since the early 1980s, though policy has become more predictable because the Fed now announces the probable trend of future target rate changes. As Paul Volcker, the former Fed chairman, argued nearly two decades ago:

> *The appeal of a simple rule is obvious. It would simplify our job at the Federal Reserve, make monetary policy easy to understand, and facilitate monitoring of our performance. And if the rule worked, it would reduce uncertainty. . . . But unfortunately, I know of no rule that can be relied on with sufficient consistency in our complex and constantly evolving economy.*[3]

So far, we have looked at active stabilization policy, which focuses on shifts in the aggregate demand curve, and passive stabilization policy, which relies more on natural shifts in the short-run aggregate supply curve. In the final section in this chapter, we will focus on an additional model, the Phillips curve, to shed more light on the relationship between aggregate demand and aggregate supply in the short and long runs.

THE PHILLIPS CURVE

At one time, policy makers thought they faced a fairly stable long-run trade-off between inflation and unemployment. This view was suggested by the research of New Zealand economist A. W. Phillips, who in 1958 published an article that examined the historical relation between inflation and unemployment in the United Kingdom.[4] Based on about 100 years of evidence, his data traced out an inverse relationship between the unemployment rate and the rate of change in nominal wages (serving as a measure of inflation). This relationship implied that the opportunity cost of reducing unemployment was higher inflation, and the opportunity cost of reducing inflation was higher unemployment.

[3]Former Federal Reserve Chairman Paul Volcker, before the Committee on Banking, Finance, and Urban Affairs, U.S. House of Representatives, August 1983.
[4]A. W. Phillips, "Relation Between Unemployment and the Rate of Change in Money Wage Rates in the United Kingdom, 1861–1957," *Economica* 25 (November 1958): 283–299.

The possible options with respect to unemployment and inflation are illustrated by the hypothetical **Phillips curve** in Exhibit 5. The unemployment rate is measured along the horizontal axis and the inflation rate along the vertical axis. Let's begin at point *a*, which depicts one possible combination of unemployment and inflation. Fiscal or monetary policy could be used to stimulate output and thereby reduce unemployment, moving the economy from point *a* to point *b*. Notice, however, that the reduction in unemployment comes at the cost of higher inflation. A reduction in unemployment with no change in inflation would be represented by point *c*. But as you can see, this alternative is not available. Thus, policy makers were thought to face a difficult trade-off: They could choose either lower inflation or lower unemployment, but not both.

Although not everyone accepted the implications of the Phillips curve, policy makers in the 1960s came to believe that they faced a stable, long-run trade-off between unemployment and inflation. The Phillips curve was based on an era when inflation was low and the primary disturbances in the economy were shocks to aggregate demand. Changes in aggregate demand can be traced as movements along a given short-run aggregate supply curve. If aggregate demand increased, the price level increased, but unemployment fell. If aggregate demand decreased, the price level decreased, but unemployment increased. With appropriate demand-management policies, government policy makers could choose any point along the Phillips curve.

The 1970s proved this view wrong in two ways. First, some of the biggest disturbances were adverse *supply* shocks, such as those created by oil embargoes and worldwide crop failures. These shocks shifted the aggregate supply curve leftward. A reduction in aggregate supply led to both higher inflation *and* higher unemployment. This stagflation was at odds with the Phillips curve. Second, economists learned that when short-run equilibrium output exceeds potential output, an expansionary gap opens. As this gap is closed by a leftward shift of the short-run aggregate supply curve, greater inflation *and* higher unemployment result—again, an outcome inconsistent with a Phillips curve.

The combination of high inflation and high unemployment resulting from stagflation and the closing of expansionary gaps can be represented by an outcome such as point *d* in Exhibit 5. By the end of the 1970s, increases in inflation and unemployment suggested either that the Phillips curve had shifted outward or that it no longer described economic reality. The situation called for a reexamination of the Phillips curve, which led to a distinction between the short-run Phillips curve and the long-run Phillips curve.

EXHIBIT 5

Hypothetical Phillips Curve

Points *a* and *b* lie on the Phillips curve and represent alternative combinations of the inflation rate and the unemployment rate that are attainable as long as the curve itself does not shift. Points *c* and *d* are off the curve; they are not attainable combinations.

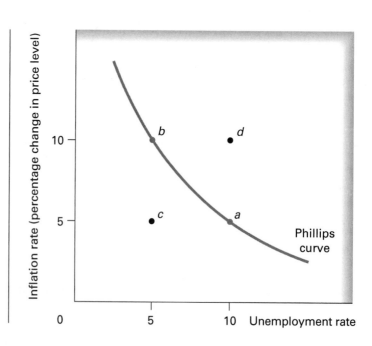

<interactive>**video**

ASK THE INSTRUCTOR: IS THE PHILLIPS CURVE A RELIABLE BASIS FOR STABILIZATION POLICY?

The Short-Run Phillips Curve

To discuss the underpinnings of the Phillips curve, we must return to the short-run aggregate supply curve. Let's begin by assuming that the price level this year is reflected by a price index of, say, 100. Suppose that people expect prices to be about 3 percent higher next year. So the price level expected for next year is 103. Workers therefore negotiate wage contracts based on an expected price level of 103. As the short-run aggregate supply curve in panel (a) of Exhibit 6 indicates, if AD is the aggregate demand curve and the price level is 103, as expected, output equals the economy's potential GDP, shown here to be $10.0 trillion. Recall that when the economy produces its potential GDP, unemployment is at the natural rate.

The short-run relationship between inflation and unemployment is presented in panel (b) of Exhibit 6 under the assumption that people expect the inflation rate to be 3 percent. The unemployment rate is measured along the horizontal axis and the inflation rate along the vertical axis. Panel (a) shows that when the inflation rate is 3 percent, the economy produces its potential GDP. When the economy produces its potential GDP, unemployment is at the natural rate, which we assume to be 5 percent in panel (b). The combination of 3 percent inflation and 5 percent unemployment is reflected by point a in panel (b), which corresponds to point a in panel (a).

What if aggregate demand turns out to be greater than expected, as indicated by AD'? In the short run, the greater demand results in equilibrium at point b, with a price level of 105 and an output level of $10.1 trillion. Since the price level is greater than the level reflected in wage contracts, the inflation rate is also greater than expected. Specifically, the inflation rate turns out to be 5 percent, not 3 percent. Output now exceeds potential, so the unemployment rate falls below the natural rate to 4 percent. This combination of a higher inflation rate and a lower level of unemployment is depicted by point b in panel (b), which corresponds to point b in panel (a).

What if aggregate demand turns out to be lower than expected, as indicated by AD''? In the short run, the lower demand results in equilibrium at point c, where the price level of 101 is lower than the level expected in labor contracts and output of $9.9 trillion is below potential GDP. With a lower-than-expected price level, the inflation rate is 1 percent rather than the expected 3 percent. With output below the economy's potential, the unemployment rate is 6 percent, which exceeds the natural rate. This combination of lower-than-expected inflation and higher-than-expected unemployment is reflected by point c on the curve in panel (b).

Note that the short-run aggregate supply curve in panel (a) can be used to establish the inverse relationship between the inflation rate and the unemployment rate illustrated in panel (b). This latter curve is called a **short-run Phillips curve**, which is generated by the intersection of alternative aggregate demand curves along a given short-run aggregate supply curve. *The short-run Phillips curve is based on labor contracts that reflect a given expected price level, which implies a given expected rate of inflation.* The short-run Phillips curve in panel (b) is based on an expected inflation rate of 3 percent. If inflation turns out as expected, unemployment equals the natural rate. If inflation is higher than expected, unemployment in the short run falls below the natural rate. If inflation is lower than expected, unemployment in the short run exceeds the natural rate.

The Long-Run Phillips Curve

If inflation is higher than expected, output can exceed the economy's potential in the short run but not in the long run. Labor shortages and worker dissatisfaction with shrinking real wages will lead to higher wage agreements in the next round of negotiations. The short-run aggregate supply curve will shift leftward until it passes through point d in panel (a) of Exhibit 6, returning the economy to its potential level of output. Point d corresponds to a higher price level, and so a higher rate of inflation. But notice that the higher inflation is no longer associated with reduced unemployment.

With the closing of the expansionary gap, the economy experiences both higher unemployment and higher inflation. At point d in panel (a), the economy produces its potential GDP, which means unemployment equals the natural rate. This combination of the natural rate of unemployment and higher inflation is depicted by point d in panel (b). The unexpectedly higher aggregate demand curve has no lasting effect on output or unemployment. Note that whereas points a, b, and c are on the same short-run Phillips curve, point d is not.

EXHIBIT 6

Relationship Between the Short-Run Aggregate Supply Curve and the Short-Run Phillips Curve

If people expect a price level of 103, which is 3 percent higher than the current level, and if *AD* is the aggregate demand curve, then the price level will actually be 103 and output will be at the potential rate. Point *a* in both panels represents this situation. Unemployment will be at the natural rate, 5 percent.

If aggregate demand is higher than expected (*AD'* instead of *AD*), the economy in the short run will be at point *b* in both panels. If aggregate demand is less than expected (*AD"* rather than *AD*), short-run equilibrium will be at point *c;* the price level, 101, will be lower than expected, and output will be below the potential rate. The lower inflation rate and higher unemployment rate are shown as point *c* in panel (b). In panel (b), points *a, b,* and *c* trace the short-run Phillips curve.

In the long run, the actual price level equals the expected price level. Output is at the potential level, $10.0 trillion, in panel (a), and unemployment is at the natural rate, 5 percent, in panel (b). Points *a, d,* and *e* represent that situation; they lie on the vertical long-run Phillips curve.

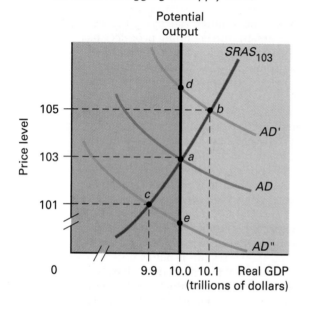

(a) Short-run aggregate supply curve

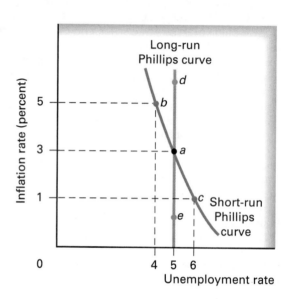

(b) Short-run and long-run Phillips curves

To trace the long-run effects of a lower-than-expected price level, let's return to point *c* in panel (a), where the actual price level is below the expected level, so output is below potential GDP. If firms and workers negotiate lower money wages (or if the growth in nominal wages trails inflation), the short-run aggregate supply curve will shift rightward until it passes through point *e*, where the economy returns once again to its potential level of output. Both inflation and unemployment will fall, as reflected by point *e* in panel (b).

Note that points *a, d,* and *e* in panel (a) depict long-run equilibrium points, in the sense that the expected price level equals the actual price level. At those same points in panel (b), the expected inflation rate equals the actual rate, so unemployment equals the natural rate. We can connect points *a, d,* and *e* in the right panel to form what is called the **long-run Phillips curve.** *When employers and workers have the time and the ability to adjust fully to any unexpected change in aggregate demand, the long-run Phillips curve is a vertical line drawn at the economy's natural rate of unemployment.* As long as prices and wages are flexible, the rate of unemployment, in the long run, is independent of the rate of inflation. *Thus, according to proponents of this type of analysis, in the long run, policy makers cannot choose between unemployment and inflation. They can choose only among alternative rates of inflation.*

The Natural Rate Hypothesis

The natural rate of unemployment is the rate that is consistent with the economy's potential level of output, which we have discussed extensively already. An important idea that emerged from this reexamination of the Phillips curve is the **natural rate hypothesis,** which states that in the long run, the economy tends toward the natural rate of unemployment. This natural rate is largely independent of the level of the *aggregate demand* stimulus provided by monetary or fiscal policy. Policy makers may be able to push the economy temporarily beyond its natu-

EXHIBIT 7

Short-Run Phillips Curves Since 1960

Each curve represents the U.S. unemployment-inflation rate combination for a given period. Notice that the short-run Phillips curve has shifted as inflation expectations have changed.

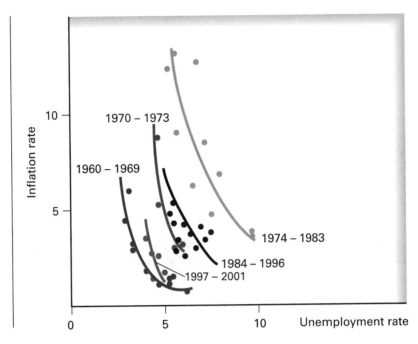

ral, or potential, rate of production, but only if the public does not anticipate the resulting level of aggregate demand and the resulting price level. The natural rate hypothesis implies that *regardless of policy makers' concerns about unemployment, the policy that results in low inflation is generally going to be the optimal policy in the long run.*

Evidence of the Phillips Curve

What has been the actual relationship between unemployment and inflation in the United States? In Exhibit 7, each year since 1960 is represented by a point, with the unemployment rate measured along the horizontal axis and the inflation rate measured along the vertical axis. Superimposed on these points is a series of short-run Phillips curves showing patterns of unemployment and inflation during what turns out to be five distinct periods since 1960. Remember, each short-run Phillips curve is drawn for a given *expected rate of inflation.* A change in inflationary expectations shifts the short-run Phillips curve.

The clearest trade-off between unemployment and inflation occurred between 1960 and 1969; the points for those years fit neatly along the curve. In the early part of the decade, inflation was low but unemployment relatively high; as the 1960s progressed, unemployment declined but actual inflation increased. The inflation rate during the decade averaged only 2.5 percent, and unemployment averaged 4.8 percent.

The short-run Phillips curve shifted to the right for the period from 1970 to 1973, when inflation and unemployment each climbed to an average of 5.2 percent. In 1974, sharp increases in oil prices and crop failures around the world reduced aggregate supply, which sparked another shift in the Phillips curve. During the 1974–1983 period, inflation averaged 8.2 percent and unemployment 7.5 percent. After two recessions in the early 1980s, the short-run Phillips curve shifted leftward. Average inflation for 1984–1996 fell to 3.7 percent and average unemployment fell to 6.1 percent. Finally, data for 1997 to 2001 suggest a new, lower short-run Phillips curve, with average inflation of only 2.4 percent and average unemployment of 4.5. Thus, the Phillips curve shifted rightward between the 1960s and the early 1980s. Since then, the Fed has learned more about how to control inflation, thereby shifting the Phillips curve back to about where it started in 1960s.

CONCLUSION

This chapter examined the implications of active and passive policy. The important question is whether the economy is essentially stable and self-correcting when it gets off track or essentially unstable and in need of active government intervention. Advocates of active policy

believe that the Fed or Congress should reduce economic fluctuations by stimulating aggregate demand when output falls below its potential level and by dampening aggregate demand when output exceeds its potential level. Advocates of active policy argue that government attempts to insulate the economy from the ups and downs of the business cycle may not be perfect but are still better than nothing. Some activists also believe that high unemployment may be self-reinforcing, because some unemployed workers lose valuable job skills and grow to accept unemployment as a way of life, as may have happened in Europe.

Advocates of passive policy, on the other hand, believe that discretionary policy may contribute to the cyclical swings in the economy, leading to higher inflation in the long run with no permanent boost in either output or employment. This group favors passive rules for monetary policy and automatic stabilizers for fiscal policy.

The active-passive debate in this chapter has focused primarily on monetary policy because discretionary fiscal policy, until quite recently, had been hampered by large federal deficits that ballooned the national debt. The debate between active and passive policy has simmered down in the last decade because of the generally strong performance of the U.S. economy. In the next chapter, we will take a closer look at the federal budget and consider the recent revival of discretionary fiscal policy.

endofchaptermaterial

- Summary
- Questions for Review
- Problems and Exercises

- Experiential Exercises
- Wall Street Journal Exercise

Take the Post-Test to assess your overall understanding of the key ideas in this chapter. The Post-Test provides a comprehensive selection of exam-style questions addressing the main topics and concepts of the chapter. At the completion of each Post-Test, you will receive a score and instructive feedback on how you answered each question, and a direct link to the part of the chapter addressed in the question. Take the Post-Test as often as you need to—a record of your progress for each attempt is kept for you to revisit and gauge your improvement. And each Post-Test is randomly generated, so every attempt is new.

CHAPTER 32

Federal Budgets and Public Policy

How big is the federal budget, and where does the money go? Why does the federal budget seem like such a tangled web? In what sense is the federal budget process at odds with discretionary fiscal policy? How is a sluggish economy like an empty restaurant? Why has the federal budget been in deficit most years, and why did a surplus finally materialize in 1998? What is the federal debt, and who owes it? Answers to these and other questions are examined in this chapter, which examines federal budgeting in theory and practice.

The word *budget* derives from the Old French word *bougette,* which means "little bag." The annual federal budget is now over $2,000,000,000,000—$2 trillion a year. That's big money! If this "little bag" contained $100 bills, it would weigh more than 22,000 *tons!* These $100 bills could fill more than 750 trailer trucks. They could paper over a 12-lane highway stretching from northern Maine to southern California. This budget could cover every U.S. family's mortgage and car payments every month of the year. If President Bush's sole function were to pay the bills by signing million-dollar checks, he would have to sign four checks a minute, 24 hours a day, 365 days a year to keep up with federal spending.

Government budgets have a tremendous impact on the economy. Government outlays at all levels amount to about 30 percent relative to GDP. Our focus in this chapter will be the federal budget, beginning with an examination of the federal budget process. We then look at the source of the deficits and how they became surpluses. We also examine the impact of our national debt and implications of paying off that debt. Topics discussed in this chapter include:

Take the Pre-Test to assess
your initial knowledge of the
key ideas in this chapter.
The Pre-Test provides
exam-style questions
addressing the main topics
and concepts of the chapter.
At the completion of each
Pre-Test, you will receive a
score and instructive feedback on how you answered
each question, and a direct
link to the part of the chapter addressed in the question. Take the Pre-Test as
often as you need to—a
record of your progress for
each attempt is kept for you
to revisit and gauge your
improvement.

- The budget process
- Rationale for deficits
- Impact of deficits
- Crowding out and crowding in
- The miraculous budget surplus
- The burden of the federal debt

<interactive>exercise

ECONDEBATE ONLINE: TAXES, SPENDING, AND DEFICITS

<interactive>update

- ECONDATA ONLINE: TAXES, SPENDING, AND DEFICITS
- ECONLINKS ONLINE: ECONOMICS WEB LINKS
- ECONNEWS ONLINE: TAXES, SPENDING, AND DEFICITS

THE FEDERAL BUDGET PROCESS

The **federal budget** is a plan for government outlays and revenues for a specified period, usually a year. Federal *outlays* include both government purchases (which we have referred to as
G) and transfer payments. Exhibit 1 shows the composition of federal outlays by major category since 1960. As you can see, the share of the budget going to national defense dropped

EXHIBIT 1 |

Defense's Share of Federal Outlays Declined Since 1960 and Redistribution Increased

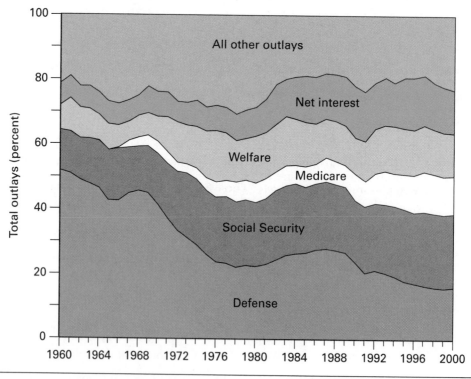

Sources: *Economic Report of the President,* January 2001, Table B-80; and the Office of Management and Budget. For the most
recent year, go to http://w3.access.gpo.gov/eop/.

from over half in 1960 to only 17 percent in 2000. Social Security's share has grown every decade. Medicare, medical care for the elderly, was introduced in the 1960s and has grown every year. In fact, Social Security and Medicare, programs aimed primarily at the elderly, now account for 34 percent of federal outlays. For the last two decades, welfare spending, which consists of cash and in-kind transfer payments, has remained at about 14 percent of federal outlays. And 12 percent of the budget pays interest on the national debt. So 48 percent, or nearly half the federal budget, redistributes income (Social Security, Medicare, and welfare); 17 percent goes to defense; 12 percent services the national debt; and the remaining 23 percent is left for everything else—from environmental protection to federal prisons and education.

ECONNEWS ONLINE: THE BUSH BUDGET

The President's Role in the Budget Process

Before 1921, the federal budget played a minor role in the economy, amounting to less than 3 percent of GDP except during wartime. Federal agencies made budget requests directly to Congress, bypassing the president entirely. Legislation in 1921 created the Office of Management and Budget (OMB) to examine agency requests and help the president develop a budget proposal. The Employment Act of 1946 created the Council of Economic Advisers to forecast the economy and assist the president in formulating an appropriate fiscal policy. By the mid-1970s, the president had in place the staff and support to put together a budget proposal.

Developing the president's budget usually begins a year before it is submitted to Congress, with each agency preparing a budget request. The congressional budget cycle begins in late January or early February, once Congress gets *The Budget of the United States Government,* a pile of books detailing the president's spending and revenue proposals for the upcoming fiscal year. The *fiscal year* runs from October 1 of one year to September 30 of the following year. At this stage, the president's budget is little more than detailed suggestions for congressional consideration. From the Council of Economic Advisers, Congress gets the *Economic Report of the President,* which offers the administration's view of the economy and includes any fiscal policy recommendations for fostering "maximum employment, production, and purchasing power."

NETBOOKMARK: SPEAKOUT.COM AND THE CENTER ON BUDGET AND POLICY PRIORITIES

The Congressional Role in the Budget Process

Once the president's budget hits Congress, budget committees in both the House and the Senate rework it until they agree on total outlays, spending by major category, and expected revenues. This agreement, called a **budget resolution,** establishes a framework to guide spending and revenue decisions and to discipline the many congressional committees and subcommittees that authorize spending. The budget cycle is supposed to end September 30, and by the start of the new fiscal year on October 1, Congress should have developed a detailed plan for spending along with revenue projections. Thus, the federal budget has a congressional gestation period of about nine months—though, as noted, the president's budget usually begins taking shape a year before it's submitted to Congress.

The size and composition of the budget and the difference between outlays and revenues measure the budget's fiscal impact. *When outlays exceed revenues, the budget is in deficit. A deficit stimulates aggregate demand in the short run but reduces national saving, which in the long run could impede economic growth. Alternatively, when revenues exceed outlays, the budget is in surplus. A surplus dampens aggregate demand in the short run but enhances domestic saving, which in the long run could promote economic growth.*

Problems with the Federal Budget Process

The federal budget process sounds good on paper, but it does not work that well in practice. There are several problems.

Continuing Resolutions Instead of Budget Decisions. Congress often ignores the budget timetable. Because deadlines are frequently missed, budgets typically run from year to year based on **continuing resolutions,** which are agreements to allow agencies, in the absence of an approved budget, to spend at the rate of the previous year's budget. Poorly conceived programs continue through sheer inertia; successful programs cannot expand. On occasion, the president must temporarily shut down some agencies because not even the continuing resolution could be approved on time. For example, in late 1995 and early 1996, most government offices closed for 27 days.

Overlapping Committee Authority. Overlapping budget authority among the many congressional committees requires the executive branch to defend the same section of the president's budget before several committees in both the House and the Senate. Thus, top officials end up spending much of their time testifying before assorted committees rather than running their agencies. Because several committees have jurisdiction over the same area, no committee really has final authority, so matters often remain unresolved even after extensive committee deliberations.

Lengthy Budget Process. You can imagine the difficulty of using the budget as a tool of fiscal policy when the budget process takes so long. Given that the average recession lasts less than a year and that budget preparations begin more than a year and a half before the budget takes effect, planning discretionary fiscal measures to smooth economic fluctuations is difficult. That's one reason why attempts to stimulate an ailing economy often seem so halfhearted; by the time Congress agrees on a fiscal remedy, the economy has often rebounded on its own.

Uncontrollable Budget Items. Congress has only limited control over much of the budget. *About three-fourths of federal budget outlays are determined by existing laws.* For example, once Congress establishes eligibility criteria, **entitlement programs,** such as Social Security and Medicare, take on lives of their own, with each annual appropriation simply reflecting the amount required to support the expected number of entitled beneficiaries. Congress has no say in such appropriations unless it chooses to change benefits or eligibility criteria. Most entitlement programs have such politically powerful constituencies that Congress is reluctant to mess with the structure.

No Separate Capital Budget. Congress approves a single budget that mixes together *capital* items, like a new federal building, with *current* outlays, like employee payrolls. Budgets for businesses and for state and local governments usually distinguish between a *capital budget* and an *operating budget.* The federal government, by mixing the two, offers a fuzzier picture of what's going on.

Overly Detailed Budget. The federal budget is divided into thousands of accounts and subaccounts, which is why it fills volumes. To the extent that the budget is a way of making political payoffs, such micromanagement allows elected officials to reward friends and punish enemies with great precision. For example, the 2001 budget included $176,000 for the Reindeer Herders Association in Alaska, $400,000 for the Southside Sportsman Club in New York, and $5 million for an insect-rearing facility in Mississippi. By budgeting in such detail, Congress tends to lose the big picture. When economic conditions change or when there is a shift in the demand for certain kinds of publicly provided goods, the federal government cannot easily reallocate funds from one account to another. Detailed budgeting not only is time consuming but also reduces the flexibility of the budget as a tool for discretionary fiscal policy and is susceptible to great abuse.

Possible Budget Reforms

Several reforms have been suggested to improve the budget process. First, the annual budget could be converted into a two-year budget, or *biennial budget.* As it is, Congress spends nearly all of the year working on the budget. The executive branch is always dealing with three budgets: administering an approved budget, defending a proposed budget before congressional committees, and preparing the next budget for submission to Congress. With a two-year budget, Congress would not be continually involved with budget deliberations, and executive branch heads could focus more on running their agencies (many states have adopted two-year budgets). A two-year budget, however, would require longer-term economic forecasts of the economy and would be even less useful than a one-year budget as a tool of discretionary fiscal policy.

Another possible reform would be to simplify the budget document by concentrating only on major groupings and eliminating line items. Each agency head would receive a total budget, along with the discretion to allocate that budget in a manner consistent with the perceived demands for agency services. The drawback is that agency heads may have different priorities than those of elected representatives.

A final reform is to sort federal spending into an operating budget and a capital budget. A *capital budget* would include spending on physical capital such as buildings, highways, computers, and other public infrastructure. An *operating budget* would include spending on the payroll, building maintenance, computer paper, and other ongoing expenses.

THE FISCAL IMPACT OF THE FEDERAL BUDGET

When annual government outlays—that is, government purchases plus transfer payments—exceed annual government revenue, the result is a *budget deficit,* a term you are already acquainted with. Although the federal budget was in surplus from 1998 to 2001, before that it had been in deficit every year but one since 1960 and in all but eight years since 1930. And the average deficit grew from less than 1 percent relative to GDP in the 1960s to more than 4 percent in the 1980s and the first half of the 1990s. To place deficits in perspective, let's first examine the economic rationale for deficit financing.

The Rationale for Deficits

Deficit financing has been justified for outlays that increase the economy's productivity—capital outlays for investments such as highways, waterways, and dams. The cost of these capital projects should be borne in part by future taxpayers, who will also benefit from these investments. Thus, there is some justification for government borrowing to finance capital projects and for future taxpayers helping to pay for them. State and local governments often issue debt to fund capital projects, such as schools. But, as noted already, the federal government does not budget capital projects separately, so there is no explicit link between federal deficits and capital budgets.

Before the Great Depression, federal deficits occurred only during wartime. Because wars involved much hardship, public officials were understandably reluctant to increase taxes much to finance war-related spending. Deficits incurred during wars were largely self-correcting, however, because government spending dropped after a war.

The Depression led John Maynard Keynes to argue that public spending should offset any drop in private spending. As you know by now, Keynes said a federal budget deficit would stimulate aggregate demand. As a result of the Depression, automatic stabilizers were also introduced, which increased public outlays during recessions and decreased them during expansions. The deficit therefore increases during recessions because, as economic activity slows, unemployment rises, increasing government outlays for unemployment benefits and for other transfer payments. Furthermore, tax revenues decline during recessions. For example, corporate tax revenue fell 10 percent during the 1990–91 recession, while welfare spending jumped 25 percent. An economic expansion is the other side of the coin. As business activity picks up, so do jobs, personal income, and corporate profits, causing federal revenue to swell. With more people employed, fewer people need unemployment benefits and welfare programs. Thus, during an expansion, federal revenue increases more than federal spending, thereby reducing a deficit or increasing a surplus.

Budget Philosophies and Deficits

Several budget philosophies have emerged over the years. Fiscal policy prior to the Great Depression aimed at maintaining an **annually balanced budget,** except during wartime. Since tax revenues rise during expansions and fall during recessions, an annually balanced budget means that spending increases during expansions and declines during recessions. But such a pattern magnifies fluctuations in the business cycle, overheating the economy during expansions and increasing unemployment during recessions.

A second budget philosophy calls for a **cyclically balanced budget,** meaning that budget deficits during recessions are covered by budget surpluses during expansions. Fiscal policy dampens swings in the business cycle without increasing the national debt. Nearly all states have established "rainy day" funds to build up budget surpluses during the good times for use during bad times.

A third budget philosophy is **functional finance,** which says that policy makers should be concerned less with balancing the budget annually, or even over the business cycle, and more with ensuring that the economy produces its potential output. This philosophy argues that one of the federal government's primary responsibilities is to promote stability at the economy's potential level of output. If the budgets needed to keep the economy operating at its potential involve chronic deficits, so be it. Since the Great Depression, budgets in this country have seldom balanced. *Although budget deficits have been larger during recessions than during expansions, the federal budget has been in deficit in all but a dozen years since 1930.*

ASK THE INSTRUCTOR: SHOULD WE AMEND THE CONSTITUTION TO REQUIRE A BALANCED BUDGET?

Deficits Since 1980

As noted in earlier chapters, in 1981 President Reagan secured a three-year budget agreement that included a large tax cut along with increases in defense spending. Supply-side economists argued that tax cuts would stimulate enough economic activity to keep tax revenues from falling. Unspecified spending cuts in the 1981 budget were supposed to erase a projected deficit, but Congress never made the promised cuts. Moreover, overly optimistic revenue projections— so-called "rosy scenarios"—were built into the budget. For example, the budget projected that real GDP would grow by 5.2 percent in 1982, but instead the economy fell into a recession, cutting output 2.0 percent that year. The recession triggered automatic stabilizers, reducing revenues and increasing spending still more. The deficit in 1982 amounted to 4 percent of GDP—at the time one of the largest peacetime deficits ever.

President Reagan's budget strategy during the 1980s called for defense increases but no new taxes and no cuts in Social Security. The deficit climbed to 6 percent of GDP in 1983. In short, the president and Congress cut tax rates but not expenditures. *Relative to GDP, federal revenues declined but federal spending increased.* Exhibit 2 shows federal revenues minus outlays relative to GDP since 1970. As the economy improved during the 1990s, the deficit decreased and then disappeared, turning into a surplus by 1998. That's the short history of modern deficits. Now let's consider why the federal budget was in deficit so long.

EXHIBIT 2

After Decades of Deficits, the U.S. Federal Budget Was in Surplus from 1998 to 2001

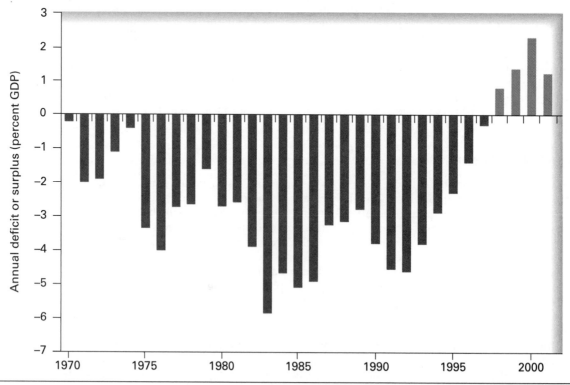

Sources: *Economic Report of the President,* January 2001, Tables B-1 and B-78; and the Office of Policy and Management. For the latest data, go to http://w3.access.gpo.gov/eop/.

Why Did Deficits Persist So Long?

As we have seen, huge deficits came from a combination of tax cuts and spending increases. But why has the budget been in deficit for all but 12 years since 1930? The most obvious answer is that, unlike legislatures in 49 states, Congress is not required to balance the budget. But why does Congress like deficits? One widely accepted model of the public sector assumes that elected officials try to maximize their political support, including votes and campaign contributions. Voters like public spending programs but hate paying taxes, so spending programs win support and taxes lose it. Because of this asymmetry, candidates try to maximize their chances of getting elected and reelected by offering a budget that is long on benefits but short on taxes—in other words, they promote a deficit. Moreover, members of Congress push their favorite programs with little concern about the overall budget. For example, Senator Trent Lott of Mississippi was able to include $1.5 billion in the 2000 budget for an amphibious assault ship to be built in his hometown of Pascagoula. The Navy never even asked for the ship.

Deficits, Surpluses, Crowding Out, and Crowding In

What effect do federal deficits and surpluses have on interest rates? Recall that interest rates affect investment, a critical component of economic growth. What's more, year-to-year fluctuations in investment are the primary source of shifts in aggregate demand. Let's look at the impact of government deficits and surpluses on investment.

Suppose the federal government increases spending without raising taxes, thereby increasing the budget deficit or reducing the surplus. How will this affect national savings, interest rates, and investment? An increase in the government deficit or a decrease in the surplus reduces the supply of national savings, leading to higher interest rates. Higher interest rates discourage, or *crowd out,* some private investment, reducing the stimulating effect of the government's deficit. The extent of **crowding out** is a matter of debate. Some argue that although government deficits may displace some private-sector borrowing, discretionary fiscal policy will result in a net increase in aggregate demand, leading to greater output and employment in the short run. Others believe that the crowding out is more extensive, so borrowing from the public in this way will result in little or no net increase in aggregate demand and output.

Although crowding out is likely to occur to some degree, there is another possibility. If the economy is operating well below its potential, the additional fiscal stimulus provided by a higher government deficit or a smaller surplus could encourage firms to invest more. Recall that an important determinant of investment is business expectations. Government stimulus of a weak economy could put a sunny face on the business outlook. As expectations grow more favorable, firms become more willing to invest. This ability of government deficits to stimulate private investment is sometimes called **crowding in,** to distinguish it from crowding out. For nearly a decade, the Japanese government has pursued deficit spending as a way of getting that flat economy going, but without much success.

Were you ever unwilling to patronize a restaurant because it was too crowded? You simply did not want to put up with the hassle and long wait and were thus "crowded out." As that baseball-player-turned-philosopher Yogi Berra said, "No one goes there nowadays. It's too crowded." Similarly, large government deficits may "crowd out" some investors by driving up interest rates. On the other hand, did you ever pass up an unfamiliar restaurant because the place seemed dead—it had few customers? Perhaps you wondered why so few people chose to eat there. If you had seen just a few more customers, you might have stopped in—you might have been willing to "crowd in." Similarly, businesses may be reluctant to invest in a seemingly lifeless economy. The economic stimulus resulting from deficit spending could encourage some investors to "crowd in."

The Twin Deficits

To finance the huge deficits of the 1980s, the U.S. Treasury had to sell a lot of bonds, pushing up market interest rates. With U.S. interest rates relatively high, foreigners were more willing to buy dollar-denominated bonds. To buy them, foreigners had to exchange their currencies for dollars. This greater demand for dollars caused the dollar to appreciate relative to foreign currencies during the first half of the 1980s. The rising value of the dollar made foreign goods cheaper in the United States and U.S. goods more expensive abroad. Thus, U.S. imports increased and U.S. exports decreased, so the foreign trade deficit increased.

The higher trade deficits meant that foreigners were accumulating dollars. With these dollars, they purchased U.S. assets, including U.S. government bonds, and thereby helped fund the giant federal deficits. The increase in funds from abroad in the 1980s and first half of the 1990s was both good news and bad news for the U.S. economy. The supply of foreign funds increased investment spending in the United States over what would have occurred in the absence of these funds. Ask people what they think of foreign investment in their town; they will likely say it's great. But the foreign supply of funds to some extent simply offsets a decline in U.S. saving. Such a pattern could pose serious problems in the long run. The United States has surrendered a certain amount of control over its economy to foreign investors. And the return on foreign investments in the United States flows abroad.

The Miraculous Budget Surplus

Exhibit 3 summarizes the federal budget since 1970, with outlays relative to GDP shown as the red line and revenues as the blue line. When outlays exceed revenues, as was the case until quite recently, the federal budget is in deficit, measured each year by the vertical distance between the blue and red lines. The pink shading shows the annual deficit as a percent of GDP. In the early 1990s, outlays started to decline relative to GDP, while revenues increased. This shrank the deficit and, by 1998, created an annual budget surplus, as indicated by the blue shading. Specifically, the deficit in 1990, which amounted to 3.8 percent relative to GDP, became a surplus by 1998, amounting to 0.8 percent relative to GDP. This surplus increased to 2.4 percent in 2000 before slipping to 1.2 percent in 2001. What turned a hefty deficit into a surplus, and why has the surplus slipped lately?

Tax Increases. With concern about the deficit growing, Congress and President George H. W. Bush agreed in 1990 to a package of spending cuts and tax increases aimed at trimming budget deficits. Ironically, those tax increases not only may have cost President Bush reelection in 1992 (because it violated his 1988 election promise of "no new taxes"), but they also began the groundwork for erasing the budget deficit, for which President Clinton was able to take credit. For his part, President Clinton increased taxes on high-income households in 1993, boosting the top marginal tax rate from 31 percent to 40 percent. The economy also enjoyed a vigorous recovery during the 1990s, fueled by rising worker productivity, growing consumer spending, globalization of markets, and the strongest stock market in history. As Fed Chairman Alan Greenspan noted, "we built a tax structure on the assumption that the economy would grow over time at rates around those seen from the early 1970s to the mid-1990s, and this structure has generated considerably more revenue as the economy's underlying growth rate has risen."[1]

EXHIBIT 3

During the 1990s, Federal Outlays Declined Relative to GDP and Revenues Increased, Turning Deficits into Surpluses

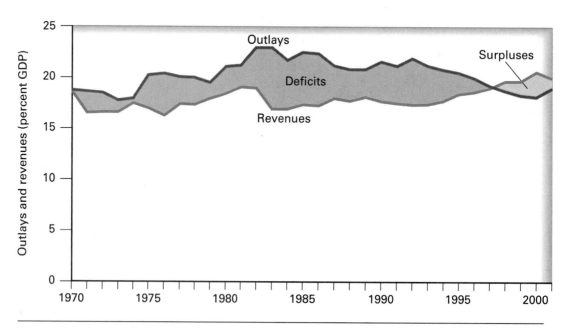

Sources: *Economic Report of the President,* January 2001, Tables B-1 and B-78; and the Office of Management and Budget. For the latest data, go to http://w3.access.gpo.gov/eop/.

[1]"The Paydown of Federal Debt," remarks by Federal Reserve Chairman Alan Greenspan before the Bond Market Association, White Sulphur Springs, West Virginia, 27 April 2001, at http://www.federalreserve.gov/boarddocs/speeches/2001/20010427/default.htm.

The combined effects of higher taxes on the rich and a strengthening economy raised federal revenue from 17.8 percent of GDP in 1990 to 20.3 percent in 2000.

Slower Growth in Federal Outlays. Because of spending discipline imposed by the 1990 legislation, growth in federal outlays slowed compared with those in the 1980s. What's more, the collapse of the Soviet Union reduced U.S. military commitments abroad. Between 1990 and 2000, military personnel levels dropped one-third and defense spending, in real terms, dropped 30 percent. An additional impetus for slower spending growth came from Republicans, who attained congressional majority in 1994. Between 1994 and 2000, domestic spending grew little in real terms. Another beneficial development was the drop in interest rates, which fell to their lowest level in 30 years, saving billions in interest charges on the national debt. In short, federal outlays dropped from 21.6 percent relative to GDP in 1990 to 17.9 percent in 2000.

A Reversal of Fortune in 2001. Thanks to the tax-rate increases and the strong economy, revenues gushed into Washington, growing an average of 8.4 percent per year between 1993 and 2000. Meanwhile, federal outlays remained in check, growing only 3.5 percent per year. By 2000, that combination created a federal budget surplus of $236 billion, quite a turnaround from a deficit that had topped $290 billion only eight years earlier. But in 2001, unemployment increased, the stock market sank, and terrorists crashed jets and spread anthrax. All this had the effect of slowing federal revenues and accelerating federal spending. To counter the recession and cope with terrorism, Congress and the president cut taxes and increased federal programs. The federal budget surplus fell by half between 2000 and 2001. The surplus was projected to turn into a deficit in 2002. After several years of deficit, the long-term budget picture eventually brightens.[2]

But the long-term budget forecast is not quite as rosy as it might appear. More than half the projected surpluses come from the Social Security program, as discussed in the following case study.

ECONDEBATE ONLINE: HOW SHOULD THE U.S. BUDGET SURPLUS BE USED?

\<interactive\>update

ECONNEWS ONLINE: A DISAPPEARING ACT

| CASE**STUDY** | Reforming Social Security and Medicare |

● *Public Policy*

Social Security is a federal redistribution program established during the Great Depression that collects payroll taxes from current workers and their employers to pay pensions to current retirees. Benefits to the more than 40 million recipients in 2001 averaged $10,140 for individual retirees and $16,920 for couples. For the first 50 years of the program, whenever tax revenues exceeded the cost of the program, Congress raised benefits, expanded eligibility, or spent the surplus on something else. Medicare, a program established in the 1960s to provide short-term medical care for the elderly, is also funded by a payroll tax. Social Security and Medicare are credited with helping reduce the poverty level among people aged 65 and older from more than 30 percent in 1960 to 10 percent in 2000—a rate as low or lower than that of any other age group.

In the early 1980s, policy makers began to recognize the tremendous impact that baby boomers would have on such a pay-as-you-go program. When baby boomers begin retiring around 2010, pension and Medicare costs are projected to explode. To address this increase, reforms adopted in 1983 raised the payroll tax rate, expanded the tax base by the rate of inflation, gradually increased the retirement age from 65 to 67, increased the penalty for early

[2]"Revised Budgetary Outlook and Principles for Economic Stimulus," Senate and House Budget Committees, 4 October 2001.

retirement, and offered incentives to delay retirement. These reforms ensured that revenues would exceed costs at least while baby boomers were in the workforce. To help pay for baby boomer retirements, the 1983 reform began accumulating the resulting surplus in trust funds. It is the annual surplus from Social Security and Medicare programs that accounted for most of the current and projected surpluses in the federal budget.

But here's the problem: Both programs are projected to go broke. Without reforms, the growth in beneficiaries and higher medical costs per beneficiary will bankrupt the Medicare Trust Fund by 2029. At that point, Medicare taxes will cover just 62 percent of projected outlays. The Social Security Trust Fund is projected to go broke in 2039, when tax receipts will cover only 73 percent of projected pension outlays. Things get worse after that, as retirees live longer and fewer new workers enter the labor force. In 2000, there were 3.4 workers per beneficiary. By 2030 only 2.1 workers will support each beneficiary. The huge sucking sound will be Social Security and Medicare deficits amounting to nearly a trillion dollars a year. By 2056, Medicare spending will exceed Social Security, and Medicare costs are projected to keep on rising, growing from 2.2 percent of GDP in 2000 to 8.5 percent by 2075.

What to do, what to do? Social Security has been called the "third rail" of American politics: electrically charged and untouchable. Lobbying groups supporting Social Security are so well organized and senior voter participation is so high that any legislator who proposes limiting benefits or increasing payroll taxes risks instant electrocution. So far, the only proposals being pushed would cost revenue in the near term. With regard to Medicare, President George W. Bush proposed a new prescription-drug benefit and budgeted $153 billion for it over the next 10 years. Democrats, calling that plan "grossly inadequate," proposed spending more like $400 billion on it. With regard to Social Security, President Bush wants younger workers offered the opportunity to invest a small portion of their Social Security taxes in the stock market or some other asset. The argument is that such an investment over the long run would yield a higher return than young workers can currently expect from the Social Security program. Diverting payroll taxes to private investment may ultimately contribute to a long-term solution, but the near-term cost is to reduce the flow of revenue supporting this pay-as-you-go plan. To some extent, Bush's 2002 budget proposal recognized this and included $600 billion over 10 years to shore up Social Security.

In summary, Social Security and Medicare have reduced poverty among the elderly, but the program will grow more costly as the elderly population grows and as the flow of young people into the workforce slows. Something has to give if the benefits are to be available for your retirement.

\<interactive\>exercise

- **eACTIVITY: REFORMING SOCIAL SECURITY AND MEDICARE**
- **ECONDEBATE ONLINE: WILL SOCIAL SECURITY SURVIVE INTO THE 21ST CENTURY?**

Sources: John Schwartz, "Social Security Checks to Rise 2.6%," *New York Times,* 20 October 2001; David Rosenbaum, "The President's Budget: Putting Faith in Discipline," *New York Times,* 10 April 2001; Charles Zwick and Peter Lewis, "Apocalypse Not: Social Security Crisis Is Overblown," *Wall Street Journal,* 11 April 2001; "Status of the Social Security and Medicare Programs: A Summary of the 2001 Annual Report," Social Security and Medicare Boards of Trustees, 19 March 2001, at http://www.ssa.gov/OACT/TRSUM/trsummary.html; and the Concord Coalition at http://www.concordcoalition.org/.

The Relative Size of the Public Sector in the United States

So far, we have focused on the federal budget, but a fuller picture should include state and local governments as well. Exhibit 4 shows government outlays at all levels relative to GDP in 10 industrial economies in 1993 and in 2000. Government outlays in the United States in 2000 were 29.3 percent relative to GDP, the smallest share in the group. This is down from 34.1 percent in 1993, a year when only Japan among the 10 industrial economies had a smaller government. Between 1993 and 2000, government outlays relative to GDP shrank in 9 of the 10 industrial economies; the average dropped from 45.2 percent to 39.6 percent. Why the drop? The demise of the Soviet Union in the early 1990s reduced defense outlays in major economies, and the failure of the socialist experiment shifted sentiment more toward private markets, thus diminishing the role of government. What's more, growing prosperity since 1993 meant less demand for government as a source of fiscal stimulus or income redistribution.

The exception to the trend toward less government is Japan, where real estate and stock market prices crashed in 1990, crushing consumer confidence and hobbling the economy for

EXHIBIT 4 |

Government Outlays as a Percentage of GDP Declined Between 1993 and 2000 in
Major Industrial Economies Except Japan

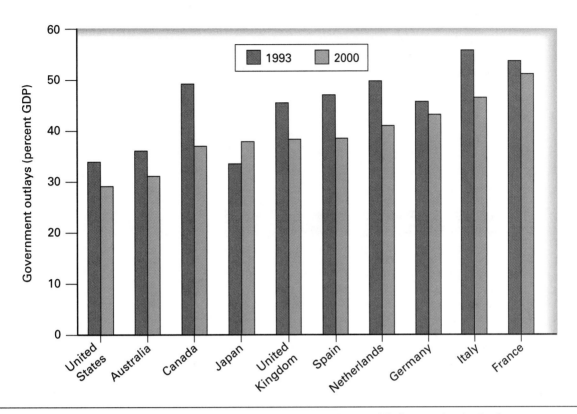

Sources: *OECD Economic Outlook,* Vol. 69 (June 2001), Annex Table 28. For the latest data, go to http://www.oecd.org/eco/eco/.

the last decade. With Japanese consumers unwilling to spend, the government has tried to stimulate demand with capital projects. Government outlays relative to GDP in Japan rose from 33.7 percent in 1993 to 38.2 percent in 2000. Capital programs were financed by larger and larger deficits, which accumulated into growing debt. Despite the stepped-up role for government, unemployment in Japan doubled from 2.5 percent in 1993 to 5.0 percent in 2000. Japan remains the most troubled major economy in the world.

So, except for Japan, the relative size of governments declined in major economies around the world between 1993 and 2000. But, a softening world economy in 2001 punctuated by terrorist attacks on America temporarily reversed the trend toward a shrinking government, especially in the United States, where spending growth exceeded federal revenue growth.

Let's turn our attention to an unintended consequence of decades of federal deficits—a sizable federal debt.

THE NATIONAL DEBT

Federal deficits add up. It took 39 presidents, six wars, the Great Depression, and more than 200 years for the federal debt to reach $1 trillion, as it did in 1981. It took only 3 presidents and another 15 years for that debt to triple in real terms, as it did by 1996. Ironically, the biggest growth in debt occurred primarily under President Reagan, who was elected on a promise to balance the budget.

The federal deficit is a flow variable measuring the amount by which outlays exceed revenues in a particular year. The federal debt, or the **national debt,** is a stock variable measuring the accumulation of past deficits, the total amount owed by the federal government. This section puts the national debt in perspective by looking at (1) changes over time, (2) U.S. debt levels compared with those in other countries, (3) interest on the debt, and (4) the prospect of paying off the debt. Note that the national debt ignores the projected liabilities of Social

Chapter 32 Federal Budgets and Public Policy

551

Security, Medicare, or other federal retirement programs. If these programs were included, the national debt would triple.

In talking about the national debt, we should distinguish between the gross debt and debt held by the public. The *gross debt* includes U.S. Treasury securities purchased by various federal agencies. Since this is debt the federal government owes to itself, policy analysts often ignore it and focus on *debt held by the public,* which includes debt held by households, firms, banks (including Federal Reserve Banks), and foreign entities. As of 2001, the gross federal debt stood at about $5.8 trillion, and the debt held by the public stood at $3.4 trillion.

One way to measure debt over time is relative to the economy's production and income, or GDP (just as a bank might compare the size of a mortgage to a borrower's income). Exhibit 5 shows federal debt held by the public relative to GDP. The cost of World War II ballooned the debt to over 100 percent relative to GDP in 1946. By 1980, it had dropped to 26 percent. But huge deficits in the 1980s and early 1990s nearly doubled debt to 49 percent by 1993. Since then, the favorable developments already discussed cut debt to 34 percent relative to GDP by 2001. Thus, between 1946 and 2001, the federal debt held by the public dropped more than two-thirds relative to GDP.

ASK THE INSTRUCTOR: HOW BIG IS THE NATIONAL DEBT?

An International Perspective on Public Debt

How does government debt in the United States compare with debt levels in other countries? Exhibit 6 compares the net government debt in the United States relative to GDP with those of nine other industrial countries. *Net debt* includes outstanding liabilities of federal, state, and local governments minus government financial assets, such as loans to students and farmers, securities, cash on hand, and foreign exchange on reserve. Despite the increase in federal debt since 1980, the United States ranks in the middle for industrial countries, with net debt in 2000 for all levels of government combined amounting to 43 percent of GDP. Australia was the low-

EXHIBIT 5

Federal Debt Held by the Public as a Percentage of GDP: 1946 to 2001

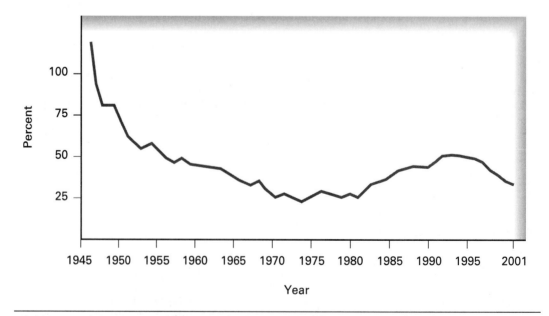

Source: *Economic Report of the President,* January 2001, the Joint Economic Committee, U.S. Congress. To compute the latest data, go to http://w3.access.gpo.gov/eop/.

EXHIBIT 6

Relative to GDP, U.S. Net Public Debt Is About Average for Major Economies

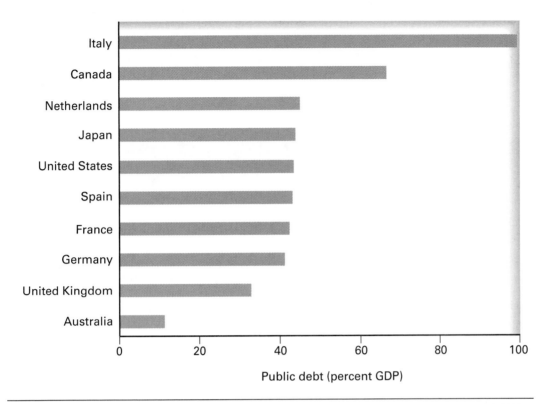

Public debt (percent GDP)

Source: *OECD Economic Outlook,* 68 (June 2001), Annex Table 35. Figures are for net debt at all levels of government in 2000.

est at 11 percent, and Italy was the highest at 100 percent. Because political power in Italy is fragmented across a dozen parties, a national government can be formed only through a fragile coalition of parties that cannot withstand the voter displeasure from hiking taxes or cutting public spending. Thus, deficits in Italy persisted until quite recently, adding to an already high national debt. Lately, as a condition for joining the European Monetary Union, member countries have been forced to reduce their federal deficits. Italy, for example, went from a deficit that was 9 percent relative to GDP in 1994 to a balanced budget in 2000.

Interest on the National Debt

Purchasers of federal securities range from individuals who buy $25 U.S. savings bonds to institutions that buy $1 million Treasury bonds. Because most federal securities are short term, the national debt "turns over" rapidly—nearly half the debt is refinanced every year. With more than $150 billion coming due each month, debt service payments are quite sensitive to movements in interest rates. Based on a $3.4 trillion debt held by the public, an increase of 1 percentage point in the nominal interest rate ultimately increases annual interest costs by about $34 billion. Interest payments on the national debt have increased from 8 percent of the federal budget in 1978 to 12 percent in 2001.

Who Bears the Burden of the Debt?

Deficit spending is a way of billing future taxpayers for current spending. The national debt raises moral questions about the right of one generation of taxpayers to bequeath to the next generation the burden of its borrowing. To what extent do budget deficits shift the burden to future generations? Let's examine two arguments about the burden of the debt.

We Owe It to Ourselves. It is often argued that the debt is not a burden to future generations because, although future generations must service the debt, those same generations receive the debt service payments. It's true that if U.S. citizens forgo present consumption to buy

bonds, they or their heirs will receive the interest payments, so debt service payments will stay in the country. Thus, future generations will both pay the interest on the debt and receive those same interest payments. In that sense, the debt is not a burden on future generations. It's all in the family, so to speak.

Foreign Ownership of Debt. But the "we owe it to ourselves" argument does not apply to that portion of the national debt purchased by foreigners. Foreigners who buy U.S. government bonds forgo present consumption and are paid back in the future. An influx of foreign savings reduces the amount of current consumption that Americans must sacrifice to finance the national debt. *A reliance on foreigners, however, increases the burden of the debt on future generations because future debt service payments no longer remain in the country.* Foreigners own about 20 percent of all federal debt.

<interactive>**video**

CNN VIDEO: "A MATTER OF PRIORITIES"

Crowding Out and Capital Formation

As we have seen, government borrowing can drive up interest rates, crowding out some private investment by making it more costly. The long-run effect of deficit spending depends on how the government spends the borrowed funds. If additional government outlays are oriented toward investments like better interstate highways and a more educated workforce, the public investment may be as productive as any private investment forgone. Thus, there may be no harmful effects on the economy's long-run productive capabilities. If, however, the additional borrowed dollars go toward current consumption, such as farm subsidies or federal retirement programs, less capital formation will result. With less investment today, there will be a smaller endowment of capital equipment and technology, slowing the growth of labor productivity in the future. As a case in point, between 1992 and 2000, the federal budget went from a big deficit to a big surplus. Real private investment, which had not changed during the deficit years of 1987 to 1992, doubled from 1992 to 2000. Thus, private investment increased as the federal deficit turned into a surplus.

Ironically, despite the large federal deficits of the 1980s and early 1990s, public investments in roads, bridges, and airports—so-called *public capital*— declined, perhaps because a growing share of the federal budget went toward income redistribution. In 1970, the value of the nation's public infrastructure was about 50 percent of GDP; this figure has since declined to about 40 percent. Some argue that declining investment in the public infrastructure serves as a drag on productivity growth. For example, the failure to invest sufficiently in airport safety and efficiency and in the air traffic control system has led to congested airports and flight delays, a problem compounded by the terrorist hijackings of September 2001.

Therefore, government deficits of one generation can affect the standard of living of the next. Note again that our current measure of the national debt does not capture all burdens passed on to future generations. As mentioned earlier, if the unfunded liabilities of government retirement programs, such as Social Security, were included, this would triple the national debt. A model that considers some intergenerational issues of public budgeting is discussed in the following case study.

CASE**STUDY**	An Intergenerational View of Deficits and Debt
	● *Public Policy*

Robert Barro, a Harvard economist, has developed a model that assumes parents are concerned about the welfare of their children who, in turn, are concerned about the welfare of *their* children, and so on for generations. Thus, the welfare of all generations is tied together. According to Barro, parents concerned about future generations will reduce the burden of federal debt on future generations and thus reduce the potential stimulative effect of deficit spending.

Here's his argument. When the government incurs deficits, this keeps current taxes lower than they would otherwise be, but taxes in the future must increase to service the resulting debt. If there is no regard for the welfare of future generations, then the older people are, the more attractive debt becomes relative to current taxes. Older people can enjoy the benefits of public spending now but will not live long enough to help finance the debt through higher taxes or lower public benefits.

But parents can undo the harm that deficit financing imposes on their children by consuming less now and saving more. As governments substitute deficits for taxes, parents will consume less and save more to increase gifts and bequests to their children. If increases in household saving just offset increases in federal deficits, deficit spending will not increase aggregate demand because the decline in consumption will negate the fiscal stimulus provided by deficits. This intergenerational transfer offsets the future burden of higher debt and neutralizes the effect of deficit spending on aggregate demand, output, and employment.

The large budget deficits caused in part by tax cuts in the early 1980s seem to provide a natural experiment for testing Barro's theory. The evidence fails to support his theory because the large federal deficits coincided with lower, not higher, saving rates. Yet defenders of Barro's view say that maybe the saving rate was low because people were optimistic about future economic growth, an optimism reflected by the strong growth in stock market averages during the 1990s. Or maybe the saving rate was low because people believed the tax cuts would result not in higher future taxes but in lower government spending, as President Reagan promised.

But there are other reasons to question Barro's theory. First, individuals without children may be less concerned about the welfare of future generations. Second, his theory assumes that people are well informed about federal spending and tax policies and about the future consequences of current policies; most people, however, seem to know little about such matters. One survey found that few adults polled had any idea about the size of the federal deficit. In the poll taken of 1,000 adults in 1995, when the federal deficit was $164 billion, only 1 in 10 said correctly that the deficit was between $100 billion and $400 billion.

\<interactive\>exercise

eACTIVITY: AN INTERGENERATIONAL VIEW OF DEFICITS AND DEBT

Sources: Robert J. Barro, "The Ricardian Approach to Budget Deficits," *Journal of Economic Perspectives* 3 (Spring 1989); Jay Mathews, "How High Is the Deficit, the Dow? Most in Survey Didn't Know," *Hartford Courant,* 19 October 1995; and David Rosenbaum, "Congress Agrees on Final Details of Tax-Cut Bill," *New York Times,* 26 May 2001.

Paying Off the Debt

As noted in an earlier chapter, labor productivity during 1996 and 2001 grew two-thirds faster on average than it did during the previous two decades, thus contributing to higher federal revenues that helped create budget surpluses. Most observers, including Fed Chairman Greenspan, expect labor productivity to continue growing at the higher recent rate, which is one reason why Congressional budget committees, even after the terrorist attacks, were still projecting the federal budget to eventually show a surplus.[3]

What impact do surpluses have on the economy? In the short run, a federal surplus could reduce aggregate demand, which could worsen a recession but relieve inflationary pressure during good times. A budget surplus would also increase the national saving rate, which should reduce interest rates and thus stimulate investment in the long run. Greater investment would, over time, provide more capital per worker, which would enhance labor productivity and income, thus boosting tax revenue. Therefore, a federal budget surplus could be self-reinforcing. If the surplus were used to pay down the national debt, over time, the cost of servicing the remaining debt would be reduced, gradually freeing up budget dollars for tax cuts, for other public spending programs, or, still more, to pay down the national debt.

In 2001, Fed Chairman Greenspan said, "Current forecasts suggest that under a reasonably wide range of possible tax and spending policies, the resulting surpluses will allow the Treasury debt held by the public to be paid off."[4] But he also felt that eliminating public debt has a small downside. Treasury debt provides an asset that is free of credit risk—a characteristic that is attractive to many investors, particularly during times of economic and financial turbulence. Treasury securities also offer a benchmark for pricing riskier debt. Greenspan says that

---

[3]"Revised Budgetary Outlook and Principles for Economic Stimulus," Senate and House Budget Committees, 4 October 2001.
[4]"The Paydown of Federal Debt," remarks by Federal Reserve Chairman Alan Greenspan before the Bond Market Association, White Sulphur Springs, West Virginia, 27 April 2001, at http://www.federalreserve.gov/boarddocs/speeches/2001/20010427/default.htm.

eliminating Treasury debt will remove something of economic value and will require that significant adjustment be made as financial markets seek an alternative. The Federal Reserve will have to adjust to the loss of Treasury debt. The Fed is already experimenting with other relatively riskless securities, including those issued by other federal agencies, by municipal governments, and even by foreign governments.

Most observers expect that federal deficits will return once baby boomers begin to retire after 2010, because of the higher outlays for Social Security and Medicare (as discussed on the first case study). Even though both programs have been building reserves in trust funds, this has been largely a paper exercise because surpluses in these programs have been used to purchase Treasury debt. As these securities mature, the Treasury will have to come up with the money to pay the trust funds. Most expect the Treasury at that point to simply issue more debt to retire existing debt. As Treasury Secretary Paul O'Neill said, the trust fund has "no assets"; the U.S. Treasury bonds it holds are merely government IOUs.[5]

CONCLUSION

John Maynard Keynes introduced the idea that federal deficit spending is an appropriate fiscal policy when private aggregate demand is insufficient to achieve potential output. The federal budget has not been the same since. Beginning in 1960, the federal budget was in deficit every year but one until 1998. And beginning in the early 1980s, huge federal deficits dominated the fiscal policy debate, tripling the national debt in real terms and putting discretionary fiscal policy off limits. But after peaking at $290 billion in 1992, the deficit came down because of higher tax rates on high-income households, reduced federal outlays (especially for defense), and a rip-roaring economy fueled by faster labor productivity growth and a dazzling stock market. The softening economy of 2001 and the terrorist attacks put discretionary fiscal policy back in the picture.

<interactive>exercise

READING IT RIGHT: WALL STREET JOURNAL EXERCISE

endofchaptermaterial

- **Summary**
- **Questions for Review**
- **Problems and Exercises**

- **Experiential Exercises**
- **Wall Street Journal Exercise**

Take the Post-Test to assess your overall understanding of the key ideas in this chapter. The Post-Test provides a comprehensive selection of exam-style questions addressing the main topics and concepts of the chapter. At the completion of each Post-Test, you will receive a score and instructive feedback on how you answered each question, and a direct link to the part of the chapter addressed in the question. Take the Post-Test as often as you need to—a record of your progress for each attempt is kept for you to revisit and gauge your improvement. And each Post-Test is randomly generated, so every attempt is new.

[5]David Wessel, "Notes on Riding the Third Rail," *Wall Street Journal,* 5 July 2001.

CHAPTER 33

<interactive>
text

International Finance

What does a "strong dollar" mean? Why do U.S. consumers favor a strong dollar while U.S. producers have mixed feelings? Should we worry when we hear about rising U.S. trade deficits? And what about the new European currency, the euro? Answers to these and other questions are explored in this chapter, which focuses on international finance.

A U.S. firm shopping for a German printing press will be quoted a price in euros. Suppose that machine costs 1 million euros. How many dollars is that? The cost in dollars will depend on the current exchange rate. When buyers and sellers from two countries trade, two currencies are usually involved. Supporting the flows of goods and services are flows of currencies that connect all international transactions.

The *exchange rate* between two currencies—the price of one in terms of the other—is the means by which the price of a good produced in one country translates into the price paid by a buyer in another country. The willingness of buyers and sellers to strike deals therefore depends on the rate of exchange between currencies. In this chapter we examine the international transactions that determine the relative value of one currency in terms of another. Topics discussed in this chapter include:

- Balance of payments
- Trade deficits and surpluses
- Foreign exchange markets

- Purchasing power parity
- Flexible exchange rates
- Fixed exchange rates

557

- International monetary system
- Bretton Woods agreement
- Managed float

\<interactive\>**exercise**

ECONDEBATE ONLINE: INTERNATIONAL FINANCE

\<interactive\>**update**

- ECONDATA ONLINE: INTERNATIONAL FINANCE
- ECONLINKS ONLINE: ECONOMICS WEB LINKS
- ECONNEWS ONLINE: INTERNATIONAL FINANCE

BALANCE OF PAYMENTS

A country's gross domestic product measures the flow of economic activity that occurs within that economy during a given period. To account for dealings abroad, countries also keep track of their international transactions. A country's *balance of payments,* as introduced in Chapter 4, summarizes all economic transactions that occur during a given period between residents of that country and residents of other countries. *Residents* include individuals, firms, and governments.

International Economic Transactions

The balance of payments measures economic transactions that occur between countries, whether they involve goods and services, real and financial assets, or transfer payments. Because it reflects the volume of transactions that occur during a particular period, usually a year, the balance of payments measures a *flow.*

Some transactions included in the balance of payments do not involve payments of money. For example, if *Time* magazine ships a new printing press to its Australian subsidiary, no payment occurs, yet an economic transaction involving another country has taken place and must be included in the balance of payments. Similarly, if CARE sends food to Africa or the Pentagon provides military assistance to Saudi Arabia, these transactions must be captured in the balance of payments. So remember, although we speak of the *balance of payments,* a more descriptive phrase would be the *balance of economic transactions.*

Balance-of-payments accounts are maintained according to the principles of *double-entry bookkeeping,* in which entries on one side of the ledger are called *credits,* and entries on the other side are called *debits.* As we will see, the balance of payments consists of several individual accounts; a deficit in one or more accounts must be offset by a surplus in the other accounts. Since total credits must equal total debits, there is a *balance* of payments. During a given period, such as a year, the inflow of receipts from the rest of the world, which are entered as credits, equals the outflow of payments to the rest of the world, which are entered as debits. The next few sections describe the major accounts in the balance of payments.

\<interactive\>**example**

NETBOOKMARK: U.S. INTERNATIONAL ACCOUNTS

\<interactive\>**video**

ASK THE INSTRUCTOR: HOW DO WE PAY FOR IMPORTS?

The Merchandise Trade Balance

The *merchandise trade balance*, a term introduced in Chapter 4, equals the value of merchandise exports minus the value of merchandise imports. The merchandise account reflects trade in goods, or tangible products (stuff you can drop on your toe), like French wine and U.S. computers, and is often referred to simply as the *trade balance*. The value of U.S. merchandise exports is listed as a credit in the U.S. balance-of-payments account because U.S. residents must *be paid* for the exported goods. The value of U.S. merchandise imports is listed as a debit in the balance-of-payments account because U.S. residents must *pay* foreigners for imported goods.

If the value of merchandise exports exceeds the value of merchandise imports, there is a *surplus* in the merchandise trade balance, or, more simply, a *trade surplus*. If the value of merchandise imports exceeds the value of merchandise exports, there is a *deficit* in the merchandise trade balance, or a *trade deficit*. The merchandise trade balance, which is reported monthly, influences foreign exchange markets, the stock market, and other financial markets. The trade balance depends on a variety of factors, including the relative strength and competitiveness of the domestic economy compared with other economies and the relative value of the domestic currency compared with other currencies.

U.S. merchandise trade since 1960 is depicted in Exhibit 1, where exports (the blue line) and imports (the red line) are expressed as a percentage of GDP. During the 1960s, exports exceeded imports, so there were trade surpluses, shaded in blue. Since 1976, imports have exceeded exports every year, resulting in trade deficits, shaded in pink. Trade deficits as a percentage of GDP have increased steadily during the last decade, growing from 1.3 percent in 1991 to 4.6 percent in 2000, when it reached a record $452.2 billion. Notice that exports as a percentage of GDP dipped during the 1980s, when the value of the dollar rose sharply relative to other currencies (more on this later).

The Balance on Goods and Services

The merchandise trade balance focuses on the flow of goods, but services are also traded internationally. *Services* are intangibles, such as transportation, insurance, banking, consulting, and tourism. Services also include the income earned from foreign investments less the income

EXHIBIT 1

Relative To GDP, U.S. Imports Have Topped Exports Since 1976, and the Trade Deficit Has Widened

Source: *Economic Report of the President,* January 2001; and the Bureau of Economic Analysis. Figures exclude military transactions. For the latest trade data, go to http://www.bea.doc.gov/bea/di1.htm.

earned by foreigners from their investment in the U.S. economy. Services are often called "invisibles" because they are not tangible. The value of U.S. service exports, like when an Irish tourist visits New York City, is listed as a credit in the U.S. balance-of-payments account because U.S. residents receive payments for these services. The value of U.S. service imports, like when a computer specialist in India enters data for an insurance company from Connecticut, is listed as a debit in the balance-of-payments account because U.S. residents must pay for the imported services.

The **balance on goods and services** is the value of exports of goods and services minus the value of imports of goods and services. U.S.-produced goods and services that are sold or otherwise provided to foreigners form part of U.S. output and income. Conversely, imports of goods and services form part of the nation's current expenditures—part of consumption, investment, and government purchases. Allocating imports to each expenditure component is an accounting nightmare, so we usually just subtract imports from exports to yield *net exports*. Thus, U.S. gross domestic product in a given year sums consumption, investment, government purchases, and net exports. Because the United States exports more services than it imports, the balance on services has been in surplus for the last three decades, so the balance on goods and services has not been as negative as the merchandise trade balance.

Unilateral Transfers

Unilateral transfers consist of government transfers to foreign residents, foreign aid, personal gifts to friends and relatives abroad, personal and institutional charitable donations, and the like. Money sent abroad by a U.S. resident to friends or relatives would be included in U.S. unilateral transfers and would be a debit in the balance-of-payments account. For example, immigrants to the United States often send money to families back home. **Net unilateral transfers** equal the unilateral transfers received from abroad by U.S. residents minus unilateral transfers sent to foreign residents by U.S. residents. U.S. net unilateral transfers have been negative each year since World War II, except for 1991, when the U.S. government received sizable transfers from foreign governments to help pay their share of the Persian Gulf War. In 2000, net unilateral transfers averaged about $500 per U.S. household.

The United States places no restrictions on the amount of money sent out of the country.[1] Other countries, particularly developing countries, strictly limit the amount of money that may be sent abroad. More generally, many developing countries, such as China, restrict the convertibility of their currency into other currencies.

When we add net unilateral transfers to the exports of goods and services minus the imports of goods and services, we get the **balance on current account,** which is reported quarterly. Thus, *the current account includes all transactions in currently produced goods and services plus net unilateral transfers.* It can be negative, reflecting a current account deficit; positive, reflecting a current account surplus; or zero.

ECONDATA ONLINE: CURRENT ACCOUNT BALANCE

The Capital Account

The current account records international transactions involving the flows of goods (including capital goods), services, and unilateral transfers. When economists talk about capital, they typically mean the physical goods employed to produce goods and services. But sometimes *capital* is just another word for *money*—money to acquire financial assets, such as stocks, bonds, and bank balances, and money to buy foreign land, housing, plants, equipment, and other physical assets. The **capital account** records international transactions involving foreign assets and liabilities. For example, U.S. residents purchase foreign securities to earn a higher rate of return and to diversify their portfolios. U.S. capital flows out when Americans buy foreign assets. Foreign capital flows in when foreigners buy U.S. assets.

Between 1917 and 1982, the United States ran a deficit in the capital account, meaning that U.S. residents purchased more foreign assets than foreigners purchased assets in the United

---

[1]Federal authorities do, however, require reporting the source of cash exports of $10,000 or more. This measure is aimed at reducing money laundering overseas.

States. The net income from these foreign assets improved our balance on current account. But in 1983, for the first time in 65 years, high real interest rates in the United States (relative to those in the rest of the world) resulted in foreigners purchasing more assets in the United States than U.S. residents purchased abroad. Since 1983, U.S. imports of capital have exceeded exports of capital nearly every year, meaning there has been a surplus in our capital account.

Americans owe foreigners more and more each year. *The United States is now the world's largest net debtor nation.* This is not as bad as it sounds, since foreign purchases of assets in the United States add to America's productive capacity and promotes employment. But the return on these assets flows to foreigners, not to Americans. Note that capital inflows and outflows are not considered imports or exports, because they reflect the purchase of existing real capital and financial assets rather than the purchase of currently produced goods and services.

The Statistical Discrepancy

As we have seen, the U.S. balance of payments records all transactions between U.S. residents and foreign residents during a specified period. It is easier to describe this record than to compile it. Despite efforts to capture all international transactions, some go unreported. For example, the government has difficulty monitoring cross-border shopping or illegal drug trafficking. But as the name *balance of payments* suggests, debits must equal credits—the entire balance-of-payments account must by definition be in balance. To ensure that the two sides balance, a residual account called the *statistical discrepancy* was created. An excess of credits in all other accounts is offset by an equivalent debit in the statistical discrepancy account, or an excess of debits in all other accounts is offset by an equivalent credit in the discrepancy account. So you might think of the statistical discrepancy as the official "fudge factor." The statistical discrepancy provides analysts with both a measure of the net error in the balance-of-payments data and a means of satisfying the double-entry bookkeeping requirement that total debits equal total credits.

Deficits and Surpluses

Nations, like households, operate under a cash-flow constraint. Expenditures cannot exceed income plus cash on hand and borrowed funds. We have distinguished between *current* transactions, which are the income and expenditures from exports, imports, and unilateral transfers, and *capital* transactions, which reflect international investments and borrowing. Any surplus or deficit in one account must be balanced by surpluses or deficits in other balance-of-payments accounts. The current account has been in deficit since 1982, meaning that the sum of U.S. imports of goods and services plus unilateral transfers to foreigners has exceeded the sum spent by foreigners on our exports and sent as unilateral transfers to us.

Exhibit 2 presents the U.S. balance-of-payments statement for 2000. All transactions requiring payments from foreigners to U.S. residents are entered as credits, indicated by a plus sign (+), because they result in an inflow of funds from foreign residents to U.S. residents. All transactions requiring payments to foreigners from U.S. residents are entered as debits, indicated by a minus sign (−), because they result in an outflow of funds from U.S. residents to foreign residents. As you can see, surpluses in the capital account and in the statistical discrepancy offset a deficit in the current account.

Foreign exchange is the currency of another country that is needed to carry out international transactions. A country runs a deficit in its current account when the amount of foreign exchange that country gets from exporting goods and services and from receipts of unilateral transfers falls short of the amount needed to pay for its imports and to make unilateral transfers. The additional foreign exchange required must come from a net capital inflow (borrowing from abroad, foreign purchases of domestic stocks and bonds, foreigners buying a steel plant in Pittsburgh or a ski lodge in Aspen, and so forth). If a country runs a current account surplus, the foreign exchange received from selling exports and from unilateral transfers received exceeds the amount required to pay for imports and to make unilateral transfers. This excess foreign exchange could be held in a bank account, converted to the domestic currency, or used to purchase foreign stocks, bonds, or other foreign assets, such as a shoe plant in Italy or a villa on the French Riviera.

When all transactions are considered, the balance of payments must always balance, though specific accounts usually do not. A deficit in a particular account should not necessarily be viewed as a source of concern, nor should a surplus be a source of satisfaction. The deficit in the U.S. current account in recent years has been offset by a surplus in the capital account. As a result, foreigners are acquiring more claims on U.S. assets, resulting in an outflow of wealth from the United States.

EXHIBIT 2

U.S. Balance of Payments: 2000 (billions of dollars)

Item	
Current Account	
1. Merchandise exports	+772.2
2. Merchandise imports	−1,224.4
3. Trade balance (1 + 2)	−452.2
4. Service exports	+646.4
5. Service imports	−584.7
6. Goods and services balance (3 + 4 + 5)	−390.5
7. Net unilateral transfers	−54.2
8. Current account balance (6 + 7)	−444.7
Capital Account	
9. Outflow of U.S. capital	−581.0
10. Inflow of foreign capital	+1,024.2
11. Capital account balance (9 + 10)	+443.2
12. Statistical discrepancy	+1.5
TOTAL (8 + 11 + 12)	**0.0**

Source: *Survey of Current Business,* U.S. Department of Commerce, July 2001. For the latest data, go to http://www.bea.doc.gov/.

<interactive>video

CNN VIDEO: "THE TROUBLES WITH TRADE"

FOREIGN EXCHANGE RATES AND MARKETS

Now that you have some idea about international flows, we can take a closer look at the forces that determine the underlying value of the currencies involved. Let's begin by looking at exchange rates and the market for foreign exchange.

Foreign Exchange

Foreign exchange, recall, is foreign currency needed to carry out international transactions. The **exchange rate** is the price of a unit of one currency required to purchase a unit of another currency. Exchange rates are determined by the interaction of the households, firms, private financial institutions, governments, and central banks that buy and sell foreign exchange. The exchange rate fluctuates to equate the quantity of foreign exchange demanded with the quantity supplied. Typically, foreign exchange is made up of bank deposits denominated in the foreign currency. When foreign travel is involved, foreign exchange may consist of foreign paper money.

The foreign exchange market incorporates all the arrangements used to buy and sell foreign exchange. This market is not so much a physical place as a network of telephones and computers connecting large banks all over the world. Perhaps you have seen pictures of foreign exchange traders in New York, Frankfurt, London, or Tokyo in front of computer screens amid a tangle of phone lines. The foreign exchange market is like an all-night diner—it never closes. A trading center is always open somewhere in the world.

We will consider the market for the euro in terms of the dollar. But first a bit about the euro. For decades the nations of Western Europe have tried to increase their economic cooperation and trade. These countries believed they would be more productive and more competitive with the United States if they acted less like a dozen separate economies and more like the 50 United States, with a single set of trade regulations and one currency. Imagine the hassle involved if each of the 50 states had its own currency.

In January 2002, euro bills and coins entered circulation in the 12 European countries adopting the new common currency. The big advantage of a common currency is that Europeans no longer have to change money every time they cross a border or trade with other countries in the group. Again, the inspiration for this is the United States, arguably the most successful economy in world history.

So the euro is now the common currency in the *euro area, euro zone,* or *Euroland,* as it has been called. The price, or exchange rate, of the euro in terms of the dollar is the number of dollars required to purchase one euro. An increase in the number of dollars needed to purchase a euro indicates a weakening, or a **depreciation,** of the dollar. A decrease in the number of dollars needed to purchase a euro indicates a strengthening, or an **appreciation,** of the dollar. Put another way, a decrease in the number of euros needed to purchase a dollar is a depreciation of the dollar, and an increase in the number of euros needed to purchase a dollar is an appreciation of the dollar.

Since the exchange rate is a price, it is determined using the conventional tools of supply and demand: The equilibrium price of foreign exchange is the one that equates quantity demanded with quantity supplied. To simplify the analysis, let's suppose that the United States and Euroland make up the entire world, so the supply and demand for euros is the supply and demand for foreign exchange from the U.S. perspective.

The Demand for Foreign Exchange

U.S. residents need euros to pay for goods and services produced in Euroland, to buy assets there, to make loans to Euroland, or simply to send cash gifts to friends or relatives there. Whenever U.S. residents need euros, they must buy them in the foreign exchange market, which could be their local bank, paying for them with dollars.

Exhibit 3 depicts a market for foreign exchange—in this case, euros. The horizontal axis shows the quantity of foreign exchange, measured here in millions of euros. The vertical axis shows the price per unit of foreign exchange, measured here as the number of dollars required to purchase one euro. The demand curve D for foreign exchange conveys the inverse relationship between the dollar price of the euro and the quantity of euros demanded, other things assumed constant. Some of the factors assumed constant along the demand curve are the incomes and preferences of U.S. consumers, the expected inflation rates in the United States and Euroland, the euro price of goods in Euroland, and interest rates in the United States and Euroland. People have many reasons for demanding foreign exchange, but in the aggregate, the lower the dollar price of foreign exchange, other things constant, the greater the quantity demanded.

A drop in the dollar price of foreign exchange, in this case the euro, means that fewer dollars are needed to purchase each euro, so the dollar prices of Euroland products (like German cars, Italian shoes, tickets to Disneyland-Paris, and Euroland securities), which have price tags listed in euros, become cheaper. The cheaper it is to buy euros, the lower the dollar price of Euroland products to U.S. residents, so the greater the quantity of euros demanded by U.S. residents, other things constant. For example, a cheap enough euro might persuade you to tour Rome, climb the Austrian Alps, wander the museums of Paris, or crawl the pubs of Dublin.

EXHIBIT 3

The Foreign Exchange Market

The fewer dollars needed to purchase 1 unit of foreign exchange, the lower the price of foreign goods and the greater the quantity of foreign goods demanded. The greater the demand for foreign goods, the greater the amount of foreign exchange demanded. The demand curve for foreign exchange slopes downward. An increase in the exchange rate makes U.S. products cheaper for foreigners. The increased demand for U.S. goods implies an increase in the quantity of foreign exchange supplied. The supply curve of foreign exchange slopes upward.

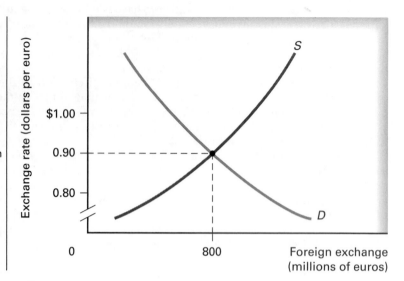

The Supply of Foreign Exchange

The supply of foreign exchange is generated by the desire of foreign residents to acquire dollars—that is, to exchange euros for dollars. Residents of Euroland want dollars to buy U.S. goods and services, to buy U.S. assets, make loans in dollars, or make cash gifts in dollars to their U.S. friends and relatives. Europeans supply euros in the foreign exchange market to acquire the dollars they need. An increase in the dollar-per-euro exchange rate, other things constant, makes U.S. products cheaper for foreigners because foreign residents need fewer euros to get the same number of dollars. For example, suppose a Dell computer sells for $900. If the exchange rate is $0.90 per euro, that computer costs 1,000 euros; if the exchange rate is $1.00 per euro, it costs only 900 euros. The number of Dell computers demanded in Euroland increases as the dollar-per-euro exchange rate increases, other things constant, so more euros will be supplied on the foreign exchange market to buy dollars.

The positive relationship between the dollar-per-euro exchange rate and the quantity of euros supplied on the foreign exchange market is expressed in Exhibit 3 by the upward-sloping supply curve for foreign exchange (again, euros in our example). The supply curve is drawn assuming that other things remain constant, including Euroland incomes and preferences, expectations about the rates of inflation in Euroland and the United States, and interest rates in Euroland and the United States.

Determining the Exchange Rate

Exhibit 3 brings together the supply and demand for foreign exchange to determine the exchange rate. At a rate of $0.90 per euro, the quantity of euros demanded equals the quantity supplied—in our example, 800 million euros. Once achieved, this equilibrium rate will remain constant until a change occurs in one of the factors that affect supply or demand. If the exchange rate is allowed to adjust freely, or to *float*, in response to market forces, the market will clear continually, as the quantities of foreign exchange demanded and supplied are equated.

What if the initial equilibrium is upset by a change in one of the underlying forces that affect supply or demand? For example, suppose an increase in U.S. income causes Americans to increase their demand for all normal goods, including those from Euroland. An increase in U.S. income will shift the U.S. demand curve for foreign exchange to the right, as Americans seek more euros to buy more Italian marble, Dutch chocolate, French couture, German machines, and euro securities.

This increased demand for euros is shown in Exhibit 4 by a rightward shift of the demand curve for foreign exchange. The supply curve does not change because an increase in U.S.

EXHIBIT 4 |

Effect on the Foreign Exchange Market of an Increase in Demand for Euros

The intersection of supply curve *S* and demand curve *D* determines the exchange rate. At an exchange rate of $0.90 per euro, the quantity of euros demanded equals the quantity supplied. An increase in the demand for euros from *D* to *D'* leads to an increase in the exchange rate from $0.90 to $0.92 per euro.

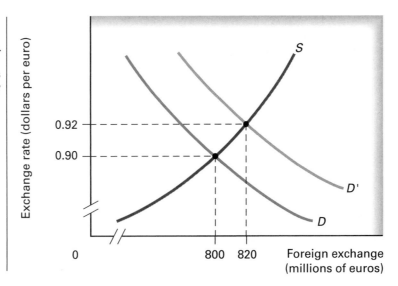

income should not affect Eurolanders' willingness to supply euros. The shift of the demand curve from *D* to *D'* leads to an increase in the exchange rate from $0.90 per euro to $0.92 per euro. Thus, the euro increases in value, or appreciates, while the dollar falls in value, or depreciates. The higher exchange value of the euro prompts some Eurolanders to purchase more American products, which are now cheaper in terms of the euro.

To review: Any increase in the demand for foreign exchange or any decrease in its supply, other things constant, causes an increase in the number of dollars required to purchase one unit of foreign exchange, which is a depreciation of the dollar. On the other hand, any decrease in the demand for foreign exchange or any increase in its supply, other things constant, causes a reduction in the number of dollars required to purchase one unit of foreign exchange, which is an appreciation of the dollar.

Arbitrageurs and Speculators

Exchange rates between specific currencies are nearly identical at any given time in markets around the world. For example, the dollar price of a euro is the same in New York, Frankfurt, Tokyo, London, Zurich, Hong Kong, Istanbul, and other financial centers. **Arbitrageurs**—dealers who take advantage of any difference in exchange rates between markets by buying low and selling high—ensure this equality. Their actions help to equalize exchange rates across markets. For example, if one euro costs $0.89 in New York but $0.90 in Frankfurt, an arbitrageur could buy, say, $10,000,000 worth of euros in New York and at the same time sell them in Frankfurt for $10,112,359, thereby earning $112,359 minus the transaction costs of the trades.

Because an arbitrageur buys and sells simultaneously, relatively little risk is involved. In our example, the arbitrageur increased the demand for euros in New York and increased the supply of euros in Frankfurt. These actions increased the dollar price of euros in New York and decreased it in Frankfurt, thereby squeezing down the differential. Exchange rates may still change because of market forces, but they tend to change in all markets simultaneously.

The demand and supply of foreign exchange arises from many sources—from importers and exporters, investors in foreign assets, central banks, tourists, arbitrageurs, and speculators. **Speculators** buy or sell foreign exchange in hopes of profiting by trading the currency at a more favorable exchange rate later. By taking risks, speculators aim to profit from market fluctuations—they try to buy low and sell high. In contrast, arbitrageurs take less risk, since they *simultaneously* buy currency in one market and sell it in another.

Finally, people in countries suffering from economic and political turmoil, such as those in Russia, Indonesia, and the Philippines, may buy *hard* currency as a hedge against the depreciation and instability of their own currencies. The dollar has long been accepted as an international medium of exchange. It is also the currency of choice in the world markets for oil and illegal drugs. But the euro eventually may challenge that dominance, in part because the largest euro denomination, the 500 euro note, is worth nearly five times a $100 bill, the top U.S. note. So it would be five times easier to smuggle currency using euro notes than it would be using U.S. dollars.

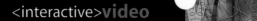

CNN VIDEO: "THE UPS AND DOWNS OF THE EURO"

Purchasing Power Parity

As long as trade across borders is unrestricted and as long as exchange rates are allowed to adjust freely, the **purchasing power parity (PPP) theory** predicts that the exchange rate between two currencies will adjust in the long run to reflect price-level differences between the two currency regions. *A given basket of internationally traded goods should therefore sell for about the same around the world (except for differences reflecting transportation costs and the like).* Suppose a basket of internationally traded commodities that sells for $9,000 in the United States sells for 10,000 euros in Euroland. According to the purchasing power parity theory, the equilibrium exchange rate should be $0.90 per euro. If this were not the case—if the exchange rate were, say, $0.80 per euro—then the basket of goods could be purchased in Euroland for 10,000 euros and sold in the United States for $9,000. The $9,000 could then be exchanged for 11,250 euros, yielding a profit of 1,250 euros, or $1,125 (= 1,250 × $0.90), minus any transaction costs. Selling dollars and buying euros will drive up the dollar price of euros.

The purchasing power parity theory is more of a long-run predictor than a day-to-day indicator of the relationship between changes in the price level and the exchange rate. For example, a country's currency generally appreciates when its inflation rate is relatively low compared with the rates in other countries and depreciates when its inflation rate is relatively high. Likewise, a country's currency generally appreciates when its real interest rates are higher than those in the rest of the world, since foreigners are more willing to buy and hold investments denominated in that currency. As a case in point, the dollar appreciated during the first half of the 1980s, when real U.S. interest rates were relatively high, and depreciated in the early 1990s, when real U.S. interest rates were relatively low.

Because of trade barriers, central bank intervention in exchange markets, and the fact that many products are not traded or are not comparable across countries, the purchasing power parity theory usually does not explain exchange rates at a particular point in time. For example, if you went shopping in London, you would soon notice a dollar does not buy as much as it does in the United States. The following case study considers the purchasing power parity theory in light of the price of Big Macs around the globe.

CASE**STUDY**	The Big Mac Price Index
	● *Bringing Theory to Life*

As you have already learned, the PPP theory says that, in the long run, the exchange rate between two currencies should move toward the rate that equalizes the prices in each country of an identical basket of internationally traded goods. A lighthearted test of the theory has been developed by the *Economist* magazine, which compares prices around the world for a "market basket" consisting simply of one McDonald's Big Mac—a product that, though not internationally traded, is essentially the same in more than 100 countries. The *Economist* begins with the price of a Big Mac in the local currency and then converts that price into dollars based on the exchange rate prevailing at the time. A comparison of the dollar price of Big Macs across countries offers a crude test of the PPP theory, which predicts that these prices should move toward equality in the long run.

Exhibit 5 lists the dollar price of a Big Mac on January 8, 2001, in each of 27 surveyed countries plus the average of the 12 countries in the euro area. By comparing the price of a Big Mac in the United States (shown as a green bar) with prices in other countries, we can derive a crude measure of whether particular currencies are undervalued or overvalued relative to the dollar. For example, because the price of a Big Mac in Israel, at $3.52, was 38 percent higher

EXHIBIT 5

On January 8, 2001, the U.S. Price of a Big Mac Exceeded Prices in Most Other Countries

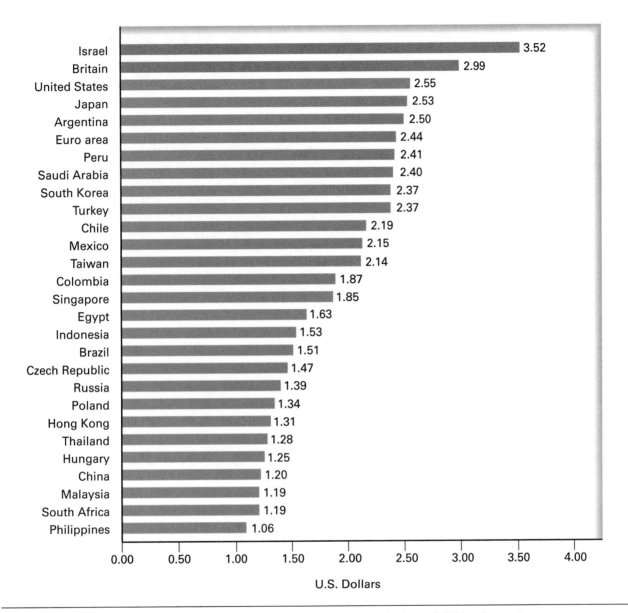

Source: "Burgernomics," *Economist,* 11 January 2001. Prices are converted into dollars using the January 8, 2001, exchange rate.

than the U.S. price of $2.55, the Israeli shekel appeared overvalued compared to the dollar. The same approach suggests that the British pound was 17 percent overvalued. But Israel and Britain (shown as red bars) were the exceptions. Because the dollar was relatively "strong" at the time of the survey, Big Macs were cheaper everywhere else on the list (shown as blue bars). The cheapest Big Mac was in the Philippines, where government instability depressed the local currency, the peso, cutting the Big Mac to $1.06, or 58 percent below the U.S. level.

Thus, Big Mac prices in 2001 ranged from 38 percent above to 58 percent below the U.S. price. This seems like a rejection of the PPP theory, but that theory relates only to traded goods. The Big Mac is not traded internationally. A large share of the total cost of a Big Mac is rent, which varies substantially across countries. Taxes and trade barriers, such as a tariff on beef, may also distort local prices. Likewise, prices for some goods vary across the United States even though we all use dollars here. For example, housing prices in the Northeast and the West Coast are higher than in the Midwest and the South. Still, a check during the last decade indicates that Big Mac prices have been slowly converging over the years in a manner consistent with the PPP theory; the range of high and low prices has squeezed down. In 1995, for example, the highest price of a Big Mac around the world was five times the lowest price; in 2001, the highest price was only 3.3 times the lowest price.

<interactive>exercise

eACTIVITY: THE BIG MAC PRICE INDEX

Sources: "Burgernomics," *Economist,* 11 January 2001; "Big Mac Currencies," *Economist,* 15 April 1995; Peter Liu and Paul Burkett, "Instability in Short-Run Adjustments to Purchasing Power Parity: Results for Selected Latin American Countries," *Applied Economics* 27 (October 1995): 973–83; and the McDonald's Corporation Web site at http://www.mcdonalds.com.

Flexible Exchange Rates

For the most part, we have been discussing a system of **flexible exchange rates,** with rates determined by supply and demand. Flexible, or *floating,* exchange rates adjust continually to the myriad forces that buffet the foreign exchange market. Consider how the exchange rate is linked to the balance-of-payments accounts. Debit entries in the current and capital accounts increase the demand for foreign exchange, resulting in a depreciation of the dollar. Credit entries in these accounts increase the supply of foreign exchange, resulting in an appreciation of the dollar.

Fixed Exchange Rates

When exchange rates are flexible, government officials usually have little direct role in foreign exchange markets. But if government officials try to set exchange rates, active and ongoing central bank intervention is necessary to establish and maintain these **fixed exchange rates.** Suppose the European Central Bank selects what it thinks is an appropriate rate of exchange between the dollar and the euro. It attempts to *fix,* or to "peg," the exchange rate within a narrow band around the particular value selected. If the value of the euro threatens to climb above the maximum acceptable exchange rate, monetary authorities must sell euros and buy dollars, thereby keeping the dollar price of the euro down. Conversely, if the value of the euro threatens to drop below the minimum acceptable exchange rate, monetary authorities must sell dollars and buy euros in foreign exchange markets. This increased demand for the euro will keep its value up relative to the dollar. Through such intervention in the foreign exchange market, monetary authorities can stabilize the exchange rate, keeping it within the specified band.

If monetary officials must keep selling foreign exchange to maintain the pegged rate, they risk running out of foreign exchange reserves. When this threat occurs, the government has several options for eliminating the exchange rate disequilibrium. First, the pegged exchange rate can be increased, which is a **devaluation** of the domestic currency. (A decrease in the pegged exchange rate is called a **revaluation.**) Second, the government can attempt to reduce the domestic demand for foreign exchange directly by imposing restrictions on imports or on capital outflows. China and many other developing countries do this. Third, the government can adopt contractionary fiscal or monetary policies to reduce the country's income level, increase interest rates, or reduce inflation relative to that of the country's trading partners, thereby indirectly decreasing the demand for foreign exchange. Several Asian economies, such as South Korea and Indonesia, pursued such policies to stabilize their currencies in 1998. Finally, the government can allow the disequilibrium to persist and ration the available foreign reserves through some form of foreign exchange control.

Now that we have concluded our introduction to the theories of international finance, let's examine how it works in practice.

DEVELOPMENT OF THE INTERNATIONAL MONETARY SYSTEM

From 1879 to 1914, the international financial system operated under a **gold standard,** whereby the major currencies were convertible into gold at a fixed rate. For example, the U.S. dollar could be redeemed at the U.S. Treasury for one-twentieth of an ounce of gold. The British pound could be redeemed at the British Exchequer, or treasury, for one-fourth of an ounce of gold. Since each British pound could buy five times as much gold as each dollar, one British pound exchanged for $5.

The gold standard provided a predictable exchange rate, one that did not vary as long as currencies could be redeemed for gold at the announced rate. But the money supply in each country was determined in part by the flow of gold between countries, so each country's monetary policy was influenced by the supply of gold. A balance-of-payments deficit resulted in a loss of gold, which theoretically caused a country's money supply to drop. A balance-of-payments surplus resulted in an increase in gold, which theoretically caused a country's money supply to rise. The supply of money throughout the world also depended on the vagaries of gold discoveries. When gold production did not keep pace with the growth in economic activity, the price level dropped. When gold production exceeded the growth in economic activity, the price level rose. For example, gold discoveries in Alaska and South Africa in the late 1890s expanded the U.S. money supply, leading to inflation.

The Bretton Woods Agreement

During World War I, many countries could no longer convert their currencies into gold, and the gold standard eventually collapsed, disrupting international trade during the 1920s and 1930s. Once an Allied victory in World War II appeared certain, the Allies met in Bretton Woods, New Hampshire, in July 1944 to formulate a new international monetary system. Because the United States had a strong economy and was not ravaged by World War II, the dollar was selected as the key reserve currency in the new international monetary system. All exchange rates were fixed in terms of the dollar, and the United States, which held most of the world's gold reserves, stood ready to convert foreign holdings of dollars into gold at a rate of $35 per ounce. Even though exchange rates were fixed by the Bretton Woods agreement, *other* countries could adjust *their* exchange rates relative to the U.S. dollar if they found a chronic disequilibrium in their balance of payments—that is, if a country faced a large and persistent deficit or surplus.

The Bretton Woods agreement also created the **International Monetary Fund (IMF)** to set rules for maintaining the international monetary system, to standardize financial reporting for international trade, and to make loans to countries with temporary balance-of-payments problems. Today, a revolving fund of $300 billion is lent to troubled economies around the world, including Russia, Brazil, Indonesia, and South Korea. Headquartered in Washington, D.C., the IMF has more than 180 member countries and a staff of 2,500 drawn from around the world.

<interactive>exercise

ECONDEBATE ONLINE: WHAT ARE THE PROS AND CONS OF INTERNATIONAL MONETARY FUND (IMF) INVOLVEMENT WITH GLOBAL ECONOMIES?

The Demise of the Bretton Woods System

During the latter part of the 1960s, inflation began heating up in the United States. Higher U.S. prices meant that those exchanging foreign currencies for dollars at the official exchange rates found these dollars bought less in U.S. goods and services. Because of U.S. inflation, the dollar had become *overvalued* at the official exchange rate, meaning that the gold value of the dollar exceeded the exchange value of the dollar. With the dollar overvalued, foreigners redeemed more dollars for gold. To halt this outflow of gold, the United States in August 1971 stopped exchanging gold for dollars. In December 1971, the world's 10 richest countries met in Washington and devalued the dollar by 8 percent. The hope at the time was that this devaluation would put the dollar on firmer footing and would save the "dollar standard." With prices rising at different rates around the world, however, an international monetary system based on fixed exchange rates was doomed.

In 1971, U.S. merchandise imports exceeded merchandise exports for the first time since World War II. When the trade deficit tripled in 1972, it became clear that the dollar was still overvalued. In early 1973, the dollar was devalued another 10 percent, but this did not quiet foreign exchange markets. The dollar, for three decades the anchor of the international monetary system, suddenly looked vulnerable, and speculators began betting the dollar would fall even more. Dollars were exchanged for German marks because the mark appeared to be the most stable currency. Monetary officials at the Bundesbank, Germany's central bank, exchanged marks for dollars in an attempt to defend the official exchange rate and prevent an appreciation of the mark. Why didn't Germany want the mark to appreciate? This would make German goods more expensive abroad and foreign goods cheaper in Germany, thereby reducing German exports and increasing German imports. So the mark's appreciation would reduce German output and employment. But after selling $10 billion worth of marks, the Bundesbank gave up defending the dollar. As soon as the value of the dollar was allowed to float against the mark, the Bretton Woods system, already on shaky ground, collapsed.

The Current System: Managed Float

The Bretton Woods system has been replaced by a **managed float system,** which combines features of a freely floating exchange rate with sporadic intervention by central banks as a way of moderating exchange rate fluctuations among the world's major currencies. Most smaller countries, particularly developing countries, still peg their currencies to one of the major currencies (such as the U.S. dollar) or to a "basket" of major currencies. What's more, in developing countries, private international borrowing and lending are severely restricted; some governments allow residents to purchase foreign exchange only for certain purposes. In some countries, different exchange rates apply to different categories of transactions.

Major criticisms of flexible exchange rates are that they are inflationary, since they free monetary authorities to pursue expansionary policies, and that they have often been volatile, especially since the late 1970s. This volatility creates uncertainty and risk for importers and exporters, increasing the transaction costs of international trade and thus reducing its volume. Furthermore, exchange rate volatility can lead to wrenching changes in the competitiveness of a country's export sector. These changes in competitiveness cause swings in employment, resulting in louder calls for import restrictions. For example, the exchange rate between the Japanese yen and the U.S. dollar has been relatively unstable, particularly because of international speculation.

Policy makers are always on the lookout for an international monetary system that will perform better than the current managed float system, with its fluctuating currency values. *Their ideal is a system that will foster international trade, lower inflation, and promote a more stable world economy.* International finance ministers have acknowledged that the world must find an international standard and establish greater exchange rate stability.

The wild swings in exchange rates that sometimes occur with flexible exchange rates have caused policy makers to intervene to reduce undesirable fluctuations, as discussed in the following case study about recent financial troubles in Asia.

CASE**STUDY**	The Asian Contagion
	● *The World of Business*

It started in Thailand in early 1997, when a booming economy ran into trouble. Speculators began betting that the Thai currency, the baht, was in for a fall. The Thai central bank tried to defend the baht's value by buying baht and selling foreign reserves. At the time, the baht's value was tied to the U.S. dollar. As the central bank's foreign reserves dwindled, the government decided in July 1997 to let the baht float. It lost 40 percent of its value against the dollar in a matter of weeks. With the baht worth so much less, Thai businesses and the government had difficulty repaying foreign loans, most of which had to be paid back in dollars.

The crisis prompted a $17 billion bailout of Thailand, supervised by the International Monetary Fund (IMF) and aimed at helping Thailand pay back some foreign debts. But problems in Thailand deepened, as outside credit agencies continued to downgrade Thai debt. Falling currency values soon spread to neighboring Indonesia, Malaysia, and South Korea, as the so-called Asian Contagion ripped through the region, cutting real GDP in each of these countries more than 5 percent in 1998. Indonesia was one of the hardest hit, with output falling 20 percent over 18 months. Note that a plunging currency value is not so much the source of economic instability as a reflection of other problems in the economy, such as falling exports and an unstable banking sector due to bad loans. Indonesia and South Korea were forced to seek IMF assistance. Indonesia was promised $40 billion in loans and South Korea $58 billion, the most costly rescue package in IMF history. In exchange for the aid, both countries agreed to cut government spending and open up their markets to foreign goods and foreign investors.

In Japan, where the economy had been struggling since 1990, matters worsened. In November 1997, four large financial institutions went bankrupt, the yen suffered its biggest drop against the dollar in years, and the stock market continued its eight-year slide. As discussed in an earlier case study, one big problem overhanging the Japanese economy was more than a trillion dollars worth of bad debts in the banking system. Banks had extended real estate loans during the booming 1980s. But when property values crashed, the loans could not be repaid, so the banks were in trouble. Japan, the second-largest economy in the world (after the United States), is by far the largest economy in Asia. A weakened Japan threatened the fragile economies of Asia as they tried to recover from financial chaos. A weakened Japan meant the country would buy less from its Asian neighbors, and a weakened yen meant Japanese exports would be cheaper on world markets, thus undercutting exports from elsewhere in Asia.

Faced with growing problems in Asia, the U.S. government joined forces with the Japanese government to intervene in currency markets and spent $2 billion buying yen. By increasing the demand for yen, the U.S. intervention reversed the slide in the yen's value. In one day, the yen-per-dollar exchange rate appreciated 5 percent. As the yen appreciated further against the dollar, the Japanese economy stabilized. By 2001, output in the other economies affected by the Asian Contagion was growing. But uncertainty continues, particularly in Thailand, Indonesia, and Japan, where bad bank loans remain on the books, undermining confidence in the banking system.

<interactive>exercise

- eACTIVITY: THE ASIAN CONTAGION
- READING IT RIGHT: WALL STREET JOURNAL EXERCISE

Sources: "Asian Economies: The East Is in the Red," *Economist,* 19 May 2001; "Emerging Market Indicators," *Economist,* 13 October 2001; "Stocks Stumble Across Asia as Yen Hits Lowest Since '90," *Wall Street Journal,* 11 June 1998; "Proposed Law in Thailand Will Create Company to Handle Bank's Bad Loans," *Wall Street Journal,* 7 May 2001; and *OECD Economic Outlook* 69 (June 2001).

CONCLUSION

The United States is very much a part of the world economy, not only as the largest exporter but also as the largest importer. Although the dollar remains the unit of transaction in many international settlements—OPEC, for example, still states oil prices in dollars—wild gyrations of exchange rates have made those involved in international finance wary of putting all their eggs in one basket. The international monetary system is now going through a difficult adjustment period as it continues to grope for a new source of stability three decades after the collapse of the Bretton Woods agreement.

endofchaptermaterial

- **Summary**
- **Questions for Review**
- **Problems and Exercises**

- **Experiential Exercises**
- **Wall Street Journal Exercise**

Take the Post-Test to assess your overall understanding of the key ideas in this chapter. The Post-Test provides a comprehensive selection of exam-style questions addressing the main topics and concepts of the chapter. At the completion of each Post-Test, you will receive a score and instructive feedback on how you answered each question, and a direct link to the part of the chapter addressed in the question. Take the Post-Test as often as you need to—a record of your progress for each attempt is kept for you to revisit and gauge your improvement. And each Post-Test is randomly generated, so every attempt is new.

Post-Test